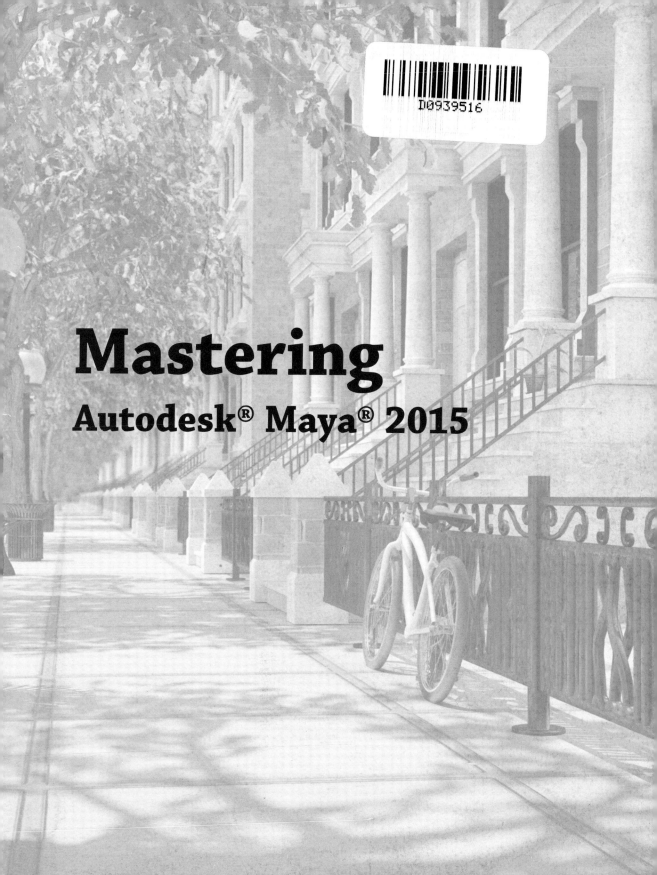

Mastering
Autodesk® Maya® 2015

Mastering

Autodesk® Maya® 2015

Todd Palamar

AUTODESK.
Official Press

SYBEX®
A Wiley Brand

Acquisitions Editor: Mariann Barsolo
Development Editor: Candace Cunningham
Technical Editor: Chip Weatherman
Production Editor: Eric Charbonneau
Copy Editor: Liz Welch
Editorial Manager: Pete Gaughan
Vice President and Executive Group Publisher: Richard Swadley
Associate Publisher: Chris Webb
Book Designers: Maureen Forys, Happenstance Type-O-Rama with Judy Fung
Proofreaders: Sarah Kaikini and Jen Larsen, Word One New York
Indexer: Ted Laux
Project Coordinator, Cover: Patrick Redmond
Cover Designer: Wiley
Cover Image: Courtesy of Todd Palamar

Copyright © 2014 by John Wiley & Sons, Inc., Indianapolis, Indiana
Published simultaneously in Canada

ISBN: 978-1-118-86251-3
ISBN: 978-1-118-86253-7 (ebk.)
ISBN: 978-1-118-86257-5 (ebk.)

Library of Congress Control Number: 2014937182

Dear Reader,

Thank you for choosing *Mastering Autodesk Maya 2015*. This book is part of a family of premium-quality Sybex books, all of which are written by outstanding authors who combine practical experience with a gift for teaching.

Sybex was founded in 1976. More than 30 years later, we're still committed to producing consistently exceptional books. With each of our titles, we're working hard to set a new standard for the industry. From the paper we print on to the authors we work with, our goal is to bring you the best books available.

I hope you see all that reflected in these pages. I'd be very interested to hear your comments and get your feedback on how we're doing. Feel free to let me know what you think about this or any other Sybex book by sending me an email at contactus@sybex.com. If you think you've found a technical error in this book, please visit http://sybex.custhelp.com. Customer feedback is critical to our efforts at Sybex.

Best regards,

Chris Webb
Associate Publisher
Sybex, an Imprint of Wiley

Acknowledgments

I would like to thank Eric Keller, whose work on previous editions has built a foundation for this edition. Thanks also to Chip Weatherman, our technical editor. Chip's fresh perspective was much appreciated.

I would also like to thank all the people from Wiley, and a special thanks to Mariann Barsolo and Candace Cunningham for having such great attitudes. Their management and editing skills are superior.

About the Author

Todd Palamar is a 23-year veteran in the computer animation industry. After transitioning early in his career from traditional special effects to computer-generated imagery, Todd did effects work for several direct-to-video movies. He later went on to work on numerous video games, including Sega of Japan's coin-operated title *Behind Enemy Lines,* as well as *Dukes of Hazzard* and *Trophy Buck 2* for the Sony PlayStation console. For six years, Todd taught at Full Sail University in Winter Park, Florida. During this time, he received numerous accolades as an outstanding educator. Todd currently runs his own company, Surrealistic Producing Effects, making and distributing movies. Todd has written several books, among them *Maya Cloth for Characters* (Surrealistic Producing Effects, 2008), *Maya Studio Projects: Dynamics* (Sybex, 2009), and *Maya Studio Projects: Photorealistic Characters* (Sybex, 2011). The breadth of his experience has allowed him to work on location-based entertainment, military simulations, television commercials, and corporate spots. You can see more of Todd's work on his company's website, www.speffects.com.

Contents at a Glance

Contents

Introduction

The Autodesk® Maya® program is big. It is really, really huge. The book you hold in your hands and all the exercises within it represent a mere sliver of what can be created in Maya. Mastering Maya takes years of study and practice. I have been using Maya almost every day since 1999, and I'm still constantly facing new challenges and making new discoveries.

This book is meant to be a guide to help you not only understand Maya, but also learn about Maya. The title *Mastering Autodesk Maya 2015* implies an active engagement with the software. This book is packed with hands-on tutorials. If you're looking for a quick-reference guide that simply describes each and every button, control, and tool in the Maya interface, turn to the Maya documentation that comes with the software. This book is not a description of Maya; it is an explanation illustrated with practical examples.

The skills you acquire through the examples in this book should prepare you for using Maya in a professional environment. To that end, some features, such as lighting and rendering with mental ray®, nDynamics, Fluids, and Maya Muscle, have received more emphasis and attention than others. Features that have not changed significantly over the past few versions of the software, such as Maya Software rendering, standard Maya shaders, and older rigging techniques, receive less attention since they have been thoroughly covered elsewhere.

When you read this book and work through the exercises, do not hesitate to use the Maya help files. We won't be insulted! The Maya documentation has a very useful search function that allows you to find complete descriptions of each control in the software. To use the help files, click the Help menu in the Maya menu interface. The documentation consists of a large library of Maya resources, which will appear in your default web browser when you access the help files. Experienced Maya artists never hesitate to use the help files to find out more information about the software; there is no shame in asking questions! In addition, hovering over a tool or setting will give you a brief description. Features new to Maya, highlighted in green throughout the interface, have links to larger descriptions as well as movies.

Who Should Buy This Book

This book is written for intermediate Maya users and users who are advanced in some aspects of Maya and want to learn more about other facets of the program. The book is intended to be used by artists who are familiar with Maya and the Maya interface or who have significant experience using similar 3D packages. If you have used older versions of Maya, this book will help you catch up on the features in Maya 2014.

If you have never used Maya or any other 3D software on a computer before, this book will be too challenging, and you will quickly become frustrated. You are encouraged to read

Introducing Autodesk Maya 2015, by Dariush Derakhshani (Sybex, 2014) or to read through the tutorials in the Maya documentation before diving into this book.

You should be familiar with the following before reading this book:

◆ The Maya interface.

◆ Computer image basics such as color channels, masking, resolution, and image compression.

◆ Computer animation basics such as keyframes, squash and stretch, and 3D coordinate systems.

◆ Standard Maya shaders, such as the Blinn, Phong, Lambert, Layered, and Anisotropic materials, as well as standard textures, such as Fractal, Ramp, Noise, and Checker.

◆ Lighting and rendering with standard Maya lights and the Maya software rendering engine.

◆ The basics of working with NURBS curves, polygon surfaces, and NURBS surfaces.

◆ Your operating system. You need to be familiar with opening and saving files and the like. Basic computer networking skills are helpful as well.

What's Inside

The topics in this book move in a progressive order from introductory to complex. They also loosely follow a typical production pipeline for starting and completing assets. The following are brief explanations of the contents of each chapter.

There is also a companion website, which is home to all the project files and samples referenced in the book, as well as bonus chapters on MEL scripting and toon shading. Go to www.sybex.com/go/masteringmaya2015 and click the Downloads tab to access the files.

◆ **Chapter 1: Working in Autodesk Maya** This chapter discusses how to work with the various nodes and the node structure that make up a scene. Using the Hypergraph, Outliner, Hypershade, Attribute Editor, and Connection Editor to build relationships between nodes is demonstrated through a series of exercises.

◆ **Chapter 2: Introduction to Animation** This chapter demonstrates basic rigging with inverse kinematics as well as animating with keyframes, expressions, and constraints. Animation layers are explained.

◆ **Chapter 3: Hard-Surface Modeling** This chapter introduces the various types of surfaces with which you can model. It walks you through numerous approaches for modeling parts of a bicycle.

◆ **Chapter 4: Organic Modeling** This chapter focuses on building a humanoid mesh, using polygon and subdivision surface techniques. Smooth mesh polygons, creasing, and soft selection are demonstrated on various parts of the model.

◆ **Chapter 5: Rigging and Muscle Systems** This chapter explains joints, expands on inverse kinematics, and covers smooth binding and proper rigging techniques. Maya Muscle is introduced and demonstrated on a character's leg.

◆ **Chapter 6: Animation Techniques** This chapter takes you through the numerous deformation tools available in Maya. Creating a facial-animation rig using blend shapes is demonstrated, along with texture deformers, nonlinear deformers, and the geometry cache. We also take a look at importing motion capture.

◆ **Chapter 7: Lighting with mental ray** This chapter demonstrates a variety of lighting tools and techniques that can be used when rendering scenes with mental ray. Indirect lighting using global illumination, Final Gathering, and the Physical Sun and Sky network are all demonstrated.

◆ **Chapter 8: mental ray Shading Techniques** This chapter describes commonly used mental ray shaders and how they can be employed to add material qualities to the space helmet created in Chapter 3. Tips on how to use the shaders together as well as how to light and render them using mental ray are offered.

◆ **Chapter 9: Texture Mapping** This chapter demonstrates how to create UV texture coordinates for a giraffe. Applying textures painted in other software packages, such as Adobe Photoshop, is discussed, as are displacement and normal maps and subsurface scattering shaders.

◆ **Chapter 10: Paint Effects** This chapter provides a step-by-step demonstration of how to create a custom Paint Effects brush as well as how to animate and render with Paint Effects.

◆ **Chapter 11: Rendering for Compositing** This chapter introduces render layers and render passes, which can be used to split the various elements of a render into separate files that are then recombined in compositing software.

◆ **Chapter 12: Introducing nParticles** This chapter provides numerous examples of how to use nParticles. You'll use fluid behavior, particle meshes, internal force fields, and other techniques to create amazing effects.

◆ **Chapter 13: Dynamic Effects** This chapter demonstrates a variety of techniques that can be used with nCloth to create effects. Traditional rigid body dynamics are compared with nCloth, and combining nCloth and nParticles is illustrated.

◆ **Chapter 14: Hair and Clothing** This chapter discusses how to augment your Maya creatures and characters using XGen, Maya nHair, and nCloth. Using dynamic curves to create a rig for a dragon's tail is also demonstrated.

◆ **Chapter 15: Maya Fluids** This chapter explains how 2D and 3D fluids can be used to create smoke, cloud, and flame effects, and provides a demonstration of how to render using the Ocean shader. Bifrost is introduced as a way of creating liquid simulation.

◆ **Chapter 16: Scene Management and Virtual Filmmaking** This chapter provides an in-depth discussion of the Maya virtual camera and its attributes. A number of exercises provide examples of standard and custom camera rigs. Stereo 3D cameras are also introduced. References and the Asset Editor are also introduced. These features aid with large Maya projects that are divided between teams of artists.

◆ **Appendix A: The Bottom Line** This appendix contains all of the solutions from the Master It section at the end of each chapter.

◆ **Appendix B: Autodesk Maya 2015 Certification** This appendix contains the Autodesk Maya 2015 Certified Professional Objectives table that lists the topic, exam objective, and chapter where the information can be found.

NOTE Go to www.autodesk.com/certification to find information about the Maya 2015 Certified Professional exam covered in this book, as well as other Maya certification exams.

Conventions

Navigating in Maya is slightly different in the Windows and Mac operating systems. You can navigate the Hypergraph by using the same hot-key combination you use in the viewport: Alt+MMB-drag/Option+MMB-drag pans through the Hypergraph workspace, and Alt+RMB-drag/Option+RMB-drag zooms in and out. (MMB refers to the middle mouse button, and RMB refers to the right mouse button.)

It is also important to note that Maya uses three digits for values listed within its tools and editors. The book may only show one or two digits when the last one or two digits are 0.

FREE AUTODESK SOFTWARE FOR STUDENTS AND EDUCATORS

The Autodesk Education Community is an online resource with more than five million members that enables educators and students to download—for free (see website for terms and conditions)—the same software used by professionals worldwide. You can also access additional tools and materials to help you design, visualize, and simulate ideas. Connect with other learners to stay current with the latest industry trends and get the most out of your designs. Get started today at www.autodesk.com/joinedu.

How to Contact the Author

You can contact author Todd Palamar with questions, comments, or concerns through his website at www.speffects.com, where you can see other books and productions on which he has worked.

Sybex strives to keep you supplied with the latest tools and information you need for your work. Please check this book's website at www.sybex.com/go/masteringmaya2015, where we'll post additional content and updates that supplement this book should the need arise.

Chapter 1

Working in Autodesk Maya

The Autodesk® Maya® working environment has evolved to accommodate the individual artist as well as a team of artists working in a production pipeline. The interface presents tools, controls, and data in an organized fashion to allow you to bring your fantastic creations to life easily.

Understanding the way Maya organizes data about the objects, animations, textures, lights, dynamics, and all the other elements contained within the 3D environment of a scene is essential to understanding how the interface is organized. Maya uses what's known as the Dependency Graph to keep track of the various packets of data, called nodes, and how they affect each other. Any single element of a Maya scene consists of multiple nodes connected in a web, and each one of these nodes is dependent on another. The Maya interface consists of editing windows that allow you to connect these nodes in an intuitive way and edit the information contained within each node.

There is usually more than one way to accomplish a task in Maya. As you grow comfortable with the interface, you'll discover which editing windows best suit your working style.

This chapter is a brief overview of what professionals need to understand when working in Maya. You'll learn what types of nodes you'll be working with and how they can be created and edited in Maya. You'll also learn how to work with projects and scene data as well as the various windows, panels, and controls that make up the interface. This will help you, whether you are working alone or as part of a team of artists.

This chapter is about working with nodes, but it is not meant to be a comprehensive guide to each and every control in Maya. You will find that information in the Maya documentation. If you've never used Maya before, I strongly encourage you to read the Maya documentation as well as *Introducing Autodesk Maya 2015*, by Dariush Derakhshani (Sybex, 2014).

In this chapter, you will learn to:

- ◆ Understand transform and shape nodes

- ◆ Create a project

Creating and Editing Nodes

A Maya *scene* is a system of interconnected nodes that are packets of data. The data within a node tells the software what exists within the world of a Maya scene. The nodes are the building blocks that you, as the artist, put together to create the 3D scene and animation that will finally be rendered for the world to see. So if you can think of the objects in your scene, their motion, and their appearance as nodes, think of the Maya interface as the tools and controls you use to connect those nodes. The relationship between these nodes is organized by the *Dependency Graph (DG)*, which describes the hierarchical relationship between connected nodes. The interface provides many ways to view the graph, and these methods are described in this chapter.

Any given workflow in Maya is much like a route on a city map. There are usually many ways to get to your destination, and some of them make more sense than others depending on where you're going. In Maya, the best workflow depends on what you're trying to achieve, and there is typically more than one possible ideal workflow.

There are many types of nodes in Maya that serve any number of different functions. All the nodes in Maya are considered DG nodes. Let's say you have a simple cube and you sub-divide it once, thus quadrupling the number of faces that make up the cube. The information concerning how the cube has been subdivided is contained within a DG node that is connected to the cube node.

A special type of DG node is the *directed acyclic graph (DAG)* node. These nodes are made of two specific types of connected nodes: transform and shape. The arrangement of DAG nodes consists of a hierarchy in which the shape node is a child of the transform node. Most of the objects you work with in the Maya viewport, such as surface geometry (cubes, spheres, planes, and so on), are DAG nodes.

To understand the difference between the transform and shape node types, think of a trans-form node as describing where an object is located and a shape node as describing what an object is.

The simple polygon cube in Figure 1.1 consists of six flat squares attached at the edges to form a box. Each side of the cube is subdivided twice, creating four polygons per side. That basically describes what the object is, and the description of the object would be contained in the shape node. This simple polygon cube may be 4.174018 centimeters above the grid, rotated 35 degrees on the x-axis, and scaled four times its original size based on the cube's local x- and y-axes and six times its original size in the cube's local z-axis. That description would be in the transform node.

FIGURE 1.1
A shape node describes the shape of an object and how it has been constructed; a transform node describes where the object is located in the scene.

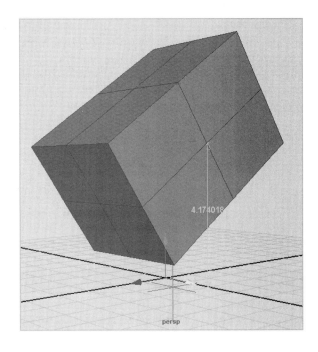

Maya has a number of workspaces that enable you to visualize and work with the nodes and their connections. The following sections describe how these workspaces work together when building a node network in a Maya scene.

Using the Hypergraph

The *Hypergraph* is a visual representation of the nodes and their connections in Maya. A complex scene can look like an intricate web of these connections. When you need to know how a network of nodes is connected, the Hypergraph gives you the most detailed view. There are two ways to view the Hypergraph:

◆ The *hierarchy view* shows the relationships between nodes as a tree structure.

◆ The *connections view* shows how the nodes are connected as a web.

You can have more than one Hypergraph window open at the same time, but you are still looking at the same scene with the same nodes and connections.

This short exercise gives you a sense of how you would typically use the Hypergraph:

1. Create a new Maya scene.

2. Create a polygon cube by choosing Create ➢ Polygon Primitives ➢ Cube.

3. You will be prompted to draw a polygon on the grid by dragging on the grid (see Figure 1.2). Drag a square on the grid, release the cursor, and then drag upward on the square to turn it into a three-dimensional cube. Release the mouse button to complete the cube. At this point, feel free to make your own decisions about the size and position of the cube on the grid.

FIGURE 1.2
Maya prompts you to draw the base of the cube on the grid in the scene.

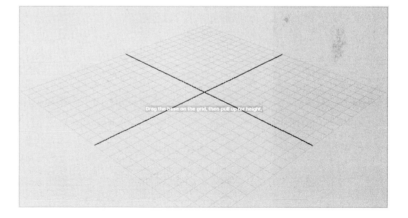

Drag the base on the grid, then pull up for height.

4. Select the cube in the viewport, and choose Window ➢ Hypergraph: Hierarchy to open the Hypergraph in hierarchy mode. You'll see a yellow rectangle on a black field labeled pCube1. The rectangle turns gray when deselected.

5. Move the mouse over the rectangle labeled pCube and then right-click. Choose Rename from the pop-up window. Rename the cube **myCube**.

6. Select myCube and, from the Hypergraph menu, choose Graph ➢ Input And Output Connections. This switches the view to the connections view just as if you had originally opened the Hypergraph by choosing Window ➢ Hypergraph: Connections. It's the same Hypergraph, but the view mode has changed, allowing you to see more of the scene.

When you graph the input and output connections, you see the connected nodes that make up an object and how the object appears in the scene. In the current view, you should see the myCube node next to a stack of connected nodes labeled polyCube1, myCubeShape, and initialShadingGroup, as shown in Figure 1.3. (The nodes may also be arranged in a line; the actual position of the nodes in the Hypergraph does not affect the nodes themselves.)

FIGURE 1.3
The node network appears in the Hypergraph. This shape node (myCubeShape) is connected to two other nodes, whereas the transform node (myCube) appears off to the side.

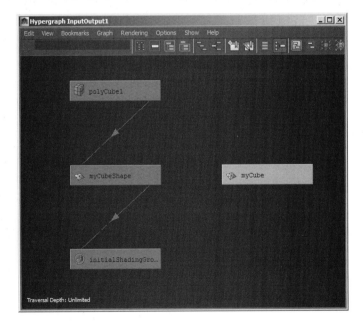

NAVIGATING THE HYPERGRAPH

You can navigate the Hypergraph by using the same hot-key combination you use in the viewport: Alt+MMB-drag/Option+MMB-drag pans through the Hypergraph workspace, and Alt+RMB-drag/Option+RMB-drag zooms in and out. (MMB means clicking with the middle mouse button, and RMB means clicking with the right mouse button.) Selecting a node and pressing the **f** hot key focuses the view on the currently selected node. It is also possible to zoom in using the scroll wheel on your mouse.

The myCube node is the transform node. The myCubeShape node is the shape node. In the Hypergraph, the shape and transform nodes are depicted as unconnected; however, there is an implied connection, as you'll see later. This is demonstrated when you rename the myCube node; the shape node is renamed as well.

In Maya, the construction history feature stores a record of the changes used to create a particular node. The polyCube1 node is the construction history node for the myCubeShape node. When you first create a piece of geometry, you can set options to the number of subdivisions, spans, width, height, depth, and many other features that are stored as a record in this history node. Additional history nodes are added as you make changes to the node. You can go back and change these settings as long as the history node still exists. Deleting a history node makes all the previous changes to the node permanent (however, deleting history is undoable). Use the following steps to guide you through the process of modifying history nodes:

1. Keep the Hypergraph open, but select the cube in the viewport.

2. Change the menu set in the upper left of the main interface to Polygons.

3. Press the 5 key on the keyboard to switch to shaded mode. Choose Mesh ➢ Smooth. The cube will be subdivided and smoothed in the viewport.

   In the Hypergraph you'll see a new polySmoothFace1 node between the polyCube1 node and the myCubeShape node (see Figure 1.4). This new node is part of the history of the cube.

FIGURE 1.4
Performing a smooth operation on the cube when construction history is activated causes a new polySmoothFace1 node to be inserted into the node network.

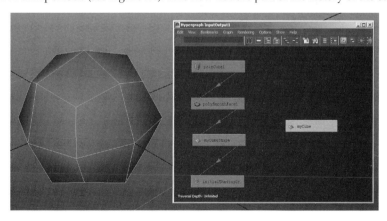

4. Select the polySmoothFace1 node, and delete it by pressing the Backspace key on the keyboard. The cube will return to its unsmoothed state.

5. Select the transform node (myCube), and press the **s** hot key. This creates a keyframe on all the channels of the transform node. A keyframe stores the current attribute values at a particular time on the timeline. Animation is created by interpolating between key-framed values.

You'll see a new node icon appear for each keyframed channel with a connection to the transform node (see Figure 1.5).

FIGURE 1.5
The attributes of myCube's transform node have been keyframed. The keyframe nodes appear in the Hypergraph.

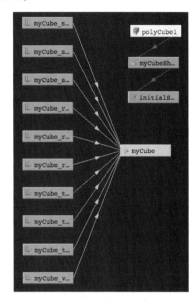

6. Hold the cursor over any line that connects one node to another. A label appears describing the output and input attributes indicated by the connection line.

WORKING WITH HISTORY

Over the course of a modeling session, the history for any given object can become quite long and complex. This can slow down performance. It's a good idea to delete history periodically on an object by selecting the object and choosing Edit ➤ Delete By Type ➤ History. You can also choose to delete the history of all the objects in the scene at once by choosing Edit ➤ Delete All By Type ➤ History. Once you start animating a scene using deformers and joints, you can use the Delete By Type ➤ Non-Deformer History option, which will remove the construction history nodes while preserving connections to animation nodes such as deformers.

You can turn off the history globally by clicking the Construction History toggle switch on the status line, as shown here:

Connecting Nodes with the Node Editor

Connections between nodes can be added, deleted, or changed using the Hypergraph and the Connection Editor. Introduced in Maya 2013, the Node Editor combines the features of the Hypergraph, Hypershade, and Connection Editor into a single graphical interface. Maya 2015 brings numerous changes and enhancements.

When you open the Node Editor you are presented with an empty, grid-lined space. To view a selected node, you must choose the type of connections you wish to graph: input, output, or both. After establishing a graph, you can add additional nodes by choosing the icon with three nodes and a red plus symbol from the Node Editor toolbar.

Every node has a series of ports for connecting attributes between nodes. By default, the nodes are shown in Simple mode, meaning none of their attributes or other ports are shown. In Simple mode, you can click on the dot on either side of the node to access a pop-up menu for a node's input or output connections. When unconnected, the superport is white. After connecting, the port takes on the color of the connected attribute. You do not always have to use the superport and subsequent pop-up menu to make connections. You can expose the lesser ports by changing the nodes' display from their simple, default display to Connected, exposing the connected attributes, or to Full mode. Click the icon in the lower-right corner of each node to change its display. You can also press 1, 2, or 3 on the keyboard, with the node selected, to change its mode. To change all of the nodes' modes at once, use the Edit menu at the top left of the Node Editor. The Full mode allows you to see all of the connectable ports (see Figure 1.6).

FIGURE 1.6
The various display modes, starting with locator1 in default, nurbsSphere1 in full, and locator2 in Connected mode

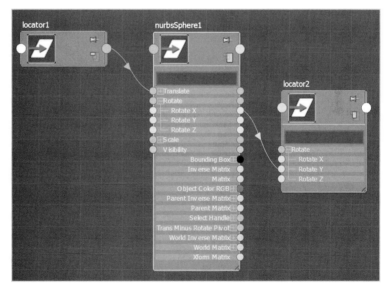

Like with all editors in Maya, you can customize the colors of the Node Editor using the Windows ➤ Settings/Preferences ➤ Color Settings window. The Attribute Type rollout under the Node Editor rollout allows you to change the color of the various types of connections.

The following steps walk you through the basic uses of the Node Editor and how to make connections:

1. Start a new Maya scene.

2. Create a locator in the scene by choosing Create ➢ Locator. A simple cross appears at the center of the grid in the viewport. This locator is a simple nonrendering null that indicates a point in space. Locators are handy tools that can be used for a wide variety of things in Maya.

3. Press the **w** hot key to switch to the Move tool; select the locator at the center of the grid, and move it out of the way.

4. Press the **g** hot key to create another locator. The **g** hot key repeats the last action you performed, in this case the creation of the locator.

5. Create a NURBS sphere in the viewport by choosing Create ➢ NURBS Primitives ➢ Sphere. If you have Interactive Creation selected, you'll be prompted to drag on the grid in the viewport to create the sphere; otherwise, the sphere will be created at the center of the grid based on its default settings.

6. Move the sphere away from the center of the grid so that you can clearly see both locators and the sphere.

7. Use the Select tool (hot key = **q**) to drag a selection marquee around all three objects.

8. Open the Node Editor by choosing Window ➢ Node Editor. A grid is drawn in the workspace. The grid can be toggled on or off by choosing the grid-visibility button (circled in Figure 1.7) from the Node Editor's toolbar. Choose the Input and Output Connections button, also circled in Figure 1.7, to graph your selection.

FIGURE 1.7
The input and output connections of the two locators and the sphere are graphed in the Node Editor.

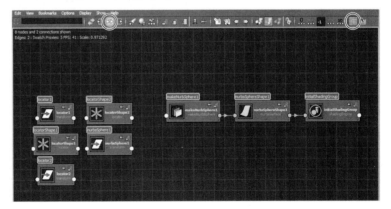

At the bottom of the screen are the two transform nodes for locator1 and locator2. locatorShape1 and locatorShape2 are the shape nodes for the locators. nurbsSphere1 is the transform node for the NURBS sphere. And nurbsSphereShape1 is the shape node for the sphere; it's connected to makeNurbSphere1, which is the history node, and to initialShadingGroup. The initialShadingGroup node is the default shading group that is applied to all geometry; without this node, the geometry can't be shaded or rendered. When you apply a new shader to an object, the connection to initialShadingGroup is replaced with a connection to the new shader. A *shader* is a node that determines how a surface appears in Maya, as well as how it reacts to virtual lights.

9. In the Node Editor, use Alt+RMB to zoom in and out. Notice how the name bar that sits on top of each node scales with the camera, enabling you to view long names regardless of your camera view.

10. Select the locator1, locator2, and nurbsSphere1 transform nodes, and drag them away from the other nodes so that you can work on them in their own space. To keep your graph neat, you can use snap to grid to align your nodes with the grid.

11. Click the white superport on the right side of the locator1 node. This is the output.

12. From the pop-up menu, choose Translate ➤ Translate. A yellow wire extends from the translate node (see Figure 1.8). The wire can be connected to a white port on another node.

FIGURE 1.8
Use the wire to connect the output of one node to the input of another.

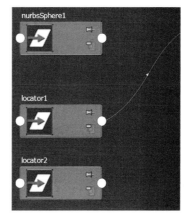

13. Connect the yellow wire to the left side of the nurbsSphere1 node by clicking on its white superport and choosing Translate from the pop-up menu. You can connect the yellow wire to either side of a node. The connection will be the same. A green wire shows the finished connection.

You can also choose Other from the pop-up menu. Doing so brings up the Input Selection window. The window lists the attributes of the node. Any of the attributes that have a plus sign next to them can be expanded to reveal nested attributes. For instance, find the Translate attribute and expand it by clicking the plus sign. (The term *translate* in Maya refers to an object's position. When you use the Move tool to change the position of an object in 3D space, you are "translating" the object.) You'll see that Translate has Translate X, Translate Y, and Translate Z. This means that you can choose either to select the Translate attribute, which will automatically use all three nested attributes as the input connection, or to expand Translate and choose one or more of the nested Translate X, Y, or Z attributes as the input connection. In some situations, a connection becomes unavailable (grayed out), indicating that the connection between the two attributes cannot be made, usually because the connection is not appropriate for the selected attributes (see Figure 1.9).

FIGURE 1.9
The Input Selection
window specifies
which attributes
can be connected
between nodes.

14. In the viewport, switch to wireframe mode if you are not already in it. You can do this by pressing **4** on the keyboard or by clicking the wireframe icon on the icon bar at the top of the viewport window; the wireframe icon is the wireframe cube.

15. In the viewport, you'll notice that the sphere has snapped to the same position as the locator. Select the sphere, and try to move it using the Move tool (hot key = **w**). The sphere is locked to the locator, so it cannot be moved. Select the locator, and try to move it; the sphere moves with the locator. The output of the locator's Translate attributes is the input for the sphere's Translate.

INCOMING CONNECTIONS

In wireframe view, an object will be highlighted in purple if it has an incoming connection from the selected object.

---

16. Click on the nurbsSphere1 node and press 3 to display the node's attributes in full. Click the plus sign next to Rotate to expand the Rotate rollout. Repeat the procedure for locator2.

17. Click on the right-side port or output for RotateX on nurbsSphere1.

18. Drag the yellow wire to the left side (the input side) of locator2 and connect it to RotateY. The yellow wire turns cyan to match the color of its port of origin and the connection is made. The difference in color indicates rotational values as opposed to numeric values, like those used by the translate and scale attributes.

19. In the viewport, select the sphere and switch to the Rotate tool (hot key = **e**).

20. Drag up and down on the red circle of the tool to rotate the sphere around its x-axis. The locator rotates around its y-axis.

Using the Node Editor to Make Simple Connections

The Node Editor is perfect for making one-to-one relationships between attributes on two nodes. In other words, the value of the output connection needs to equal exactly the value of the input connection. You can also create nodes from inside the editor by using the RMB and subsequent marking menu.

The Node Editor can get cluttered quickly. To combat a messy graph, you can pin your nodes to their current position and size regardless of regraphing. The pushpin icon in the upper-left quadrant of the node (top-right corner on Mac) allows you to toggle the pinning feature. You can also select Options ➢ Pin All Nodes By Default or RMB-click in the Node Editor to access the option through the marking menu.

New!

It is also possible to reduce the number of attributes displayed in each node to help simplify your view. To activate Edit Custom Attribute List, RMB-click on a port of a node you wish to customize. In edit mode, the node is divided by a yellow bar. The attributes above the yellow bar are the ones that display. Those below the yellow bar are hidden. You can click on an attribute to hide or unhide it. Attributes can also be rearranged by MMB-dragging to a new location within the node. To accept your changes, RMB-click on the node's graphic and deselect Edit Custom Attribute List. You can then press **4** to see your edited node. To revert the node to its original settings, RMB-click on any attribute in edit mode and choose Revert from the context menu.

Experiment with making connections between the various attributes with the Node Editor. You can break a connection by selecting and dragging the arrow along the wire into empty space. Notice the changes in the port colors when making or breaking connections.

Creating Node Hierarchies in the Outliner

**CERT
OBJECTIVE**

The Outliner shows a hierarchical list of the nodes in the scene in a form similar to the outline of a book. It is another way to view the transform and shape nodes in a scene and a way to create hierarchical relationships between nodes through parenting. The Outliner does not show the connections between nodes like the Hypergraph does; rather, it shows the hierarchy of the nodes in the scene. To see how this works, try the following exercise:

1. Open `miniGun_v01.ma` from the `Chapter1/scenes` directory at the book's web page (`www.sybex.com/go/masteringmaya2015`). The scene consists of a minigun model in three parts.

2. Open the Outliner by choosing Window ➢ Outliner.

OUTLINER LAYOUT PRESETS

The Outliner can be opened as a separate panel or, like many of the panels in Maya, it can be opened in a viewport. A popular window arrangement is to split the viewports into two views, with the left view set to the Outliner and the right view set to the perspective view. You can open this arrangement by going to the menu bar in a viewport window and choosing Panels ➢ Saved Layouts ➢ Persp/Outliner. You can also click the third layout button on the left side of the interface just below the toolbox (as shown here).

3. At the top of the Outliner is a menu bar. In the Display menu, make sure DAG Objects Only is selected and Shapes is deselected (see Figure 1.10).

FIGURE 1.10
The Display menu at the top of the Outliner

In the Outliner, you'll see three nodes listed—gunBarrels, housing, and mount—in addition to the four default cameras and several set nodes (don't worry about the set nodes). These are the three transform nodes for the pieces of the minigun. Select each node, and you'll see the corresponding part highlighted in the perspective view. At the moment, each piece is completely separate and unconnected.

4. Select the housing node, and switch to the Rotate tool (hot key = **e**).

5. Rotate the objects; nothing else is affected. Try translating housing using the Move tool (hot key = **w**); again, nothing else is affected.

6. Use Undo (hot key = **Ctrl/Cmd+z**) a few times until the housing node returns to its original location and orientation.

7. In the Outliner, select the gunBarrels object. Then Ctrl/Cmd+click the housing object, and choose Edit ➤ Parent (hot key = **p**) from the main Maya menu at the top.

Parenting one object to another means that you have made one transform node the child of the second. When an object is a child node, it inherits its position, rotation, scale, and visibility from the parent node. When you have multiple objects selected, the last object selected becomes the parent. In the Outliner, you'll notice that the housing node has a plus sign beside it and the gunBarrels node is not visible. The plus sign indicates that the node has a child node.

8. Click the plus sign next to the housing node to expand this two-node hierarchy. The gunBarrels node is now visible as the child of the housing node.

9. Select the housing node, and try rotating and translating it. The gunBarrels node follows the rotation and translation of the housing node (see Figure 1.11).

FIGURE 1.11
When the gunBarrels node is made a child of the housing object, it inherits changes made to the housing object's transform node.

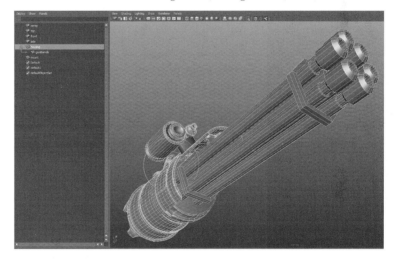

Unlike the situation presented in the "Connecting Nodes with the Node Editor" section earlier in this chapter, the rotation and translation of the gunBarrels object are not locked to the rotation and translation of the housing node; rather, as a child, its rotation, translation, scale, and visibility are all relative to that of its parent.

10. Select the gunBarrels node, and try rotating and translating the object; then rotate and translate the housing node. You'll see the gun barrels maintain their position relative to the housing node. You could create an animation in which the gun barrels rotate on their own z-axis to spin around while firing, at the same time the housing node is animated, rotating on all three axes in order to aim.

11. Press Undo a few times (hot key = **Ctrl/Cmd+z**) until both the housing and gunBarrels objects are back to their original positions.

12. In the Outliner, select the housing node, and MMB-drag it on top of the mount node. This is a way to parent objects quickly in the Outliner.

13. Click the plus signs next to the mount and housing nodes in the Outliner to expand the hierarchy. The lines indicate the organization of the hierarchy; the gunBarrels node is parented to the housing node, which is parented to the mount node.

SHIFT+CLICK TO EXPAND THE HIERARCHY

You can expand an entire hierarchy with one click in the Outliner. Just Shift+click the plus sign for the hierarchy you want to expand.

---

14. Select the mount node, and choose Edit ➤ Duplicate (hot key = **Ctrl/Cmd+d**). This makes a copy of the entire hierarchy. The duplicated mount node is named mount1.

15. Select the mount1 node, and switch to the Move tool (hot key = **w**). Pull on the tool's red arrow to move the duplicate along the x-axis about two units.

16. Select the mount node, and then Ctrl/Cmd+click the mount1 node in the Outliner.

17. Choose Edit ➤ Group (hot key = **Ctrl/Cmd+g**) to group these two nodes under a single parent node.

A group node is a transform node that has no shape node. It's just a location in space used to organize a hierarchy. Like a parent node, its children inherit its rotation, translation, scale, and visibility.

18. Select the group1 node, and Shift+click the plus sign next to it in the Outliner to expand the group and all its children.

19. Double-click the label for the group1 node in the Outliner to rename it; rename the group **guns**.

RENAMING NODES

You'll notice that the duplicate mount node has been renamed mount1 automatically. Nodes on the same level of the hierarchy can't have the same name. The child nodes do have the same name, and this is usually a bad idea. It can confuse Maya when more complex connections are made between nodes. Whenever you encounter this situation, you should take the time to rename the child nodes so that everything in the scene has a unique name.

---

20. Select the mount1 node in the guns hierarchy, and choose Modify ➤ Prefix Hierarchy Names.

21. In the pop-up window, type **right_**. This renames the top node and all its children so that "right_" precedes the name. Do the same with the other mount node, but change the prefix to **left_**.

CERT OBJECTIVE

22. Select the guns group, and choose Modify ➤ Center Pivot. This places the pivot at the center of the group. Try rotating the guns group, and you'll see both guns rotate together (see Figure 1.12).

FIGURE 1.12
The guns group
is rotated as a
single unit.

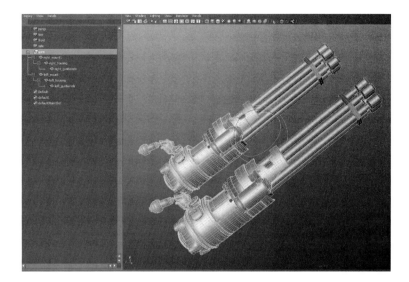

Each member of the hierarchy can have its own animation, so both gun barrels can rotate around their z-axes as they fire, the two housing nodes could be animated to aim in different directions, and the two guns could rotate as one unit, all at the same time. The entire group can be parented to another node that is part of a vehicle.

Displaying Options in the Outliner

There are several options in the Outliner for displaying nodes and their hierarchical arrangements. You can see that the default perspective, top, side, and front cameras are visible as nodes at the top of the Outliner. Also, a number of sets, such as the defaultLightSet, appear at the bottom of the Outliner. These sets are mainly used for organization of data by Maya and are usually not directly edited or altered.

1. In the Display menu of the Outliner, select the Shapes option to display the shape nodes of the objects. The shape nodes appear parented to their respective transform node. You can select either the transform node or the shape node in the Outliner to select the object.

ACCESSING OUTLINER OPTIONS

You can right-click in the Outliner to access the Outliner's display options quickly, rather than use the menu at the top of the Outliner.

---

2. In the Display menu, activate the visibility of attributes by selecting the Attributes (Channels) option.

   Each node now has an expandable list of attributes. Most of the time you may want this option off because it clutters the Outliner and there are other ways to get to these attributes. Ultimately, how you use these options is up to you.

3. Turn off the Attributes display, and turn off the DAG Objects Only option. This allows you to see all the nodes in the scene in the Outliner list, as opposed to just the DAG nodes.

DAG stands for "directed acyclic graph," and DAG objects are those that have both a shape and a transform node. It's not crucial to understand exactly what directed acyclic graph means as long as you understand that it is an arrangement in which a shape node is parented to a transform node. When you turn off DAG Objects Only in the Outliner, you'll see all the nodes in the Maya scene appear. Many of these are default utility nodes required to make Maya function, such as the layerManager node or the dynController1 node. Many other nodes appear when you create a new node or connection. An example of this is a keyframe or an expression node.

When you turn off DAG Objects Only, the list can get quite long. To find a node quickly, type the node's name in the field at the very top of the Outliner. This hides all nodes except the named node. Clearing the field restores the visibility of all nodes in the Outliner (see Figure 1.13).

FIGURE 1.13
The Outliner can display shape nodes as well as other types of nodes in the scene.

Additional viewing options are available in the Show menu, which contains options for displaying only nodes of a certain type. Throughout this book, the Outliner will be used extensively, so you'll have lots of practice working with this panel.

4. In the Display menu of the Outliner, turn the DAG Objects Only option back on. Save the scene as `minGun_v02.ma`.

To see a finished version of the scene, open `miniGun_v02.ma` from the `chapter1\scenes` directory on the book's web page.

SEARCHING FEATURES IN THE OUTLINER

A complex scene in Maya can easily have hundreds of nodes. Just one character often has associated geometry, dozens of animation controls, joints, textures, and so on. Add another character to the scene with its own set of node networks, and the Outliner can become very cluttered very quickly. Establishing an organized naming system for the nodes in your scenes has many benefits, one of which is that you can use the search feature in the Outliner to filter what is displayed, thus making it easy to access the nodes you need. Take the time to name your nodes in such a way as to make searching easy. The following illustrates how the search feature can be used in a complex scene.

Let's say you have a scene with two complex characters, one named Larry and the other named Cecil. Both characters have similar rigs that use NURBS curves to control their animation rigs, and both have geometry, joints, shaders, and so on. When naming the nodes associated with each character, you make sure that all Larry nodes start with the name "larry." So, Larry's skin geometry might be named `larry_SKIN_GEO`, whereas his clothes would use names like `larry_PANTS_GEO`. Using capital letters in this case is purely a personal preference; the important thing is that the name of each node starts with `larry_`. Cecil would use the same convention; his skin geometry would be `cecil_SKIN_GEO`, and his pants would be `cecil_PANTS_GEO`. You end the names using GEO so that you know that this is a geometry node.

The controls for the animation rig use names like `larry_LEFT_HAND_wrist_CTRL1`, `larry_SPINE_CTRL1`, and `larry_NECK_CTRL1`. You get the idea. You can see that each of these nodes belongs to Larry, nodes for the left side of the body are clearly identified, the associated body part is identified, and they end with the letters CTRL. The same goes for Cecil.

Now here's where this type of organization, or something similar, is helpful in the Outliner. At the top of the Outliner is a blank field. To filter the nodes listed in the Outliner, you need to type some text and either precede or follow the text with an asterisk (*). The asterisk tells Maya to show all nodes that use the text before or after the asterisk in the name. So if you want to see all nodes associated with Larry, type **larry***. If you want to see all the control nodes for both Cecil and Larry, type ***CTRL***. In this case, there may be text before and after the CTRL letters, so use an asterisk before and after CTRL. If you want to see the controls associated with Cecil's hands, type **cecil*HAND***, and so on.

The following images show variations on how to search through the Outliner with this method. If nothing appears in the Outliner when you type some text, check to see whether the asterisk is in the right place. To find one specific node, type its full name without the asterisk.

continues

(continued)

The Channel Box

The term *channel* is, for the most part, interchangeable with *attribute*. You can think of a channel as a container that holds the attribute's value. The *Channel Box* is an editor that lists a node's attributes for quick access. The Channel Box displays the node's attributes, which are most frequently keyframed for animation.

The Channel Box is located on the right side of the screen when the view mode at the end of the status bar is set to show the Channel Box/Layer Editor (see Figure 1.14).

FIGURE 1.14

The icon in the upper right of the interface toggles the visibility of the Channel Box/ Layer Editor.

Two tabs on the very right side of the screen allow you to switch quickly between the Channel Box and the Attribute Editor, as shown in Figure 1.15. (The Attribute Editor is discussed in detail later in this chapter.) These tabs are visible when both the Attribute Editor icon and the Channel Box icon are activated on the status bar in the upper-right corner of the interface.

This exercise gives a quick tour of how to work in the Channel Box:

1. Create a new scene in Maya, and create a NURBS sphere on the grid (Create ➤ NURBS Primitives ➤ Sphere). You'll be prompted to draw the sphere on the grid if the Interactive Creation mode is on; if not, the sphere will appear at the center of the grid. Either option is fine.

FIGURE 1.15
The two tabs on
the right side of
the screen allow
you to switch
quickly between
the Channel
Box and the
Attribute Editor.

2. Make sure that the Channel Box is visible on the right side of the screen. To do this,
click the icon at the farthest right of the status bar (shown earlier in Figure 1.14). This is
a toggle to display the Channel Box. Click it until the Channel Box appears, as shown in
Figure 1.16.

FIGURE 1.16
The Channel
Box displays the
channels for
the currently
selected object.

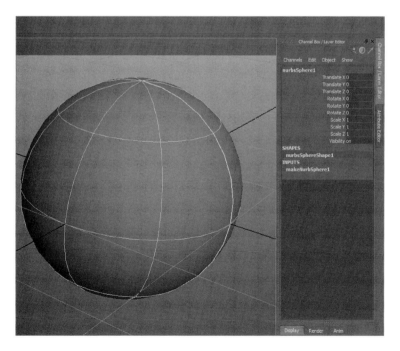

3. The Channel Box will list the currently selected object. Select the sphere, and you'll see nurbsSphere1 appear. The list below it shows the attributes for the nurbsSphere1's transform node.

 The lower half of the Channel Box lists the connections to this node. You'll see the name of the associated shape node under SHAPES, and below this a section for the inputs. In this case, the input is the history node, named makeNurbSphere1, which contains the original settings used to create the sphere. If you delete history on the sphere, these attributes will no longer be accessible.

4. In the upper section of the Channel Box, under nurbsSphere1, try selecting the fields and inputting different values for Translate, Scale, and Rotate. The sphere updates its position, size, and orientation.

5. In the Visibility channel, select the word On in the field, and type **0**. The sphere disappears. Input the value **1**, and it reappears. Visibility is a Boolean, meaning it is either on or off, 1 or 0.

6. Select the Translate X field so that it is highlighted. Shift+click the Rotate Z value, and all the values in between are also selected.

7. Type **0** in the Translate X field while they are selected, and press the Enter key. Doing so sets all the Translate and Rotate values to the same value, places the sphere at the center of the grid, and returns it to its original orientation (see Figure 1.17).

FIGURE 1.17
You can quickly "zero out" the Translate and Rotate channels by Shift+clicking their fields and entering 0.

8. In the makeNurbSphere section under INPUTS, highlight the Start Sweep channel. Enter a value of **90**, and the sphere opens up. If this is hard to see, switch to shaded mode by pressing **5** on the keyboard. You're altering the construction history of the sphere so that it is no longer a closed surface.

9. Select the word Sections so that it is highlighted in blue. MMB-drag back and forth in the viewport. Doing so creates a virtual slider so that you can change the value of the field interactively instead of numerically. This should work for all the channels (at least, most of the time).

10. Set the timeline to frame 1 by clicking on the far left of the time slider where it is labeled 1, and press the **s** hot key. You'll see all the channels turn orange, indicating that they have been keyframed. The **s** hot key keyframes all the available channels.

11. Move the timeline to frame 24, and change some settings both on the transform node (the upper half of the Channel Box) and under makeNurbSphere1 in the INPUTS section.

12. Press the **s** hot key again to set another key. Play the animation, and you'll see the sphere update based on the keyframed changes.

If the animation seems to play too quickly, you need to change the preferences so that playback matches the frame speed of the animation. To do so, choose Windows ➤ Settings/Preferences ➤ Preferences. In the Preferences window, choose Time Slider on the left column and set PlayBack Speed to Real-Time [24 FPS].

The **s** hot key keyframes everything, even those channels you may not need to keyframe. You can use the Channel Box to keyframe specific channels.

13. Rewind the timeline, and choose Edit ➤ Keys ➤ Delete Keys to remove all the keyframes on the sphere.

14. Highlight Translate X and Shift+click Translate Z so that the translation channels are all selected.

15. Right-click these values, and choose Key Selected (see Figure 1.18).

FIGURE 1.18
Right-click the selected channels, and choose Key Selected to keyframe just those specific channels.

16. Move to frame 24, and enter different values in the Translate fields.

17. Shift+click the Translate fields in the Channel Box, right-click, and choose Key Selected. This places a keyframe on just the selected channels—often a cleaner and more efficient way to work because you're placing keyframes only on the channels you need to animate and not on every keyable channel, which is what happens when you use the **s** hot key. Now try playing the animation.

BE THRIFTY WITH KEYFRAMES

Creating extra, unnecessary keys leads to a lot of problems, especially when you start to refine the animation on the Graph Editor (discussed in Chapter 2, "Introduction to Animation." Keyframes also can increase the scene size (the amount of storage space the scene uses on disk). Be cheap with your keyframes, and use the Key Selected feature to keyframe only the channels you need. Avoid using the **s** hot key to create keys on everything.

18. To remove keys, you can highlight the channels, right-click, and choose Break Connections. This removes any inputs to those channels. The values for the current keyframe will remain in the channels.

The channels are color-coded to show what kind of input drives the channel:

◆ Pink indicates a keyframe.

◆ Purple indicates an expression.

◆ Yellow indicates a connection (as in a connection from another node or channel, made in the Connection Editor or Node Editor).

◆ Brown indicates a muted channel.

◆ Gray means the channel is locked.

LOCKING AND MUTING CHANNELS

You can mute a channel by right-clicking it and choosing Mute Selected from the context menu. When you mute a channel, the keyframes on that channel are temporarily disabled; as long as the channel is muted, the animation will not update. This is useful when you want to disable the keyframes in a channel so that you can focus on other aspects of the animation. Locking a channel is another option available when you right-click selected channels in the Channel Box. A locked channel prevents you from adding keyframes to a channel regardless of whether it has been animated. Creating animation is examined further in Chapter 2.

The Channel Box will be explored throughout the book and used frequently, particularly in the chapters concerning animation.

The Attribute Editor

The Attribute Editor is a tabbed panel that gives detailed information and access to a node's attributes. The tabs at the top of the editor allow you to move between the attributes of all the upstream (input) and downstream (output) connected nodes. This exercise gives a brief tour of how to use the Attribute Editor:

1. Create a new scene in Maya. Create a polygon cube on the grid (Create ➤ Polygon Primitives ➤ Cube).

2. Select the cube, and open its Attribute Editor. There are several ways to do this:

◆ Right-click and hold the right mouse button over the cube, and choose pCube1 from the marking menu.

◆ Select the cube, and choose Window ➤ Attribute Editor.

◆ Click the Show/Hide Attribute Editor icon in the upper right of the Maya interface (Figure 1.19).

FIGURE 1.19
The Show/Hide
Attribute Editor
icon resides in
the upper-right
corner of the
Maya interface.

- ◆ Press Ctrl+a on the keyboard. This toggles between Channel Box and Attribute Editor
  if they're docked.

3. With the Attribute Editor open, choose the pCube1 tab at the top (Figure 1.20). The panel
that opens contains the attributes for the cube's transform node, much like the upper section of the Channel Box described in the previous section. It also contains options for setting limits on the transform attributes.

FIGURE 1.20
The Attribute
Editor contains
tabs that allow
you to move
through the con-
nected nodes of
a network.

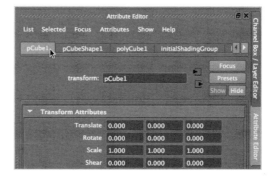

Many of the settings can be accessed through the Attribute Editor's rollout panels. These
are collapsible sections of grouped settings.

4. In the Attribute Editor, on the pCube1 tab, click the triangle next to mental ray. This
reveals mental ray–specific settings related to the cube. Note that there are subsections
under mental ray that are also collapsible.

5. Choose the pCubeShape1 tab at the top of the Attribute Editor. This tab contains settings
related to the shape node. For example, expand the Render Stats section and you'll see a
list of settings that control how the shape will appear in a render.

6. Choose the polyCube1 tab, and you'll see the construction history settings. If you delete
history on the cube, this tab will no longer appear.

7. Expand the Poly Cube History rollout. If you right-click any of the fields, you get a menu
that offers options such as expressions, key setting, or locking, much like the fields in the
Channel Box (Figure 1.21).

FIGURE 1.21
Right-clicking
an attribute field
reveals a menu
with options for
animating the
attribute value.

8. In the Subdivisions Width field, highlight the text and type =. Doing so lets Maya know that you want to add an expression to the field.

CUSTOMIZING THE ATTRIBUTE EDITOR

There are several ways to customize the Attribute Editor. The menu displayed by right-clicking on any field contains the Hide Attribute Control option. Choosing this removes the attribute from view. To display it, choose Show ➤ Show Attributes, and then choose the hidden attribute you want to show. For greater control, you can create an XML-based template file. Maya automatically reads XML files placed in the scripts\AETemplates folder of your Maya install directory. You can then choose the template from the Attribute Editor's menu Show ➤ Set Current View or Show ➤ Set Global View.

---

9. Complete the expression by typing **9*2** after the equals sign (see Figure 1.22); then press the Enter key. Doing so adds an expression to this attribute that makes the Subdivisions Width value equal to 18. Note that the field turns purple and the slider can no longer be moved.

FIGURE 1.22
You can enter
simple math-
ematical expres-
sions directly
into a field in the
Attribute Editor.

Note that a new tab called expression1 is added to the top of the Attribute Editor; this is a new expression node that is now part of the cube's node network.

If the number of connected nodes is too large to fit within the tab listing at the top, you can use the two arrow buttons to the right of the tabs to move back and forth between the tab listings. Likewise, if not all connections are visible, you can use the Go To Input and Go To Output Connection buttons to the right of the field indicating the node name.

The Notes field at the bottom is useful for typing your own notes if you need to keep track of particular settings or leave a message for yourself or other users (see Figure 1.23). You can collapse this section by dragging the bar above it downward, thus making more room for the other settings in the Attribute Editor.

FIGURE 1.23

Messages can be entered in the Notes section at the bottom of the Attribute Editor.

The Attribute Editor is the workhorse panel of Maya. Throughout this book we will use it constantly. Make sure you are comfortable with the core concepts of how to switch between node settings using the tabs as well as how to change the available values.

LOAD ATTRIBUTES

You can use the Load Attributes button at the bottom of the Attribute Editor if the attribute display needs to be refreshed. Maya automatically updates the editor when new attributes are added, but occasionally it misses an update and needs to be refreshed.

Working with Shader Nodes in the Hypershade

The *Hypershade*, as the name suggests, is similar in function to the Hypergraph. It gives a visual display of how nodes in a Maya scene are connected. The Hypershade is mostly concerned with shaders—nodes used to define the color and material properties of renderable objects in a scene. These include materials (also known as shaders), textures, lights, cameras, and shading utilities. However, it is not unusual to use the Hypershade Work Area to make connections between other types of nodes as well. In this exercise, you'll use the Hypershade to connect several types of nodes.

1. Create a new scene in Maya. Create a NURBS cone on the grid. You'll be prompted to draw the cone on the grid if Interactive Creation mode is on; if it is not, the cone will appear at the center of the grid. Either option is fine.

2. Switch to smooth-shaded mode by pressing **6** on the keyboard, or click the Smooth Shade All and Textured icons on the viewport's menu bar (see Figure 1.24).

FIGURE 1.24
The Maya viewport
menu bar allows
you to choose
between shading
modes by toggling
buttons.

3. Open Hypershade by choosing Window ➢ Rendering Editors ➢ Hypershade.

The Hypershade Editor is made up of several frames. On the left side is a list and a visual menu of the nodes you can create in Hypershade. The list is divided into sections for the Maya nodes, mental ray nodes, and a customizable list for your own favorites at the very top. Clicking a category in the list filters the node-creation buttons to the right of the list, which helps to cut down on the amount of time you need to hunt for specific nodes. To add a node to the Favorites list, MMB-drag the node button from the right on top of the Favorites menu. You can also search through the nodes by typing in the field at the very top of the list. For example, typing **mia** in this field filters the node creation buttons so that all the mia (mental images architectural) nodes are displayed (see Figure 1.25).

FIGURE 1.25
The text field at the top
of the Create tab allows
you to filter the list of
buttons. MMB-dragging
a button on top of
the Favorites section
adds the node to the
Favorites.

The right side of the Hypershade contains a visual display of the nodes in the scene at the top and the Work Area at the bottom (see Figure 1.26). The upper section is organized by tabs named Materials, Textures, Utilities, Rendering, Lights, Cameras, Shading Groups, Bake Sets, Projects, and Asset Nodes. If you want to access all the file textures used in the scene, you can choose the Textures tab to see them listed with preview icons.

4. On the left side of the Hypershade, click Surface in the list of Maya nodes. Click the Blinn button to create a new Blinn material.

You can see the new blinn1 material listed on the Materials tab; it also appears in the Work Area.

FIGURE 1.26
The Hypershade organizes render nodes and offers a workspace for constructing render node networks. This image shows an example of a shader network graphed in the Work Area.

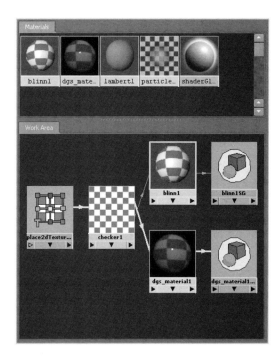

HYPERSHADE TABS

If tabs appear to be missing, you can revert to the default tab layout by choosing Tabs ➤ Revert To Default Tabs, as shown here. This clears the current tabs and replaces them with the default Materials, Textures, Utilities, Rendering, Lights, Cameras, and other default tabs. You can use the Tabs menu to create your own custom tabs and determine which tabs you want visible and in what order.

DEFAULT SCENE MATERIALS

All Maya scenes start with three materials already created: lambert1, particleCloud1, and shaderGlow1. The lambert1 material is the default material applied to all newly created geometry, the particleCloud1 material is a special material reserved for particle-cloud objects, and the shaderGlow1 node sets the glow options for all shaders in the scene.

---

5. Select the blinn1 material in the Work Area and, from the menu at the top of the Hypershade, choose Graph ➤ Input And Output Connections. This displays all the upstream and downstream nodes connected to blinn1. Upstream nodes are nodes that plug into a node and affect its attributes; downstream nodes are ones that are affected by the node.

   The blinn1SG node is a downstream node known as a *shader group*, connected to blinn1. All materials have a shader group node connected to them. This node is a required part of the network that defines how the shader is applied to a surface, and it is often used when creating complex mental ray shader networks and overrides (see Figure 1.27).

FIGURE 1.27
Shaders all have shading group nodes attached, which define how the shader is applied to the geometry.

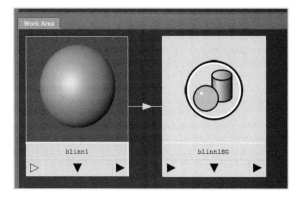

6. In the viewport, select the cone. You can apply the blinn1 material to the cone in three ways:

   ◆ MMB-drag the material icon from the Hypershade on top of the cone in the viewport window.

   ◆ Select the cone, right-click the blinn1 node in the Hypershade, and choose Assign Material To Selection (see Figure 1.28).

   ◆ Right-click the surface in the viewport, and choose Assign New Shader to create a new shader, or choose Assign Existing Material to assign a shader you've already created.

7. In the Work Area of the Hypershade, select the blinn1 node. This opens the Attribute Editor for the Blinn shader if it's not open already. This is where you can adjust the settings that define the look of the material.

FIGURE 1.28
Right-click a shader, and drag upward on the marking menu to choose Assign Material To Selection.

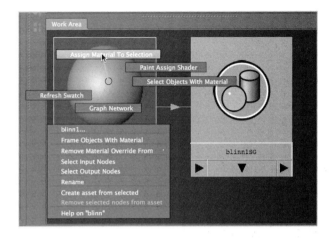

USE THE SHELF BUTTONS TO CREATE A NEW SHADER

You can assign a new material to a surface using the buttons in the rendering shelf at the top of the Maya interface (shown here). If you select an object and click one of these buttons, a new shader is created and assigned to selected objects. If no objects are selected, it just creates a new shader, which you'll find on the Materials tab of the Hypershade.

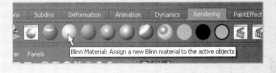

8. In the Attribute Editor for the blinn1 node, rename the material **coneShader** by typing in the field at the top of the editor.

9. Click the checkered box to the right of the Color slider. This opens the Create Render Node window (see Figure 1.29).

10. Select 2D Textures from the list on the left, and click the Grid button on the right side of the panel to create a grid texture; this is applied to the color channel of the cone, and it is visible on the cone in the viewport when textured and smooth-shaded mode is on (hot key = **6**) (see Figure 1.30).

11. Select coneShader in the Work Area of Hypershade, and right-click its icon. Choose Graph Network. You'll see that the coneShader node now has the grid1 texture node as well as the place2dTexture1 node attached (see Figure 1.31).

12. Click the place2dTexture1 node in the Work Area, and its attributes will be displayed in the Attribute Editor.

13. Type **0.5** in the first field next to Coverage and press Enter. This reduces the coverage of the grid texture in U space by one-half.

FIGURE 1.29
Click the checkered box next to the Color slider to open the Create Render Node window.

FIGURE 1.30
The grid texture appears on the cone when the perspective view is set to shaded mode.

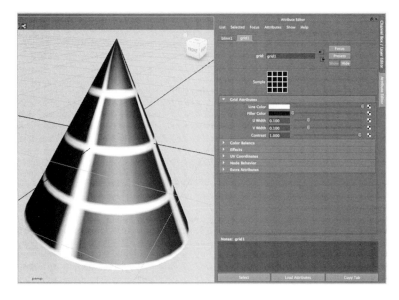

FIGURE 1.31
Applying the grid
texture to the color
channel of the
coneShader adds
two new nodes to
the shader network.
Graph the input and
output connections
to see these nodes in
the Hypershade.

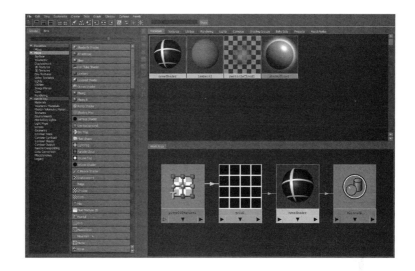

NURBS UV TEXTURE COORDINATES

NURBS surfaces have their U and V texture coordinates based on the parameterization of the surface, unlike polygon meshes, which require defined UV coordinates. You can use the attributes in the place2dTexture1 node to position textures on NURBS surfaces.

14. Select the grid1 node in the Work Area of the Hypershade to open its settings in the Attribute Editor.

15. Expand the Color Balance rollout, and click the color swatch next to Default Color. This opens the Color History. Set the color to **red**.

DEFAULT COLOR

The default color of the texture is the color "behind" the grid texture. Any part of the surface that is not covered by the grid (based on the settings in the place2dTexture1 node) will use the default color.

16. In the left panel of the Hypershade, select 2D Textures in the Maya list, and click the Ramp button to create a ramp node. At the moment, it is not connected to any part of the coneShader network. This is another way to create render nodes in the Hypershade.

NAVIGATING THE HYPERSHADE WORK AREA

You can zoom in or out while in the Work Area of the Hypershade by holding down the Alt button while RMB-dragging; likewise, you can pan by holding the Alt button down while MMB-dragging.

17. Select the grid1 texture to open its settings in the Attribute Editor.

18. In the Work Area of the Hypershade, MMB-drag the ramp texture from the Work Area all the way to the color swatch next to the Filler Color in the grid's Attribute Editor. Hold the MMB while dragging; otherwise, you'll select the ramp texture, and the Attribute Editor will no longer display the grid1 texture attributes (see Figure 1.32). If the Connection Editor pops up as a result of dragging, you can just click Close.

FIGURE 1.32
A texture node can be MMB-dragged from the Hypershade into an attribute slot in the Attribute Editor.

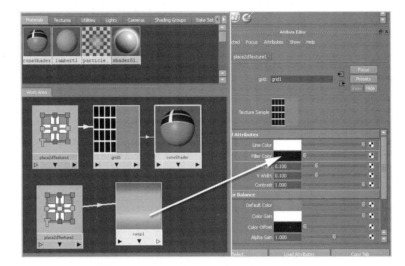

19. Select the coneShader node in the Work Area of the Hypershade, and choose Graph ➤ Input And Output Connections from the Hypershade menu. In the Work Area, you can see that the ramp texture is connected to the grid1 texture. The grid1 texture is connected to the coneShader, and the shader is connected to the blinn1SG node (see Figure 1.33).

FIGURE 1.33
The coneShader network has grown with the addition of new nodes.

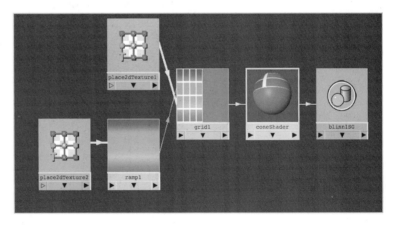

GRAPHING SHADER NETWORKS

You can graph the shader network at any time to refresh the view of the connected nodes in the Work Area. Just right-click the node you want to graph and choose Graph Network, or click the Input And Output Connections button at the top of the Hypershade (shown here). More options for displaying the network are available in the Graph menu at the top of the Hypershade.

20. Select the blinn1SG node, and graph its input and output connections. The cone's shape node appears (if the Bottom Caps option was on in the Creation options for the NURBS cone, you'll see a second shape node for the cone's bottom cap surface). The blinn1SG node is also connected to the render partition and the light linker, which defines the lights used to light the cone (see Figure 1.34).

FIGURE 1.34
The shape nodes for the cone are included in the graph when the input and output connections of the blinn1SG node are graphed.

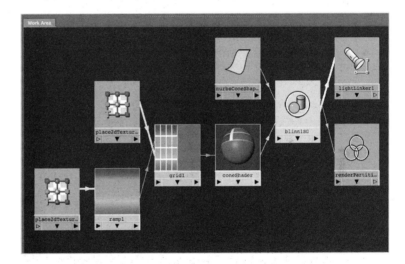

The Hypershade is a powerful and easy-to-use editor. You can build complex networks of nodes quickly, just like rearranging building blocks. You can see how nodes are connected by holding the mouse pointer over the lines that connect the nodes.

The previous sections of this chapter revealed to you the many ways Maya nodes can be displayed, connected, and edited in a Maya scene. Make sure that you are comfortable with the basics of working with the editors described. You will rely on them heavily throughout the book, and by working through the various exercises, you will gain proficiency in using them.

Creating Maya Projects

Organization is the key to creating a successful animation. Whether you are working by yourself or with others in a production pipeline, you'll want to know where to find every file related to a particular project, whether it's a scene file, a texture map, an image sequence, or a particle disk cache. To help you organize all the files you use to create an animation, Maya offers you the option of easily creating a Maya project, which is simply a directory with subfolders where each file type related to your scenes can be stored.

Creating a New Project

Creating a new project is simple. Projects can be created on your computer's primary hard drive, a secondary drive, or a network drive. The scene files used for each chapter in this book are stored in their own project directories at www.sybex.com/go/masteringmaya2015. Maya uses a default project directory when one has not been specified. This is located in your My Documents\maya\projects folder in Windows. As an example, you'll create a project directory structure for the examples used in this chapter.

1. Start a new Maya scene. You'll note that an empty scene is created when you start Maya.

2. Choose File ➤ Project Window.

3. The Project Window dialog box opens. Click the New button to the right of the Current Project field. In the Current Project field, type **Mastering_Maya_Chapter01** (see Figure 1.35).

FIGURE 1.35
The Project Window dialog box lets you set the location of a new project directory and determine its directory structure on your hard drive.

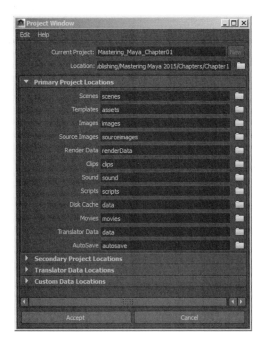

4. To the right of the Location field, click the folder icon to browse your computer. The Select Location window opens and lets you determine where on your computer or network you want the project to be stored, or you can simply type the path to the directory. The project folder can be a subfolder of another folder if you like.

In the Primary Project Locations section, you'll see a large number of labeled fields. The labels indicate the various types of files a Maya scene may or may not use. The fields indicate the path to the subdirectory where these types of files will be located.

When you click the New button as mentioned in step 3, Maya automatically fills in all the fields (see the right side of Figure 1.36).

FIGURE 1.36

Clicking the New button fills in all the fields with the preferred default file structure in Maya (right side of the image). The directory structure is created on the specified drive (left side of the image).

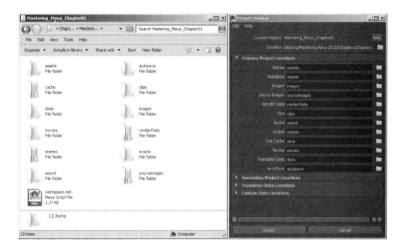

The fields contain the name of the subdirectory relative to the project file. So when you choose to use the default settings, all Maya scene files (files with the .mb or .ma file extension) will be stored in a folder labeled Scenes. The path to that folder will be, in this example, Mastering_Maya_Chapter01\Scenes.

EDITING DEFAULT FILE LOCATIONS

If you decide you want to store the scene files in a different directory, you can type the path to that directory in the field or click the folder icon to the right of the field to set a different folder path.

---

5. Click Accept. Maya will take a few moments to create the project directory and all subfolders on the specified drive.

6. Use your computer's file browser to locate the new project; then expand the folder, and you'll see all the subfolders.

Editing and Changing Projects

You may not need to use every folder Maya creates for you, or you may decide to change where Maya looks for elements such as file textures. If you're working on a number of projects, you may need to switch the current project. All of these options are available in the Maya File menu.

1. To edit the current project, choose File ➢ Project Window. The Project Window dialog box opens with all the paths to the project subdirectories. You can type a new directory path in any one of these fields or click the folder icon to browse your computer's directory. Then click the Accept button. If a folder does not already exist, Maya will create it for you.

RELINKING FILES AFTER CHANGING PROJECT SETTINGS

If you edit the project, Maya will look in the newly specified folders from this point on, but files used prior to editing the project will not be copied or moved. You'll need to move these files using the computer's file browser if you want Maya to find them easily after editing the project.

---

2. To switch projects, you can choose File ➢ Set Project or choose a project listed in the Recent Projects menu.

When working on a project with a number of other animators, you can choose to share the same project, which is a bit risky, or each animator can create their own project directory structure within a shared folder. The latter approach is a little safer because it prevents two people from having the same project open or overwriting each other's work. Later in this book, you'll learn how multiple animators can share parts of the scene using file references.

It is possible to work on a scene file outside the current project. This happens usually when you forget to set the project using the File ➢ Set Project option. Make a habit of setting the current project each time you start to work on a scene; otherwise, linked files such as textures, dynamic caches, and file references can become broken, causing the scene to behave unpredictably (which is a nice way of saying that the scene will fall apart and possibly crash Maya).

While working with the project files for this book, you'll want to copy the entire project to your local drive and then use the Project Window dialog box to choose the corresponding chapter project directory as the current project. This way, all the linked files in the scenes should behave correctly and the exercises will function.

OVERRIDING PROJECT SETTINGS

You can choose to override a project setting for an individual scene element. For instance, by default Maya looks to the sourceimages directory for file textures. However, when you create a file texture node, you can use the Browse button to reference a file anywhere on your machine or the network. This is usually not a great idea; it defeats the purpose of organizing the files in the first place and can easily lead to broken links between the scene and the texture file. It's a better idea to move all file textures used in the scene to the sourceimages directory or whatever directory is specified in your project settings.

The Bottom Line

Understand transform and shape nodes.   DAG nodes have both a transform node and a shape node. The transform node tells where an object is located; the shape node describes how it is made. Nodes can be parented to each other to form a hierarchy.

> **Master It**   Arrange the nodes in the `miniGun_v03.ma` file in a hierarchical structure so that the barrels of the guns can rotate on their z-axis, the guns can be aimed independently, and the guns rotate with the turret.

Create a project.   Creating a project directory structure keeps Maya scene files and connected external files organized to ensure the animation project is efficient.

> **Master It**   Create a new project named Test, but make sure the project has only the scene, source images, and data subfolders.

Chapter 2

Introduction to Animation

Computer animation has revolutionized the way stories are told. Whether the animation is used for entertainment, to advertise a product, or to demonstrate a complex scientific principle, the ability to construct virtual three-dimensional objects and then manipulate their movements over time has given the artist an unprecedented amount of power. Creative Autodesk® Maya® users will find that there are few limits to what they can accomplish through animation.

Animation in Maya is accomplished through a wide variety of tools and techniques. The goal of this chapter is to show you how to use the tools in Maya to animate the attributes of various nodes. Gaining an understanding of how you can solve problems in Maya is essential to telling your story through computer animation.

In this chapter, you will learn to:

- ◆ Use inverse kinematics

- ◆ Animate with keyframes

- ◆ Use the Graph Editor

- ◆ Preview animations with a playblast

- ◆ Animate with motion paths

- ◆ Use animation layers

Using Joints and Constraints

Most of this chapter is devoted to exercises that animate a simple mechanical bug model. Animation and rigging are closely related skills. *Rigging* is the process where controls are created to allow you to manipulate the three-dimensional objects in order to generate animation. Even if you don't intend to do much of your own rigging, you'll have an easier time understanding how to animate if you know what goes into creating a rig. Chapter 5, "Rigging and Muscle Systems," delves into more advanced rigging concepts. In this chapter, you'll learn basic tools and techniques for rigging to get you started.

Joint Basics

A *joint* is the basic animation control. It is essentially a point in space connected by a virtual bone, symbolized by an elongated pyramid. The geometry is bound to the joints in a process known as *skinning*. The skinned geometry is then deformed when the joints are moved to create such effects as the bend in an elbow or a knee.

When you are rigging mechanical objects and robots, it's not always necessary to use joints; you can parent the parts of the object together in an organized fashion and then set keyframes directly on the geometry. (This is demonstrated in Chapter 1, "Working in Autodesk Maya.") However, because of the built-in hierarchy of joints as well as the many animation controls available, using joints can make rigging and animating mechanical objects easier, even if you don't intend to bind or skin the geometry so that it is deformed by the joints.

You create joints using the Joint tool (from the Animation menu set, choose Skeleton ➤ Joint Tool). A joint is represented by a simple wire sphere. As noted before, when one joint is connected to another, the space between the two joints is bridged with a wireframe pyramid shape referred to as a *bone*. The broad end of the bone is placed next to the parent joint, and the pointed end of the bone is pointed toward the child joint (see Figure 2.1).

FIGURE 2.1
Two joints are placed on the grid with a bone between them.

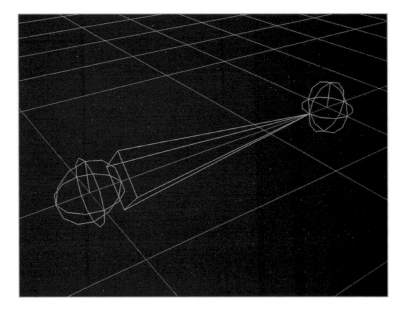

Joints are most often animated by rotating the parent joint or using *inverse kinematics*, which orients the joints based on the position of a goal called an *end effector*. This topic is discussed later in this chapter, in the section "Inverse Kinematics." Joints can also be animated by placing keyframes on Translate or Scale channels. This approach, however, is slightly less common.

Joints are usually placed in a hierarchical relationship known as a *joint chain*. Joint chains can have many branches and numerous controls, depending on the complexity of the model. A series of joint chains is known as a *skeleton*.

A joint is a type of deformer that typically influences the shape of nearby components depending on how the components of the geometry are bound, or skinned, to the joints. Since the bug in these examples is mechanical, the joints do not need to deform the geometry of the model. You can simply parent the pieces of the leg geometry to the individual joints. Skinning geometry to joints is explored further in Chapter 5.

Point Constraints

A *point constraint* uses the world space position of one object to control the world space position of another object. World space coordinates tell exactly where an object is in relation to the rest of the scene. This is different from object space coordinates, which are relative to the object's initial position.

For instance, if you move an object on the grid, the Translate channels in the Channel Box indicate where an object is in object space. If you freeze the transformations on an object (Modify ➤ Freeze Transformations) after moving the object, its Translate (and Rotate) channels become 0 in X, Y, and Z (Scale channels become 1 in X, Y, and Z), and its current position is now its starting position in object space.

If you create a joint in a scene and then reposition it and freeze transformations, you'll notice that the Rotate channels all become 0 for its new orientation; however, the Translate channels are not affected by freeze transformations. If you want to place a joint exactly at the position of another object, you can't rely on the object's Translate channels as an accurate description of the object's location in world space. One way to get around this is to use a point constraint to position the joint according to the object's world space coordinates.

Aim Constraints

An *aim constraint* constrains the orientation of an object relative to the position of one or more other objects. The following steps show you how to add aim constraints and use them to control parts of a mechanical bug:

1. Open the `mechBugRig_v01.ma` scene from the `chapter2\scenes` directory at the book's web page (`www.sybex.com/go/masteringmaya2015`).

2. Turn on the display layer for BODY; turn off the LEGS layer so that the legs are hidden and the body is displayed.

3. Create a locator (Create ➤ Locator), and name it **eyeAimLoc**.

4. Set eyeAimLoc's Translate X, Y, and Z channels to **0**, **0**, and **2**, respectively.

5. In the Outliner, expand the mechanicalBug ➤ Bug ➤ bugBody group.

6. MMB-drag eyeAimLoc into the bugBody group under mechanicalBug ➤ Bug.

7. Select eyeAimLoc, and choose Modify ➤ Freeze Transformations so that the Translate channels become 0, 0, and 0.

8. Expand the frontBody group, the head group, and the face group.

9. Select eyeAimLoc, and Ctrl/Cmd+click the eyeBase group (see Figure 2.2).

10. From the Animation menu set, choose Constrain ➤ Aim Options.

11. In the Aim Constraint Options dialog box, choose Edit ➤ Reset Settings to return the settings to the default.

12. Set the Aim Vector fields to **0**, **0**, and **1** so that the aim vector is set to the z-axis (see Figure 2.3).

FIGURE 2.2
Select the eyeAim-
Loc locator and the
eyeBase object in
the Outliner.

FIGURE 2.3
The Aim Constraint
Options window

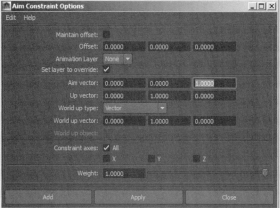

13. Click Apply to create the constraint.

14. Move the locator around in the scene, and you'll see that the eyes follow it (see Figure 2.4). Because the locator is parented to the bugBody, when you animate the bug, the locator will move with it.

FIGURE 2.4
The eyes follow
the position of the
eyeAimLoc locator.

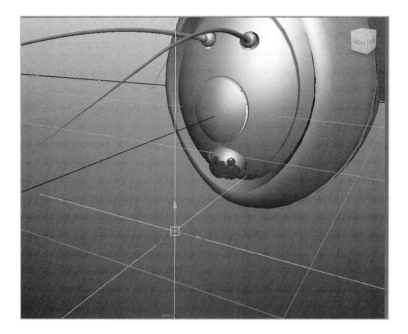

FIGURE 2.4
The eyes follow
the position of the
eyeAimLoc locator.

15. Create two new locators named **leftAntennaAimLoc** and **rightAntennaAimLoc**.

16. Set leftAntennaAimLoc's Translate X, Y, and Z to **1**, **0**, and **3**, respectively, and set right-AntennaAimLoc's Translate X, Y, and Z to **-1**, **0**, and **3** likewise.

17. Freeze transformations for both locators.

18. Shift+click both locators, and group them together. Name the group **antennaAim**. Leave the pivot point for the group at the center of the grid.

19. In the Outliner, MMB-drag antennaAim into the bugBody group.

20. Expand the antennaAim group, and make sure the face group is expanded as well (in the bugBody/frontBody/head group).

21. Use an Aim constraint tool to constrain the leftAntenna to the leftAntennaAimLoc locator and the rightAntenna to the rightAntennaAimLoc locator.

When you move each antennaAimLoc locator, the antennae follow; when you rotate the antennaAim group, the locators move and the antennae follow. This gives you a way to animate the antennae separately and together (see Figure 2.5).

22. Save the scene as `mechBugRig_v02.ma`.

To see a version of the scene up to this point, open the `mechBugRig_v02.ma` scene from the `chapter2\scenes` directory at the book's web page.

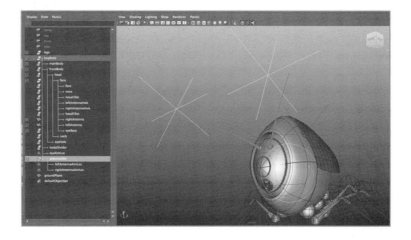

Inverse Kinematics

Kinematics is the study of the motion of objects. This is related to, but distinguished from, dynamics in that kinematics studies only the way in which objects move and not the cause of the objects' motion. In 3D computer graphics, the term *kinematics* describes how joints can be moved to animate objects and characters. There are two main types of kinematics: forward kinematics and inverse kinematics.

The term *forward kinematics* refers to a situation in which each joint in the chain inherits the motion of its parent joint. Thus if you have four joints in a chain, when you rotate the root, the three child joints move based on the rotation of the root. When you rotate the second joint, the third and fourth joints inherit the motion of the second (see Figure 2.6).

FIGURE 2.6
When using for-
ward kinematics,
each joint inherits
the rotation of its
parent.

Forward kinematics can be useful in many situations; for instance, they are often used for basic arm animation for characters. However, they can be tedious and difficult to work with for other types of animation, particularly when you are animating the legs of a character walking or jumping. Constant adjustments have to be made to ensure that, as the root joints are animated, the limbs of the character do not penetrate the floor or slide during a walk cycle.

Inverse kinematics (IK) cause the joints in a chain to orient themselves based on the position of a goal known as the *end effector* (see Figure 2.7). Inverse kinematics can be a more intuitive technique than forward kinematics in many situations. When used on legs, the Sticky option for inverse kinematics can prevent joints from penetrating the floor or sliding during a walk cycle.

When animating an IK chain, you can simply change the position of the end effector using the IK Handle tool, and all the joints in the chain will orient themselves based on the position of the end effector. The end effector itself is positioned using the IK Handle; the end effector is not actually visible or selectable in the viewport (it can be selected in the Hypergraph window).

FIGURE 2.7
Inverse kinematics cause the joints in a chain to rotate based on the position of a goal.

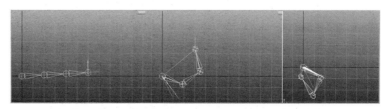

There are controls for blending between forward and inverse kinematics known as FK/IK Blend. You can switch between forward and inverse kinematics and even blend between the two. This topic is covered in more detail in Chapter 5.

The kinematic controls work very well for many standard situations. Most professional riggers prefer to create their own custom controls and solutions. Creating custom controls is discussed in Chapter 5. In this section, a basic, simple IK technique is used on the legs of the mechanical bug. This technique makes animating the legs easier and more intuitive because you only need to worry about the position of a single goal when animating all the parts of one of the legs.

IK Handle Tool

CERT OBJECTIVE

In this section, you'll add inverse kinematics to each of the legs on the mechanical bug:

1. Continue with the scene from the previous section, or open the `mechBugRig_v02.ma` scene from the `chapter2\scenes` directory at the book's web page.

2. In the Layer Editor, turn off Visibility for the body layer.

3. From the Animation menu set, choose Skeleton ➤ IK Handle Tool options.

4. In the Tool Settings dialog box, set the Current Solver option to ikSCsolver. This is the Single Chain solver that works well for simple joint chains, such as the legs in this bug.

   The other option is the Rotate Plane solver (ikRPsolver). This solver has extra controls that can be used to solve joint-flipping problems, which can occur with more complex joint arrangements. If you create an IK Handle using the ikSCsolver and your joints behave unpredictably, try switching to the ikRPsolver. (You can do this after creating the handle using the menu options in the IK Handle's Attribute Editor.) The various types of IK solvers are discussed in Chapter 5, "Rigging and Muscle Systems."

   In general, when adding inverse kinematics to a joint chain using the IK Handle tool, you don't want the joints to be aligned in a straight line. There should be at least a small bend in the joint chain. This helps the solver figure out how the joints should bend as they attempt to rotate based on the position of the end effector. It's also a good idea to freeze transformations on the joints so that their X-, Y-, and Z-rotation channels are set to 0 before adding the IK Handle (in the `mechBug_v03.ma` scene, this has already been done).

5. Turn on Solver Enable, and turn off Snap Enable.

Snap Enable causes the IK Handle to snap back to the position of the end joint when you release it. You'll create a custom handle using a curve, so this option should be off.

6. Turn on Sticky.

Sticky keeps the IK Handle's position constant as you pose the rest of the skeleton. This option is very useful for keeping feet from moving through the floor when animating the other parts of the skeleton (see Figure 2.8).

FIGURE 2.8
The settings for the IK Handle tool

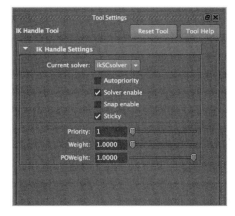

7. The other settings can be left at their defaults. With the IK Handle tool activated, click the frontLeftLegJoint (the joint at the root of the front left leg); then click the joint at the end of the frontLeftLeg chain. The IK Handle appears at the end of the joint chain (see Figure 2.9).

FIGURE 2.9
The IK Handle tool creates a handle and adds the IK solver for the front left leg.

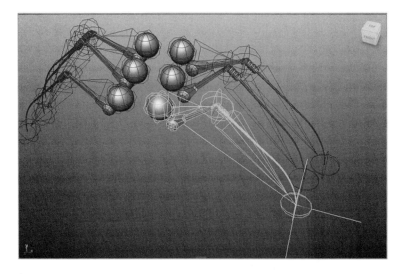

8. Try moving the IK Handle; you'll see the rest of the joint rotate based on the position of the handle.

9. Click Undo until the IK Handle returns to its original location.

It's usually a good idea to use a curve or another easily selectable object as a control for the IK Handle. This makes it easy to select the handle directly in the scene without having to hunt around in the Outliner.

10. Create a NURBS circle with Interactive Creation turned off (Create ➤ NURBS Primitives ➤ Circle).

11. In the Channel Box for the NURBS circle, expand the makeNurbCircle 1 section under INPUTS. This gives you access to the shape node settings for the circle. Set the radius to **0.4**.

12. Position the circle at the same location of the IK Handle by snapping it in place.

13. Select the nurbsCircle1, and rename it **frontLeftFootCtrl**.

14. Choose Modify ➤ Freeze Transformations so that the current position of the curve becomes its home position.

15. Select the frontLeftFootCtrl curve, and Ctrl/Cmd/Shift+click the ikHandle1.

16. Create a point constraint so that the handle is constrained to the frontLeftFoot circle (Constrain ➤ Point).

17. You can turn off visibility of the ikHandle1 object. To move the leg, select the frontLeftLegCtrl circle and move it around. To reset its position, set its Translate X, Y, and Z channels to **0**.

18. Repeat steps 2 through 17 to create controls for the other five legs. (The options for the IK Handle tool should already be stored, so you can just activate the tool and use it to add IK to the other legs.)

19. When you have finished making the controls for the other legs, select the control circles and group them. Name the group **legsControlGroup**.

20. Select the legsControlGroup group, and choose Modify ➤ Center Pivot. This places the pivot of the group at the center of the controls.

21. Make another NURBS circle; name the circle **legsCtrl**.

22. Position the circle at the same location of the legsControlGroup's pivot.

23. Freeze transformations on the legsCtrl.

24. Select the legsCtrl circle, and Ctrl/Cmd/Shift+click the legsControlGroup.

25. Choose Constrain ➤ Parent Options.

26. In the Parent Constraint Options dialog box, make sure Maintain Offset is on, and both Translate and Rotate are set to All.

27. Click Apply to create the constraint. The Parent constraint constrains both the translation and the rotation of one object to another.

Now you have a selectable control for moving all the legs as well as each individual leg. This will mean less time hunting around in the Outliner.

COLOR-CODING CONTROLS

You can create different colors for the NURBS curve you use as a control. To do so, open the Attribute Editor for the curve, and expand the Object Display rollout and then the Drawing Overrides rollout. Click Enable Overrides, and use the Color slider to choose a new color for the circles. This helps them stand out in the scene.

---

28. Finally, you can straighten up the Outliner by grouping the IK Handles. Name the group **feetIKHandles**.

29. Group the legs and bugBody together, and name this group **bug**.

30. Save the scene as `mechBugRig_v03.ma`.

To see a version of the scene up to this point, open the `mechBugRig_v03.ma` scene from the `chapter2\scenes` directory at the book's web page.

Creating a Master Control

To finish the rig, you can create a selectable control to animate the position and the rotation of the bugBody and then group all the parts of the bug together so that it can be moved easily or scaled in the scene.

1. Continue with the scene from the previous section, or open the `mechBugRig_v03.ma` scene from the `chapter2\scenes` directory at the book's web page.

2. Create a new display layer named **controls**.

3. Turn off the visibility of the legs and body display layers.

4. Select the NURBS circles, and add them to the controls layer.

5. Turn off the visibility of the controls layer so that the scene is blank.

6. Turn on the visibility of the grid, and turn on Snap To Grids.

7. Choose Create ➢ CV Curve Tool Options. Set Curve Degree to 1 Linear.

8. Switch to the top view, and use the curve to draw a shape like the one in Figure 2.10. The shape should be a cross with an arrowhead at each end.

9. Press Enter to complete the curve.

10. Choose Modify ➢ Center Pivot, and name the curve **bodyCtrl**.

11. Scale the bodyCtrl curve in X, Y, and Z to **0.35**.

FIGURE 2.10
Create a cross with an arrowhead at each end using a linear CV curve.

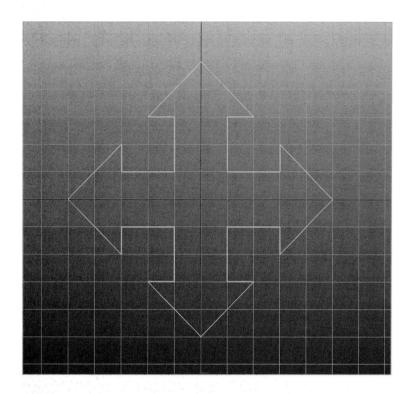

12. Freeze transformations on the curve.

Next you want to move the curve above the body so that you can easily select it. This curve controls the translation and rotation of the bugBody. However, you want to keep the pivot point of the control at the center of the bugBody. Since you snapped the curve to the center of the bugBody, the pivot point of the curve is at the same position as the bugBody. So, how do you move the curve without moving the pivot point? Simple—you move all of the CVs of the curve above the bugBody. This method moves the curve without changing its pivot point.

13. Select the bodyCtrl curve, and switch to CV Selection mode (right-click the curve and choose Control Vertex).

14. Drag a selection marquee over all the CVs of the curve.

15. Turn the visibility of the body back on. Using the perspective view, switch to the Move tool and drag up on the y-axis to position the CVs of the curve above the body. Since the pivot point has not changed, it doesn't matter how high you place the curve above the bug; it just has to be easily selectable (see Figure 2.11).

16. Select the bodyCtrl curve in the Outliner, and Ctrl/Cmd+click the bug group.

FIGURE 2.11
Move the CVs of the bodyCtrl curve above the bugBody; the pivot point of the curve remains at the center of the bugBody.

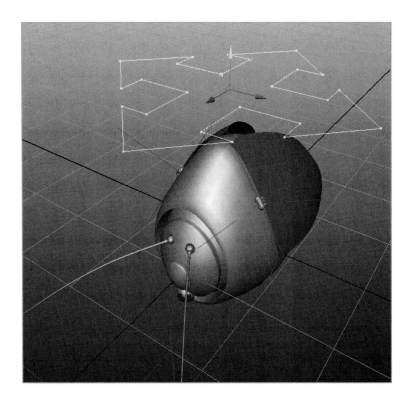

17. Choose Constrain ➤ Parent Options. In the Parent Constraint Options dialog box, make sure Maintain Offset is selected and Translate and Rotate are set to All. Create the constraint.

    The parent constraint constrains both the translation and rotation of one object to another object.

18. Turn on the LEGS layer.

19. Select the bodyCtrl curve, and try moving and rotating it. The legs stay on the ground (within a certain range).

    At this point, you should have a nice set of simple controls for both the body and the legs of the bug. All this work will make animating the bug a much more pleasant experience.

20. Finally, select all of the nodes except the ground plane and cameras. Group them together. Name the group **mechanicalBug**.

21. Add the bodyCtrl curve and the three locators for the eyes and antenna controls to the controls layer.

22. Save the scene as **mechBugRig_v04.ma**.

To see a version of the scene up to this point, open the `mechBugRig_v04.ma` scene from the `chapter2\scenes` directory at the book's web page (Figure 2.12).

FIGURE 2.12
The completed bug
rig is ready for
animation.

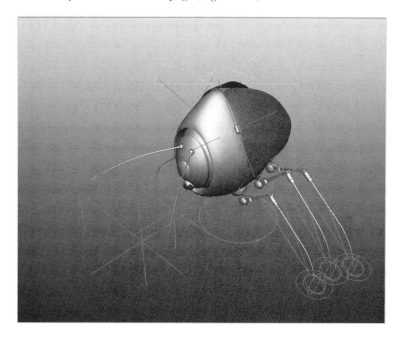

One last control you can add to the bug is a selectable rotational control for the antennaAim group. Use the same techniques used to create the bodyCtrl curve. The `mechBug_v01.ma` scene has an example of this control.

Keyframe Animation

The simplest way to animate an object in Maya is to use keyframes. A *keyframe* records the value of an attribute at a point in time on the timeline. When two keyframes are set for an attribute at different points in time, Maya interpolates the value between the two keyframes on the time-line, and the result is an animation.

Keyframes can be set on almost any attribute in Maya. You can use keyframes to animate an object's position, the color of the shader applied to the object, the visibility of the object, whether the object becomes dynamic, and so on.

Now that you have a rig for the mechanical bug that can be animated, you can get to work bringing it to life.

Creating Keyframes

In this exercise, you'll see the various ways you can set and manipulate keyframes in the Maya interface.

The mechanical bug in this scene has been rigged using the techniques discussed in the first part of the chapter. The major difference is that a circle has been added between the two antenna controls that you can select and animate to control both antennae at the same time.

The controls are color-coded so that they are more organized visually. The visibility of the joints is turned off in the Show menu of the perspective view; however, they are still present in the scene.

FRAME RATE

When you begin an animation, it's always a good idea to set the frame rate in the Maya preferences. The default frame rate is 24 frames per second, which is standard for film. To change the frame rate, choose Window ➤ Settings/Preferences ➤ Preferences. In the Preferences window, select Settings from the list of Categories, and then choose Frame Rate from the Time drop-down list.

Keyframes can be placed on the individual channels of an object using the Channel Box. It's usually a good idea to keyframe on the channels that need to be animated rather than all of the channels and attributes of an object. To keyframe individual channels, follow these steps:

1. Open the mechBug_v01.ma scene in the chapter2\scenes directory at the book's web page.

2. In the perspective view, select the blue bodyCtrl curve above the bug (the curve that looks like a cross with an arrowhead on each end).

3. Move the current frame in the timeline to frame 20 by clicking and dragging the timeline marker until the marker is at frame 20. Alternatively, type **20** in the box to the far right of the timeline.

4. With the bodyCtrl selected, highlight the Translate Y channel in the Channel Box by clicking it; then right-click and choose Key Selected from the context menu (see Figure 2.13).

FIGURE 2.13
Set a keyframe on the Translate Y channel of the bodyCtrl.

5. Set the timeline to frame 48.

6. Use the Move tool to pull the bodyCtrl curve up to about two units, and set another keyframe on the Translate Y channel. The keys are represented on the timeline by a thin red vertical line (see Figure 2.14).

FIGURE 2.14
Keyframes are represented on the timeline by a thin red vertical line.

7. Rewind and play the animation. You'll see the bug start moving upward on frame 20 and stop on frame 48.

For the most part, setting keyframes is pretty straightforward. If you want to set a keyframe on all the Translate channels at the same time, the hot key is **Shift+w**. To set a keyframe on all Rotate channels at once, use **Shift+e**. To set a keyframe on all the Scale channels at once, use **Shift+r**.

PLAYBACK SPEED

You can change the playback speed of the animation in Maya in the timeline Preferences window. (You can also access these options quickly by right-clicking the timeline and choosing a playback-speed option from the context menu.) Open the options by choosing Window ➤ Settings/ Preferences ➤ Preferences. Choose Time Slider from the list of categories. The Playback Speed menu allows you to choose the playback speed.

You can choose Play Every Frame, Real-Time (24 frames per second), Half (12 frames per second), or Twice (48 frames per second), or you can set a custom playback speed. Generally, the most useful speeds are Play Every Frame and Real-Time. If there are dynamics in the scene (such as particles, nCloth, rigid bodies, and so on), set this option to Play Every Frame so that the dynamics calculate correctly. You can set the Max Playback Speed as well so that the animation speed cannot exceed a certain rate. Setting Max Playback Speed to Free means the animation will play back as fast as your processor allows, which can be faster than the final rendered animation.

Auto Keyframe

The Auto Keyframe feature automatically places keyframes on an object when a change is made to one of its attributes. For Auto Keyframe to work, the attribute must already have an existing keyframe. To turn Auto Keyframe on, click the key icon to the right of the timeline. This exercise shows you how to use Auto Keyframe:

1. On the timeline for the mechBug_v01.ma scene, set the current frame to **20**.

An easy way to do this is to use the Step Back One Frame or Step Forward One Frame button to the right of the timeline. The hot keys for moving back and forth one key are **Alt/Option+,** (comma) and **Alt/Option+.** (period).

2. Shift+click all six of the small purple leg-control circles below the bug's feet (see Figure 2.15).

FIGURE 2.15
Select the leg-control circles.

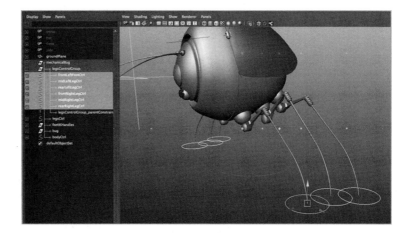

3. With the control circles selected, press **Shift+w** to place a keyframe on the Translate channels for all the selected curves.

4. Click the Key icon to the far right of the timeline to turn on Auto Keyframe.

5. Set the timeline to frame **40**.

6. Select each of the circles, and move them in toward the center (see Figure 2.16).

7. When you play the animation, you'll see that the legs move inward without you having to set a keyframe in the Channel Box.

8. Save the scene as `mechBug_v02.ma`.

To see a version of the scene up to this point, open the `mechBug_v02.ma` scene from the `chapter2\scenes` directory at the book's web page.

HANDLE WITH CARE

Using Auto Keyframe is a matter of personal preference. You can easily set unwanted keys on an object by mistake when using this feature, so remember to use it with caution.

Moving and Scaling Keyframes on the Timeline

CERT
OBJECTIVE

You can reposition keys on the timeline interactively by selecting the key markers and sliding them back and forth:

1. Continue with the scene from the previous section, or open the `mechBug_v02.ma` scene from the `chapter2\scenes` directory at the book's web page.

FIGURE 2.16
Move the leg-
control circles in
toward the center of
the bug.

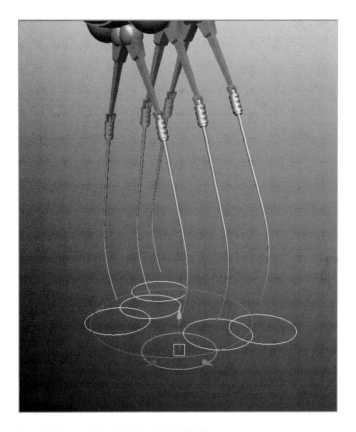

2. In the Perspective window, select the blue bodyCtrl curve.

3. Hold down the Shift key, and drag a selection directly on the timeline. You'll see a red area appear as you drag. Keep dragging this area so that it covers both keyframes set on the bodyCtrl curve (see Figure 2.17).

FIGURE 2.17
Hold down the Shift
key and drag the
timeline to select a
range of keys.

4. To move the keys forward or backward in time, drag the two arrows at the center of the selection. Drag these arrows to move the keys so that the first key is on frame 10.

   To scale the keys, drag one of the arrows on either side of the selection. The other end of the selection acts as the pivot for the scaling operation; you may need to reposition the keys on the timeline again after scaling.

5. Scale the keys down by dragging the arrow on the right end of the selection toward the left.

6. After scaling the keys, drag the arrows at the center to reposition the keys so that the animation starts on frame 10.

7. Save the scene as `mechBug_v03.ma`.

SNAP KEYS

As you scale and move keys, you'll notice that a keyframe can be positioned on the fraction of a key. In other words, a key might end up on frame 26.68. You can fix this by choosing Edit ➤ Keys ➤ Snap Keys Options. In the Snap Keys Options dialog box, set the value for Snap Times To A Multiple Of to **1** and set Snap to Times. You can apply this to selected objects—or all objects, selected channels, or all channels—and define the time range. You can also right-click selected keyframes on the timeline and choose Snap. This automatically snaps keyframes to the nearest integer value.

You can move an individual key by Shift+clicking the key marker on the timeline and then dragging the arrows to move the key.

Repositioning and scaling keys directly on the timeline is usually good for simple changes. To make more sophisticated edits to the animation, you can use the Graph Editor discussed later in the chapter, in the section, "Additional Editing Tools."

When you play the animation, you'll see that the bug jumps up fairly quickly and much sooner than before. You'll also notice that the animation of the legs has not changed.

Spend a few minutes practicing these techniques on each of the legs objects. Changes made to the position of the keyframes affect selected objects. You can edit each legsCtrl circle separately or all of them at the same time.

To see a version of the scene up to this point, open the `mechBug_v03.ma` scene from the `chapter2\scenes` directory at the book's web page.

Copy, Paste, and Cut Keyframes

There are a number of ways you can quickly copy, paste, and cut keyframes on the timeline and in the Channel Box:

1. Continue with the scene from the previous section, or open the `mechBug_v03.ma` scene from the `chapter2\scenes` directory at the book's web page.

2. Select the bodyCtrl curve in the perspective view.

3. On the timeline, Shift-drag a selection over both of the keyframes.

4. Right-click the selection, and choose Copy (see Figure 2.18).

5. Deselect the keys by clicking the timeline, move to frame 70, right-click the timeline, and choose Paste ➤ Paste.

The keys for the Translate Y channel are pasted on the timeline at frame 70. If you play the animation, you'll see that the bug jumps up, moves back down, and then jumps up again.

Other options include the following:

Paste Connect Pastes the copied key with an offset starting at the value of the previous key

Cut   Removes the keyframes from the timeline but copies their values to the clipboard so that they can be pasted anywhere on the timeline

Delete   Removes the keys

Delete FBIK   Deletes the Full Body IK keys

You can copy and paste keys from two different channels by using the options in the Channel Box.

FIGURE 2.18
You can copy key-
frames directly
onto the timeline.

6. Select the bodyCtrl curve in the perspective view.

7. In the Channel Box, right-click the Translate Y channel.

8. Choose Copy Selected (see Figure 2.19).

FIGURE 2.19
You can copy key-
frames using the
menu options in the
Channel Box.

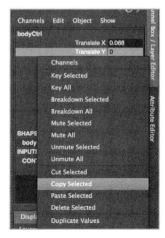

9. Highlight the Translate Z channel, right-click, and choose Paste Selected.

This pastes the values (including keyframes) copied from the Translate Y channel to the Translate Z channel. The starting point of the pasted keyframes is based on the current time in the timeline. When you play the animation, the bug moves forward as it moves up. The forward motion will be offset (in time) depending on the current frame in the timeline.

You can also cut and delete keyframes in the Channel Box. The Duplicate keyframe operation allows you to copy keyframes from one object to another:

1. Create a NURBS sphere, and set its Translate X to **5**.

2. Shift+click the bodyCtrl curve.

3. Right-click the Translate Y channel, and choose Duplicate Values.

   This connects the keyframes on the Translate Y channel of the bodyCtrl curve to the NURBS sphere. If you change the values of these keys, both the bodyCtrl curve and the sphere will reflect the changes made to the keys.

When duplicating keyframes, the order in which you select the objects is important. Select the object you want to use as the source of the duplicate keyframes last. If you graph the objects on the Hypergraph, you'll see that the same keyframe nodes are attached to both objects.

The Graph Editor

The timeline and the Channel Box offer a few basic controls for creating and editing keyframes. However, when you're refining an animation, the controls in the Graph Editor offer greater flexibility as well as visual feedback on the interpolation between keyframes. To open the Graph Editor, choose Window ➢ Animation Editors ➢ Graph Editor. You can also set a viewport to the Graph Editor view.

The Graph Editor can be synchronized to the Channel Box. When in sync, selecting an attribute from the Channel Box also selects it in the Graph Editor. You can also synchronize the timeline with the Channel Box, limiting the displayed keyframes to your selection. Turning both of these options on allows you to manipulate keys easily using all three tools. These features can be toggled through the Channel Box under the Channels menu.

THE GRAPH EDITOR AXES

The Graph Editor is a two-dimensional display of the animation in a scene (shown here). The Graph Editor has two axes: x and y. The x-, or horizontal, axis typically displays the time of the scene in frames. As you move from left to right on the graph, time moves forward. Moving from right to left means going backward. It is possible to go into negative keyframe values if you create keys to the left of the zero marker.

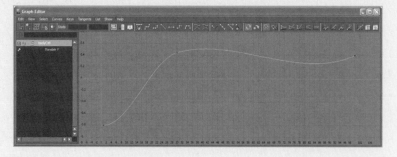

The y-, or vertical, axis displays the values of the keys in units for translation and scale and in degrees (or radians, depending on the setting in the rotation settings in the preferences) for rotation. The higher you go on the y-axis, the higher the value of the key. Of course, anything below the zero line indicates negative values.

Animation Curves

CERT
OBJECTIVE

Animation curves visually describe how the values between two keyframes are interpolated over time. A keyframe is represented by a point on the curve. The portion of the curve on the graph to the left of a keyframe represents the animation before the key, and the line and the portion on the right represent the animation after the key. The keys themselves have handles that can be used to fine-tune the shape of the curve and thus the behavior of the animation both before and after the key. The shape of the curve to the left of the key is known as the *incoming tangent* (or in tangent), and the shape of the curve to the right of the key is known as the *outgoing tangent* (or out tangent). This is shown in Figure 2.20.

FIGURE 2.20
The curves on the Graph Editor represent the interpolation of values between keyframes for a selected object.

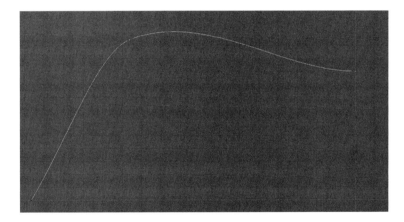

Each animated channel has its own curve on the graph. You can use the menu in the Graph Editor to edit the keys and change the way the curves are displayed on the Graph Editor.

In this exercise, you'll use the Graph Editor to refine a simple animation for the mechanical bug. In this animation, the bug will leap in the air, hover for two seconds, lean forward, and then fly off the screen in a gentle arc. You'll start by setting keys on the Translate channels of the bug. To make things easier, you'll use Auto Keyframe.

The setting applied to the tangents of the curves specifies the overall shape of the curve before and after each key. You can apply a tangent setting to one or more selected keys on the graph, and the in and out tangents can also have their own settings.

The settings are listed in the Tangents menu in the Graph Editor and are also represented visually by the icons at the top of the Graph Editor. Clicking one of these icons or applying a setting from the Tangents menu changes the interpolation of the selected key(s) or tangent handles (see Figure 2.21).

FIGURE 2.21
The icons for the tangent settings at the top of the Graph Editor

When you are blocking out an animation, you'll often find the Stepped or StepTangents setting useful. Stepping the tangent eliminates the interpolation between keys so that an object's animated values do not change between keyframes; instead, the animation appears to pop instantly from key to key. Using stepped keys when you block out the animation gives you a clear idea of how the object will move without the additional motion that can be added by curved tangents.

1. Open the mechBug_v01.ma scene from the chapter2\scenes directory at the book's web page. This is the original rigged bug without the keyframes you added in the previous sections.

2. Open the Preferences window by choosing Window ➤ Settings/Preferences ➤ Preferences.

3. Click the Animation category under Settings.

4. Make sure Auto Key is enabled. Click Save to save the preferences (see Figure 2.22).

FIGURE 2.22
The animation preferences are established in the Preferences window.

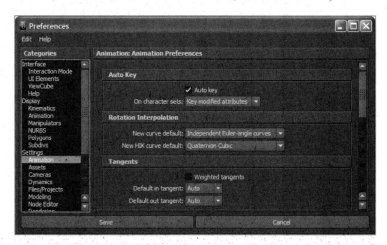

5. Set the length of the timeline to 120.

6. Set the current frame to 20.

7. RMB-click the timeline, and check Enable Stepped Preview.

8. Select the blue bodyCtrl curve in the perspective view.

9. Press **Shift+w** and **Shift+e** to set keyframes on the Translate and Rotate channels, respectively.

   When you are blocking out the animation, the only object that needs to be keyframed at this point is the bodyCtrl curve.

10. Set the timeline to frame 25, and move the bodyCtrl curve down so that the Translate Y channel is about -0.78.

11. Set the timeline to frame 35.

12. Drag up on the bodyCtrl curve until the Translate Y channel is around 7 units.

13. Set the timeline to 45.

14. Rotate the bodyCtrl slightly, and move the bug a little forward and to the side. This gives the bug a slight wobble as it hovers. Try these settings:

    Translate X: **-0.68**

    Translate Y: **4.968**

    Translate Z: **0.532**

    Rotate X: **-11**

    Rotate Y: **7**

    Rotate Z: **10**

    Many of these values were arrived at by simply moving and rotating the bodyCtrl curve in the scene. You can use these exact values or something that's fairly close. Most of the time when blocking in the animation you'll move the objects in the scene rather than type in precise values, but the keyframe values are included here as a rough guide. Remember, right now the only object being keyframed is the bodyCtrl curve.

15. Set the frame to 60. The bug is starting to turn as it decides which way to fly. Rotate it to the left a little and add a bit more variation to its position. Try these settings:

    Translate X: **-0.057**

    Translate Y: **4.677**

    Translate Z: **-1.283**

    Rotate X: **-18**

    Rotate Y: **20**

    Rotate Z: **-13**

16. Move the time slider to frame 79. Now the bug is starting to fly away. Rotate it so it is facing downward slightly. Try these settings:

    Translate X: **1.463**

    Translate Y: **3.664**

    Translate Z: **-0.064**

    Rotate X: **31**

    Rotate Y: **35**

    Rotate Z: **1.5**

17. Set the time slider to frame 95. The bug is beginning its flight, so it turns more to the left and dips down a little. Try these settings:

Translate X: **4.421**

Translate Y: **3.581**

Translate Z: **1.19**

Rotate X: **1.5**

Rotate Y: **46**

Rotate Z: **2**

18. In the final keyframe on frame 120, the bug is flying away. Try these settings:

Translate X: **11.923**

Translate Y: **9.653**

Translate Z: **6.794**

Rotate X: **49**

Rotate Y: **62**

Rotate Z: **24**

19. Play back the animation a few times. You'll see the bug pop from one position to another. Make changes if you like, but try not to add any more keys just yet. It's best to use as few keys as possible; you'll let the curves do all the work in a moment.

20. Select the red legsCtrl circle, and keyframe its Translate channels so that it follows the flight of the bug. To keep it interesting, place the keys at different frames than the bodyCtrl curve. Remember to set an initial keyframe before using Auto Keyframe.

You can set keys on the individual foot controls, but at this point let's keep things simple and focus on just the bodyCtrl curve and the translation of the legsCtrl curve.

21. From the perspective view, choose Panels ➤ Saved Layouts ➤ Persp/Graph/Outliner so that the interfaces are split between the perspective in the Outliner and the Graph Editor.

22. Select the bodyCtrl curve, and hold the cursor over the Graph Editor.

23. Press the **f** hot key so that you can see all the animation curves for the bodyCtrl object. Since the timeline is set to preview stepped tangents, they look like straight lines in a stepped pattern (see Figure 2.23).

24. Save the scene as **mechBug_v04.ma**.

To see a version of the scene up to this point, open the mechBug_v04.ma scene in the chapter2\scenes folder at the book's web page.

FIGURE 2.23
The Graph Editor is
in its own panel in
the interface; the
keys for the
bodyCtrl curve
appear as straight
lines.

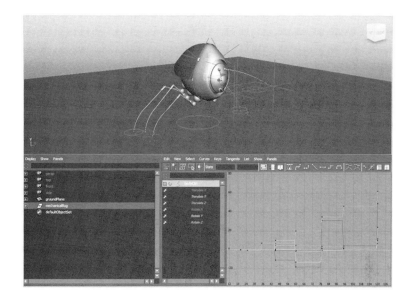

GHOSTING

Ghosting is a way to visualize how an object changes over time in space, as shown here. It is analogous to "onion skinning" in traditional animation, where you can see how the object looks in the animation several steps before and/or after the current frame.

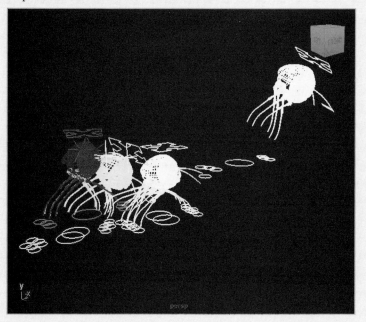

continues

> *(continued)*
>
> To activate ghosting, select an animated object and choose Animate ➤ Ghost Selected Options. In the Ghost Options dialog box, after choosing a specific ghosting type, you can specify the number of frames to display before and/or after the current frame. You can also choose to display specific frames. To remove the ghosting, select the object, and choose Animate ➤ Unghost Selected, or Animate ➤ Unghost All.

Editing Animation Curves

At this point, you're ready to start refining the animation curves using the tangent tools. Keep things simple and add keys only when absolutely necessary.

1. Continue with the scene from the previous section, or open the mechBug_v04.ma scene from the chapter2\scenes directory at the book's web page.

2. In the Layer Editor, turn off the visibility of the LEGS layer so that you can just focus on the animation of the body.

3. Select the bodyCtrl curve and, in the Graph Editor, drag a selection marquee over all the translation and rotation keys.

4. Uncheck Enable Snapped Preview in the timeline, and then test how the animation looks when different tangent types are applied to the keys.

5. On the toolbar of the Graph Editor, click the second tangent icon, or choose Tangents ➤ Spline. This changes all the selected key tangents to splines.

6. Play the animation, and observe how the bug moves as it jumps, hovers, and flies away.

7. In the Graph Editor, zoom in closely to the selected keys.

   You'll notice that spline tangents add a bit of overshoot to some of the keys, as shown in Figure 2.24, which results in a smooth, natural motion. However, in some cases this may add extra motion where you don't want it. It depends on how much precise control you want over the animation.

FIGURE 2.24
Switching to spline tangents adds a slight overshoot to the animation curves. Notice how the curve dips below the lowest value of some of the keyframes.

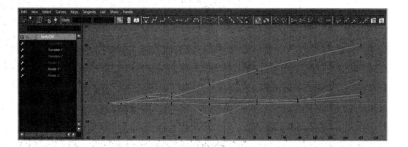

8. Try switching to the clamped-type tangent (the third tangent icon, or choose Tangents ➤ Clamped).

Clamped tangents are very similar to spline tangents; in fact, you'll notice a difference between spline and clamped tangents only when two values in a curve are very close together. Clamped tangents remove any overshoot that may cause sliding or slipping in an object. In the current animation example, you won't see much of a difference at all except for a couple of keyframes (see Figure 2.25).

FIGURE 2.25
Clamped tangents are similar to spline tangents except for values that are very close. Here, spline tangents (top image) are converted to clamped tangents (bottom image).

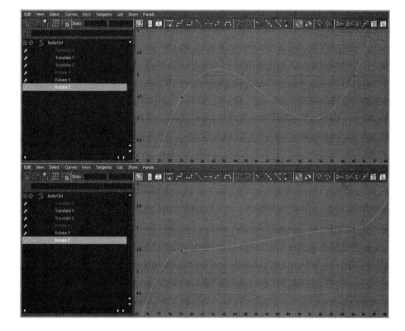

9. Now, switch to the Auto-type tangent (the first tangent icon, or choose Tangents ➤ Auto).

Auto tangents ensure smooth transitions between keys without overshooting the maximum or minimum values. The tangent is automatically adjusted when a key is moved. You can see its effect by translating a key to a different frame. Watch the tangent handle adjust as it gets closer to another key. This is the default tangent type for new keys.

Aside from auto, spline, clamped, and stepped tangents, you can also try using one of the following tangent types. A single curve can use any combination of tangent types as well.

Linear Tangents   Create straight lines between keyframes, resulting in a sharp and direct motion.

Flat Tangents   Make the tangents completely horizontal. Flat keyframes are useful when you want to create a slow ramping effect to the values, known as *easing in* or *easing out*. Easing in means that the animation curve starts out flat and then gradually becomes steeper; easing out is the opposite.

Plateau Tangents   Create smooth curves between keyframes. However, the overshoot that occurs with spline and clamped tangents is eliminated so that the peaks of each curve do not go beyond the values you set when you create the keyframes. Plateau tangents offer a good balance between smooth motion and control.

When keys are selected, the tangent icon is highlighted in the Graph Editor toolbar. If multiple keys are selected with different tangent types, none of the icons are highlighted.

10. With all the keys selected in the Graph Editor, click the last tangent icon, or choose Tangents ➤ Plateau to switch to plateau-type tangents. Once an overall tangent type is established, you can edit the tangents and values of individual keys.

A good place to start editing the animation is the initial leap that occurs at frame 20.

11. Make sure that you can see both the Graph Editor and the body of the bug in the perspective view. The bugCtrl object should be selected so that you can see its animation curves.

12. In the left column of the Graph Editor, highlight Translate Y to focus on just this individual curve.

The leap has a slight anticipation where the bug moves down slightly before jumping in the air. At the moment, the motion is uniform, making it look a little uninteresting. You can edit the curve so that the bug leaps up a little faster and sooner. Start by moving the third keyframe closer to the second.

13. Select the third keyframe, and click the Move Nearest Picked Key icon (the first icon on the far left of the toolbar) or use the **w** hot key. To move the key, MMB-drag to the left (see Figure 2.26). To constrain the movement horizontally so that its value is not changed (only its time), hold the Shift key while dragging with the MMB.

FIGURE 2.26
Move the third keyframe on the bodyCtrl's Translate Y channel to the left, closer to the second keyframe.

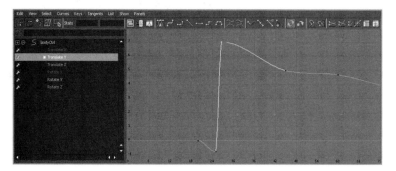

You can enter numeric values into the Stats fields for precise control. The first field is the keyframe's time in frames; the second field is the value for the keyframe.

14. Slide the keyframe to the left so that it is close to the second keyframe; the curve in between should become more of a straight line. If you want the keys to snap to whole values, select the key and choose Edit ➤ Snap.

There are two magnet icons on the toolbar of the Graph Editor (see Figure 2.27; these may be visible only when the Graph Editor is maximized). These icons turn on horizontal and vertical snapping, respectively. The keyframes are then snapped to the grid in the Graph Editor.

FIGURE 2.27
The magnet icons turn on horizontal and vertical snapping.

15. You can change the shape of the curves by editing the tangents directly:

   a. Drag a selection box around the handle to the right of the third key.

   b. Press the **w** hot key to switch to the Move tool.

   c. MMB-drag upward to add overshoot to the out-tangent (see Figure 2.28).

FIGURE 2.28
MMB-drag the tangent handles to edit the curve shape directly.

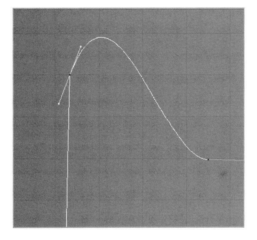

16. You'll notice that, as you drag upward on the tangent handle, the handle on the opposite side of the key moves downward, maintaining the shape of the curve through the key. You can break the tangency of the curve handles if you want a different interpolation for the in- and out-tangents:

   a. Drag a selection around both handles of the second key on the Translate Y channel.

   b. Choose Keys ➤ Break Tangents to break the tangency of the handles. The in-tangent is now colored teal, and the out-tangent is colored magenta.

   c. Drag a selection handle around the in-tangent, and MMB-drag it upward so that there is a slight bump and then a sharp dip in the curve (see Figure 2.29).

FIGURE 2.29
When you break
the tangency of the
handles, you can
move the tangent
handles on either
side of the keyframe
independently of
each other.

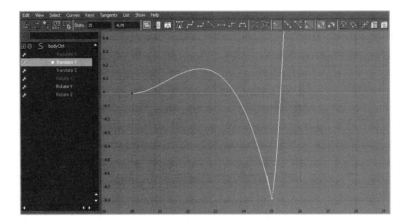

When you play the animation, the bug moves up slightly, moves down quickly, and then leaps into the air. You can unify the tangents by choosing Keys ➤ Unify Tangents. The angle of the tangents will not change, but you won't be able to edit the in- and out-tangent independently until you break the tangents again.

17. Save the scene as **mechBug_v05.ma**.

To see a version of the scene up to this point, open the mechBug_v05.ma scene from the chapter2\scenes directory at the book's web page.

Weighted Tangents

You can convert the tangents to weighted tangents, which means you can further refine the in- and out-tangents by pulling on the tangent handles.

1. Continue with the scene from the previous section, or open the mechBug_v05.ma scene from the chapter2\scenes directory at the book's web page.

2. Select the bodyCtrl curve and, in the Graph Editor, select the Translate Y channel to isolate the curve.

3. Press the **f** hot key so that the entire curve fits in the Graph Editor.

4. Drag a selection around the fourth key, and use the MMB to drag it down a little to create a slight dip in the curve (see the upper-left image of Figure 2.30).

5. With the key selected, choose Curves ➤ Weighted Tangents. The ends of the handles are extended. When a key is converted to a weighted tangent, all the keys on the curve also become weighted tangents.

6. Select the handles, and choose Keys ➤ Free Tangent Weight. The handles turn to small squares, indicating that the tangents can be pulled (the upper-right image of Figure 2.30).

7. MMB-drag the handles left or right to extend the length of the handles; notice the change in the shape of the curve (the lower-left image of Figure 2.30).

FIGURE 2.30
FIGURE 2.30
Weighted tangents
allow you to edit
the curves by pull-
ing and pushing the
tangent handles.

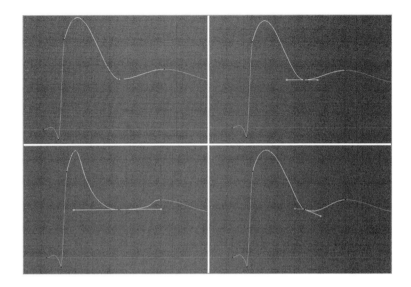

8. Break the tangents on the selected handles (Keys ➢ Break Tangents).

9. Push the handle on the left of the fourth key toward the right to shorten the incoming tangent.

10. Pull the outgoing tangent of the fourth keyframe down and to the right (the lower-right image of Figure 2.30).

11. Play the animation, and see how changing the length of the handles affects the way the bug jumps.

12. Save the scene as **mechBug_v06.ma**.

To see a version of the scene up to this point, open the mechBug_v06.ma scene from the chapter2\scenes folder at the book's web page.

Additional Editing Tools

In addition to moving keyframes and tangents, you can use the Region tool to stretch and shrink a number of selected keys at once:

1. Continue with the scene from the previous section, or open the mechBug_v06.ma scene from the chapter2\scenes directory at the book's web page.

2. Select the bodyCtrl curve in the perspective view, and enter the Graph Editor.

3. Press the **f** hot key so that all the curves are visible on the editor.

4. Choose the Region tool from the Graph Editor toolbar (see Figure 2.31).

5. Drag a selection marquee over all the keys from frame 60 to the end of the animation. A box is drawn around the keys. You can stretch or shrink the box to change the distance between selected keys.

FIGURE 2.31
The Region tool
is the fourth icon
from the left in
the Graph Editor
toolbar.

6. Increasing the scale horizontally slows down the animation; decreasing the horizontal scale speeds up the animation (see Figure 2.32). Drag the right manipulation handle of the Region tool to the right a little to extend the animation and slow it down after the fourth keyframe.

FIGURE 2.32
The Region tool
stretches or shrinks
the distances
between selected
keys on the graph.

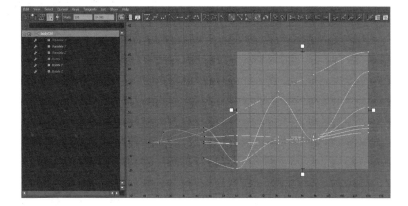

If you want to scale just the values, you can drag up or down. Small changes made with the Region tool can have a significant effect, so use this tool with caution.

Another way to edit the keys is to use the Lattice Deform Keys tool.

7. With the keys still selected, choose Edit ➤ Transformation Tools ➤ Lattice Deform Keys Tool. Doing so creates a lattice deformer around the selected keys. You can also choose the icon to the left of the Region Tool.

8. Click and drag the points and lines of the lattice to change its shape (see Figure 2.33). This is a good way to add a little variation to the animation.

To change the number of rows and columns in the lattice, open the Tool Settings dialog box while the Lattice Deform Keys tool is active. If the lattice does not update properly when you change the settings in the Tool Settings dialog box, try reselecting the keys in the Graph Editor.

The Retime Keys Tool, the fifth icon in the Graph Editor toolbar, lets you retime segments of animation. By adjusting markers placed in the graph view, you can move keyframes or entire segments of animation. Moving a marker pushes the unmarked keys outward without affecting their timing.

1. Select one or more animation curves in the Graph Editor.

2. Click the Retime Tool icon in the Graph Editor toolbar.

FIGURE 2.33
The Lattice Deform Keys tool creates a lattice around selected keys to manipulate groups of selected keys.

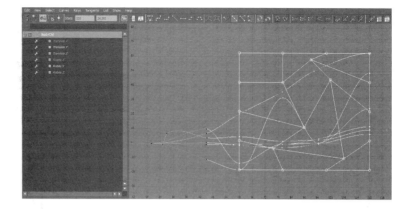

3. Double-click the LMB to place a marker in the graph view. A single marker will retime the entire curve. Add additional markers to retime specific areas.

4. LMB-click the middle section of the placed marker and drag to move keys.

5. RMB-click the solid yellow line at the top of the marker to lock the frames in between two markers (Figure 2.34).

FIGURE 2.34
Lock the keys in between two markers.

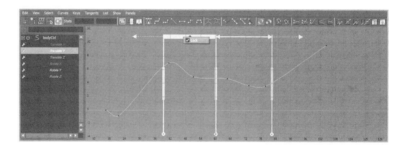

6. Slide the locked area as one whole section, or move other markers outside of the locked area.

7. Delete a marker by clicking the X at the bottom of the marker.

The Insert Keys tool inserts a key in one or more animation curves. To use this tool, follow these steps:

1. Select one or more animation curves in the Graph Editor.

2. Click the Insert Key icon in the Graph Editor toolbar.

3. MMB-click the curve.

The Add Keys tool, located under the Keys menu, is similar to the Insert Keys tool except that wherever you click the Graph Editor is then used as the value for the added key. Both tools require that you MMB-click the Graph Editor. Regardless of the tool you use, the tangent of the new key is based on your animation preferences.

You can copy and paste keys on the graph; pasted keys are placed at the current location on the timeline. This means that if you select a group of keys that start at frame 40 and then move the timeline to frame 60 and paste, the keys will be pasted at frame 60. For more precise copying and pasting, use the Copy and Paste options in the Graph Editor's Edit menu.

Practice editing the keys on the Graph Editor for the bodyCtrl curve (both Translate and Rotate channels). When you're happy with the animation, edit the keys set on the legCtrl circle.

If you decide to use Auto Keyframe when refining the animation for other parts of the robot, switch the default in-tangent and out-tangent to Spline, Clamped, or Plateau in the Preferences dialog box. Otherwise, Maya inserts stepped keyframes while Auto Keyframe is on, which can be frustrating to work with at this point.

You can add natural-looking motion to the way the bug hovers by shifting the keys placed on the different channels back and forth in time so that they don't occur on the same frame (see Figure 2.35).

To see a version of the scene where the keys have been edited, open the mechBug_v07.ma scene in the chapter2\scenes directory at the book's web page.

Breakdowns and In-Betweens

A *breakdown* is a special type of helper keyframe. The breakdown itself is just like a keyframe; what makes it special is how the breakdown affects the other keys on the curve. When you insert a breakdown and then move keys before or after the breakdown, the position of the breakdown moves as well to maintain a proportional relationship with the other keys on the curve. Normally, when you move a keyframe, the other keys are not adjusted.

Try this short exercise to understand how breakdowns work:

1. Continue with the scene from the previous section or open the mechBug_v07.ma scene from the chapter2\scenes directory at the book's web page.

2. Turn off the visibility of the LEGS layer so that you can focus on just the bug body.

3. Select the blue bodyCtrl curve, and open the Graph Editor.

4. Select the Translate Y channel so that it is isolated on the graph.

5. Drag a selection around the third key on the graph.

6. Switch to the Move tool (hot key = **w**). Hold the Shift key, and MMB-drag back and forth on the graph. The key's movement is restricted to a single axis. The other keys on the graph do not move; this is the normal behavior for keys.

7. Drag a selection around the second and fourth keys on the graph.

8. From the menu in the Graph Editor, choose Keys ➤ Convert To Breakdown.

You won't notice any difference in the keys themselves or their tangent handles. The color of the key tick mark on the graph changes to green, but other than that, it looks and acts the same.

9. Drag a selection around the third key on the graph, and try moving it back and forth.

FIGURE 2.35
Shift the keys for the various channels back and forth in time so that they don't occur on the same frame. This creates a more natural motion.

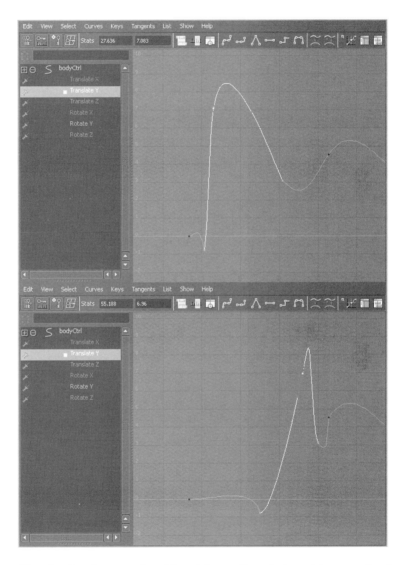

This time you'll notice that the second and fourth keys adjust their position to maintain a proportional relationship in the shape of the curve with the changes made to the third key. The same behavior occurs if you change the first key (see Figure 2.36).

FIGURE 2.36
Breakdowns are special keys that maintain the proportions of the curve when neighboring keys are edited.

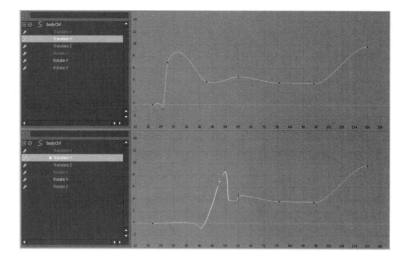

You can convert any key to a breakdown using the Keys menu. To insert a breakdown, set the timeline to the frame where you want the breakdown, right-click one or more channels in the Channel Box, and choose Breakdown Selected. You can add a breakdown to all the channels by choosing Breakdown All.

Breakdowns are useful for adding precise animation to an object's channels without affecting the tangents of the surrounding keys. This can be important if you have perfected an animation but need to make a small change to a single key.

An *in-between* is a point on the curve that does not have a keyframe. In other words, each frame between two keys is known as an in-between. When you add an in-between, you shift all the keys to the right of the current point in the timeline one frame to the right. When you remove an in-between, you shift all the keys to the left.

BUFFER CURVES

Buffer curves are a Graph Editor tool designed to let you experiment with variations of animation curves without losing any of the work you've done. To use a buffer curve, follow these steps:

1. Select the animated object, and open the Graph Editor.

2. In the Graph Editor, choose View ➢ Show Buffer Curves to enable the visibility of these curves.

3. Select the curve you want to edit, and choose Curves ➢ Buffer Curve Snapshot. This places a copy of the selected curve into memory.

4. Make changes to the curve.

The Buffer Curve appears in a dark gray color on the Graph Editor, which is visible as you edit the curve. The default color scheme Maya uses for the Graph Editor can make the gray color of the buffer curve difficult to see. You can change the color of the Graph Editor:

a. Choose Window ➢ Settings/Preferences ➢ Color Settings.

b. In the Colors editor, select Animation Editors.

c. Adjust the Graph Editor Background setting so that it is light gray.

This should allow you to see the buffer curve more easily.

5. To swap between the edited curve and the buffer curve, choose Curves ➤ Swap Buffer Curve.

6. To turn off Buffer Curves when you have finished editing, go to the View menu in the Graph Editor and turn off Show Buffer Curves.

Pre- and Post-Infinity

The Pre- and Post-Infinity settings can be used to create simple repeating motions quickly. To animate the flapping wings, you can set three keyframes and then set the Post-Infinity settings to Cycle.

1. Open the mechBug_v07.ma scene from the chapter2\scenes directory at the book's web page to clear any changes you made to the scene file.

2. Set the timeline to frame 10.

3. In the perspective view, zoom in closely to the body of the bug; on its left side, select the small piece of geometry that holds the wing to the body. The object is called leftWingMotor (see Figure 2.37).

FIGURE 2.37
Select the leftWing-
Motor object on the
side of the bug.

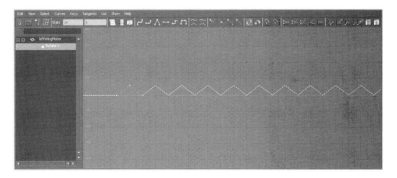

4. Right-click the Rotate X channel in the Channel Box, and choose Key Selected.

5. Set the frame in the timeline to frame 12. Set Rotate X to **60**, and create another keyframe.

6. Set the timeline to frame 14, set Rotate X to **0**, and create another keyframe.

7. With the leftWingMotor selected, open the Graph Editor.

8. Select Rotate X in the window on the left of the Graph Editor, and press the **f** key so that the editor focuses on the animation curve for this channel.

9. Select all the keys, and choose Tangents ➤ Linear to convert the curve to linear tangents.

10. Zoom out a little in the Graph Editor.

11. With the curve selected, choose Curves ➤ Post Infinity ➤ Cycle.

12. Choose View ➤ Infinity in the Graph Editor. The cycling keyframes are shown as a dotted red line on the graph (see Figure 2.38).

FIGURE 2.38
You can view how the keyframes will cycle by choosing View ➤ Infinity. The animation curve after the last keyframe is shown as a dotted line.

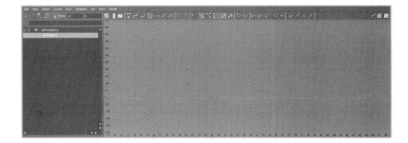

13. Play the animation in the perspective view. The wing starts flapping in frame 10; it continues to flap at the same rate for the rest of the animation.

To make the wing flap faster, simply scale the keyframes.

14. Repeat steps 7 through 12 for the rightWingMotor.

15. Save the animation as **mechBug_v08.ma**.

To see a version of the animation up to this point, open the mechBug_v08.ma scene from the chapter2\scenes directory at the book's web page.

The Pre-Infinity options work just like the Post-Infinity options, except the cycling occurs before the first keyframe. The Oscillate option cycles the keyframes backward and forward.

Cycle With Offset cycles the animation curve with an offset added to the cycle based on the value of the last keyframe (see Figure 2.39).

FIGURE 2.39
Cycle With Offset adds an offset to the cycle based on the value of the last keyframe.

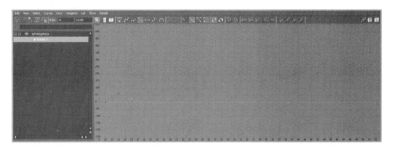

The Linear option extends the curve, based on the tangency of the final keyframe, into infinity. Thus if you want the bug to continue to fly upward forever, you can select the Translate Y channel and set Post Infinity to Linear.

GRAPH EDITOR VIEWING OPTIONS

Here are several options that can make working in the Graph Editor a bit easier:

Stacked Curves   The Stacked Curves option in the View menu separates the view of each curve of the selected object and stacks them vertically (as shown here). This may make it easier to see what's going on with each curve than in the default view, which overlays the curves in a single view.

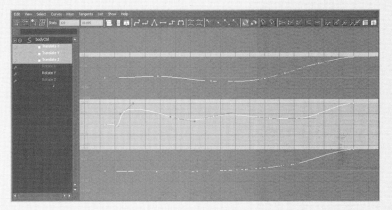

Pin Channel   The Pin Channel option in the Curves menu keeps the animation curve of a selected channel in the Graph Editor. Normally the curves displayed in the Graph Editor update as you select different objects in the scene. When you pin a channel, it stays visible regardless of what else is selected. You can activate this by clicking the pin icon in the list of channels on the left side of the Graph Editor.

Display Normalized   The Display Normalized Option in the View menu fits the selected animation curve within a range between –1 and 1. This affects how the animation is displayed but does not affect the actual values of the animation. In some cases, you may want to think of an animation curve's values in terms of a percentage; by normalizing the curve, you can think of the values between 0 and 1, as 0 to 100 percent.

You can also change the color of selected animation curves by choosing Edit ➢ Change Curve Color Options. A color swatch appears in the Change Curve Colors Options dialog box, enabling you to pick a custom color.

continues

(continued)

Classic Toolbar   The Classic toolbar can be turned off and swapped for a simplified version by using the View menu. Numerous icons are removed and/or shuffled from the toolbar, giving you a more streamlined version.

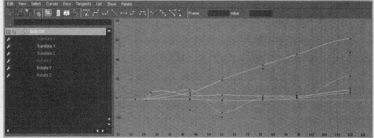

Playblast and FCheck

A *playblast* is a way to create an unrendered preview of an animation. When you create a playblast, Maya captures each frame of the animation. The frames can be stored temporarily or saved to disk. You should always use playblasts to get a sense of the timing of the animation. What you see in the Maya viewport window is not always an accurate representation of how the final animation will look.

FCheck (or Frame Check) is a utility program that ships with Maya. This program plays back a sequence of images with some simple controls. When you create a playblast, you have the option of viewing the sequence in your operating system's media player or in FCheck. FCheck is usually the better choice because of its simplicity and support for a variety of image formats.

This exercise will show you how to preview an animation using a playblast and FCheck:

1. Open the `mechBug_v08.ma` scene from the `chapter2\scenes` directory at the book's web page.

2. Choose Window ➢ Playblast Options.

3. In the Playblast Options dialog box, set Time Range to Time Slider. Set Format to avi, for Windows Media or qt for QuickTime.

4. Set Display Size to From Window, and set Scale to **1.0** (see Figure 2.40).

5. Click Playblast to record the image sequence. In the case of the bug animation, this should take only a few seconds. A scene that has a lot of dynamics or a lot of geometry may take longer.

Once the playblast is complete, FCheck should open automatically and play the sequence. You can also open a sequence in FCheck by choosing (from the main Maya menu bar) File ➢ View Sequence.

In the FCheck window, the movie-viewing controls are at the top of the menu bar. The Alpha and Z Depth display options work only for rendered sequences that have alpha or Z Depth channels included.

FIGURE 2.40
The options for a
playblast

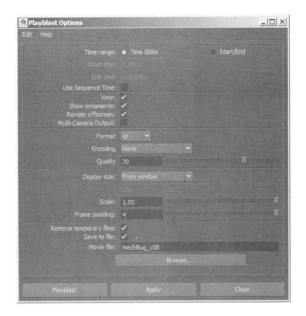

FIGURE 2.40
The options for a
playblast

In Windows, you can scrub back and forth in the animation by clicking and dragging
directly on the image in FCheck. You can also RMB-drag on the image to draw quick notes and
annotations. The notes remain on the frame as long as FCheck is open (see Figure 2.41). You can
use FCheck's File menu to save and load animation sequences.

FIGURE 2.41
FCheck is a util-
ity program that
plays back image
sequences. In
Windows, you can
draw on the frames
displayed in FCheck
using the RMB.

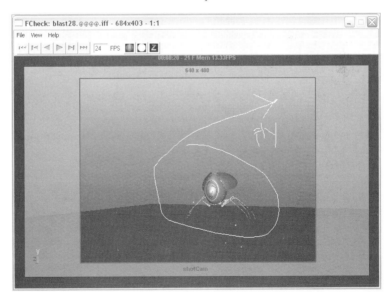

The Mac version of FCheck uses a separate control panel called FCheck Info. You can scrub
through the movie by dragging left or right in the window. In the Mac version, you cannot draw
on the images as you can with the Windows version. The Mac version may also display a blank

image for a minute or so while it loads the sequence into memory. Once it has loaded, press the **t** hot key to see the sequence play at the correct frame rate; otherwise, the sequence may play too quickly.

Driven Keys

Driven keys are keyframes that are driven by the attributes of another object rather than time. Standard keyframes describe a change for an object's attribute at two different points in time. For example, a cube may have a Translate Y value of 0 at frame 10 and a Translate Y value of 30 at frame 50. When the animation is played, the cube moves up 30 units between frames 10 and 50. When you create driven keys, you create a relationship between any two attributes. For example, you could have the Rotate X channel of a cone control the Translate Y channel of a cube. Thus when the cone's Rotate X is at 0 degrees, the Translate Y channel of the cube is at 0. When the Rotate X channel of the cone is 90 degrees, the Translate Y channel of the cube is at 50. The cone is referred to as the *driving object*, and the cube becomes the *driven object*. You can even have the attribute of one object drive one or more attributes on the same object.

Driven keys are often used in rigging to automate the animation of parts of the model, which saves a lot of time and tedious keyframing when animating the rest of the model.

Creating a Driven Key

In this section, you'll create driven keys to automate the walking motion of the mechanical bug's legs so that, when the bug moves forward or backward on its z-axis, the legs automatically move:

1. Open the `mechBugWalk_v01.ma` scene from the `chapter2\scenes` directory at the book's web page.

2. In the perspective view, use the Show menu to turn off the visibility of the joints so that it's easier to select the leg controls. Make sure the Tangents settings in the Animation Preferences are set to Flat for both Default In and Default Out tangents.

   Driven keys are set through a separate interface. You'll set up the walk cycle for one leg and then copy and paste the keys to the others.

3. From the Animation menu set, choose Animate ➤ Set Driven Key ➤ Set. The Set Driven Key window opens.

   The upper part of the Set Driven Key window lists the driver object (there can be only one at a time) and its attributes. The bottom part of the window lists the driven objects (there can be more than one at a time) and their attributes. The first step is to load the driver and driven objects. Figure 2.42 shows the Set Driven Key window with objects loaded already; you'll load the objects and attributes in the next few steps.

4. Select the bodyCtrl curve, and click the Load Driver button.

5. Select the frontLeftFootCtrl curve, and click Load Driven.

   To create the walk cycle for the front left leg, the Z translation of the bodyCtrl curve will drive the Z translation of the front left foot (making it move forward) and the Y translation of the front left foot (making it move up as it moves forward). You need to create the first key to establish the starting position of the front left leg.

FIGURE 2.42
The Set Driven Key interface lists the driver objects at the top and the driven objects on the bottom.

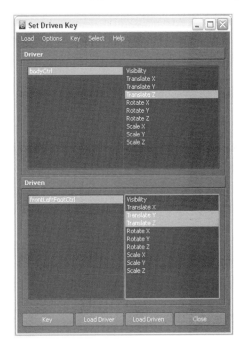

6. Select the frontLeftFootCtrl curve, and set its Translate Z channel to **-1**.

7. In the Set Driven Key window, select Translate Z in the upper-right corner; this indicates the Translate Z of the bodyCtrl curve as selected in the upper left of the box.

8. Shift+click the Translate Y and Translate Z channels in the lower right; this indicates the Translate Z and Translate Y of the frontLeftFootCtrl curve (see Figure 2.42).

9. Click the Key button at the bottom of the Set Driven Key window.

   When you click the Key button, the current value for the channel selected in the upper right is the driver for the values of the channels in the lower right.

   ◆ The Translate Z of bodyCtrl is set to **0**.

   ◆ The Translate Z of frontLeftFootCtrl is set to **-1**.

   ◆ The Translate Y of frontLeftFootCtrl is set to **0**.

   A keyframe relationship is set up between the Translate Z of bodyCtrl and the Translate Z and Translate Y of frontLeftFootCtrl. When frontLeftFootCtrl is selected, its Translate Y and Translate Z channels are colored pink in the Channel Box, indicating a keyframe has been set on these channels.

10. Select the bodyCtrl curve again, and set its Translate Z to **1**.

11. Select the frontLeftFootCtrl curve, and set its Translate Z to **1** and its Translate Y to **0.8**.

12. Make sure that, in the Set Driven Key window, the Translate Z channel is selected in the upper right and both the Translate Y and Translate Z channels are selected in the lower right.

13. Click the Key button again to set another key. Enter the following settings:

Translate Z of bodyCtrl: **2**

Translate Z of frontLeftFootCtrl: **3**

Translate Y: **0**

14. Click the Key button again.

15. Set the Translate Z of bodyCtrl to **4**. Don't change either setting for Translate Z or Translate Y of frontLeftFootCtrl. Set another key.

The IK applied to the front left leg keeps it stuck in place, which makes the walk cycle easy to animate.

16. In the perspective view, try moving the bodyCtrl rig back and forth on the y-axis. You'll see the front left foot take a step.

17. Save the scene as `mechBugWalk_v02.ma`.

To see a version of the scene up to this point, open the `mechBugWalk_v02.ma` scene from the `chapter2\scenes` directory at the book's web page.

Looping Driven Keys

To make the foot cycle, you can use the Pre- and Post-Infinity settings in the Graph Editor:

1. Continue with the scene from the previous section, or open the `mechBugWalk_v02.ma` scene from the `chapter2\scenes` directory at the book's web page.

2. Select the frontLeftFootCtrl curve, and open the Graph Editor (Window ➢ Animation Editors ➢ Graph Editor).

3. In the left column, select the Translate Y and Translate Z channels.

You'll see the animation curves appear on the graph. Since these are driven keys, the horizontal axis does not represent time; rather, it is the Translate Z channel of the bodyCtrl curve. So, as the graph moves from left to right, the value of the bodyCtrl's Translate Z channel increases. Moving from right to left, the value decreases.

4. In the Graph Editor menu, choose View ➢ Infinity. You can now see the Pre- and Post-Infinity values for the curves.

5. Select the green Translate Y curve. Choose Curves ➢ Pre Infinity ➢ Cycle. Then choose Curves ➢ Post Infinity ➢ Cycle.

By doing this, you create a repeating cycle for Translate Y. The foot moves up and down in the same pattern as the bodyCtrl curve moves back and forth. The Translate Z channel is a little different. Since it is moving along the z-axis in space, you need to offset the value for each step so that the foot continues to step forward.

6. Select the blue Translate Z curve, and choose Curves ➤ Pre Infinity ➤ Cycle With Offset. Then choose Curves ➤ Post Infinity ➤ Cycle With Offset. The dotted line on the graph shows how the Translate Z channel moves up in value with each cycle (see Figure 2.43).

FIGURE 2.43
The Pre- and Post-Infinity values of the Translate Z channel are set to Cycle With Offset so that it continually steps as the bug is moved back and forth.

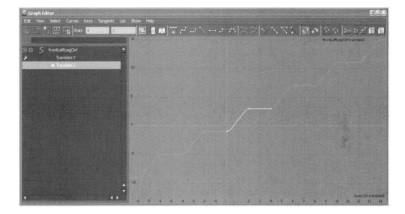

7. Move the bodyCtrl curve back and forth on the z-axis, and you'll see that the front left leg now walks with the bug.

8. Save the scene as `mechBugWalk_v03.ma`.

To see a version of the scene up to this point, open the `mechBugWalk_v03.ma` scene from the `chapter2\scenes` directory at the book's web page.

Copying and Pasting Driven Keys

The trick at this point is to create the same driven key arrangement for the other five legs in the easiest way possible. You can achieve this using Copy and Paste. The important thing to remember is that to paste driven keys from a channel on one object to another, you should have one driven key already created for the target objects.

1. Continue with the scene from the previous section, or open the `mechBug_v03.ma` scene from the `chapter2\scenes` directory at the book's web page.

2. From the Animation menu set, choose Animate ➤ Set Driven Key ➤ Set to open the Set Driven Key window.

3. Select the bodyCtrl curve, and load it as the driver.

4. Select all the leg-control curves except frontLeftLegCtrl.

5. Click the Load Driven button.

6. Make sure the Translate Z channel of the bodyCtrl curve is at **0**. Set the Translate Z of the five leg control curves to **-1**.

7. Select the Translate Z channel in the upper right of the Set Driven Key window. In the lower left, make sure all the leg control curves are selected.

8. Select the Translate Y and Translate Z channels in the lower right (see Figure 2.44).

FIGURE 2.44
Set an initial driven key on the Translate Y and Translate Z channels of the five remaining legs.

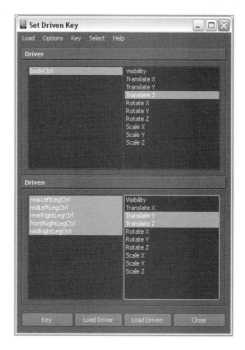

9. Click the Key button to create an initial key for the five legs. You can close the Set Driven Key window.

10. Make sure the bodyCtrl curve's Translate Z channel is at **0**. Select the frontLeftFootCtrl curve. In the Channel Box, highlight the Translate Y and Translate Z channels. Right-click, and choose Copy Selected.

11. Deselect frontLeftFootCtrl curve. Shift+click the five other leg control curves.

12. Highlight the Translate Y and Translate Z channels, right-click, and choose Paste Selected.

When you move the bodyCtrl curve back and forth, the other legs take one step. You need to loop the driven keys of the other legs in the Graph Editor.

13. Select the leg control circles for the five remaining legs, and open the Graph Editor.

14. Ctrl/Cmd+click the Translate Y channels of all the leg controls in the left column of the editor.

15. Drag a selection over the keys on the graph, and choose Curves ➤ Pre Infinity ➤ Cycle and then Curves ➤ Post Infinity ➤ Cycle.

16. Ctrl/Cmd+click the Translate Z channel for each of the leg controls in the Graph Editor.

17. Drag a selection around the keys on the graph, and choose Curves ➤ Pre Infinity ➤ Cycle With Offset and then Curves ➤ Post Infinity ➤ Cycle With Offset.

18. Drag the bodyCtrl curve back and forth on the Graph Editor. All the legs take a step; however, they all do so at the same time, which looks a little silly.

19. To create a more convincing walk cycle for the bug, select each leg control, and open the Graph Editor.

20. Select the keys on the graph, and use the Move tool to slide them a little backward or forward in time so that each leg has its own timing (see Figure 2.45).

FIGURE 2.45

Add variation to the movement of the legs by sliding the keys for each leg control on the Graph Editor.

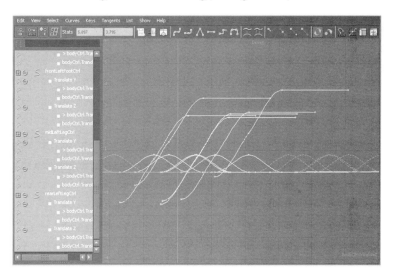

As you change the position of the Translate Z keys on the Graph Editor, you may also need to slide the curves up or down a little to make sure that they remain within the proper leg-length range as they step. You can generally figure out the proper setting through experimentation.

21. Save the scene as `mechBugWalk_v04.ma`.

Creating a walk cycle this way is a little tricky, and it will take some practice. You can set keyframes on the Translate Z channel of the bodyCtrl curve so that the bug walks forward and then adjust the position of the legCtrl curves as the animation plays. You can also change the position for the keyframes on the Graph Editor for pairs of legs so that the midLeftLegCtrl, frontRightLegCtrl, and rearRightLegCtrl all move together, alternating with the remaining leg controls. Study the finished version of the walking bug in the `mechBugWalk_v04.ma` scene in the `chapter2\scenes` directory at the book's web page to see how this walk cycle was accomplished.

Real World Scenario

SET-DRIVEN FINGERS

When it comes to rigging humanoid fingers, set-driven keys are a great solution. By adding custom attributes (discussed in Chapter 5), you can set up Channel Box attributes to provide individual finger control as well as group control to quickly create common gestures such as a pointing finger or a balled-up fist.

Motion-Path Animation

CERT
OBJECTIVE

You can animate the movement of an object by attaching the object to a curve and then sliding down the length of the curve over time. This is known as *motion-path animation*. To create a motion path, perform the following steps:

1. Open the mechBugPath_v01.ma scene from the chapter2\scenes directory at the book's web page.

2. Turn on the grid display, and choose Create ➤ CV Curve Tool ➤ Options.

3. In the options, make sure that Curve Degree is set to Cubic.

4. Draw a curve on the grid using any number of points; make sure that the curve has some nice twisty bends in it.

5. Right-click the curve, and choose Control Vertex.

6. Use the Move tool to move the CVs of the curve up and down so that the curve is three-dimensional (see Figure 2.46).

FIGURE 2.46
Draw and shape a curve in the scene.

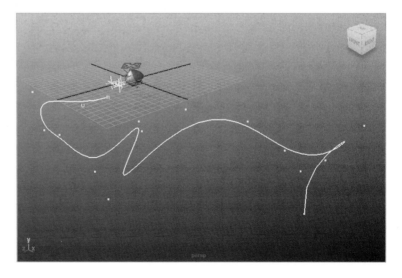

7. In the Outliner, select the mechanicalBug group, and Ctrl/Cmd+click the curve.

8. From the Animation menu set, choose Animate ➤ Motion Paths ➤ Attach To Motion Path ➤ Options.

9. In the options, choose Edit ➤ Reset to reset the options. Do the following:

Set Front Axis to Z.

Turn on Follow.

Enable Bank.

Set Bank Limit to **30**.

10. Click Attach to attach the bug to the curve (see Figure 2.47).

FIGURE 2.47
The options for Attach
To Motion Path

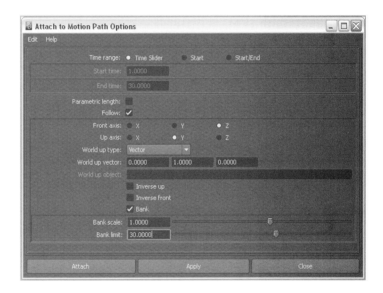

The default Time Range is set to Time Slider so that the bug will travel the length of the curve based on the current length of the time slider (200 frames in this scene). You can change this after the motion path is created.

The Follow option orients the animated object so that the front axis follows the bends in the curve. The Bank option adds a rotation on the z-axis around bends in the curve to simulate banking.

11. Play the animation. The bug follows the path (see Figure 2.48).

FIGURE 2.48
The bug is attached to the motion-path curve. As the animation plays, the bug travels along the length of the curve.

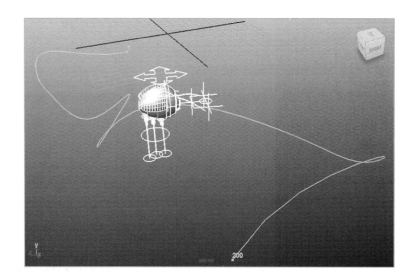

At this point, the animation looks a little silly; the other parts of the bug need to be animated, which you can do using the techniques described in this chapter. By attaching the mechanical-Bug group as opposed to the bodyCtrl group, you now have the option of adding animation to the bodyCtrl curve to provide variation in the movement of the bug as it flies along the curve.

You can change the rate at which the bug flies along the curve by editing the motionPath1 node's U Value attribute on the Graph Editor:

1. In the Outliner, select the mechanicalBug group.

2. In the Channel Box under Inputs, select motionPath1.

3. Choose Window ➢ Animation Editors ➢ Graph Editor to open the Graph Editor.

4. In the left column, select the motionPath1 U Value attribute, and press the **f** hot key to focus the graph on its animation curve.

5. Use the graph-editing tools to edit the curve.

6. Save the scene as **mechBugPath_v02.ma**.

To see a version of the scene up to this point, open the mechBugPath_v02.ma scene in the chapter2\scenes directory at the book's web page.

Motion Trails

You can animate the movement of an object and then create an editable motion trail. To create an editable motion trail, perform the following steps:

1. Open the mechBugTrail_v01.ma scene from the chapter2\scenes directory at the book's web page. The mechanical bug has already been animated with basic movement.

2. In the Outliner, select the mechanicalBug group.

3. Choose Animate ➤ Create Editable Motion Trail. A curve is created with white cubes, representing the bug's keyframes (see Figure 2.49).

FIGURE 2.49
A motion trail is created based on the bug's keyframes.

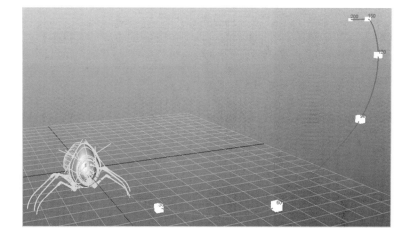

4. Click a white cube to select it. Use the Move tool to reposition a keyframe. When a keyframe is moved, notice how other keyframes are affected. This is based on the type of tangent the animation curves have. If you change the tangent type in the Graph Editor, the motion trail updates as well (see Figure 2.50).

FIGURE 2.50
A step tangent is used on the Translate Y channel.

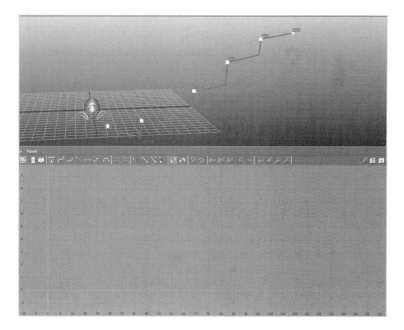

5. Move the keyframes to smooth out the motion trail.

6. Right-click the trail to bring up its marking menu. Choose Show Frame #s (see Figure 2.51).

FIGURE 2.51
Use the marking menu to show the frame numbers.

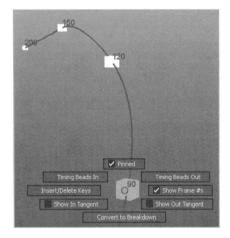

7. Open the marking menu again, and choose Insert/Delete Keys. In this mode, you can click anywhere on the curve to insert a key. Place a key somewhere between frames 60 and 90.

8. Translate the key further out into the positive Z-direction.

9. Choose Insert/Delete Keys from the marking menu again. Hold Shift, and click frame 90 to delete it.

To see a version of the scene up to this point, open the mechBugTrail_v02.ma scene in the chapter2\scenes directory at the book's web page.

Animating Constraints

You can constrain an object to more than one node. The weighting of the constraint strength can be blended between the two nodes and even animated. This is a great technique for solving difficult animation problems, such as a character picking up and putting down an object.

Dynamic parenting refers to a technique in which the parenting of an object is keyframed. In this exercise, you'll animate the mechanical bug sitting on a moving object for a few moments before flying off along a motion path.

This scene has the bug rigged and sitting at the origin of the grid. A cattail is bobbing up and down in the breeze. Above the cattail, a curve defines a motion path (see Figure 2.52).

A locator named bugLanded is constrained to one of the joints of the cattail using a parent constraint. On the motion path is another locator named bugFly. To make the bug sit on the moving cattail, you'll create a parent constraint between the bug and the bugLanded locator:

1. Open the `mechBugConstrain_v01.ma` scene from the `chapter2\scenes` directory at the book's web page.

FIGURE 2.52
The scene contains
an animated cattail
and a motion path.

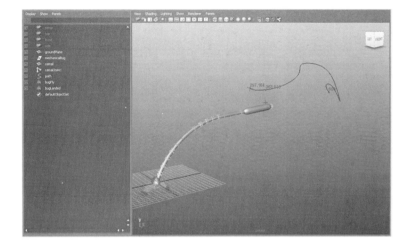

FIGURE 2.52
The scene contains
an animated cattail
and a motion path.

2. In the Outliner, select the bugLanded locator, and Ctrl/Cmd+click the mechanicalBug group.

3. From the Animation menu set, choose Constrain ➤ Parent Options.

4. In the Parent Constraint Options dialog box, turn off Maintain Offset. Leave Translate and Rotate set to All.

5. Click Add to make the constraint (see Figure 2.53).

FIGURE 2.53
The options for the
parent constraint

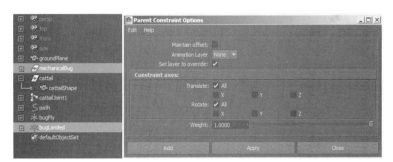

The mechanical bug now appears on the end of the cattail. You can reposition the bug on the cattail using the bodyCtrl and legCtrl curves.

6. In the Layer Editor, turn on the Controls layer.

7. Select the blue bodyCtrl curve, and pull it upward to move the bug up above the end of the cattail.

8. Turn on wireframe view.

9. Select the red legCtrl circle, and move it upward with the Move tool so that the legs are positioned on the end of the cattail. (Use the Show menu in the viewport to turn off the visibility of Joints so that you can easily see the geometry.)

10. Position each of the small purple leg-control circles so that the bug's legs are posed on the end of the cattail geometry (see Figure 2.54).

FIGURE 2.54
Pose the legs using the legCtrl curves so that the bug is standing on the cattail.

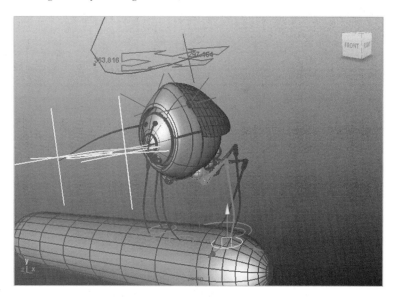

11. Play the animation. You'll see the bug sticking to the cattail as it moves up and down.

12. Set the timeline to frame 320.

13. In the Outliner, select the bugFly locator, and Ctrl/Cmd+click the mechanicalBug.

14. Create another parent constraint; the same options should be applied automatically when you create the constraint.

   When you play the animation, you'll see that the bug is floating between the two locators, thus inheriting a blend of their animation. This is because the strength of both constraints is at 1 (or full strength).

15. Set the timeline to frame 353. This is a point where the two locators are very close, and it is a good time for the bug to start to fly off.

16. In the Outliner, expand the mechanicalBug group. Select the mechanicalBug_parentConstraint1 node.

17. In the Channel Box, set Bug Fly W1 to **1** and Bug Landed W0 to **0**. The bug reorients itself to match the orientation of the bugFly locator.

18. Shift+click both the Bug Landed W0 channel and the Bug Fly W1 channel in the Channel Box (see Figure 2.55). Right-click, and choose Key Selected.

FIGURE 2.55
Set the weights of the parent constraint and add a keyframe.

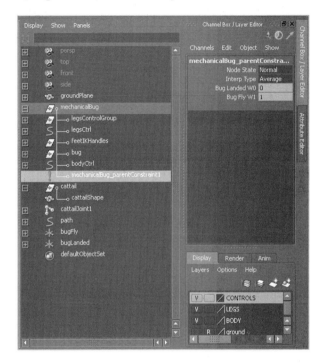

19. Set the timeline to **347**.

20. Reverse the values of the two weights so that Bug Landed W0 is at **1** and Bug Fly W1 is at **0**.

21. Set another keyframe.

22. Rewind and play the animation. You'll see the bug sitting on the cattail as it bobs up and down. At frame 347, the bug switches to the motion path and flies off.

23. With the mechanicalBug_parentConstraint1 node selected, open the Graph Editor.

24. Select the Bug Landed W0 and Bug Fly W1 channels on the left column of the Graph Editor, and press the **f** hot key to focus on their animation curves.

25. Use the curve-editing tools to fine-tune the animation so that the transition between the cattail and the motion path is smoother. This usually takes a fair amount of experimentation (see Figure 2.56).

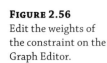

FIGURE 2.56
Edit the weights of
the constraint on the
Graph Editor.

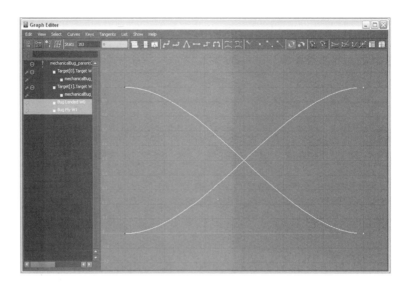

26. Save the scene as **mechBugConstrain_v02.ma**.

In some cases, you can create a smoother transition by extending the length of time between the keyframed weight values. It depends on what type of motion you are trying to achieve and your personal taste.

As shown in the mechBugConstrain_v02.ma scene from the chapter2\scenes directory at the book's web page, you can also animate the bodyCtrl curve and the leg controls to lend a more believable motion to the bug as it takes flight.

Animation Layers

Animation layers separate the keyframe data applied to objects in the scene so that you can create variations of animations for approval from a director, blend different versions of an animation together for a higher level of control, or organize the animated parts of an animation. This section is a tour of how animation layers work and some of the ways they can be applied in a scene. There is a great amount of flexibility in how animation layers can be used; no doubt you will create your own preferred animation-layer workflow after a bit of practice.

Creating an Animation Layer

In this section, you'll create a simple dancing motion for the mechanical bug. Animation layers take some getting used to, so you'll start with a simple animation.

1. Open the mechBugLayers_v01.ma scene from the chapter2\scenes directory at the book's web page.

2. Set the current frame on the timeline to **1**.

3. Select the blue bodyCtrl curve above the bug, and set its Translate Y channel to **-0.5**.

4. Create a keyframe for this channel.

5. Set the current frame to 20, set Translate Y to **0.5**, and create another keyframe.

6. Create three more keyframes for the bodyCtrl curve:

   Frame 40 Translate Y: **-0.5**

   Frame 60 Translate Y: **0.5**

   Frame 80 Translate Y: **-0.5**

   When you play the animation, the bug bobs up and down.

7. In the Layer Editor in the lower-right corner of the screen below the Channel Box, click the Anim tab. This switches the Layer Editor to Animation layers as opposed to Display or Render layers.

8. Choose Layers ➢ Create Empty Layer. Two layers appear. The new layer is AnimLayer1, and the default BaseAnimation layer is at the bottom.

   In the perspective view, nothing has changed regardless of which layer is selected.

9. Double-click AnimLayer1, and rename it **bounce** (see Figure 2.57).

FIGURE 2.57

Create a new animation layer in the scene, and rename it bounce.

10. Select the bodyCtrl curve.

11. In the Animation Layer Editor, select the bounce layer, RMB-click it, and choose Add Selected Objects. This adds just the bodyCtrl curve.

    Notice that all the channels in the Channel Box are now yellow. You'll also notice that, in the INPUTS section under the Channel Box for the bodyCtrl curve, bounce has been added to the list of inputs.

    When creating an animation layer, you have the option of creating the layer from selected objects in the scene or copying an existing layer (using the options in the Layers menu). When you copy a layer, the keyframes are also copied to the new layer. The Layer Editor has a lot of options you'll explore as you go through the next few exercises.

12. Select the bounce layer, and a green circle appears on the right. This indicates that the layer is active.

13. Play the animation. It looks the same as before. Notice that there are no keyframe tick marks on the timeline.

14. Select the BaseAnimation layer; the tick marks reappear. So, what does this mean?

Each layer has its own set of keyframes for the objects in that particular layer. The bounce layer has no keyframes yet, so what you're seeing when you play the animation are the keyframes set on the BaseAnimation layer. The way in which the keyframes on one layer interact with the keys on another depends on the layer's Mode and Accumulation settings.

You can also choose Layers ➤ Selected Objects to create a new layer based on the selected objects. The keyframes set on the object are removed from the current selected layer and added to the new layer created from the Extract operation.

Layer Mode

The mode of a layer can be either Additive or Override. Additive layers blend the values of the keys together so that the resulting animation is a combination of the two layers. Using the Additive mode, you can add changes to the animation without affecting the original keyframes on the BaseAnimation layer.

When a layer is set to Override mode, the animation on that layer overrides the animation on the layers below it. Override mode is a good way to create different "takes" or versions of an animation without affecting the original BaseAnimation layer.

Follow the next steps to see how these modes work:

1. In the Layer Editor, select the bounce layer.

2. Choose (from the menu in the Layer Editor) Layers ➤ Layer Mode ➤ Override. When you play the animation, the bug no longer moves.

If you switch to the BaseAnimation layer, you can see the keyframes on the timeline, but the bug still doesn't move. This is because even though the bounce layer is not selected, it is overriding the BaseAnimation layer.

3. In the Layer Editor, click the Mute Layer button on the bounce layer (see Figure 2.58). The Mute Layer button temporarily disables the layer. When you click Play, you'll see the bug move up and down again.

FIGURE 2.58
The Mute Layer button temporarily disables a layer.

4. Turn the Mute Layer button off, and then play the animation. The bug should stop moving.

5. Select the bounce layer, and drag the Weight slider slowly to the left as the animation plays (see Figure 2.59).

Figure 2.59
The Weight slider determines the amount of influence the layer has over the animation.

As you drag the Weight slider left, the influence of the overriding layer decreases, and you can see the bug start to move up and down again. When the weight is at 0, the overriding layer has no more influence. The K button to the right of the Weight slider sets a keyframe on the Weight value so that you can animate the strength of the weight over time.

6. Set the Weight for the bounce Layer to **1**, and make sure the layer is not muted. When you play the animation, you should see no motion.

7. Select the bodyCtrl curve, and set the following keyframes on the Translate Y channel:

    Frame 1 Translate Y: **-0.05**

    Frame 10 Translate Y: **0.5**

8. With the bodyCtrl curve selected, open the Graph Editor and select the Translate Y channel.

9. Drag a selection around the keys, and choose Curves ➢ Post Infinity ➢ Oscillate.

    When you play the animation, the bug bounces a little faster. As you lower the Weight setting for the layer, you'll see the slower-bouncing motion of the BaseAnimation layer.

    If you turn off the Passthrough option in the Layers ➢ Layer Mode menu, the animation of the lower layers does not pass through the upper layers, so as you lower the Strength value you'll see the bouncing stop as the Weight value approaches 0.

10. RMB-click on the bounce layer, and set Layer Mode to Additive, as shown in Figure 2.60.

Figure 2.60
When Layer Mode is set to Additive, the animation of the two layers is combined.

11. Set the Weight setting of the bounce layer to **1**, and play the animation.

    You can see that the resulting animation is now a combination of the keyframe values on the bounce and BaseAnimation layers. (The Passthrough option has no effect on additive layers.)

    When the mode is set to Additive, the keyframe values from the top layer are added to the layers below; in this case, the values of the Bounce layer are added to the values in the BaseAnimation layer. As you alter the Weight slider for additive layers, this decreases the layer's keyframe values. Keep in mind that the layer only affects the keyframe values of the objects that it contains.

12. In the Options menu of the Layer Editor, choose the Turn On Ghosts Manually option.

13. Click the Ghost/Color Layer button (its icon looks like a little man on a red background) in the BaseAnimation layer. This creates a ghost of the animated objects on this layer so that you can compare it with the animation on other layers. In this case, you'll see a red copy of the bodyCtrl curve moving according to the keyframes set on the BaseAnimation layer. The icon switches so that you'll see two men on the button. One represents the ghost of the other.

14. Rewind the animation, and select the bodyCtrl curve.

15. In the Layer Editor, choose Create Layer From Selected. Name the new layer **rock**, and set its mode to Override.

16. Select the rock layer. In the Channel Box, highlight the Rotate X, Y, and Z channels, and set a keyframe on these channels.

17. Turn on the Auto Keyframe feature by clicking the key icon to the right of the timeline.

18. Set the timeline to various points in the animation, and use the Rotate tool to rotate the bug, making it do a happy little dance.

19. Rewind and play the animation. You'll see the bug move around.

Experiment with the weight of the rock layer; try setting its mode to Additive, and observe the result.

By varying the weight, you get a pretty good dancing action (for a mechanical bug) fairly easily.

20. Save the scene as `mechBugLayers_v02.ma`.

To see a version of the scene up to this point, open the `mechBugLayers_v02.ma` scene from the `chapter2\scenes` folder at the book's web page.

USE ANIMATION LAYERS FOR DRIVEN KEYS

Layers can be created for other types of keyframe animation, such as driven keys. For instance, you can create a layer where driven keys make the legs of the bug appear to crawl forward as the bodyCtrl moves along the z-axis and then a second layer where a new set of driven keys makes the bug appear to crawl sideways as the bodyCtrl moves along the x-axis.

Other Options in the Layer Editor

The Layer Editor includes other options as well:

Lock Layer   Click the padlock icon to the left of the layer. When this is active, you cannot add keyframes to the layer. This is helpful if you use Auto Keyframe because it prevents you from accidentally changing the animation on a layer.

Solo Layer   Click the horizontal bar icon to left of the layer. This temporarily disables the animation of other layers so that you can focus on just the soloed layer. (More than one layer can be in solo mode.)

Mute Layer   This button disables animation on the selected layer.

Ghost/Color Layer   This button creates a ghost of the animated objects on the layer. You can change the color of the ghost by right-clicking the ghosting button and choosing a color from the context window.

Zero Key Layer   The Zero Key Layer is a way to edit a small portion of an animation using an animation layer. Select an object in the layer, and click the Zero Key Layer icon in the upper left of the Layer Editor to create a starting point on the timeline for the edit. Then move the timeline to a later point in the animation, and click the Zero Key Layer icon again. Any keyframes you set on the object between these two points in time will not be offset from the original animation.

You can change the order of layers by clicking the up and down arrows in the upper right of the Layer Editor window. The order of layers affects how the animation behaves. For instance, an override layer overrides animation on the layers below it but not above it. You can stack additive layers above, and Override Layer adjusts their weighting and rearranges their order to create different variations on the animation.

The Layer Accumulation settings under Layers ➤ Scale Accumulation determine how scaling and rotation are calculated when two or more layers that have animated scaling and rotation are combined.

The animated scaling on two layers can be added or multiplied depending on the Layer Accumulation setting.

Euler and quaternion are two different methods for calculating rotation. Euler is the standard method used in Maya. If the combination of rotation animation on two different layers leads to an unexpected result, try switching to quaternion in the Layer Accumulation settings.

Euler vs. Quaternion Rotation

Euler rotation (pronounced oiler) is calculated based on three angle values (X, Y, and Z) plus the order in which the angles are calculated. This is the standard method for calculating rotation in Maya, and it works in most cases. Euler rotation is prone to the problem of Gimbal Lock, where two of the axes overlap and lead to the same result.

Quaternion rotation uses a more complex algorithm that helps it avoid Gimbal Lock problems. When Rotation is set to Quaternion, Maya calculates the animation of rotation by using the X, Y, Z animation curves to create a fourth curve (W), which represents the rotation in quaternion units.

Layer Hierarchy

You can create a hierarchical relationship between animation layers. This is useful as an organizational tool and can speed up your workflow as you animate. Creating a hierarchy means parenting one or more animation layers to another. When you mute or solo the parent layer, all the child layers are also muted or soloed. Likewise, the Weight and Mode settings of the parent can affect the child layers. When animation layering becomes complex, you can use the hierarchy to enable, disable, and rearrange the layers quickly.

1. Continue with the scene from the previous section, or open the `mechBugLayers_v02.ma` scene from the `chapter2\scenes` folder at the book's web page.

2. In the Animation Layer Editor, mute the rock and bounce layers. You'll notice that the bug still bounces. This is because of the keyframes set on the BaseAnimation layer.

3. Before creating a hierarchy for the layers, you can quickly move the animation on the BaseAnimation layer to its own new layer.

   a. Select the bodyCtrl curve and the BaseAnimation layer.

   b. Right-click the BaseAnimation layer.

   c. Choose Extract Selected Objects.

   Extracting the bodyCtrl object from the BaseAnimation layer creates a new animation layer that contains the bodyCtrl curve and its animation. At the same time, the keyframes from the bodyCtrl curve are removed from the BaseAnimation layer. If you mute all the layers except BaseAnimation, the bug no longer moves when you play the animation.

4. Name the new layer **bounce1**, and rename bounce as **bounce2**.

5. Make sure bounce1 is below bounce2. Mute all the layers (see Figure 2.61).

FIGURE 2.61
Copy the BaseAnimation layer, rename it bounce1, and move it below the other layers. Mute all layers.

6. In the Layer Editor, choose Layers ➤ Create Empty Layer. Name the new layer **legAnim**.

7. Select the circle under the front-left leg.

8. In the Layer Editor, choose Layers ➤ Create From Selected. Name the new layer **FLeftLegAnim**.

9. MMB-drag FLeftLegAnim on top of the legAnim layer to make it a child of this layer. A small black triangle appears, and the FLeftLegAnim layer is indented above the legAnim layer (see Figure 2.62).

10. Repeat steps 7 through 9 for the front-right leg circle. Name the new layer **FRightLegAnim**.

11. Select the FLeftLegAnim layer and, in the perspective view, select the circle under the front-left leg.

12. In the Channel Box, Shift+click all the channels except the Translate channels.

13. Right-click, and choose Remove From Selected Layers (see Figure 2.63).

14. With the FLeftLegAnim layer selected, set a keyframe on the left leg-control circle's Translate channels. Then use the Auto Keyframe feature to create an animation of the leg moving up and down as if it's tapping out a little beat.

FIGURE 2.62
The FLeftLegAnim
layer is parented to
the legAnim layer.

FIGURE 2.63
Remove the Rotate and
Scale channels from
the animation layer.

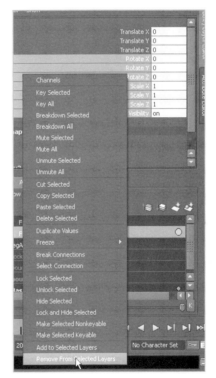

15. Switch to the FRightLegAnim layer, and create a similar animation for the front-right leg.

16. When you have a nice animation going for both layers, unmute the other layers and play the animation.

17. Click the gray triangle on the legAnim layer to collapse the layer.

Experiment with the Weight setting of the legAnim layer. The Weight value of the parent layer applies to both child layers as well. This is also true for the Layer Mode, Mute, and Solo settings.

18. Save the scene as `mechBugLayers_v03.ma`.

You can create further nested layers within the hierarchy. Each child layer can have its own Mode setting. To keep things simple, you can use empty layers as parent layers. The empty parent layers can be used to set the Weight and Mode operations of the child layers. If the parent layer is empty, you don't have to worry about how the animation in a parent layer is blended with the child layers.

To see a version of the scene up to this point, open the `mechBugLayers_v03.ma` scene from the `chapter2\scenes` folder at the book's web page.

Merging Layers

You can merge the animation of two layers into a single animation layer:

1. Continue with the scene from the previous section, or open the `mechBugLayers_v03.ma` scene from the `chapter2\scenes` folder at the book's web page.

2. In the Animation Layer Editor, Shift+click the bounce2 and bounce1 layers.

3. Choose Layers ➢ Merge Layers Options.

4. In the Merge Layers Options dialog box, set the Merge To option to Bottom Selected Layer.

5. Set Layers Hierarchy to Selected and Result Layer Mode to Additive.

6. Turn on the Smart Bake option.

   When you merge two or more layers, the animation of the objects on the layers is baked. You can choose to sample the baked keyframes based on the Sample By value. For instance, if you set Sample By to 1, the object on the resulting baked layer will have a keyframe placed on the animated channels for every frame of the animation. A setting of 2 creates a key on every other frame. The Smart Bake option creates a curve from the combined animation layers with fewer keyframes. The Increase Fidelity setting increases the accuracy of the resulting animation curve to represent better the combined animation of the two layers. The Sample By option is more accurate but creates a lot of keyframes, which can be hard to edit. The Smart Bake option works well when there are fewer layers or the animation is simple.

   You can bake a parent layer and all its child layers into a single layer. You can also choose to delete the original layers or keep them. Figure 2.64 shows the options for merging layers.

7. Click Apply to merge the layers. A new layer named Merged_Layer is created. Rename the new layer **bounce**.

8. Select the bounce layer.

9. In the perspective view, select the bodyCtrl and open the Graph Editor. You'll see the merged animation curve in the Graph Editor (see Figure 2.65).

10. Save the scene as **mechBugLayers_v04.ma**.

To see a version of the scene, open the `mechBugLayers_v04.ma` scene in the `chapter2\scenes` folder at the book's web page.

FIGURE 2.64
The options for
merging layers

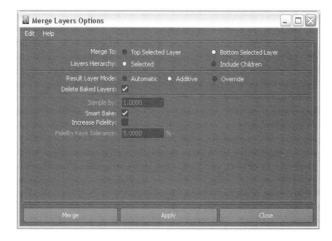

FIGURE 2.65
The merged anima-
tion curve is dis-
played in the Graph
Editor.

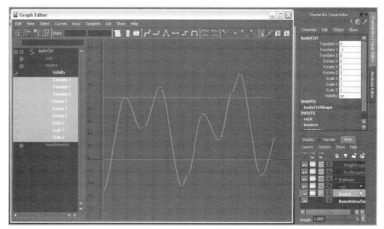

CAMERA SEQUENCING

Maya 2012 introduced the Ubercamera to the Camera Sequencer, which gave you the ability to play all of your individual camera sequences through a single camera. Maya 2013 added the ability to use weighted curves on your keyframed cameras. For more information on these tools, refer to the CameraSequencer.mov movie file included in the BonusMovies folder at the book's web page.

Grease Pencil

New!

The Grease Pencil tool allows you to draw on a viewport as if it were glass. Using a virtual marker, you can quickly create nondestructive sketches, scribbles, or lines of action to help describe your scene. Whatever your markings may be, you can keyframe them throughout your scene and on any camera. This tool is great for roughing out future poses for characters and allows you to work in a more traditional way. The following steps take you through the Grease Pencil tool's common attributes:

1. Open the `mechBugTrail_v02.ma` scene from the `chapter2\scenes` folder at the book's web page.

2. In the perspective view, click the Grease Pencil tool icon on the Viewport menu (Figure 2.66). The Grease Pencil toolbar appears.

FIGURE 2.66
The Grease Pencil icon is positioned under the Lighting menu.

3. Make sure you are at frame 0 and click the Add Frame icon (a gray page graphic with a red plus sign on top) on the Grease Pencil toolbar. Clicking this icon creates a keyframe at the current time and turns the icon gray. A small blue box is displayed at frame 0 on the timeline (see Figure 2.67). Since we haven't drawn anything yet, this is an empty frame.

FIGURE 2.67
The Add Frame icon is the first one on the Grease Pencil toolbar.

4. Move the timeline to frame 30. You have three instruments to choose from: a pencil, marker, or a soft pencil. Using the marker, draw an arrow in the direction of the motion path. Press **b** to change the brush size. Notice that drawing in the viewport automatically creates a keyframe. Figure 2.68 shows an example.

5. Move the timeline to frame 90. Notice the previously drawn arrow is ghosted. Choose the pencil and change the color to green by clicking the color swatch. Draw another arrow in the direction of the motion path.

6. Move the timeline to frame 150. Choose the soft pencil and change the color to red. Draw another arrow.

7. Play the animation to see the arrows pop up throughout the animation. You can toggle the preframe ghosting if desired or use the eraser to fine-tune your drawings.

FIGURE 2.68
Draw an arrow with
the marker.

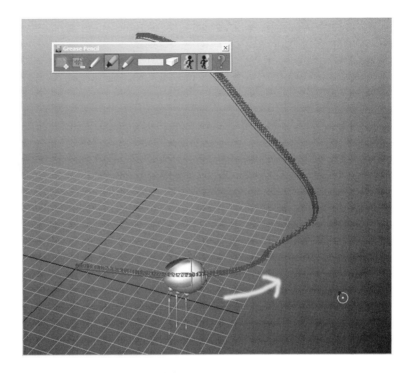

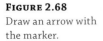

FIGURE 2.68
Draw an arrow with
the marker.

The Bottom Line

Use inverse kinematics.   Inverse kinematics creates a goal object, known as an end effector, for joints in a chain. The joints in the chain orient themselves based on the translation of the goal. The IK Handle tool is used to position the end effector.

    Master It   Create an inverse kinematic control for a simple arm.

Animate with keyframes.   A keyframe marks the state of a particular attribute at a point in time on the timeline. When a second keyframe is added to the attribute at a different point in time, Maya interpolates the values between the two keyframes, creating animation. There are a number of ways to edit keyframes using the timeline and the Channel Box.

    Master It   Create a number of keyframes for the Translate channels of a simple object. Copy the keyframes to a different point in time for the object. Try copying the keyframes to the Scale channels. Try copying the keys to the Translate channels of another object.

Use the Graph Editor.   Sophisticated animation editing is available using the animation curve-editing tools on the Graph Editor.

    Master It   Create a looping animation for the mechanical bug model using as few keys as possible. The bug should leap up repeatedly and move forward with each leap.

Preview animations with a playblast. A playblast is a tool for viewing the animation as a flipbook without actually rendering the animation. FCheck is a utility program that is included with Maya. Playblasts can be viewed in FCheck.

Master it Create a playblast of the mechBugLayers_v04.ma scene.

Animate with motion paths. Motion paths allow you to attach an object to a curve. Over the course of the animation, the object slides along the curve based on the keyframes set on the motion path's U Value.

Master It Make the bug walk along a motion path. See whether you can automate a walk cycle based on the position along the path.

Use animation layers. Using animation layers, you can add new motion that can override existing animation or be combined with it.

Master It Create animation layers for the flying bug in the mechBug_v08.ma scene in the chapter2\scenes folder at the book's web page. Create two layers: one for the bodyCtrl curve and one for the legsCtrl curve. Use layers to make the animation of the wings start with small movements and then flap at full strength.

Chapter 3

Hard-Surface Modeling

Creating 3D models in computer graphics is an art form and a discipline unto itself. It takes years to master and requires an understanding of form, composition, anatomy, mechanics, and gestures. It's an addictive art that never stops evolving. With a firm understanding of how the tools work, you can master the art of creating 3D models.

The Autodesk® Maya® software supports three types of surfaces: polygon, NURBS, and subdivisions. Each is quite different and has its strengths and weaknesses. There are few restrictions when working with polygons, and for this reason they are more popular than NURBS and Subdivisions as a modeling tool. Ultimately, NURBS and Subdivision surfaces can be converted to polygons, allowing you to take advantage of the strengths of both. This chapter walks you through the different components of each surface type. With a solid understanding of the surfaces, various techniques are demonstrated for building hard surface models. We'll use all three surface types to create a bicycle.

In this chapter, you will learn to:

◆ Understand polygon geometry

◆ Understand NURBS surfaces

◆ Understand subdivision surfaces

◆ Employ image planes

◆ Model with NURBS surfaces

◆ Model with polygons

Understanding Polygon Geometry

Polygon geometry refers to a surface made up of polygon faces that share edges and vertices. A *polygon face* is a geometric shape consisting of three or more edges. *Vertices* are points along the edges of polygon faces, usually at the intersection of two or more edges.

Many tools are available that allow you to make arbitrary changes (such as splitting, removing, and extruding) to polygon faces. Polygons are versatile. They can be used to create hard-surface models, such as vehicles, armor, and other mechanical objects, as well as organic surfaces, such as characters, creatures, and other natural objects. Before you get started working on the bicycle, it's a good idea to gain an understanding of the basic components of a polygon surface.

Polygon Vertices

A *polygon* is a surface constructed using three or more points known as *vertices*. The surface between these vertices is a *face*. A *mesh* is a series of faces that share two or more vertices. The most common way to create a polygon surface is to start with a primitive (such as a plane, sphere, or cube) and then use the numerous editing tools to shape the primitive gradually into the object that you want to create.

When all the vertices of a polygon are along a single plane, the surface is referred to as *planar*. When the vertices are moved to create a fold in the surface, the surface is referred to as *nonplanar* (see Figure 3.1). It's usually best to keep your polygon surfaces as planar as possible. This strategy helps you avoid possible rendering problems, especially if the model is to be used in a video game. As you'll see in this chapter, you can use a number of tools to cut and slice the polygon to reduce nonplanar surfaces.

FIGURE 3.1
Moving one of the vertices upward creates a fold in the surface.

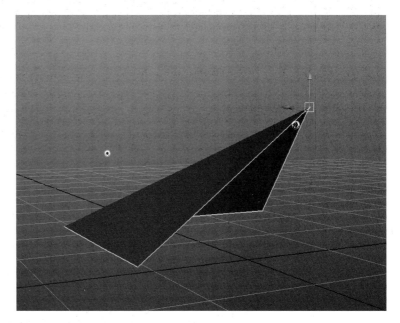

Polygon Edges

The line between two polygon vertices is an *edge*. You can select one or more edges and use the Move, Rotate, and Scale tools to edit a polygon surface. Edges can also be flipped, deleted, or extruded. Having this much flexibility can lead to problematic geometry. For instance, you can extrude a single edge so that three polygons share the same edge (see Figure 3.2).

This configuration is known as a *nonmanifold surface*, and it's a situation to avoid. Some polygon-editing tools in Maya do not work well with nonmanifold surfaces, and they can lead to rendering and animation problems. Another example of a nonmanifold surface is a situation where two polygons share a single vertex but not a complete edge, creating a bow-tie shape (see Figure 3.3).

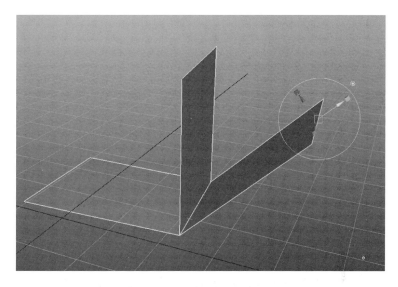

Polygon Faces

The actual surface of a polygon is known as a *face*. Faces are what appear in the final render of a model or animation. There are numerous tools for editing and shaping faces, which are explored throughout this chapter and the next one.

Take a look at Figure 3.4. You'll see a green line poking out of the center of each polygon face. This line indicates the direction of the face normal; essentially, it's where the face is pointing.

The direction of the face normal affects how the surface is rendered; how effects such as dynamics, hair, and fur are calculated; and other polygon functions. Many times, if you are experiencing strange behavior when working with a polygon model, it's because there is a problem with the normals (see Figure 3.5). You can usually fix this issue by softening or reversing the normals.

FIGURE 3.4
The face normals are indicated by green lines pointing from the center of the polygon face.

FIGURE 3.5
The normal of the second polygon is flipped to the other side.

Two adjacent polygons with their normals pointing in opposite directions is a third type of nonmanifold surface. Try to avoid this configuration.

Working with Smooth Polygons

There are two ways to smooth a polygon surface: you can use the Smooth operation (from the Polygons menu set, choose Mesh ➤ Smooth), or you can use the Smooth Mesh Preview command (select a polygon object, and press the **3** key).

When you select a polygon object and use the Smooth operation in the Mesh menu, the geometry is subdivided. Each level of subdivision quadruples the number of polygon faces in the geometry and rounds the edges of the geometry. This also increases the number of polygon vertices available for manipulation when shaping the geometry (see Figure 3.6).

FIGURE 3.6
From left to right, a polygon cube is smoothed two times. Each smoothing operation quadruples the number of faces, increasing the number of vertices available for modeling.

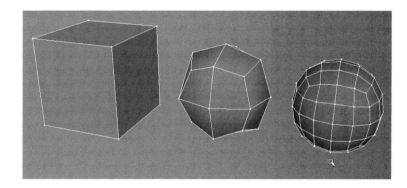

New!

When you use the smooth mesh preview, the polygon object is actually converted to a subdivision surface, or subD. Maya uses the OpenSubdiv Catmull-Clark method for subdividing the surface. You can read more about subdivision surfaces later in this chapter in the section "Using Subdivision Surfaces."

When a polygon surface is in smooth mesh preview mode, the number of vertices available for manipulation remains the same as in the original unsmoothed geometry; this simplifies the modeling process.

◆ To create a smooth mesh preview, select the polygon geometry, and press the **3** key.

◆ To return to the original polygon mesh, press the **1** key.

◆ To see a wireframe of the original mesh overlaid on the smooth mesh preview (see Figure 3.7), press the **2** key.

FIGURE 3.7
This image shows the original cube, the smooth mesh preview with wireframe, and the smooth mesh preview without wireframe.

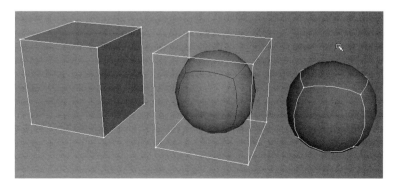

The terms *smooth mesh preview* and *smooth mesh polygons* are interchangeable; both are used in this book and in the Maya interface.

When you render polygon geometry as a smooth mesh preview using mental ray®, the geometry appears smoothed in the render without the need to convert the smooth mesh to standard polygons or change it in any way. This makes modeling and rendering smooth and organic geometry with polygons much easier.

Understanding NURBS

NURBS is an acronym that stands for Non-Uniform Rational B-Spline. As a modeler, you need to understand a few concepts when working with NURBS, but the software takes care of most of the advanced mathematics so that you can concentrate on the process of modeling.

Early in the history of 3D computer graphics, NURBS were used to create organic surfaces and even characters. However, as computers have become more powerful and the software has developed more advanced tools, most character modeling is accomplished using polygons and subdivision surfaces. NURBS are more ideally suited to hard-surface modeling; objects such as vehicles, equipment, and commercial product designs benefit from the types of smooth surfacing produced by NURBS models.

All NURBS objects are automatically converted to triangles at render time by the software. You can determine how the surfaces will be *tessellated* (converted into triangles) before rendering, and you can change these settings at any time to optimize rendering. This gives NURBS the advantage that their resolution can be changed when rendering. Models that appear close to the camera can have higher tessellation settings than those farther away from the camera.

One of the downsides of NURBS is that the surfaces themselves are made of four-sided patches. You cannot create a three- or five-sided NURBS patch, which can sometimes limit the kinds of shapes you can make with NURBS. If you create a NURBS sphere and use the Move tool to pull apart the control vertices at the top of the sphere, you'll see that even the patches of the sphere that appear as triangles are actually four-sided panels (see Figure 3.8).

FIGURE 3.8
Pulling apart the control vertices at the top of a NURBS sphere reveals that one side of each patch had been collapsed.

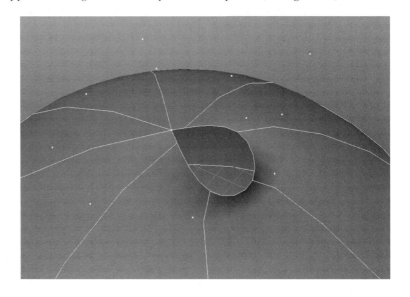

Understanding Curves

All NURBS surfaces are created based on a network of NURBS curves. Even the basic primitives, such as the sphere, are made up of circular curves with a surface stretched across them. The curves themselves can be created several ways. A *curve* is a line defined by points. The points along the curve are referred to as *curve points*. Movement along the curve in either direction is defined by its U-coordinates. When you right-click a curve, you can choose to select a curve point. The curve point can be moved along the U-direction of the curve, and the position of the point is defined by its U-parameter.

Curves also have *edit points* that define the number of spans along a curve. A *span* is the section of the curve between two edit points. Changing the position of the edit points changes the shape of the curve; however, this can lead to unpredictable results. It is a much better idea to use a curve's control vertices to edit the curve's shape.

Control vertices (CVs) are handles used to edit the curve's shapes. Most of the time you'll want to use the control vertices to manipulate the curve. When you create a curve and display its CVs, you'll see them represented as small dots. The first CV on a curve is indicated by a small box; the second is indicated by the letter *U*.

Hulls are straight lines that connect the CVs; they act as a visual guide.

Figure 3.9 displays the various components.

The degree of a curve is determined by the number of CVs per span minus one. In other words, a three-degree (or cubic) curve has four CVs per span. A one-degree (or linear) curve has two CVs per span (see Figure 3.10). Linear curves have sharp corners where the curve changes directions; curves with two or more degrees are smooth and rounded where the curve changes direction. Most of the time, you'll use either linear (one-degree) or cubic (three-degree) curves.

You can add or remove a curve's CVs and edit points, and you can also use curve points to define a location where a curve is split into two curves or joined to another curve.

The *parameterization* of a curve refers to the way in which the points along the curve are numbered. There are two types of parameterization:

Uniform Parameterization   A curve with uniform parameterization has its points evenly spaced along the curve. The parameter of the last edit point along the curve is equal to the number of spans in the curve. You also have the option of specifying the parameterization range between 0 and 1. This method is available to make Maya more compatible with other NURBS modeling programs.

Chord Length Parameterization   Chord length parameterization is a proportional numbering system that causes the length between edit points to be irregular. The type of parameterization you use depends on what you are trying to model. Curves can be rebuilt at any time to change their parameterization; however, this will sometimes change the shape of the curve.

You can rebuild a curve to change its parameterization (using the Surfaces menu set under Edit Curves ➢ Rebuild Curve). It's often a good idea to do this after splitting a curve or joining two curves together, or when matching the parameterization of one curve to another. By rebuilding the curve, you ensure that the resulting parameterization (Min and Max Value attributes in the curve's Attribute Editor) is based on whole-number values, which leads to more predictable results when the curve is used as a basis for a surface. When rebuilding a curve, you have the option of changing the degree of the curve so that a linear curve can be converted to a cubic curve, and vice versa.

FIGURE 3.9
The top image shows a selected curve point on a curve, the middle image shows the curve with edit points displayed, and the bottom image shows the curve with CVs and hulls displayed.

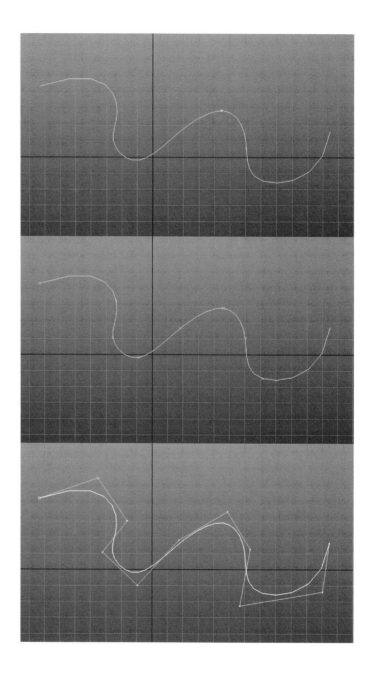

FIGURE 3.10
A linear curve has sharp corners.

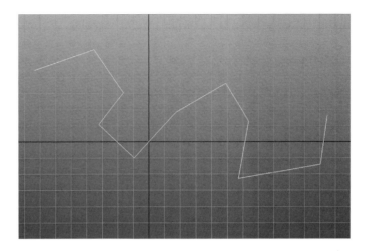

BÉZIER CURVES

Bézier curves use handles for editing, as opposed to CVs that are offset from the curve. To create a Bézier curve, choose Create ➤ Bezier Curve. Each time you click the perspective view, a new point is added. To extend the handle, LMB-drag after adding a point. The handles allow you to control the smoothness of the curve. The advantage of Bézier curves is that they are easy to edit, and you can quickly create curves that have both sharp corners and rounded curves.

IMPORTING CURVES

You can create curves in Adobe Illustrator and import them into Maya for use as projections on the model. For best results, save the curves in Illustrator 8 format. In Maya, choose File ➤ Import ➤ Options, and choose Adobe Illustrator format to bring the curves into Maya. This is often used as a method for generating logo text.

Understanding NURBS Surfaces

NURBS surfaces follow many of the same rules as NURBS curves since they are defined by a network of curves. A primitive, such as a sphere or a cylinder, is simply a NURBS surface lofted across circular curves. You can edit a NURBS surface by moving the position of the surface's CVs (see Figure 3.11). You can also select the *hulls* of a surface, which are groups of CVs that follow one of the curves that define a surface (see Figure 3.12).

NURBS curves use the U-coordinates to specify the location of a point along the length of the curve. NURBS surfaces add the V-coordinate to specify the location of a point on the surface. Thus a given point on a NURBS surface has a U-coordinate and a V-coordinate. The U-coordinates of a surface are always perpendicular to the V-coordinates of a surface. The UV coordinate grid on a NURBS surface is just like the lines of longitude and latitude drawn on a globe.

FIGURE 3.11
The shape of a NURBS surface can be changed by selecting its CVs and moving them with the Move tool.

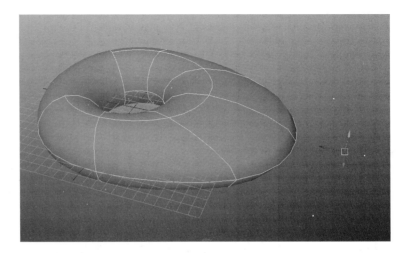

FIGURE 3.12
Hulls can be selected and repositioned using the Move tool.

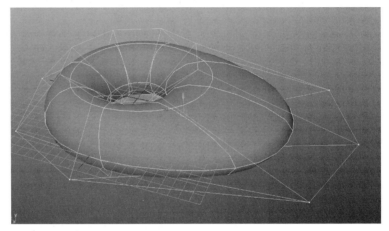

Just like NURBS curves, surfaces have a degree setting. Linear surfaces have sharp corners (see Figure 3.13), and cubic surfaces (or any surface with a degree higher than 1) are rounded and smooth. Often a modeler will begin a model as a linear NURBS surface and then rebuild it as a cubic surface later (Edit NURBS ➤ Rebuild Surfaces ➤ Options).

You can start a NURBS model using a primitive, such as a sphere, cone, torus, or cylinder, or you can build a network of curves and loft surfaces between the curves or any combination of the two. When you select a NURBS surface, the wireframe display shows the curves that define the surface. These curves are referred to as *isoparms*, which is short for "isoparametric" curve.

A single NURBS model may be made up of numerous NURBS patches that have been stitched together. This technique was used for years to create CG characters, but now most artists favor polygons or subdivision surfaces. When you stitch two patches together, the tangency must be consistent between the two surfaces to avoid visible seams. It's a process that often takes some practice to master (see Figure 3.14).

FIGURE 3.13
A linear NURBS
surface has sharp
corners.

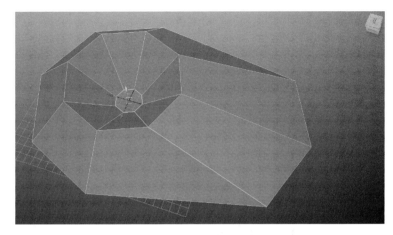

FIGURE 3.14
A character is cre-
ated from a series
of NURBS patches
stitched together.

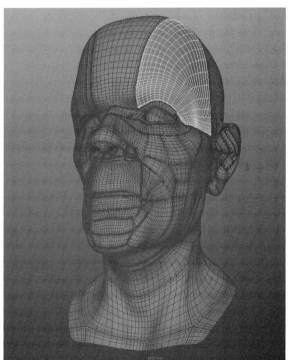

LINEAR AND CUBIC SURFACES

A NURBS surface can be rebuilt (Edit NURBS ➤ Rebuild Surfaces ➤ Options) so that it is a cubic
surface in one direction (either the U direction or the V direction) and linear in the other (either
the U direction or the V direction).

Surface Seams

Many NURBS primitives have a seam where the end of the surface meets the beginning. Imagine a piece of paper rolled into a cylinder. At the point where one end of the paper meets the other there is a seam. The same is true for many NURBS surfaces that define a shape. When you select a NURBS surface, the wireframe display on the surface shows the seam as a bold line. You can also find the seam by selecting the surface and choosing Display ➤ NURBS ➤ Surface Origins (see Figure 3.15).

FIGURE 3.15
The point on a NURBS surface where the seams meet is indicated by displaying the surface origins.

U Surface Origin

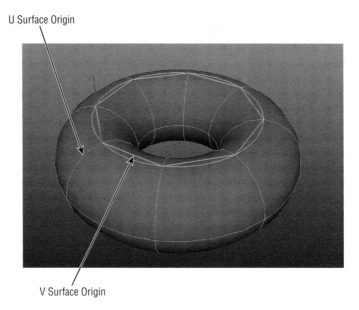

V Surface Origin

The seam can occasionally cause problems when you're working on a model. In many cases, you can change the position of the seam by selecting one of the isoparms on the surface (right-click the surface and choose Isoparm) and choosing Edit NURBS ➤ Move Seam.

NURBS Display Controls

You can change the quality of the surface display in the viewport by selecting the surface and pressing **1, 2,** or **3** on the keyboard:

◆ Pressing the **1** key displays the surface at the lowest quality, which makes the angles of the surface appear as corners.

◆ Pressing the **2** key gives a medium-quality display.

◆ Pressing the **3** key displays the surface as smooth curves.

None of these display modes affects how the surface will look when rendered, but choosing a lower display quality can help improve performance in heavy scenes. The same display settings apply for NURBS curves as well. If you create a cubic curve that has sharp corners, remember to press the **3** key to make the curve appear smooth.

Using Subdivision Surfaces

CERT
OBJECTIVE

The Maya subdivision surfaces are very similar to the polygon smooth mesh preview. The primary distinction between smooth mesh preview and subdivision surfaces (subDs) is that subdivision surfaces allow you to subdivide a mesh to add detail only where you need it. For instance, if you want to sculpt a fingernail at the end of a finger, using subDs you can select just the tip of the finger and increase the subdivisions. Then you have more vertices to work just at the fingertip, and you can sculpt the fingernail.

Most subD models start out as polygons and are converted to subDs only toward the end of the modeling process. You should create UV texture coordinates while the model is still made of polygons. They are carried over to the subDs when the model is converted.

So why are subDs and smooth mesh preview polygons so similar, and which should you use? SubDs have been part of Maya for many versions. Smooth mesh preview polygons have only recently been added to Maya; thus, the polygon tools have evolved to become very similar to subDs. You can use either type of geometry for many of the same tasks; it's up to you to decide when to use one rather than another.

When you convert a polygon mesh to a subdivision surface, you should keep in mind the following:

◆ Keep the polygon mesh as simple as possible; converting a dense polygon mesh to a subD significantly slows down performance.

◆ You can convert three-sided or *n*-sided (four-or-more-sided) polygons into subDs, but you will get better results and fewer bumps in the subD model if you stick to four-sided polygons as much as possible.

◆ Nonmanifold geometry is not supported. You must alter this type of geometry before you are allowed to do conversion.

Employing Image Planes

CERT
OBJECTIVE

Image planes refer to implicit surfaces that display an image or play a movie. They can be attached to a Maya camera or free-floating. The images themselves can be used as a guide for modeling or as a rendered backdrop. You can alter the size of the planes, distorting the image, or use Maintain Pic Aspect Ratio to prevent distortion while scaling. Image planes can be rendered using Maya software or mental ray. In this section, you'll learn how to create image planes for Maya cameras and how to import custom images to use as guides for modeling a bicycle.

It's not unusual in the fast-paced world of production to be faced with building a model based on a single view of the subject. You're also just as likely to be instructed to blend together several different designs. You can safely assume that the concept drawing you are given has been approved by the director. It's your responsibility to follow the spirit of that design as closely as possible with an understanding that the technical aspects of animating and rendering the model may force you to make some adjustments. Some design aspects that work well in a two-dimensional drawing don't always work as well when translated into a three-dimensional model. Building a hard-surface model from real-world photos, like we'll do with the bicycle, can be easier if you know that all the pieces and parts have been designed to fit together.

Image planes are often used as a modeling guide. They can be attached to a camera or be free floating and have a number of settings that you can adjust to fit your own preferred style. The following exercise walks you through the steps of adding multiple image planes.

1. Create a new scene in Maya.

2. Switch to the Front view. From the Create menu, choose Free Image Plane (see Figure 3.16).

FIGURE 3.16

Use the View menu in the panel menu bar to add an image plane to the camera.

3. A dialog box will open; browse the file directory on your computer, and choose the `bicycleFront.jpg` image from the `chapter3\sourceimages` directory at the book's web page (`www.sybex.com/go/masteringmaya2015`).

4. The front-view image opens and appears in the viewport. Select the image plane, and open the Attribute Editor (see Figure 3.17).

5. In the Image Plane Attributes section, you'll find controls that change the appearance of the plane in the camera view. Make sure the Display option is set to In All Views. This way, when you switch to the perspective view, the plane will still be visible.

   You can set the Display mode to RGB if you want just color, or to RGBA to see color and alpha. The RGBA option is more useful when the image plane has an alpha channel, and it is intended to be used as a backdrop in a rendered image as opposed to a modeling guide. There are other options, such as Luminance, Outline, and None.

   The Color Gain and Color Offset sliders can be used to change the brightness and contrast. By lowering the Color Gain and raising the Color Offset, you can get a dimmer image with less contrast.

6. The Alpha Gain slider adds some transparency to the image display. Drag this slider left to reduce the opacity of the plane.

   Other options include using a texture or an image sequence. An image sequence may be useful when you are matching animated models to footage.

FIGURE 3.17
The options for the image plane are displayed in the Attribute Editor.

ARRANGING IMAGE PLANES

In this example, the image plane is attached to the side-view camera in Maya, but you may prefer to create a second side-view camera of your own and attach the image plane to that. It depends on your own preference. Image planes can be created for any type of camera. In some cases, a truly complex design may require creating orthographic cameras at different angles in the scene.

If you want to have a concept drawing or other reference images available in the Maya interface, you can create a new camera and attach an image plane using the reference image. Then set the options so that the reference appears only in the viewing camera. Every time you want to refer to the reference, you can switch to this camera, which saves you the trouble of having the image open in another application.

7. Currently, the shape node of the image plane is selected. Select the image in the viewport to select the plane's transform node.

8. Select the Move tool (hot key = t). Translate the image plane in the y-axis to place the bike's tires on top of the XZ plane (see Figure 3.18).

9. Rename the image plane to **frontImage**.

FIGURE 3.18
Position the image
plane to sit on top
of the grid plane.

10. Switch to the front camera, and use Panels ➢ Orthographic ➢ New ➢ Back to create
    another camera.

11. Create another image plane and import the `bicycleBack.jpg` image.

12. Move the new image plane in the y-axis to the same value as the first image plane. The
    two images should now overlap. This can cause the image to pop or flicker at certain
    angles as the graphics card fights over which image to display. Move backImage to –0.1 in
    the z-axis to prevent the flickering.

13. Rename the image plane to **backImage**.

14. With both images aligned and their alpha gain set to 1.0, you can tumble the camera in
    the perspective view to see the front and back of the bike. Lowering the alpha gain will
    cause the images to overlap from every angle. Although this might be distracting at first,
    a lower alpha gain allows you to see your modeled geometry from all angles. Select both
    image planes and in the Channel Box set the Alpha Gain to **0.5**.

IMAGE DISTORTION

Photographs will always have a certain amount of image distortion. This is natural lens distortion and is unavoidable. When modeling based on photographs, keep in mind the true shape of
an object. For instance, in the bicycle photographs the tires do not look completely round due to
image distortion. However, you can assume the tires are round and should be modeled as such.

Modeling NURBS Surfaces

To start the model of the bike, begin by creating the bicycle frame from extruded curves:

1. Continue with the scene from the previous section, or open the `bicycle_v01.ma` scene from the `chapter3\scenes` folder at the book's web page. Make sure the images are visible on the image planes. You can find the source files for these images in the `chapter3\sourceimages` folder.

2. Choose Create ➢ CV Curve Tool.

3. By default the CV curve tool will create a curve with a degree of 3. This is suitable to create smooth rounded curves. Draw a curve for each bar of the bicycle frame (Figure 3.19). Use as few CVs as you can to accurately capture the form of the frame. Remember with a degree of 3 you will need a minimum of four CVs for the curve to be valid.

FIGURE 3.19
Draw six curves to represent each bar on the bicycle frame.

4. You can extrude another curve along these ones to generate geometry. Choose Create ➢ NURBS Primitives ➢ Circle. If you have Interactive Creation selected in the NURBS Primitives menu, you will be prompted to draw the circle on the grid. (I find Interactive Creation a bit of a nuisance and usually deselect it.) Draw the circle to the approximate width of a bicycle frame's bar.

5. Select the NURBS circle. Hold C on the keyboard, to activate Snap To Curve, and MMB-drag on the uppermost curve. Drag the circle to the start of the curve. Select the Rotate tool (hot key = **e**). Rotate the circle to make it perpendicular to the frame curve (see Figure 3.20).

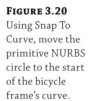

FIGURE 3.20
Using Snap To Curve, move the primitive NURBS circle to the start of the bicycle frame's curve.

SNAP TO CURVE

Snapping to a curve can be tricky. Make sure none of the axes are active on the translate manipulator. An active (yellow_) axis will prevent the object to be snapped from moving in any axis except the one that is highlighted. All three axes should be their respective colors. The MMB is required to snap. A good practice is to MMB-drag somewhere along the intended curve and then drag the snapped object to the desired position.

---

6. Switch to the Surfaces menu and Shift+click the frame curve.

7. Open the options for Surfaces ➤ Extrude. The goal is to extrude the circle into a tube along the chosen path, in this case the frame curve. By default Style is already set to Tube. The rest of the options should match those shown in Figure 3.21. Click Extrude to apply the settings and close the window.

The resulting NURBS surface is a direct product of the curves used to create it. The number of control vertices in the curves is the same number of control points in the respective direction on the NURBS surface. Figure 3.22 shows the CVs of the NURBS circle. Notice how they align perfectly with the isoparms of the NURBS tube.

8. The resulting tube is probably not the right diameter. Select the original NURBS circle. Select the Scale tool (hot key = **r**). Scale the circle to the correct size of the bike frame. Notice the size of the tube updates simultaneously through its history connection to the creation curves.

The original curve created for the frame can also be adjusted. Modifying its control vertices can help in shaping the tube to match the reference material. You can also move the components to change the length of the surface.

FIGURE 3.21
The settings for the
Extrude options

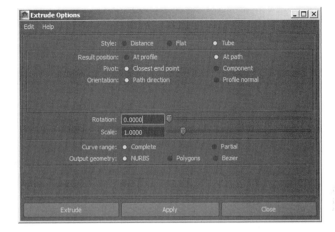

FIGURE 3.21
The settings for the
Extrude options

FIGURE 3.22
The curves' components are used
to determine
the components
of the extruded
NURBS surface.

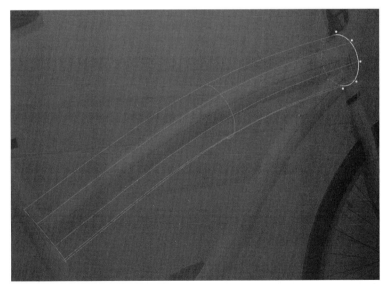

MANIPULATING COMPONENTS

Selecting construction curves can be difficult since they sit directly under a surface. You can activate the geometry selection mask along the status bar, but this will not prevent the surface's components from being selected. Instead, assign the surface to a layer and then make that layer a template.

9. The frame is not one diameter from start to finish. It narrows closer to the bike seat. With the NURBS circle still selected, click the extrude1 node under the OUTPUTS section of the Channel Box. Change the Scale value to alter its diameter (see Figure 3.23).

FIGURE 3.23
The Scale attribute in the extrude1 history node allows you to taper the extrusion.

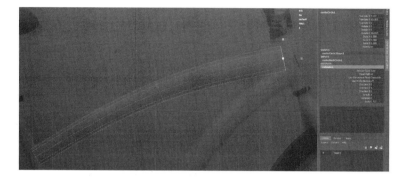

10. Not all of the bars in the frame reside in the same plane. The fork that holds the front tire extends out from the frame in order to compensate for the width of the tire. You can modify the curve before or after you extrude the surface.

Create a NURBS circle and snap it to the start of the fork. Rotate the circle perpendicular to the fork's curve. Figure 3.24 shows the positioning.

FIGURE 3.24
Position a new NURBS circle at the top of the fork curve.

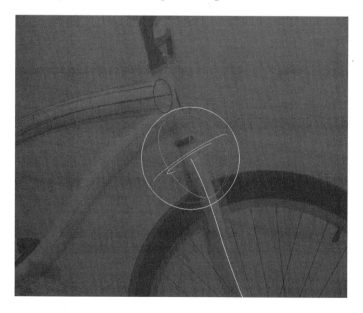

11. Extrude the circle along the fork curve by selecting first the circle and then the fork curve. Use the same settings from Figure 3.21. Maya will remember your previous settings so there shouldn't be a need to make any adjustments. Figure 3.25 shows the extruded surface.

FIGURE 3.25
Extrude the fork for the front tire.

12. Scale the NURBS circle to match the diameter of the fork.

13. Add the fork geometry to a layer and make that layer a template.

14. Select the fork curve. RMB-click over the curve and choose Control Vertex from the marking menu.

15. Translate the control vertices to match the shape of one side of the fork. Use additional reference images from the chapter3\sourceimages folder as needed.

16. Moving CVs on the curve yields predictable results on the extruded surface except when you move the U CV. Altering the U changes the direction of the curve, causing the NURBS circle to no longer be perpendicular to the fork's curve. Figure 3.26 shows the resulting malformation in the extrusion.

To fix the shape of the extrusion after modifying the U CV, rotate the circle so that it is perpendicular to the fork's curve again. Figure 3.27 shows the corrected fork geometry.

17. Once the surface is shaped, you might notice the isoparms are not evenly spaced. You may even have a pinching around the area bend in the fork geometry (see Figure 3.28).

FIGURE 3.26
The extruded surface
is shearing as a result
of changing the posi-
tion of the *U* CV.

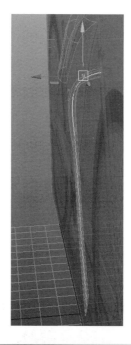

FIGURE 3.27
The orientation of
the NURBS circle has
been corrected, elimi-
nating any shearing.

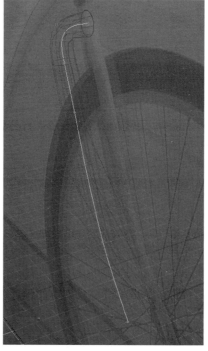

FIGURE 3.28
Pinching can occur around areas with a high degree of curvature.

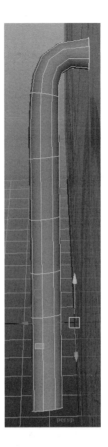

You can fix these issues by rebuilding the original fork curve. With the history still intact, the changes to the original curve will affect the NURBS surface.

Select the fork curve and open its Attribute Editor. Choose the curveShape node. Make note of the number of spans. In this example there are six.

18. Choose Edit Curves ➤ Rebuild Curve ➤ Options. Change the number of spans to a value higher than the number of spans in the curve itself. In this example the spans are set to 8. Click Apply to test the settings. If needed, change the number of spans and apply the settings again.

Two things happen to the surface. First, the number of spans is increased. Second, the CVs are redistributed to be uniformly spaced. Figure 3.29 shows the corrected surface.

FIGURE 3.29
The number of spans
in the construction
curve was rebuilt
from six to eight.

NURBS COMPONENT COORDINATES

When you select CVs on a NURBS curve or surface, you'll see a node in the Channel Box labeled CVs (Click To Show). When you click this, you'll get a small version of the Component Editor in the Channel Box that displays the position of the CVs in local space—this is now labeled CVs (Click To Hide)—relative to the rest of the sphere. The CVs are labeled by number. Notice also that moving them up in world space actually changes their position along the z-axis in local space.

19. Continue extruding and shaping the rest of the parts to the bike frame.

20. Save the scene as **bicycle_v02.ma**.

To see a version of the scene to this point, open the bicycle_v02.ma scene from the chapter3\scenes directory at the book's web page.

Lofting Surfaces

A *loft* creates a surface across two or more selected curves. It's a great tool for filling gaps between surfaces or developing a new surface from a series of curves. In this section, you'll create the bicycle seat from a series of curves.

1. Continue with the scene from the previous section or open the bicycle_v02.ma scene from the chapter3\scenes directory at the book's web page.

2. Create a free image plane using the seat.jpg file from the chapter3\sourceimages directory at the book's web page. Transform the image plane to roughly match the scale and position of the seat in the front image plane. Use Figure 3.30 as a guide.

FIGURE 3.30

Add a new image plane to use as reference for the seat.

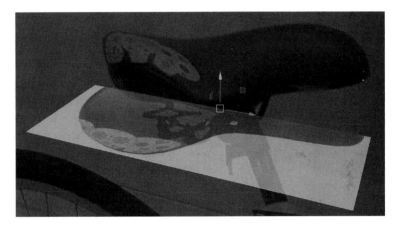

3. Starting a lofted surface from scratch can be daunting at first. The trick is to not worry about matching the shape. Instead create a series of curves, loft the surface, and through construction history match the shape.

Looking at the shape of the seat, you can estimate that you will need about eight control vertices to define the seat's contours. Choose Create ➤ CV Curve Tool. Make sure you are using a curve degree of 3. From the front viewport, draw a curve with eight CVs around the thickest part of the seat. Starting at the thickest point ensures you will have enough CVs to accurately define the surface (see Figure 3.31).

4. Using multiple viewports, shape the curve to roughly match the outline of the seat. You are not going for accuracy. You just want to give the curve some shape in all three axes. Eventually you will mirror the geometry since the seat is symmetrical. Therefore the curve can start along the center line of the seat or on the XY plane. Also, plan on leaving the bottom open. Use Figure 3.32 as a guide.

FIGURE 3.31
Draw a curve at
the thickest part
of the seat.

FIGURE 3.32
Shape the curve
to loosely match
the bike seat.

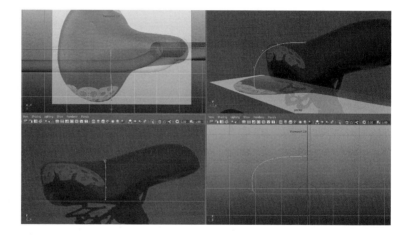

5. With the curve selected, choose Edit ➢ Duplicate (or press Ctrl/Cmd+d) to make a standard duplicate of the curve.

6. Move the curve a unit in either direction.

7. Scaling the curve is a quick way to match the contour of the seat shape. The most effective way to scale the curve and maintain its position along the center line is to move the curve's pivot point to its start.

Hold D on the keyboard to enter pivot mode and hold C to activate Snap To Curve. MMB-click on the curve and drag the pivot point to the start of the curve. Translate the curve to the top of the seat. Scale the curve in the y- and z-axes to match the height and width of the bicycle seat.

8. Repeat steps 5 through 7 to get a total of eight curves (see Figure 3.33).

FIGURE 3.33
Transform the curves to match the reference images.

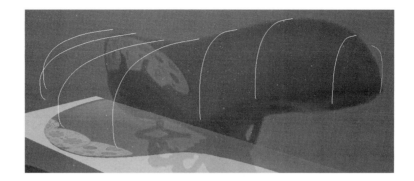

Leave the back of the seat open. It will be easier to close at a later time. Rotate the curve for the front of the seat 90 degrees.

9. Select the curves from front to back. The selection order dictates the direction of the surface as well as the lofting order. Selecting curves out of order will result in a loft that overlaps itself.

10. Choose Surfaces ➤ Loft ➤ Options. In the Loft Options dialog box, make sure the degree of the loft is set to Cubic.

11. Click the Loft button. Figure 3.34 shows the lofted surface.

FIGURE 3.34
The duplicated curves are selected in order from right to left, and then a loft surface is created.

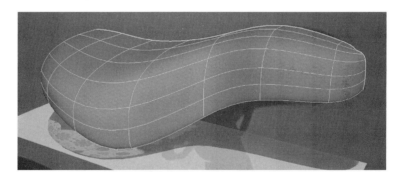

12. With the basic surface created, you can now select individual curves and modify the shape interactively. To facilitate shaping the curves, add the surface to a referenced layer. You can also select all the curves and press F8 to enter global component mode (see Figure 3.35). Global component mode allows you to adjust the components of every object you select instead of on a per model basis.

13. Name the new surface **seat**. When you're happy with the result, save the model as **bicycle_v03.ma**.

To see a version of the scene to this point, open the bicycle_v03.ma scene from the chapter3\scenes directory at the book's web page.

FIGURE 3.35
The CVs of the loft, selected and repositioned to match the reference images

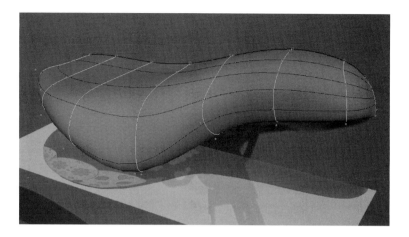

Attaching Surfaces

Once half of the model is shaped, you can mirror it to the other side and attach the surfaces together. The following steps take you through the process.

1. Continue with the scene from the previous section, or open the `bicycle_v03.ma` scene from the `chapter3\scenes` folder at the book's web page.

2. The construction history is no longer needed. Select the seat and choose Edit ➢ Delete By Type ➢ History.

3. Select all of the curves and delete them.

4. Select the seat. Choose Edit ➢ Duplicate Special ➢ Options. Group the duplicate under World and set the scale to **–1.0** in the z-axis (see Figure 3.36). Make sure the seat's pivot point is located along the XY plane; you'll scale from the pivot. Choose Duplicate Special to apply the settings and close the window.

FIGURE 3.36
Use these settings to create a mirror image of the seat.

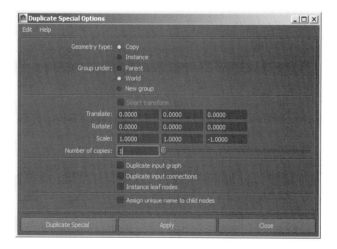

Mirroring Objects

When you've completed changes for one side of a NURBS model, you can mirror them to the other side:

1. Create a group for the parts you want to mirror; by default, the pivot for the new group will be at the center of the grid.

2. Select the group and choose Edit ➢ Duplicate Special.

3. Set Scale X of the duplicate to **–1.0** to mirror across the x-axis.

When you create the duplicate, you can freeze transformations on the objects and ungroup them if you like.

---

5. Select the mirrored duplicate and original seat.

6. Choose Edit Nurbs ➢ Attach Surfaces ➢ Options. You can choose from two different attachment methods. The first, Connect, will attach the two surfaces and preserve the existing shape. Blend will average the control vertices being attached. For the bike seat, choose Blend to create a smooth transition between the two surfaces. Uncheck Keep Originals and click Attach. Figure 3.37 shows the settings.

Figure 3.37
The options for
Attach Surfaces

7. The two halves are now one. Notice the front and back of the surface did not attach. This is because a NURBS surface must have four sides. Delete the node's history and freeze its transforms.

8. You can continue to make adjustments to the surface to match the reference material by modifying its components. There are only two component types you can manually adjust: hulls and control vertices.

9. Save the scene as **bicycle_v04.ma**.

To see a version of the scene to this point, open the bicycle_v04.ma scene from the chapter3\scenes directory at the book's web page.

REVOLVED SURFACES

Revolves are useful for creating cylindrically shaped objects from a single curve. You can quickly create a complex surface and continue to modify it through its construction history. The following example walks you through the process of creating a wine glass:

1. Use the CV Curve tool to draw the profile of a wine glass. The image here shows a completed curve:

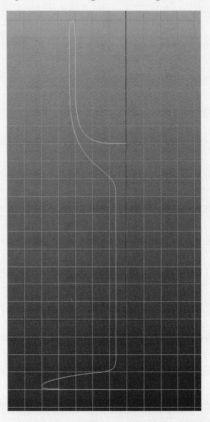

2. Choose Surfaces ➤ Revolve. The following image shows the resulting revolved surface:

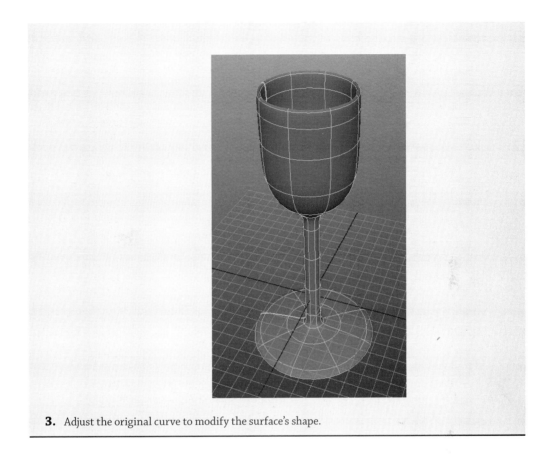

3. Adjust the original curve to modify the surface's shape.

Converting NURBS Surfaces to Polygons

Today's production pipelines demand a high degree of flexibility. NURBS excel at creating smooth contours but are not easily combined into complex objects. You can use a NURBS surface to start a polygon model combining the strengths of both NURBS and polygon-modeling tools. You have built multiple pieces of the bike using NURBS surfaces. To take the models to the next level, we'll convert from NURBS to polygons.

1. Continue with the scene from the previous section, or open the `bicycle_v04.ma` scene from the `chapter3\scenes` folder at the book's web page.

2. Select the bicycle seat.

3. Choose Modify ➤ Convert ➤ NURBS To Polygons ➤ Options.

4. Maya provides numerous tessellation methods for converting NURBS to polygons. For the bike the best method is going to be control points. Control points works well since we controlled the number of points through the curves used to create the surfaces. Figure 3.38 shows the selected options.

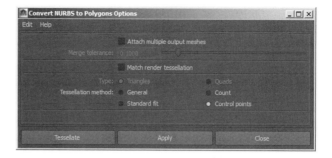

NURBS TESSELLATION METHODS

In addition to control points, Maya offers three other tessellation methods for converting your NURBS surfaces to polygons. General divides the geometry based on the number of U and V values you enter. You can think of this as the number of contiguous edges that will wrap around your model. Count allows you to enter a target value for the number of polygons. The geometry will be subdivided to the closest possible value. Last, Standard Fit allows you to establish a criterion for subdividing the model. Standard Fit will continue to tessellate the model until that criterion is met.

5. Converting the bike seat results in a linear polygon surface (see Figure 3.39). It might look as if you wasted your time shaping the model; however, you can enable smooth mesh preview by pressing **3** on the keyboard.

FIGURE 3.39
The NURBS surface converted to polygons

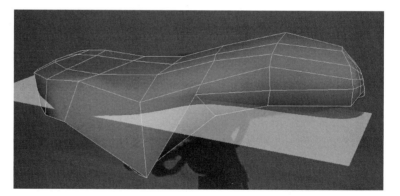

6. Name the new surface **seat**. Save the model as **bicycle_v05.ma**.

7. Convert the rest of the NURBS surfaces in the scene using the same settings.

To see a version of the scene to this point, open the bicycle_v05.ma scene from the chapter3\scenes directory at the book's web page.

Modeling with Polygons

Maya 2015 brings lots of significant changes to the polygon tools. The Modeling Toolkit, first introduced in Maya 2014, has been further integrated into the Maya global polygon toolset. The polygon menus have been restructured for better organization and to include tools from the toolkit. In addition, several tools, like Bevel and Boolean operations, have been reworked for improved performance and stability.

When dealing with hard-surface objects, you want to stay away from pushing and pulling vertices manually. This generates uneven and inaccurate contours. In general, hard-surface objects are made in factories, where precision is essential to the completion of a product. Modeling can be a numbers game. Aligning parts with the same number of edges/faces makes the modeling process a lot easier. With that, it is beneficial to start a model using primitive objects as opposed to building polygon geometry from scratch. Primitive surfaces provide consistent geometry and can be easily modified through their construction history.

Using Booleans

A *Boolean operation* in the context of polygon modeling creates a new surface by adding two surfaces together (union), subtracting one surface from the other (difference), or creating a surface from the overlapping parts of two surfaces (intersection). Figure 3.40 shows the results of the three types of Boolean operations applied to a polygon torus and cube.

FIGURE 3.40
A polygon torus and cube have been combined using union (left), difference (center), and intersection (right) operations.

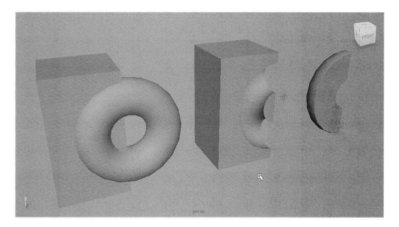

Maya 2015 uses a new carve library for its Boolean operations. The workflow is the same, but the results are improved. Regardless, Booleans are complex operations. The geometry created using Booleans can sometimes produce artifacts in the completed model, so it's best to keep the geometry as simple as possible. It's also beneficial to align the edges of one surface with that of another in order to reduce the number of extra divisions that may result.

In this section, you'll use Boolean operations to weld the different parts of the bike frame together:

1. Continue with the scene from the previous section, or open the `bicycle_v05.ma` scene from the `chapter3\scenes` folder at the book's web page.

2. Select the two largest pipes of the bike frame. The ends of the pipes intersect each other by the handle bars. You can use an intersection to weld these two pipes together. Prior to performing the Boolean operation, the ends need to be cleaned up. Select the end vertices of both pipes (see Figure 3.41).

FIGURE 3.41
Select the ends of the two largest parts of the bike frame.

3. Open the options for the Scale tool by double-clicking its icon in the toolbox. The icon is a cube with four red arrows emanating from it.

4. Select Discrete Scale and set the step size to **1.0**. The Scale tool will now snap to a value of 1.

5. The goal is to make both ends flush with each other and to maintain the angle of the bottom pipe. Change the orientation of the manipulator by matching a point from the lower pipe. Under the Scale Settings rollout, click Set To Point. The manipulator is now oriented properly.

6. Scale the selection in the y-axis until the vertices are flush with each other. Figure 3.42 shows the results.

7. The open edges at either end of the pipes will prevent the Boolean from welding the two objects cleanly. The polygon faces that overlap will remain since neither surface is a closed volume. To close the ends, choose Mesh ➤ (Shape) Fill Hole.

8. You can now use the Boolean tool on the two objects. With both surfaces selected, choose Mesh ➤ (Combine) Booleans ➤ Intersection. Figure 3.43 shows the results of the Boolean.

FIGURE 3.42
Scale the ends of the pipe to make them flush with each other.

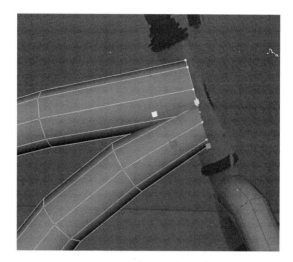

FIGURE 3.43
Use Intersection to join the two parts of the frame together.

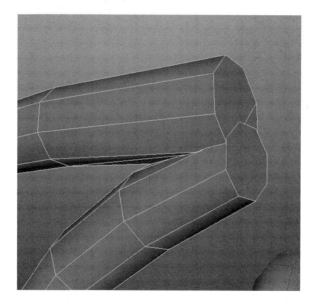

9. To bring the fork together with the large pipes of the frame, create a primitive polygon cylinder using the tool's default settings (see Figure 3.44).

10. Position the cylinder to match the reference material. Use the settings in Figure 3.45 to alter the construction history of the cylinder.

FIGURE 3.44
Create a polygon
cylinder.

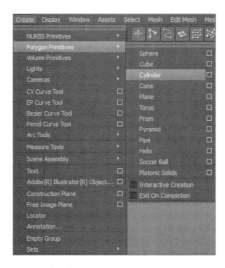

FIGURE 3.45
Position and alter
the cylinder's con-
struction history.

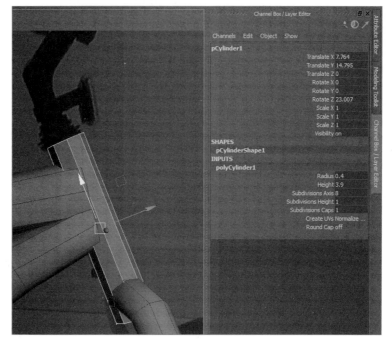

11. Before intersecting the parts, match up the geometry to avoid overlap and extra divisions. Scaling the ends of the pipe until the vertices reside inside the primitive cylinder works best. Use Figure 3.46 for reference.

12. It also helps if additional geometry is added to give the Boolean a better surface to cut into. Select the primitive cylinder and choose Mesh Tools ➤ (Edit) Insert Edge Loop Tool.

13. Using the default settings of the tool, LMB-click on the cylinder at the approximate location where the two frame pipes have been welded together (see Figure 3.47). Release the mouse button when you are happy with the edge loop's placement.

FIGURE 3.46
Scale the ends of the frame pieces to fit inside the primitive cylinder.

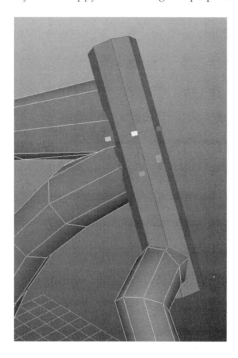

FIGURE 3.47
Insert an edge loop into the cylinder.

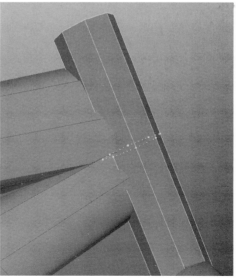

14. Add two more edge loops on either side of the inserted edge loop. Align them with a corresponding edge from the frame. Use Figure 3.48 as a guide.

FIGURE 3.48
Insert two more edge loops into the cylinder.

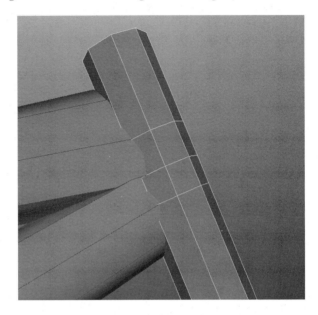

15. Select the frame, fork, and cylinder. The order is irrelevant. Choose Mesh ➤ (Combine) Booleans ➤ Union. Figure 3.49 shows the results.

16. Delete the history and save your scene as **bicycle_v06.ma**.

To see a version of the scene to this point, open the bicycle_v06.ma scene from the chapter3\scenes directory at the book's web page.

Cleaning Topology

Topology refers to the arrangement of polygon edges on a surface. The versatility of polygons allows you to alter components freely, which can result in bad topology. As a result, the polygons often require a bit of work to maintain their integrity. In this section, we'll look at multiple tools for adding and removing polygon components.

1. Continue with the scene from the previous section, or open the bicycle_v06.ma scene from the chapter3\scenes folder at the book's web page.

2. The Boolean applied in the previous section has left numerous *n*-sided polygons and overlapping edges. You can clean these up quickly with the Target Weld tool. Choose Mesh Tools ➤ (Edit) Target Weld Tool. RMB-click over the geometry and choose Vertex. A red circle shows up around the closest vertex to your mouse as a preselection highlight (see Figure 3.50).

FIGURE 3.49
Use a union
Boolean to weld
all three parts
together.

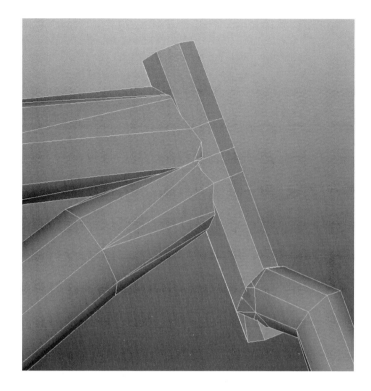

FIGURE 3.50
A preselection high-
light is activated
when using the
Target Weld tool.

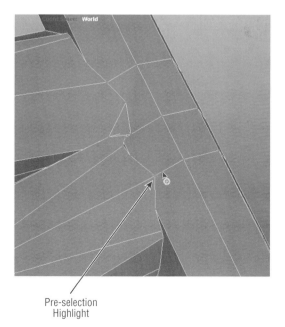

Pre-selection
Highlight

3. The difference between a stray vertex and a vertex with good topology is that a stray vertex does not conform to the existing structure of the geometry. LMB-click on a stray vertex and drag to a vertex with good topology. A line is displayed between the two vertices.

   Notice how the good edges define the structure. Eliminating the vertices surrounding them will have little impact on the surface shape.

4. Work your way around the frame connection points. Only do one side or half of the geometry. Eventually the clean side will be mirrored across. Figure 3.51 shows the bicycle frame after the stray vertices have been welded to existing vertices.

FIGURE 3.51
The bike frame has been cleaned of stray vertices.

5. You can also eliminate the edges that are creating triangles on the surface. Having them gone will make modifying the surface easier and make the surface smoother, especially with smooth mesh preview (see Figure 3.52).

FIGURE 3.52
The triangle-forming edges have been removed.

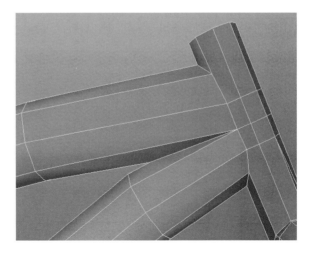

There are two ways you can delete an edge. The first is to simply select the edge and press Delete on the keyboard. The second is to select the edge and choose Edit Mesh ➢ (Edge) Delete Edge/Vertex or press Ctrl+Delete. The difference between the two methods is that the latter will delete any non-winged vertices associated to the edge. Go through the area you cleaned and remove the triangle edges. Only Delete on the keyboard should be necessary.

Non-winged Vertices

Vertices that are attached to two or fewer edges are called *non-winged vertices*. These vertices can be deleted, whereas "winged" vertices—those connected by more than two edges—cannot.

---

6. Use the Boolean tools for the rest of the bike frame and clean the topology. Add more cylinders as needed. Remember, you need to do only one side.

To see a version of the scene to this point, open the `bicycle_v07.ma` scene from the `chapter3\scenes` directory at the book's web page.

Creating Your Own Polygons

Primitives are a great place to start modeling, but some shapes are too irregular to make with primitives. You can build your own polygon shapes to begin a model. The following section walks you through the process of building the odd-shaped tire hanger of the rear tire.

1. Continue with the scene from the previous section, or open the `bicycle_v07.ma` scene from the `chapter3\scenes` folder at the book's web page. Half of the bike frame has been removed for simplicity.

2. Choose Mesh Tools ➢ (Edit) Create Polygon Tool.

3. Using the tool's defaults, LMB-click to create the basic shape of the tire hanger. Leave out the round tab at the top-left corner (see Figure 3.53). When finished, press Enter to complete the shape.

4. When you're building a round shape from scratch, there is no need to try to draw a circle. Instead, start with a primitive object, like a cylinder or sphere, to get a rounded object. You can then integrate the rounded shape into your object. For the tab, create a primitive cylinder.

5. Transform the cylinder to match the size and location of the screw hole in the tab. Use Figure 3.54 as reference.

6. Select all the faces of the cylinder except for one end. Press Delete to remove the geometry, leaving a polygonal disc (see Figure 3.55).

7. With the disc selected, choose Modify ➢ Center Pivot. The pivot point is forced into the middle of the disc.

8. Snap the disc to the XY grid plane. You can use the hot key **x** to snap to grid.

9. To complete the tab, RMB-click over the geometry and select Edge. Double-click any of the exterior edges to select the entire outer loop.

FIGURE 3.53
Use the Create
Polygon tool to draw
out a custom shape.

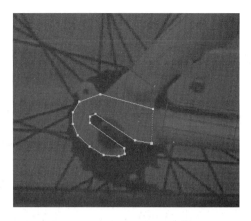

FIGURE 3.54
Position a primi-
tive cylinder in
the screw hole of
the tab.

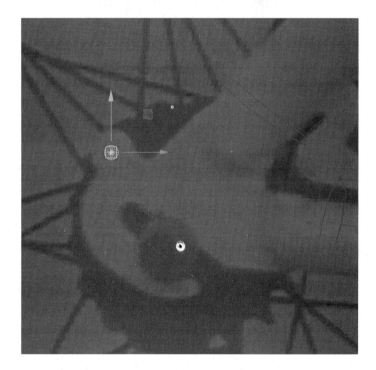

10. Choose Mesh Tools ➤ (Edit) Extrude Tool. Extrude the edge selection to match the outer size of the metal tab (see Figure 3.56).

11. Delete the faces for half of the disc. Do not include any of the faces on the interior circle.

12. Select the border edges from the side of the disc you deleted. You can select the row of edges by clicking on the first edge and then double-clicking on the last.

FIGURE 3.55
Delete the faces
of a cylinder to
create a disc.

FIGURE 3.56
Extrude the
edges of the
polygon disc.

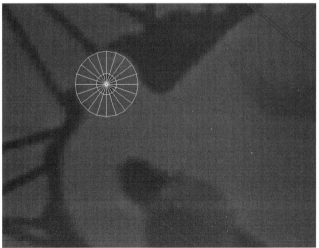

13. Choose Extrude. Do not move the extrusion. Choose the Move tool and open its tool options. You want to translate the newly extruded edges in a linear direction that matches the center line of the disc. To do this, select Set To Edge under the Move tool settings. Click on the center edge. The Move tool updates to the new orientation.

14. Translate the edge selection to where it meets the polygon edge of the tire hanger, as shown in Figure 3.57.

FIGURE 3.57
Translate the edges in the x-axis to meet the edge of the tire hanger.

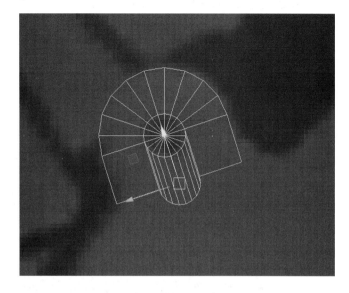

15. Open the Scale tool options. Set the orientation of the Scale tool to the same edge from step 13. Scale the edge selection with a discrete scale of **1.0** to make the edges coplanar. Figure 3.58 shows the results.

FIGURE 3.58
Scale the edges to make them coplanar.

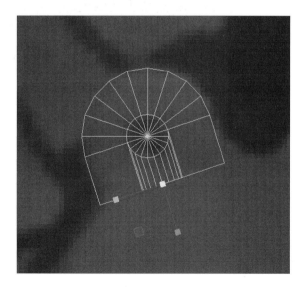

16. You can now delete the interior faces that make up the hole of the tab. To quickly select the faces, RMB-click over the geometry and choose Vertex. Click the center vertex of the interior disc. Hold Ctrl+RMB over the geometry and from the marking menu choose To Faces ➤ To Faces. Delete the selected faces.

To see a version of the scene to this point, open the `bicycle_v08.ma` scene from the `chapter3\scenes` directory at the book's web page.

Multi-Cut Tool

The Multi-Cut tool allows you to divide polygon faces. You can use it to make simple divisions, from one vertex to another, or to cut through multiple edges all at once. You are also allowed to draw divisions inside existing faces as long as you end up on an adjacent edge. The Multi-Cut tool effectively replaces the Interactive Split Polygon tool. Figure 3.59 shows an example.

FIGURE 3.59
With the Multi-Cut tool, you can draw divisions inside existing faces.

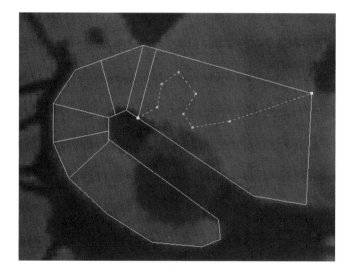

The following steps walk you through adding divisions with the Multi-Cut tool:

1. Continue with the scene from the previous section, or open the `bicycle_v08.ma` scene from the `chapter3\scenes` folder at the book's web page.

2. The tab and custom polygon shape need to be merged together. Before you can do this, their components must match. Select the custom polygon shape.

3. Choose Mesh Tools ➤ (Edit) Multi-Cut Tool. LMB-click on the inside loop and then again on the outside edge to create a division. RMB-click to complete the division. You can also press Enter to complete the cut. Use Figure 3.60 as a guide.

4. Continue to add divisions to the surface. You need enough divisions, around six, to create a circular shape. The tire hanger has two circular shapes: one on the inside and one on the outside. Use the Multi-Cut tool to connect the two half circles (see Figure 3.61).

FIGURE 3.60
Use the Multi-Cut tool to add a division to the custom polygon shape.

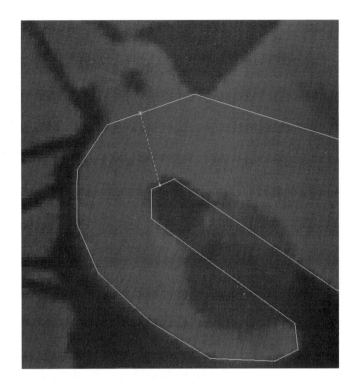

FIGURE 3.61
Add divisions to round out the interior and exterior of the tire hanger.

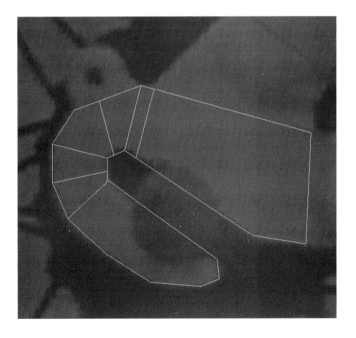

5. Use the Multi-Cut tool to remove the remaining *n*-gons on the surface. You can click and hold on an edge to drag the division along the length of the edge to be divided. Holding Shift snaps the division to 10-percent increments. Figure 3.62 shows the new divisions.

FIGURE 3.62
Divide the geometry to get rid of any *n*-gons.

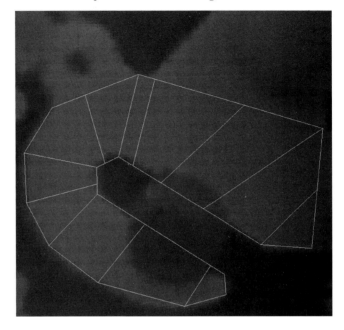

To see a version of the scene to this point, open the `bicycle_v09.ma` scene from the `chapter3\scenes` directory at the book's web page.

Combining and Merging Geometry

Typically it's best to build complex parts as individual pieces and then bring them all together to form a single object. The tire hanger is made up of two separate pieces. To join them into one, you will use a combination of tools. The following steps take you through the process:

1. Continue with the scene from the previous section, or open the `bicycle_v09.ma` scene from the `chapter3\scenes` folder at the book's web page.

2. Select the tab and custom polygon shape. Choose Mesh ➤ Combine. The two separate objects are now a single node.

3. Delete the node's history and rename the node to **tireHanger**.

COMBINE AND SEPARATE

Combining does not merge any geometry. It merely makes multiple nodes into a single node. As long as the geometry is not connected by any components, you can split the combined components back into individual nodes using Mesh ➤ (Separate) Separate.

---

4. Select the four vertices that make up the center of the tab and polygon shape (see Figure 3.63).

FIGURE 3.63
Select the middle vertices by the connection point of the combined object.

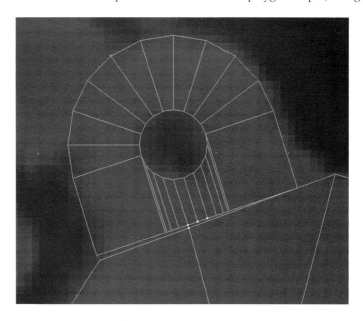

5. Choose Edit Mesh ➤ Merge Components To Center.

6. Select the remaining vertices on one side of the tab. Use Target Weld to drag the entire selection to the left corner vertex of the custom polygon shape. Figure 3.64 shows the end result.

FIGURE 3.64
Weld half of the vertices to a single vertex.

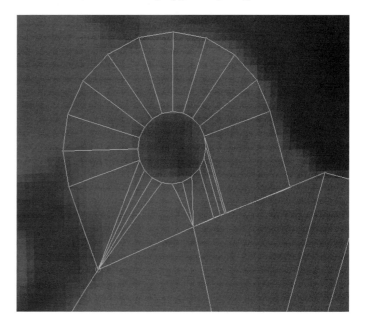

7. Repeat step 6 for the other side of the tab shape.

8. Shape the geometry to match the reference material. Save your scene as **bicycle_v10.ma.**

To see a version of the scene to this point, open the bicycle_v10.ma scene from the chapter3\scenes directory at the book's web page.

Bridge Polygon

The Bridge tool appends a series of polygons between border edges. The border edges must reside on the same node before the Bridge tool will work. The Bridge tool can make quick work of connecting the tire hanger to the frame of the bike. To use the Bridge tool, follow these steps:

1. Continue with the scene from the previous section, or open the bicycle_v10.ma scene from the chapter3\scenes folder at the book's web page.

2. Select the tire hanger. Extrude the geometry in the local z-axis to 0.1.

3. Center the object's pivot. Snap the object to the center line of the frame, as Figure 3.65 shows.

FIGURE 3.65
Snap the tire hanger to the center line of the bike frame.

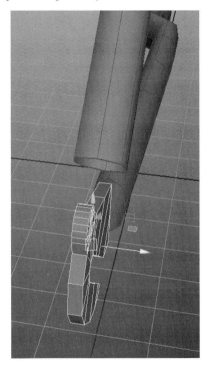

4. To bridge between two objects, the border edges you want to bridge must have the same number of edges. With the tireHanger node selected, choose Mesh Tools ➤ (Edit) Insert Edge Loop ➤ Options.

5. Under Settings in the Insert Edge Loop tool, check Multiple Edge Loops. Change the number of edge loops to **1**. Setting a value of 1 is a quick trick to insert a loop in the center of your selection. Click on any edge along the thickness of the tire hanger (see Figure 3.66). Release the mouse button to insert the loop.

FIGURE 3.66
Insert an edge loop
down the middle of
the thickness of the
tire hanger.

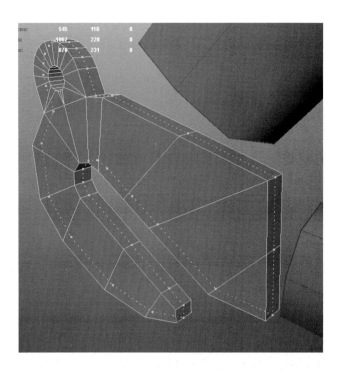

6. Select the four faces next to the lowest bar on the bike frame and delete them. This creates a border edge. Use Figure 3.67 for reference.

FIGURE 3.67
Delete the four
faces closest to
the lower bar of
the bike frame.

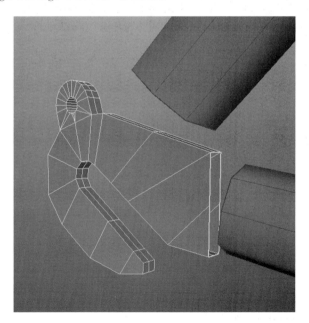

DISPLAY COMPONENTS

You can visualize border edges per object by opening the object's Attribute Editor and expanding the Mesh Component Display rollout. You can select the Display Borders option as well as change the Border Width display.

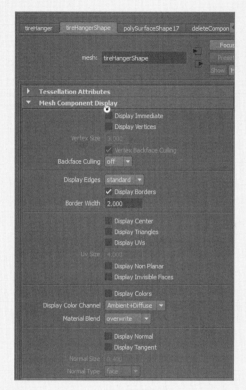

7. Select the frame and tire hanger. Combine the objects into a single node.

8. RMB-click on the object and choose Edge from the marking menu.

9. Double-click both border edges, as shown in Figure 3.68.

FIGURE 3.68
Select the bor-
der edges.

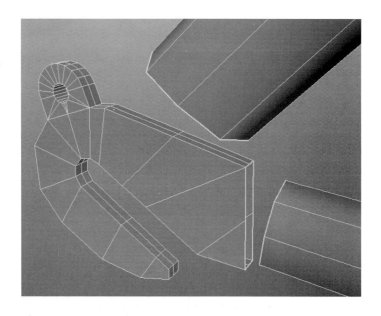

10. Choose Edit Mesh ➤ (Edge) Bridge. The defaults create too much geometry. In the Channel Box or Attribute Editor, change Divisions to **1** (see Figure 3.69).

FIGURE 3.69
Change the
number of divi-
sions in the
bridge to 1.

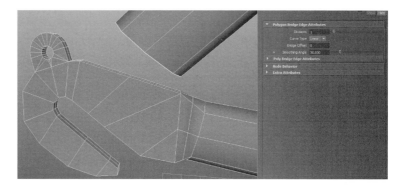

11. Repeat the steps 5 through 9, omitting step 6, to bridge the upper part of the bike frame. Figure 3.70 shows the finished product. Save your scene as **bicycle_v11.ma.**

FIGURE 3.70
Bridge the top section of the frame.

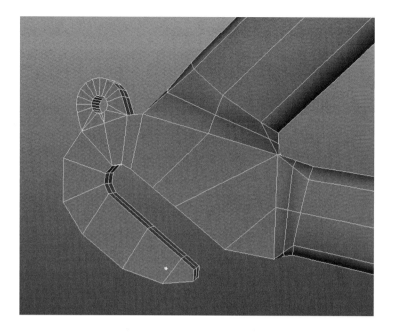

BRIDGE OFFSET

Bridging edges do not always line up perfectly. Often the bridge will appear twisted as a result of appending edges together that are not directly in line with one another. To correct this, use the bridge offset. You can click on the channel in the Channel Box and then MMB-click in the viewport to cycle through edge values to find the desired results.

To see a version of the scene to this point, open the `bicycle_v11.ma` scene from the `chapter3\scenes` directory at the book's web page.

Mirror Cut

The Mirror Cut tool creates symmetry in a model across a specified axis. The tool creates a cutting plane. Any geometry on one side of the plane is duplicated onto the other side and simultaneously merged with the original geometry.

In the options for Mirror Cut, you can raise the Tolerance, which will help prevent extra vertices from being created along the center line of the model. If you raise it too high, the vertices near the center may be collapsed. You may have to experiment to find the right setting.

1. Continue with the scene from the previous section, or open the `bicycle_v11.ma` scene from the `chapter3\scenes` directory at the book's web page.

2. Select the bike frame, and choose Mesh ➤ (Mirror) Mirror Cut. A plane appears down the center of the bike frame's geometry.

3. Set the Translate Z channel of mirrorCutPlane1 to **0.0**. The mirrored geometry is extended.

DISAPPEARING OR GREEN POLYGONS

It may look as though polygons disappear when you use the Mirror Cut tool. It might just be that Maya is not displaying them correctly. If this happens to you, choose the default material icon from the Viewport menu. The icon is a sphere that is half shaded in gray and half a checkerboard. This forces everything in the viewport to use the default material.

In the Outliner, several new nodes have been created. These include the mirrorCutPlane1 and the mirroredCutMesh1 group. The frame has been renamed to polySurface18 (see Figure 3.71).

FIGURE 3.71
Mirror the frame across the z-axis using the Mirror Cut tool.

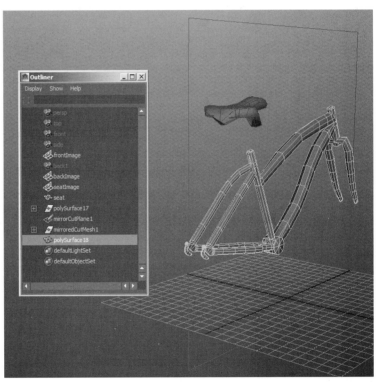

4. Select the polySurface18 node, and choose Edit ➤ Delete By Type ➤ History. This removes the group nodes that were created. Select the mirrorCutPlane1 node, and delete it.

5. Name the polySurface18 node **frame**.

To see a version of the scene to this point, open the bicycle_v12.ma scene from the chapter3\scenes directory at the book's web page.

The rest of the bike can be modeled using the methods and techniques outlined in this chapter. When approaching a new piece, ask yourself if there is a primitive object that closely matches the surface shape or even a portion of the surface shape. For instance, the bike tire can be created quickly using a primitive polygon torus. You can use the following settings for the torus's construction history.

Radius: **6.21**

Section Radius: **0.52**

Subdivision Axis: **30**

Subdivisions Height: **8**

Figure 3.72 shows the finished version of the bike. You can also open the `bicycle_final.ma` scene from the `chapter3\scenes` directory at the book's web page.

FIGURE 3.72
The finished version of the bicycle

The Bottom Line

Understand polygon geometry.   Polygon geometry consists of flat faces connected and shaped to form three-dimensional objects. You can edit the geometry by transforming the vertices, edges, and faces that make up the surface of the model.

Master It   Examine the polygon primitives in the Create ➢ Polygon Primitives menu.

Understand NURBS surfaces.   NURBS surfaces can be created by lofting a surface across a series of curves. The curve and surface degree and parameterization affect the shape of the resulting surface.

Master It   What is the difference between a one-degree (linear) surface, a three-degree (cubic) surface, and a five-degree surface?

Understand subdivision surfaces. Any polygon object can be converted to a subdivision surface directly from its Attribute Editor. Maya offers three different methods for subdivision.

Master It Convert a polygon model to a subdivision surface model. Examine how the polygon object changes in shape.

Employ image planes. Image planes can be used to position images for use as a modeling guide.

Master It Create image planes for side, front, and top views for use as a model guide.

Model with NURBS surfaces. A variety of tools and techniques can be used to model surfaces with NURBS. Hard-surface/mechanical objects are well-suited subjects for NURBS surfaces.

Master It Create the spokes of the bike.

Model with polygons. Booleans can be a great way to quickly cut holes into polygon surfaces. It is important, however, to establish a clean surface for the Boolean to cut into or intersect with. When you're using multiple objects, doing so becomes even more important.

Master It Create the hub for all of the bicycle spokes to come into. Each spoke should have its own hole.

Chapter 4

Organic Modeling

Organic modeling uses the same basic tools required for hard modeling. However, the demand on the tools is greater. Organic-looking surfaces are much harder to generate than most factory-built objects. Organic surfaces require nature's imperfections and long continuous surfaces that blend back into themselves.

This chapter focuses on creating the base shape of a generic human female—generic because the main goal is not to model specific details of an individual but to convey proper edge flow and structure that can support anatomy. Following these principles will allow you to adapt the methods to create other life forms, such as a quadruped or ape.

In this chapter, you will learn to:

♦   Implement box modeling

♦   Employ build-out modeling

♦   Sculpt polygons

♦   Use retopology tools

Implement Box Modeling

Box modeling is the technique of using the polygon-modeling tools to shape a basic cube into a more complex object. Once the form is established, you can add more geometry to create detail. Over the years, as computer power and modeling tools have improved, the box model has also evolved into a more rounded shape. To begin a human form, you will start with a smoothed cube. This allows you to pull out the necessary amount of geometry for good *surface flow*.

Surface flow refers to the orientation of your polygon edges. Ideally you want to have uniformly spaced edges or polygon faces of equal size. Your edges should be perpendicular to each other, creating square faces. Poor surface flow can result in poor deformation. The fewer the polygons, the more important surface flow becomes.

TOPOLOGY

Topology is a big concern when modeling surfaces that will be animated using deformers. Character modelers spend a great deal of time perfecting the topology of their models so that they work well when animated.

The best way to start is to create some orthographic drawings based on the sketch. You can use these as a guide in the Autodesk® Maya® software to ensure that the placement of the model's parts and the proportions is consistent. Sometimes the concept artist creates these drawings for you; sometimes you need to create them yourself. (And sometimes you may be both modeler and concept artist.) When creating the drawings, it's usually a good idea to focus on the major forms, creating bold lines and leaving out most of the details. A heavily detailed drawing can get confusing when you're working in Maya. You can always refer to the original concept drawing as a guide for the details. Since there is only one view of the design, some parts of the model need to be invented for the three-dimensional version. Figure 4.1 shows the orthographic drawings for this project.

FIGURE 4.1
Simplified drawings have been created for the front and side views of the concept.

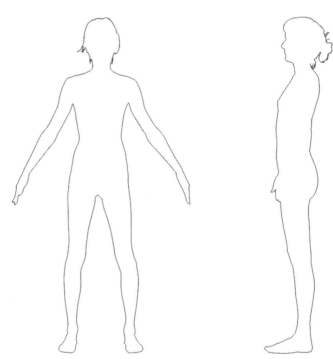

After you create the orthographic drawings, your first task is to bring them into Maya and apply them to image planes. You can do so by following the instructions outlined in Chapter 3, "Hard-Surface Modeling," in the section "Employing Image Planes."

Shaping Using Smooth Mesh Polygon Geometry

In this section, you'll create the basic shape of the torso for the human character using the Extrude tool and smooth mesh polygon geometry.

1. Open the torso_v01.ma scene from the chapter4\scenes directory at the book's web page (www.sybex.com/go/masteringmaya2015). The scene contains two free image planes, each set up with a different view of the female reference material. If the image files are missing from the scene and you get an error, you may have to remap the images onto the image planes.

2. Choose the Create ➤ Polygon Primitives ➤ Cube options and in the resulting window accept the default options.

3. Select the cube, and name it **torso**. Position and scale the torso so that it roughly matches the position of the torso in the side view.

4. Set the channels as follows:

    Translate X: **0**

    Translate Y: **16.356**

    Translate Z: **0**

    Scale X: **3.782**

    Scale Y: **3.782**

    Scale Z: **3.782**

5. With the cube selected, choose Mesh ➤ (Shape) Smooth. Use the default settings. Figure 4.2 shows the progress so far.

FIGURE 4.2
A smoothed poly-gon cube placed roughly in the same position as the torso in the side view

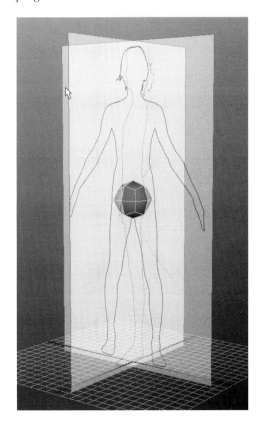

6. With the torso selected, press the **3** key to switch to smooth mesh preview. The edges of the shape become rounded. With smooth mesh preview enabled, the object is essentially a sphere.

SMOOTH MESH PREVIEW SETTINGS

By default, smooth mesh preview displays the smoothing at two divisions, as if you had applied a smoothing operation to the geometry twice. You can change the display settings on a particular piece of polygon geometry by selecting the object and choosing Display ➤ Polygons ➤ Custom Polygon Display. These settings are also located under the Smooth Mesh rollout on the shape node in the Attribute Editor. At the bottom of the Custom Polygon Display Options dialog box, you'll find the Smooth Mesh rollout. Changing the value of the Division Levels slider sets the number of subdivisions for the smooth mesh preview. You can also select the Show Subdivisions option to see the subdivisions on the preview displayed as dotted lines. The options are applied to the selected object when you click the Apply button. Be aware that a high Division Levels setting slows down the performance of playback in Maya scenes.

Additional controls are available under the Extra Controls rollout. Lowering the Continuity slider decreases the roundness of the edges on the preview. You can also choose to smooth the UVs and preserve Hard Edges and Geometry borders.

7. Open the Modeling Toolkit by clicking the vertical tab on the right side of the screen. Choose the Select tool (see Figure 4.3). Clicking on any of the transformation tools automatically activates the toolkit. It also sets your component selection to Multi-Component mode.

FIGURE 4.3
Click the Select tool in the Modeling Toolkit.

8. The Modeling Toolkit has a symmetry function that allows you to work on half of the model while the other half automatically updates. To use this feature, first select a single edge along the object's center line. There is no need to change your component selection since you are in Multi-Component mode.

9. Click the Symmetry button in the Modeling Toolkit. The name of the object now appears below the Symmetry button.

10. With the Symmetry feature active, you only need to work on half of the model. This includes making selections as well. With that in mind, select the four faces as shown in Figure 4.4.

FIGURE 4.4
Select four faces on the right side of the shape.

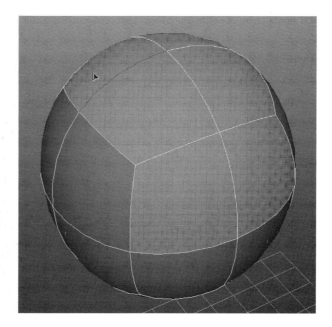

11. Switch to the front view. Select the Extrude button under the Mesh Editing Tools rollout of the Modeling Toolkit. Click and drag to pull the extrusion out in the local z-axis. Pull the faces until they reach the border of the drawing (see Figure 4.5).

EXTRUDE IN THE MODELING TOOLKIT

When you choose the Extrude tool, you are given an additional rollout based on your current selection. By default, Face Extrude is set to Local Z. You can choose another option from the rollout or use the tool's marking menu by pressing Ctrl+Shift and then RMB-clicking in the viewport. Dragging with the LMB affects the active option.

FIGURE 4.5
Extrude the
selected faces to
match the reference
material.

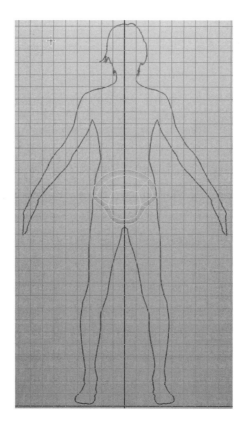

12. Switch to the Scale tool. The hot key **r** works with the Modeling Toolkit. Scale down the extruded faces in the y-axis. The Scale tool stops automatically when the faces are flattened (see Figure 4.6).

FIGURE 4.6
Scale the faces in
the y-axis.

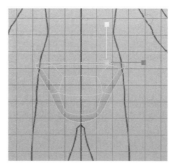

13. Switch to the perspective view, and shape the surface to roughly match the drawing. Use the Move tool to push and pull vertices. Remember, only half of the model needs to be adjusted. The Symmetry feature allows you to select a vertex from either side of the model. Figure 4.7 shows the pelvis after it has been shaped.

FIGURE 4.7
Shape the vertices of the pelvis with the Move tool.

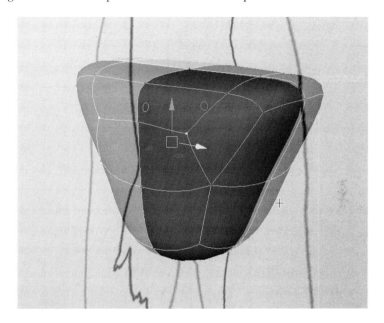

SMOOTH MESH VERTEX DISPLAY

As you select vertices using the Move tool, you'll notice that the handle of the Move tool is offset from the selected vertices. If you find this confusing, press the 2 key to see a wireframe cage of the original mesh. Then you'll see the actual positions of the vertices on the unsmoothed version of the surface.

---

14. Select the four faces that make up the top of the surface, as shown in Figure 4.8.

15. Select Extrude and drag the extrusion to 1.0 unit. The Extrude tool remembers the value used in the last extrusion. You may end up dragging the extrusion back down in order to achieve the proper height. Figure 4.9 shows the relative placement for the extrusion.

FIGURE 4.8
Choose the faces
at the top of the
pelvis.

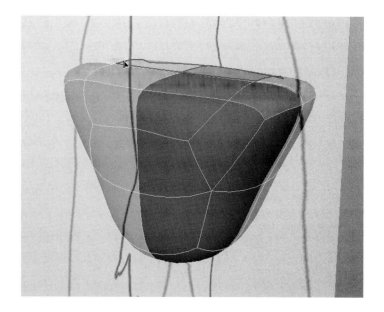

FIGURE 4.9
Extrude the top of
the torso upward in
the y-axis.

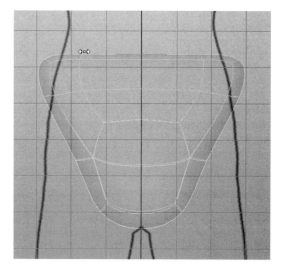

16. Scale the extruded faces in the x-axis to fit them with the reference material. The faces
below the new extrusion might be outside the reference material shape. This is okay for
now. Smooth mesh preview can cause the shape to change as you continue to extrude
faces; therefore, making subtle changes this early in the modeling process may be a waste
of time.

17. Save the scene as **`torso_v02.ma`**.

To see a version of the scene to this point, open the `torso_v02.ma` scene from the `chapter4\scenes` directory at the book's web page.

18. Continue with the scene from step 17, or open the `torso_v02.ma` scene from the `chapter4\scenes` directory at the book's web page. If you load a previously saved scene, you will need to reestablish symmetry. Look to steps 9 and 10 if you need help.

19. Before continuing with the torso, extrude the leg. Select four faces along the hip line. Use Figure 4.10 for reference.

FIGURE 4.10
Select the four faces needed to extrude the leg.

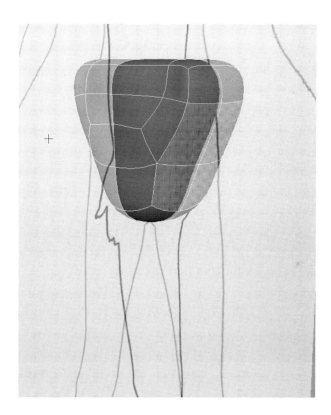

20. Before continuing with the body, extrude the leg. Select four faces along the hip line. Use Figure 4.11 for reference.

21. Translate and rotate the extruded leg to match the reference material (see Figure 4.12).

22. Continue to shape the torso at the vertex level. Use multiple viewports to get the correct contours (see Figure 4.13).

FIGURE 4.11
Extrude the leg in
the local z-axis.

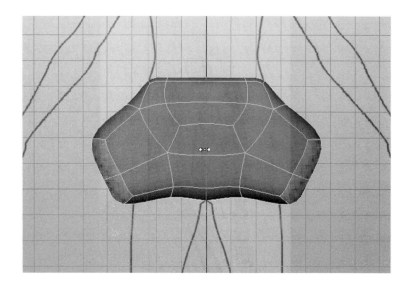

FIGURE 4.12
Shape the end of
the leg extrusion to
match the reference
material.

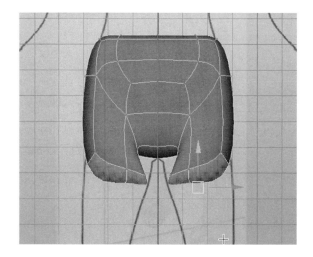

FIGURE 4.13
Shape the torso in
multiple views.

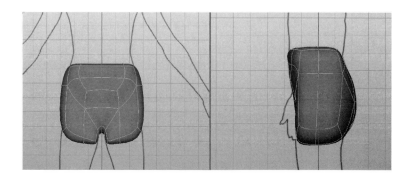

23. You can now focus your attention on the upper body. Select the faces at the top of the pelvis.

24. Extrude the faces up to the waist (see Figure 4.14).

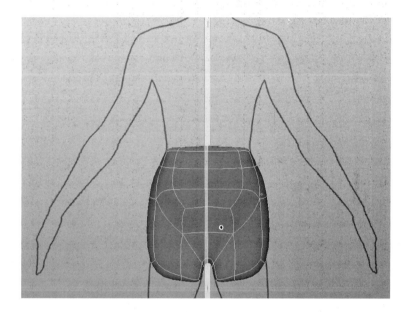

25. You can use the Extrude tool options to help shape the extrusion. Hold Ctrl+Shift RMB to open the marking menu and choose Offset. Click and drag to decrease the width of the geometry. Reduce the size of the extrusion until it matches the reference image.

26. The Extrude tool remains active until you click on another tool. To add another extrusion, Shift-drag to pull the extrusion up in the local z-axis. The Extrude tool always defaults to the local z-axis upon creation.

27. After releasing the mouse button, you can click again to use Offset to increase the width of the extrusion.

28. Hold Shift and extrude another level. Raise the geometry up to the armpit. Figure 4.15 shows the progress of the torso.

29. Save the scene as **torso_v03.ma**.

To see a version of the scene to this point, open the torso_v03.ma scene from the chapter4\scenes directory at the book's web page.

30. Continue with the scene from step 29, or open the torso_v03.ma scene from the chapter4\scenes directory at the book's web page. If you load a previously saved scene, you will need to reestablish symmetry. Again, look to steps 9 and 10 if you need help.

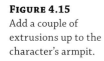

FIGURE 4.15
Add a couple of
extrusions up to the
character's armpit.

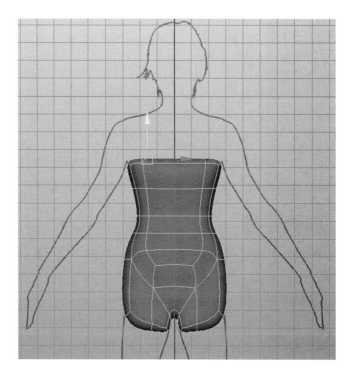

31. You can now extrude the shoulder. This is critical to getting proper edge flow. The direction of the geometry needs to change in order to accommodate the arm. Select the two faces, one in front and one in back, closest to the armpit.

32. If you are continuing from your own scene, you may want to click the Reset Settings button before extruding. This changes the Extrude options back to their default values, thus preventing unpredictable results.

33. Extrude the faces halfway into the shoulder.

34. Translate and rotate the extruded faces so the edges are perpendicular to the length of the arm (see Figure 4.16).

35. Add another extrusion to complete the shoulder. If the faces you are extruding from are at the proper angle, you may not need to adjust the new extrusion. The goal is to have four faces that can be extruded for the arm.

36. There is a large dip in the middle of the chest. Select all of the faces making up this U-shaped structure. There are six faces total on one side. Use Figure 4.17 as a guide.

FIGURE 4.16
Position the extrusion so faces can be extruded down the length of the arm.

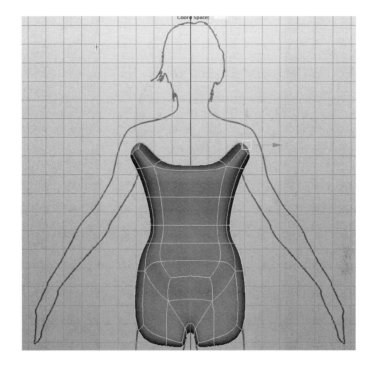

FIGURE 4.17
Select the faces in the middle of the torso.

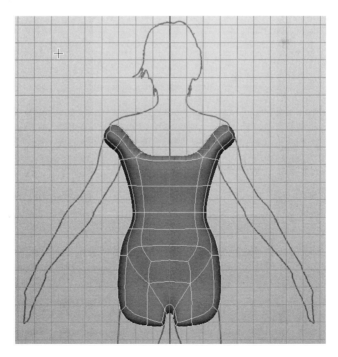

37. Extrude the faces up to the start of the neck. Scale the selection in the y-axis to flatten geometry.

38. Translate the selection so the geometry is on the shoulder line (see Figure 4.18).

FIGURE 4.18
Position the geometry to line up with the shoulders.

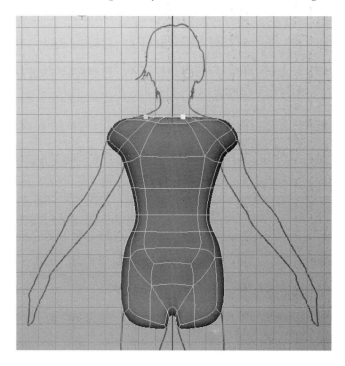

39. You can now go back and shape the geometry to match the reference material. When shaping the neck area, push the vertices outward to leave four faces total to be extruded up into the neck.

ARTISTIC JUDGMENT

Keep in mind that the main goal of this segment of the chapter is to become comfortable with the task of modeling with smooth preview. Creating a perfect representation of the reference image or an exact duplicate of the example model is not as important as gaining an understanding of the differences between normal polygons and smooth polygons.

In the real world, you would use your own artistic judgment when creating a model based on a drawing; there's no reason why you can't do the same while working through this chapter. The concept images are based off a real person. As you shape the geometry, do not forget how familiar you are with the subject. Consider your own body and the contours that describe your shape.

---

40. Save the scene as **torso_v04.ma**.

To see a version of the scene to this point, open the `torso_v04.ma` scene from the `chapter4\ scenes` directory at the book's web page.

The surface flow for the torso is complete. The edges have been configured in such a way that adding additional edge loops will wrap around the body and contribute to the surface shape where needed (see Figure 4.19). For instance, adding a loop down the length of the left leg will create a loop that crosses over the right leg and back again. The goal is to prevent additional geometry from extending to other parts of the body in a nonsymmetrical manner. This keeps the detail local to the location you are adding it to.

FIGURE 4.19
The selected faces show the geometry's surface flow.

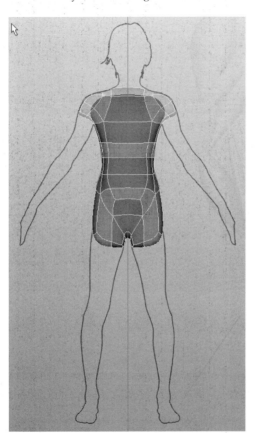

Connect Components

In the previous section, you used the Extrude tool to build upon a simple shape to create a model with good surface flow. You can now insert geometry logically and not worry about edge loops spiraling out of control. When you're using the box modeling technique, Connect Components offers some nice advantages. The following steps take you through the process of adding a leg to the character:

1. Continue with the scene from the previous section, or open the `torso_v04.ma` scene from the `chapter4\scenes` directory at the book's web page.

2. Establish symmetry through the Modeling Toolkit.

3. Select the two edges that divide the four faces at the bottom of the leg. Shift the edges using the Move tool to center them within the leg. You want to keep the faces as square as possible.

4. Select the four faces associated with the edges.

5. Extrude the edges down to the character's kneecap.

6. Extrude the faces again and drag them to the character's ankle (see Figure 4.20).

FIGURE 4.20
Extrude faces to create the ankles.

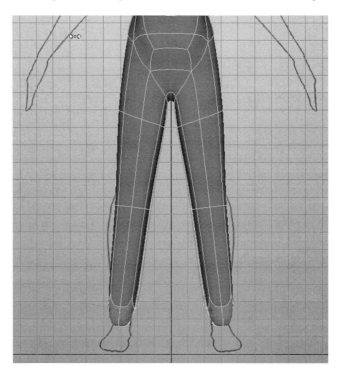

7. Select the edge loop above the knee. Choose a face, hold down Shift, and double-click the next face in the loop. The entire loop is selected.

8. Choose Edit Mesh ➢ Connect Components ➢ Options.

9. Select the Insert With Edge Flow option. Doing so tells the new components to obey the curvature of the mesh. Click Connect to insert an edge loop (see Figure 4.21).

For illustration purposes, the edge loop on the character's right leg was added without edge flow turned on. Notice how the new loop, on the character's left leg, actually bulges out, similar to how the leg is on the reference material. You can alter the effects of the edge flow through the Channel Box by clicking on the polyConnectComponents history node. Click the words Adjust Edge Flow. MMB-click and drag in the viewport to interactively adjust the value. The value ranges from 0 to 1; however, you can type in any value, positive or negative. The default value of 1 should be sufficient.

FIGURE 4.21
To insert an edge
loop, click Connect.

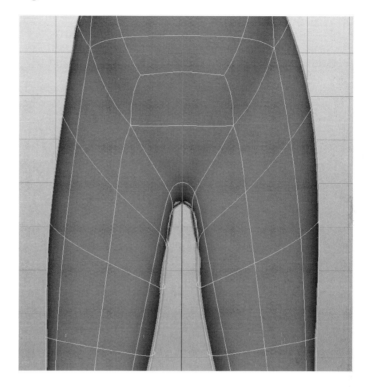

10. Save the scene as **torso_v05.ma**.

To see a version of the scene to this point, open the torso_v05.ma scene from the chapter4\ scenes directory at the book's web page.

Slide Edge Tool

Good surface flow contributes to the shape of the model. When making changes to an organic character, you often want to keep the existing shape but relocate an edge loop. Using the transformation tools, like Move and Rotate, can disrupt the shape of the surface because they cannot follow surface contours in their movement. The Slide Edge tool allows you to keep the shape while you move edges. The following steps take you through the process:

1. Continue with the scene from the previous section, or open the torso_v05.ma scene from the chapter4\scenes directory at the book's web page.

2. Establish symmetry through the Modeling Toolkit.

3. Select the edge loop directly below the knee.

4. Use Connect Components with the Insert With Edge Flow option selected to insert an edge loop. Figure 4.22 shows the new loop.

FIGURE 4.22
Add another edge loop.

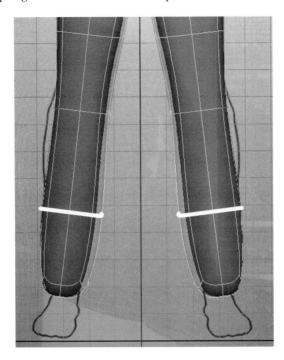

5. RMB-click over the geometry and choose Edge from the marking menu. Double-click to select the added loop.

6. Choose Mesh Tools ➤ (Edit) Slide Edge Tool.

7. MMB-click and drag the loop up toward the knee. Try to line it up with the largest part of the calf muscle on the reference material. Notice as you slide the loop it retains the shape of the surface.

8. Open the Channel Box. Click the top polyConnectComponent node under the Inputs section.

9. Change the Adjust Edge Flow value to **2.0**.

10. The Slide Edge Tool remains active. You can continue to slide the edge as needed. Figure 4.23 shows the final position of the edge loop.

11. Save the scene as **torso_v06.ma**.

To see a version of the scene to this point, open the torso_v06.ma scene from the chapter4\ scenes directory at the book's web page.

FIGURE 4.23
Slide the edge loop
to fit with the calf
muscle.

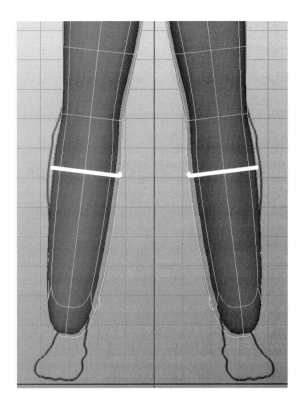

Offset Edge Loops

Sometimes you need to add an edge loop on either side of an existing loop. The center line of the character is a great example.

1. Continue with the scene from the previous section, or open the `torso_v06.ma` scene from the `chapter4\scenes` directory at the book's web page.

2. Establish symmetry through the Modeling Toolkit.

3. Choose Mesh Tools ➤ Offset Edge Loop Tool Options.

4. Select the Insert With Edge Flow option and click Enter Tool And Close. The smooth preview mode automatically switches to smooth with cage.

5. Make sure you have multi-components or edges selected.

6. Click on the center line of the character. Drag the mouse to position the two new loops (see Figure 4.24).

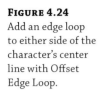

FIGURE 4.24
Add an edge loop to either side of the character's center line with Offset Edge Loop.

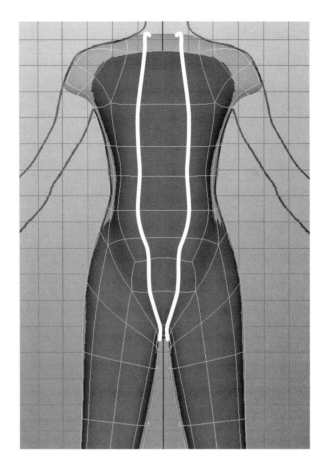

7. Save the scene as **torso_v07.ma**.

To see a version of the scene to this point, open the torso_v07.ma scene from the chapter4\ scenes directory at the book's web page.

Employ Build-out Modeling

The build-out method of modeling is similar to box modeling in that you are using the Extrude tool to create new geometry. The major difference, however, is that you start with planar geometry instead of a closed volume like the primitive cube. In this section the character's head is roughed out using the build-out method. As with the torso, the focus is on the tools and not on creating detail in the model.

1. Open the head_v01.ma scene from the chapter4\scenes directory at the book's web page. The scene contains two free image planes, each set up with a different view of the character's head.

2. Switch to the front view. Choose Mesh Tools ➢ Create Polygon Tool.

3. Draw a polygon around the shape of the eye. When you first start any surface, keep in mind that less is more. Try creating the shape of the eye with as few points as possible. Use Figure 4.25 as reference.

FIGURE 4.25
Use the Create Polygon tool to draw out the shape of the eye.

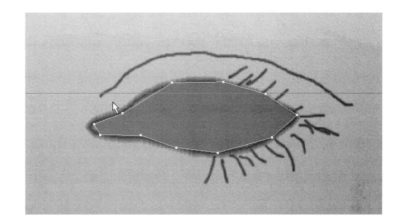

4. Double-click the border edge to select the loop.

5. Choose Edit Mesh ➢ (Edge) Extrude. Change the Offset value to **0.03**. This creates the skin that conforms to the eyeball.

6. Press **g** to repeat the last command. Another extrusion is added.

7. Change its Offset value to **0.05** and translate the extrusion to **0.07** in the local z-axis. Pulling the geometry back helps form the upper eyelid (see Figure 4.26).

FIGURE 4.26
Add another extrusion to form the upper eyelid.

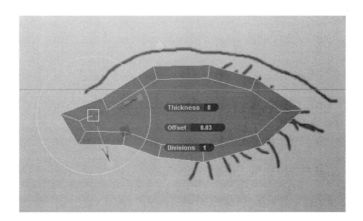

8. The interior face of the eye is a large n-gon. Press **3** to activate smooth mesh preview. Figure 4.27 (left) shows how poorly the mesh divides as a result of the n-gon. Select the face and delete it. Compare the surface shape without the n-gon on the right side of Figure 4.27.

FIGURE 4.27
N-gons smooth
poorly and should
not be used (left).
The geometry with-
out the *n*-gon is
much better shaped
(right).

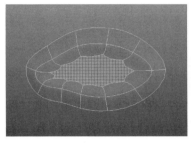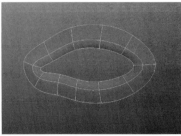

FIGURE 4.27
N-gons smooth
poorly and should
not be used (left).
The geometry with-
out the *n*-gon is
much better shaped
(right).

9. Save the scene as **head_v02.ma**.

To see a version of the scene to this point, open the head_v02.ma scene from the chapter4\
scenes directory at the book's web page.

Extrude Along a Curve

By default, the Extrude tool uses a selected curve to extrude geometry along. The option is
ignored if no curve is selected. You can extrude along a curve using edges or faces. As with most
of the tools in Maya, you can modify the extrusion after you apply the tool or any time up until
you delete the geometry's history. Next you'll use the Extrude tool to shape the character's laugh
line:

1. Continue with the scene from the previous section, or open the head_v02.ma scene from
   the chapter4\scenes directory at the book's web page.

2. Use the Create Polygon tool to build a single-quad face in the middle of the character's
   chin. Align the face so that it sits on the positive X side of the world's YZ plane (see Figure
   4.28).

FIGURE 4.28
Create a single-
quad face for the
chin.

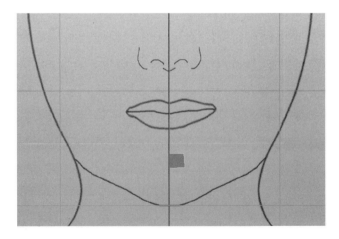

3. Draw a cubic curve from the polygon's edge, around the mouth, and up and over the
   nose. Use Figure 4.29 for reference.

FIGURE 4.29
Draw a curve to plot the laugh line.

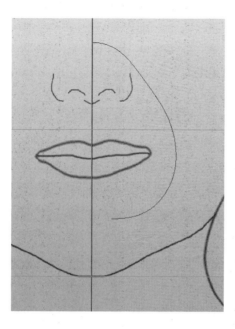

4. Custom shapes always default to the grid plane in which you are creating them. The quad face and curve sit in the middle of the world. Switch to the side view and align the face and curve with the reference material, as in Figure 4.30.

FIGURE 4.30
Shape the laugh line to match the character reference in the side view.

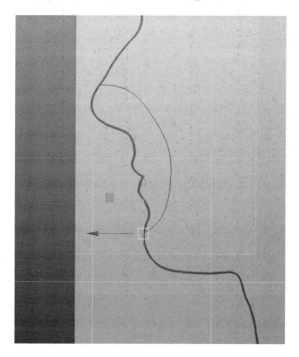

TWEAK MODE

You can activate tweak mode for the Move tool by choosing Tweak/Marquee from the Modeling Toolkit. This option is located under the Move tool icon at the top of the toolkit. When this option is selected, any component you touch is nudged in the direction of the mouse-pointer movement. Note that the Move tool manipulator is not displayed when you're in tweak mode. You can also use the hot key ` (the tilde/back quote key) to active tweak mode.

5. Select the quad's edge that you want to extrude and then select the curve.

6. Choose Edit Mesh ➤ (Edge) Extrude. Use the default options. Extruding along a curve is already active.

7. With only one division, the geometry is stretched from the beginning of the curve to its end. Increase the divisions to **10** to accurately follow the curve. Figure 4.31 shows the divided extrusion.

FIGURE 4.31
Increasing the extruded divisions helps the geometry follow the curve.

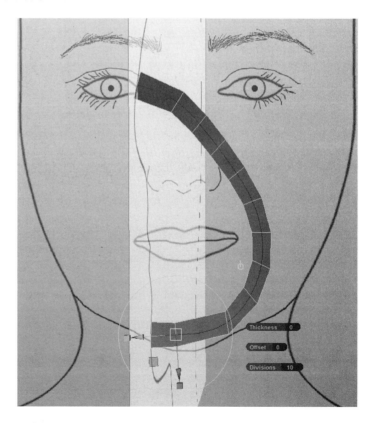

8. The divisions are unevenly distributed due to poor parameterization of the curve. Select the curve and switch to the Surfaces menu.

9. Choose Edit Curves ➤ Rebuild Curve Options.

10. In addition to the defaults, select NumSpans. Doing so keeps the current number of spans but redistributes them so they will be evenly spaced. Figure 4.32 shows the corrected geometry.

FIGURE 4.32
Rebuild the curve using the same number of spans in the curve.

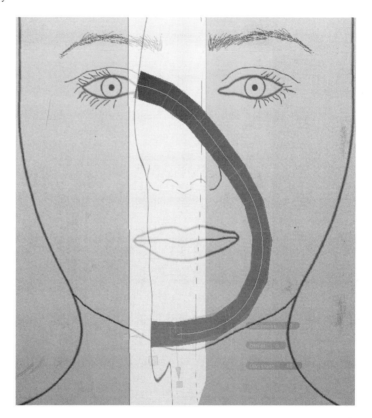

11. Move the eye geometry up to its position on the reference material.

12. Select the laugh line and the eye geometry. Delete the history of both objects.

13. Choose Mesh ➤ Combine.

14. Select two edges from the eye loop and the two edges across from the eye loop on the laugh line.

15. Choose Edit Mesh ➤ (Edge) Bridge. The two pieces of geometry are now connected.

16. Change Bridge Divisions to **2**. Adding two extra divisions keeps the face size consistent with the size of the existing geometry. Figure 4.33 shows the completed bridge.

FIGURE 4.33
Use two divisions
for the bridge.

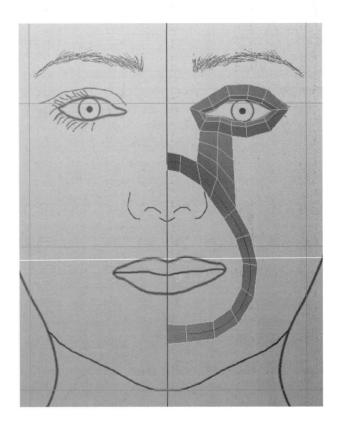

17. Save the scene as **head_v03.ma**.

To see a version of the scene to this point, open the head_v03.ma scene from the chapter4\
scenes directory at the book's web page.

Building each landmark of the face and then connecting it to existing geometry helps maintain good surface flow. It also permits finer control and allows you to work on isolated local
regions. You do not have to worry about added geometry having a negative impact on another
area. You can test configurations and densities prior to bringing the pieces together. Using these
techniques, you can build the entire head.

Sculpting Polygons

Once you complete the base mesh, you can start adding specific detail to your model. Pushing
and pulling a single vertex is time consuming and often leads to lumpy-looking surfaces. Maya
offers several ways to deal with groups of components.

Soft Select Tool

Soft Selection is an option you can use with the regular transformation tools. Move, Rotate, and
Scale have rollout options in the toolbox to control various aspects of the Soft Select tool. The

Modeling Toolkit also offers these options. Let's look at some common uses and functionalities of the tool:

1. Open the `female_v01.ma` scene from the `chapter4\scenes` directory at the book's web page.

2. Select the geometry and focus the camera on the character's middle finger.

3. Choose the Move tool from the Modeling Toolkit. Expand the Soft Selection rollout and choose Soft Select.

   When you choose Soft Select, the surface turns yellow and black. The colors indicate the strength of the tool's falloff. The falloff is dictated by the curve in the graph of the Soft Selection rollout.

4. Set Falloff Radius to **0.10.**

5. As you move your mouse, the falloff radius travels across the surface. Position the mouse over the middle finger. Notice how the falloff extends to other fingers (see Figure 4.34, left). This is a result of using the Volume falloff mode.

6. Change the falloff to Surface. Soft Select now obeys the surface, removing any effect it had on the other fingers (see Figure 4.34, right).

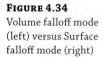

FIGURE 4.34
Volume falloff mode (left) versus Surface falloff mode (right)

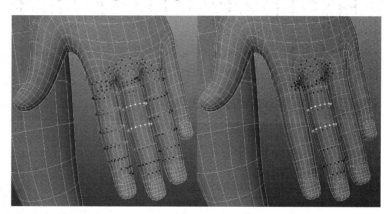

You can use the hot key **b** to interactively change the falloff radius.

Real World Scenario

POLYGON MODELING WITH PAINT EFFECTS

Paint Effects is most often used for creating large plants, trees, and other natural and organic objects. However, Paint Effects is not limited to these types of objects by any means. You can easily adapt the procedural approach used to create Paint Effects strokes to create details, such as wires and hoses used for mechanical objects. You can convert the strokes into NURBS surfaces or polygons and incorporate them into your models.

continues

(continued)

In addition, since the converted surface created from the Paint Effects stroke still has a connection to the original stroke, you can use the Paint Effects controls to add detail and even animate the surface.

Paint Effects requires a bit of bouncing around between settings, which can be a little disconcerting at first. With some practice, you'll get the hang of it. It helps to understand how Paint Effects brushes work. Creating and designing Paint Effects brushes is discussed in detail in Chapter 10, "Paint Effects."

Sculpting Polygons Using Artisan

The Artisan interface is a Maya editing system that simulates using a brush to sculpt surfaces and paint attribute values. Artisan works best when used with a digital tablet and stylus, but it will also work with a standard mouse.

In modeling mode, Artisan can be used to sculpt polygon, NURBS, and subdivision surface geometry. In other parts of this book, you'll see how Artisan can also be used to paint weights for deformers, edit texture maps, and paint the strength of nParticle force fields emitted by surfaces.

For the most part, the Artisan modeling controls are the same whether you are working with polygons, NURBS surfaces, or subdivision surfaces. In this section, you'll be introduced to Artisan as you sculpt detail on the female character.

The Artisan sculpting brushes work very well for creating details such as folds in fabric or muscle definition. In this section, you'll use the sculpting tools to give definition to the character's arms.

1. Open the `female_v02.ma` scene from the `chapter4\scenes` directory at the book's web page.

2. Choose Modify ➤ Convert ➤ Smooth Mesh Preview To Polygons. The amount of geometry is increased so you have more vertices to sculpt with.

CONVERTING SMOOTH MESH PREVIEW TO POLYGONS

Converting a smooth mesh preview to polygons produces the same result as selecting the object, pressing the **1** key to deactivate smooth mesh preview, and then performing a Smooth operation (Mesh Smooth). However, if you have a creased edge on a smooth-mesh-preview surface, the crease will be carried over to the converted polygon model. The same is not true when you use the Smooth operation.

3. Make sure the surface is selected. You must have something selected before using the Sculpt Geometry tool. You can only choose nodes or vertices to sculpt on.

4. Choose Mesh Tools ➤ (Edit) Sculpt Geometry Tool Options to activate the Artisan brush-based interface. The settings in the Tool Settings dialog box control how the brush works as you sculpt the surface. At the top of the dialog box are the basic controls:

Radius(U) and Radius(L)   These settings define the range for the radius of the brush. If you are using a digital tablet and stylus, you can change the radius based on the amount of pressure you apply to the brush. The Radius(U) setting is the upper limit of the radius; Radius(L) is the lower limit of the radius. If you are using a mouse, only the Radius(U) value is used. You can also set the Radius(U) value interactively by holding down the **b** key while dragging left or right on the surface in the viewport. The radius of the brush is represented by a red circle (see Figure 4.35).

FIGURE 4.35
The settings for the Artisan brush-based sculpting tool. The circle represents the radius of the brush.

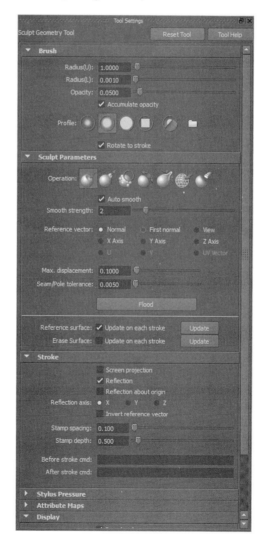

By default, the pressure you apply to the brush affects only the opacity of the stroke. If you want the pressure to control the radius of the brush, or both the radius and the opacity at the same time, scroll down to the Stylus Pressure settings and select from the choices in the Pressure Mapping menu.

Opacity   This setting determines the strength of the change created by the brush. When you use Artisan to sculpt geometry, Opacity modifies the Max Displacement setting found in the Sculpt Parameters section. If Max Displacement is set to 1 unit and Opacity is set to 0.1, each stroke displaces the surface 0.1 units. If Accumulate Opacity is selected, each time a single stroke passes over itself, the surface is displaced further. Setting Opacity to 0 means that the stroke has no effect on the surface.

Profile   This setting determines the shape of the brush tip. The first two icons on the left lend a soft edge to the brush. This is more apparent when the geometry is dense and has a lot of points that can be displaced. The second two icons produce a hard edge to the brush: one is circular, and the other is square. By clicking the Browse button, you can load a grayscale image to use as the brush shape, which is activated by the fifth icon. The Rotate To Stroke option rotates the image as you draw, so it always points in the direction of the stroke.

Sculpt Parameters   This section contains the settings for how the surface will react to the brush strokes. The Operation buttons cause the brush to push down, push up, smooth, relax, pinch, slide, or erase the stroke. Smooth and Relax are very similar.

Smooth   Smooth averages the position of the vertices. Oversmoothing will result in a flattened surface. In addition to softening details, it is good for untangling vertices that are too close or overlapping each other. You can also use Auto Smooth to have the other operations smooth as you sculpt.

Relax   Relax averages the bumpiest areas of the surface while maintaining the overall shape of the surface. If the surface vertices are already dispersed evenly across the surface, the Relax brush will have no effect.

Slide   Slide moves vertices along the shape of your existing surface. Slide does not work with Reflection turned on.

Reference Vector   This setting determines the direction of the change sculpted on the surface. When it is set to Normal, the vertices are displaced in the direction of their normal. When it is set to First Normal, all the vertices are displaced in the direction of the normal of the first vertex affected by the stroke. View displaces the vertices based on the current view, and the X Axis, Y Axis, and Z Axis options restrict displacement to the specified axis. If you hold down the Ctrl key while painting, it will invert the direction of the displacement.

Flood   This button fills the entire object based on the Operation, Reference Vector, Opacity, and Max. Displacement settings. You can use it to smooth or relax the whole object after making changes or to inflate or shrink the entire object.

Reflection   These options, found in the Stroke rollout, are similar to the Reflection options found in the Move tool, and they are useful when sculpting symmetrical objects.

5. In the Sculpt Geometry Tool options, set Radius(U) to **0.25** and Opacity to **0.1**.

6. Click the first icon in the Profile section and the first icon in the Operation section.

7. Set Reference Vector to Normal, and Max. Displacement to **0.1**.

8. Expand the Stroke rollout and select Reflection.

9. If you are using a digital tablet and a stylus, select Stylus Pressure from the Stylus Pressure rollout, and set Pressure Mapping to Both.

10. In the Display rollout, choose the options Draw Brush While Painting and Draw Brush Feedback so that you can see how the brush changes based on the amount of pressure applied to the pen on the tablet. You may also want to deselect Show Wireframe so that the wireframe display does not obscure your view of the changes made on the brush.

11. Paint some strokes on the character's shoulder. Create the musculature of the deltoid muscles. Work your way down the arm into the bicep. You can hold the Ctrl key down while you paint on the surface to invert the direction of the displacement. When you hold the Shift key while painting, the brush mode switches to smooth.

    As you paint, experiment with the options for the Artisan brush settings. You can also enter smooth mesh preview on the surface by pressing the **3** key.

12. Add definition to the neck and sculpt the collarbone by using the Relax and Smooth operations to even out the lumps and bumps. Then switch to the Pinch operation to help define the area between muscle groups and bone (see Figure 4.36).

FIGURE 4.36
Sculpt muscle definition into the character's arm.

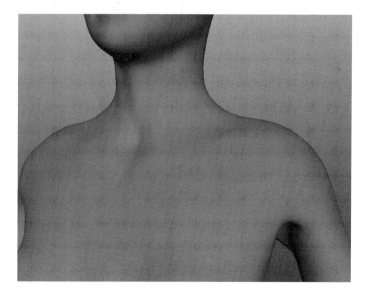

13. Save the scene as **female_v03.ma**.

To see a version of the scene to this point, open the female_v03.ma scene from the chapter4\ scenes directory at the book's web page.

Use Retopology Tools

These days, character models are rarely created in Maya. The Autodesk® Mudbox® software and Pixologic's ZBrush digital sculpting programs, among others, are an important part of the character-creation pipeline. Because of their intuitive digital-sculpting tools and capacity for working with dense meshes, they're often used to add changes and detail to models started in Maya. For more information, take a look at *Introducing ZBrush*, by Eric Keller (Sybex, 2008) and *Introducing Mudbox*, by Ara Kermanikian (Sybex, 2010).

Highly detailed, sculpted models are impractical to take through the production pipeline. Instead, the high-resolution model is rebuilt with new geometry to a lower, more manageable resolution, using the high-resolution model as reference. This process is called *retopologizing*. Retopologizing the model affords you complete control over the surface flow, enabling you to add edge loops where they can support the model's detail the best.

Importing and Exporting

Maya allows you to establish a connection between Maya and Mudbox. Doing so lets you make changes to the object in Maya and have the changes carry over to Mudbox without having to reload the geometry. For this operation to work, the same versions of Maya and Mudbox must be installed. Here are the steps to connect the two programs:

1. Select the polygon object to send to Mudbox.

2. Choose File ➤ Send To Mudbox. Several options are available from this menu, including the following:

   ◆ Send As A New Scene

   ◆ Update Current Scene

   ◆ Add To Current Scene

   ◆ Select Previously Sent Objects

3. After you choose one of the options, a connection indicator is displayed to the right of the status bar. Maya and Mudbox are now connected.

A caveat to this process is that Mudbox does not support multiple materials. If geometry is sent to Mudbox with multiple materials, Mudbox will read only the first material and ignore the others.

You can also send the geometry from Mudbox back to Maya. Mudbox sculpting layers can be exported as Maya blend shapes.

Maya also supports numerous translators to export and import geometry. The FBX file format, considered an interchange file format, allows you to exchange geometry as well as animation, joints, weighting, and other assets between 3D applications, like the Autodesk® 3ds Max® and Autodesk® Softimage® software. You can use DXF, OBJ, VRML2, and OpenFlight file formats to move geometry in and out of Maya.

To access the available translators, you can use File ➤ Import Options. In the Options window, change File Type to match the desired extension. If the extension is not present, you will need to load the proper translator plug-in by choosing Window ➤ Settings/Preferences ➤ Plug-in Manager. For exporting geometry, choose File ➤ Export All or File ➤ Export Selection.

Alembic Cache Files

Maya also supports Alembic cache files. Alembic is an open source interchange framework developed by Lucasfilm and Sony Pictures Imageworks. Alembic essentially "bakes" geometry, capturing vertex positions and animated transforms. It efficiently stores this information without the overhead of tools or procedures used to create them. As a result, you get an optimized version of the original animated or nonanimated object. You can take advantage of the Alembic format by using it to import dense meshes that ordinarily would be too costly to display. The following steps show you how to convert a dense mesh to an Alembic cache:

1. Most of the import tools in Maya are plug-ins. For this example, make sure the objEport .mll, abcExport.mll, and abcImport.mll plug-ins are loaded.

2. Choose Window ➤ Settings/Preferences ➤ Plug-in Manager.

3. Select Loaded and Auto Load for the following plug-ins:

   AbcExport.mll

   AbcImport.mll

4. Starting with a new scene, choose File ➤ Import. Load hand_v01.obj from the chapter4\ scenes directory at the book's web page. Notice the size of the file is 934 MB.

5. Select the hand and choose Pipeline Cache ➤ Alembic Cache ➤ Export Selection To Alembic.

6. Set Cache Time Range to Current Frame. Choose Export All.

7. Save the Alembic file as **hand.abc**.

8. Choose File ➤ New to clear the scene.

9. You can now import the hand back into Maya in its optimized format. Choose Pipeline Cache ➤ Alembic Cache ➤ Import Alembic. Load hand.abc. Notice the size of the file is 272 MB.

10. Save the scene as **hand_v01.ma**.

To see a version of the scene to this point, open the hand_v01.ma scene from the chapter4\ scenes directory at the book's web page.

Slide on Surface

Now that you have an optimized version of the high-resolution hand, you can manipulate it inside of Maya without lag. To begin retopologizing the hand, you can use primitive cylinders for each of the fingers. The following steps show you how to conform one piece of geometry to another:

1. Continue with the scene from the previous section, or open the hand_v01.ma scene from the chapter4\scenes directory at the book's web page.

2. Select the hand and place it on a layer. Turn its visibility off.

3. Choose Create ➤ Polygon Primitives ➤ Cylinder.

4. Change the following settings in the Channel Box for the polyCylinder's construction history:

Radius: **0.8**

Height: **2.5**

Subdivision Axis: **8**

Subdivision Height: **4**

Subdivision Caps: **2**

Round Cap: **On**

5. Use the following coordinates to position the cylinder over the index finger:

Translate X: **4.049**

Translate Y: **-2.561**

Translate Z: **1.487**

Rotate X: **9.183**

Rotate Y: **9.82**

Rotate Z: **-163.704**

6. Select the top two rows of faces on the cylinder and delete them (see Figure 4.37).

FIGURE 4.37
Delete the top section of the cylinder.

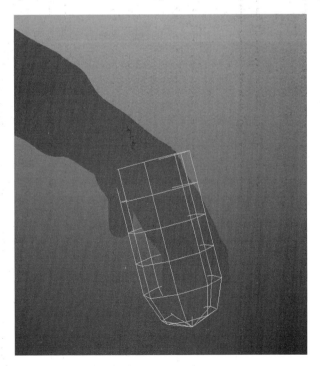

7. Select the hand and choose the Make Live Surface icon from the Snap Tool section of the Status Line. The Make Live Surface icon is the large magnet furthest to the right in the Snap Tool section. The hand turns green.

8. Select the cylinder and choose the Move tool from the Modeling Toolkit.

9. Selecting any component on the surface of the cylinder activates the *slide on surface* functionality. Select all of the cylinder's vertices. When you position the cursor over the Move icon of the cylinder, you will see the word *slide* appear. Click and drag the Move tool in any direction. The cylinder snaps to the surface of the hand (see Figure 4.38).

FIGURE 4.38

Use the Move tool to force the surface to snap to the hand.

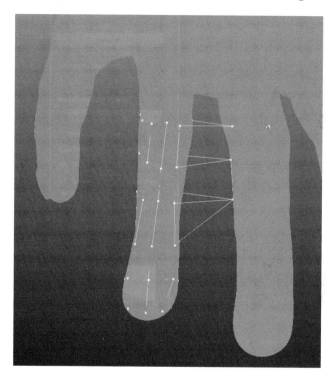

10. Several of the vertices snapped to the middle finger. Select the stray vertices and translate them in the z-axis until they pop over to the index finger.

11. You can now manipulate any component type and it will stick to the live surface. Manipulate the cylinder's geometry to fit the details of the finger. Don't worry about making the geometry look nice. Simply get the edge loops on each cylinder perpendicular to the fingers of the live surface.

12. Repeat the process for the other four fingers. Figure 4.39 shows the results.

13. Save the scene as **hand_v02.ma**.

To see a version of the scene to this point, open the hand_v02.ma scene from the chapter4\ scenes directory at the book's web page.

FIGURE 4.39
Shape four more cylinders for the other fingers.

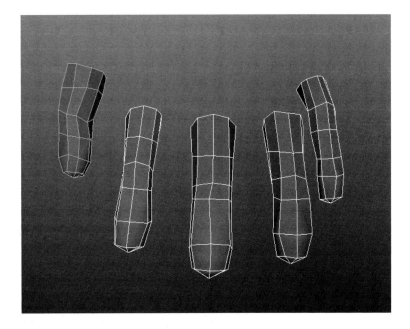

Quad Draw

New!

Quad Draw allows you to rapidly generate polygon faces that can conform to another surface. The following procedure uses Quad Draw to retopologize a high-resolution zombie hand:

1. Continue with the scene from the previous section, or open the hand_v02.ma scene from the chapter4\scenes directory at the book's web page.

2. Select the fingers and choose Mesh ➢ Combine.

3. Delete the history of the finger geometry.

4. Select the hand and make it a live surface.

5. Select the fingers and open the Modeling Toolkit. Choose Quad Draw from the Mesh Editing Tools rollout. The wireframe of the finger geometry turns black (see Figure 4.40).

6. The finger geometry may not be evenly spaced on the live surface. Quad Draw has a Relax feature built into the tool. Hold Shift and LMB-drag on the index finger to relax the geometry. Hold **b** and LMB-drag left or right to change the size of the area of influence for the Relax operation.

Quad Draw has its own marking menu. You can access it by holding Ctrl+Shift and RMB-clicking. Options on the marking menu allow you to force the Relax operation to be applied to interior vertices, border vertices, or both. By default, Relax is set to Auto Lock. Auto Lock uses the type of vertex you click on first, interior or border, to determine what the Relax operation will affect.

FIGURE 4.40
With the finger geometry selected, choose Quad Draw from the Modeling Toolkit.

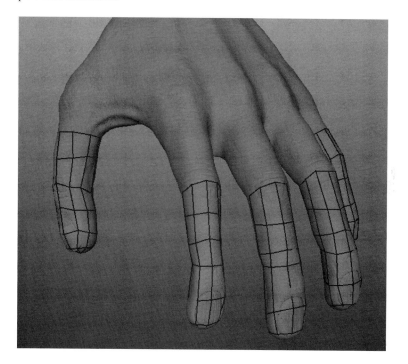

7. Relax the border vertices and interior vertices for all the fingers.

8. Hold Ctrl+Shift and RMB-click over the index finger geometry. Choose Extend:Edge Loop from the marking menu.

9. Hold Tab and LMB-click to extend the edge loop up the length of the finger. Add two extensions to complete the finger length.

10. Repeat the process of extending the finger geometry for each of the fingers (see Figure 4.41).

11. You want to connect the thumb and index finger together. The flow of the geometry on the end of the thumb may be going in the wrong direction. MMB-drag a component, vertex, or edge to slide it into the proper position. Use Figure 4.42 as a guide.

FIGURE 4.41
Extend the edge
loops on each of the
fingers.

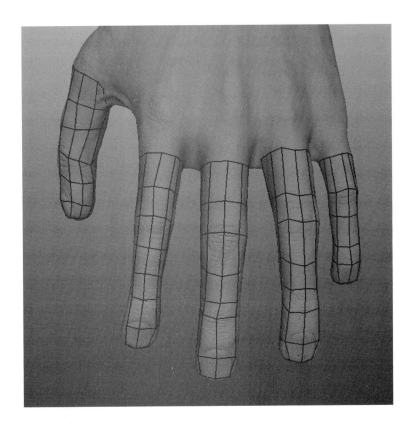

FIGURE 4.42
Shift the surface
flow of the thumb
to align with the
index finger.

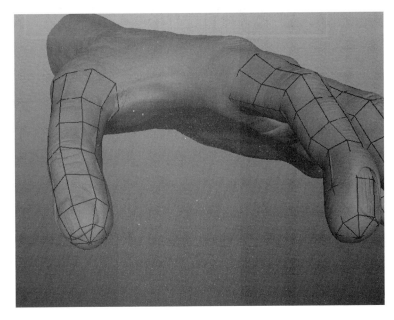

12. Hold Shift and hover over the empty space between the thumb and index finger. A green polygon fills in the area. Depending on the position of your mouse, you may need to move around a little to get the proper quad. LMB-click to create the face. Add another face directly above (see Figure 4.43).

FIGURE 4.43
Hold Shift to generate quads between existing faces.

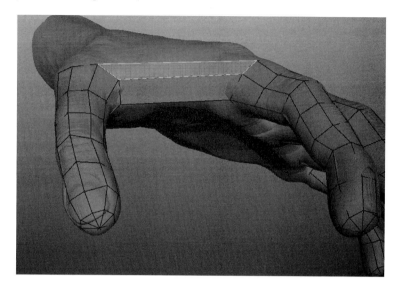

13. Ctrl+click to insert an edge loop. Add a total of three edge loops (see Figure 4.44). You can hide the live surface hand at this point if it becomes distracting.

FIGURE 4.44
Insert three edge loops between the thumb and index finger.

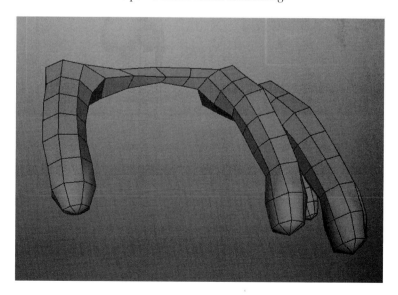

14. Holding Shift, fill in the polygons between each of the fingers.

15. Using Tab, extend the top loop of the index finger. While extending the loop, drag the selection toward the faces you added in step 13. The corner vertex will automatically weld when it comes close to another vertex (see Figure 4.45)

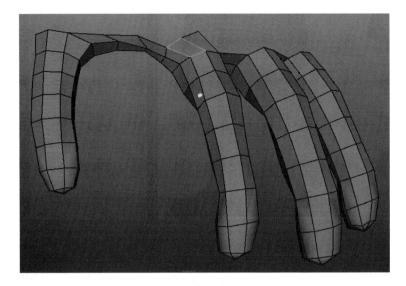

16. Quad Draw also allows you to move components without having to select them. Moving the mouse over the geometry displays the preselection highlight. LMB-drag to move the component when it is highlighted. Shift the new vertices toward the interior of the hand to make the faces evenly spaced (see Figure 4.46).

17. Extend the fingers and the geometry in between each finger by one face loop. If the geometry does not automatically weld while extending a loop, you can LMB-drag the component to its desired location. When the components get close enough, they will automatically weld.

18. At this point you can extend the entire edge loop that wraps around the hand. Extend the loop three times to match the geometry to the geometry of the thumb (see Figure 4.47).

While you are extending the loops, be sure to check that the new vertices are not welding to any unwanted locations. If you continue to drag the loop, the weld will break. After each extension, you may want to use the Relax operation to keep the geometry uniformly spaced.

19. You can continue to extend loops to complete the hand retopology or use another technique available with Quad Draw. LMB-click on the live surface hand where you want to place a vertex. A green dot will appear (see Figure 4.48).

FIGURE 4.46
Make the edges of
the new geometry
evenly spaced.

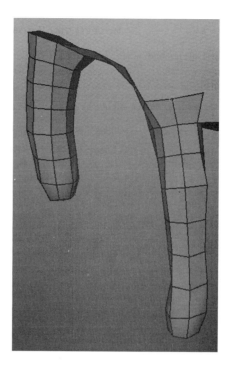

FIGURE 4.47
Extend the geome-
try from the fingers
three times.

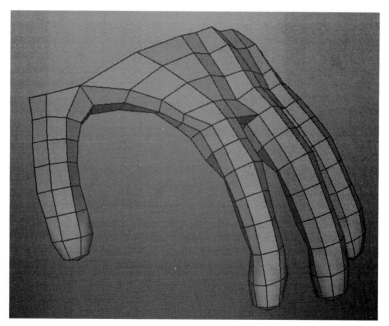

FIGURE 4.48
Click to create a
green dot where you
want a new vertex.

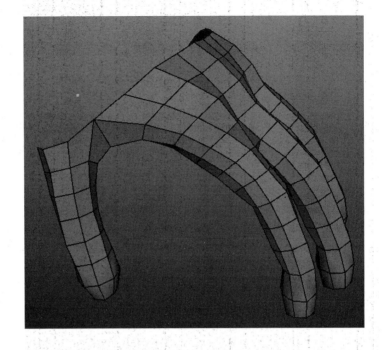

FIGURE 4.49
Drag in the empty
space to draw new
faces.

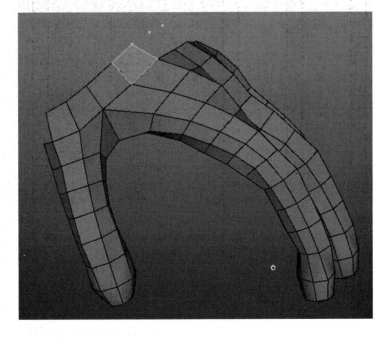

20. Add several more green dots. Keep in mind that you are creating vertices and that you want them to be in alignment with your existing geometry.

21. You can now hold Shift and LMB-drag over the empty space between the dots and geometry to draw new faces (see Figure 4.49). You can press and hold Ctrl+Shift and LMB-click to delete components.

22. Save the scene as **hand_v03.ma**.

To see a version of the scene to this point, open the hand_v03.ma scene from the chapter4\ scenes directory at the book's web page.

Reduce

The Reduce tool can remove unneeded vertices without affecting an object's general shape. Specific controls allow you to keep borders, hard edges, or creases. The following steps take you through the process of reducing a polygon mesh:

1. Open the reduce1.ma scene from the chapter4\scenes folder at the book's web page.

2. Select the hand and choose Mesh ➤ Reduce.

3. Select Keep Original and click Apply.

4. A duplicate hand is created. Click the Wireframe On Shaded icon in the viewport.

5. Select either glove and open its Attribute Editor. Click the polyReduce1 tab.

6. Make sure Reduction Method is set to Percentage and change the percentage to **93.0**. The model is reduced quickly and efficiently (see Figure 4.50).

FIGURE 4.50
The polygons for the model on the left have been reduced.

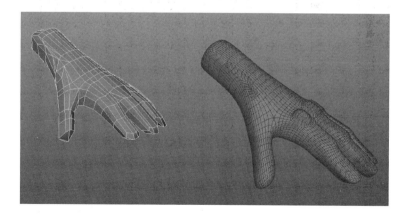

You can change Reduction Method to Vertex Count or Triangle Count and the values will automatically adjust without affecting the reduced surface. To see a version of the reduced glove, open the reduce2.ma scene from the chapter4\scenes directory at the book's web page.

The Bottom Line

Implement box modeling. Box modeling allows you to start with a simple primitive that you can extrude to create a complex form.

Master It Starting from a smoothed cube, use box modeling techniques to create a head.

Employ build-out modeling. From a single polygon, you can extrude edges to create smaller sections of a larger object.

Master It Use the build-out method to model an ear.

Sculpt polygons. Artisan is a brush-based modeling and editing toolset. Using Artisan, you can sculpt directly on the surface of geometry.

Master It Use Artisan to sculpt dents into a surface.

Use retopology tools. Highly detailed, sculpted models are impractical to take through the production pipeline. Instead, the high-resolution model is *retopologized* to a lower, more manageable resolution.

Master It Use Quad Draw to create a low-polygon game model of the hand in hand_v01.ma.

Chapter 5

Rigging and Muscle Systems

Rigging is the process of creating an organized system of deformers, expressions, and controls applied to an object so that it can be easily and efficiently animated. A good rig should intuitively allow an animator to concentrate on the art of animation without the technical aspects of rigging getting in the way. In addition, a good rig should be well organized so that it can easily be changed, repurposed, or fixed if there is a problem.

Rigging as a practice is continually evolving in the industry. New technologies, concepts, and approaches emerge every day and are widely discussed and debated among professional technical directors throughout the world. Although this chapter offers advice on how best to approach creating part of a character rig in the Autodesk® Maya® program, its main purpose is to help you understand how the tools work so that you can approach creating your own rigs and adapting rigging practices from others.

The first part of this chapter explores techniques for creating efficient character rigs. There are many approaches to rigging characters; the main focus of these exercises is to build an understanding of how the Maya toolset works so that you can adapt it to your preferred rigging workflow. We provide additional tips and tricks that can help you avoid common rigging pitfalls.

The second portion of the chapter is devoted to Maya Muscle, a plug-in designed to create realistic deformations for character rigs. The muscle system works with skeletons to simulate the qualities of flesh and skin.

The focus of this chapter is to rig and weight a giraffe. You will create controls to operate its legs and spine. Regardless of the character—in this case a giraffe—the concepts are the same. The typical pipeline is to build a skeleton, create the rig, and then weight the geometry.

In this chapter, you will learn to:

- ♦ Create and organize joint hierarchies
- ♦ Use Human Inverse Kinematics rigs
- ♦ Apply skin geometry
- ♦ Use Maya Muscle

Understanding Rigging

CERT OBJECTIVE

Today's characters are more complex than ever. Even the simplest are expected to have a full range of motion and perform as if they actually existed. To achieve this level of realism, numerous tools and techniques are applied. In this chapter, you'll build a realistic giraffe.

The most common types of rigs are created using joint deformers. In character animation, a skeletal system is created from joints to match the basic shape of the character. A joint is represented by a simple wireframe sphere. Joints are connected by bones, which are represented by a wireframe pyramid. When one joint is parented to another joint, the bone is aligned so that the pointed end of the pyramid points to the child joint (see Figure 5.1).

FIGURE 5.1
Joints are positioned based on the shape of the object they are meant to deform.

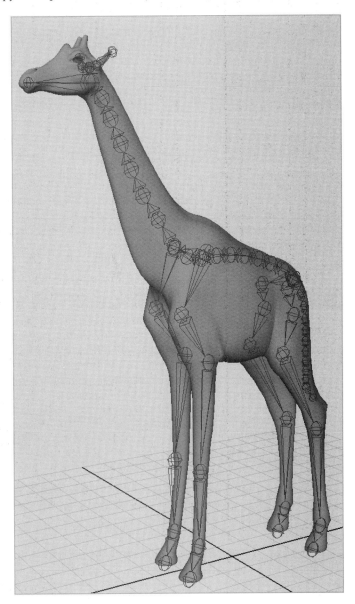

The geometry of the character is bound or skinned to the joints so that the joints deform the geometry—making knees bend, wrists twist, fingers clench, and so on. Each joint in a hierarchy exerts influence over each vertex of the geometry, pushing or pulling it in one direction or another. The amount of influence exerted on a vertex by a joint is controlled through weighting.

Once geometry has been skinned to a skeleton of joints, a system of controls is created to make animating the joints as simple as possible. Controls can be created from locators or curves or any other node that can be selected in the viewport. These nodes then control the movement of joints via expressions, utility nodes, constraints, or driven keys. You used a simple control system in Chapter 2, "Introduction to Animation," to rig a mechanical bug model.

In addition, other types of deformers are often applied to the geometry to compensate for the shortcomings of simple joint deformations. Influence objects, lattice deformers, Maya Muscle, and other tools and techniques are often used to create believable motion and to simulate the properties of flesh and tissue for characters.

Creating and Organizing Joint Hierarchies

The Joint tool creates a joint each time you click the scene. As long as the Joint tool is active, each time you click the scene, a new joint is added and parented to the previous joint, forming a simple hierarchy known as a *joint chain*. To exit the Joint tool, press the Enter key on the keyboard. This is useful if you need to finish one joint chain and then start another.

You can create branches of joints by parenting joint chains to intermediate joints in the initial chain. Parenting the branches and groups of joint chains lets you quickly create sophisticated joint hierarchies known as *skeletons*.

Because many skeletons can become quite complex, they should be properly organized and named so that animators and other riggers (referred to as *technical directors* in some instances) can easily access and understand the skeleton and all of its various parts.

The orientation of joints relative to their parent joints must be consistent throughout the skeleton to achieve proper functionality. The default orientation of a joint, established when the joint is added to a chain, is often incorrect and can lead to problems such as gimbal lock.

GIMBAL LOCK

Gimbal lock is a situation in which a joint or object achieves a rotation that causes two of the rotation axes to overlap. When this occurs, the rotations for the overlapping axes are the same, which prevents the joint from rotating in three dimensions. Two of the rotational axes are so close that, when rotated along either axis, the resulting motion is the same.

Skeletons are built by using the Joint tool. The goal is to create joints to mimic the functionality of a real skeleton. It is not always necessary to replicate every single bone in your character. Often you can create the same effect of the real thing through a reduced number of joints. Some other cases require the addition of joints that don't exist at all to achieve the effect you are after. Either way, it's important to remember the goal of a skeleton is to provide the necessary structure for a character to move—in other words, to provide whatever it takes in the most efficient manner possible.

New!

1. Open the `giraffe_v01.ma` scene from the `chapter5\scenes` folder at the book's web page (`www.sybex.com/go/masteringmaya2015`). The scene contains a polygon giraffe.

2. Switch to the side view. The first part of the skeleton to draw is the giraffe's front leg.

DRAWING JOINTS

Although joints can be drawn in any view, it is best to use an orthographic view. When joints are started in the perspective, their origin is unpredictable. You can, however, draw joints onto an existing skeleton in the perspective view. The origin of the new joints resides in the same plane as the joint to which it is being connected, as determined by the camera's view.

---

3. Switch to the Animation menu set, and choose Skeleton ➢ Joint Tool.

JOINT SYMMETRY

In the Joint tool options, there is a setting to turn Symmetry on or off. Having symmetry on automatically creates a mirrored duplicate of your joints. When you are using joint symmetry, the mirrored joints are attached via a symmetry constraint. After placing your joints, you can delete the constraints. We'll keep Symmetry off for the giraffe skeleton to take advantage of some different tools later in the chapter.

---

4. Click the Snap To Projected Center icon, located to the right of Snap To Point. This new feature snaps any object to the relative center of a geometric object. In this case, it is being used to center the joints within the giraffe's leg.

5. To keep the joints visible through the geometry, choose Shading ➢ X-Ray Joints from the viewport's menu.

6. Starting just below the neck, begin drawing five joints down the length of the leg. You can reposition the joints as you go. If you hold the LMB, instead of clicking you can move the joint to position it better. After you release the button, use the MMB to make other alterations. Continue clicking with the LMB until all five joints are drawn. When you're done, press Enter to complete the operation. Use Figure 5.2 as a reference.

   It's important to have a slight rotation for the knee if you decide to use inverse kinematics later. (*Inverse kinematics* is a special type of control mechanism for animating the joints; this topic will be discussed later in the chapter.)

   When you create inverse kinematics, Maya needs a hint as to how you want the joint to bend when the IK Handle is moved. For now, make sure that there is an angle in the joint chain at the location of the knee (joint3).

7. Using the down-arrow key, pick-walk through the skeleton's hierarchy to reposition the rest of the joints. This method of moving the joints works fine as long as you move the joints in order.

If you go back up the hierarchy, any changes made to a joint affect all the joints underneath it. To avoid this, with a joint selected, press Insert or Home on the keyboard to activate the joint's pivot point. You can now move the joint independently.

Holding the **d** key also activates the joint's pivot point. Figure 5.3 shows the joint's final position in the front view.

FIGURE 5.2
Draw five joints for the giraffe's front leg.

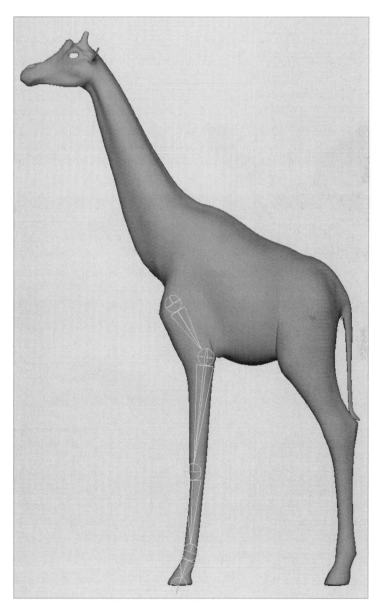

FIGURE 5.3
Move the joints
in the front view.

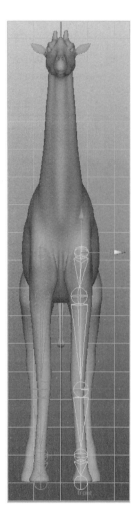

8. Repeat the procedure for the left hind leg. You can use the Joint tool marking menu to make adjustments to your joint settings if needed by pressing Ctrl/Cmd+Shift+RMB. Use Figure 5.4 for reference.

9. Next is the giraffe's spine. Switch to the side view.

10. You want the spine joints to be evenly spaced. This ensures that the geometry receives an even distribution of influence from the joints. Move off into empty space, and snap nine joints to the grid.

JOINT DISPLAY SIZE

You can change the display size of the joints in the viewport window by choosing Display ➤ Animation ➤ Joint Size.

FIGURE 5.4
Draw the bones
for the left
hind leg.

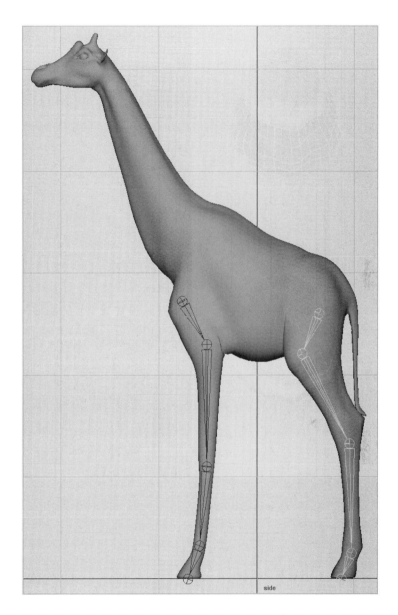

11. Translate the root of the snapped joints just above the giraffe's tail. The spine is much longer than the giraffe's geometry.

a. To maintain its uniform size, Shift+click each joint, starting with the tip and ending with the root.

b. Select the Scale tool. The manipulator is displayed at the location of the last joint selected.

c. Scale the skeleton in the z-axis until the tip is above the front leg's second joint.

12. Rotate each joint to get the proper curve in the spine. Use Figure 5.5 as a guide.

13. The joints for the neck and tail are created in a similar fashion. Repeat the procedure, placing 11 joints in the tail and 8 in the neck. Figure 5.6 shows the finished skeleton parts.

FIGURE 5.5
Rotate the joints to give curvature to the spine.

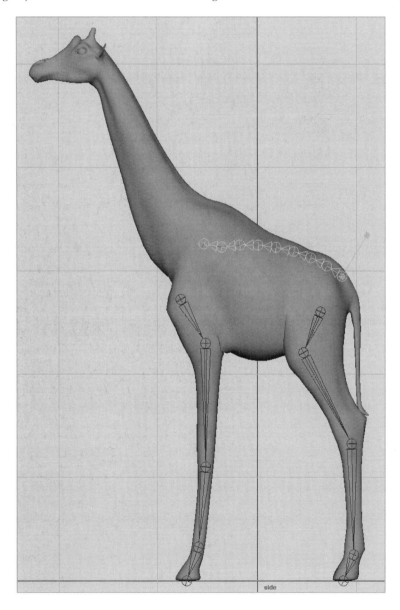

FIGURE 5.6
Create the neck
and tail.

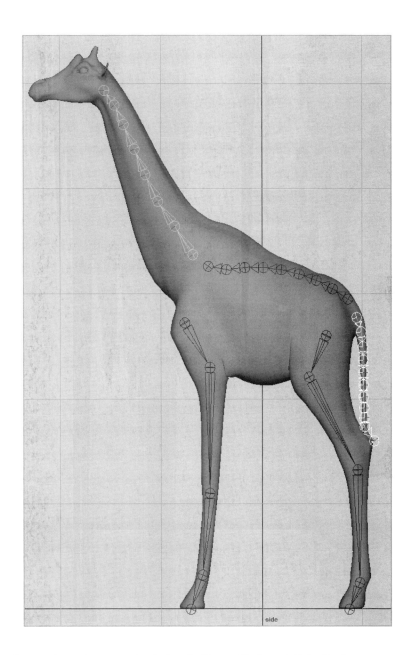

14. The only remaining joints are in the head. Choose Skeleton ➢ Joint Tool.

15. With the Joint tool active, click the last neck joint.

16. Click the end of the head. The head joint is automatically connected to the neck.

17. Finish up the head by adding ears (see Figure 5.7).

FIGURE 5.7
Finish the head
by adding two
more joints for
the ears.

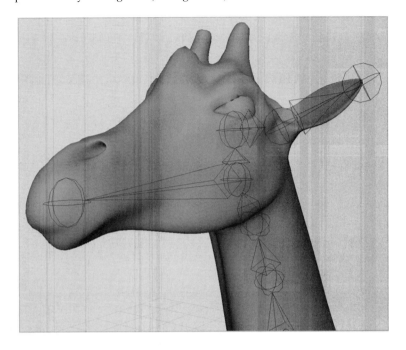

18. It's now time to attach the front leg to the spine. You need to add one more joint, which would be the equivalent of the human clavicle, in between the spine and front leg. Create and position a single joint above the left leg, equal in height to the spine. Position it using Figure 5.8 as a guide.

19. Select the root of the left leg. Hold Shift, and choose the newly created clavicle joint.

20. Press the **p** key to parent the joints.

21. Select the clavicle joint, and parent it to the second-to-last spine joint.

22. Repeat steps 18–21 for the hind leg. Instead of a clavicle, create a hipbone. Use Figure 5.9 as reference.

23. Finish up by parenting the tail to the root of the spine.

24. Save the scene as **giraffe_v02.ma**.

To see a version of the scene up to this point, open the giraffe_v02.ma scene from the chapter5\scenes directory at the book's web page.

FIGURE 5.8
Create a clavicle joint.

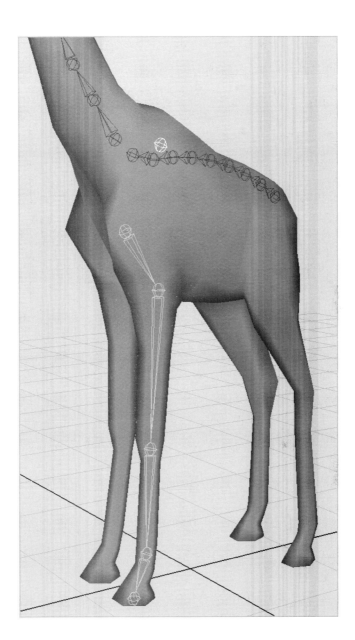

Orienting Joints

By default, a joint's rotation axis automatically adjusts so that the x-axis always points down the length of the bone to the next joint in the chain. This behavior can be turned off using the Move tool or by choosing Skin ➤ Edit Smooth Skin ➤ Move Skinned Joints Tool. As with most nodes in Maya, you can also change the way a joint rotates. This is done for numerous reasons:

◆ To make sure the orientation of the joint is aligned with its bone. (When you freeze the transforms on a joint, the joint orientation will match the joint's parent and not the bone.)

◆ To help avoid gimbal lock.

◆ To change the orientation for effect or specific control. For instance, you can have the left leg rotate in unison with the right leg when both are rotated simultaneously. By altering the right leg's orientation, you can have the legs rotate opposite one another in a scissor-like fashion when rotated simultaneously.

FIGURE 5.9
Create a hip joint, and parent the joints together.

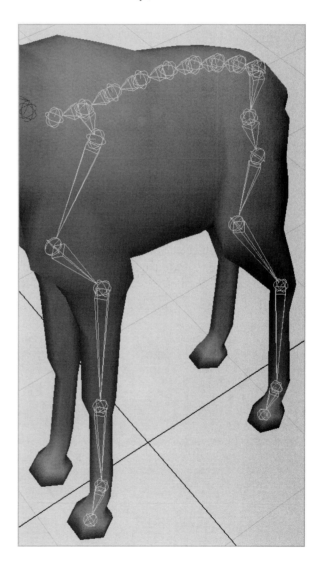

Typically, orientation is done prior to binding your geometry to the skeleton. This is to prevent your geometry from inheriting any transformations. However, Maya does provide tools, such as Move Skinned Joints, to orient joints after they have been attached to geometry.

Typically, each joint is oriented so that the x-axis of its rotation is aimed along the length of the joint. The axis points down toward the child joint.

CERT OBJECTIVE

1. Continue with the scene from the previous section, or open the `giraffe_v02.ma` scene from the `chapter5\scenes` directory at the book's web page.

2. Select the skeleton's root, and freeze transformations on Translate, Rotate, and Scale. You want to make sure all the joints have a rotation of **0** and a scale of **1**. The translation cannot be zeroed, so it doesn't matter if it is included in the operation.

3. With the root still selected, open the options of the function Skeleton ➤ Orient Joint. By default, the Orient Joint function affects child joints when applied to a parent. Since you are starting at the root of the skeleton and working your way down, you can leave this option selected.

4. Keep all the default settings. The Toggle Local Axis Visibility button hides or makes visible the local axes for any selected joint, and it is useful for checking the accuracy of your joint's orientation without you having to leave the tool.

5. Choose Orient; Figure 5.10 shows the resulting Orient Joint options.

FIGURE 5.10
Use the Orient Joint tool to force the x-axis down the length of the bone.

The rotation axis of each joint should be consistent throughout the skeleton to ensure predictable behavior. Ideally, the red x-axis should be pointing down the length of the joint, and the rotation of the green y-axis and the blue z-axis should match throughout the skeleton as much as possible. There will be exceptions to this based on the requirements of the skeleton or your own personal preference. In general, consistency is the most important aspect to watch out for.

6. Check all the joints for consistency. Some of the joints may not have oriented properly based on their position in the world. If that's the case, reorient the joint by deselecting Orient Children Of Selected Joints in the Orient Joint options. Toggle the joints' local axes to double-check your work.

7. Save the scene as **`giraffe_v03.ma`**.

To see a version of the scene up to this point, open the `giraffe_v03.ma` scene from the `chapter5\scenes` directory at the book's web page.

Naming Joints

When creating a skeleton, you need to be extremely conscientious about how you name the joints. Clear, concise naming helps everyone involved in the animation understand how the rig is set up and how each joint is supposed to function. When naming joints, use a prefix such as L_ to indicate the left side and R_ to indicate the right side. If a joint is meant to be used as a control, use a suffix such as _CTRL. The advantage of being consistent with prefixes and suffixes is that you can easily search and replace the prefix or suffix if it needs to be changed on a large number of joints.

1. Continue with the scene from the previous section, or open the `giraffe_v03.ma` scene from the `chapter5\scenes` folder at the book's web page.

2. Open the Outliner, and select each of the joints making up the spine, starting with the root joint. Use Figure 5.11 as a guide.

3. Click the icon next to the input field on the status line.

4. Choose Rename. Type **spine** and press Enter. Maya changes the name and automatically increments the numbering.

5. Rename the neck and tail the same way.

NAMING THE LAST JOINT

It is a good idea to name the last joint of a hierarchy something different. For instance, rename the last joint on the tail to **tailtip**. These joints are typically not weighted; therefore, it's good practice to differentiate them from the rest of the skeleton.

---

6. Naming the legs is more of a manual process since each joint should be named differently. Starting from the top of the front leg, name the joints as follows (be sure to include the underscore).

QUADRUPED BONE NAMES

Anatomically the front leg of a quadruped animal has the same bones as a human arm. As such they are also named the same. Therefore when naming the bones, the "front leg" of the giraffe is named as an arm. This also helps cut down on duplicate names with numerous prefixes:

> **clavicle_**
>
> **shoulder_**
>
> **upperarm_**
>
> **forearm_**
>
> **forefoot_**
>
> **forefoottip_**

Then name the hind leg's joints:

hip_

thigh_

upperleg_

lowerleg_

hindfoot_

hindfoottip_

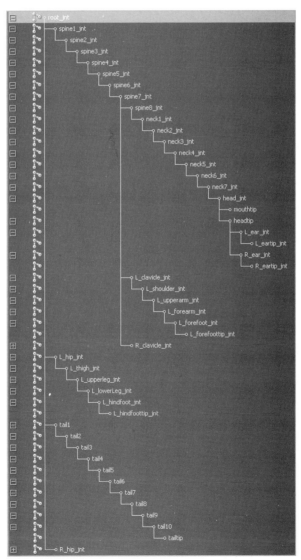

FIGURE 5.11
Name each of the joints to make its purpose clear and to keep it organized.

7. To prevent the leg-joint names from having a conflict from left to right and to organize your naming structure better, add a prefix to all the names. Select the root joint of both legs. Choose Modify ➤ Prefix Hierarchy Names. In the input field, enter **L_**.

It is also a good idea to add a suffix to the joints to prevent confusion further along in the rigging process.

8. Select all the joints to the legs.

9. Choose Modify ➤ Search And Replace Names.

10. In the Search For field, enter _.

11. In the Replace field, enter **_jnt**.

12. Click Replace.

The underscore you added to the names is swapped out with _jnt, and the names are now complete.

You could have easily typed **_jnt** as you were creating each of the names. The main point of the preceding step was to familiarize you with the Search And Replace tool. In addition, if you are renaming numerous nodes or are unsure of your naming convention, you can add an underscore to make altering the name of multiple objects easier.

Refer back to Figure 5.11 to see the final hierarchy and names.

13. Save the scene as **giraffe_v04.ma**.

AUTOMATING RENAMING

Michael Comet, a modeling/rigging artistic/technical director at Pixar Animation Studios and the original creator of Maya Muscle, has bottled these tools' functionalities to take them a step further. He offers an easy-to-use script called cometRename that can handle all of your renaming needs. You can download it at www.comet-cartoons.com/maya.html.

To see a version of the scene up to this point, open the giraffe_v04.ma scene from the chapter5\scenes directory at the book's web page.

Mirroring Joints

The Mirror Joint command is used to duplicate part of the skeleton across a specified axis. It's identical to using Joint Symmetry during the creation of a joint but has the added advantages of renaming and grouping to an existing hierarchy. For example, if a joint chain is parented to part of the skeleton or the collarbone is connected to the spine, the mirrored joint chain is parented to the same joint in the spine.

1. Continue with the scene from the previous section, or open the giraffe_v04.ma scene from the chapter5\scenes directory at the book's web page.

2. Select L_clavicle_jnt.

3. Choose Skeleton ➤ Mirror Joint ➤ Options.

4. In the options, set Mirror Across Axis to YZ, and set Mirror Function to Behavior.

Behavior is usually the best option when building character skeletons. When this option is enabled, corresponding joints on either side of the central axis rotate the same way. So if both shoulder joints are selected and rotated, both arms will rotate forward toward the chest, producing a mirror image across the central axis. The Orientation option means that, when corresponding joints are rotated the same amount on the same axis, one of the arms will have the opposite behavior of the other.

5. In the Replacement Names For Duplicated Joints section, set Search For to **L_** and Replace With to **R_** (see Figure 5.12). This automatically renames the joint chains based on what you put in these fields. In this case, the front leg on the giraffe's right side will use the prefix R_ .

FIGURE 5.12
Duplicate joints are automatically renamed with the search and replace options.

6. Click the Apply button to mirror the leg.

7. Repeat the process for the hind leg and the ear.

8. Save the scene as `giraffe_v05.ma`.

To see a version of the scene up to this point, open the `giraffe_v05.ma` scene from the `chapter5\scenes` directory at the book's web page.

Rigging the Giraffe

As mentioned at the beginning of the chapter, today's rigs must be robust. Many different tools and aspects of Maya come together when character rigging. Inverse kinematics (IK) was introduced in Chapter 2 , where you created a simple mechanical bug using IK Handles and basic techniques. In this section, you'll explore inverse kinematics a little further as well as some of the specialized IK rigging tools Maya offers.

As discussed in Chapter 2, *kinematics* is the study of the motion of objects. There are two main types of kinematics:

Forward Kinematics   This refers to a situation in which each joint in the chain inherits the motion of its parent joint.

Inverse Kinematics   This causes the joints in a chain to orient themselves based on the position of a goal known as the *end effector.*

In this section, you'll learn in more detail how to set up and use inverse kinematics.

IK Legs

Maya uses several types of solvers to calculate how the bones orient themselves based on the position of the end effector. In Chapter 2, you used the Single-Chain solver, which is a simple solver with a few controls.

1. Open the `giraffe_v05.ma` scene from the `chapter5\scenes` directory at the book's web page.

2. From the Animation menu set, choose Skeleton ➤ IK Handle Tool ➤ Options.

3. In the options, set Current Solver to Rotate-Plane Solver and leave the other settings at the defaults (see Figure 5.13).

FIGURE 5.13
Choose Rotate-Plane Solver in the IK Handle Settings options.

4. With the IK Handle tool active, click L_upperarm_jnt, and then click L_forefoot_jnt. You'll see a line drawn between the first joint you clicked and the second joint. The line is known as the *IK Handle Vector*. You can also see a line that runs through the joint chain (see Figure 5.14).

   Inverse kinematics controls can be applied to any joints in the chain, not just between the root and the end joint.

   In the Outliner, you'll see that a node named effector1 has been added at the end of the chain. Also, a node named ikHandle1 appears in the Outliner.

5. Switch to the perspective view, select ikHandle1 in the Outliner, and move it around. Notice how the joint chain reacts. Notice also that, in some positions, the joints flip around to try to match the position of the IK Handle.

   In the Attribute Editor for ikHandle1, look on the IK Handle Attributes tab. The two main settings for the IK Handle are Snap Enable and Sticky:

   ◆ When Snap Enable is on, the IK Handle snaps back to the end joint.

   ◆ The Sticky setting keeps the joints oriented toward the goal when the root joint is moved. This is useful for legs, because it keeps the feet from sliding on the floor.

The difference is obvious:

a. Move L_upperarm_jnt while Sticky is off.

b. Use Undo to return the joint to its original position.

c. Set the Stickiness setting to Sticky.

d. In the Outliner, select L_shoulder_jnt and move the joint around; note how the chain remains oriented toward the IK Handle.

e. Set Stickiness back to off before continuing.

FIGURE 5.14

Attach the IK Handle to the joint chain by clicking the two end joints in the chain. Inverse kinematics is indicated by a line between the two selected joints.

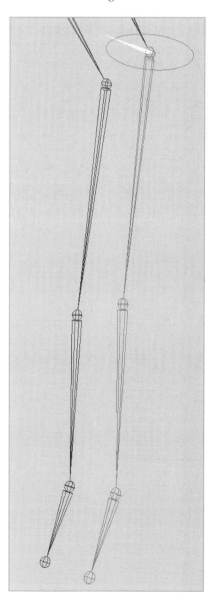

To animate a joint chain with inverse kinematics, you set keyframes on the IK Handle, not the joints. In most situations, you'll want to constrain the IK Handle to another type of control object, such as a curve. The control is keyframed, and the IK Handle is constrained to the control so that it inherits the animation of the control. Constraining the IK Handle to another node produces the same effect as the Stickiness option. Let's add a simple control handle to the front leg.

An ideal animation rig should be easy to understand and animate. This means the controls should be clearly labeled and easy to select directly in the viewport window. With any handle, the animator should be able to enter **0** in all the translation channels for the controls to return the rig to the start position if needed. IK Handles use world space coordinates, so setting their translation channels to **0** moves a handle to the origin. One common solution to this problem is to constrain the handle to a locator, which can then be used to animate the handle. You can set a start position for the control and then freeze transformations on it so that, when the translation channels are set to 0, the control moves to the start position and brings the IK Handle along.

1. Choose File ➢ Import. Import `sphereHandle.ma` from the `chapter5\scenes` directory at the book's web page.

   The imported sphere was created by duplicating the surface curves of a low-resolution NURBS sphere. The multiple curves were cut and reattached into a single continuous curve. When designing your own control handle, you can always overlap the curve onto itself. You will not notice a performance hit by using a few extra control vertices.

2. Snap the sphere to the center of L_forefoot_jnt.

3. Freeze the transforms, and rename it to **L_FrontLeg_CTRL**.

4. With the sphere selected, Shift+click the IK Handle.

5. Choose Constrain ➢ Point ➢ Options.

6. Reset the tool settings from the Edit menu to make sure you are using the defaults. Add the constraint.

7. Add a Single-Chain handle from L_forefoot_jnt to L_forefoottip_jnt. The Single-Chain handle functions differently, and it is not affected as the Rotate-Plane handles are when they are constrained.

8. Turn on Sticky to keep the handle fixed.

9. Parent the Single-Chain handle to the sphere.

10. Save the scene as **`giraffe_v06.ma`**.

To see a version of the scene up to this point, open the `giraffe_v06.ma` scene from the `chapter5\scenes` directory at the book's web page.

FK Blending

Once the constraint is added, new joints appear over the leg. These joints are a representation of a forward kinematics chain. Maya automatically applies FK to any IK chain. Figure 5.15 shows a combination of joints.

FIGURE 5.15
The FK joints are
drawn larger than
the IK joints.

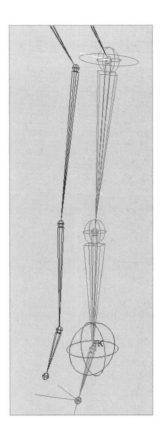

The FK joints are displayed larger than the IK joints to help differentiate between the two. You can control how both are displayed by choosing Window ➢ Settings/Preferences ➢ Preferences and then selecting Kinematics in the Display category. Essentially the two joints are the same. They do not have separate nodes, but they can be controlled independently.

The IK Handle inherently has an IkBlend attribute. When it is set to 1, the IK solver is 100 percent active. When set to 0, FK is 100 percent active. It is possible to blend the effects of both by using any value in between. As with the IK Handle, you do not want to keyframe the FK joints directly. Instead, you can assign handles to each joint. Let's do that next:

1. Open the `giraffe_v06.ma` scene from the `chapter5\scenes` directory at the book's web page.

2. Choose Create ➢ NURBS Primitives ➢ Circle.

3. Snap the circle to L_forearm_jnt.

4. Scale the circle uniformly to **0.25**.

5. Freeze the transforms, and delete its history.

6. Change the name of the circle to **L_forearm_FK**.

7. With the circle selected, Shift+click L_forearm_jnt.

8. Choose Constrain ➤ Orient ➤ Options.

9. In the Orient options, select Maintain Offset. Make sure all the axes are constrained, and choose Add.

Rotating L_forearm_FK won't do anything yet. To see the effects of the handle, set the IkBlend attribute to **0** and then rotate the handle. After testing it, be sure to return the handle's rotate values to **0**.

10. Duplicate L_forearm_FK, and rename it to **L_upperarm_FK**.

11. With L_upperarm_FK selected, Shift+click L_upperarm_jnt.

12. Choose Constrain ➤ Orient using the same options from step 9 (see Figure 5.16).

FIGURE 5.16
Use primitive
NURBS circles for
FK Handles.

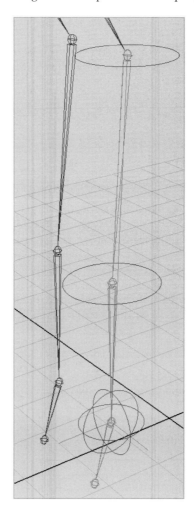

When you rotate L_upperarm_FK, with IkBlend set to 0, you will notice that L_forearm_FK is left behind. A point constraint will fix this.

13. Select L_forearm_jnt.

14. Shift+click L_forearm_FK.

15. Choose Constrain ➢ Point Tool Options. Make sure the options are set to default, and click Add.

16. Save the scene as `giraffe_v07.ma`.

To see a version of the scene up to this point, open the `giraffe_v07.ma` scene from the `chapter5\scenes` directory at the book's web page.

Rotate Plane Solver

The Rotate Plane solver (RP solver) differs from the Single-Chain solver in that the end effector matches the position of the IK Handle but not the rotation. Instead, the rotation of the chain is controlled using a special disc-shaped manipulator that can be keyframed if needed. The RP solver is more predictable and used most often, especially when creating skeletons for characters. The RP solver is similar to the SC solver except that an additional circular icon appears, indicating the pole vector for the chain. The pole vector determines the direction of rotation for the joints as they attempt to reach the IK Handle (see Figure 5.17).

You can select the IK Handle (ikHandle2 in the example), and turn on the Show Manipulators tool. Using this tool, you can do the following:

◆   Rotate the blue disc to adjust the rotation of the chain

◆   Change the numeric values in the Channel Box using the Twist channel

The pole vector of the chain is indicated by the white triangle in the rotate plane indicator at the start point of the IK chain. Changing the pole vector also changes the orientation of the chain. The pole vector determines the angle of the rotate plane for the RP solver. This can be used to control unwanted flipping while animating the IK Handle.

The Twist attribute is directly related to the pole vector. In general, you'll want to adjust the pole vector to orient the chain properly and then use the Twist attribute to solve any flipping problems you may encounter while animating.

The pole vector of an IK Handle can be constrained to another node, just like the IK Handle. Controlling the pole vector through a separate node allows you to zero out the transforms and gives you a visual representation in the viewport. Let's add one to the front leg:

1. Open the `giraffe_v07.ma` scene from the `chapter5\scenes` directory at the book's web page.

2. The pole vector can be controlled just like the IK Handle. Choose File ➢ Import, and select `poleVectorHandle.ma` from the `chapter5\scenes` directory at the book's web page. Rename the imported handle to **L_Leg_PV**.

3. With point snapping on, move L_Leg_PV on top of L_upperarm_jnt. Turn off point snapping.

FIGURE 5.17
The RP solver adds an additional control to determine how the chain rotates as it attempts to match the position of the IK Handle.

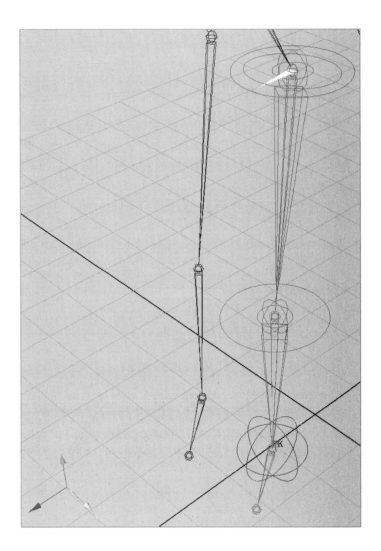

4. Select L_Leg_PV and choose Modify ➢ Freeze Transformations. This will zero out the channels in the Translate XYZ.

5. Open the IK Handle's Attribute Editor.

6. Choose Copy Tab at the bottom of the window.

7. From the copied window, open the IK Solvers Attributes tab and find the Pole Vector XYZ coordinates (see Figure 5.18).

8. Copy the Pole Vector's XYZ coordinates to the L_Leg_PV Translate XYZ. The values of the pole vector place the handle along the same vector. This prevents the pole vector from shifting or being altered from its vector when it will eventually be constrained to the handle.

By adding an Aim constraint, you force the pole vector handle always to orient in the same direction of the forearm joint. This does not provide any necessary functionality—only a better visual representation.

FIGURE 5.18
Find the Pole Vector attributes in the Attribute Editor.

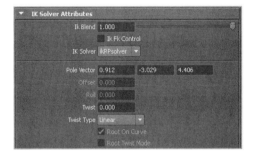

9. Select L_forearm_jnt.

10. Shift+click L_Leg_PV. Choose Constrain ➢ Aim Tool Options.

11. Change the options to match those in Figure 5.19, and click Add.

FIGURE 5.19
Set the Aim constraint options.

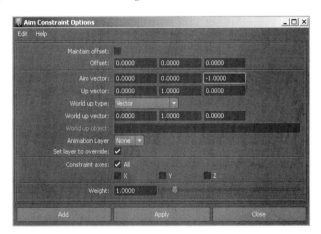

The pole vector handle is too close to the joints. This will cause the joint chain to flip a lot when the IK Handle is moved around.

12. Select L_FrontLeg_PV, and translate it in the Z to about 4.0 units.

13. Find L_FrontLeg_PV in the Outliner or Hypergraph.

14. Attached to it is the Aim constraint. Select and delete it.

15. Select L_FrontLeg_PV, and freeze the transforms.

16. With L_FrontLeg_PV still selected, choose the leg's IK Handle.

17. Add a pole vector constraint by choosing Constrain ➢ Pole Vector. You can see the connection, as shown in Figure 5.20, if you select the IK Handle.

FIGURE 5.20
Use a Pole Vector constraint to control the pole vector of the front leg's IK Handle.

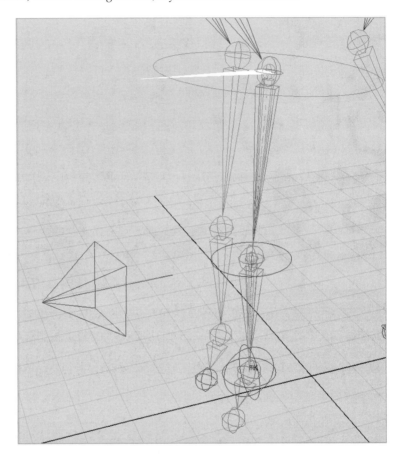

18. Save the scene as **giraffe_v08.ma**.

To see a version of the scene up to this point, open the giraffe_v08.ma scene from the chapter5\scenes directory at the book's web page.

Creating Custom Attributes

CERT OBJECTIVE

You have added several control handles to the leg. The IK and FK Handles have overlapping functionality. When the leg is under full control of the IK, there is no need to see the FK controls;

likewise, when the FK is in full control, there is no need to see the IK controls. You can add an attribute that will toggle between the two without any direct input from the user. Using utility nodes and custom attributes can add a tremendous amount of flexibility and power to your rig. The next exercise creates a custom attribute and, based on its value, turns off or on the visibility of your controls:

1. Open the `giraffe_v08.ma` scene from the `chapter5\scenes` directory at the book's web page. The scene picks up where the previous exercise left off.

2. Select L_FrontLeg_CTRL.

3. Choose Modify ➢ Add Attribute. The Add Attribute window is displayed. Type **IKBlend** for the Long Name and change the settings to match those in Figure 5.21. Make sure the Make Attribute option is set to Keyable and the Data Type option is set to Float.

FIGURE 5.21
Add an attribute called IkBlend to L_FrontLeg_CTRL.

4. Click OK to add the attribute.

   You can also access the Add Attribute window through the Channel Box by choosing Edit ➢ Add Attribute.

5. Look in the Channel Box with L_FrontLeg_CTRL selected and you'll see the new channel named IkBlend. The attribute exists but has no functionality.

6. Select L_FrontLeg_CTRL and L_Forearm_FK, and choose Window ➢ Hypergraph: Connections (see Figure 5.22).

FIGURE 5.22
The node's up-
and downstream
connections are
displayed in the
Hypergraph.

7. In the Hypergraph window, choose Rendering ➤ Create Render Node.

8. With the Create Render Node window open, choose Utilities from the Maya menu.

9. After the window updates, select Condition. A condition node is created in the Hypergraph.

   A condition node sets up an if...else statement. In this exercise, you want the condition to state that if IkBlend is 1, then the visibility of the FK Handles is off. Furthermore, if IkBlend is less than 1, the FK Handles visibility is on.

10. MMB-click L_FrontLeg_CTRL, and drag it onto Condition1. Notice when you drag the mouse, a plus sign is displayed. This lets you know you are performing an action.

11. After you release the MMB, choose Other from the pop-up menu. The Connection Editor opens with the first and second nodes preloaded (see Figure 5.23).

FIGURE 5.23
The Connection
Editor shows
attributes of the
two nodes to be
connected.

12. Choose IkBlend from the bottom of the left-side list (L_FrontLeg_CTRL).

13. In the right-side list (Condition1), select firstTerm. The two attributes are now connected, with IkBlend driving the values of the firstTerm attribute. Leave the Connection Editor open.

14. Open condition1's Attribute Editor. Use Figure 5.24 for the rest of the settings.

FIGURE 5.24
Change the
values of the
Condition node.

- ◆ The First Term setting is the variable; its value determines if and what action needs to be taken.

- ◆ The Second Term setting is what the First Term is compared against.

- ◆ Operation specifies how the comparison should be executed.

- ◆ True and False are what should happen based on the condition. In this case, if the condition is true and IkBlend is less than 1, the resulting value will be 1. If it is greater than 1, or false, the resulting value will be 0.

You need only one channel to make this operation work. Use the first attribute, which is defined as Color Red. The other two channels, blue and green, have been set to 0 simply to avoid confusion.

15. With Condition1 selected, choose Reload Left in the Connection Editor.

16. Select L_forearm_FK, and choose Reload Right.

17. Select OutColorR from Condition1 and Visibility from L_forearm_FK.

The connection is complete. You can test it by opening L_FrontLeg_CTRL in the Channel Box and setting the IkBlend attribute to anything less than 1.

18. Connect the same OutColorR of Condition1 to the visibility of L_upperarm_FK. Now they both turn on or off simultaneously. Figure 5.25 shows the connected nodes in the Hypergraph.

FIGURE 5.25
The connections
are displayed in
the Hypergraph.

19. Save the scene as **giraffe_v09.ma**.

To see a version of the scene up to this point, open the `giraffe_v09.ma` scene from the `chapter5\scenes` directory at the book's web page.

SET DRIVEN KEYS

Set Driven Keys are an invaluable asset to character rigging. You can further control the leg of the giraffe by driving the rotation of L_clavicle_jnt and L_shoulder_jnt with Z-rotation from L_upper-arm_jnt. These bones have a limited specific amount of movement and therefore can be automated with the motion of the leg.

Spline IK

The IK Spline solver uses a curve to control the rotation of the joints. This is ideal for long snaking chains and tails. The solver can generate a curve or use an existing curve. The CVs of the curve become the manipulators for the joint chain. Usually it's a good idea to create clusters for the CVs of the curve and animate CVs of the curve indirectly using the clusters. In the next example, you'll use a spline IK to control the giraffe's spine:

1. Open the `giraffe_v10.ma` scene from the `chapter5\scenes` directory at the book's web page. The scene has been continued from the previous exercise; all of the legs have been rigged.

2. Choose Skeleton ➤ IK Spline Handle Tool Options.

3. Select Auto Create Curve, and deselect Auto Simplify Curve to prevent Maya from reducing the number of control vertices in the spline. Use Figure 5.26 to confirm your settings.

FIGURE 5.26
Create an IK Spline Handle with these options.

4. With the IK Spline Handles tool active, choose root_jnt and then spine8_jnt. The tool autocompletes and connects the spine chain to a curve. If you grab a CV and move it, you can see the spine's motion, as Figure 5.27 demonstrates.

RIGGING THE GIRAFFE | **237**

Figure 5.27
The CVs of the spline are used to manipulate the spine's joints.

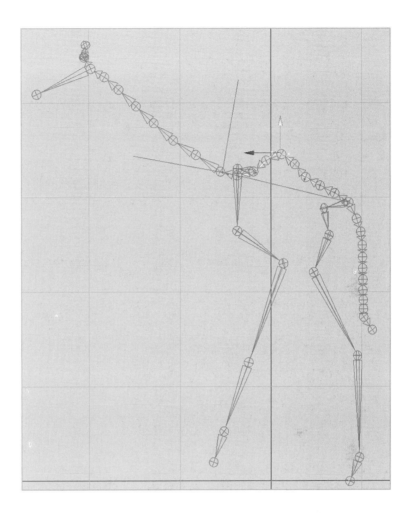

5. Select the curve, and switch to the Surfaces menu set.

6. Choose Edit Curves ➤ Selection ➤ Cluster Curve. Doing so automatically places clusters on each CV of the curve (see Figure 5.28). When animating the curve, you should keyframe the clusters and not the CVs of the curve. For more information on clusters, consult Chapter 6, "Animation Techniques."

   The cluster handles are created with their translates and rotates set to 0, which is perfect for animating. However, cluster handles have a low selection priority, making them difficult to deal with, especially in a complex rig. As with the other handles, it is best to create a custom controller to operate the clusters.

7. Choose Create ➤ NURBS Primitive ➤ Circle.

8. Rename the handle to **shoulder_CTRL**, and snap it to spine7_jnt.

FIGURE 5.28
Each CV of the
spline is now
attached to a
cluster handle.

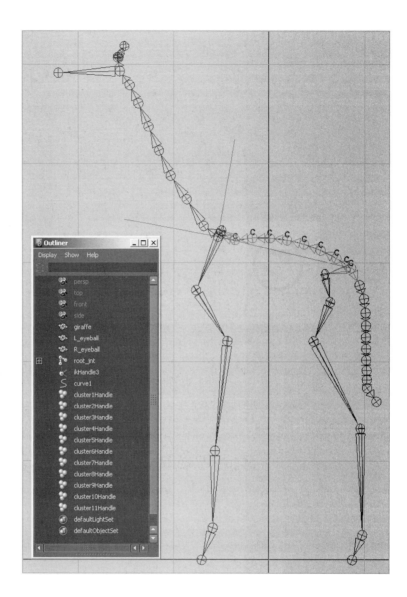

9. Scale the handle uniformly to 0.7.

10. Duplicate shoulder_CTRL, and rename it to **torso_CTRL**.

11. Translate torso_CTRL to be centered between spine5_jnt and spine4_jnt. Scale it uniformly to 0.5.

12. Duplicate torso_CTRL, and rename it to **hip_CTRL**.

13. Snap hip_CTRL to spine1_jnt. Figure 5.29 shows the position of the three circles.

FIGURE 5.29
Position three
NURBS circles along
the giraffe's spine.

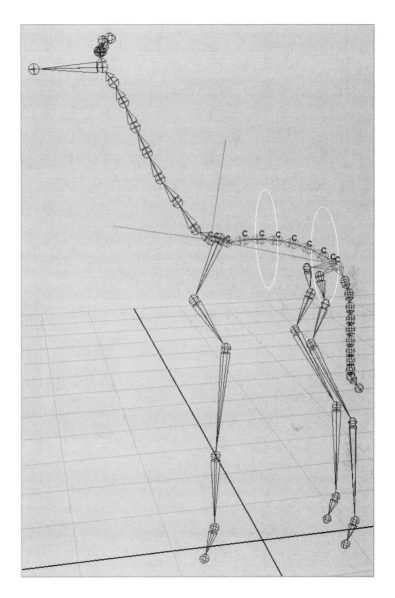

The cluster handles will not react through a parent-child relationship because the Relative feature is selected. In addition, parenting the cluster handles and getting them to move with the character results in unwanted deformations and double transformations on the spline curve. Instead, the cluster handles are constrained to the NURBS curves.

14. Select hip_CTRL, and Shift+click cluster1Handle.

15. Choose Constrain ➤ Parent Options.

16. Select Maintain Offset, and make sure All is selected for Translate and Rotate. Figure 5.30 shows the settings. Repeat this step for the next three cluster handles.

FIGURE 5.30
Add a Parent con-
straint to the first
four cluster handles.

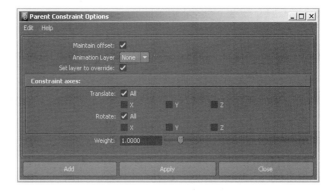

17. Select torso_CTRL, and add the same Parent constraint from step 16 to clusterHandle 5, 6, 7, and 8.

18. Select shoulder_CTRL, and add the same Parent constraint from step 16 to clusterHandle 9, 10, and 11.

19. Grab hip_CTRL, and move it around. Notice how joints pull away from the curve and the other control handles. Figure 5.31 shows an example of this.

This is undesirable and causes major problems while animating. The fix is to point-constrain each control to the one before it. However, constraining a handle directly would lock out the translation and prevent you from keyframing it. Empty group nodes are used instead, and the control handles are parented to them.

20. Choose Create ➤ Empty Group or Ctrl/Cmd+g. null1 is created. Change its name to **torso_GRP.**

21. Snap torso_GRP to spine4_jnt. Freeze the transforms.

22. Select hip_CTRL and then torso_GRP.

23. Choose Constrain ➤ Point Options.

24. Check Maintain Offset, and make sure all axes are being constrained. Click Apply.

25. Select torso_CTRL, and make it a child of torso_GRP.

26. Choose Create ➤ Empty Group.

27. Change the null's name to **shoulder_GRP.**

28. Snap shoulder_GRP to spine7_jnt. Freeze the transforms.

29. Select torso_CTRL and then shoulder_GRP.

30. Choose Constrain ➤ Point Options.

FIGURE 5.31
The joints pull away
from the curve,
causing undesirable
effects.

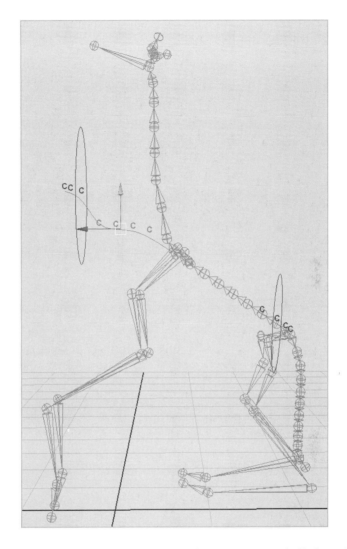

31. Select Maintain Offset, and make sure all axes are being constrained. Click Apply.

32. Move the hip_CTRL again and look at the differences the groups and constraints have made. Figure 5.32 shows the results of these actions.

33. Save the scene as `giraffe_v11.ma`.

To see a version of the scene up to this point, open the `giraffe_v11.ma` scene from the `chapter5\scenes` directory at the book's web page.

IK Spline Handles come with an extra feature called Twist. Although this attribute shows up on other types of IK Handles, it affects only the spline IK. Ultimately, the giraffe's final rig will not have any IK Handles visible, since control for all of them is being passed to a custom handle. Keeping in line with this, you can add the twist of the spline IK to a custom attribute on the shoulder control.

FIGURE 5.32
Shoulder and torso
controls follow along
with the hip control.

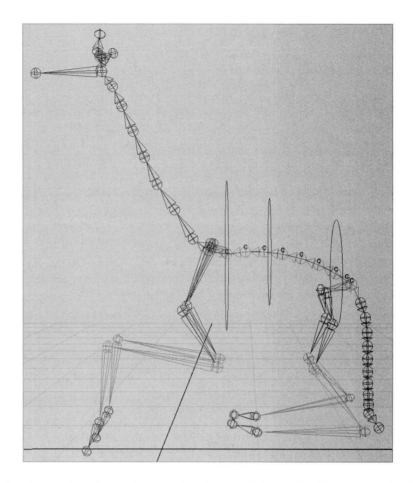

You can apply what you have learned to complete the rest of the giraffe. If you get stuck, take a look at the complete giraffe in the scene `giraffe_v12.ma` in the `chapter5\scenes` directory at the book's web page.

Human Inverse Kinematics

Human Inverse Kinematics (HIK) is used for full-body inverse kinematics. This system creates IK Handles that control an entire biped or quadruped skeleton rather than using multiple IK chains on individual limbs. It is a powerful system capable of producing smooth animations quickly. In addition, the time it takes to set up a full-body IK skeleton is a fraction of the time needed to create your own rig. HIK is a plug-in, but it is loaded automatically by default.

Perhaps the greatest strength of the HIK system is its ability to retarget animations from one character to another. Characters of different sizes and proportions can swap motions. Animation layers can be used to create nondestructive offsets to fix any discrepancies between the characters' movements.

Skeleton Generator

The HIK tools allow you to create a custom skeleton and rig or use the system's Skeleton Generator. Bipedal or quadrupedal characters can be created, but all must be in a T-pose or T-stance looking toward the positive z-axis. The HIK system also requires a standard set of 15 bones. The following example takes you through the steps to create a bipedal character:

1. Start with a new scene in Maya. From the Animation module choose Skeleton ➢ HumanIK. The Character Controls panel opens.

   The Character Controls panel contains the Character Controls button (top-left corner) and three sections: Create, Define, and Import. Clicking the Character Controls button reveals the full set of options available for the Character Controls.

2. Choose Create ➢ Skeleton from the Character Controls button or from the first section of the Character Controls panel. A large biped skeleton is created in the viewport, and the Character Controls panel is refreshed with a new set of options.

3. Change the Character Scale to make the character about 10.5 units tall. Altering the Character Scale slider always ends with the scale setting returning to 1.0. To achieve a height of 10.5 units, enter a scale of **0.07**.

   Figure 5.33 shows the skeleton created with the HIK Skeleton Generator and scaled to 10.5 units.

FIGURE 5.33

A skeleton generated by the HIK Skeleton Generator

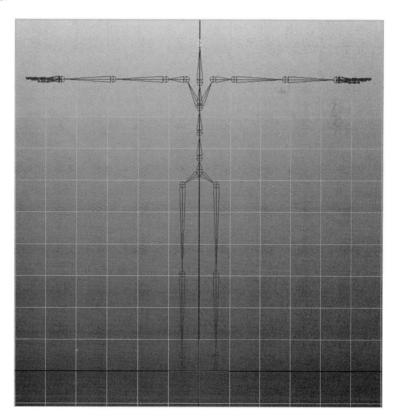

4. In the Skeleton section of the Character Controls panel, check Lower–Arms to add roll bones to the characters' forearms.

You can customize the existing skeleton further by adding or taking away toes, spine joints, and numerous other bones. You can also modify the bones directly to fit your character by translating and rotating the bones in the viewport.

After the skeleton is made, it must be characterized by the HIK system; *characterizing* a skeleton means mapping each joint to a corresponding joint within the HIK system. Once that's done, the HIK solver can understand your skeleton and you can apply a control rig. Since you used the built-in Skeleton Generator, you do not need to map the bones.

5. With any bone selected, click the Character Controls button and choose Create ➤ Control Rig. This automatically locks the skeleton from further changes. The Character Controls panel is updated again and a control rig is added to the skeleton (see Figure 5.34). Save the scene as **hikCharacter_v01.ma**.

FIGURE 5.34
The control rig is added to the skeleton.

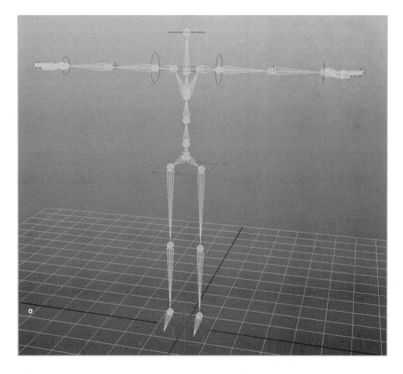

To see a version of the scene up to this point, open the hikCharacter_v01.ma scene from the chapter5\scenes directory at the book's web page.

Character Controls

The HIK system comes with a Character Controls panel (see Figure 5.35) that allows you to select the control handles of your character quickly and easily and to toggle between, FK, IK, and full body IK. You can also click the encircled arrows to see exploded views of the hands and feet.

FIGURE 5.35

The Character Controls panel

HIK   IK   FK

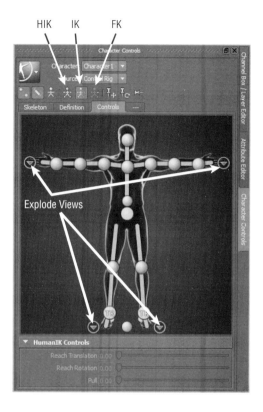

Within the Character Controls panel is a row of icons located above the Skeleton, Definition, and Controls tabs. The first two icons allow you to toggle the visibility of the FK handles and bones. The next icon toggles the visibility of the full body skeleton. By default, this is turned off. Go ahead and choose the Show/Hide Skeleton icon to display the full-body skeleton. It appears under the FK bones. Click the Show/Hide FK icon to turn the FK bones off.

The next three icons—Full Body, Body Part, and Selection—control the functionality of the control handles on the character. Starting in reverse order, the Selection icon allows you to move a handle without having the bones follow along. The next, Body Part, treats the bones connected to the selected handle as an ordinary IK system. Choose this icon, and select the left wrist handle. You can select the wrist handle through a viewport or from the humanoid image within the Character Controls panel. Use the Move tool to see how it affects the skeleton. Use Undo to return the skeleton back to its default position. Now select the Full Body icon, and move the wrist handle again. Notice the difference (see Figure 5.36).

Whether you animate a body part or the full body, the effectors will always appear synchronized by default in the viewport. The effectors' position is the final solved animation. You can turn the synchronization off or on by clicking the Character Controls button and choosing Edit ➤ Control Rig ➤ Align Control Rig.

FIGURE 5.36
The left wrist handle is translated with Full Body IK turned on.

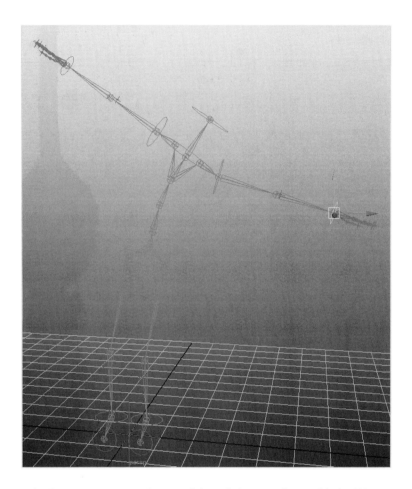

The HIK system also has separate control over roll-bone behavior. If you added roll bones, you can alter the way rotation is distributed to them. The following steps take you through the process:

1. Continue with the scene from the previous exercise, or load hikCharacter_v01.ma scene from the chapter5\scenes directory at the book's web page. Select Character1_Ctrl_LeftWristEffector, and open its Attribute Editor.

2. In the Attribute Editor, choose the HIKproperties1 tab. Open the Roll & Pitch rollout.

3. Set the Left Forearm Roll to **0.5**. With a 0.5 value, the left forearm joint will rotate approximately half the amount of the left wrist effector's rotation.

4. Set the Left Elbow Roll to **0.2**. With a 0.2 value, the elbow joint will rotate approximately 20 percent of the left wrist effector's rotation. This will also cause the left forearm to rotate 20 percent less than what was stated in step 3.

5. Rotate the left wrist effector in the x-axis. Select each joint along the forearm to see how the roll attributes affected their values.

At any time, you can return your character or parts of your character to their stance pose by clicking the Character Control button and choosing Edit ➤ Control Rig ➤ Stance Pose. The selection mode, set in the Character Controls panel, dictates whether the full body is returned to the stance pose or whether only the selected body parts are.

You can customize the character interface by adding your own image or moving the location of the effectors within the interface. This is achieved by editing the XML configuration files located in the `Program Files\Autodesk\Maya2015\resources\CharacterControls` directory. In the same directory is a `DefaultImages` folder containing all the images needed for the interface.

Interoperability

You can send Human IK characters to the Autodesk® MotionBuilder® software by choosing File ➤ Send To MotionBuilder. The One-Click plug-in included with Maya must be loaded and MotionBuilder must be installed on your computer in order for this menu to appear. This feature allows you to send new scenes or update individual elements to MotionBuilder. You can also establish a live connection and stream animation from MotionBuilder on to your character in Maya. Streaming animation can be done using an HIK rig or custom rig of your own design.

You can convert bipedal character animation toolkit (CAT) rigs from the Autodesk® 3ds Max® software into FK representations on a human IK skeleton in Maya. You can make changes to the character in Maya, and then send it back to 3ds Max as an updated CAT character. You can also choose to "bake" the animation of your HIK character for greater interoperability. (Baking is the process of transferring information from one source to another.) Click the Character Control button in the Character Controls panel; you can choose to bake the animation to the skeleton or control rig. The baking options update automatically depending on your selection, enabling you to bake the full body, body part, custom rig, or live skeleton.

Skinning Geometry

Skinning geometry is the process in which geometry is bound to joints so that, as the joints are rotated or translated, the geometry is deformed. The terms *skinning* and *binding* are interchangeable. There are two types of skinning: smooth binding and interactive skin binding (an extension of smooth binding).

Polygon and NURBS geometry can be bound to skeletons; however, polygon geometry often produces more predictable results. In this section, you will continue with the giraffe, which is polygon geometry.

When geometry is smooth-bound to a skeleton, each vertex of the geometry receives a certain amount of influence from the joints in the skeleton. The amount of weight value of the joints determines the amount of influence each vertex receives from a joint. By default, the values are normalized, ranging from 0 to 1, where 0 is no influence and 1 is full (or 100 percent) influence. Weight values can be normalized in two different ways: Post (the default method) or Interactive. Post weights are calculated only when the bound mesh is deformed, preventing previously weighted vertices from being changed. Interactive normalization sets the weight value exactly as you enter it, forcing the weights to always total 1.0. When you bind geometry to a skeleton, the vertex weights are set automatically based on the options you specify in the Smooth Bind command. In most situations, the weights of the geometry require further editing after executing the Smooth Bind command.

HEAT-MAP BINDING

Heat-map binding emits weight values from the joint or influence object onto the surrounding mesh. Hotter or higher values are given to vertices closest to the influence object. The further a vertex is from an influence object, the cooler or lower the weight value. Heat-map binding works only on polygon meshes and can fail if your mesh has nonmanifold geometry or badly shaped faces. In addition, if your joints are located outside of the mesh, the joint will have no influence on the geometry.

When binding geometry to the skeleton, make sure the rotations of the joints in the skeleton are all at 0. This means that if an IK Handle has been added to the skeleton, you should select and disable the handle (choose Skeleton ➤ Disable Selected IK Handles) and then set the joint-rotation channels to 0. Bind the skin to the joints and re-enable the IK Handle (choose Skeleton ➤ Enable Selected IK Handles).

The pose the skeleton is in when you bind the geometry is known as the *bind pose*. If at some point you need to detach and reattach the geometry to edit the geometry, you must be able to return to the bind pose easily. Do so by selecting the skeleton's root joint and choosing Skin ➤ Go To Bind Pose.

Editing the skin weights is usually accomplished through three tools:

Interactive Skin Binding Tool First, this tool enables you to alter the area of influence rapidly by each joint.

Paint Skin Weights Next, you can refine your weights further with this tool. It employs the Artisan brush interface to set weights interactively.

Component Editor You can also edit the weight values directly for selected vertices using the Component Editor. The Component Editor gives you precise control over each vertex and the exact amount of weight it receives.

Editing skin weights can be a difficult and occasionally frustrating process. In the upcoming exercise, you'll learn a few tips that can help make the process a little easier and faster.

Interactive/Smooth Binding

Maya automatically assigns skin weights to each vertex of the geometry as it is bound to the joints. There are options for assigning these weights based on the vertices' proximity to the joints and the number of joints that can influence any particular vertex. Even so, after binding, you'll need to edit the weights using the Paint Skin Weights tool. If the geometry is very dense—meaning that it has a lot of vertices—this process can take a while.

Interactive skin binding uses an adjustable volume to define smooth skin weights. The volumes can be moved and shaped to fit your character's geometry, all the while giving you instant feedback on how the vertices are being influenced.

Weighting the Giraffe

You don't use just one tool when weighting a character. Numerous tools and techniques are applied to achieve maximum performance. In this exercise, you will weight the giraffe with an interactive skin bind:

1. Open the `giraffe_v11.ma` scene from the `chapter5\scenes` directory at the book's web page. The scene has a complete version of the giraffe's rig.

2. Select root_jnt and the giraffe's mesh.

3. Choose Skin ➤ Bind Skin ➤ Interactive Skin Bind Options.

Notice that you can choose to bind the entire joint hierarchy or just selected joints. In this example, you'll bind the entire hierarchy.

BROKEN-JOINT SKELETONS

Keep in mind that you also have the option of binding only selected joints. In some circumstances, this can be quite useful. For example, if you set up what is known as a *broken-joint* skeleton, which uses additional bones outside the main skeleton hierarchy as deformers, these additional joints are usually constrained to the main hierarchy using parent constraints. When you use parent constraints, the joints "float" outside the main hierarchy, giving them a level of freedom of movement to create special deformation effects. (Sometimes floating joints are used for facial animation instead of or in addition to blend shape deformers.) When skinning a broken rig to the skeleton, select the floating joints along with the joints in the main hierarchy when the smooth bind operation is performed.

Here are the relevant settings:

Bind Method   The bind method determines how joints influence vertices, by either following the skeleton's hierarchy or simply using whichever joint is the closest. The hierarchy of the giraffe is complete and calls for every bone to be weighted; however, for the tips, use Closest In Hierarchy.

Include Method   The include method dictates which vertices are included in the initial volumes. Your options are Closest Volume and Minimum Weight. Choosing Minimum Weight opens an additional option to set the length of the volume. By default this is 0.25, causing each volume to be 25 percent longer than the bone to which it is attached. Most characters will have a different area of influence based on its location. For instance, the giraffe's knee needs to have a smaller falloff compared to the torso. Choose Closest Volume.

You can use two types of volumes—a cylinder or a capsule:

◆   A cylinder will deliver a hard edge.

◆   The capsule is rounded at its ends, providing a smoother falloff.

Keep the capsule turned on.

Skinning Method   The skinning method has the greatest impact on your bind. You can use Classic Linear, Dual Quaternion, or a blend of both.

◆   Classic Linear does not preserve volume and produces a visible shrinking of the geometry.

◆   Dual Quaternion provides the most suitable deformations for realistic characters. It preserves the volume of a mesh when a joint is twisted or rotated.

Take a look at Figure 5.37 to see the differences between the two.

FIGURE 5.37
The Classic Linear
skinning method is
applied to the joints
on the left and Dual
Quaternion is applied
on the right.

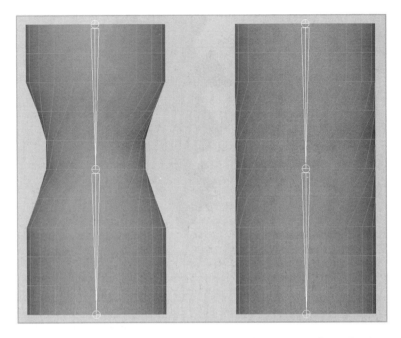

The last two settings relate to how many influences a single vertex can have. It is important to remember that joints are not the only nodes that can be bound to geometry. Other geometry can also be used, and it is therefore considered an influence as well. Most weighted objects do not require more than four influences per vertex, which is the default. In addition, a lot of game engines have a hard limit of four influences on a single vertex. After binding, you can keep the influences locked to four by selecting Maintain Max Influences. This is particularly useful when weighting geometry for an environment outside of Maya, such as a game engine. Keep the default settings for the giraffe (see Figure 5.38).

FIGURE 5.38
Bind the giraffe
geometry to its
skeleton.

4. Choose Bind Skin.

Keep in mind that all the weighting can be altered after the bind has been applied. These settings merely give you a place to start and typically require a lot of fine-tuning. Furthermore, you can change these settings through the skinCluster node that is attached to the bound geometry (see Figure 5.39).

RIGID BINDING

With rigid skinning, you can have only a single joint influence each vertex. Therefore, you must use a flexor, which is a lattice deformer, around the bone to achieve a smooth deformation effect. The typical pipeline for using Rigid Binding is as follows:

1. Select a skeleton and geometry.

2. Choose Skin ➤ Bind Skin ➤ Rigid Bind.

3. Edit joint deformation by selecting a joint and adding a flexor, Skin ➤ Edit Rigid Skin ➤ Create Flexor.

4. Shape the flexor to the desired deformation.

FIGURE 5.39
The skinCluster node holds all the settings from the initial binding options.

The giraffe's initial bind is established; now it's time to fine-tune its weighting. Traditionally, modifying weighted geometry has been like feeling your way around in the dark. The Interactive Skin Bind tool not only sheds light on each and every vertex, but it does so with precision and ease of use. The Interactive Skin Bind tool allows you to massage the weights quickly to an acceptable level.

5. Start with the giraffe's front legs to get used to the controls. Select L_upperarm_jnt. If it isn't active already, choose Skin ➤ Edit Smooth Skin ➤ Interactive Skin Bind Tool. By default, two volumes are displayed. The only interactive one is the volume on the selected joint. The second volume is a reflection that is attached to R_upperarm_jnt. The reflection is displayed based on the Reflection tool settings and operates the same way as it does with the transformation tools (see Figure 5.40).

Each volume can be translated, rotated, and shaped. A heat-style color graph is used to illustrate the joint's influence, with red being the highest amount of influence and blue being the least. A few color presets are provided along with the ability to change the color graph any way you would like.

The capsule's manipulator is also color-coded. Red, green, and blue are used to represent the three axes, respectively. Depending on which part of the manipulator you grab, the shape of the capsule is altered. For the most part, each axis scales the selected ring uniformly.

6. Use the LMB and grab the top, red horizontal ring.

7. Resize it to decrease the amount of influence.

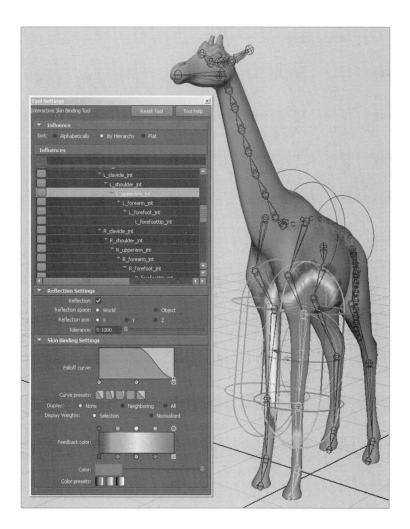

8. Repeat this operation for the lower ring.

9. In addition to changing the capsule's shape, you can use the traditional Move And Rotate manipulator (scale is based on the volume) to fit the capsule better to the geometry. The manipulator is located in the center of the capsule. Looking at the front of the giraffe, translate and rotate the capsule for a better fit. Do the same for its profile. Figure 5.41 shows the adjusted capsule.

10. Visible interactivity has been limited so far because the giraffe is in its original bind pose position. Translate the leg **1.0** in the Z and **0.5** in the Y.

11. Select L_upperarm_jnt. Notice that the geometry in the middle of the bone appears to be sagging (see Figure 5.42). This is an indication that the geometry is not weighted to 1 at those particular vertices. However, the heat map shows full influence. Use the up arrow to go to the preceding joint, L_shoulder_jnt.

12. L_shoulder_jnt overlaps the L_upperarm_jnt, causing the problem. Use the down arrow to return to L_shoulder_jnt.

Maya is displaying the non-normalized weight of the joint; therefore, the color displayed is red. What you are actually seeing is the combined weight value of both joints.

FIGURE 5.41
Translate and rotate the capsule to encompass the leg geometry.

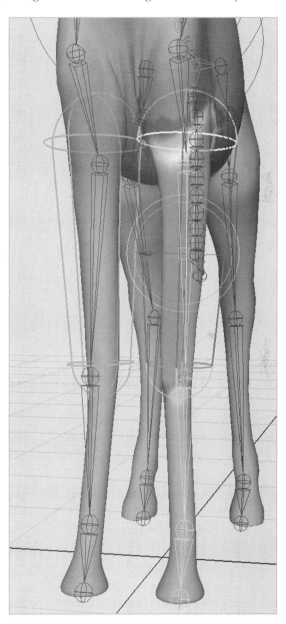

13. In the tool settings for Interactive Skin Bind, find Display Weights. It is located above the color graph. Change it to Normalized. You can now see the true weight value of the joint.

14. Use the up arrow to go back to L_shoulder_jnt.

FIGURE 5.42
The geometry in the middle of the bone is sagging even though the volume shows the hottest influence.

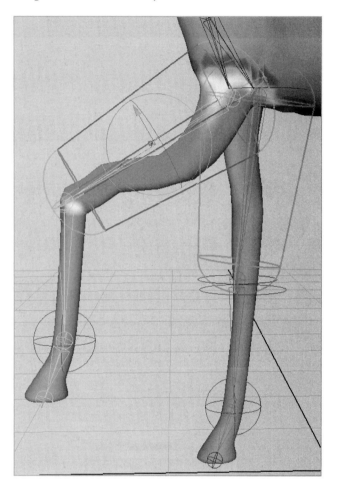

15. Modify the volume to fit its bone better. You can hold Shift while moving the red rings to scale the entire volume uniformly. If you hold Shift while adjusting the green or blue rings, the effects are local to that ring. Figure 5.43 shows the results of the new volume shape.

16. Save the scene as `giraffe_v12.ma`.

To see a version of the scene up to this point, open the `giraffe_v12.ma` scene from the `chapter5\scenes` directory at the book's web page.

FIGURE 5.43
Modifying L_shoulder_jnt's volume fixes the upper arm (front leg).

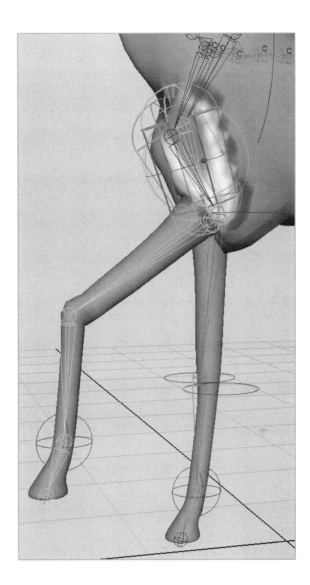

New!

SMOOTH BIND WEIGHTING

You can also simulate the functionality of Interactive Skinning by using Smooth Bind and Weight Distribution. Under the Smooth Bind options, change the Weight Distribution to Neighbors. This keeps weights from being distributed beyond joints that are not in close proximity. Normalize weights must be set to Interactive to use this option. Furthermore, only joints with weight are considered.

Geodesic Voxel Binding

New!

Maya 2015 brings a new binding method for smooth binds called *geodesic voxel binding*. This binding method creates a voxel representation of your mesh. A *voxel* is a volumetric pixel (described in more detail in Chapter 15, "Fluid Simulation"). The distance from the joint or influence object is calculated through the volume to determine the falloff. As a result, geodesic voxel binding provides greater accuracy and smoother results. If you are binding multiple meshes, the voxelization treats them as a single volume.

Geodesic voxel binding is superior to the other binding methods since it is based on the true volume of the object. Essentially the skeleton is aware of the object's shape, helping to prevent things like arms being weighted to legs and finger weights bleeding over into other fingers. The drawback, however, is that it takes considerably longer to perform the initial bind. Binding with Closest In Hierarchy happens almost instantaneously, whereas you might wait minutes for geodesic voxel binding to complete. Increasing the voxel resolution with a geodesic bind also increases the computation time. Characters with detailed skeletons will most likely require a higher resolution, but the default value of 256 is suitable for most situations.

In a side-by-side comparison of binding methods, the differences may not be readily apparent. Take a look at Figure 5.44. The hand was bound to its skeleton using the default binding values for each of the different binding methods. The geodesic voxel bind is on the left. Look at how smoothly the geometry deforms while retaining its original shape. The Closest In Hierarchy method averages the weighting, causing the deformations to soften the details of the model. You can notice this on the interior angle of the bent finger. Its closest competition is the heat map bind (right). With heat map binding, however, the geometry is pinching, almost to the point of interpenetration. In addition, heat map binding does not support all geometry types like nonmanifold geometry and can fail as a result.

FIGURE 5.44
The three different binding methods are compared: geodesic (left), Closest In Hierarchy (middle), and heat map (right).

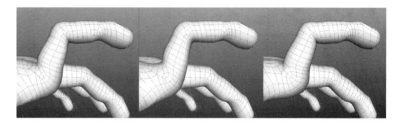

Geodesic voxel binding is part of the Smooth Bind options. Use the following steps to apply the method:

1. Open the `giraffe_v11.ma` scene from the `chapter5\scenes` directory at the book's web page.

2. Select root_jnt and the giraffe's mesh.

3. Choose Skin ➤ Bind Skin ➤ Smooth Bind Options.

4. Set the Bind Method to Geodesic Voxel. Figure 5.45 shows all of the options associated with Smooth Bind.

FIGURE 5.45
The options for Smooth Bind

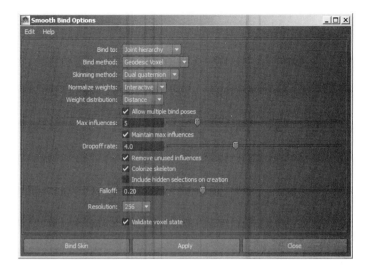

Painting Skin Weights

The Interactive Skin Bind tool takes you far into the weighting process. However, the weights still need work. To make the skin move properly, you need to edit the weight values of the vertices. You can do so by using the Paint Weights tool. To maximize the benefits of painting weights, your geometry should have good UVs. These are explained in Chapter 9, "Texture Mapping." This exercise demonstrates techniques for painting weights on various parts of the giraffe:

1. Continue with the scene from the previous section, or open the `giraffe_v12.ma` scene from the `chapter5\scenes` directory at the book's web page.

2. Move the giraffe leg up again to see the effects of painting weights interactively.

3. Translate the leg **1.0** in the Z and **0.5** in the Y.

4. In the viewport, switch to smooth-shaded mode (hot key = **6**).

5. Select the giraffe geometry, and choose Skin ➢ Edit Smooth Skin ➢ Paint Skin Weights Tool. Make sure the Tool Options window is open.

   The geometry turns black except for the area around the joint listed in the Influence section of the Paint Skin Weights Tool window. The geometry is color-coded:

   ◆ White indicates a joint weight value of 1 (100 percent).

   ◆ Black indicates a joint weight value of 0.

   ◆ Shades of gray indicate values between 0 and 1 (see Figure 5.46).

FIGURE 5.46

The Paint Skin Weights tool color-codes the geometry based on the amount of weight influence each joint has for each vertex of the skinned geometry.

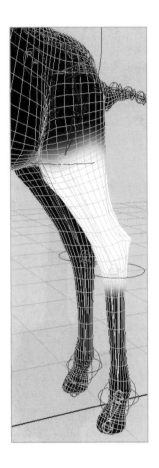

You can also switch to the same gradient color ramp used in the Interactive Skin Bind tool.

The Paint Skin Weights tool uses the Artisan brush interface. As you paint on the model, the operation selected in the Paint Weights section determines how the brush edits the weights. You can replace, add, smooth, or scale weights in the areas you paint on the model. The easiest way to approach weight painting is to stick to only the Add and Smooth operations.

Each vertex on the model receives a value up to 1 from all the joints on the model. The total weight values must equal 1 so, if a selected vertex receives a value of 0.8 from a particular joint, the remaining weight value (0.2) must come from another joint in the chain. Usually this remaining weight value comes from a joint close by the vertex, as determined by Maya. This is where things can get tricky. If you paint on a vertex using the Replace operation with a value of 0.5 for a particular joint, the remaining 0.5 weight value is distributed among the other joints in the chain. This can lead to some strange and unpredictable results. If instead you use the Add operation with very low values, you can carefully increase a joint's influence over a vertex without worrying about Maya assigning the remaining weight values to other joints in the chain.

New!

6. The area you want to paint is the armpit of the front-left leg (or arm). To prevent other areas from receiving or transferring weight during the painting process, you can lock the weights on specific joints. We will need to alter the weights from spine5_jnt down to L_forefoottip_jnt. Choose these bones by holding Shift and selecting the first joint and then the last joint in the Influences section of the Paint Weights tool.

7. Choose the Invert Selection icon from the under the Influences section. It is the last icon to the right. Next, click on any one of the selected bones' lock icon. This will lock all of the selected joints. You can also RMB-click on a joint to bring up a menu with locking commands.

8. To expedite the process, force the Paint Weights tool to display only the joints for which you want to paint influence. To do this, hold Ctrl (Cmd on the Mac) and pick each joint with which you want to work in the Influences section of the Paint Weights tool. You can also use Shift to select the first and last joints to highlight a group.

9. With your joints selected, click the tack/pin icon in the upper-right corner of the Influences section (see Figure 5.47).

FIGURE 5.47
Reduce the number of joints displayed in the Paint Weights tool by pinning them.

10. Choose L_upperarm_jnt from the influences.

11. Set Paint Operation to Replace and Value to **0.0**.

12. Paint the area being pulled by the arm that belongs to the torso. To resize your brush, use the **b** key. Use Figure 5.48 for reference.

13. Once you have separated the torso skin from arm skin, use the Smooth operation to clean the weights.

    The giraffe has a bone jutting out in this location. A lot of the weights are still being used by the torso.

14. Set the paint value to **0.1**.

15. Use the Add operation to move the weights more onto the upper arm.

16. When finished, go back over the arm again with the Smooth operation. Figure 5.49 shows the progress so far.

FIGURE 5.48
Paint a weight of 0 to remove the influence of the arm.

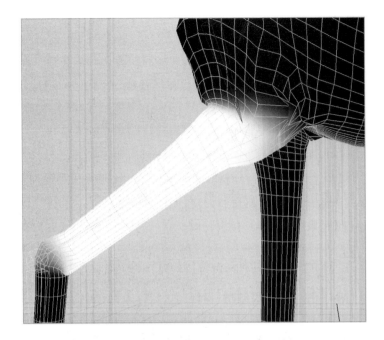

FIGURE 5.49
The skin weighting has been smoothed.

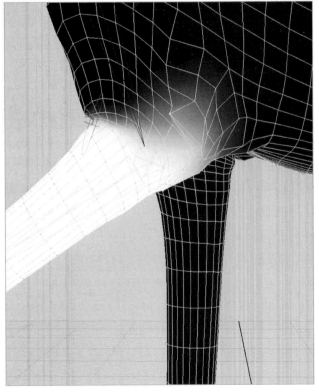

A few vertices are still being unruly.

17. Change Paint Tool Mode to Select, and choose two or three of the worst vertices. You can also choose Paint Select.

Toward the top of the Paint Skin Weights window is a Tools section. The middle icon is the Weight Hammer tool. This tool assigns an average of the weights around the selected vertices. Figure 5.50 shows the same area from Figure 5.47 after the Weight Hammer tool was applied.

FIGURE 5.50
The skin weights have been cleaned up with the Weight Hammer tool.

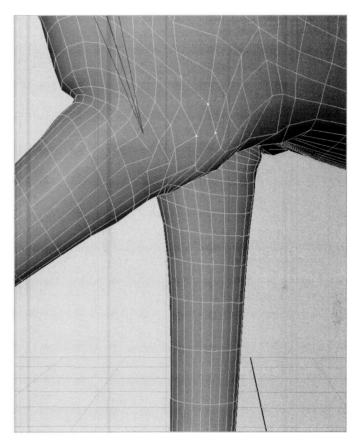

18. You can continue to paint the skin weights with the joints posed. This is an excellent way to get visual feedback as you edit the weights.

19. Save the scene as `giraffe_v13.ma`.

To see a version of the scene up to this point, open the `giraffe_v13.ma` scene from the `chapter5\scenes` directory at the book's web page.

Editing Skin Weights in the Component Editor

CERT
OBJECTIVE

In some cases, you may want to edit the skin weights by entering a precise numeric value. To do this, follow these steps:

1. Switch to component mode, and select the vertices you need to edit directly.

2. Choose Window ➤ General Editors ➤ Component Editor.

3. On the Smooth Skins tab, you'll see a spreadsheet that lists each joint's influence for each of the selected vertices (see Figure 5.51). You can change these values by directly entering numbers into the spreadsheet.

FIGURE 5.51
You can use the Component Editor to enter numeric weight values for the joints.

Remember that each vertex must have a total weight value of 1, so if you set a value lower than 1, the remaining value will be assigned to a different joint. You can turn on the Hold option to lock a vertex's weight value so that Maya will not change the value automatically.

Copying Skin Weights

You can copy the weights from the low-resolution model to the high-resolution model. It does not matter that the vertices do not perfectly match, because the overall weighting can easily be transferred. This reduces the difficulty of editing the initial weights on the high-resolution model.

Copying weights is extremely useful when you have a lot of characters to weight. Once you are happy with one character, you can copy its weights onto another character, even if the dimensions are not the same. The Copy Weights tool copies weighting information based on proximity. As long as the vertices are close to one another, the weights are transferred regardless of vertex density or geometry shape. It is even possible to move the bones of the weighted objects to match the new object more closely. The source does not matter. Of course, the closer the two are in shape and size, the better the end results.

Mirroring Skin Weights

You can copy weight values from one side of a symmetrical character to another using the Mirror Skin Weights command. This technique greatly reduces the amount of time you'd spend painting weights and ensures consistency in weighting for both sides of a character. First select the mesh, and then choose Skin ➤ Edit Smooth Skin ➤ Mirror Skin Weights ➤ Options. In the options, you can choose which axis the weights are mirrored across.

The Maya Muscle System

Maya Muscle tools deform the surface of geometry much like other types of deformers. They simulate the behavior of actual muscles and can be driven by the rotation of joints or expressions. Muscles are similar to the influence objects, but they offer better control for deforming the skinned geometry surface. Much of the purpose and functionality of influence objects is replaced by Maya Muscle, so this edition of *Mastering Autodesk Maya* does not discuss influence objects.

The Maya Muscle deformer is actually a surface that can be manipulated while connected to the deformed geometry. The muscle objects can create complex deformations by allowing for multiple end shapes per muscle.

Muscle objects can slide beneath the deformed geometry to create special effects, and muscles also have properties that allow movement such as jiggle, force, and collision.

Understanding the Maya Muscle System

The Maya Muscle system is a collection of deformation tools that can work independently or in concert to deform geometry so that it looks like muscles are bulging and stretching beneath skin. The primary system has three main deformer types:

Capsules   Capsules are simple skin deformers used as replacements for joints. It is necessary to use capsules because standard Maya joints cannot work directly with the muscle deformer. Capsules are shaped like a simple pill. The basic capsule shape cannot be changed. However, it can be scaled to simulate the basic shape of muscles.

Bones   Bones are skin deformers that have been converted from regular polygon geometry. Because of this, bones can be almost any shape you need. The term *bones* in this sense should not be confused with the standard bones, which are the shapes that connect joints. The Maya Muscle system uses the term bones because these deformers are useful for simulating the movement of specially shaped bones—such as the scapula—beneath skin.

Muscles   Muscles are skin deformers created from NURBS surfaces. The muscle deformers are designed to replicate the behavior of real-life muscles. To achieve this, they have two connection points at either end, which are attached to the character's rig. So, for example, when the character moves/bends his arm, the connection points move closer together, creating a bulging/squashing effect. When the character extends his arm, the connection points move farther apart, creating a stretching effect. The transition between squashing and stretching is automatically eased in and out, so the deformer's movements are smooth.

Any of these muscle deformers can be bound to the character's skin geometry using one of the various types of weighting available. Weighting muscle deformers to geometry is similar to using smooth binding to connect geometry to Maya joints. The weighting types include Sticky, Sliding, Displacement, Force, Jiggle, Relax, and Smooth. The following sections demonstrate using muscle deformers with Sticky weighting, which is similar to smooth binding, discussed earlier in this chapter.

To use a muscle system, you must first create the muscle objects (capsule, bone, or muscle), apply the muscle deformer to the character's skin, connect the specific muscle objects (capsule, bone, or muscle) to the deformer, and then use a weighting type to bind it to determine how the deformer affects the character's skin using one of the available weighting types.

It is important to understand that, when you use the Maya Muscle system, the character's skin geometry must be bound to objects that have the cMuscleObject shape node. In other words, you must either replace or convert any existing joints with capsules or Maya Muscle bones. You can also transfer any existing skin weights created for Maya joints to the muscle system.

In the following exercises, you'll add the Maya Muscle system to the giraffe.

Using Capsules

Capsules are similar to Maya joints, except that their shape can be used to influence the deformation of the character's skin geometry. It's also necessary to replace existing joints with capsules or polygon bones to use the Maya Muscle deformer.

This scene picks up where the painting weights exercise left off. The geometry is smooth-bound to the rig, and the weights for the joints have been cleaned up.

The Maya Muscle plug-in may not be loaded. If you do not see the Muscle menu in the Animation menu set, you'll need to load the plug-in using the Plug-in Manager.

1. Open the `giraffe_v13.ma` scene from the `chapter5\scenes` directory at the book's web page.

2. Choose Window ➢ Settings/Preferences ➢ Plug-in Manager.

3. In the Plug-in Manager window, select the Loaded and Auto Load options next to `MayaMuscle.mll` (see Figure 5.52).

FIGURE 5.52
Load the Maya Muscle plug-in using the Plug-in Manager.

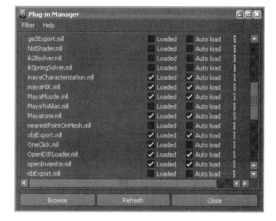

Once the plug-in is loaded, you should see the Muscle menu in the Animation menu set. (The Muscle menu actually appears in all the menu sets; for the moment, though, you should be using the Animation menu set.)

4. Choose Edit ➢ Select All By Type ➢ Joints.

5. Go through the selection, and deselect all the tip joints.

6. With only the joints selected, choose Muscle ➢ Muscle/Bones ➢ Convert Surface To Muscle/Bone. The joints automatically convert to capsules, and polygon geometry automatically converts to polygon bones. In this case, you should not have any polygon geometry selected.

   It is important to make sure that the joints are oriented properly. We discussed this earlier in the chapter in the "Orienting Joints" section. In the example scene, the joints have been oriented so that the x-axis points along the length of the bone toward the child joint.

7. When you execute the conversion command, you'll be asked to specify which axis points down the length of the joints. This is used to orient the capsules. Since the joint rig is set up to use the x-axis, choose X-Axis from the pop-up window.

8. The capsules on the right side of the skeleton are flipped. This is a result of mirroring the skeleton. The joints have the proper orientation, but the capsules do not. To change this, select each capsule of the right legs and the right ear, and go to the Channel Box for the capsule's shape node. Change the capsule axis to Neg X-Axis.

   You can edit the attributes of the capsule in the SHAPES section of the capsule's Channel Box. At the bottom of the shape node list, you can determine the display quality of the capsule. The nSegs and nSides settings change the number of divisions in the capsule, but these settings do not affect how the capsule deforms the skin. nSegs sets the number of segments along the length the capsule; nSides sets the number of divisions around the axis of the capsule.

9. Spend a few minutes editing the size of capsules. The volume of the capsules doesn't need to overlap the skin as the Interactive Skin Bind volumes did, so you can use a small radius size for the capsules.

10. Save the scene as `giraffeMuscles_v01.ma`.

To see a version of the scene up to this point, open `giraffeMuscles_v01.ma` from the `chapter5\scenes` directory at the book's web page.

Converting joints to capsules is the easiest way to prepare an existing rig for use with Maya Muscle. The Convert Surface To Muscle/Bone command works only on selected joints and surfaces. You can also create individual capsules using the Muscle ➢ Muscle/Bones ➢ Make Capsule and Muscle ➢ Muscle/Bones ➢ Make Capsule With End Locator commands. You can add a capsule to a rig by parenting the capsule or its end locators to parts of the rig.

Creating a Muscle Using the Muscle Builder

The Muscle Builder is designed to create muscle deformers easily and quickly. In this section, you'll create several generic muscles for the left hind leg using the Muscle Builder.

This window allows you to create and edit simple muscle shapes for the skeleton. To make the muscle, you'll first specify the Attach objects. These are the parts of the skeleton where each end of the muscle will be attached. Once you create the muscle, you can edit its shape using the controls in the Muscle Builder:

1. Continue with the scene from the previous section, or open the `giraffeMuscles_v01.ma` scene from the `chapter5\scenes` directory at the book's web page.

2. Choose Muscle ➢ Simple Muscles ➢ Muscle Builder to open the Muscle Builder window.

3. Select L_upperleg_jnt.

4. In the Muscle Builder window, click the <<< button to the right of the Attach Obj 1 field. This loads the L_upperleg_jnt capsule into this field.

5. Select the L_lowerleg_jnt capsule, and load it into the Attach Obj 2 field (see Figure 5.53).

6. Click the Build/Update button to create the muscle.

   The nSpans, nSegs, Width, and Falloff sliders determine the shape of the muscle's surface. nSpans and nSegs determine the number of spans and segments that the NURBS muscle surface will use. Falloff determines how the ends of the muscle taper at each end; a lower setting creates less of a taper. Width determines the overall width of the muscle shape. As long as the AttachObj fields are still filled out, you can interactively adjust the muscle.

7. Use the settings from Figure 5.53 to size the muscle to the leg.

If you can't achieve the position you are after with the sliders, you can click the AttachObj 1 or AttachObj 2 button. Doing so selects the appropriate node for manual positioning using the normal transform tools. The Muscle object appears in the perspective view attached to the skeleton, as shown in Figure 5.54. You'll see that a new NURBS surface named cMuscleBuilder_surf1 has been created along with two new cameras named MuscleBuilderCamera and MuscleBuilderCameraSide. The cameras are used in the Muscle Builder.

FIGURE 5.53
Specify the two Attach objects in the Muscle Builder window.

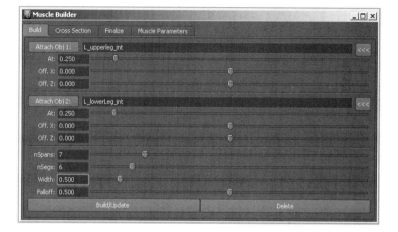

8. Save the scene as **giraffeMuscles_v02.ma**.

To see a version of the scene up to this point, open the giraffeMuscles_v02.ma scene from the chapter5\scenes directory at the book's web page.

CAPSULE VISIBILITY

To make things easier to see, the capsules have been hidden in the viewport. They are considered locators, and they can be deselected from the Show menu in the viewport.

MUSCLE-SURFACE NAME

Do not change the default name of the muscle surface (cMuscleBuilder_surf1) while working in the Muscle Builder. You'll have an opportunity to change the name when you convert the surface into a deformer. If you change the name of the surface before converting the surface to a muscle, the Muscle Builder will not be able to perform the conversion properly.

FIGURE 5.54
The muscle surface
appears attached
to the skeleton.

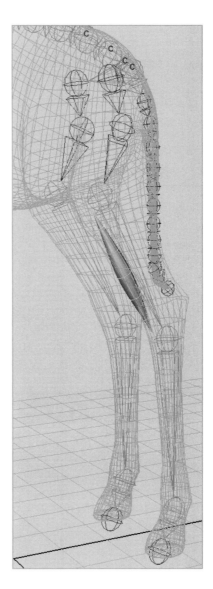

To place the muscle properly, you should check an anatomy reference. Some experimentation is required to place the muscle and achieve realistic motion and deformation. The settings applied to the muscle may look exaggerated in Maya, but this may be necessary to create a realistic deformation.

1. Switch to the Cross Section tab in the Muscle Builder. In this section of the window, the curves that control the shape of the muscle surface are listed on the left. (If you have loaded the saved scene or reloaded your own, it's necessary to choose Update from the Build section of the Muscle Builder. You must enter the same information from

Figure 5.53 to keep the muscle from changing.) Two camera views allow you to select the curves and move them to shape the overall muscle.

2. To edit the position of one of the circles, select one or more of the curves listed on the left and then use the Move tool to reposition the curve. Movements of each control circle are limited to the x- and y-axes.

You can move the circles in the perspective view as well as in the cross-section view of the Muscle Builder (see Figure 5.55).

FIGURE 5.55
You can use the cross-section views to edit the shape of the muscle.

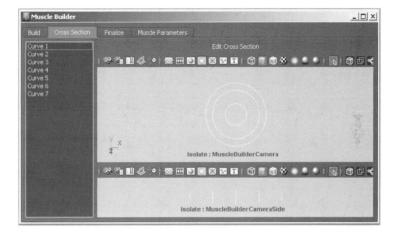

At this point, you may also find that the initial placement needs adjusting. You can go back and forth between the Cross Section tab and the Build tab to finalize the muscle's position.

MUSCLE SHAPE

Even though you have complete control over the shape of the muscle, it is best to keep it close to its original shape. Altering the muscle too much can result in awkward deformations. Muscles deform the skin to which they're attached based on the position of their control vertices, making muscle shape very important. However, you can paint influence on the skin to minimize the shape's impact.

When you have finished editing the basic shape of the muscle, you are ready to convert it to a muscle deformer. This action is performed on the Finalize tab of the Muscle Builder.

3. Leave Num Controls set to **3**, and set Type to Cube. (You can choose Curve or Null as well—whichever you prefer.)

If you need to mirror the muscle to the opposite side of the body, you can choose a mirror axis from the Create Mirror Muscle options. You can use the Search and Replace fields to replace prefixes such as L (for left) with R (for right) on the mirrored objects.

4. Click the Convert To Muscle button to create the deformer.

5. In the pop-up box, you will be warned that further changes cannot be made to the muscle using the interface controls. You'll also be prompted to name the muscle. Name it **L_legbicep** (see Figure 5.56).

FIGURE 5.56
You are prompted to name the muscle when you click the Convert To Muscle button.

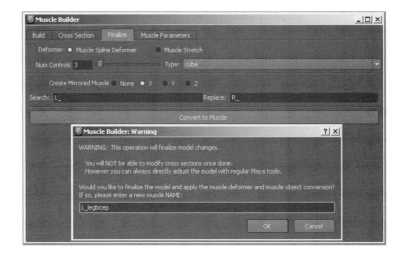

CHANGING MUSCLES

You can still change the shape of a muscle after you finalize it by altering the muscle surface's controls vertices. All the normal components used with NURBS, such as hulls and CVs, can be modified.

When you finalize the muscle, the original surface is grouped with its controls. Control cubes appear at either end of the muscle and in the center. These can be used to fix position and rotation problems.

6. Add several more generic muscle shapes to fill in the leg and gluteus maximus areas. Figure 5.57 shows the addition of five more muscles.

7. Save the scene as **giraffeMuscles_v03.ma**.

To see a version of the scene up to this point, open the giraffeMuscles_v03.ma scene from the chapter5\scenes directory at the book's web page.

Editing Muscle Parameters

Muscle parameters determine how the muscle behaves as the joints are animated. If you select L_HindLeg_CTRL and move it around, you'll see that the muscles stretch and squash.

FIGURE 5.57
Add five more muscles to the hind end of the giraffe.

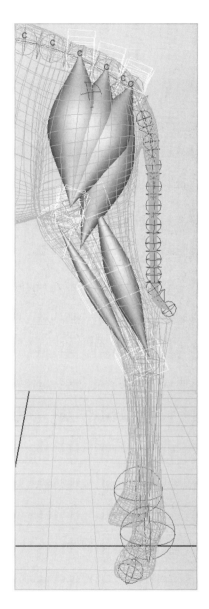

Many of the settings in the Muscle Parameters section can be changed in the Channel Box or Attribute Editor. To refine how the muscle reacts to motion, you need to have the Muscle Builder open.

1. Continue with the scene from the previous section, or open the giraffeMuscles_v03.ma scene from the chapter5\scenes folder at the book's web page. If it is not open already, choose Muscle ➤ Simple Muscles ➤ Muscle Builder to open the Muscle Builder interface.

2. In the Muscle Parameters Settings tab, go to the Muscle Object Settings section and set Draw to Muscle. If this is set to Off, you'll see the deformer, but changes made to the Squash and Stretch settings will not be displayed.

   The first step to editing the muscle's behavior is to establish its default stretch and squash shapes based on the movement of the leg.

   The giraffe's leg is positioned in the animal's default stance and default pose in Maya. You can use this pose to establish the default shape of the bicep muscle. Since the giraffe is standing, you would assume that the muscle is engaged and slightly flexed.

3. Select the shape node of the muscle or muscles you want to affect. In this case, you will be working with just the left leg bicep. In `giraffeMuscles_v03.ma`, the node is named cMuscleSplineL_legbicep.

4. In the Muscle Builder interface under the Spline Length Settings section, click the Set Current As Default button.

5. In the perspective view, select L_HindLeg_CTRL, and translate it to **2.0** in the Y and **−3.2** in the Z. This stretches the L_bicep muscle to its extreme pose.

6. Select the muscle shape node and, in the Muscle Builder, click the Set Current As Stretch button.

7. Set the L_HindLeg_CTRL to **2.0** in the Translate Y and **4.0** in the Translate Z to push the leg toward the chest.

8. Select the muscle shape node and, in the Muscle Builder, click the Set Current As Squash button.

9. Proceed with the rest of the leg muscles. You can move the leg forward and set all the squash positions for those muscles that would be flexed. You do not have to do one muscle at a time. The Muscle Builder affects whichever muscle is selected. Figure 5.58 shows the combination of squashed and stretched muscles.

   The settings in the Stretch Volume Presets section determine how the shape muscle deformer transitions between extreme poses. To set this properly, animate the leg so that you can adjust the settings and see the results as the leg moves.

10. Set the Time Slider to 100 frames.

11. Select L_HindLeg_CTRL, and create a short animation where the locator moves back and forth, causing the leg to bend and straighten. Use the same values from steps 5 and 7 as your in-between frames.

12. Select the bicep muscle in the viewport.

13. Play the animation, and make sure the Muscle Builder is still open. As the leg moves, you may see some jiggling in the muscle; that's part of the Jiggle settings, which you'll edit in the next few steps.

14. As the leg moves back and forth, click the Small, Medium, and Large buttons. Notice the change in the muscle's size and behavior as you switch between presets.

FIGURE 5.58
Set the squash and
stretch of each
muscle.

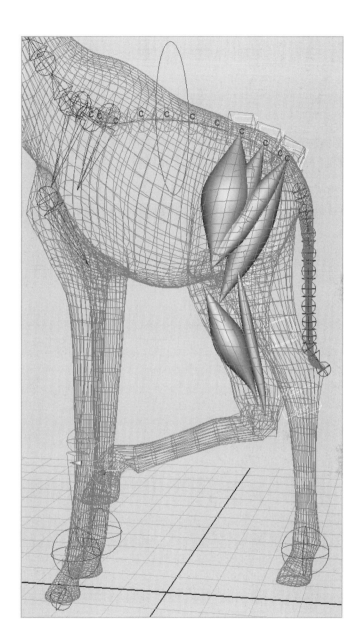

FIGURE 5.58
Set the squash and
stretch of each
muscle.

15. You can edit the numeric values in the START, MID, and END fields to fine-tune the behavior. It's usually easiest to start by loading one of the presets and then make small changes to the values.

When you're happy with how the muscle is shaped as it moves, you can move on to editing the Jiggle motion.

16. While the animation plays, click the Default, Light, Medium, Heavy, and OFF buttons in the Jiggle Presets section. Observe the difference in behavior as each preset is applied.

17. You can fine-tune the behavior of the jiggling by editing the numeric values in the START, MID, and END fields for Jiggle, Cycle, and Rest:

    ♦ Jiggle is the intensity of jiggle.

    ♦ Cycle is the frequency of jiggle oscillation.

    ♦ Rest is the time it takes for the muscle to come to a stop.

    The Dampen settings add a damping effect as the muscle reaches extreme poses.

18. Be sure to remove any animation applied to the controls.

19. Save the scene as **giraffeMuscles_v04.ma**.

To see a version of the up scene to this point, open the giraffeMuscles_v04.ma scene from the chapter5\scenes directory at the book's web page.

Converting the Smooth Skin to a Muscle System

Now that the muscles have been set up and are working properly, you can apply them to the giraffe geometry so that it deforms the character's skin. Applying the deformer to the geometry involves weighting the skin to the muscles. This is similar in concept to smooth-binding geometry to joints. In fact, you can convert the skin weights painted earlier in the chapter to the muscle system.

1. Continue with the scene from the previous section, or open the giraffeMuscles_v04.ma scene from the chapter5\scenes directory at the book's web page.

2. Select the giraffe geometry.

3. Choose Muscle ➢ Skin Setup ➢ Convert Smooth Skin To Muscle System.

4. Maya asks whether you want to delete or disable the skin weights applied to the arm. Choose Disable. (You can delete the weights if you want to, but it may be a good idea to keep the weights in the scene in case they are needed later.)

5. Maya asks you to choose the axis for the capsules. Choose the x-axis to match the orientation of the capsules. Converting the skin takes a few moments (denser geometry takes longer to process); you'll see a dialog box that displays the progress of the calculation.

    This takes the smooth skin joint weights that were painted on the geometry and converts them to muscle weights. However, only the capsules are included. If you move L_HindLeg_CTRL, you'll notice that the muscles do not yet deform the skin. They need to be attached to the skin and weighted before they will work.

6. Select all the muscle objects and the giraffe skin. (The muscle objects are the NURBS muscle surfaces.)

7. Choose Muscle ➢ Muscle Objects ➢ Connect Selected Muscle Objects.

8. A dialog box asks you to set the Sticky Bind Maximum Distance value. Choose Auto-Calculate. Each muscle is calculated.

 The muscles are now connected to the skin geometry. However, the muscles still will not affect the geometry until the weights are painted for each muscle.

9. Switch to shaded view.

10. Select the giraffe mesh, and choose Muscle ➤ Paint Muscle Weights.

11. The geometry becomes color-coded to indicate the weight strength of each muscle listed in the Muscle Paint window. Make sure the weight type is set to Sticky.

12. Scroll to the bottom of the list in the Muscle Paint window, and select L_glute1. The geometry turns black, indicating there is no weight for this muscle.

13. Use L_HindLeg_CTRL to pose the arm as you paint weight values for the glutes.

14. Set Weight to **0.1** and Operation to Add.

15. Paint over the area of the glute to start adding weights.

 ◆   Low-weight values are blue.

 ◆   Higher-weight values are green, orange, and red.

 You can also set the Paint Skin Weights tool to paint in Gray.

16. Paint L_glute2 as well. Figure 5.59 shows the results of painting the weights.

 Keep in mind that the muscles do not have to fit perfectly under the skin. They are not rendered with the character, so penetration is okay. The important part is how the skin looks and reacts.

17. When you have finished painting the weights, close the window.

18. Create another animation for L_HindLeg_CTRL so that you can see the muscle in action as it deforms the skin.

19. If you need to change muscle parameters, such as the Jiggle attributes, select the muscle and choose Muscle ➤ Simple Muscle ➤ Set Muscle Parameters. Use the settings in the Muscle Parameters tab to adjust the muscle quality.

20. Save the scene as `giraffeMuscles_v05.ma`.

To see a version of the scene up to this point, open the `giraffeMuscles_v05.ma` scene from the `chapter5\scenes` directory at the book's web page.

Sliding Weights

Sliding weights are used to create the effect of skin sliding over bones and muscle. In this example, you'll make the skin at the top of the hind leg a little loose by painting sliding weights.

1. Continue with the scene from the previous section, or open the `giraffeMuscles_v05.ma` scene from the `chapter5\scenes` directory at the book's web page.

2. Select the giraffe mesh.

3. In the Channel Box, select the cMuscleSystem1 node under INPUTS.

4. Set Enable Sliding to On. This is an easy step to forget, but if you don't enable sliding weights on the character's skin, you won't see the sliding effects.

5. With the giraffe mesh selected, choose Muscle ➤ Paint Muscle Weights.

6. Choose the L_glute1 from the list of muscle objects.

7. Set Weights to Sliding and the operation to Add. Set Weight to **0.5**.

8. Paint the muscle area.

9. Switch to L_glute2, and paint its sliding weight also.

10. Select L_HindLeg_CTRL, and move the control handle back and forth to see the effects of the sliding weights.

11. Save the scene as **giraffeMuscles_v06.ma**.

To see a version of the scene up to this point, open the giraffeMuscles_v06.ma scene from the chapter5\scenes directory at the book's web page.

Creating the anatomy for an entire character takes good research and a lot of time. The muscle system is versatile enough to let you add muscles only where they are needed. You can add them gradually to the skin and test them as you go. It is not necessary to fill the skin with muscles. To learn more, check out the book *Maya Studio Projects: Photorealistic Characters* (Sybex, 2011).

The Bottom Line

Create and organize joint hierarchies.   A joint hierarchy is a series of joint chains. Each joint in a chain is parented to another joint, back to the root of the chain. Each joint inherits the motion of its parent joint. Organizing the joint chains is accomplished by naming and labeling the joints. Proper orientation of the joints is essential for the joints to work properly.

Master It   Create a joint hierarchy for a giraffe character. Orient the joints so that the x-axis points down the length of the joints.

Use Human Inverse Kinematics rigs.   Human Inverse Kinematics (HIK) creates IK Handles that control an entire bipedal or quadrupedal skeleton rather than using multiple IK chains on individual limbs.

Master It   Define the giraffe skeleton, and apply the HIK system to it.

Apply skin geometry.   Skinning geometry refers to the process in which geometry is bound to joints so that it deforms as the joints are moved and rotated. Each vertex of the geometry receives a certain amount of influence from the joints in the hierarchy. This can be controlled by painting the weights of the geometry on the skin.

Master It   Paint weights on the giraffe model to get smooth-looking deformations on one side of the model. Mirror the weights to the other side.

Use Maya Muscle.   Maya Muscle is a series of tools designed to create more believable deformations and movement for objects skinned to joints. Capsules are used to replace Maya joints. Muscles are NURBS surfaces that squash, stretch, and jiggle as they deform geometry.

Master It   Use Maya Muscle to create muscles for the hind leg of the giraffe. Use the muscle system to cause skin bulging and sliding.

Chapter 6

Animation Techniques

As you learned in Chapter 1, "Working in Autodesk Maya," objects in an Autodesk® Maya® scene have both a transform node and a shape node. The transform node contains data related to where the object is in a scene, its orientation, and its scale. The shape node contains data about the form of the object. If you want to animate an object moving around in a scene, usually you'll keyframe the translation, rotation, and scale of the transform node. If you want to animate the shape of an object, such as the facial expressions of a character, you can use a *deformer*, which is a type of animation control applied to the shape node of an object. Deformers are extremely versatile, and they can be used for both modeling and animation and as part of an animation rig.

This chapter explores different ways to animate geometry. From creating facial expressions to applying motion capture, Maya offers thousands of ways to bring your creations to life.

In this chapter, you will learn to:

- ◆ Work with deformers

- ◆ Add jiggle movement to an animation

- ◆ Animate facial expressions

- ◆ Animate nonlinear deformers

- ◆ Apply motion capture

Working with Deformers

New! Deformers can be applied to any object in Maya that has control vertices or control points. There is no limit to how many deformers you can have on a single object. Deformers can be layered on top of one another and applied to individual faces, edges, or vertices.

ShrinkWrapping Geometry

New! The ShrinkWrap deformer allows one piece of geometry to influence another. The target object or deforming object will take on the shape of a source object. Essentially, the components of the deforming object wrap around the shape of the source object. Many different effects can be achieved with this deformer since the position of both objects play a part and can be animated.

In this section, you'll use the ShrinkWrap deformer to form the features of a character's face on a glass mirror:

1. Open the shrinkWrap_v01.ma scene from the chapter6\scenes directory at this book's web page (www.sybex.com/go/masteringmaya2015). The scene contains a model of a floor mirror and a simplistically rigged head.

2. In the persp view, select the glass model, and Shift+click the head geometry.

3. Choose Create Deformers ➢ Shrinkwrap.

4. Select the group1 node and translate the node 2.0 units in the z-axis. The mirror reacts to the head's proximity (see Figure 6.1).

FIGURE 6.1
As the head gets close to the mirror, the mirror's geometry snaps to the head's contours.

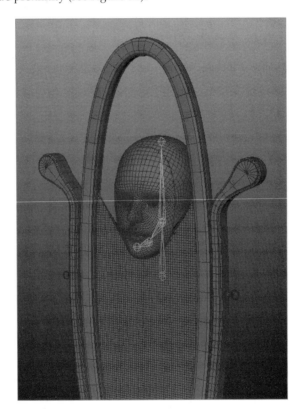

5. Select the glass and open its Attribute Editor.

6. Choose the shrinkwrap1 node.

7. Change the Projection setting to Vertex Normals. The geometry of the glass is now projected along the head's vertex normals. Figure 6.2 shows the results.

FIGURE 6.2
Use vertex normals for the projection method.

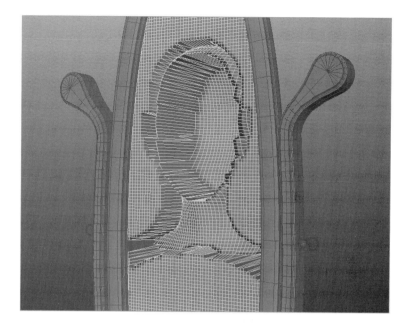

8. Check Reverse under the shrink attributes. Reverse forces the wrapping object to use the opposite side of the surface to perform the projection (bidirectional uses both sides of the surface). Figure 6.3 shows the ShrinkWrap settings.

FIGURE 6.3
The ShrinkWrap settings in the Attribute Editor.

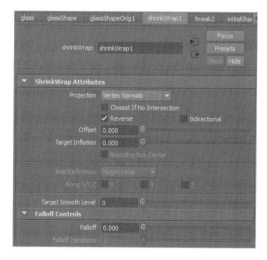

9. To help see the ShrinkWrap effects, turn off the visibility of the HEAD layer.

10. Click Play on the Time Slider to make the animation on the head appear on the glass geometry. Figure 6.4 shows the last frame.

FIGURE 6.4
Changes to the shape of the character's head cause the glass geometry to deform

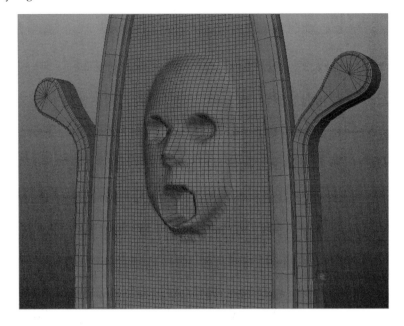

11. Save the scene as **shrinkWrap_v02.ma**.

To see a version of the scene to this point, open the shrinkWrap_v02.ma scene from the chapter6\scenes directory at the book's web page.

Using Textures to Deform Objects

New!   The texture deformer allows you to deform geometry based on an applied texture. This is similar to the effects of rendering a displacement map, discussed in Chapter 9, "Texture Mapping." The difference, however, is the results can be seen instantly. Furthermore, you can adjust or animate the texture deformer in real time.

The texture deformer works only with existing geometry. You must have enough faces/vertices to support the amount of detail in your texture in order for the effect to look correct. The geometry is deformed regardless of its density, but it may lack the details contained in the texture. In this exercise, you'll use the texture deformer to add multiple deformations to the glass of a floor mirror:

1. Open the textureDeformer_v01.ma scene from the chapter6\scenes folder at the book's web page. The scene contains a polygon model of a floor mirror.

2. Select the glass object.

3. Switch to the Polygons menu set. Choose Select ➤ Select Border Edge Tool. The glass geometry is switched to component mode automatically.

4. Double-click on the border edge of the glass geometry. Change your viewport to display the wireframe to make selecting the border edge easier.

5. Choose the select tool from the Toolbox to deactivate the Select Border Edge Tool. Ctrl/Cmd+RMB-click on the border edge of the glass geometry and convert the selection to vertices through the marking menu.

6. Hold Shift and draw a marquee around the entire mirror to invert your selection. All of the interior vertices of the glass geometry are now selected.

7. Switch to the Animation menu set. With the interior vertices selected, choose Create Deformers ➤ Texture Deformer. The texture deformer is applied to the highlighted vertices and the texture deformer manipulator is created (see Figure 6.5).

FIGURE 6.5
The texture deformer is applied to the current selection.

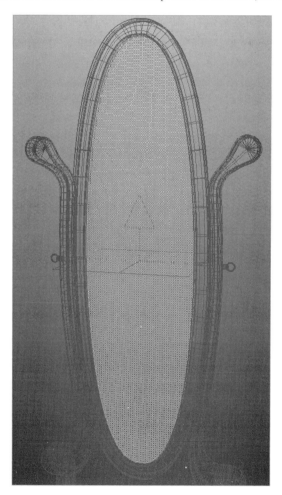

8. Select the texture deformer manipulator and open its Attribute Editor. Choose the texture Deformer1 tab.

9. Click the Create Render Node icon for the Texture attribute (see Figure 6.6).

10. In the Create Render Node window, choose File from the right-side node list. Choose the sourceimages folder of the current project, and open the vector displacement map

vortex_vdm.exr. Vector displacement maps contain depth and directional information that can shape geometry. The creation of vector displacement maps and the EXR file format are discussed in Chapter 9.

11. The texture deformer is rotated so that its effects are pushing the geometry in the y-axis. Select textureDeformerHandle1. Rotate the handle to 90.0 in the x-axis (see Figure 6.7).

FIGURE 6.6
Click the Create Render Node icon in the texture deformer's Attribute Editor.

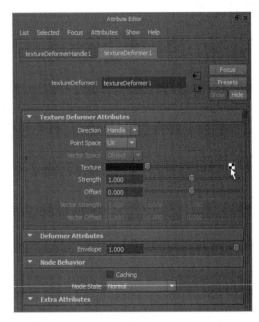

FIGURE 6.7
Once oriented properly, the texture shapes the geometry.

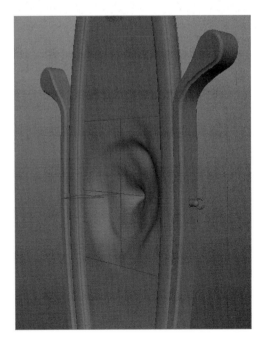

12. The texture map is deforming the glass surface but not to its fullest potential. Open textureDeformerHandle1's Attribute Editor. Choose the textureDeformer1 tab. Change the Direction attribute to Vector and Vector Space to Tangent (see Figure 6.8).

FIGURE 6.8
Change the texture space to use the depth and directional data of the vector displacement.

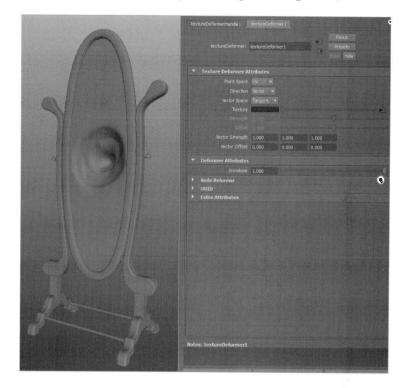

13. You can animate the channels of any texture map applied to your texture deformer as well as the channels of the texture deformer itself. Under the Texture Deformer Attributes rollout, set Vector Strength to **0.0** in the y-axis. RMB-click in the field and choose Set Key from the context menu.

14. Go to frame 24.

15. Set Vector Strength to **2.0** in the y-axis and set another key.

16. Play the animation to see a hole open up in the middle of the glass.

To see a version of the scene to this point, open the textureDeformer_v02.ma scene from the chapter6\scenes directory at the book's web page.

The texture deformer is extremely powerful since you are limited only by the texture you connect to it. You can use logos for raised print or patterns to create realistic surface features. It is important to note that the texture deformer works only with existing geometry. It does not add anything to the object it is applied to. Therefore, intricate textures will require a greater amount of geometry in order for them to deform a surface properly (see Figure 6.9).

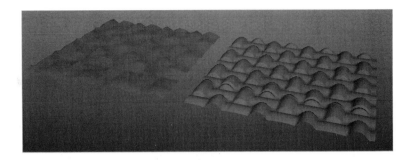

Animating Facial Expressions Using Blend Shapes

As the name suggests, a blend shape deformer blends, or *interpolates*, between variations of a
geometric form. A blend shape deformer uses one or more blend shape targets. These *targets* are
duplicates of the original model that have been modified using a variety of modeling techniques.

Animating facial expressions for characters is usually accomplished through the use of blend
shapes. Although this is not the only way to animate expressions and speech, it is the most common because it is relatively straightforward to set up and animate. In this section, you'll learn
how to create blend shape targets, paint blend shape weights, create a blend shape deformer, and
build a simple facial-animation rig.

You create the blend shape deformer by selecting the targets and the original model and
choosing Create Deformers ➤ Blend Shape. The deformer controls consist of sliders—one for
each blend shape target. The original model is animated by moving and keyframing the sliders.
As the value of a slider moves between 0 and 1, Maya interpolates the change, blending between
the original shape and the target shape. The duplicate model is known as the *blend shape target*,
and the original model is known as the *base mesh*.

You should understand a few things about how blend shapes work before you set up a facial-
animation rig. First, blend shapes always move in a straight line when interpolating the change
between the original model and the blend shape target. Think of how your eyelids move when
you blink. Your eyelid is a flap of skin that moves over the spherical shape of your eyeball. If you
make a dot on the edge of your eyelid with a marker (don't do this—just imagine it) and then
follow the path of that dot from a side view, the dot moves in an arc as your eyelid closes.

If you have a model of a face with the eyes open and a blend shape target with the eyes
closed, when you create the blend shape deformer and then animate the eyes closing, instead
of moving in an arc the eyelids will move in a straight line from the open position to the closed
position. Most likely the eyelid geometry will pass through the eyeball geometry, creating a
less-than-convincing blinking behavior. The middle eye in Figure 6.10 shows the results of
blending the first and last eyelid shape together. Understanding that the blend shape deformer

moves in a linear direction from one state to the next is important if you are to develop a solution for this problem.

FIGURE 6.10
Blend shape deformations move in a straight line, which can cause problems for certain types of facial movements, such as blinking eyelids.

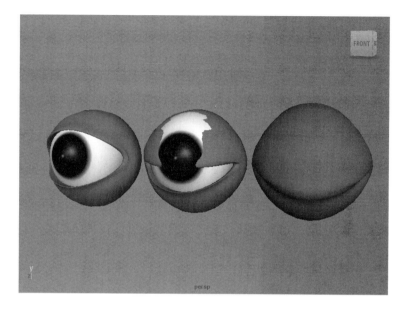

Real World Scenario

POINT ORDER CHANGES ON IMPORT

It is a fairly common practice to export a polygon model from Maya as an OBJ-format file for editing in another 3D program, such as ZBrush or the Autodesk® Mudbox® software. When the edited object is imported back into Maya, the vertex order can change if the options are not set correctly in the Import Options box. The model may have exactly the same number of points as the original, but when you use the imported model as a blend shape target and animate the deformer, the model suddenly becomes mangled.

When you import an OBJ-format model into Maya, always remember to select the Single Object option or make sure Use Legacy Vertex Ordering is *off* when importing an OBJ file made up of multiple objects. (These options are available when File Type is set to OBJ.) If the option is set to Multiple Objects and Use Legacy Vertex Ordering is selected, the point order of the model can change, which would cause major problems when using the imported model as a blend shape target.

continues

(continued)

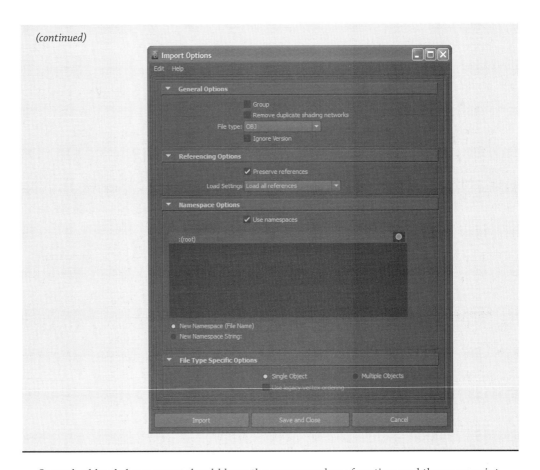

Second, a blend shape target should have the same number of vertices and the same point order as the original geometry. Vertices on polygons and control vertices (CVs) on NURBS geometry are numbered in a specific order. You can see the numbers listed in the Script Editor when the vertices are selected. If the number of points and the order of the points on a blend shape target do not match the original, the deformer will not be created, or it will behave strangely (see Figure 6.11). It is possible to use a blend shape target that has a different number of vertices than the base mesh; however, this can lead to unpredictable results.

FIGURE 6.11
When the point order of the base mesh and the blend shape target do not match, strange results can occur when the deformer is applied.

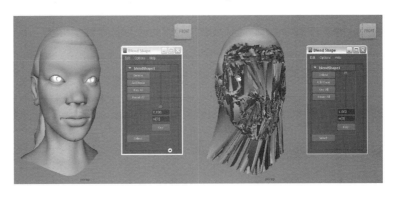

Third, when deforming a model with more than one blend shape target, the changes created by the targets are added together. So if you have one blend shape target in which a face is smiling and a second target in which the face is frowning, you may think that one target cancels the other. In fact, setting both blend shape targets to full strength creates a strange result on the base mesh because the smile and the frown will be added together (see Figure 6.12).

FIGURE 6.12
A smile shape and a frown shape are added together to create a very strange expression.

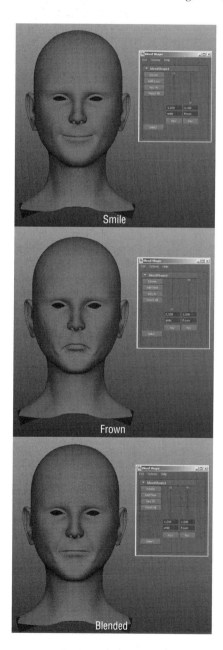

Creating Blend Shape Targets

The first step in setting up a blend shape facial animation rig is to model the actual blend shapes based on the base mesh. The final rig works something like the controls for a puppet. Rather than animate blend shape targets using a happy face model and a sad face model, you want the blend shape target models built so that they allow you to isolate individual muscle movements. This will give you the most control when animating. When animating a smile, you'll have controls for the mouth, eyelids, eyebrows, cheeks, and more, so you have the option of animating a smile with brows up for a happy character and a smile with brows down for a menacing character. In addition, you want to isolate the sides of the face so that the corner of one side of the mouth can be animated separately from the corner of the other side of the mouth.

When creating blend shape targets, it's best to think in terms of what the muscle is doing rather than a particular expression. The same targets are used to animate speech and emotion. So, rather than creating a blend shape target for a smile and a blend shape target for the "eeeee" sound, you want to make a single blend shape target that pulls back a corner of the mouth. Then this blend shape target combined with muscle movements created for other targets can be used for smiling, saying "cheeeese," or doing both at the same time.

In this exercise, you'll create blend shape targets for a character's mouth that can be used for widening the lips as in a smile as well as narrowing the lips as in a kiss. These two shapes (mouthWide and mouthNarrow) will then be separated into four shapes (leftMouthWide, leftMouthNarrow, rightMouthWide, and rightMouthNarrow).

1. Open the amanda_v01.ma scene from the chapter6\scenes directory at the book's web page. This scene shows a basic polygon head.

USING STANDARD FACIAL FEATURES

It's a good idea to have models of the teeth and hair included in the scene when creating blend shape targets, even if they are just temporary versions. It makes modeling the shape changes easier. Teeth play a big role in the way the mouth is shaped when moving, so it's good to have some kind of guide available while making blend shape targets. A simple hair shape is useful as a visual indicator for where the hairline starts when you are working on shapes for the brow.

---

2. Select the amanda model, and duplicate it (Ctrl/Cmd+d). Move the duplicate to the side, as shown in Figure 6.13. Name the duplicate **mouthWide**.

   By default, blend shape deformers calculate only shape node–level changes. In other words, only changes made on the vertex level are considered. You can move, rotate, and scale the targets without affecting the base mesh—unless you specify otherwise in the deformer options. This will be discussed further later in the chapter.

3. Select the Move tool, and open the Tool Settings dialog box for the tool. Under the Symmetry Settings, activate Symmetry and set Symmetry Axis to X.

4. Turn on Soft Select, and set Falloff Mode to Surface. Set Falloff Radius to **0.10**, and add a point to the Falloff Curve value. Set Interpolation to Spline, and adjust the curve to look like Figure 6.14.

FIGURE 6.13
A duplicate of the
original head model
is created.

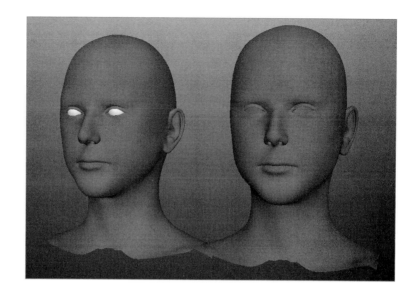

FIGURE 6.14
The settings for the
Move tool

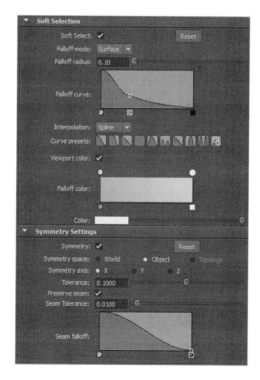

  5. Select and then RMB-click the mouthWide geometry, and choose Vertex to switch to vertex selection mode.

6. Select a vertex at the corner of the mouth, as shown in Figure 6.15. You'll see the vertices colored, indicating the Soft Selection radius and falloff. Carefully start moving the corner to the side and back toward the ear.

FIGURE 6.15
The vertices are color-coded to indicate the falloff strength and radius of the Move tool when Soft Select is enabled.

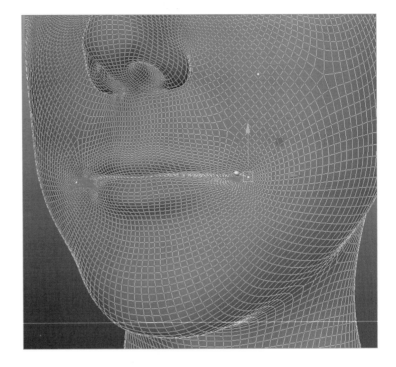

7. Open the Modeling Toolkit. Select and then right-click the mouthWide geometry, and choose Edge to switch to edge selection mode.

8. Choose a single edge from the center line of the model. Select Symmetry from the Modeling Toolkit.

9. RMB-click on the mouthWide geometry and choose Vertex to switch to vertex selection mode.

10. Choose the Move tool from the Modeling Toolkit.

11. Under Transform Constraints, select Surface. By enabling Surface, you allow the transformed vertices to follow the contours of the surface. This helps maintain the shape and volume of your geometry. In terms of blend shape targets, it essentially gives the geometry a solid core to move points along.

12. Check Soft Selection in the Soft Selection rollout. Choose Surface with a value of **0.08**, as shown in Figure 6.16.

FIGURE 6.16
The settings from
the Modeling
Toolkit.

The muscles in the face work in concert to create facial expressions. Most of the face muscles are designed to convey emotion, aid with speech, and keep food in your mouth while you eat. Muscles work in groups to pull parts of the face in various directions like a system of pulleys. When you smile or grimace, the corners of your mouth are pulled back toward the ears by several muscles working together.

Cartoons often simplify the smile by drawing the corners of the mouth upward into a U shape. However, in reality the corners of the mouth move upward only a small degree. The illusion of perspective makes it look as though the mouth is forming a U. The smile shape is not a U shape, but rather the lips are stretched in a nearly straight line across the teeth. To refine the smile, follow these steps:

A. It will take a little work to form the smile shape on the face. Use a mirror for reference. Keep in mind that as the lips are pulled across the teeth, they are stretched and lose volume, giving them a thinner appearance.

As you work, make adjustments to the settings on the Move tool, and change the Falloff Radius and Falloff Curve values as needed.

B. When the corners of the mouth are pulled back, adjust other parts of the face near the corners and on the lips, but don't go too far beyond the area of the mouth. Remember, you are making an isolated change in the shape of the mouth, not a complete facial expression.

C. In addition to the Move tool, the Artisan brush is useful for sculpting changes in the model. To activate this tool, select the mouthWide model, and choose (from the Polygons menu set) Mesh ➤ Sculpt Geometry Tool. To ensure that the changes you make affect both sides of the model, make sure the Reflection option is activated in the Stroke section. To make the changes a mirror reflection, check Invert Reference Vector.

You can also restrict the effects of your brush by changing the Reference Vector setting under Sculpt Parameters. Setting it to the x-axis allows you to stretch the lips lengthwise without pushing them in any other axis.

Use a combination of the preceding tools to create the mouth shape. The final wide mouth shape should look like a fake smile because there are no changes in the other parts of the face. It's a good idea to build a little overshoot into your blend shape targets so that you have a wider range with which to work when animating (see Figure 6.17).

FIGURE 6.17
The base model (left) and the completed smile blend shape target (right)

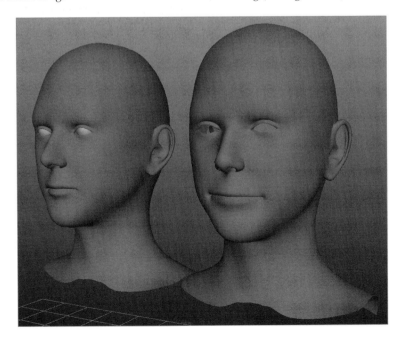

13. Save the scene as **amanda_v02.ma**.

    To see a version of the scene to this point, open the amanda_v02.ma scene from the chapter6\scenes directory at the book's web page.

    The next blend shape is the opposite of the smile. For this shape, the mouth needs to be pulled in from the corners.

14. Create another duplicate of the amanda model. Name the duplicate **mouthNarrow**. Move it to the model's right side.

15. Use the Move tool and the Artisan brush to push the sides of the mouth toward the center of the face. The lips should bulge up in the center.

    As the lips push together and bulge at the center, there is a slight curling outward. Those parts of the upper and lower lips that touch in the neutral pose become exposed, and the flesh of the lips rolls outward (but just slightly).

16. Use the Rotate tool with Soft Select to help create this rolling outward effect. Figure 6.18 shows the finished narrow mouth blend shape target, the base mesh, and the smile blend shape target, respectively.

FIGURE 6.18
The completed narrow mouth blend shape target, the base mesh, and the smile blend shape target

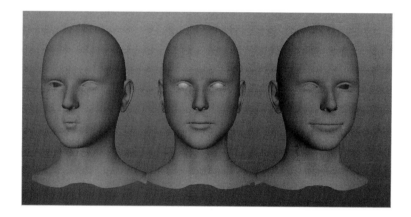

17. Once you are satisfied with the two mouth shapes, save the scene as **amanda_v03.ma**.

    To see a version of the scene up to this point, open the amanda_v03.ma scene from the chapter6\scenes folder at the book's web page.

SURFACE VS. VOLUME SOFT SELECT

To move the vertices of the lips separately, use Soft Selection in Surface mode. To move parts of the lips together, use Soft Selection in Volume mode.

Creating Blend Shapes

To create the blend shape deformer, select all the targets first and then choose the base mesh. Next select the Blend Shape deformer from the Deformers menu in the Animation menu set. In this section, you'll create the deformer using the mouthWide and mouthNarrow shapes.

1. Continue with the scene from the previous section, or open the amanda_v03.ma scene from the chapter6\scenes folder at the book's web page.

2. Shift+click the mouthWide model and the mouthNarrow model; then Shift+click the amanda model.

3. Switch to the Animation menu set, and choose Create Deformers ➢ Blend Shape Options. In the Create Blend Shape Options dialog box, choose Reset Settings from the Edit menu to set the options to the default settings. You want Origin set to Local; this means that only shape node–level changes will be used on the deformer. If the target can be moved, scaled, or rotated, it will not affect how the deformer is applied.

4. Name the blend shape deformer **amandaFace** (see Figure 6.19). Click Create to make the deformer.

FIGURE 6.19
The options for the blend shape deformer

5. To test the deformer, choose Window ➢ Animation Editors ➢ Blend Shape. A small pop-up window appears with two sliders. These are the controls for the blend shape deformers.

6. Move the sliders up and down, and see how they affect the model (see Figure 6.20). Try putting both sliders at **1** to see the shapes added together. Also try setting the values to negative values or values beyond 1.

7. Save the scene as **amanda_v04.ma**.

To see a version of the scene to this point, open the amanda_v04.ma scene from the chapter6\scenes directory at the book's web page.

Painting Blend Shape Weights

At this point, you have two blend shapes available for animating, mouthWide and mouthNarrow. You may decide that you want additional blend shape targets for the same mouth shape but restricted to just one side of the mouth. This gives you more options for animating a wider variety of facial movements. One easy way to create these additional targets is to use blend shape weighting as a shortcut for making additional blend shape target models from the symmetrical facial poses that you've already created.

1. Continue with the scene from the previous section, or open the amanda_v04.ma scene from the chapter6\scenes directory at the book's web page.

2. Select the amanda model, and choose Edit Deformers ➢ Paint Blend Shape Weights Tool ➢ Options.

3. The model turns completely white, and the options open in the Tool Settings box.

   In the Target box is the list of all the current blend shapes applied to the model. The white color on the model indicates that the blend shape weight is at full strength.

4. Open the blend shape control window by choosing Window ➢ Animation Editors ➢ Blend Shapes. Set the mouthWide slider to **1** so that you can see the deformer applied to the model (see Figure 6.21).

FIGURE 6.20
The blend shapes are controlled using the blend shape sliders.

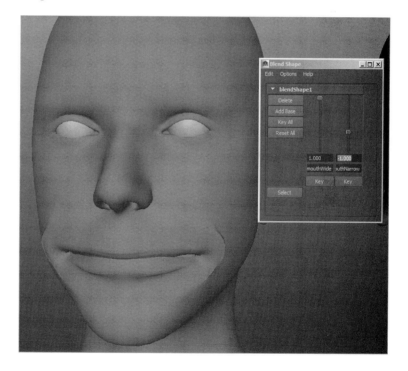

5. In the Paint Blend Shape Weights Tool dialog box, set Paint Operation to Replace and Value to **0**. Click the Flood button. This floods the model with a zero-weight value. The model turns black, and the effect of the mouthWide deformation disappears.

6. Set Value to **1**, and paint the area around the mouth on the model's left side. As you paint, you'll see the left side move into the mouthWide shape within the area painted white (see Figure 6.22).

FIGURE 6.21
Activating the
Paint Blend Shape
Weights tool turns
the model white,
indicating that
the selected tar-
get in the options
is applied at full
strength to all the
model's vertices.

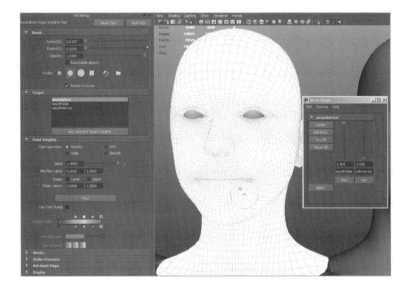

FIGURE 6.22
As the weights are
painted, the side of
the mouth moves
into the mouthWide
shape.

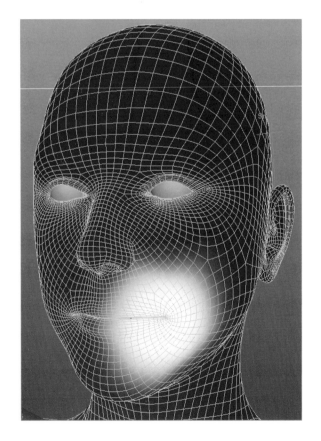

EMPLOYING THE USE COLOR RAMP OPTION

You can receive even more detailed visual feedback by activating the Use Color Ramp option. This assigns a gradient of colors to the values painted on the vertices. You can customize these colors by changing the colors in the Weight Color option, or you can use one of the preset gradients.

7. When you think you have painted enough of one side of the mouth, select the amanda model and duplicate it (Ctrl/Cmd+d). Move the duplicate up and off to the side, and name it **mouthLeftWide**. (Remember to name the deformers based on the character's left or right side, not your left or right.)

8. Select the amanda model again, and choose Edit Deformers ➤ Paint Blend Shape Weights Tool.

9. Flood the model with a zero value again, set Value to **1**, and this time paint the mouth area on the model's right side.

10. Duplicate the model again, and move the duplicate model up and away from the amanda model. Name this duplicate **mouthRightWide**.

11. Select the amanda model again, and choose Edit Deformers ➤ Paint Blend Shape Weights Tool. Set Value to **1**, and flood the model to return the weight for the mouth-Wide shape to 1.

    The two duplicate models will look somewhat strange; this is a very unusual expression (see Figure 6.23). You can use the Artisan brush and the Move tool to make the mouth look more natural, but try to restrict your edits to one side of the mouth or the other. Remember that this particular mouth movement will probably be accompanied by other shape changes during animation, which will make it look more natural. Most likely these shapes will not be used at their full strength, but it's good to model a little overshoot into the shape to expand the range of possible movements.

12. Save the scene as `amanda_v05.ma`.

To see a version of the scene to this point, open the `amanda_v05.ma` scene from the `chapter6\` `scenes` directory at the book's web page.

ADDING JOINTS

Some facial movements, such as opening and closing the jaw, blinking the eyes, and moving the tongue, are better suited to joint rigs than to blend shape targets. In the end, the final rig will use a combination of deformers to create the full range of facial movements.

FIGURE 6.23
Two new blend
shape targets have
been created using
the Paint Blend
Shape Weights tool.

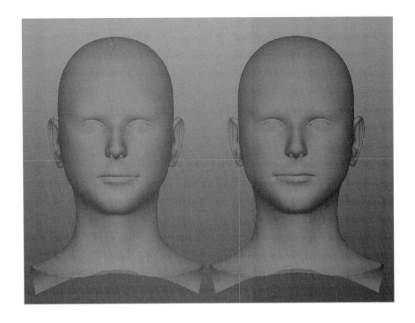

Adding Targets

You can add the new targets to the existing blend shape deformer as follows:

1. Continue with the scene from the previous section, or open the amanda_v05.ma scene from the chapter6\scenes directory at the book's web page.

2. Select the amanda model, and choose Window ➤ Animation Editors ➤ Blend Shape to open the blend shape controls.

3. Choose the mouthRightWide target, and Shift+click the amanda model. Choose Edit Deformers ➤ Blend Shape ➤ Add. You'll see a new slider appear in the blend shape controls.

4. Repeat step 3 for the mouthLeftWide target (see Figure 6.24).

FIGURE 6.24
Sliders are added
to the blend shape
control window
as the additional
targets are added to
the deformer.

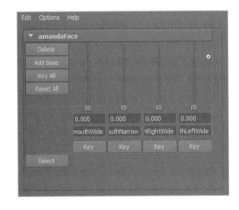

5. Save the scene as **amanda_v06.ma**.

To see a version of the scene to this point, open the amanda_v06.ma scene from the chapter6\ scenes directory at the book's web page.

Test the slider controls in the Blend Shape window. You can continue to edit the blend shape targets after they have been added to the deformer. You may want to make additional changes to improve the expressions and the movement between shapes. Remember that, at this point, it's fine to have some strange-looking expressions. The final rig may have dozens of blend shape targets that all work together to create various expressions and facial movements. As long as you have the blend shape targets available, you can continue to refine the expressions by editing the targets.

You can quickly create new blend shape targets from existing targets. This can be helpful when you are making targets that represent small or subtle muscle movements. To do this, make an expression by experimenting with the values in the Blend Shape control panel, use the Paint Blend Shape Weights tool to fine-tune, and then duplicate the deformed base mesh to create a new target. You can then add the target to the blend shape node, giving you more sliders and more targets to work with. In a production situation, a realistic blend shape may consist of hundreds of targets.

DEFORMER ORDER

When using blend shapes with joints or other deformers, you may have to change the position of the deformer in the deformer order. If you're getting strange results when you animate blend shapes, you may need to rearrange the deformer in the list of inputs. To do so, right-click the base mesh, and choose Inputs ➤ All Inputs from the marking menu. In the list of input operations, you can MMB-drag any of the deformers up and down the list to change its position. You also have the option of setting the blend shape order on the Advanced tab of the options when you create the blend shape deformer.

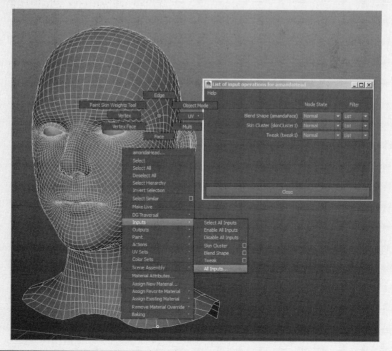

Animating a Scene Using Nonlinear Deformers

The nonlinear deformers include the bend, flare, sine, twist, squash, and wave deformers. The names of the deformers give a pretty good indication of what they do. They work well for creating cartoonish effects, and they even do a decent job of faking dynamic effects, saving you from the extensive setup many dynamic simulations require. All the nonlinear deformers work the same way. The deformer is applied to a surface, a lattice, components, or a group of surfaces, and then parameters are edited to achieve the desired effect. The parameters can be animated as well. You can use nonlinear deformers in combination with each other and with other deformers.

In this section, you'll use nonlinear deformers to animate a jellyfish bobbing in the ocean. You'll use just a few of the deformers to create the scene, but since they all work the same way, you can apply what you've learned to the other nonlinear deformers in your own scenes.

Creating a Wave Deformer

The wave deformer creates a ring of sine waves like a circular ripple in a puddle. To create the gentle bobbing up and down of a jellyfish, you'll animate the parameters of a wave deformer.

1. Open the `jellyfish_v01.ma` scene from the `chapter6\scenes` directory at the book's web page.

   This scene contains a simple jellyfish model. The model consists of the body of the jellyfish and its tendrils. All the surfaces are NURBS. The tendrils, which were created by converting Paint Effects strokes to NURBS surfaces, are grouped together and then grouped again with the body (see Figure 6.25).

FIGURE 6.25
The jellyfish model is created from groups of NURBS surfaces.

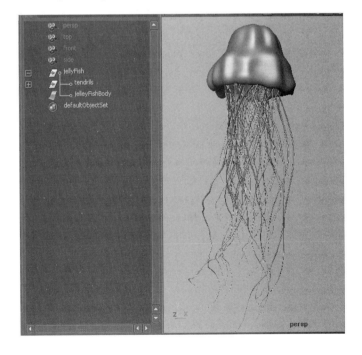

2. Select the jellyFish group in the Outliner. Switch to the Animation menu set, and choose Create Deformers ➤ Nonlinear ➤ Wave. The deformer appears as a single line. In the Outliner, you'll see that a new wave1Handle node has been created.

3. Select wave1Handle, and open its Attribute Editor. Click the wave1 tab. The tab contains the parameters for the deformer.

4. Set Amplitude to **0.041**. The Amplitude increases the height of the sinusoidal wave. This is displayed in the wireframe deformer handle in the viewport. Notice that the jellyfish is now distorted.

5. Set Wavelength to **0.755**; this decreases the distance between the peaks and valleys of the sine wave, creating a long, smooth type of distortion (see Figure 6.26).

FIGURE 6.26
The settings on the wave1 tab change the shape of the wave deformer.

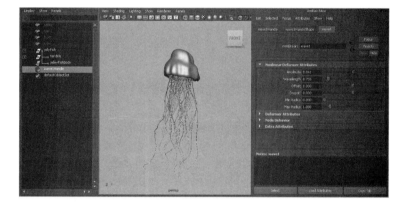

6. Use the following settings to position the wave handle at the center of the jellyfish body:

   Translate X: **0**

   Translate Y: **0.787**

   Translate Z: **−0.394**

7. Set all three Scale channels to **30**.

8. To animate the bobbing motion, create a simple expression that connects the Offset value to the current time. Open the Attribute Editor for wave1Handle to the wave1 tab. In the field next to Offset, type **=time** and press the Enter key.

9. Set Min Radius to **0.1**. If you switch to wireframe display, you'll see that a gap has appeared at the center of the deformer handle.

   The deformer now affects only the areas between the edge of the min radius and the outer edge of the deformer. You can set a range of deformation by adjusting the Min and Max Radius sliders. *Dropoff* reduces the amplitude of the deformer at the outer edges of the range. Setting Dropoff to **−1** would reduce the amplitude at the center of the deformer.

10. Save the scene as **jellyfish_v02.ma**.

To see a version of the scene up to this point, open the `jellyfish_v02.ma` scene from the `chaper6\scenes` directory at the book's web page.

Squashing and Stretching Objects

The squash deformer can both squash and stretch objects. It works well for cartoony effects. In this section, you'll add it to the jellyfish to enhance the bobbing motion created by the wave deformer.

1. Continue with the scene from the previous section, or open the `jellyfish_v02.ma` scene from the `chapter6\scenes` directory at the book's web page.

2. Switch to the Animation menu set.

3. Select the jellyFish group in the Outliner, and choose Create Deformers ➤ Nonlinear ➤ Squash. A node named squash1Handle appears in the Outliner. In the perspective view, the squash handle appears as a long line with a cross at either end.

4. Select squash1Handle in the Outliner, and set the Translate channels to the following:

   Translate X: **0**

   Translate Y: **1.586**

   Translate Z: **0**

5. Select the squash1Handle, and open the Attribute Editor to the squash1 tab. The Low and High Bound sliders set the overall range of the deformer. Leave Low Bound at –1, and set High Bound to **0.5** (see Figure 6.27).

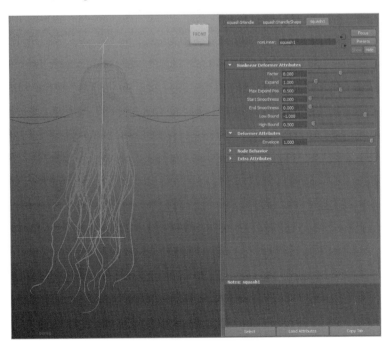

FIGURE 6.27
The squash deformer settings appear in the Attribute Editor.

PAINT WEIGHTS FOR NONLINEAR DEFORMERS

You can paint weights on all the nonlinear deformers. This painting feature works in the same way as painting weights on blend shapes and clusters. To access the tool, choose Edit Deformers ➤ Paint Nonlinear Weights Tool.

You can animate any of the settings to add motion to the jellyfish. In this case, you'll add an expression to the Factor setting of squash1. Setting Factor to a positive value stretches the object; setting Factor to a negative value squashes the object. For the jellyfish, animating between squash and stretch helps make the model appear as though it's floating in water. You can use a sine function as part of an expression that smoothly animates the Factor value between positive and negative values:

1. In the Factor field, type **`squash1.factor=0.25*(sin(time*2));`** and press the Enter key.

   Multiplying `time` by 2 speeds up the animation of the values. Multiplying the entire expression by 0.25 keeps the range of values between -0.25 and 0.25. Going beyond this range deforms the jellyfish a bit too much.

   Factor controls the vertical displacement created by the squash deformer; the Expand setting controls the horizontal displacement created by the effect.

2. Set Expand to **2**. Set Max Expand Pos to **0.78**. This places the vertical position of the center of the effect along the length of the deformer.

3. Save the scene as **`jellyfish_v03.ma`**.

To see a version of the scene to this point, open the `jellyfish_v03.ma` scene from the chapter6\scenes directory at the book's web page.

Twisting Objects

The twist deformer twists an object around a central axis. You'll add this to the jellyfish to create some additional motion for the tendrils.

1. Continue with the scene from the previous section, or open the `jellyfish_v03.ma` scene from the chapter6\scenes directory at the book's web page.

2. In the Outliner, expand the jellyFish group and select the tendrils group.

3. Choose Create Deformers ➤ Nonlinear ➤ Twist. A new twist1Handle node will appear in the Outliner.

4. Select twist1Handle in the Outliner, and set the Translate channels to the following:

   Translate X: **0**

   Translate Y: **-18**

   Translate Z: **0**

5. Open the Attribute Editor for twist1Handle to the twist1 tab.

Just like for the squash deformer, you can specify the range of the effect of the deformer using the Low Bound and High Bound sliders:

1. Set Low Bound to **-1** and High Bound to **0.825**.

   The Start Angle and End Angle values define the amount of twist created along the object. If you move the End Angle slider, the top of the tendrils spin around even if they are outside the High Bound range. Moving the Start Angle slider twists the tendrils at their ends, which is more like the effect you want. You can use a simple noise expression to create a smooth type of random oscillation between values. Since the Start Angle is specified in degrees, you can multiply the noise expression by 360 to get a full range of twisting motion.

2. In the Start Angle field, type `=360*(noise(time*0.1));`. Multiplying `time` by 0.1 slows down the motion of the twisting.

3. Rewind and play the animation. You're on your way to creating an interesting jellyfish motion (see Figure 6.28).

FIGURE 6.28
The jellyfish is animated using a number of nonlinear deformers.

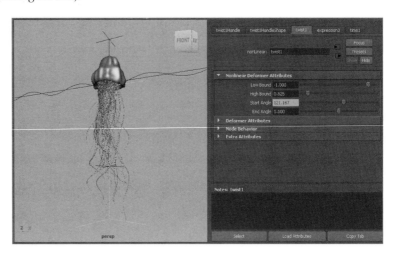

4. Save the scene as **jellyfish_v04.ma**.

To see a version of the scene to this point, open the `jellyfish_v04.ma` scene from the `chapter6\scenes` directory at the book's web page.

Real World Scenario

UNDULATING BACTERIA

While working on a creepy animation sequence for the closing titles of a feature film, one of the authors of an earlier edition of this book, Eric, was asked to create hairy microbes floating in a cellular environment. The art director wanted the bacteria encased in an undulating membrane. To do this, Eric combined nonlinear deformers and a blend shape. Using a blend shape, he transferred the animation of the undulating membrane from a copy of the bacteria to the animated version of the bacteria. You can try this yourself using the following steps:

1. Create a model of a bacterium. Usually, a rounded elongated cube with a lot of divisions does a good job.

2. Create a duplicate of the bacterium geometry.

3. Animate the original geometry floating in an environment or slinking along an animation path.

4. Apply a series of deformers to the duplicate geometry to make the surface undulate and throb.

5. Select the deformed duplicate and the animated original, and choose Create Deformers ➤ Blend Shape. Set the value of the Blend Shape on the animated bacterium to **1**. The deformations applied to the duplicate are now transferred to the original.

Using this setup, you won't need to worry about grouping the nonlinear deformers or parenting them to the animated original. You can move the duplicate and its deformers out of camera view and continue to edit the animation by changing the settings on the duplicate's deformers.

Creating a Jiggle Effect

A jiggle deformer is a simple way to add a jiggling motion to deformed objects. Jiggle deformers do not have the same level of control as dynamic systems, such as nucleus, fluids, or hair. Jiggle deformers are best used as a substitute for dynamics when the situation requires just a little jiggly motion.

Applying Jiggle Deformers

There aren't very many options for creating jiggle deformers. To apply a jiggle deformer, select the object you want to jiggle and create the deformer. In this section, you'll add the jiggle to the jellyfish:

1. Continue with the scene from the previous section, or open the jellyfish_v04.ma scene from the chapter6\scenes directory at the book's web page.

2. Select the jellyFish group in the Outliner. Choose Create Deformers ➤ Jiggle Deformer ➤ Options.

3. In the Create Jiggle Deformer Options dialog box, set Stiffness to **0.1** and Damping to **0.8**. A higher Stiffness setting creates more of a vibrating type of jiggle; lowering the Stiffness value makes the jiggle more jellylike.

4. Click Create to make the deformer. You won't see any new nodes appear in the Outliner because the Display option is set to DAG Objects Only.

   If you turn off the DAG Objects Only option in the Outliner, you'll see that a jiggle deformer is created for each surface. A jiggle cache is created to aid in the calculation and playback of the scene (Figure 6.29).

FIGURE 6.29
A node for each
jiggle deformer
applied to the sur-
faces appears in the
Outliner.

5. Rewind and play the scene; you'll see that the jellyfish has a jiggling motion, especially in the tendrils.

If you want to edit the settings of all the jiggle deformers at once (since there are so many tendrils, a lot of deformer nodes were created), disable the DAG Objects Only option in the Outliner's Display menu, Shift+click all the jiggle nodes (not the jiggle cache nodes), and then edit the settings in the Channel Box. When you have multiple objects selected, editing the settings in the Channel Box applies the settings to all the selected objects. This is not true when you are working in the Attribute Editor.

Painting Jiggle Weights

The jiggle effect looks good in the area of the tendrils, but it's a little too strong on the top of the jellyfish body. You can edit the weights of the deformer interactively using the Paint Jiggle Weights tool:

1. Select the jellyFishBody node in the Outliner, and choose Edit Deformers ➤ Paint Jiggle Weights Tool.

2. In the Tool Settings dialog box, set Paint Operation to Replace and Value to **0**. Paint the area at the top of the jellyfish body.

3. Set Paint Operation to Smooth, and click the Flood button a few times to smooth the overall weighting (see Figure 6.30).

FIGURE 6.30

Paint the weights of the jiggle deformer on the top of the jellyfish body, and then smooth them using the Flood button.

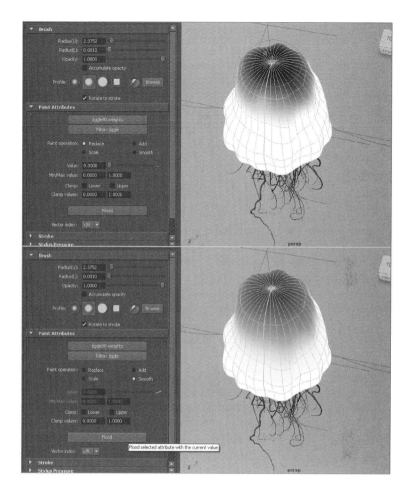

4. Rewind and play the animation. The jiggling is not quite as strong on the top of the jellyfish.

5. Save the scene as **jellyfish_v05.ma**.

To see a version of the scene to this point, open the jellyfish_v05.ma scene from the chapter6\scenes directory at the book's web page.

SETTING THE PLAYBACK SPEED

If the jellyfish seems to explode during playback, it is probably because you have the timeline playback preferences set to Real Time. Change the playback speed to Play Every Frame. You can access these settings by clicking the icon next to the key at the bottom-right corner of the interface or through the preferences (Windows ➤ Settings/Preferences ➤ Time Slider).

Optimizing Animations with the Geometry Cache

When you create a geometry cache for animated geometry, a series of files written to your computer's hard drive store the position of each of the points of the specified geometry over time. Geometry caches are used to optimize the performance of an animation. As your scenes become filled with complex animated characters that interact with environments and effects, playback performance can get bogged down, making the scene frustrating to work with. By using geometry caches, you can store that animation data on the hard drive as a separate file, thus freeing up resources so that your computer can more easily play the animation and ensuring that you'll have a much easier time working on other aspects of the scene, such as lighting, effects, or other animated elements.

Once you create a geometry cache, you can add more deformers and animation to the cached geometry and even alter the playback speed of the cached geometry.

In this section, you'll get a sense of how you can use a geometry cache by creating one for the jellyfish animated in the previous section. Then you'll see how you can use the geometry cache settings to slow the playback of the jellyfish so that the floating motion looks more natural. This is just one example of a creative use of the geometry cache.

Creating a Geometry Cache

The motion-deformed jellyfish looks pretty good as a simple animation. However, after all the deformers have been combined and the jiggle has been added, the motion looks a little too fast for a convincing deep-sea environment. Obviously, you can continue to edit the expressions used on the deformers, but in this section you'll take a shortcut by using a geometry cache.

1. Continue with the scene from the previous section, or open the `jellyfish_v05.ma` scene from the `chapter6\scenes` directory at the book's web page. To create a geometry cache, you need to select the geometry nodes; selecting group nodes or parents of the geometry nodes won't work.

2. In the Outliner, hold the Shift key and click the plus sign next to the jellyfish group to expand this group and the tendrils group at the same time.

3. Shift+click all the tendril objects and the jellyFishBody surface.

4. From the Animation menu set, choose Geometry Cache ➢ Create New Cache ➢ Options.

5. In the Create Geometry Cache Options dialog box, use the Cache Directory field to specify a directory for the cache. By default, the cache is created in the `Data` folder for the current project. If you will be rendering across computers on a network, make sure all the computers have access to the directory that contains the cache.

6. Name the cache **jellyfish**. Set File Distribution to One File and Cache Time Range to Time Slider.

7. Click Create to make the cache. Maya will play through the animation and write the cache files to disk.

8. When Maya has completed the cache, it should automatically be applied to the jellyfish. To prove this, you can select the deformers in the scene, delete them, and then play back the animation. The jellyfish should still bob up and down.

Editing the Cache Playback

Once the cache has been created, you can use the settings in the cache node to change the speed of the playback. This will create a more believable motion for the jellyfish.

1. Select any of the surfaces in the jellyfish (not the jellyfish group node), and open the Attribute Editor.

2. Switch to the jellyfishCache1 tab. Set the Scale attribute to **5**. This scales the length of the animation to be five times its original length, thus slowing down the speed of playback (see Figure 6.31).

FIGURE 6.31

The options for the geometry cache playback

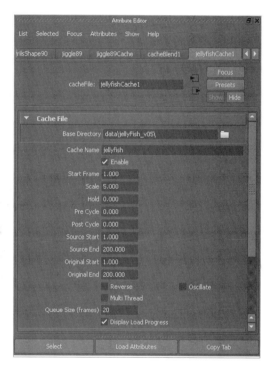

3. Set the length of the timeline to **1000**. The original 200-frame animation has been scaled to 1,000 frames.

4. Create a playblast. You'll see that the jellyfish is now much slower and looks more like an undersea creature.

   Once you have created a cache, you can add other deformers, animate the movement of the jellyfish group, and even make animated copies.

5. Select the jellyFish group, and choose Edit ➢ Duplicate Special ➢ Options.

6. In the Duplicate Special Options dialog box, set Geometry Type to Instance. Click Duplicate Special to create the copy.

7. Move the copy away from the original, and rotate it on its y-axis so that it does not look exactly like the original.

8. Make a few more copies like this to create a small jellyfish army. Play back the animation to see the army in action (see Figure 6.32).

FIGURE 6.32
Duplicates of the original jellyfish are created to make a small jellyfish army.

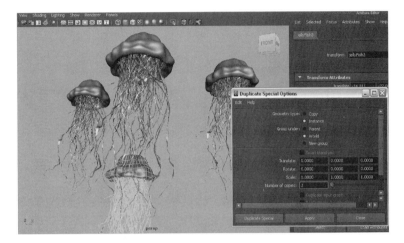

To create variations among the jellyfish, you can create three or four original jellyfish animations that have differences in their deformer settings and create a different cache for each. Then create several sets of instances for each jellyfish. Position them strategically in the camera view, and vary their Y-rotations.

Applying Motion Capture

Capturing the motion of a real person used to require tens of thousands of dollars and enough floor space to park a jet. Nowadays, all you need is an Xbox Kinect to have your own motion-capture system. If the Kinect isn't appealing, don't worry—there are hundreds of motion-capture files you can download, most of which are free. Motion capture has become extremely available. In the following example, we'll take a look at how to apply existing motion capture to the Human Inverse Kinematics (HIK) character rig you created in Chapter 5, "Rigging and Muscle Systems."

1. Open the `hikCharacter_v01.ma` scene from the `chapter6\scenes` directory at the book's web page.

2. Choose Window ➤ General Editors ➤ Visor.

THE VISOR

The Visor is a central library within Maya that allows you to access presets, example files, and other assets. The tabs at the top of the Visor let you browse and then choose the various types of assets. Much of the time you'll use the Visor to select a Paint Effects brush discussed in Chapter 10, "Paint Effects."

3. In the Visor, click on the Mocap Examples tab.

4. Maya comes with numerous motion-captured files. MMB-click walksit.ma and drag the file into a viewport.

5. The scene file is imported into your existing scene. You probably won't see anything show up. This is because the imported assets are much bigger than the HIK character. Press **a** to frame all. Figure 6.33 shows the extreme differences between the two character rigs.

FIGURE 6.33
The imported motion capture example is much larger than the HIK rig.

6. Choose Skeleton ➢ Human IK to open the Character Controls window.

7. In the Character Controls window, make sure Character is set to Character1. Change Source to MocapExample. Use Figure 6.34 as a guide.

FIGURE 6.34
Apply the motion-
capture example by
changing the source
in the Character
Controls window.

8. The character updates with the motion capture. Zoom out if you can't see the skeleton anymore.

9. The animation is 122 frames long. Change the timeline to match and then click Play to watch the motion. The HIK now uses the motion of the motion-capture example regardless of the difference in scale between the two skeletons.

10. The motion capture is applied directly to the HIK skeleton, bypassing the control handles. You can bake the animation to the controllers. Under the Character Controls menu button (the large blue icon in the upper-left corner), choose Bake ➤ Bake To Control Rig. The default options work perfectly for this example.

Maya creates a key at every frame. When done, the control rig is automatically applied to the character. You can now play the animation as you did before.

With the motion applied to the control rig, you can add animation on top of an animation layer or to the control handles directly. To see a version of the final scene, open the `mocap_v01.ma` scene from the `chapter6\scenes` directory at the book's web page.

The Bottom Line

Work with deformers. Maya has a multitude of deformers that can be used to animate or model any object with control points. Deformers provide real-time results, making them easy and flexible to work with.

Master It Create a planet with a terrain filled with craters.

Animate facial expressions. Animated facial expressions are a big part of character animation. It's common practice to use a blend shape deformer to create expressions from a large number of blend shape targets. The changes created in the targets can be mixed and matched by the deformer to create expressions and speech for a character.

Master It Create blend shape targets for the amanda character. Make an expression where the brows are up and another where the brows are down. Create a rig that animates each brow independently.

Animate nonlinear deformers. Nonlinear deformers apply simple changes to geometry. The deformers are controlled by animating the attributes of the deformer.

Master It Animate an eel swimming past the jellyfish you animated in this chapter.

Add jiggle movement to an animation. Jiggle deformers add a simple jiggling motion to animated objects.

Master It Add a jiggling motion to the belly of a character.

Apply motion capture. Maya comes with several motion-capture animations. You can access them through the Visor.

Master It Switch between multiple motion-capture examples on the same character.

Chapter 7

Lighting with mental ray

To achieve professional-quality, realistic renders in the Autodesk® Maya® program, you need to master the mental ray® render plug-in that comes with Maya. mental ray is a complex rendering system that is incorporated through the Maya interface. Learning how to use it properly and efficiently takes time, study, and practice. Chapter 8, "mental ray Shading Techniques," Chapter 9, "Texture Mapping," and Chapter 11, "Rendering for Compositing," discuss various aspects of working with mental ray.

This chapter is concerned with using mental ray lighting tools and techniques to create realistic renders. Options available within mental ray allow you to achieve a wide variety of effects. You won't need to use all of them in every case, but a good understanding of what is available will help you make better decisions when approaching a lighting problem in a scene.

In this chapter, you will learn to:

- ◆ Use shadow-casting lights

- ◆ Render with global illumination

- ◆ Render with Final Gathering

- ◆ Use image-based lighting

- ◆ Render using the Physical Sun and Sky network

- ◆ Understand mental ray area lights

Shadow-Casting Lights

You can create two types of shadows in mental ray: cast shadows and ambient occlusion. Several methods are available for creating them. Any combination of cast shadows and ambient occlusion can be used in a mental ray scene:

Cast Shadows   Cast shadows are created when an object blocks the rays of light coming from a light source. Cast shadows are the most familiar type of shadow. They are a good indication of the type, location, and orientation of the light source casting the shadow.

Ambient Occlusion   Ambient occlusion occurs when indirect light rays are prevented from reaching a surface. Ambient occlusion is a soft and subtle type of shadowing. It's usually found in the cracks and crevices of 3D objects and scenes.

In this section, you'll create and tune cast shadows using lights in mental ray. Ambient occlusion is discussed later in the chapter, in the sections "Indirect Lighting: Global

Illumination" and "Indirect Illumination: Final Gathering," as well as in Chapter 11, "Rendering for Compositing."

REVIEW MAYA LIGHTS

Before starting this chapter, you should be familiar with the basics of using lights in Maya. You should understand how to create, position, and edit standard Maya lights (spotlight, directional light, point light, area light, and volume light). Using Maya Software as a renderer is not covered in this book. Maya Software settings have not changed significantly in several years, whereas mental ray's implementation in Maya continues to develop and expand. In a professional setting, you will be expected to understand how to render with mental ray, so this book is devoted to helping you achieve the necessary understanding and skill for using mental ray.

A light source in a Maya scene casts either raytrace or depth map shadows. When you create a light in Maya, its shadows are set to raytrace by default. You can use depth map and raytrace shadows together in the same scene, but each light can cast only one or the other type of cast shadow.

Shadow Preview

When you create a shadow-casting light in a Maya scene, you can preview the position of the shadow in the viewport window.

This scene shows a bicycle. The shaders used for the vehicle are simple standard Maya Blinn materials. When you're setting up lights for a scene, it's usually a good idea to use simple shaders as you work. This makes test rendering faster, and it also keeps the focus on how the lighting will work within the composition. Later, as you refine the lighting of the scene, you can add more complex shaders and textures.

1. Open the `bicycle_v01.ma` scene from the `chapter7chapter7\scenes` folder at the book's web page (www.sybex.com/go/masteringmaya2015).

2. Create a spotlight by choosing Create ➤ Lights ➤ Spot Light.

   To position the spotlight, use the Move and Rotate tools. You can also look through the light as if it were a camera, which is often a faster and easier way to place the light in the scene.

3. Select the spotlight and, from the viewport panel menu, choose Panels ➤ Look Through Selected. Use the Alt/Option+MMB and the Alt/Option+RMB key combinations to move the view so that you can see the model from above (see Figure 7.1).

4. The green circle at the center of the view represents the cone angle of the spotlight. Open the Attribute Editor for the spotLight1 object, and click the spotLightShape1 tab. Set Cone Angle to **90**. The light from the spotlight now covers more area in the scene.

5. In the Panels menu, choose Lighting ➤ Shadows; this option is available only when Use All Lights has been activated. Choose Use All Lights through the menu or press 7 on the keyboard.

   You won't see any shadows until you activate shadows for the lights in the scene.

6. Select the spotLight1 object, open its Attribute Editor, and click the spotLightShape1 tab.

7. Expand the Shadows section, and activate Use Depth Map Shadows. A preview of the shadow appears on the ground plane (Figure 7.2).

FIGURE 7.1
View the scene from the position of the spotlight.

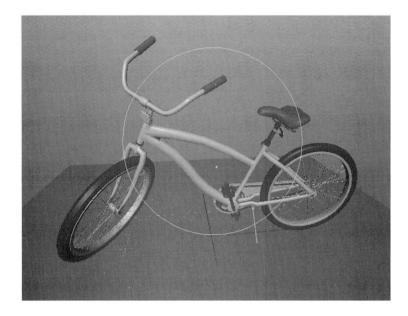

FIGURE 7.2
Activate a preview of the spotlight's shadow in the scene.

8. Select the spotlight, and use the Move and Rotate tools to change its position and rotation. Observe the changes in the preview. The preview will most likely slow down the performance of Maya, so use this feature only when you are positioning lights.

9. Scroll to the top of the spotlight attributes, and set Type to Directional. (The shadow preview works only for spotlights and directional-type lights.) Notice the difference in the shape of the shadow.

10. Switch Type back to Spotlight, and set the cone angle back to **90**.

11. Save the scene as `bicycle_v02.ma`.

To see a version of the scene, open the `bicycle_v02.ma` file from the `chapter7\scenes` folder at the book's web page.

Depth Map Shadows

Depth map shadows (also known as *shadow maps*) are created from data stored in a file that is generated at render time. The file stores information about the distance between the shadow-casting light and the objects in the scene from the light's point of view. Depth map shadows usually take less time to render than raytrace shadows and produce excellent results in many situations.

When using mental ray, you can choose to use the native depth map shadows in Maya or mental ray's own depth map format. In this exercise, you will compare the results produced using various depth map shadow settings.

Using the mental ray Plug-In

The implementation of mental ray in the Maya interface is admittedly not intuitive. Remember that mental ray is a separate program that is integrated into Maya, which is why it seems very scattered. Understanding this can help you cope with the strangeness of mental ray's Maya integration. Be prepared for some convoluted workflow practices as well as a certain level of redundancy, because mental ray has its own version of many common Maya nodes.

---

1. Open the `streetCorner_v01.ma` scene from the `chapter7\scenes` folder at the book's web page. This scene shows a section of a city street corner.

   All of the objects in the scene have been assigned to lambert1. Using a simple Lambert shader speeds up the render and allows you to focus on how the shadows look on the surfaces without the distraction of reflections and specular highlights.

2. Open the Render Settings window (Window ➤ Rendering Editors ➤ Render Settings), and make sure mental ray is the selected option in the Render Using menu.

Loading mental ray

If mental ray does not appear in the Render Using list, you'll need to load the plug-in listed in the preferences. Choose Window ➤ Settings/Preferences ➤ Plug-in Manager. At the bottom of the list of plug-ins, make sure there's a check mark in the box next to `Mayatomr.mll` (or `Mayatomr.bundle` on a Mac) in the Loaded and Auto Load columns. You'll see that mental ray now appears in the Render Using drop-down menu.

---

3. Switch to the Quality tab; then go to the menu bar at the top of the Render Settings window and choose Presets ➤ Load Preset to load the Production preset (see Figure 7.3).

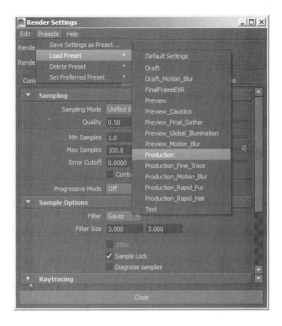

UNIFIED SAMPLING

Unified Sampling greatly streamlines the rendering quality in mental ray by giving you a single Quality slider that adaptively controls image quality. This simplifies tuning the quality of your render and offers increased performance. To use the options provided in previous versions of Maya, choose the Legacy Sampling mode.

4. Open the Attribute Editor for spotLight1, and click the spotLightShape1 tab.

5. Scroll down to the Shadows section; Depth Map Shadows should be activated. Turn this option on whenever you want to use depth map shadows.

6. Choose Window ➤ Rendering Editors ➤ Render View to open the Render View window, where you can preview your renders as you work. As you create renders, you can store the images and compare them with previous renders.

7. From the Render View menu, choose Render ➤ Render ➤ streetCornerCam.

You'll see the render appear in the window after a few seconds. By default, the quality of depth map shadows is pretty poor. With some tweaking, you can greatly improve the look of the shadows.

The shadow is generated using a special depth file, which is an image. As such, the image has a resolution that is controlled by the Resolution slider. When the resolution is low, you can see a grainy quality in the shadows, as shown in Figure 7.4.

FIGURE 7.4
The default depth map shadows have a grainy quality.

To improve the look of the shadow, you can balance the resolution with the filter size:

1. Set Resolution to **2048** and Filter Size to **0**.

2. Create a test render in the render view, and store the image in the Render View window (in the Render View menu, choose File ➤ Keep Image In Render View). The shadow is improved and relatively free from artifacts.

3. Set Resolution to **512** and Filter Size to **4**.

4. Create a test render, store the render in the Render View window, and use the scroll bar at the bottom of the render view to compare the two images (see Figure 7.5).

FIGURE 7.5
Two renders using depth map shadows. The left side uses a high-resolution map with no filtering; the right side uses a low-resolution map with high filtering.

Using a low resolution (such as 512) and a high filter size (such as 4), as shown on the right side of Figure 7.5, creates soft shadows, the kind you might expect on an overcast day. One weakness in using a high filter size is that the blurring is applied to the entire shadow. In reality, shadows become gradually softer as the distance increases between the cast shadow and the shadow-casting object.

The Use Mid Dist feature is enabled by default. This option corrects banding artifacts that can occur on curved and angled surfaces. The Mid Dist Map is a second image file that records the points midway between the first and second surfaces encountered by the light. The second image is used to modify the depth information of the original depth map file to help eliminate banding artifacts.

The Bias slider provides a similar function for eliminating artifacts. The slider adjusts the depth information in the depth map file. Increasing the bias pushes surface points closer to the shadow-casting light to help eliminate artifacts. This transformation of surface points occurs in the depth map file, not in the actual geometry of the scene.

If you are encountering artifacts on the surface of objects and Use Mid Dist is enabled, you can use the Bias slider to reduce the artifacts. Change the bias values in small increments as you create test renders. If the bias is too high, you'll see a gap between the shadow-casting object and the shadow.

The Use Auto Focus setting automatically adjusts the objects within the field of the light's viewable area to the maximum size of the shadow map resolution. Thus if from the light's point of view an object is surrounded by empty space, the light will zoom into the object in the depth map image. This helps optimize the use of the pixels within the depth map image so that none are wasted. It's usually a good idea to leave this setting enabled when using spotlights; however, you may encounter a different situation with other types of lights.

Now try this:

CERT OBJECTIVE

1. Set Resolution of the depth map to **512** and Filter Size to **0**.

2. Scroll up in the Attribute Editor, and set the light Type to Directional.

3. Create a test render.

The shadow is very blocky when the light is switched to directional (see Figure 7.6).

FIGURE 7.6
Depth map shadows cast by directional lights appear very blocky.

When you use spotlights, the size of the viewable area from the light's point of view is restricted by the cone angle and the distance between the light and the subject. When you use directional lights, the size of the viewable area is always adjusted to fit all the objects in the scene. This is because directional lights do not factor in their position in the scene when calculating shadows, only their orientation.

In this situation, you can use the new Shadow Map Camera feature described in the next section, "mental ray Shadow Map Overrides."

mental ray Shadow Map Overrides

The mental ray overrides offer settings that are similar to those for the standard Maya shadow maps. In addition to the Resolution setting, there are Samples and Softness settings. The Softness setting is similar to the Filter Size attribute for Maya shadow maps. You can click the Take Settings From Maya button to load the settings created for standard Maya shadow maps automatically into the mental ray attributes.

1. Open the `streetCorner_v02.ma` scene from the `chapter7\scenes` folder at the book's web page. In the Render Settings window, make sure Render Using is set to mental ray. Switch to the Quality tab, and make sure the Production preset is loaded.

2. Select the spotlight, and open the Attribute Editor to the spotLightShape1 tab. In the Shadows section, make sure Use Depth Map Shadows is on.

3. Scroll down to the Attribute Editor, expand the mental ray rollout, and expand the Shadows section under mental ray.

4. Check the Use mental ray Shadow Map Overrides box. This activates the Shadow Map Overrides section, giving you access to mental ray controls for shadow maps.

5. Set Resolution to **2048** and Softness to **0.025**.

6. Create a test render. Store the image in the Render View window. The render is similar to the results seen before—in other words, it's very grainy.

7. Set Samples to **64**, and create another test render. The graininess is reduced without significantly impacting the render time. Store the image in the render view.

USE SHADOW MAP CAMERA FOR DIRECTIONAL LIGHTS

The Use Shadow Map Camera feature is designed to solve the problem of rendering shadow maps with directional lights in scenes that have large areas of geometry, such as a ground plane that stretches off into the distance. To use this feature, follow these steps:

1. Enable the Use mental ray Shadow Map Overrides check box in the mental ray section of the directional light's Attribute Editor.

2. Click the Take Settings From Maya button. Doing this will automatically copy the settings from the Maya Depth Map Shadows settings. It will also automatically fill in the name for the Shadow Map camera settings.

3. Enable the Use Shadow Map Camera check box near the bottom of the Shadow Map Overrides section. Decrease the Camera Aperture setting, and increase the Camera Resolution setting. Test the render, and adjust the settings until the desired result is achieved.

Detail shadow maps are a more advanced type of shadow map that stores additional information about the surface properties of shadow-casting objects. This information includes surface properties such as transparency. The render takes longer, but the shadows are improved.

8. Set Shadow Map Format to Detail Shadow Map (see Figure 7.7), and create another render.

FIGURE 7.7
Enable Detail Shadow Map in the mental ray Shadows settings.

9. Use the scroll bar at the bottom of the render view to compare this render with the previous two renders (Figure 7.8).

FIGURE 7.8
The street corner is rendered with Samples set to 1 (left image), Samples set to 64 (middle image), and Detail Shadow Map enabled (right image).

10. Save the scene as **streetCorner_v03.ma**.

Rendering with Detail Shadow Maps enabled will take more time, but the quality is improved. Detail shadow maps are more sensitive to changes in the Softness setting in the Shadow Map Overrides rollout. There are also additional Samples and Accuracy settings in the Detail Shadow Maps rollout that can be used to tune the quality of the maps. You can use the Shadow Map File Name field to set a name for saved shadow maps and then reuse the shadow maps to improve render time as long as the lights or shadow-casting objects are not animated. The settings for saving shadow maps are found in the Shadows section of the Render Settings window on the Quality tab.

The bottom line is that when using depth map shadows, you can use a number of options to improve the quality of the shadows. The goal is to strike a balance between render time and quality.

To see a version of the scene up to this point, open the streetCorner_v03.ma scene from the chapter7\scenes folder at the book's web page.

Raytrace Shadows

Raytrace shadows are created by tracing the path of light rays from the light source to the rendering camera. Using raytrace shadows produces more accurate results but often takes a little more time and processor power to calculate (although this has become less of an issue in recent years because of improvements in computer processor speeds).

These are some advantages raytrace shadows have over shadow maps:

◆ Raytrace shadows created with area lights become softer and lighter as the distance increases between the shadow and the shadow-casting object.

◆ Raytrace shadows can be accurately cast from transparent, refractive, and colored objects.

◆ Raytrace shadows support indirect lighting methods.

To activate raytrace shadows, make sure Raytracing is enabled on the Quality tab of the mental ray Render Settings window, and enable Use Ray Trace Shadows for the light. When you choose the Production quality preset for mental ray, Raytracing is enabled by default (see Figure 7.9).

FIGURE 7.9
Raytracing is enabled in the mental ray Render Settings window, and Use Ray Trace Shadows is enabled for the light.

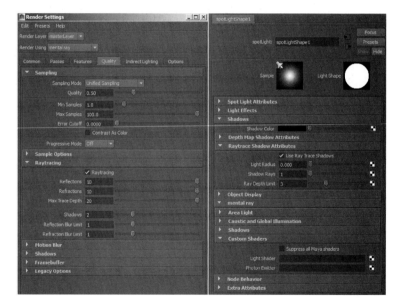

Raytrace shadows are typically very crisp when enabled. To add softness to the shadow, increase the Shadow Rays and Light Radius values in the Raytrace Shadow Attributes section. In Figure 7.10, you can see how increasing the Light Radius and Shadow Rays values adds softness to the shadow. The render in the left image uses a Light Radius of 0 and a Shadow Rays setting of 1. The render in the right image has a Light Radius of 3, and Shadow Rays is set to 20. Notice that the blurring on the shadow increases as the distance between the shadow and the shadow-casting object increases.

FIGURE 7.10
Add softness to
raytrace shadows by
increasing the Light
Radius and Shadow
Rays settings.

The Light Radius setting is giving the light a random position within the given radius for each pixel of shadow. Since the position of directional lights is of no consequence, their shadows are softened with a channel called Light Angle, which randomizes the angle of the light.

Increase the Ray Depth Limit value when you need a shadow to be visible in reflections. Each level of the Ray Depth Limit corresponds to the number of raytrace bounces the light will calculate before the shadow is no longer visible. (see Figure 7.11).

FIGURE 7.11
When Ray Depth
Limit is set to 1, the
shadow is not vis-
ible in the reflection
(left image). When
it is set to 2, the
shadow is visible
(right image).

UMBRA AND PENUMBRA

The *umbra* of a shadow is the area that is completely blocked from the light source. The *penumbra* is the transition from a lighted area to the umbra. Crisp shadows have a very small penumbra; soft shadows have a large penumbra.

Indirect Lighting: Global Illumination

In reality, when a ray of light hits an opaque surface, it is either absorbed or reflected (or a little of both) by the surface. If the light ray is reflected, it reenters the environment and continues to bounce off reflected surfaces until it is absorbed by another surface. Objects illuminated by reflected light are thus lit indirectly.

As light rays bounce around in an environment, fewer of them reach the parts that are hidden in corners, cracks, and crevices. The lack of light in these areas creates a type of shadowing known as *ambient occlusion*. You can see ambient occlusion shadowing in the crevices of the photograph in Figure 7.12.

FIGURE 7.12
Ambient occlusion refers to the shadowing effect seen in the crevices of this photograph.

mental ray has three methods for simulating indirect lighting and ambient occlusion shadowing: the Global Illumination, Final Gathering, and Ambient Occlusion shaders. You can use them separately or together depending on what you are trying to achieve in your render.

In this section, you'll get some hands-on experience working with global illumination; the next section covers Final Gathering. Using ambient occlusion will be discussed along with ambient occlusion render passes in Chapter 11.

Global illumination simulates photons of light bouncing off geometry in a Maya scene. It is a two-step process. In the first step, the photon-emitting light shoots out photons into a scene. A photon map is created that records the position of the photons and their intensities in three-dimensional space. Then the area is searched for surfaces that intersect the photons, those surfaces are illuminated based on the intensities of the intersecting photons, and the diffuse value of the shader is applied to the surface. Glossy, black, or reflective surfaces with no diffuse value will not be affected by global illumination; a diffuse value must be present.

The second part of the process is the actual rendering of the image. The photon map is stored in a data structure known as a *Kd-Tree*. During rendering, the energy values are averaged over a given radius in the Kd-Tree, and these values are interpolated to create the look of light bouncing off the diffuse surfaces. The great thing about this method is that once you have perfected the look of the global illumination, if the elements of the scene are fairly static, you can save the photon map and reuse it in the scene, cutting down on the amount of time required to render each frame.

In this exercise, you'll use global illumination to light a simple kitchen scene. There are no textures or colors in the scene, so you can focus specifically on how global illumination reacts with surfaces.

1. Open the `hospitalRoom_v01.ma` scene from the `chapter7\scenes` folder at the book's web page. In the scene, a camera named renderCam has already been created and positioned.

2. Create a directional light, and place it outside the window.

3. Rotate the light so that it's shining in the window (the position of a directional light does not affect how it casts light—only the rotation does—but it's convenient to have it outside the window). Use these settings in the Channel Box:

   Rotate X: **−141.753**

   Rotate Y: **22.931**

   Rotate Z: **15.26**

4. Create a test render in the render view using the renderCam camera. The image should look very dark except for the light shining through the blinds of the window.

5. Open the Render Settings window, and switch to the Indirect Lighting tab.

6. Expand the Global Illumination rollout, turn on Global Illumination, and use the default settings (see the left side of Figure 7.13).

7. In the Attribute Editor settings for directionalLightShape1, expand the mental ray rollout and, under Caustic And Global Illumination, activate Emit Photons (as in the right side of Figure 7.13).

FIGURE 7.13
Activate Global Illumination in the Render Settings window, and activate Emit Photons in the light's Attribute Editor.

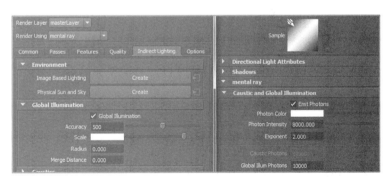

8. Create another test render. The resulting render should look pretty horrible.

Using a directional light is a perfectly reasonable choice for creating the look of light coming through a window. The light rays cast by a directional light are parallel, which simulates the way light from a distant source, such as the sun, behaves. However, directional lights tend to have an overexposed quality when used as photon-casting lights (see Figure 7.14). This is because the photons cast from a photon-emitting light need to have both a direction and a position. Directional lights have only a direction (based on the rotation of the light), so the light often casts too many photons, and artifacts can result. It's a good practice to avoid directional lights altogether as photon-casting light. The best types of lights to use are area, spot, and point. Area lights tend to work the best since they cast light from a sizable area as opposed to a point in space.

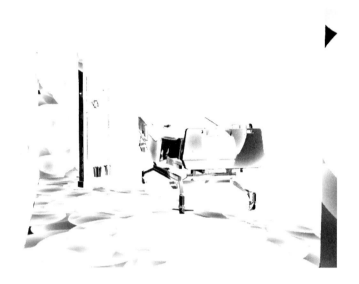

The photon-casting properties of a light are completely separate and unrelated to the light's intensity. In practice, it's often a good idea to use one light to cast direct light as well as to create cast shadows, and another light to create the indirect light.

If you are in a situation where the same light is casting direct and indirect illumination, raising the intensity can cause the area around the light to become overexposed. In this situation, you may want to use two lights placed near each other. One light should cast only direct light (that is, Cast Photons is disabled), and the other light should have 0 Intensity but Cast Photons enabled, as follows:

1. In the Attribute Editor for the directional light, turn off Emit Photons in the Caustic And Global Illumination settings. Rename the light **Sun**.

2. Create an area light (Create ➢ Lights ➢ Area Light).

3. Place the light near the wall opposite the window. Name the light **Bounce**. You can use these settings in the Channel Box:

   Translate X: **5.323**

   Translate Y: **12.614**

   Translate Z: **-39.104**

   Rotate Y: **-90**

   Scale X: **11.119**

Scale Y: **10.476**

Scale Z: **1**

4. Open the Attribute Editor for Bounce. Turn off Emit Diffuse and Emit Specular.

5. In the mental ray rollout, turn on Emit Photons.

6. Create a test render of the scene, and store the image in the Render View window.

   The render is a big improvement. The default settings still require some tuning, but it looks less like a nuclear blast.

GLOBAL ILLUMINATION AND SCALE

Global illumination is sensitive to the scale of the objects in a scene. If you continue to get blown-out results using other types of lights as photon emitters, try uniformly increasing the scale of the objects in the scene.

---

7. The image looks a little weird because there is sunlight coming through a black window. To create a quick fix for this, select renderCam and open its Attribute Editor.

8. In the Environment tab, set the Background Color to white. Create another test render (see Figure 7.15).

FIGURE 7.15
Photons are cast from an area light placed opposite the window, inside the room. When the background color for the camera is set to white, the area outside the window is white.

9. Save the scene as **hospitalRoom_v02.ma**.

To see a version of the scene up to this point, open the hospitalRoom_v02.ma scene from the chapter7\scenes folder at the book's web page.

Tuning Global Illumination

Adjusting the look of the global illumination requires editing the settings in the area light's Attribute Editor and in the Render Settings window. The settings work together to create the effect. Often, you'll tune the lighting of the scene by adjusting and readjusting the various settings until you get the best result you can.

1. Continue with the scene from the previous section, or open the hospitalRoom_v02.ma file from the chapter7\scenes folder at the book's web page.

2. Take a look at the area light's settings under Caustic And Global Illumination:

   Emit Photons This option turns on the photon-casting property of the light.

   Photon Color This option adds color to the actual photons.

   Photon Intensity This option controls the energy of the photons as they are shot into the room and how they are reflected from various sources.

   Exponent This option controls the photon decay rate. A setting of 2 is consistent with the inverse square law, which states that the intensity of light is inversely proportional to the square of the distance from the source. A setting of 2 would be analogous to setting a light's Decay rate to Quadratic. This setting simulates how light works in the real world. Setting Exponent to 1 is analogous to setting a light's Decay setting to Linear, which is closer to how light from distant bright sources, such as the sun, decays.

   Global Illum Photons This option specifies the number of photons cast into the room by the photon-casting light. Increasing this value often aids in the look of the effect. The more photons you add, the longer the render can take in some cases.

3. The indirect lighting looks a little blown out. Lower Photon Intensity to **5000**.

   The blotchy quality on the wall is caused because there are not enough photons being cast by the light. Increasing the number of photons creates more overlapping and thus smoothes the look of the light as it reflects from the surface. Be aware that increasing the number of photons in the scene doesn't cast more light into the scene. The intensity is simply shared by more photons.

4. Set Global Illum Photons to **25000**. Create a test render (see Figure 7.16).

MORE IS NOT ALWAYS BETTER

Each situation demands its own settings to create the ideal look of indirect lighting. Sometimes increasing Global Illum Photons beyond a certain level will make the renders look just as blotchy as a low setting. It's best to experiment to find the right setting for your scene.

---

5. Open the Render Settings window, and click the Indirect Lighting tab. Take a look at the Global Illumination settings:

   Global Illumination This option turns on global illumination calculations. Some mental ray presets, such as Preview Global Illumination, activate this option when chosen. Notice the Caustics check box; this activates the caustics calculations, which are separate from global illumination, as you'll see later in this chapter.

Accuracy This option specifies an overall level of accuracy in the global illumination calculations. If this option is set to 1, the photons are not blended together at all, and you can see the individual photons (see Figure 7.17). Generally, it's a good idea to keep Accuracy between 250 and 800 for most situations.

FIGURE 7.16
By decreasing Photon Intensity and increasing Global Illum Photons, you improve the lighting.

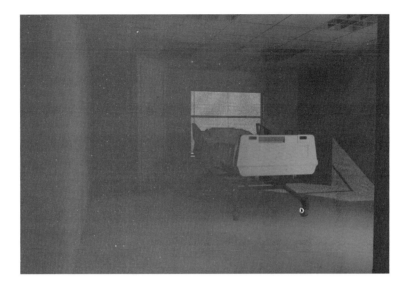

FIGURE 7.17
Lowering the Accuracy setting in the Render Settings window reveals the individual photons as they are reflected on surfaces.

Scale This option acts as a global brightness control for the global illumination effect.

Radius This option controls the radius of the actual photons. When the option is set to 0, mental ray determines the radius of the photons based on the requirements of the scene. The radius is not actually 0. Increasing the radius can smooth the photons;

however, too large an area can cause color bleeding and a loss of detail in the shadows, leading to a blurry, undefined sort of look.

Merge Distance   This option specifies a distance in world space within which overlapping photons are merged. The option is used to reduce the size of photon maps and decrease render times. You should raise this setting by very small increments. It can increase the blotchy look of the render.

6. Click the color swatch next to Scale to open the Color Chooser.

7. Make sure the mode of the Color Chooser is set to **HSV**. Set the value (V) to **1.5**, and create another test render (see Figure 7.18). This is a good way to brighten the overall global illumination effect without raising the Photon Intensity value on one or more lights.

FIGURE 7.18
Raising the Scale value to 1.25 in the Color Chooser window brightens the overall effect of global illumination.

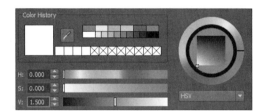

8. Save the scene as **hospitalRoom_v03.ma**.

To see a version of the scene up to this point, open the hospitalRoom_v03.ma scene from the chapter7\scenes folder at the book's web page.

Rendering with global illumination requires a lot of testing and tuning. At a certain point, you'll need to combine the techniques with other indirect lighting tools such as Final Gathering to perfect the look.

Working with Photon Maps

Photon maps are generated during a mental ray render using global illumination. They store the position, energy, color, and other data associated with the photons cast during rendering. The map can be saved to disk and reused to cut down on render time. This, in fact, eliminates the first stage of rendering with global illumination on subsequent renders.

Of course, if there is a lot of animation in the scene, reusing the same map will not always work, but in a scene such as the current one, it can be quite helpful.

To save a photon map, type a name for the map in the Photon Map File field (found in the Photon Map section on the Indirect Lighting tab of the Render Settings window) and create a render (do not add a file extension to the name). When you want to reuse the same map, deselect Rebuild Photon Map. The map is stored in the renderData\mentalray\photonMap folder with the .pmap extension. When you want to overwrite the map, simply select Rebuild Photon Map.

Remember to turn on Rebuild Photon Map when you make changes to the scene. Otherwise, the scene will not update correctly as you create test renders.

The Enable Map Visualizer option is a way to visualize how the photons are cast in the scene. When you enable this option and create a global illumination render, you'll see dots spread around the scene in the camera view, representing the distribution of photons cast by the light.

1. In the Render Settings window, type **test** in the Photon Map File field (found in the Photon Map section of the Indirect Lighting tab).

2. Select Rebuild Photon Map and Enable Map Visualizer.

3. Open the render view, and create a test render from the renderCam camera.

4. Close the render view when the render is complete. Look at the perspective view in Maya. You should see the geometry covered in dots representing the distribution of photons created by the bounce light.

5. Choose Window ➤ Rendering Editors ➤ mental ray ➤ Map Visualizer. The options in the resulting dialog box allow you to customize the look of the Visualizer in the perspective window (see Figure 7.19).

FIGURE 7.19
The Map Visualizer allows you to see how the photons are cast in the scene.

6. To remove the dots, select the mapViz1 node in the Outliner and delete it. Doing so will not affect the render or the saved photon map.

The dots in the scene can be colored based on the Photon Color setting of the light; you can use this to diagnose how each photon-casting light is affecting the scene. Also, if you save more than one photon map, you can load and view them using the Enable Map Visualizer option. Use the Map File Name dialog box to load saved maps.

Another way to visualize the photons in the scene is to use the Diagnose Photon menu in the Photon Map section of the Indirect Lighting tab of the Render Settings window. When you choose a setting from this menu and create a render, the shaders in the scene are replaced with a single shader colored to indicate either the photon density or the irradiance of surfaces in the scene.

IRRADIANCE

You can find the Irradiance controls in the mental ray rollout in standard Maya shaders applied to objects. The slider is a multiplier used to adjust how a particular surface responds to the total amount of incoming light energy (or radiant power) from the surroundings.

By raising the value of Irradiance, the surface is affected by the color in the Irradiance Color slider. You can lower the value of the Irradiance Color slider to eliminate any areas on the shader that may appear too bright or blown out. You can also change the hue of the irradiance color to change the color of the indirect lighting on all surfaces that have the shader applied. Remember to keep these settings as consistent as possible between shaders in a given scene to avoid incoherence in the lighting.

Color Bleeding

When light is reflected from a colored surface, the color of that surface affects the color of the light reflecting from it. mental ray's global illumination simulates this property.

1. Open the `hospitalRoom_v04.ma` scene from the `chapter7\scenes` folder at the book's web page. This scene has a bucket added close to where the sunlight strikes the floor and the wall.

2. The model has a Lambert shader applied with bright red set for the color. Create a test render. You'll see the red color bleed onto the surrounding area.

Color bleeding is a part of global illumination and occurs automatically when colored objects are near the photon-emitting lights.

Importons

Importons are very similar to photons. Importons are emitted from the camera and bounce toward the light. Photons are emitted from the lights and bounce toward the camera, so importons actually move in the opposite direction of photons. You can use importons to improve the quality of global illumination maps.

You can find the Importons controls in the Importons section of the Indirect Lighting tab of the Render Settings window. Importons are available only when Global Illumination is enabled.

When you render using importons, mental ray first calculates the importon emission and then renders the scene. The importons are discarded when the render is completed.

The Density value of the importons controls how many importons are emitted from the camera per pixel. Generally, this value does not need to be higher than 1. The Merge Distance setting works very similarly to the Merge Distance setting used for photons. The Traverse feature maximizes the number of importons in the scene; it's generally a good idea to leave this option on.

You can improve the quality of global illumination renders by activating the Importons option. The option must be turned on in the Indirect Lighting tab in the Render Settings window and also in the Features tab of the Render Settings window.

Caustics

Global illumination simulates light reflected from diffuse surfaces. Caustics simulate light reflected from glossy and reflective surfaces as well as light that passes through refractive transparent materials. Caustics are calculated completely independently from global illumination; however, the workflow is very similar.

This exercise will show you how to set up and render using caustics. The scene contains a globe with crystalline structures emanating from the top. The globe is set on top of a metal stand. At the moment, all the objects in the scene use a simple Lambert shader.

1. Open the `crystalGlobe_v01.ma` scene from the `chapter7\scenes` folder at the book's web page.

2. In the Outliner, expand the Globe group, and select the crystal object.

3. Assign a Blinn shader to the crystal (from the Rendering menu set, choose Lighting/ Shading ➢ Assign Favorite Material ➢ Blinn).

4. Open the Attribute Editor for the Blinn material, and name it **crystalShade**.

5. Set the Color option of crystalShade to red and Transparency to a very light gray—almost white.

6. In the Specular Shading section of the Attribute Editor, use the following settings:

   Eccentricity: **0.05**

   Specular Roll Off: **1**

   Specular Color: **White**

   Reflectivity: **0.25**

7. Expand the Raytrace Options rollout, and activate Refractions; set Refractive Index to **1.2** (see Figure 7.20).

8. Create a spotlight. Select the spotlight, and choose Look Through Selected Camera.

9. Aim the spotlight so that it's looking down at the globe and stand. Position the light so that the globe fits inside the cone angle radius (the circle at the center of the screen), as shown in Figure 7.21.

CERT OBJECTIVE

FIGURE 7.20
The settings for the crystalShade shader.

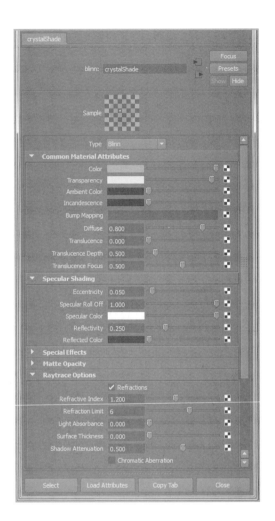

FIGURE 7.21
The scene is viewed from the spotlight. Position the light so that the cone angle fits around the globe and stand.

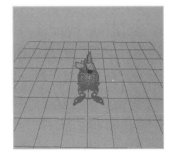

10. Switch to the perspective view. Open the Render Settings window, and set Render Using to mental ray.

11. On the Quality tab, set Quality Presets to Production.

12. In the Attribute Editor for the spotlight, turn on Use Ray Trace Shadows.

13. Create a test render of the scene using the renderCam camera.

    At the moment, caustics have not been activated. Keep this image in the render view so that you can compare it with the caustics render.

14. Open the Render Settings window, and switch to the Indirect Lighting tab.

15. Under Global Illumination, turn on Caustics. Leave Global Illumination deselected.

16. Select the spotlight. In the Attribute Editor for the spotlight, scroll down to the mental ray section. Under Caustics And Global Illumination, turn on Emit Photons.

17. Create another test render in the render view. Immediately you can see a dramatic difference in the two renders (see Figure 7.22).

FIGURE 7.22
The image on the left is rendered without Caustics enabled; the image on the right has Caustics enabled.

The light passing through the refractive surface produces a white highlight in the shadow on the floor. You can also see some of the red color of the globe reflected on the floor in a few spots. Notice, however, that the shadow is no longer transparent. The light that passes through the transparent globe is bent by the globe's refractive properties. This results in the hot spot seen at the center of the shadow. mental ray adds the bright spot on top of an opaque shadow.

18. The Caustics settings are similar to the Global Illumination settings. In the spotlight's Attribute Editor, lower Photon Intensity to **3000**. Set Caustic Photons to **80000**.

    You can adjust the color of the caustic highlight by changing the caustic photon color or by changing the color of the transparency on the crystal shader. It's probably a better idea to change the transparency color on the shader; that way, if one light is creating caustics on two different objects that are shaded with different colors, the color of the caustic photons won't clash with the color of the objects.

The Exponent setting for caustics works just like the Exponent setting for global illumination.

19. Select the crystal object, and open the Attribute Editor.

20. Click the Crystal Shade tab. Set the Transparency color to a light pink.

21. Open the Render Settings window, and click the Indirect Lighting tab. Set Accuracy for Caustics to **32**.

22. Create a test render of the scene (see Figure 7.23).

FIGURE 7.23
The scene is rendered after lowering the Accuracy and the Photon Intensity settings.

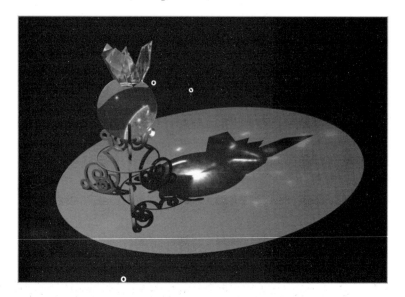

A lower Accuracy value produces sharper caustic highlights at the risk of some graininess. A higher value removes the grainy quality but softens the look of the caustics. You can also soften the look a little by setting Filter to Cone.

The Radius value can be left at 0 if you want Maya to determine the proper radius at render time. Settings lower than 1 make individual photons more visible. The Merge Distance setting merges all photons within the specified distance, which can decrease render times but remove the detail in the caustic patterns.

Caustic Light Setup

In practice, spotlights are usually the best choice for creating caustics. Area lights don't work nearly as well. The cone angle of the spotlight is reduced so that no photons are wasted; they are concentrated on the globe and stand. However, you may not want the visible edge of the spotlight cone on the floor. To fix this, you can use two spotlights—one to create the caustic photons and the other to light the scene.

1. Select the spotlight and duplicate it (Ctrl/Cmd+D).

2. Open the Attribute Editor for spotlight1:

a. Under Spotlight Attributes, turn off Emit Diffuse.

    b. Under Shadows, turn off Use Raytrace Shadows.

3. Select spotlight2, and open its Attribute Editor. Under Spotlight Attributes, turn off Emit Specular.

4. Set Cone Angle to **90**.

5. Turn off Emit Photons under Caustics And Global Illumination.

6. Create a test render of the scene. The scene looks pretty much the same, but the area of light cast by the spotlight has been widened.

7. In the Outliner, select the Stand group, and apply a Blinn shader. Name the shader **standShader**.

8. Open the Attribute Editor for standShader:

    a. Set Color to a light, bright yellow.

    b. Set Diffuse to **0.25**.

9. Under Specular Shading, apply the following settings:

Eccentricity: **0.1**

Specular Roll Off: **1**

Specular Color: **White**

Reflectivity: **0.85**

10. Create another test render. You can clearly see the light reflected off the stand and onto the floor (see Figure 7.24).

FIGURE 7.24
Apply a reflective shader to the stand, creating intricate patterns of reflected light on the floor.

11. Save the scene as **crystalGlobe_v02.ma**.

When working with caustics, you'll get more interesting results when the caustic light patterns are created from complex objects. You'll also find that the patterns created by transparent objects vary greatly when you change the Refractive Index value of the transparent shader.

To see a version of the scene up to this point, open the `crystalGlobe_v02.ma` scene from the `chapter7\scenes` folder at the book's web page.

Indirect Illumination: Final Gathering

Final Gathering is another method for calculating indirect lighting. It can be used on its own or in conjunction with global illumination. Final Gathering uses irradiance sampling and ambient occlusion to create the look of ambient and indirect lighting. When Final Gathering is enabled, rays are cast from the camera into the scene. When a ray intersects with a surface, a Final Gathering point is created that samples the irradiance value of the surface and determines how it is affected by other scene elements, such as nearby objects, lights, and light-emitting surfaces.

Final Gathering uses raytracing rather than photon casting. Each Final Gathering point that the camera shoots into the scene lands on a surface and then emits a number of Final Gathering primary rays, which gather information about the irradiance values and proximity of other scene elements. The information gathered by the rays is used to determine that the surface is shading normal at the Final Gathering point. Imagine a hemispherical dome of rays that are emitted from a point on a surface; the rays gather information about other surfaces in the scene. Like global illumination, this allows it to simulate color bleeding from nearby surfaces.

Light-Emitting Objects

One of the most interesting aspects of Final Gathering is that you can use objects as lights in a scene. An object that has a shader with a bright incandescent or ambient color value actually casts light in a scene. This works particularly well for situations in which geometry needs to cast light in a scene. For example, a cylinder can be used as a fluorescent lightbulb (see Figure 7.25). When a shader is assigned to the cylinder with a bright incandescent value and Final Gathering is enabled, the result is a very convincing lighting scheme.

In this exercise, you'll light the bicycle seen earlier in the chapter, using only objects with incandescent shaders. Polygon planes will be used as "light cards" to simulate the look of diffuse studio lighting. You'll find that it's easy to get a great-looking result from Final Gathering rendering while still using simple, standard Maya shaders.

1. Open the `bicycle_v01.ma` scene from the `chapter7\scenes` folder at the book's web page.

2. Open the Render Settings window. Make sure you are using mental ray for the renderer and click the Common tab.

3. Scroll to the bottom of the window, and expand the Render Options rollout. Make sure the Enable Default Light option is not checked.

   The Enable Default Light option is normally on so that when you create a test render in a scene with no lights, you can still see your objects. When you add a light to the scene, the default light is overridden and should no longer illuminate the objects in the scene.

However, since you won't be using actual lights in this scene, you need to deselect Enable Default Light.

FIGURE 7.25
A cylinder with an incandescent shader casts light in the scene when Final Gathering is enabled.

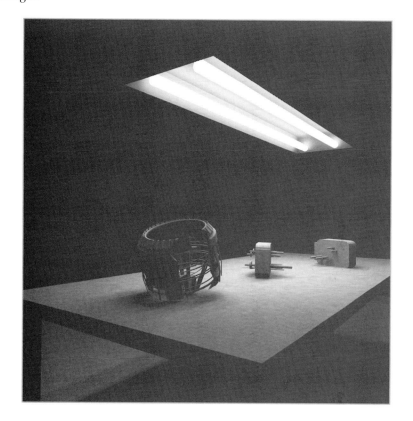

4. Switch to the Quality tab, and set Quality Presets to Production.

5. Create a quick test render using the renderCam camera. The scene should appear completely black, confirming that no lights are on in the scene.

6. Switch to the Indirect Lighting tab, scroll down, and activate Final Gathering.

7. Do another test render. The scene should still be black.

8. Select the renderCam camera in the Outliner, and open its Attribute Editor.

9. Switch to the renderCamShape tab, scroll down to the Environment section, and set Background Color to white.

10. Create another test render. Make sure renderCam is chosen as the rendering camera.

    You'll see the bicycle appear as the scene renders. There are no lights in the scene. However, the white color of the background is used in the Final Gathering calculations. You'll notice that the scene renders twice.

The Final Gathering render takes place in two stages:

a. In the first pass, Final Gathering projects rays from the camera through a hexagonal grid that looks like a low-resolution version of the image.

b. In the second stage, the Final Gathering points calculate irradiance values, and the image is actually rendered and appears at its proper quality.

You'll often notice that the first pass appears brighter than the final render.

The bicycle has simple shaders applied and no textures. The shadowing seen under the bicycle and in the details is an example of ambient occlusion that occurs as part of a Final Gathering render (see Figure 7.26).

FIGURE 7.26
The bicycle is rendered with no lights in the scene. The camera's Background Color value is used to calculate the Final Gathering points.

11. Set Background Color of renderCam to black.

12. Create a polygon plane, and apply a Lambert shader to the plane.

13. Set the Incandescence option of the plane's Lambert shader to white.

14. Use the Move and Rotate tools to position the plane above the bicycle at about a 45-degree angle. Use the following settings in the Channel Box for the plane:

Translate X: **0.0**

Translate Y: **36.0**

Translate Z: **25.0**

Rotate X: **45**

Rotate Y: **0**

Rotate Z: **0**

Scale X: **40**

Scale Y: **20**

Scale Z: **20**

15. Select the plane, and open the Attribute Editor to the pPlaneShape2 tab.

16. Expand the Render Stats rollout, and turn off Primary Visibility. This means that the plane still influences the lighting in the scene and can still be seen in reflections and refractions, but the plane itself is not seen by the rendering camera.

17. Create another test render from the renderCam camera. The bicycle appears much darker this time.

18. Select the pPlane2 shape, and open the Attribute Editor.

19. Select the tab for the plane's Lambert shader, and click the swatch next to Incandescence to open the Color Chooser.

20. Set the slider mode to HSV using the menu below the Color Chooser. Set the value slider (V) to **4**.

21. Create another test render. The bicycle should be more visible now compared to its appearance in the test render from step 17 (see Figure 7.27).

FIGURE 7.27
Raising the value of the incandescence on the shader's plane increases the illumination on the bicycle.

Using incandescent objects is a great way to simulate the diffuse light boxes used by photographers. You can easily simulate the lighting used in a studio by strategically placing incandescent planes around the bicycle. However, you'll notice that the lighting is somewhat blotchy. You can fix this using the Final Gathering settings on the Indirect Lighting tab of the Render Settings window.

The Final Gathering options in the render settings set the global quality of the Final Gathering render. Here is a brief description of what these settings do:

Accuracy This value determines the number of Final Gathering rays shot from the camera. Higher values increase render time. A value of 100 is fine for testing; a high-quality render typically uses 500 to 800 rays.

Point Density This setting determines the number of Final Gathering points generated by the rays. Increasing this value also increases quality and render time.

Point Interpolation This setting smoothes out the point calculation. Increasing this value improves the quality of the result without adding too much to render time. However, as with any smoothing operation, detail can be lost at higher values.

Primary Diffuse Scale Just like with global illumination and caustics, this scale brightens the resulting Final Gathering render.

Secondary Diffuse Bounces Enabling this option allows Final Gathering rays to bounce off a second diffuse surface before terminating. This increases realism as well as render time. Final Gathering rays do most of their work on the first or second bounce; beyond that, the calculations don't yield a significant difference.

Secondary Diffuse Scale Increasing the value of Secondary Diffuse Scale increases the influence of the Secondary Diffuse Bounces.

PER-SURFACE FINAL GATHERING SETTINGS

Individual surfaces can have their own Final Gathering settings located in the mental ray rollout in the surface's shape node. These settings will override the render settings and can be used as needed for optimizing renders.

---

22. In the Final Gathering options in your render settings, set Accuracy to **400**, Point Density to **2**, and Secondary Diffuse Bounces to **1**.

23. Create another test render (see Figure 7.28).

FIGURE 7.28
Increasing the Final Gathering values enhances the realism of the lighting.

The white polygon is reflected in the surface of the bicycle. The shader that is applied to the body is a very simple Phong-type shader, and it looks pretty good.

24. Save the scene as `bicycle_v03.ma`.

To see a version of the scene up to this point, open the `bicycle_v03.ma` scene from the `chapter7\scenes` folder at the book's web page.

Final Gathering Maps

Setting the Rebuild option (in the Final Gathering Map section of the Indirect Lighting tab of the Render Settings window) to Off causes mental ray to reuse any saved Final Gathering maps generated from previous renders. This saves a great deal of time when you are creating a final render. However, if the camera is moving and Final Gathering requires additional points for interpolation, new points are generated and appended to the saved map.

When Rebuild is set to Freeze, the scene is rendered with no changes to the Final Gathering map regardless of whether the scene requires additional points. This reduces flickering in animated sequences, but you need to make sure the scene has enough Final Gathering points generated before using the Freeze option.

If a scene has an animated camera, you can generate the Final Gathering map by rendering an initial frame with Rebuild set to On, moving the Time Slider until the camera is in a new position, and then setting Rebuild to Off and rendering again. Repeat this procedure until the path visible from the camera has been sufficiently covered with Final Gathering points. Then create the final render sequence with Rebuild set to Freeze. The following exercise demonstrates this technique:

1. Open the `bicycle_v04.ma` scene from the `chapter7\scenes` folder at the book's web page. In this scene, a camera named FGCam is animated around the bicycle.

The first 24 frames of the animation have been rendered using Final Gathering. In the Final Gathering Map section of the Render Settings window, the Rebuild attribute is set to On, so new Final Gathering points are calculated with each frame.

2. View the rendered sequence by choosing File ➢ View Sequence. The 24-frame sequence is found in the `chapter7\images` directory at the book's web page. The sequence is labeled `bicycle`. You can clearly see flickering in this version of the animation.

3. In the Final Gathering Map section, turn on Enable Map Visualizer. Set the timeline to frame 1, and create a test render using the FGCam camera.

4. When the render is complete, switch to the perspective view. In the viewport window disable Polygons in the Show menu. You can clearly see the Final Gathering points outlining the surface of the bicycle.

Notice that there are no points in the shape of the bike in areas that the camera could not see. The rays were blocked (see Figure 7.29).

5. In the Render Settings window, set Rebuild to Off. Set the timeline to **6**, and create another test render using the FGCam camera.

You'll notice that it takes less time to render, and the display of the Final Gathering points in the perspective view is updated. More points have been added to correspond with the FGCam's location on frame 6. The Final Gathering points are saved in a file named `default.fgmap`.

FIGURE 7.29
The Final Gathering
points are visible in
the scene after cre-
ating a test render.

**CERT
OBJECTIVE**

NEON LIGHTS

You can create convincing neon lights using light-emitting objects; an example is shown here. By
adding a glow effect to your incandescent shaders and rendering with Final Gathering, you can
make the neon lights look very realistic.

Here's a solid technique for creating this effect:

1. Create a series of curves to build the neon-light geometry. Shape them into letters or decorative elements.

2. Apply a Paint Effects brush to the curves to build the neon tubes.

3. Convert the brush strokes into NURBS or polygon geometry.

4. Apply a Blinn shader to the neon-tube geometry. In the incandescence channel of the shader, add a ramp texture.

5. To make the center of the tube brighter than the edges, connect a Sampler Info node to the ramp. Use the Connection Editor to connect the Facing Ratio attribute of the Sampler Info node to the V Coordinate attribute of the ramp. Make sure the ramp is set to V Ramp.

6. Edit the ramp so that its top (which corresponds to the center of the neon tube) is brighter than its bottom (which corresponds to the edges of the neon tube).

7. In the Special Effects rollout of the shader, increase the Glow Intensity setting. A value of **0.1** should be sufficient.

8. In the Hypershade, select the shaderGlow1 node, and open its Attribute Editor. Turn off Auto Exposure. This eliminates flickering problems that may occur if the scene is animated.

9. Turning off Auto Exposure causes the glow effect to be overly bright. In the Glow Attributes section of the shaderGlow1 node, lower the Glow Intensity setting. Finding the proper value takes some experimentation on a number of test renders.

   There is only one shaderGlow node for each Maya scene. This node applies the same settings to all of the glowing objects within a scene. The glow effect is a postprocess effect, so you won't see the glow applied in the render until all the other parts of the image have been rendered.

10. In the Render Settings window, make sure Renderer is set to mental ray.

11. In the Indirect Lighting tab, turn on Final Gathering.

12. Click the swatch next to Primary Diffuse Scale to open the Color Chooser. Raise the value above 1. A setting between 2 and 4 should be sufficient.

Surfaces near the neon tubes should have a high diffuse value so that they reflect the light emitted by the tubes. To see an example of neon lighting using Final Gathering, open the vegas.ma scene from the chapter7\scenes folder at the book's web page.

---

6. Make three more renders from frames 12, 18, and 24 (see Figure 7.30).

7. To speed the rendering of the Final Gathering points, on the Features tab in the Render Settings, change Render Mode to Final Gathering Only (see Figure 7.31).

8. When done rendering updates to the Final Gathering map, set Rebuild to Freeze, to prevent any more points being added.

9. Render a sequence of the first 24 frames of the animation, and compare this to the bicycle sequence. You can also view the bicycle_rebuild sequence in the chapter7\images directory at the book's web page. Be sure to set Render Mode back to Normal on the Features tab.

The flickering in the new sequence is greatly reduced using this technique.

10. Save the scene as **bicycle_v05.ma**.

To see a version of the sequence, open the `bicycle_v05.ma` scene from the `chapter7\scenes` folder at the book's web page.

FIGURE 7.30
Additional Final Gathering points are added to the existing map file each time a test render is created.

FIGURE 7.31
Changing Render Mode to Final Gathering Only saves time when creating Final Gathering points.

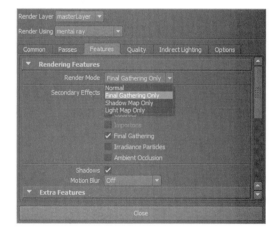

FINAL GATHERING PASS

You can render a special Final Gathering map render pass to automate the process described in the previous section. The purpose of this pass is to create a Final Gathering map for the entire scene before rendering the images. This can save time on subsequent renders if you do not need to change the lighting or if you need to recompute Final Gathering points for a specific set of frames or render layers. Once the Final Gathering map pass is created, you can specify the files generated by the pass in the Final Gathering Map section in the Indirect Lighting section of the Render Settings window. For more information on creating render passes, consult Chapter 12, "Introducing nParticles."

This system does not work if there are animated objects in the scene. If the Final Gathering map is generated and saved while an object is in one position, the same irradiance values are used on a subsequent frame after the object has moved to a new position. This can lead to a strange result. You can enable the Optimize For Animations option through the Final Gathering Mode menu in the Final Gathering Tracing section to help reduce Final Gathering flickering in scenes with animated objects.

The Diagnose Final Gathering option, in the Final Gathering Map section, color-codes the Final Gathering points so that you can easily distinguish the initial points created with the first render from points added during subsequent renders.

Other Final Gathering quality controls are found in the Final Gathering Quality and Final Gathering Tracing sections in the Indirect Lighting tab of the Render Settings window:

Optimize For Animations   Located in the Final Gather Mode menu, this option essentially automates the system described previously. It reduces flickering, but at the expense of accuracy.

Use Radius Quality Control   Located in the Final Gathering Mode menu, this setting has been largely replaced by the Point Interpolation setting. However, it can still be used if you prefer. If this option is enabled, the Point Interpolation setting is automatically disabled, and vice versa. Use Radius Quality Control corresponds to the Accuracy setting. It basically sets the sampling range for Final Gathering rays to search for irradiance information from nearby surfaces. The typical practice is to set Max Radius to 10 percent of the overall scene size and Min Radius to 10 percent of Max Radius. You also have the option of specifying the radius in terms of pixel size. These settings help reduce artifacts.

Filter   This attribute relates to using high dynamic range (HDR) images and will be discussed later in this chapter.

Falloff Start and Falloff Stop   These settings limit the distance Final Gathering rays can travel. This is especially important in a large scene where objects may be far apart. You can optimize render time by setting a range for these values. When a Final Gathering ray has reached its maximum distance as set by Falloff Stop, it samples any further irradiance and color values from the environment (set by the camera's Background Color attribute) and uses them to shade the surface. The falloff start begins a linear transition to the environment sampling, and the falloff stop is the end point for this transition as well as the farthest point a Final Gathering ray can travel. Think of the start and stop points as the beginning and end of a gradient. At the start portion of the gradient, surface sampling is at 100 percent, and the environment sampling is at 0 percent. At the stop point of the gradient, the surface sampling is at 0 percent, and the environment sampling is at 100 percent.

Adjusting the Falloff Start and Falloff Stop values can reduce render times even in an indoor scene. By default, the scene background color is black. If you set Falloff Start to 15 and Falloff Stop to 20 and render, the frame takes less time to render but comes out very dark in shadowed areas that are 15 to 20 units from a Final Gathering point. This is because the default black background is being blended into the surface color. If you feel too much detail is lost to the darkness, you can create an environment dome with a constant color or an HDR image, or you can simply set the render camera's background to a value greater than 0. Setting the value too high reduces contrast in the scene, similar to adding an ambient light. A low value between 0.25 and 0.5 should work well.

Reflections, Refractions, and Max Trace   These sliders set the maximum number of times a Final Gathering ray can be reflected (which creates a secondary ray) or refracted from reflective, glossy, or transparent surfaces. The default values are usually sufficient for most scenes.

MIDEFAULTOPTIONS NODE

You can access even more options for Global Illumination and Final Gathering settings by selecting the miDefaultOptions node. To find this node, open the Outliner and, from the Display menu, deselect DAG Options Only. Scroll down and select the miDefaultOptions node from the list, and open the Attribute Editor. You'll see the options described earlier as well as some options not otherwise available, such as separate red, green, and blue channels for Final Gathering Scale.

Using Lights with Final Gathering

The previous exercises demonstrated how Final Gathering can render a scene without lights by using only incandescent objects. However, for many situations, you'll want to combine Final Gathering with lights so that specular highlights and clear shadows are visible in the render. If you take a look outside on a sunny day, you'll see examples of direct lighting, cast shadows, indirect lighting, and ambient occlusion working together. Likewise, a typical photographer's studio combines bright lights, flashbulbs, and diffuse lights to create a harmonious composition. You'll also find that combining lights and Final Gathering produces a higher-quality render.

FINAL GATHERING AND GLOBAL ILLUMINATION

In many cases, the look of indirect lighting can be improved and rendering times can be reduced by using Final Gathering and Global Illumination at the same time. Final Gathering usually works fairly well on its own, but Global Illumination almost always needs a little help from Final Gathering to create a good-looking render. When Global Illumination and Final Gathering are enabled together, the Final Gathering secondary diffuse bounce feature no longer affects the scene; all secondary diffuse light bounces are handled by Global Illumination.

Image-Based Lighting

Image-based lighting (IBL) uses the color values of an image to light a scene. This can often be done without the help of additional lights. When you enable IBL, you have the choice of rendering the scene using Final Gathering, IBL with Global Illumination, or IBL with the mental ray Light Shader. This section will describe all three methods.

You can use high dynamic range (HDR) images with IBL. An HDR image is a 16- or 32-bit floating-point format image that stores multiple levels of exposure within a single image. Standard 8-bit formats store their color values as integers (whole numbers), whereas a 32-bit floating-point file can store colors as fractional values (numbers with a decimal). This means that the 8-bit formats cannot display a full range of luminance values, whereas the 16- or 32-bit floating-point images can. Multiple levels of exposure are available in HDR floating-point images, which can be used to create more dynamic and realistic lighting in your renders when you use IBL.

HDR images come in several formats, including HDR, OpenEXR (`.exr` extension), floating-point TIFFs, and Direct Draw Surface (DDS). Most often you'll use the HDR and OpenEXR image formats when working with IBL.

OpenEXRLoader

To view and use OpenEXR images in Maya, you'll need to enable the `OpenEXRLoader.mll` plug-in. It should be on by default, but occasionally it does not load when you start Maya. To load this plug-in, choose Window ➢ Settings/Preferences ➢ Plug-in Manager. From the list of plug-ins, select the Loaded and Auto Load boxes next to the `OpenEXRLoader.mll` plug-in (`OpenEXRLoader.bundle` on the Mac).

When an HDR image is used with IBL, the lighting in the scene looks much more realistic, using the full dynamic range of lighting available in the real world. When integrating CG into live-action shots, a production team often takes multiple HDR images of the set and then uses these images with IBL when rendering the CG elements. This helps the CG elements match perfectly with the live-action shots.

The downside of HDR images is that they require a lot of setup to create. However, you can download and use HDR images from several websites, such as `www.openfootage.net/`.

Several companies, such as Dosch Design (`www.doschdesign.com`), sell packages of HDR images on DVD that are very high quality.

HDR images are available in several styles, including angular (light probe), longitude/latitude (spherical), and vertical or horizontal cubic cross. mental ray supports angular and spherical. You can convert one style to another using a program such as Paul Debevec's HDRShop (`www.hdrshop.com`). Debevec is a pioneer in the field of computer graphics and virtual lighting. He is currently a researcher at the University of Southern California's Institute for Creative Technologies.

Enabling IBL

To use IBL in a scene, open the Render Settings window and make sure mental ray is chosen as the renderer. Switch to the Indirect Lighting tab, and click the Image Based Lighting Create button at the top of the window. This creates all the nodes you'll need in the scene to use IBL.

You can have more than one IBL node in a scene, but only one can be used to create the lighting.

IBL and Final Gathering

Using IBL with Final Gathering is similar to the concept of using light-emitting objects. When you enable IBL, a sphere is created, and you can map an HDR image to the sphere. The scene is rendered with Final Gathering enabled, and the luminance values of the image mapped to the sphere are used to create the lighting in the scene. You can use additional lights to create cast shadows and specular highlights or use IBL by itself. The following exercise takes you through the process of setting up this scenario.

You'll need a high dynamic range image (HDRI) to use for the mentalrayIbl node. You can download a number of these images free of charge from Debevec's website at www.pauldebevec .com/Probes/. Download the all_probes.zip file and unzip it; place the files in the sourceim-ages folder of your current project.

1. Open the bicycle_v01.ma scene from the chapter7\scenes folder at the book's web page.

2. Open the Render Settings window, and make sure the Render Using option is set to mental ray. Make sure the Enable Default Light option is not checked.

3. Switch to the Indirect Lighting tab, and click the Create button next to Image Based Lighting. This creates the mentalrayIbl1 node, which is a sphere scaled to fit the contents of the scene.

4. Select the mentalrayIbl1 node in the Outliner, and open its Attribute Editor.

5. Click the folder icon next to the Image Name field. Choose the building_probe.hdr image from the images you downloaded from www.pauldebevec.com/Probes/.

6. Connect this image to the mentalrayIbl node in the scene.

7. The image is in the Angular mapping style, so set Mapping to Angular.

8. Expand the Light Emission rollout and check Emit Light. Change the Quality setting to **0.5**.

    When the Emit Light option is enabled in the mentalrayIbl node, the image used for the IBL node emits light as if the image itself were made up of directional lights. Each direc-tional light gets a color value based on a sampling taken from the image mapped to the sphere. You can control the overall quality with a single slider.

9. Render a test frame to see the effects of the Light Emission (see Figure 7.32).

10. In the Render Settings window, enable Final Gathering.

11. Create a test render using the renderCam camera.

    In this case, you'll see that the image is blown out. You can also see the HDR image in the background of the scene.

FIGURE 7.32
The scene is lit using the HDR image as a light source.

12. In the Attribute Editor for the mentalrayIblShape1 node, scroll down to Render Stats, and turn off Primary Visibility.

13. Enable Adjust Final Gathering Color Effects. Doing so enables the Color Gain and Color Offset sliders. Set the Color Gain slider to a medium gray.

14. Create another test render (see Figure 7.33).

FIGURE 7.33
The settings on the mentalrayIblShape1 node are adjusted in the Attribute Editor. The scene is lit using the HDR image and Final Gathering.

15. Save the scene as **bicycle_v06.ma**.

To see a version of the scene, open the bicycle_v06.ma scene in the chapter7\scenes folder at the book's web page. Note that you will need to connect the IBL node to the building_probe .hdr image in order for this scene to render correctly.

You can see that the bicycle is now lit entirely by the HDR image. The HDR image is also visible in the reflective surfaces of the bike. If you want to disable the visibility of the reflections, turn off Visible As Environment (in the Render Stats section).

If you need to adjust the size and position of the IBL sphere, turn off the Infinite option at the top of the node's Attribute Editor. You can adjust the quality of the lighting using the Final Gathering controls in the Render Settings window.

ADDITIONAL IBL TECHNIQUES

The IBL node can be used to emit photons into the scene, both global illumination and caustics. This can be used in conjunction with Final Gathering or with global illumination alone.

You'll get better results combining global illumination with either Final Gathering or the IBL Light Shader. You can also turn on Caustics in the Render Settings window if you want create caustic light effects from a surface reflecting the IBL.

You can use the Global Illumination settings in the Render Settings window as well as the Photon Emission settings in the mentalrayIbl node to tune the look of the photons. By default, photons emitted from the IBL node are stored in the map at the moment they hit a surface. This makes the global illumination render fast and work well if global illumination is used by itself.

Physical Sun and Sky

mental ray provides a special network of lights and shaders that can accurately emulate the look of sunlight for outdoor scenes. Using the Physical Sun and Sky network requires rendering with Final Gathering. It's very easy to set up and use.

Enabling Physical Sun and Sky

To create the Physical Sun and Sky network, use the controls in the Indirect Lighting tab of the Render Settings window:

1. Open the streetCorner_v04.ma scene from the chapter7\scenes folder at the book's web page.

2. Open the Render Settings window, and make sure Render Using is set to mental ray.

3. Switch to the Indirect Lighting tab in the Render Settings window, and click the Create button for Physical Sun And Sky.

   Clicking the Create button creates a network of nodes that generates the look of sunlight. These include the mia_physicalsun, mia_physicalsky, and mia_exposure simple nodes. You'll notice that there is a directional light named sunDirection that has been added to the scene. To control the lighting of the scene, you'll change the orientation of the light. The other light attributes (position, scale, intensity, color, and so on) will not affect the lighting of the scene. To change the lighting, you need to edit the mia_physicalsky node in the Attribute Editor.

4. Select the sunDirection light in the Outliner, and use the Move tool to raise it up in the scene so that you can see it clearly. The position of the sun will not change the lighting in the scene.

5. In the Render Settings window, make sure Final Gathering is enabled. It should be turned on by default when you create the physical sun nodes.

6. Open the Render View window, and create a test render from the renderCam camera.

7. Store the rendered image in the Render View window.

The rendered image includes cast shadows from the sun, ambient occlusion created by Final Gathering, and a sky gradient in the background that is reflected in the windows of the building.

8. Select the sunDirection light, and set its Rotate X value to **-150**.

9. Create another test render, and compare it with the first.

When you change the orientation of the sunDirection light, it affects the color of the lighting as well to simulate accurately the lighting you see at different times of day.

10. Select the sunDirection node, and use the following settings:

Rotate X: **-164.156**

Rotate Y: **12.0**

Rotate Z: **4.397**

11. Select the sunDirection node in the Outliner, and open its Attribute Editor.

12. Select the mia_physicalsky1 tab. In the Shading rollout, use the following settings:

Sun Disk Intensity: **0.5**

Sun Disk Scale: **2**

Sun Glow Intensity: **0.5**

13. Create another test render. With these settings, the sun is actually visible in the sky (see the bottom image of Figure 7.34).

14. Save the scene as **streetCorner_v05.ma**.

To see a finished version of the scene, open the streetCorner_v05.ma scene from the chapter7\scenes folder at the book's web page.

PHYSICAL SUN AND SKY BACKGROUND

Note that the sky in the background of the rendered images will not appear when importing into compositing software unless you choose to ignore the alpha channel.

FIGURE 7.34
Changing the rotation of the sunDirection's light changes the lighting to emulate different times of day.

Editing the Sky Settings

To change the look of the sky in the scene, use the settings found on the mia_physicalsky node.

A number of settings in the Attribute Editor for the sunDirection node help define the color and quality of the sky and the sun in the render. Here is a brief description of some of these settings (see Figure 7.35):

Multiplier This setting adjusts the overall brightness of the sky.

R, G, and B Unit Conversions These settings adjust the coloring of the sky in the R (red), G (green), and B (blue) channels when these values are changed incrementally.

Haze This setting adds haziness to the sky.

Red/Blue Shift Use this option to shift between warm and cool lighting in a scene. Negative numbers shift colors toward blue; positive numbers shift colors toward red. The value range should be kept between –1 and 1.

Saturation The saturation is physically accurate at a value of 1.0. Changing the value to 0.0 removes the color values causing a grayscale image. Increasing it to its maximum value of 2.0 raises the color intensities.

FIGURE 7.35
The settings for changing the look of the physical sky in the render.

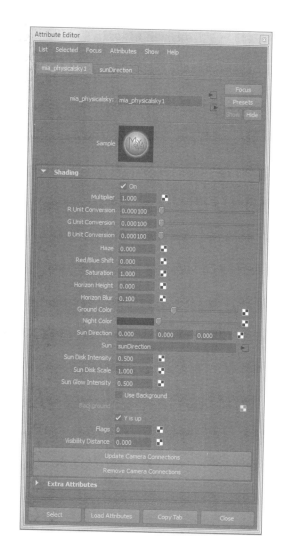

Horizon Height and Blur   These settings change the position and blurriness of the horizon line visible in the renders behind the geometry.

Ground Color   This option changes the color of the area below the horizon. Note that the horizon does appear in reflective shaders applied to the geometry in the scene.

Night Color   This option affects the color of the sky when the sun is rotated close to 180 degrees.

Sun Direction   This setting rotates the sunDirection light in the scene to change the sun direction. Fields should be left at 0.

Sun   This option connects the sun settings to a different light in the scene.

Sun Disk Intensity, Sun Disk Scale, and Sun Glow Intensity   These settings affect the look of the sun when it is visible in the render.

Use Background   This option adds a texture for the environment background. Use this setting as opposed to the standard Maya environment shaders.

Y is up   Defines which axis points to up in the world. When unchecked, the sun and sky are oriented to Z up.

Flags   This parameter is for internal testing and should always be set to 0.

Visibility Distance   Defines the distance at which the haze effect becomes hazier.

Update Camera Connections   This button adds a new renderable camera to the scene after you create the Physical Sun and Sky network. The network applies specific shaders to all of the renderable cameras in the scene when it is first created. Any new cameras added to the scene will not have these connections enabled by default. Click this button each time you add a new camera to the scene.

Remove Camera Connections   This option removes all cameras from the Physical Sun and Sky network.

If you need to delete the Physical Sun and Sky network from the scene, open the Render Settings window and click the Delete button for the Physical Sun And Sky attribute.

mental ray Area Lights

mental ray area lights are designed to create a simulation of light sources in the real world. Most lights in Maya emit light rays from an infinitely small point in space. In the real world, light sources are three-dimensional objects, such as a lightbulb or a window, that have a defined size.

Lighting a scene using standard lights, such as the point and spotlights, often requires additional fill lighting to compensate for the fact that these lights do not behave like real-world light sources. Area lights are designed as an alternative to this approach. A mental ray area light is essentially an array of spotlights. The array creates a 3D light source, which results in more realistic light behaviors, especially with regard to shadow casting. The downside is that area lights often take longer to render, so they are not always ideal for every situation.

Follow the steps in this exercise to understand how to use area lights in mental ray:

1. Open the hospitalRoom_v01.ma scene from the chapter7\scenes folder at the book's web page.

2. Create an area light (Create ➤ Lights ➤ Area Light). Position the light using the following settings:

   Translate X: **-6.842**

   Translate Y: **12.424**

   Translate Z: **-5.567**

   Rotate X: **-90**

   Scale X: **1.32**

   Scale Y: **2.736**

   Scale Z: **4.639**

3. Open the Render Settings window, and set Render Using to mental ray.

4. Open the Render View window, and create a test render from the renderCam camera.

5. Store the image in the render view.

The render looks very blown out and grainy. You can reduce the grainy quality by increasing the shadow rays used on the light. However, there is something important and potentially confusing that you should know about using a standard Maya area light with mental ray. The light as it stands right now is not actually taking advantage of mental ray area light properties. To make the light a true mental ray area light, you need to enable the Use Light Shape attribute under the mental ray rollout under the Area Light section. Until you enable this attribute, you'll have a hard time getting the area light to look realistic.

6. Open the Attribute Editor for areaLight1. Switch to the AreaLightShape1 tab.

7. In the mental ray ➤ Area Light rollout, activate Use Light Shape and create another test render (see Figure 7.36).

FIGURE 7.36
The mental ray area light is enabled when Use Light Shape is activated in the Attribute Editor.

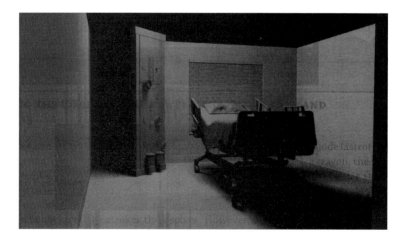

The new render is less blown out, and the shadows are much softer (although still grainy).

Unlike standard Maya area lights, the intensity of mental ray area lights is not affected by the scale of the light. To change the intensity, use the Intensity slider at the top of the Attribute Editor. The shape of the shadows cast by mental ray area lights is affected by the shape specified in the Type menu and the scale of the light.

To improve the quality of the shadows, increase the High Samples setting. The High Samples and Low Samples settings control the quality of the shadow in reflected surfaces. These can be left at a low value to improve render efficiency.

8. Set Light Shape Type to Sphere, and increase High Samples to **32**.

9. Turn on the Visible option.

10. Create a test render, and compare the render to the previous versions (see Figure 7.37).

FIGURE 7.37
The area light is
visible in the
render.

Area lights come with several different preset shapes. The Sphere type area light is similar to a point light, but instead of emitting light from an infinitely small point in space, it emits from a spherical volume, making it ideal for simulating light cast from things such as lightbulbs.

You can also create an area light that behaves like a spotlight.

11. Place an area light within each of the light fixtures in the ceiling. You can duplicate the area light and move the duplicate into a new position.

12. Create another test render (see Figure 7.38).

FIGURE 7.38
The shape of the
spotlight creates
shadows based
on the area light
settings.

13. Save the scene as **hospitalRoom_v05.ma**.

The light quality and shadow shape remain the same as in the previous renders. However, switching the light Type setting to Spotlight adds the penumbra shape you expect from a spotlight. This allows you to combine the properties of spotlights and mental ray area lights. The Visible option in the mental ray settings does not work when using a spotlight as the original light.

To see a version of the scene, open the hospitalRoom_v05.ma scene from the chapter7\ scenes folder at the book's web page.

Light Shaders

mental ray has a number of light shaders that can be applied to lights in a scene. The purpose of these shaders is to extend the capabilities of Maya lights to allow for more lighting options. When a mental ray shader is applied to a Maya light, specific attributes on the original light node are overridden. The light's attributes can then be set using the controls on the light shader node.

Some shaders, such as the Mib_blackbody and Mib_cie_d shaders, are very simple. These two shaders translate the color of the light as a temperature specified in kelvin. Other shaders are more complex, providing a number of attributes that can be used in special circumstances.

This section will discuss some of the light shaders and how you can use them in Maya scenes.

Physical Light Shader

The Physical Light shader is a type of shadow-casting light that is used in combination with indirect lighting (Final Gathering, global illumination) to create more physically accurate light behavior. There are also certain materials, such as the mental ray Architectural materials (mia), that are designed to work with physical lights (these materials are discussed in Chapter 8, "mental ray Shading Techniques").

Physical lights always cast raytrace shadows, and the falloff rate for the light obeys the inverse square law, just like lights in the real world. This law states that the intensity of light is inversely proportional to the square of the distance from the source. So, the light intensity decreases rapidly as the light travels from the source.

Physical lights are easy to set up and use. Once you are comfortable with them, consider using them whenever you use indirect lighting, such as global illumination and Final Gathering. This exercise will show you how to create a physical light. The scene has a number of standard Maya spotlights positioned to match the recessed lighting fixtures in the ceiling; six of these lights are currently hidden so that you can focus on just two of the lights. Final Gathering has been enabled for the scene.

1. Open the hospitalRoom_v05.ma scene from the chapter7\scenes folder at the book's web page.

2. Select areaLight1 and open its Attribute Editor.

3. Under mental ray, expand the Custom Shaders rollout and click the checkered box to the right of the Light Shader field.

4. From the Create Render Node pop-up, select the MentalRay Lights heading under the mental ray section (see Figure 7.39).

FIGURE 7.39

Apply the Physical Light shader to spotLight1.

5. Click the physical_light button to create a light shader. This connects the shader to the area light.

The attributes for the physical_light shader will open in the Attribute Editor. You'll see the settings for the shader:

Color The Color setting controls the color and intensity of the light by adjusting the color values in the color swatch.

Cone The Cone setting is used when the Physical Light shader is applied to mental ray spot and area spotlights to define the cone angle and penumbra. Higher values create a softer penumbra.

Threshold The Threshold setting defines a minimum illumination value. When you increase the threshold, the lighting in the scene is contracted around the brighter areas, giving you more control over the precise areas of light in the scene. This can cause hard edges to appear around the edges of light cast by spotlights even after you adjust the Cone value.

Cosine Exponent Similar to the Cone setting, the Cosine Exponent attribute contracts the area of light cast when the shader is applied to mental ray area lights. As the value of Cosine Exponent increases, the light cast by the area light becomes more focused.

6. Open the Hypershade editor.

7. Switch to the Utilities tab. (If the tabs do not appear at the top of the Hypershade, choose Tabs ➢ Revert To Default Tabs, and click OK in any warning windows that pop up.)

8. Select the spotlight2 node in the Outliner, and open its Attribute Editor.

9. MMB-drag the physicalLight1 shader from the Utilities section of the Hypershade to the Light Shader field in the mental ray section of areaLight2's Attribute Editor. This means that both area lights are connected to the same physical light shader.

10. Repeat step 9 to add the physical light shader to areaLight3 and areaLight4.

11. Create a test render from the renderCam camera (see Figure 7.40).

FIGURE 7.40
Render the scene
using a physical
light.

FIGURE 7.40
Render the scene
using a physical
light.

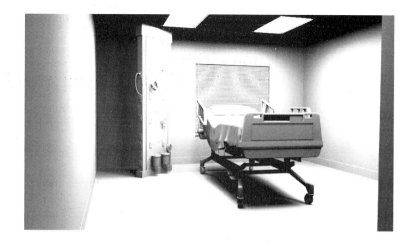

12. Store the render in the Render View window.

The lighting looks too bright. To fix this, you'll use the Color swatch value in physical_
light1's Attribute Editor. The default value for the light is 1000.

13. Click the color swatch to open the Color Chooser window. Change the lower-right menu
to HSV. Change the Value cell to **500**.

14. Create a new test render. The room is darker but the lighting looks a bit blown out, and it
does not look as though the lights are accurately lighting the room (see Figure 7.41). You
can fix this by applying a tone-mapping lens shader to the renderCam camera.

FIGURE 7.41
The physical light
shader creates a
blown-out look to
the render.

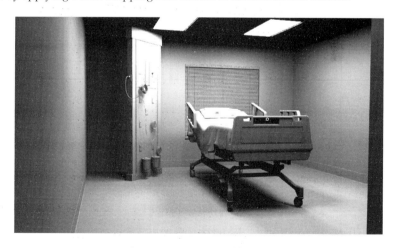

15. Save the scene as **hospitalRoom_v06.ma**.

To see a version of this scene, open hospitalRoom_v06.ma from the chapter7\scenes folder at the book's web page.

Tone Mapping

Rendering using physical lights often results in a very blown-out image. This is because computer monitors are unable to display the full range of luminance values created by physical lights. To correct this, you may need to apply a tone-mapping lens shader to the rendering camera (mia_exposure_photographic or mia_exposure_simple).

1. Continue with the scene from the previous section, or open the hospitalRoom_v06.ma scene from the chapter7\scenes folder at the book's web page.

2. Open the render settings and turn on Final Gather. Set Secondary Bounce to 1.

3. Create a test render and store the image for comparison.

4. Select the renderCam camera in the Outliner, and open its Attribute Editor.

5. Scroll down to the mental ray rollout, and click the checker icon next to Lens Shader.

6. In the Create Render Node window, select Lenses from the mental ray section.

7. Click the mia_exposure_simple button to attach a lens shader to the camera. (Lens shaders are explored further in Chapter 8.)

8. Create a test render using the renderCam camera. You'll see that the bounced light created by Final Gathering is more visible and the lights look less blown out (see Figure 7.42).

FIGURE 7.42
Applying a lens shader to the camera corrects the tonal values of the image so that it appears correct on a computer monitor.

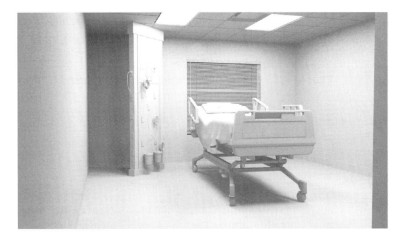

9. The room is starting to look more properly lit. Open the Attribute Editor for the physical_light1 node, and continue to adjust the Color value. To do so, click the color swatch to open the Color Chooser window. You can stick with a white color or tint the light by changing the lower-right menu to RGB and entering new values into the R, G, and B cells.

10. Save the scene as **hospitalRoom_v07.ma**.

To see a version of the scene, open the hospitalRoom_v07.ma scene from the chapter7\ scenes folder at the book's web page.

Photometric Lights and Profiles

Photometric lights allow you to attach light profiles created by light manufacturers so that you can simulate specific lights in your scenes. These profiles are often available on light manufacturers' websites. The profile itself is a text file in the IES format.

The profiles simulate the qualities of the light, such as falloff and the influence of the light fixture. A light profile can include the sconces and fixtures attached to the light itself. This is most helpful in creating accurate architectural renderings.

To use a photometric light, you can attach the Pmib_light_photometric shader to a point light and then attach the profile to the light using the Profile field in the shader's attributes. You can also skip using the shader altogether and attach the IES profile directly to the point light in the Light Profile field available in point lights.

In many cases, you'll need to adjust the shadows cast by lights using a profile to make them more realistic. Use raytrace shadows, and adjust the Shadow Rays and Light Radius values to improve the look of the shadows.

If you'd like to experiment using light profiles, you can download IES-format light profiles from www.lsi-industries.com/products/products-home.aspx. Browse to any of their lights, and you can download the IES photometrics.

BONUS MOVIES

You'll find some movies on this book's web page that cover the use of additional mental ray lighting nodes, such as the portal light and participating media. These nodes can help create atmospheric type effects like fog and light rays. You can find the movies in the bonusMovies folder.

The Bottom Line

Use shadow-casting lights. Lights can cast either depth map or raytrace shadows. Depth map shadows are created from an image projected from the shadow-casting light, which reads the depth information of the scene. Raytrace shadows are calculated by tracing rays from the light source to the rendering camera.

Master It Compare mental ray depth map shadows to raytrace shadows. Render the crystalGlobe.ma scene using soft raytrace shadows.

Render with global illumination.   Global illumination simulates indirect lighting by emitting photons into a scene. Global illumination photons react with surfaces that have diffuse shaders. Caustics use photons that react to surfaces with reflective shaders. Global illumination works particularly well in indoor lighting situations.

> **Master It**   Render the rotunda_v01.ma scene, found in the chapter7\scenes folder at the book's web page, using global illumination.

Render with Final Gathering.   Final Gathering is another method for creating indirect lighting. Final Gathering points are shot into the scene from the rendering camera. Final Gathering includes color bleeding and ambient occlusion shadowing as part of the indirect lighting. Final Gathering can be used on its own or in combination with global illumination.

> **Master It**   Create a fluorescent lightbulb from geometry that can light a room.

Use image-based lighting.   Image-based lighting (IBL) uses an image to create lighting in a scene. High dynamic range images (HDRIs) are usually the most effective source for IBL. There are three ways to render with IBL: Final Gathering, global illumination, and with the light shader. These can also be combined if needed.

> **Master It**   Render the bicycle scene using the Uffizi Gallery probe HDR image available at http://ict.debevec.org/~debevec/Probes.

Render using the Physical Sun and Sky network.   The Physical Sun and Sky network creates realistic sunlight that's ideal for outdoor rendering.

> **Master It**   Render a short animation showing the street corner at different times of day.

Understand mental ray area lights.   mental ray area lights are activated in the mental ray section of an area light's shape node when the Use Light Shape option is enabled. mental ray area lights render realistic, soft raytrace shadows. The light created from mental ray area lights is emitted from a three-dimensional array of lights as opposed to an infinitely small point in space.

> **Master It**   Build a lamp model that realistically lights a scene using an area light.

Chapter 8

mental ray Shading Techniques

A *shader* is a rendering node that defines the material qualities of a surface. When you apply a shading node to your modeled geometry, you use the shader's settings to determine how the surface will look when it's rendered. Will it appear as shiny plastic? Rusted metal? Human skin? The shader is the starting point for answering these questions. Shading networks are created when one or more nodes are connected to the channels of the shader node. These networks can range from simple to extremely complex. The nodes that are connected to shaders are referred to as *textures*. They can be image files created in other software packages or procedural (computer-generated) patterns, or they can be special nodes designed to create a particular effect.

The Autodesk® Maya® software comes with a number of shader nodes that act as starting points for creating various material qualities. The mental ray® plug-in also comes with its own special shader nodes that expand the library of available materials. Since the mental ray rendering plug-in is most often used to create professional images and animations, this book emphasizes mental ray techniques. You'll learn how to use mental ray shaders to create realistic images.

In this chapter, you will learn to:

♦ Understand shading concepts

♦ Apply reflection and refraction blur

♦ Use mia materials

♦ Understand mila shading layers

♦ Render contours

Shading Concepts

Shaders are sets of specified properties that define how a surface reacts to lighting in a scene. A mental ray material is a text file that contains a description of those properties organized in a way that the software understands. In Maya, the Hypershade provides you with a graphical user interface so that you can edit and connect shaders without writing or editing the text files themselves.

The terms *shader* and *material* are synonymous; you'll see them used interchangeably throughout this book and the Maya interface. mental ray also uses shaders to determine properties for lights, cameras, and other types of render nodes. For example, special lens shaders are applied to cameras to create effects such as depth of field.

THE MENTAL RAY PLUG-IN

mental ray is a rendering plug-in that is included with Maya. It is a professional-quality photore-alistic renderer used throughout the industry in film, television, architectural visualization, and anywhere photorealism is required.

Learning mental ray takes time and practice. Even though it's a plug-in, you'll find that it is as deep and extensive as Maya itself. mental ray includes a library of custom shading nodes that work together to extend the capabilities of mental ray. There are a lot of these nodes—many more than can be covered in this book.

When approaching mental ray as a rendering option, you can quickly become overwhelmed by the number of shading nodes in the mental ray section of the Hypershade. When these shading nodes are coupled with the mental ray–specific attributes found on standard Maya nodes, it can be difficult to know what to use in a particular situation. Think of mental ray as a large toolkit filled with a variety of tools that can be used in any number of ways. Some tools you'll use all the time, some you'll need only for specific situations, and some you may almost never use. You'll also find that, over time, as your understanding of and experience with mental ray grows, you may change your working style and use particular nodes more often. As you work with mental ray, expand your knowledge and experience through study and experimentation.

In this chapter, you'll be introduced to the most commonly used nodes, which will make you more comfortable using them in professional situations. There should be enough information in this chapter to give the everyday Maya user a variety of options for shading and rendering using mental ray. If you decide that you'd like to delve deeper into more advanced techniques, we recommend reading the mental ray shading guide that is part of the Maya documentation, as well as Boaz Livny's excellent book *mental ray for Maya, 3ds Max, and XSI* (Sybex, 2008).

Before starting this chapter, make sure that you are familiar with using and applying standard Maya shaders, such as the Lambert, Blinn, Phong, Ramp, Surface, and Anisotropic shaders. You should be comfortable making basic connections in the Hypershade and creating renders in the Render View window. You should understand how to use Maya 2D and 3D textures, such as Fractal, Ramp, and Checker. Review Chapter 7, "Lighting with mental ray," for background on lighting with mental ray. Many of the issues discussed in this chapter are directly related to lighting and mental ray lighting nodes.

This section focuses on shaders applied to geometry to determine surface quality. Three key concepts that determine how a shader makes a surface react to light are diffusion, reflection, and refraction. Generally speaking, light rays are reflected or absorbed or pass through a surface. Diffusion and reflection are two ways in which light rays bounce off a surface and back into the environment. Refraction refers to how a light ray is bent as it passes through a transparent surface. This section reviews these three concepts as well as other fundamentals that are important to understand before you start working with the shaders in a scene.

Maya Standard Shaders and mental ray Materials

The Maya standard shaders are found in the left list in the Hypershade window when you click the Surface heading under Maya (as shown here). The most often used standard shaders are Anisotropic, Blinn, Lambert, Phong, and Phong E. You can use any of these shaders when rendering with mental ray.

The mental ray materials (also referred to as *shaders*) are found in the left list in the Hypershade window when you click Materials under mental ray (as shown here). The shaders will work only when rendering with mental ray.

continues

(continued)

This chapter will discuss some aspects of working with the standard Maya shaders, but for the most part it will focus on the most often-used mental ray shaders. If you are unfamiliar with the standard shaders, we recommend you review the Maya documentation.

Diffusion

Diffusion describes how a light ray is reflected off a rough surface. Think of light rays striking concrete. Concrete is a rough surface covered in tiny bumps and crevices. As a light ray hits the bumpy surface, it is reflected back into the environment at different angles, which diffuse the reflection of light across the surface (see Figure 8.1).

FIGURE 8.1
Light rays that hit a rough surface are reflected back into the environment at different angles, diffusing light across the surface.

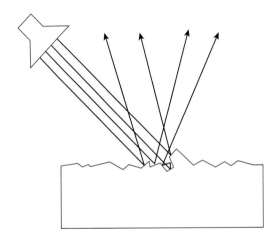

You see the surface color of the concrete mixed with the color of the lighting, but you generally don't see the reflected image of nearby objects. A sheet of paper, a painted wall, and clothing are examples of diffuse surfaces.

In standard Maya shaders, the amount of diffusion is controlled using the Diffuse slider. As the value of the Diffuse slider is increased, the surface appears brighter because it is reflecting more light back into the environment.

Reflection

When a surface is perfectly smooth, light rays bounce off the surface and back into the environment. The angle at which they bounce off the surface is equivalent to the angle at which they strike the surface—this is the *incidence angle*. This type of reflection is known as a *specular* reflection. You can see the reflected image of surrounding objects on the surface of smooth, reflective objects. Mirrors, polished wood, and opaque liquids are examples of reflective surfaces. A specular highlight is a reflection of the light source on the surface of the object (see Figure 8.2).

Logically, smoother surfaces, or surfaces that have a specular reflectivity, have less diffuse. However, many surfaces are composed of layers (think of glossy paper) that have both diffuse and specular reflectivity.

FIGURE 8.2
Light rays that hit a smooth surface are reflected back into the environment at an angle equivalent to the incidence of the light angle.

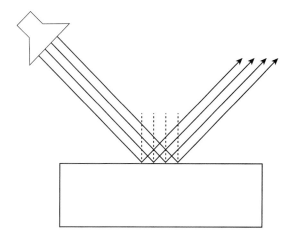

A glossy reflection occurs when the surface is not perfectly smooth but not so rough as to diffuse the light rays completely. The reflected image on a surface is blurry and bumpy and otherwise imperfect. Glossy surfaces can represent those surfaces that fit between diffuse reflectivity and specular reflectivity.

Refraction

A transparent surface can change the direction of the light rays as they pass through the surface (see Figure 8.3). The bending of light rays can distort the image of objects on the other side of the surface. Think of an object placed behind a glass of water. The image of the object as you look through the glass of water is distorted relative to an unobstructed view of the object. Both the glass and the water in the glass bend the light rays as they pass through.

FIGURE 8.3
Refraction changes the direction of light rays as they pass through a transparent surface.

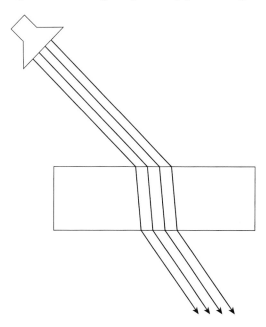

Shaders use a refractive index value to determine how refractions will be calculated. The refraction index is a value that describes the amount by which the speed of the light rays is reduced as it travels through a transparent medium, as compared to the speed of light as it travels through a vacuum. The reduction in speed is related to the angle in which the light rays are bent as they move through the material. A refraction index of 1 means the light rays are not bent. Glass typically has a refractive index between 1.5 and 1.6; water has a refractive index of 1.33.

If the refracting surface has imperfections, this can further scatter the light rays as they pass through the surface. This creates a blurry refraction.

Refraction in Maya is available only when raytracing is enabled (mental ray uses raytracing by default). The controls for refraction are found in the Raytrace section of the Attribute Editor of standard Maya shaders. A shader must have some amount of transparency before refraction has any visible effect.

The Fresnel Effect

The *Fresnel effect* is named for the nineteenth-century French physicist Augustin-Jean Fresnel (pronounced with a silent *s*). This effect describes the amount of reflection and refraction that occurs on a surface as the viewing angle changes. The *glancing angle* is the angle at which you view a surface. If you are standing in front of a wall, the wall is perpendicular to your viewing angle, and thus the glancing angle is 0. If you are on the beach looking out across the ocean, the glancing angle of the surface of the water is very high. The Fresnel effect states that as the glancing angle increases, the surface becomes more reflective than refractive. It's easy to see objects in water as you stare straight down into water (low glancing angle); however, as you stare across the surface of water, the reflectivity increases, and the reflection of the sky and the environment makes it increasingly difficult to see objects in the water.

Opaque, reflective objects also demonstrate this effect. As you look at a billiard ball, the environment is more easily seen reflected on the edges of the ball as they turn away from you than on the parts of the ball that are perpendicular to your view (see Figure 8.4).

FIGURE 8.4
A demonstration of the Fresnel effect on reflective surfaces: the reflectivity increases on the parts of the sphere that turn away from the camera.

Anisotropy

Anisotropic reflections appear on surfaces that have directionality to their roughness, which causes the reflection of light to spread in one direction more than another. When you look at the surface of a compact disc, you see the tiny grooves that are created when data is written to the disc to create the satin-like anisotropic reflections. Brushed metal, hair, and satin are all examples of materials that have anisotropic specular reflections.

The resulting stretch or compression of an anisotropic reflection is defined in U and V directions. Anisotropy works in conjunction with the UV coordinates defined on a piece of geometry. (UV texture layout will be covered in Chapter 9, "Texture Mapping").

Creating Blurred Reflections and Refractions Using Standard Maya Shaders

Standard Maya shaders, such as the Blinn and Phong shaders, take advantage of mental ray reflection and refraction blurring to simulate realistic material behaviors. These options are available in the mental ray section of the shader's Attribute Editor. As you may have guessed, since these attributes appear in the mental ray rollout of the shader's Attribute Editor, the effect created by these settings will appear only when you are rendering with mental ray. They do not work when you are using other rendering options, such as Maya Software.

Reflection Blur

Reflection blur is easy to use, and it is available for any of the standard Maya shaders that have reflective properties, such as Blinn, Phong, Anisotropic, and Ramp. This exercise demonstrates how to add reflection blur to a Blinn shader. This scene contains a model of a coffeemaker above a checkered ground plane.

1. Open the `reflectionBlur.ma` file from the `chapter8\scenes` folder at the book's web page (`www.sybex.com/go/masteringmaya2015`).

2. In the Outliner, select the glass surface from the coffeePot hierarchy. Assign a Blinn shader to the glass pot, and name the shader **glass_MAT**.

QUICKLY ASSIGN A SHADER TO A SURFACE

There are several ways to assign a shader to a surface quickly:

◆ Many standard Maya shaders are available in the Rendering shelf. You can select an object in a scene and click one of the shader icons on the shelf. This creates a new shader and applies it to the selected object at the same time. The names of the shaders appear on the help line in the lower left of the Maya interface.

◆ Another way to apply a shader is to select the object in the viewport window, right-click it, and choose Assign New Material from the bottom end of the marking menu. This will open a window with a list of material bases.

◆ You can select the object, switch to the Rendering menu set, and choose Lighting/Shading ➢ Assign New Material.

---

3. In the Common Material attributes rollout of the glass shader, set Diffuse to **0**, and set Transparency to white so that you can see inside the coffee pot.

4. In the Specular Shading rollout, set Specular Color to white and set Reflectivity to 1.

5. Change Eccentricity to **0.2** and Specular Roll Off to **0.8**. The Eccentricity setting controls the intensity of the "hot spot" of the specular highlight. The Specular Roll Off setting controls the surface's ability to reflect its surroundings; however, when raytracing, this has no effect on the reflection. In this raytraced scene, Specular Roll Off has been raised to decrease the softness of the specular highlight, giving a more glasslike appearance to the shield.

6. The mental ray renderer has already been selected in this scene. Render the scene in the Render View window from the persp camera.

7. Store the image in the Render View window.

8. Scroll down in the Attribute Editor of glass_MAT, expand the mental ray rollout, and increase Mi Reflection Blur to **2** (see Figure 8.5).

9. Create another test render, and compare this to the render in the previous step (see Figure 8.6). You can see how the reflection of the checkered pattern now appears blurred.

Mi Reflection Blur Limit sets the number of times the reflection blur itself is seen in other reflective surfaces. Increasing the Reflection Rays value increases the quality of the blurring, making it appear finer. Notice that the reflection becomes increasingly blurry as the distance between the reflective surface and the reflected object increases.

Many surfaces are more reflective than you may realize. An unpolished wooden tabletop or even asphalt can have a small amount of reflection. Adding a low reflectivity value plus reflection blurring to many surfaces increases the realism of the scene.

Refraction Blur

Refraction blur is similar to reflection blur. It blurs the objects that appear behind a transparent surface that uses refraction. This gives a translucent quality to the object we're seeing through.

1. Continue with the scene from the previous section.

2. Set the Mi Reflection Blur value of the glass shader back to **0**. Set Reflectivity to **0** as well. This way, you'll clearly be able to see how refraction blur affects the shader.

3. In the Attribute Editor of glass_MAT, expand the Raytrace Options rollout, and activate the Refractions option. Set Refractive Index to **1.2**.

FIGURE 8.5
The Reflection Blur
settings are in the
mental ray rollout
of the shader's
Attribute Editor.

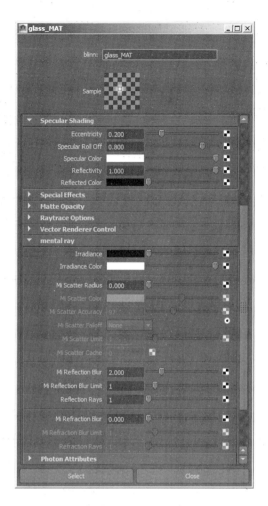

4. Render the scene from the persp camera, and store the image in the Render View window (see the left image in Figure 8.7). The objects seen through the glass become distorted because of the refraction of light as it passes through the glass.

FIGURE 8.6
The reflection on the glass pot is blurred.

FIGURE 8.7
The refracted light distorts the look of the objects behind the glass coffee pot (left image). The refracted image is then blurred (right image).

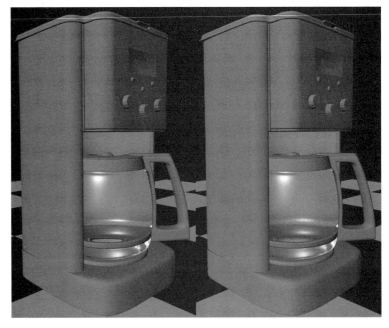

5. Expand the mental ray section of the glass_MAT's Attribute Editor. Set Mi Refraction Blur to **1**, and create another test render (see the right image in Figure 8.7).

6. Save the scene as `reflectionBlur_v02.ma`.

To see a version of the scene, open the `reflectionBlur_v02.ma` file from the `chapter8\` scenes folder at the book's web page.

Mi Refraction Blur Limit sets the number of times the refraction blur itself will be seen in refractive surfaces. Increasing the value of Refraction Rays increases the quality of the blurring, making it appear finer.

INTERACTIVE PHOTOREALISTIC RENDER PREVIEW

Interactive Photorealistic Render (IPR) preview is a mode that can be used in the Render View window. When you create a render preview using the special IPR mode, any changes you make to a shader or the lighting, or even some modeling changes in the scene, automatically update the Render View window, allowing you to see a preview of how the changes will look interactively. IPR works very well with mental ray; in fact, it supports more rendering features for mental ray than for Maya Software.

In addition, Maya offers a progressive rendering mode for IPR. This mode begins rendering with a low sampling rate and progressively increases the rate until the render reaches its final result. This rendering mode allows for fast previews without having to commit to a lengthy render time.

The workflow for creating an IPR render in mental ray is slightly different from the one for creating a Maya Software IPR. To create an IPR render, follow these steps:

1. Select the viewport you wish to render by clicking an empty portion of the viewport menu bar. Open the Render View by using the IPR button (labeled *IPR* at the right side of the status line).

2. Select a region by drawing a region box over the parts of the image you want to tune. The region renders. To avoid demanding too much memory for IPR, keep the region box as small as possible. To enable Progressive Mode, you must use Unified Sampling and set the Progressive Mode option to IPR Only in the Sampling drop-down under the Quality tab.

3. Make changes to the materials and the lighting; you'll see the image in the selected region box update as you make the changes.

4. When you are done with your tuning, stop IPR from constantly updating by clicking the IPR stop sign icon in the upper right of the Render View.

Most, but not all, mental ray features are supported by IPR. Occasionally you'll need to click the IPR button to update the render if IPR gets out of sync (or choose IPR ➤ Refresh IPR Image from the menu in the Render View window). The IPR render is a close approximation of the final render; be aware that what you see in the IPR render may look slightly different in the final render.

mental ray Shaders

mental ray has a number of shaders designed to maximize your options when creating reflections and refractions, as well as blurring these properties. Choosing a shader should be based on a balance between the type of material you want to create and the amount of time and processing power you want to devote to rendering the scene.

This section looks at a few of the shaders available for creating various types of reflections and refractions. These shaders are by no means the only way to create reflections and refractions. As discussed in previous sections, standard Maya shaders also have a number of mental ray–specific options for controlling reflection and refraction.

Once again, remember to think of mental ray as a big toolbox with lots of options. The more you understand about how these shaders work, the easier it will be for you to decide which shaders and techniques you want to use for your renders.

The mia material shader is the Swiss Army knife of mental ray shaders. It is a monolithic material, meaning that it has all the functionality needed for creating a variety of materials built into a single interface. You don't need to connect additional shader nodes into a specific network to create glossy reflections, transparency, and the like.

MENTAL RAY EXTENDED MATERIALS

The mental ray nodes that use the x suffix are more advanced (extended) versions of the original shader. Most of the advancements are in the back-end; the interface and attributes of mi_car_paint_phen and mi_car_paint_phen_x are the same. It's safe to use either version. You can upgrade the mi_car_paint_phen material by clicking the buttons in the Upgrade Shader section of the material's Attribute Editor. The x_passes materials are meant to be used with render passes. For the most part, we use the materials with the x suffix and later upgrade the material if we decide we need to use render passes. Render passes are covered in Chapter 11, "Rendering for Compositing."

---

mia stands for *mental images architectural*, and the shaders (mia_material, mia_material_x, mia_material_passes) and other lighting and lens shader nodes (mia_physicalsun, mia_portal, mia_exposure_simple, and so on) are all part of the "mental images" architectural library. The shaders in this library are primarily used for creating materials used in photorealistic architectural renderings; however, you can take advantage of the power of these materials to create almost anything you need.

The mia material has a large number of attributes that at first can be overwhelming. However, presets are available. You can quickly define the look you need for any given surface by applying a preset. Then you can fine-tune specific attributes of the material to get the look you need.

Using the mia Material Presets

The presets that come with the mia material are the easiest way to establish the initial look of a material. Presets can also be blended to create novel materials. Furthermore, once you create something you like you can save your own presets for use in other projects.

In this exercise we'll work on defining materials for the coffeemaker. The chapter8\ reference folder at the book's web page contains a photo of the appliance to help you match the look. The example scene uses the mia_physicalsunsky lighting network and Final Gathering to light the scene.

1. Open the `coffeeMaker_v01.ma` scene from the `chapter8\scenes` folder at the book's web page. The surfaces in the model have been grouped to keep the model organized.

2. Open the Hypershade window, and select Materials under the mental ray section of the list on the left of the editor.

3. Click the mia_material_x button to create a material, and name it **brushedAluminum_MAT**.

4. In the Outliner, expand the coffeePot and coffeeMaker groups. Select silverRing, control-Panel, and backing. Apply the brushed aluminum material to the objects (right-click the material in the Hypershade, and choose Assign Material To Selection).

5. Open the Attribute Editor for the brushed aluminum shader.

6. Click the Presets button in the upper right, and choose SatinedMetal ➢ Replace.

7. Open the Render View window, and create a render from the renderCam camera. The satined metal preset is near perfect. Save the render in the Render View.

8. In the Attribute Editor, scroll to the Diffuse rollout at the top.

9. Set Color to a medium gray.

10. Create another test render, and compare it with the previous render (see Figure 8.8).

FIGURE 8.8
The mia material comes with a number of presets that can provide a good starting point or complete the look of a material.

You can tweak many of the settings to create your own custom metal, but it already looks pretty good. Like with the other materials in this chapter, the Glossiness setting adds blur to the reflections. Turning on Highlights Only creates a more plastic-like material—with this option activated, the Reflection settings apply only to specular highlights.

Next you can add a black plastic material to various parts:

1. Create a new mia_material_x shader, and name it **shinyBlackPlastic_MAT**.

2. Select the following objects and assign the black plastic material:

   Backsplash

   Handle

   Knobs

   Lid

   Spout

   TopCasing

   Trim

3. Open the Attribute Editor for the plastic material.

4. Click the Presets button, and apply the GlossyPlastic preset to the shader.

5. Create another test render, and compare it to the previous renders. The reflectivity of the preset makes the black plastic look too light.

6. Change the Reflectivity to **0.5**. Figure 8.9 shows the rendered results.

FIGURE 8.9
The black plastic material is applied to all of the plastic parts of the coffeemaker.

7. Save the scene as `coffeeMaker_v02.ma`.

To see a version of the scene, open the `coffeeMaker_v02.ma` scene from the `chapter8\` scenes folder at the book's web page

Adding Shaders to Individual Polygons

Some areas of the coffeemaker's control panel are not brushed aluminum. Several polygon faces for the digital readout should have different shaders assigned to them. The following exercise demonstrates applying a shader to these areas.

1. Select the faces shown in Figure 8.10.

FIGURE 8.10

Select the faces surrounding the digital readout area.

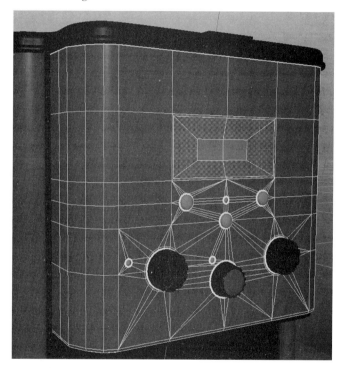

2. RMB-click the shinyBlackPlastic_MAT shader and choose Assign Material To Selection.

3. Create a new mia_material_x shader and name it **readout_MAT**.

4. Open readout_MAT's Attribute Editor. Click the Presets button, and apply the MattePlastic preset to the shader.

5. Set the Color to the following:

H: **68.571**

S: **0.167**

V: **0.329**

6. Select the two faces inside of the shiny black plastic area you selected in step 1. Assign readout_MAT to the faces.

7. Create a test render of the coffeemaker to see the new materials.

8. Repeat the process and assign the brushed aluminum shader to the inner circle of the control knob. Figure 8.11 shows the rendered results.

FIGURE 8.11
Individual faces have been assigned to different shaders for parts of the coffeemaker.

9. Create another mia_material_x using the matte plastic preset. Change its color to black and assign it to the coffeemaker's base.

10. Save the scene as **coffeeMaker_v03.ma**.

To see a version of the scene, open the coffeeMaker_v03.ma scene from the chapter8\ scenes folder at the book's web page.

Creating Thick and Thin Glass

With the mia_material shader we can simulate thickness and thinness in the material itself without creating extra geometry. This can be very useful, especially for glass surfaces.

1. Continue with the scene from the previous section, or open the coffeeMaker_v03.ma file from the chapter8\scenes folder at the book's web page.

2. In the Hypershade, create two new mia_material_x nodes. Name one **thinGlass** and the other **thickGlass**.

3. Apply the thickGlass shader to the glass object in the Outliner.

4. In the Attribute Editor for the thickGlass material, use the Preset button to apply the GlassThick preset.

5. Create a test render from the renderCam camera.

The settings to control thickness are found under the Advanced Refractions controls. Along with the standard Index Of Refraction setting, there is an option for making the material either thin-walled or solid. You also have the option of choosing between a transparent shadow and a refractive caustic that is built into the material (the caustics render when caustic photons are enabled and the light source emits caustic photons; for more information on caustics, consult Chapter 7).

6. The thick glass is more reflective by nature. The coffee pot should be made from thinner glass. Assign the thinGlass material to the glass.

7. Add the GlassThin preset to the shader.

8. Create another test render from the renderCam camera (see Figure 8.12).

FIGURE 8.12
The GlassThin pre-set is assigned to the coffeemaker.

9. Save the scene as **coffeeMaker_v04.ma**.

To see a finished version of the scene, open the coffeeMaker_v04.ma scene from the chapter8\scenes folder at the book's web page.

Other mia Material Attributes

The mia_material has a lot of settings that can take some practice to master. It's a good idea to take a look at the settings used for each preset and note how they affect the rendered image. Over time, you'll pick up some good tricks using the presets as a starting point for creating your own shaders. The following sections give a little background on how some of the settings work.

BUILT-IN AMBIENT OCCLUSION

The Ambient Occlusion option on the material acts as a multiplier for existing ambient occlusion created by the indirect lighting (Final Gathering/Global Illumination). The Use Detail Distance option in the Ambient Occlusion section can be used to enhance fine detailing when set to On. When Use Detail Distance is set to With Color Bleed, the ambient occlusion built into the mia_material factors the reflected colors from surrounding objects into the calculation.

TRANSLUCENCY

The Translucency setting is useful for simulating thin objects, such as paper, that allow some amount of light to pass through them. This option works only when the material has some amount of transparency. The Translucency Weight setting determines how much of the Transparency setting is used for transparency and how much is used for translucency. So if Transparency is 1 (and the transparency color is white) and Translucency Weight is 0, the object is fully transparent (see the plane in Figure 8.13, left). When Translucency Weight is at 0.5, the material splits the Transparency value between transparency and translucency (Figure 8.13, center). When Translucency Weight is set to 1, the object is fully translucent (Figure 8.13, right).

FIGURE 8.13
Three planes with varying degrees of translucency applied

You can also create translucent objects by experimenting with the glossiness in the Refraction settings. This can be used with or without activating the Use Translucency option. If the translucency setting does not seem to work or make any difference in the shading, try reversing the normals on your geometry (in the Polygons menu set, choose Normals ➤ Reverse).

The mia materials have a wide variety of uses beyond metal and plastic (see the sidebar "Using the mia_material to Shade Organic Objects" for one example). The materials offer an excellent opportunity for exploration. For more detailed descriptions of the settings, read the mental ray for Maya Architectural Guide in the Maya documentation.

 **Real World Scenario**

USING THE MIA_MATERIAL TO SHADE ORGANIC OBJECTS

The many settings of the mia_material can be used to create material properties well beyond what is listed in the Presets menu. In fact, the mia_material is by far my favorite shader available in Maya because of its versatility. The Translucency attributes make it ideal for shading things like leaves in a close-up, insect wings, and clothing. I've even used the material to create the look of flakes of skin as seen on a microscopic scale.

You can create these effects by mapping file textures to various channels of the mia_material. Mapping file textures is covered in depth in Chapter 9, but this example should be simple enough to follow even if you have not worked with texture maps very much.

The mia_shader has an advanced attribute called Cutout Opacity. This is like a second transparency channel that is used to map a texture to define the silhouette of an object. Here's how you can use this channel:

1. Open the `leaves_v01.ma` scene from the `chapter8\scenes` folder at the book's web page.

2. In the Hypershade editor, create a new mia_material_x shader.

3. Apply this shader to the leaf1 and leaf2 objects in the scene.

4. Create a new file texture node (select 2D Textures from under the Maya heading in the list on the left), and click the File button.

5. Open the Attribute Editor for the file1 node.

6. Click the Image Name field. Find and open the `leaf.tif` file located in the `chapter8\sourceimages` folder.

7. MMB-drag the file1 node from the Hypershade to the color swatch in the Diffuse rollout of the mia_material_x1 node's Attribute Editor.

8. Repeat step 7, but this time connect the file1 node to the color swatch in the Refraction node. This will use the file1 image, which is a picture of a leaf, to color the transparency of the leaf objects.

9. In the Reflection rollout, set Reflectivity to **0.18** and Glossiness to **0.2**.

10. In the Refraction rollout, set Transparency to **0.15**.

11. In the Translucency rollout, turn on Use Translucency. Set Color to a light gray and Weight to **0.8**.

12. Create a test render.

    These are some nice-looking translucent leaves, but there is an ugly black box around the leaf image in the texture. This is where Cutout Opacity is useful. You can easily use this channel to create the edges of the leaves based on the alpha channel stored in the original `leaf.tif` file.

13. Expand the Advanced rollout toward the bottom of the mia_material_x1 shader's Attribute Editor.

continues

(continued)

14. MMB-drag the file1 node from the Hypershade window onto the Cutout Opacity slider. This will automatically connect the alpha channel of the file1 texture to the Cutout Opacity setting.

15. Create another test render. Voilà! Translucent leaves!

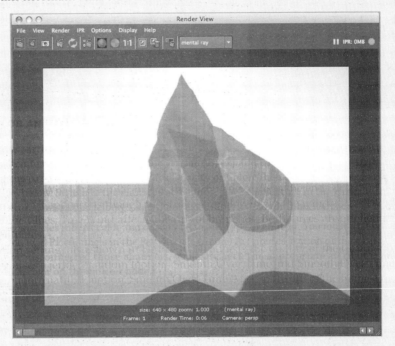

This technique is useful because the shader can be applied to very simple geometry. The planes used for the leaves can be turned into nCloth objects and have dynamic forces create their movement. (Particles and Soft Body Dynamics are covered in Chapter 13, "Dynamic Effects," and Chapter 14, "Hair and Clothing.")

There are several things you need to remember to determine whether this technique is working in your own scenes:

◆ Make sure the normals of your polygon objects are facing in the correct direction.

◆ Make sure the file texture you use for Cutout Opacity has an alpha channel.

◆ Make sure that the Transparency setting is above 0 in order for the translucency to work.

You may notice that the texture in our exercise was connected to the refraction color and not the translucency color. This is so that the shadows cast by the leaves are semitransparent. You can map a texture to the translucency color, but your shadows may appear black.

Another useful setting is the Additional Color channel in the Advanced rollout. This can be used to create incandescent effects similar to the incandescence channel on standard Maya shaders (Blinn, Phong, Lambert, and so on).

Layering Shaders

New!
Layering shaders allow you to create a shader with infinite complexity. Autodesk Maya 2015 offers mental ray's latest layering library, which includes its mila (mental image layering) shaders. The layering shaders are separate components of a traditional shader divided into separate nodes that can easily be stacked and blended on top of one another. The basic concept behind using layering shaders is: if you don't need it, don't include it. For instance, if you are creating a shader for a brick wall there is no need to include transparency settings.

Layering shaders attempt to mimic real-world physics. Therefore they should only interact with lights that are physically plausible—the light should act like a real-world light. Area lights and image-based lighting work the best with the layering shaders since their visible light corresponds with the light they actually cast. Other lights can be used, but the results may not be desirable.

The base layering shader is the mila material. It is created and assigned to geometry as any other shader would be. When you create the mila material a layer node and diffuse material are created automatically (see Figure 8.14).

FIGURE 8.14
A graphed mila material in the Hypershade

From an artistic point of view, the mila material simply collects information from its layers. It does not contribute to the actual shading of the surface it's assigned to. With that, the mila material must always have a base component. By default, the base component is a diffuse layer. This is comparable to a lambert shader. There are three variations of base components: diffuse, reflective, and transmissive or translucent (see Figure 8.15). You can change the base component at any time without affecting added layers.

Layers are added from within the mila material. Each layer is weighted. Its effect over bottom layers can be reduced by decreasing the layer's weight. After adding your first layer, you then have the option to add a mix layer. Mix layers blend the layer components together in an additive manner. For instance, mixing two diffuse layers, one red and one blue, would result in a purple diffuse shader.

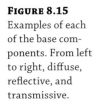

FIGURE 8.15
Examples of each of the base components. From left to right, diffuse, reflective, and transmissive.

A layer's directional weight can be controlled through three different layer types: Weighted, Fresnel, or Custom. These options are available when you create a new layer. The directional weight of a layer controls how light interacts with that layer. Choosing a type sets specific options in the layer node. Weighted is the plain version of the layer without any directional weight. Fresnel uses the Index Of Refraction value established in the layer. Custom allows you to define your own normal and grazing reflectivity. Regardless of the type of layer you choose, you can always change the settings after the layer has been created.

You can add as many components as you want to a single layer. You can also create multiple layers and connect them to a single layer, combining the effects from every component. Layering shaders are extremely versatile and unrestricted. In the next chapter, you'll create a layering network with subsurface scattering components to give a lifelike appearance to a giraffe model.

Building a Layered Car Paint Shader

In reality, car paint consists of several layers; together these layers combine to give the body of a car its special, sparkling quality. Car paint uses a base-color pigment, and the color of this pigment changes hue depending on the viewing angle. This color layer also has thousands of tiny flakes of metal suspended within it. When the sun reflects off these metallic flakes, you see a noticeable sparkling quality. Above these layers is a reflective clear coat, which is usually highly reflective (especially for new cars) and occasionally glossy. The clear coat itself is a perfect study in Fresnel reflections. As the surfaces of the car turn away from the viewing angle, the reflectivity of the surface increases.

The metallic paint material is similar to the car paint phenomenon material. In fact, you can re-create the car paint material by combining the mi_metallic_paint node with the mi_glossy_reflection node and the mi_bump_flakes node.

In this section, you'll learn how to use the car paint material by applying it to a model of a truck.

1. Open the truck_v01.ma scene from the chapter8\scenes folder at the book's web page. This scene uses the Physical Sun and Sky network for lighting.

PHYSICAL SUN AND SKY

When setting out to texture a model, sometimes we like to start by using the Physical Sun and Sky lighting model that was introduced in Chapter 7. As we develop the materials for the model, it's helpful to see how they react to physically accurate lighting. This light setup uses Final Gathering, which can add a little extra time to the rendering because the image must go through two passes: one to calculate the Final Gathering and a second to render the image. All of this is explained in detail in Chapter 7.

2. Open the Hypershade window, and select the Create ➤ mental ray Materials ➤ mila_material.

3. Open the mila_material shader's Attribute Editor. Change the Base Component to Reflective (Paint) (see Figure 8.16).

FIGURE 8.16
Use the Reflective (Paint) base component.

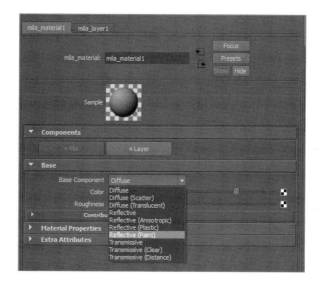

4. The truck has several shaders already applied. In the Materials tab on the right side of Hypershade, RMB-click on carParts1, and choose Select Objects With Material; this will select all the polygons on the model that use this shader.

5. Assign the mila_material shader created in step 3 to the selected parts. Parts of the truck body now appear red.

6. Rename the mila_material shader to **carPaint1_MAT**.

7. Select the faces of carParts2 shader and assign carPaint1_MAT to it.

8. Select **carPaint1_MAT** from the Hypershade. Choose the Input and Output Connections icon to graph the material's connections in the Hypershade work area (see Figure 8.17).

FIGURE 8.17
Graph the material
to expose all of its
connections in the
Hypershade.

Diffuse Parameters

At the top of the attributes, you'll find the Diffuse Parameters rollout. The settings here determine the color properties of the base pigment layer. As the color of this layer changes depending on the viewing angle, the various settings determine all the colors that contribute to this layer.

1. Set Tint Color to a darker red. Using the HSV color settings, change the value to **0.6**. Tint is the main color of the shader. If you wanted to add a texture map to apply decals to the car, you would use this channel. Figure 8.18 shows a render of the truck so far.

FIGURE 8.18
A dark red tint has
been added to the
shader.

2. Set Edge Color to a similar shade of red, but lower the value so that it is almost black. Edge Color is apparent on the edges that face away from the camera. Newer cars and sports cars benefit from a dark Edge Color setting.

Edge Color Bias specifies the amount of spread seen in Edge Color. Lower values (0.1 to 3) create a wider spread; higher values (4 to 10) create a narrower band of Edge Color.

3. Edge Weight controls the overall contribution of the edge color effect. Set this value to **10.0**. Figure 8.19 shows the rendered results.

4. Glossy Color is the color seen in the surface areas that face the light source. Change the Glossy Color settings to match the following values:

H: **360.0**

S: **0.421**

V: **0.348**

Flake Parameters

The Flake Parameters settings are the most interesting components of the shader. These determine the look and intensity of the metallic flakes in the pigment layer of the car paint:

Flake Color   Should usually be white for new cars.

Flake Weight   A multiplier for Flake Color. Higher values intensify the look of the flakes; 1 is usually a good setting for most situations.

Flake Roughness   Changes the shader from a typical Lambert style shading at 0 to a more powdery look at 1.0.

Flake Scale   Sets the size of the flakes. It's important to understand that the size of the flakes is connected to the scale of the object. If you notice that the size of the flakes is different on one part of the car compared to the others, select the surface geometry and freeze the transformations so that the Scale X, Y, and Z values are all set to 1. This will correct the problem and ensure that the flakes are a consistent size across all the parts of the car.

Flake Density   Determines the number of flakes visible in the paint. The values range from 0.0 to 1.0. In many situations, a high value means that the individual flakes are harder to see.

Flake Strength   Varies the orientation of the flakes in the paint. Setting this to 0 makes all the flakes parallel to the surface; a setting of 1 causes the flakes to be oriented randomly, making the flakes more reflective at different viewing angles.

Flake Type   Specifies different procedural patterns to define the shape of the flakes.

Flake Cell Style   Forces the pattern specified in the Flake Type setting to be represented as irregular shapes or circles.

Flake Circle Size   Increases or decreases the size of the circular pattern if Circular is chosen for the Flake Cell Style value.

5. For this exercise, use the following settings:

Flake Weight: **0.2**

Flake Scale: **0.001**

Flake Density: **0.4**

Flake Strength: **0.1**

You can see the rendered version with the new flake settings in Figure 8.20.

FIGURE 8.20
The Flake parameters have been set.

Specular Reflection Layer

A specular layer defines the look of the specular highlight on the surface. By adding a specular layer, you can make the car paint look brand-new or old and dull.

1. Select carParts1_MAT. In its Attribute Editor choose the +Layer button.

2. From the pop-up window, choose Fresnel Layer.

3. From the next pop-up window, choose Specular Reflection.

4. The layer is added to the mila_material shader. An abridged version of the specular reflection layer's attributes is displayed within the material node. Change the Fresnel IOR attribute to **1.44** to match the IOR of aluminum. Figure 8.21 shows the rendered results.

Glossy Reflection Parameters

The reflectivity of the surface is at its maximum when Reflection Color is set to white. When this option is set to black, reflections are turned off.

1. Select carParts1_MAT. In its Attribute Editor choose the +Layer button.

2. From the pop-up window, choose Fresnel Layer.

3. From the next pop-up window, choose Glossy Reflection.

4. The layer is added to the mila_material shader. Change the Fresnel IOR attribute to **1.44**.

5. To mimic the crisp reflective proprieties of metal, change the Roughness setting to **0.0**. Figure 8.22 shows the results of the glossy layer.

6. Add the carParts1_MAT to the rest of the vehicle's parts.

7. Save the scene as **truck_v02.ma**.

To see a finished version of the scene, open the truck_v02.ma file from the chapter8\scenes folder at the book's web page.

Rendering Contours

mental ray has a special contour-rendering mode that enables you to render outlines of 3D objects. This is a great feature for nonphotorealistic rendering. You can use it to make your 3D animations appear like drawings or futuristic computer displays. The end title sequence of the film Iron Man is an example of this style of rendering.

Rendering contours is easy, but it requires activating settings in several places. Furthermore, it is not supported in Unified Sampling mode; you must use Legacy Sampling mode. The following steps take you through the process of rendering with contours:

1. Open the truckContour_v01.ma scene from the chapter8\scenes folder at the book's web page. A standard Maya Lambert material is applied to the truck.

2. Open the Render Settings window, and under the Quality tab, change Sampling Mode to Legacy Sampling Mode.

3. Select the Features tab. Expand the Contours section, and click Enable Contour Rendering. This makes contour rendering possible, but you won't see any results until you activate a few more options.

4. Expand the Draw By Property Difference section. These settings define how the contours will be drawn. One of these options must be activated, or contour rendering will not take place. Click Between Different Instances. This means that lines will be drawn around each piece of geometry in the scene (see Figure 8.23).

FIGURE 8.23
To render contour lines, you must select Enable Contour Rendering and choose a Draw By Property Difference option.

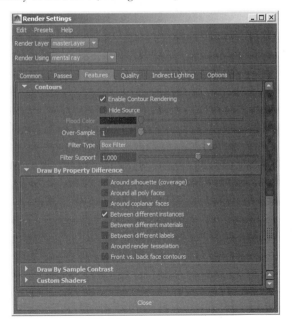

5. Open the Hypershade window, select the truck_MAT material, and graph its input and output connections.

6. In the work area of the Hypershade, select the truck_MAT2SG node that is attached to the truck_MAT shader and open its Attribute Editor. Switch to the truck_MAT2SG tab.

7. In the Contours section of the mental ray rollout in the Attribute Editor, select the Enable Contour Rendering option. Set Color to red (see Figure 8.24).

FIGURE 8.24
Contour Rendering also needs to be enabled in the shader's shading group node settings.

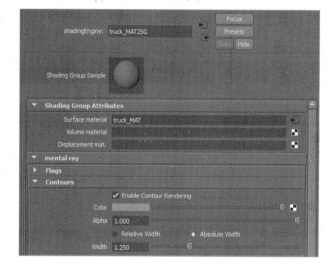

8. Create a test render in the Render View window from the renderCam camera. The contours are added after the scene renders, on top of the shaded view of the geometry.

9. Open the Render Settings window.

10. On the Features tab, in the Contours section activate Hide Source, and set Flood Color to a dark blue.

11. Create another test render (see Figure 8.25).

FIGURE 8.25
Contour rendering creates lines on top of the rendered surface. The source has been hidden, so only the lines render.

This time the original geometry is hidden, and only the contours are rendered. Flood Color determines the background color when Hide Source is activated. Oversampling sets the quality and antialiasing of the contour lines. To see a finished version of the scene, open the truckContour_v02.ma scene from the chapter8\scenes folder at the book's web page.

You can adjust the width of the contours using the controls in the Contours section of the shading group. Absolute Width ensures that the contours are the same width; Relative Width makes the width of the contours relative to the size of the rendered image.

Since each shading group node has its own contour settings, you can create lines of differing thickness and color for all the parts of an object. Just apply different materials to the different parts, and adjust the settings in each material's shading group node accordingly.

Experiment using different settings in the Draw By Property Difference section of the Render Settings window. More complex contour effects can be created by plugging one of the contour shaders available in the Create mental ray Node section of the Hypershade into the Contour Shader slot under the Custom Shaders section of the shading group node.

The Bottom Line

Understand shading concepts. Light rays are reflected, absorbed by, or transmitted through a surface. A rough surface diffuses the reflection of light by bouncing light rays in nearly random directions. Specular reflections occur on smooth surfaces; the angle at which rays bounce off a smooth surface is equivalent to the angle at which they strike the surface. Refraction occurs when light rays are bent as they are transmitted through the surface. A specular highlight is the reflection of a light source on a surface. In CG rendering, this effect is often controlled separately from reflection; in the real world, specular reflection and highlights are intrinsically related.

Master It   Make a standard Blinn shader appear like glass refracting light in the jellybeans_v01.ma scene in the chapter8\scenes folder on the book's web page.

Apply reflection and refraction blur.   Reflection and Refraction Blur are special mental ray options available on many standard Maya shading nodes. You can use these settings to create glossy reflections when rendering standard Maya shading nodes with mental ray.

Master It   Create the look of translucent plastic using a standard Maya Blinn shader.

Use mia materials.   The mia materials and nodes can be used together to create realistic materials that are always physically accurate. The mia materials come with a number of presets that can be used as a starting point for your own materials.

Master It   Create a realistic polished-wood material.

Understand mila shading layers.   The layering shaders are separate components of a traditional shader that can easily be stacked and blended on top of one another. Layered shaders allow you to add an infinite amount of detail to a single shader.

Master It   Create a mix layer and blend two colored diffuse layers together.

Render contours.   mental ray has the ability to render contours of your models to create a cartoon drawing look for your animations. Rendering contours requires that options in the Render Settings window and in the shading group for the object be activated.

Master It   Render the coffeemaker using contours.

Chapter 9

Texture Mapping

The use of two-dimensional images to add color and detail to three-dimensional objects has been a big part of computer modeling and animation from the very start. This technique is known as *texture mapping*, and it is practically an art form all its own. A well-painted texture map can add an astonishing degree of realism, especially when combined with good lighting and a well-constructed 3D model. In this chapter, you'll see how to use texture mapping in the Autodesk® Maya® software to create a photorealistic giraffe.

Texture mapping has many different levels. On one end, you add as much as you can to the map, light, reflections, and shadow. On the other end, you rely on shaders and rendering techniques and have maps that provide nothing more than shades of color.

In this chapter, you will learn to:

◆ Create UV texture coordinates

◆ Work with bump, normal, and displacement maps

◆ Create a subsurface scattering layering shader

◆ Work with Viewport 2.0

UV Texture Layout

UV texture mapping is a necessary part of completing a model. UVs provide space for painted images to be placed on your model. In Maya, using UVs goes beyond texture mapping. Having good UVs also provides you with a surface on which to paint skin weight maps, fur attributes, and simulation parameters. UV mapping has been simplified in Maya to a couple of tools, and it can be done very rapidly.

UVs are often looked at as tedious and difficult but a necessary evil. There is a lot of truth to this; however, UV mapping has a strong purpose, and it should be considered an important part of the process. UV mapping is a lot like wrapping a present, where you have a flat sheet of paper that needs to go around an awkwardly shaped object with as few seams as possible.

LINKING TEXTURE FILES

The project files in this chapter are linked to texture files found in the chapter9\sourceimages folder at the book's web page (www.sybex.com/go/masteringmaya2015). It's possible that these links may break when working with the scenes at the book's web page. You may want to copy the Chapter 9 project to your local hard drive, and make sure that the current project is set to Chapter 9. This way, when you load a premade scene and render it, the scenes should render properly.

What Are UV Texture Coordinates?

Just as x-, y-, and z-coordinates tell you where an object is located in space, u- and v-coordinates tell you where a point exists on a surface. Imagine a dot drawn on a cardboard box. The u- and v-coordinates specify the location of that dot on the surface of the box. If you unfold the box and then place a grid over the flattened box, you can plot the position of the dot using the grid. One axis of the grid is the u-coordinate; the other axis is the v-coordinate. 3D software uses u- and v-coordinates to determine how textures should be applied to 3D objects. *UV mapping* refers to the process of determining these coordinates for polygon objects. *UV layout* is a term that refers to the 2D configuration of the UVs on a surface, such as a picture of the unfolded box on a grid taken from above (see Figure 9.1). In the UV Texture Editor, u-coordinates are plotted along the horizontal axis, and v-coordinates are plotted along the vertical axis.

FIGURE 9.1
UV coordinates appear as an unfolded version of the model. They determine how textures are applied to 3D models. In this image, the coordinates tell Maya where to place the word "hello" on the cube.

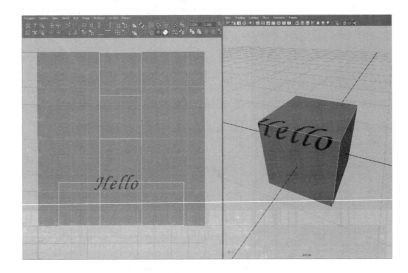

NURBS surfaces have implicit UVs; this means that the coordinates are built into the parameterization of the surface. UV texture coordinates do not have to be created for NURBS surfaces; only polygon and subdivision surfaces require mapped UVs. With regard to subdivision surfaces, it's usually best to map the UVs on a polygon version of the model and then convert that model to subdivision surfaces. The mapped UV coordinates are converted along with the polygon object.

UV maps act as a guide for the placement of images. Images can be painted in Maya on a flat canvas in 2D space or in 3D space directly on the model. Third-party software, like Adobe Photoshop, the Autodesk® Mudbox® product, or Pixologic's ZBrush, is usually employed to do the bulk of the texture work. Figure 9.2 shows a typical Photoshop texture-painting session using a snapshot of the UVs, created in Maya, as a guide.

A good UV layout will also minimize stretching, warping, and the appearance of seams between the parts of the UV map. For a character's head, a good UV layout may look a little strange, but you should be able to make out where the eyes, nose, mouth, ears, and other features are located. This is often referred to as a *human-readable UV layout* as opposed to an automatically tiled layout that functions just fine but is impossible to decipher when you are trying to paint a 2D map in Photoshop (see Figure 9.3).

FIGURE 9.2
UV coordinates are used as a guide for painting 3D model textures in digital paint programs such as Photoshop.

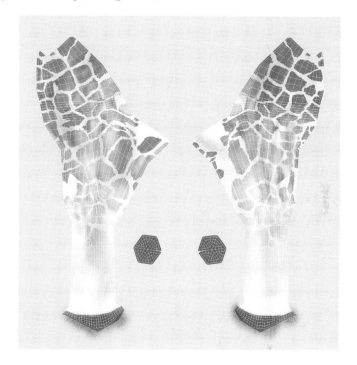

Even if you intend to create texture maps in a program such as Autodesk Mudbox, The Foundry's Mari, or ZBrush, which allow you to paint directly on a 3D model, it's a good idea to make sure you have human-readable UVs. This is especially true when you are working in a production pipeline. The textures you create in ZBrush or MAXON's BodyPaint may need to be mapped or enhanced in Photoshop. If the UVs are not human-readable, the process becomes extremely difficult.

The process of mapping UVs is typically done with a viewport and the UV Texture Editor. The interface of the UV Texture Editor is a 2D graph with menus and an icon bar at the top (see Figure 9.4). Many of the icon commands are duplicated in the menu selections in the editor window. You can also find the same tools in the Polygon menu set under Create UVs and Edit UVs. The UV Texture Editor graph is divided into four quadrants. The upper-right quadrant (shaded darker gray) is typically where you'll keep your texture coordinates. Notice the numbers on the graph; the upper-right quadrant has the positive U and V values. The values range from 0 to 1. It is possible to have coordinates existing outside this range, which is useful when creating photorealistic models, but most of the time you want to keep the coordinates within this range.

FIGURE 9.3
Human-readable
UVs bear some
resemblance to the
original 3D object
so that an artist
can easily paint
textures (top).
Automatically
tiled UVs (bottom)
will function but
are typically frag-
mented chunks of
information and
difficult for artists
to decipher.

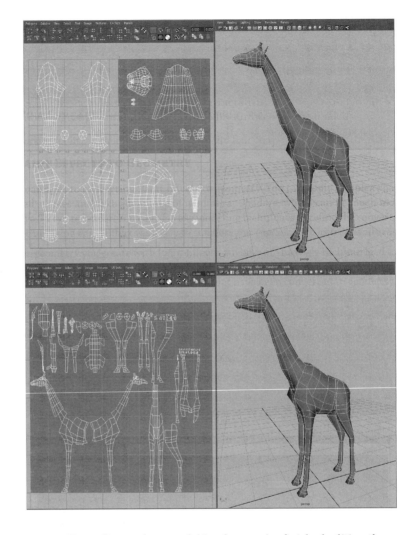

The best time to create UV coordinates for a model is when you've finished editing the model. Inserting edges, subdividing, and extruding will alter the coordinate layout and produce undesirable effects. However, to save time, if the model is symmetrical, you can lay out the UVs when the model is half-finished.

Take a look at Figure 9.5. The giraffe has been cut in half. UVs are part of the geometry. Mirroring the geometry also mirrors the UVs. Therefore, it is necessary to lay out the UVs for only half the model. When you're done, the geometry can be mirrored over, and the UVs can be finished.

FIGURE 9.4
UV Texture Editor.

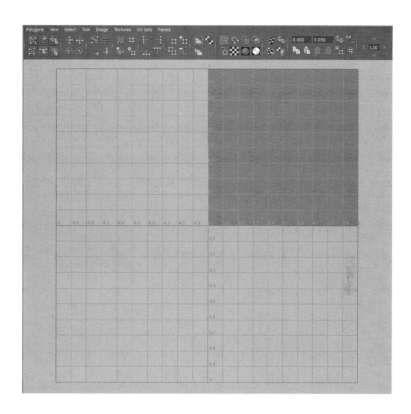

FIGURE 9.5
The giraffe has
been cut in half in
preparation for UV
mapping.

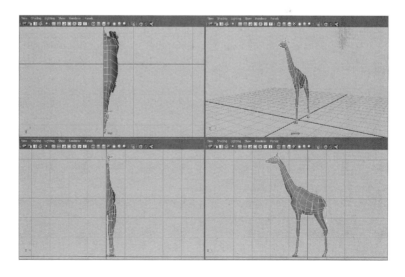

UVs are created by selecting polygon faces and projecting coordinates onto your selection. Maya has several projection methods for facilitating UV mapping. The trick is to match your projection to your selection, and vice versa. To familiarize yourself with the process, you'll take the giraffe from Chapter 5, "Rigging and Muscle Systems," and lay out the UVs for its front leg, body, and head. The following exercises walk you through the process.

Mapping the Giraffe Leg

Using the same giraffe model we worked with in Chapter 5, begin laying out its UVs, starting with its front leg. The model has been cut in half to allow mirroring later in the chapter.

1. Open the scene file `giraffeUV_v01.ma` from the `chapter9\scenes` folder at the book's web page.

2. Select the model. From a viewport menu, choose Panels ➤ Saved Layouts ➤ Persp/UV Texture Editor.

3. Legs are simple to UV-map because they match the cylindrical projection tool. Choose a group of faces on the lower half of the giraffe's front leg. Press Shift+> to increase your selection. Continue up the leg until you achieve the selection shown in Figure 9.6. (Make sure you do not select the underside of the foot.)

FIGURE 9.6
Select the faces on the front leg.

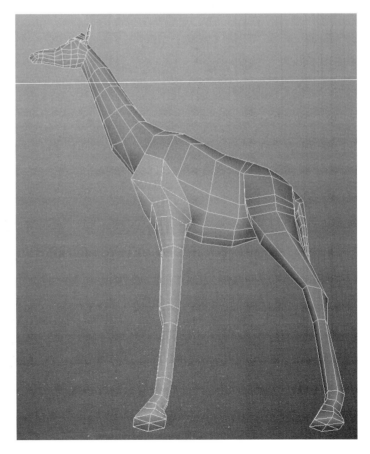

You want to make sure your selection roughly matches your projection method, in this case a cylinder. The bottom of the giraffe's foot would act as a cap if included in the selection, preventing the UVs from unfolding properly.

4. In the Polygons menu set, choose Create UVs ➤ Cylindrical Mapping. UVs are created; however, they don't look pretty (see Figure 9.7).

FIGURE 9.7
The cylindrically mapped UVs.

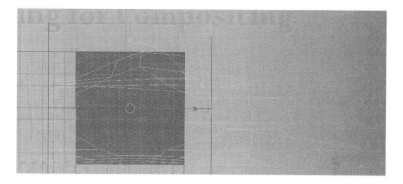

NAVIGATION IN THE UV TEXTURE EDITOR

You can move around in the UV Texture Editor just as you can in the perspective view, except that you can't tumble around, since by its nature UV texturing is a 2D process. Use Alt/Option+right-click to zoom and Alt/Option+middle-click to pan.

---

5. You need to fit the manipulator to the geometry in order to improve the quality of the UVs. It needs to be translated and rotated. To do this, find the red T at the bottom of the manipulator.

6. Click the red T to activate the combined Move/Rotate/Scale tool.

7. Translate the cylinder first in the Z direction and then rotate it. Use Figure 9.8 as reference.

FIGURE 9.8
Fit the manipulator to the leg.

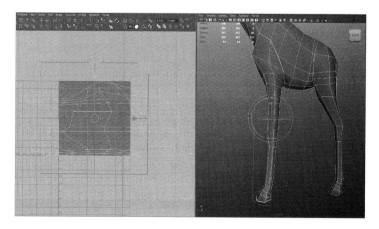

SELECTING THE PROJECTION MANIPULATOR

If you accidentally deselect the manipulator, click the polyCylProj1 node from the Channel Box. Next, click the Show Manipulator Tool icon on the toolbar.

---

8. While the faces are still selected, change them to UVs by choosing Select ➤ Convert Selection ➤ To UVs.

   When faces are selected, only those faces are shown in the UV Texture Editor. When you select UVs in whole or in part, all the mapped UVs are displayed. Moving your UV shells into empty space keeps them from overlapping.

9. Move the UV selection away from the texture space into solid gray space. You can use the Move tool from the toolbar. Moving the *UV shell* into empty space gives you more space in which to work.

10. Select a single UV, and then choose Select ➤ Select Shell or RMB-click and choose Shell from the marking menu.

11. Convert the selection to faces by choosing Select ➤ Convert Selection To Faces.

    After some experience, you will be able to look at a UV shell and determine whether it is good or needs improvement. However, to see the smallest defects, it's necessary to assign a textured pattern to the faces.

12. With the shell selected and in the perspective viewport, right-click a face and choose Assign Favorite Material from the marking menu.

13. Choose a Lambert material, and assign a checkered pattern to the Color channel.

14. Press **6** to see the texture in the viewport (see Figure 9.9).

15. Save the scene as **giraffeUV_v02.ma**.

Notice that when you move the UV coordinates around the UV Texture Editor, the checkered pattern moves but does not disappear. This is because the pattern repeats infinitely beyond the 0 to 1 range of the grid (where the image preview is seen when the Display Image button is activated). Eventually you'll move the leg back to the grid, but for now you just want to move it out of the way while you work on other parts of the giraffe.

To see a version of the scene up to this point, open the giraffeUV_v02.ma scene from the chapter9\scenes folder at the book's web page.

Unfolding UVs

New!

Once you have the basic UV layout created for the model, you can use the Unfold tool to remove any remaining overlapping UVs as well as to reduce distortion on the model. Unfolded UVs can be used at any time during the process on entire shells or just selected UVs. The Unfold command tries to make the UVs conform to the three-dimensional shape of the object.

FIGURE 9.9
The UVs stretch and warp the checkered pattern.

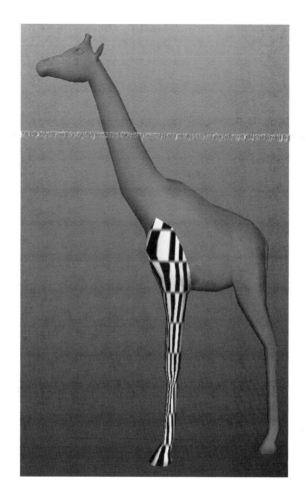

1. Continue with your file or open the `giraffeUV_v02.ma` scene from the `chapter9\scenes` folder at the book's web page. The scene picks up where the previous exercise left off.

2. Select the UV shell for the leg. Remember, you can do this quickly by selecting a single UV and choosing Select ➤ UV Shell.

3. Choose EditUVs ➤ Unfold.

4. In the Unfold UV Options dialog box, uncheck Pack. Pack forces the UVs into the 0 to 1 texture space. Since only the leg has projected UVs there is no point in fitting it to the texture space.

5. Click the Apply button, and observe the results in the perspective view, as shown in Figure 9.10. You can uniformly scale the UVs to increase the checkerboard resolution on the model.

FIGURE 9.10
The results of
unfolding the
leg UVs.

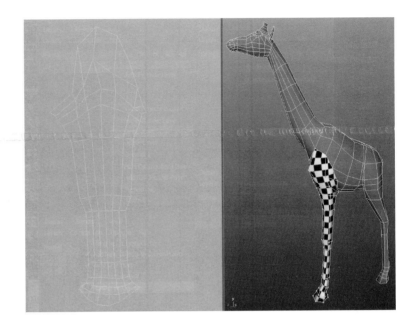

The checkered pattern looks good. The UVs are laid out nicely.

6. Save the scene as **giraffeUV_v03.ma**.

To see a version of the scene up to this point, open the giraffeUV_v03.ma scene from the chapter9\scenes folder at the book's web page.

Mapping the Giraffe Head

Generating UVs for the face, whether human or animal, is the hardest part, primarily because this is the location of the majority of the visible detail. You want to minimize warped or stretched UVs as much as possible, especially around the nose and eyes, where defining lines can become stretched, making the model appear less believable. The following exercise is one approach to mapping the head:

1. Open the giraffeUV_v03.ma scene from the chapter9\scenes folder at the book's web page or continue where you left off. The scene picks up where the previous exercise ended.

2. You want to establish a good selection, similar to the leg. Use the Select Lasso tool, and select all the head faces (see Figure 9.11).

3. Use the Paint Select tool to deselect the ears, nose interior, eye socket, and horns (see Figure 9.12). By default, the Paint Select tool is set to select. By holding Ctrl, you can reverse the operation. You also may have to change your selection to faces, which can be done by right-clicking and choosing Face from the marking menu.

FIGURE 9.11
Select the giraffe's head.

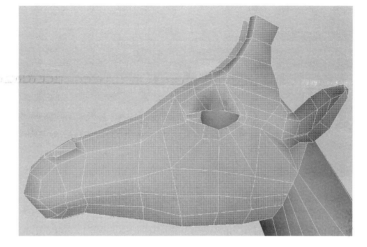

FIGURE 9.12
Deselect the ears, nose, eye socket, and horn parts of the giraffe's head.

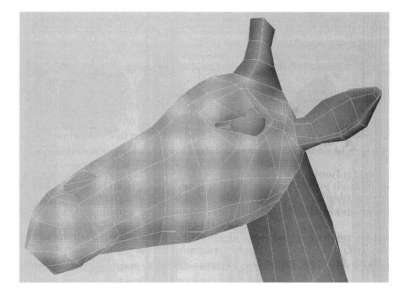

4. Choose Create UVs ➤ Cylindrical Mapping (see Figure 9.13).

5. Rotate the cylindrical projection to –90 in the X and Z directions.

6. Using the z-axis, translate the manipulator closer to the geometry.

Notice in the Channel Box it is the Projection Center X that is updated. These are the manipulator's world coordinate values. The UVs should now resemble the geometry (see Figure 9.14).

FIGURE 9.13
Use a cylindrical projection to project the UVs.

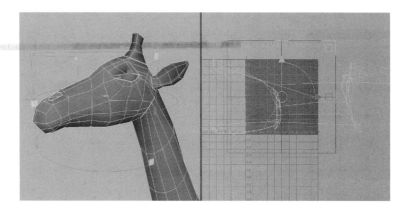

FIGURE 9.14
Translate the manipulator to correct the head UVs.

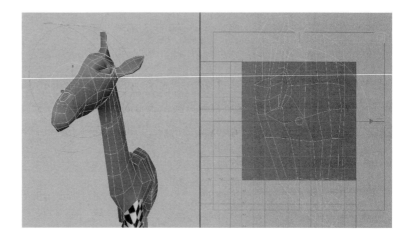

7. Assign a new material with a checkered pattern for the Color channel. (If you need help, refer to steps 12 and 13 in the "Mapping the Giraffe Leg" section's exercise.)

8. Select the shell, and translate it into empty space.

9. Choose EditUVs ➢ Unfold. The UVs are quickly shaped to remove any stretching or warping (see Figure 9.15).

FIGURE 9.15
The Unfold tool corrects the head UVs.

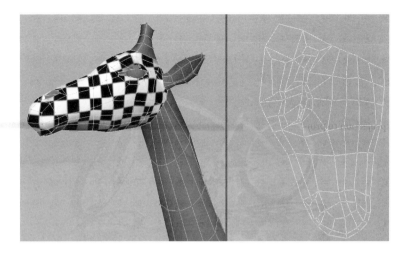

10. Save the scene as **giraffeUV_v04.ma**.

The head UVs are laid out nicely; however, including the other half does change things. The next exercise on mirroring geometry continues with the head UVs.

To see a version of the scene up to this point, open the giraffeUV_v04.ma scene from the chapter9\scenes folder at the book's web page.

Mirroring UVs

There is no way to mirror UVs only. You must mirror the geometry. The basic workflow for a symmetrical model is to lay out the UVs for one side of the model and then mirror the geometry.

1. Continue laying out the UVs for half of your model or open the giraffeUV_v05.ma scene from the chapter9\scenes folder at the book's web page. The scene has been continued from the previous exercise. All the UVs have been laid out in preparation for mirroring the geometry.

2. Select the giraffe. Choose Mesh ➢ Mirror Geometry ➢ Options. Make sure that you are mirroring across the –X direction (see Figure 9.16).

FIGURE 9.16
Set the options for the Mirror Geometry tool.

3. Click polyMirror1 in the Channel Box, and set Merge Threshold to **0.005**.

4. Open the UV Texture Editor.

It appears that none of the UVs has been mirrored. However, the mirrored UVs are sitting on top of the preexisting UVs.

5. Choose Polygon ➢ Layout.

6. Use all of the defaults except for the Scale Mode value; change it to None. Figure 9.17 shows the Layout options. Click Apply.

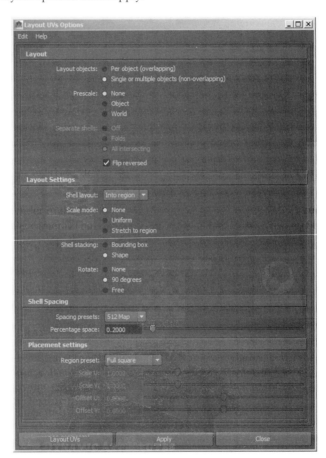

FIGURE 9.17
The Layout UVs options.

Layout is an automated process that separates and reverses any of the UV shells for you. It also arranges the UV shells into a tight square. This is beneficial when the UVs are done.

FLIPPED UVs

When creating UV texture coordinates, you need to make sure that the direction is consistent among all of the UVs; otherwise, strange artifacts can appear when the model is textured and rendered. Maya color-codes the shells to differentiate between their directions; one of the side-of-the-face shells is blue, and the other is red. You can view this by choosing Image ➤ Shade UVs.

7. Some of the UV shells can be combined into a single shell. To make working with the shells easier, you can arrange them so they sit next to their corresponding other half. Choose the Move UV Shell tool from the UV Texture Editor toolbar. It is the second icon from the left.

8. Click on a shell and drag it to empty space. The Move UV Shell tool automatically selects the shell. Move all of the shells that have a corresponding half. When done, click the Select tool on the toolbar to deactivate the Move UV Shell tool.

9. Select the edges along the top of the head. Start at one edge in front of the nose, and go all the way back to the neck. Use Figure 9.18 for reference.

FIGURE 9.18
Select edges to be
sewn together.

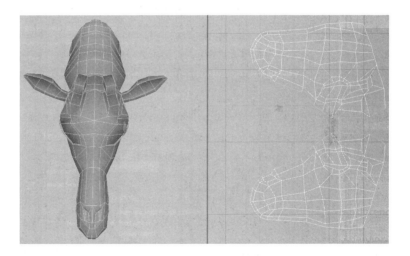

10. Choose Move And Sew UV Edges from the Polygons menu. The two halves of the head come together. Some of the UVs are overlapping along the shell's center line. Ignore this for now.

11. Move and sew the rest of the UVs in the same way.

New!

12. Once all of the halves have been sewn together, choose Unfold3D ➢ Optimize. The Optimize tool smoothes any overlap or defects in the UV shells. Figure 9.19 shows the optimized head UVs.

FIGURE 9.19
The finished head UVs.

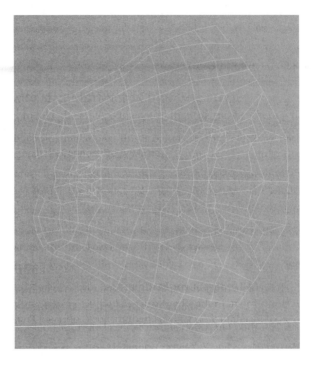

13. Save the scene as `giraffeUV_v06.ma`.

To see a version of the scene up to this point, open the `giraffeUV_v06.ma` scene from the `chapter9\scenes` folder at the book's web page.

More UV Tools

Often, UVs don't go where you want them to, leading to overlap and warping issues. Other situations call for the UVs to match existing ones or be placed precisely according to production specifications. Maya comes with several tools to assist in manipulating UVs manually.

The first is the UV Lattice tool. It creates a 2D structure with a definable set of control points, allowing you to make broad changes to groups of UVs. Figure 9.20 shows an example. You can move the lattice by its points or move an edge. The UV Lattice tool is located under the Tools menu in the UV Texture Editor.

Next is the UV Smudge tool. It works with selected UVs, making it a great choice for moving any that are overlapping. It has a similar effect to the UV Lattice tool; however, it uses a brush instead of handles. You can scale the brush size by holding down the **b** key and dragging the mouse. UV Smudge is also located under the Tools menu in the UV Texture Editor. Figure 9.21 shows the tool in action.

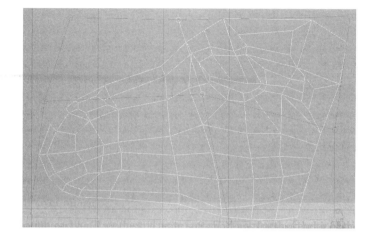

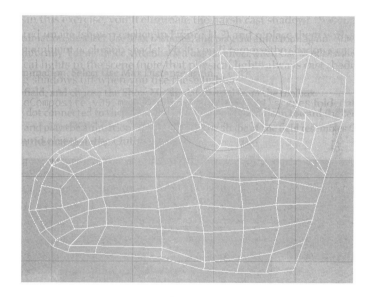

Another great tool is Automatic Mapping, which is a projection method for mapping UVs. You can use it to generate UVs quickly for hard-to-reach areas, such as the inside of a mouth or an ear canal. It is also useful for handling small parts, like teeth. Automatic mapping typically does not give you good UVs, but it saves a lot of time that would otherwise be spent selecting faces and moving manipulators. Automatic Mapping is located in the main Polygons menu set under Create UVs.

ICON HELP

Remember that if you hover over an icon with the mouse, the name of the tool will appear in the help line at the lower left of the screen. This is useful when the icon for the tool is less than intuitive.

Arranging UV Shells

The purpose of your project or model will dictate how you arrange your UV shells. If you are using your model in a game, your UVs should be condensed to the fewest maps possible. The goal is to put as many of the UV shells as you can onto a single material. Most games support multiple maps and therefore allow you to split up groups of UV shells onto multiple materials. Figure 9.22 shows the arrangement of the UV shells for the giraffe if it were going to use a single map in a game environment. The Layout tool is very effective for automatically creating this type of arrangement.

FIGURE 9.22
The UV shells are arranged into the 0 to 1 texture space in preparation for a game environment.

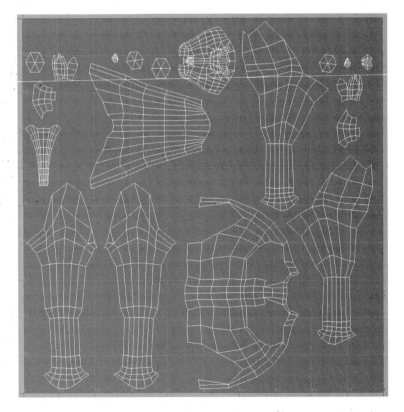

For film and other projects without real-time game restrictions, you can arrange your UVs to maximize texture space. This means a single UV shell can fill all the 0 to 1 texture space if needed. Textures are automatically repeated inside the UV Texture Editor; therefore, your UVs can be positioned outside the normalized texture space (see Figure 9.23). This makes viewing and modifying UVs easier. They can also sit on top of one another, as long as they are assigned to separate materials.

FIGURE 9.23
The UV groups are spread out and assigned to multiple materials to use more texture space.

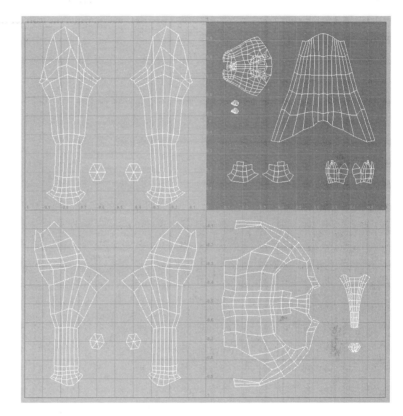

You can generate a snapshot of the UVs to serve as a guide for painting the textures in Photoshop:

1. Continue with your scene or open the `giraffeUV_v07.ma` scene from the `chapter9\` `scenes` folder at the book's web page. In the UV Texture Editor window, choose Polygons ➢ UV Snapshot.

2. In the UV Snapshot dialog box, use the Browse button to choose the folder where you want to save the file.

3. Set the size of the texture file. In this case, choose 2048.

   You can resize the document in Photoshop if you decide you need higher or lower resolution for the texture. Since the model will be seen close up, you may eventually want to increase the resolution to as high as 4096. It's usually best to keep these dimensions the same size in X and Y so that the texture is square.

4. Keep Color Value white so that the UV texture guide appears as white lines on a dark background.

   In Photoshop, you can set the UV texture snapshot on a separate layer above all the other layers and set the blend mode to Screen so that the UV texture lines appear on top of the painted textures.

5. Set the Image Format to TIFF. Notice in the filename field that there is an asterisk after the name you have entered. Change the asterisk to the file extension—in this case, to **tiff**. Click OK to generate the snapshot.

6. You can also set the UV range to grab an area other than the 0 to 1 texture space. For instance, to get a snapshot of the hind-leg UVs in the lower-left corner, you would use **–1.0** for the U and V settings (see Figure 9.24).

FIGURE 9.24
The options for taking a UV snapshot

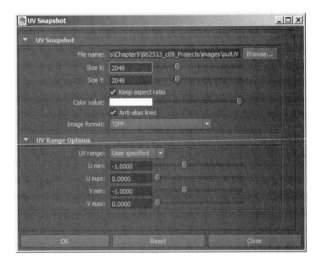

7. Open the snapshot in Photoshop or your favorite paint program, and use the UVs as a guide for painting the textures.

To see a finished version of the head with complete UV maps, open the `giraffeUV_v07.ma` file from the `chapter9\scenes` folder at the book's web page.

Additional UV Mapping Considerations

Proper UV mapping is essential for creating and applying painted textures to your polygon and subdivision surface models. However, UV mapping can also affect how your models work with other aspects of Maya. Because displacement maps are essentially textures that deform geometry, it's important that UV coordinates be created properly in order for the displacements to deform the geometry properly.

Two-dimensional procedural nodes, such as ramps, fractals, and (obviously) checkered patterns, are affected by UV mapping. When you apply a fractal to a polygon model, the seams between UV coordinates can be very obvious if the UVs are not carefully mapped. Likewise, paint effects, hair, skin weighting, and fur all rely on UV coordinates to function properly.

UVs can also be animated using keyframes. You can use this technique to create some interesting effects, especially in games, where it may be more efficient to create a repeating animated loop of UV texture coordinates than to create an animated sequence of images. To animate UVs, select the UVs in the UV Texture Editor, press the **s** hot key to create a keyframe, change their positions, and set another keyframe by pressing the **s** hot key again. You can refine the animation using the Graph Editor.

TEXTURES ON DEFORMING SURFACES

Sometimes textures can appear to move or swim on a deforming surface. You can avoid this by mapping to a UV set. However, it is not always necessary to have UVs. You can save considerable time by using a projected procedural or file texture on a surface without UVs. If the surface is deforming, the texture may shift or move around the surface as it deforms. To correct this, you can turn on the local setting in the texture node, convert the procedural to a file texture, or create a reference object.

Transferring UVs

UVs can be transferred from one object to another. This is usually done between two versions of the same object and can be useful as a tool for quickly creating UVs on a complex object. The workflow might look something like this:

1. Create a duplicate of a complex object.

2. Smooth the duplicate using an operation such as Average Vertices or the sculpting brush.

3. Generate UV coordinates for the smoothed version using any combination of methods. Smoothing out the detail makes applying UV coordinates a little easier.

4. Select the smoothed version; then Shift+click the original and choose Mesh ➢ Transfer Attributes ➢ Options.

5. Set the options so that the UVs are copied from the smoothed version to the original.

Multiple UV Sets

An object can have more than one version of the UV coordinates. These are known as *UV sets*. For instance, for a character's head, you may use one UV set to control how color information is applied to the face and another set to control how the hair or fur is applied to the head. To create multiple sets, you can use the UV Set Editor (Create UVs ➢ UV Set Editor). You can copy UVs from one set to another and link textures to different sets using the Relationship Editor (Window ➢ Relationship Editors ➢ UV Linking).

Optimizing Textures

Maya offers an optimized format that is used at render time. Textures using standard image file formats such as TIF are loaded into memory before rendering begins, which can slow down the rendering and lead to instability. Maya can convert the file texture to an optimized, uncompressed, OpenEXR format that allows Maya or mental ray® to load the texture as needed during render, which not only increases stability but also allows for the use of much larger textures.

The original file textures are still used in the scene and stored in the sourceimages folder and referenced when you work in the scene. The conversion takes place automatically, and the converted files are stored in the sourceimages/cache folder by default. When you render the scene, you'll see your file textures listed there with the .map extension. In versions of Maya prior to 2008, you had to convert file texture images to the MAP format manually by using the imf_copy utility.

To enable this automatic conversion feature, follow these steps:

1. Choose Window ➤ Settings/Preferences ➤ Preferences.

2. In the Rendering section, select Use Optimized Textures (Auto-conversion), as shown in Figure 9.25.

FIGURE 9.25
Enable the Use Optimized Textures feature in the Preferences window.

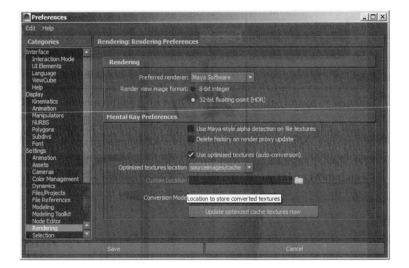

3. You can choose to use the default sourceimages/cache folder for the current project or specify a custom location. If you are rendering on a network, make sure that all render nodes can see the folder where you store the optimized file.

4. You can also choose to convert all textures or just the ones that have been assigned to shaders. To update the files, click the Update Optimize Cache Textures Now button. The files should update automatically at render time, but just in case they don't for some reason, you can use this button to force a refresh.

Bump and Normal Mapping

Bump maps, normal maps, and displacement maps are three ways to add surface detail to a model using textures. In this section, you'll learn about bump and normal maps. A discussion concerning displacement maps appears later in this chapter.

Bump maps and normal maps are similar in that they both create the impression of surface detail by using color information, stored in a 2D texture map, to alter the surface normal of an object. When the light in a scene hits the surface of an object, the color values in the texture tell the rendering engine to alter the surface normal so that the light creates a highlight or shading/shadowing. The surface geometry itself is not changed; however, the altered normal makes it look as though the geometry has more detail than it does. This saves the modeler the trouble of sculpting every single wrinkle, fold, bump, screw, or scratch into a model and keeps the geometry resolution of the model down to a level that the computer's processor can handle.

Bump and normal maps do not alter the surface geometry. This means that the part of the surface that faces the camera will appear as though it has bumps and depressions, but as the surface of the geometry turns away from the camera, it becomes apparent that the silhouette of the geometry has not been changed by the bump or normal map. Figure 9.26 demonstrates this principle.

FIGURE 9.26
This sphere has a noise texture applied as a bump map. It looks lumpy from the front, but the silhouette of the sphere is not altered by the bump map.

Bump Maps

Bump maps are simply grayscale textures, usually painted in a 2D paint program such as Photoshop. Bump maps are best used for fine detail, such as tiny wrinkles, pores, small rivets, scratches, small dents, wood grain, and so on. When texturing highly detailed characters, you can best use bump maps with displacement maps.

Any texture can be used as a bump map, including the 2D and 3D procedural textures such as Fractal, Ramp, Grid, Crater, Water, Brownian, and so on. When you place a texture in the

Bump Mapping channel of a standard Maya shader, a connection is made between the outAlpha attribute on the texture and the Bump value of the shader. These are especially useful since a lot of textures in the real world have patterns, burlap, concrete, and so on.

Normal Maps

A bump map displaces a surface normal either up or down (relative to the surface normal) based on the value of the texture. Normal maps, on the other hand, replace the normal direction with a vector stored in the RGB colors of the map. In other words, rather than pulling out a bump or pushing in a depression, the colors of the normal map change the X, Y, Z of the normal based on the RGB color of the map (see Figure 9.27).

FIGURE 9.27
The diagram shows how bump maps and normal maps affect the surface normals of a polygon in different ways.

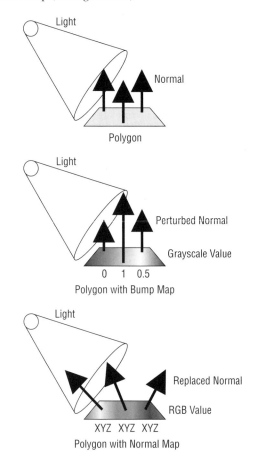

When viewed as a 2D texture in a paint program, normal maps have a psychedelic rainbow color. These colors tell Maya how the normal on the surface of the geometry should be bent at render time. It's difficult for an artist to paint a normal map because the RGB values are not intuitively applied.

There are two types of normal maps:

Object Space Maps   These are used for nondeforming objects, such as walls, spaceships, trashcans, and the like. They are calculated based on the local object space of the object. *Up* in object space means toward the top of the object. If the object is rotated upside down in world space, the top is still the top—so a robot's head is still the top of the object in object space even if it's hanging upside down.

Tangent Space Maps   These are used for deforming objects, such as characters. Tangent space maps record the normal's vector relative to the object's surface. In tangent space, *up* means up away from the surface of the object. Tangent space maps appear more blue and purple since the direction in which the normal is being bent is always relative to the surface along the tangent space z-axis. The z-axis corresponds with the blue channel (XYZ = RGB). Object space maps have more variation in color.

In practice, most artists use tangent space maps for everything. In fact, prior to Maya 2008 tangent space maps were the only type of normal maps that Maya supported. Tangent space maps work well for both deforming and nondeforming objects.

The most common way to create a normal map is to use a high-resolution, detailed version of the model as the source of the normal map and a low-resolution version of the model as the target for the map. The difference between the two surfaces is recorded in the colors of the map, which is then used to alter the appearance of the low-resolution model. This is a typical process when creating models for games where low-resolution models are required by the real-time rendering engine but the audience demands realistically detailed objects.

Creating Normal Maps

In this exercise, you'll create a normal map for the giraffe. A high-resolution version of the model will be used as the source of the map. To create a normal map in Maya, you'll use the Transfer Maps tool. This tool can be used to create a number of texture map types, including normal maps.

1. Open the `giraffeTransferMaps_v01.ma` file from the `chapter9\scenes` folder at the book's web page.

2. Look in the Display Layer panel. You'll see two layers: one labeled LORES, and the other labeled HIRES. Turn off the LORES layer, and turn on the HIRES layer. You'll see a higher-resolution detailed version of the giraffe, as shown in Figure 9.28.

3. Turn off the HIRES layer. The geometry does not need to be visible in order to extract maps. Thus if the high-resolution geometry is slowing down your computer, you can hide it.

4. Right-click the LORES layer, and choose Select Objects.

5. Under the Rendering menu set, choose Lighting/Shading ➤ Transfer Maps to open the Transfer Maps window (see Figure 9.29).

6. Expand the Target Meshes rollout. The loresGiraffeShape object is listed since it was selected when you opened the window. If it does not appear, select it and click the Add Selected button. No other objects should be listed; if they are, select them in the list, and click the Remove Selected button.

7. Expand the Source Meshes rollout, right-click the HIRES layer, and choose Select Objects.

8. Click the Add Selected button to add it to the list.

9. Expand the Output Maps section; you'll see icons representing all the types of maps that can be created.

10. Click the Normal option to add *normal map* to the list. If other types of maps are listed, click the Remove Map button in the section for the map you want to remove.

11. Click the folder next to the Normal Map field (see Figure 9.30), and set the location and filename for the location of the map that will be created.

FIGURE 9.29

The Transfer Maps window

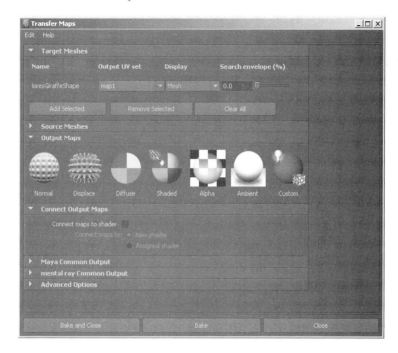

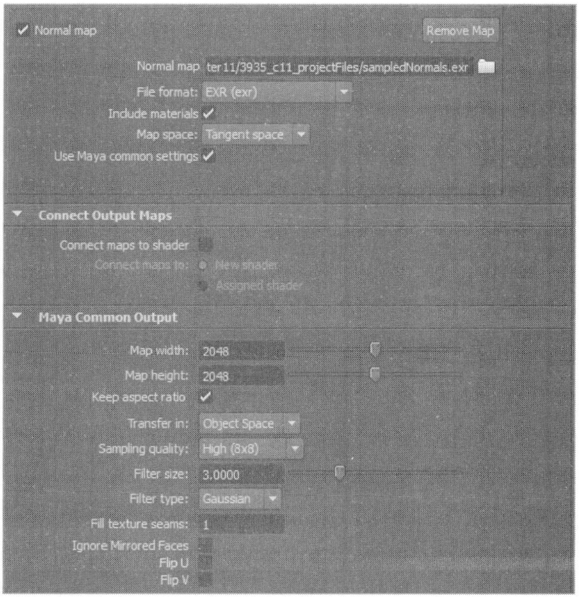

FIGURE 9.30

The transfer map's options

12. Choose the sourceimages folder of the current project, and name the file
giraffeHead_Nrml.

There are a number of file format options to choose from. The two best choices are Maya
IFF and EXR. Both are 32-bit formats that will ensure a detailed smooth map.

13. Choose EXR; this way, you can open the map in Photoshop (CS1 and higher) for viewing
if you need to. If the file extension is something other than .exr, it will be automatically
updated.

OPENEXRLOADER PLUG-IN

When using the EXR format in Maya, you'll need to make sure the OpenEXRLoader plug-in
is currently loaded; otherwise, you'll get an error when you try to connect the file to a shader.
Choose Window ➤ Settings/Preferences ➤ Plug-in Manager. In the list of plug-ins, make sure
OpenEXRLoader.mll is currently selected.

---

14. The Include Materials check box is extremely useful if you want to include a bump map
as part of the normal map. For now, deselect it since there is no bump map applied to the
high-resolution mesh material.

However, make a note of this option—you can add more detail to your normal map, such
as pores and fine wrinkles, by applying a bump texture to the shader for the high-resolution mesh object and then activating this option when using the Transfer Maps tool.

BAKING BUMP MAPS

When you bake a bump map into the normal map using the Include Materials option, the Bump
Depth setting on the shader of the source mesh will determine the intensity of the bump as it's
baked into the normal map. If you want to change this later, you'll need to adjust Bump Depth on
the source mesh and rebake the normal map.

---

15. Set Map Space to Tangent Space. You should always use tangent space maps for
characters. (And, as stated already, you can use them for any type of object.)

16. The Use Maya Common Settings check box makes the tool use the settings specified in
the Maya Common Output. If this is deselected, sliders that appear will allow you to set
the size of the map in this section. For now, keep this box selected.

17. In the Connect Output Maps settings, you can connect the map to a shader automatically.
Deselect the Connect Maps To Shader option for now.

Later in this chapter, you'll learn how to make the connection manually. Once you understand how the connection is made, you can use the Connect Maps To Shader option in the
future to make things more convenient.

18. In the Maya Common Output settings, enter the following:

  a. Set the size of the map to **2048** in width and height.

  b. Set Transfer In to Object Space, and set Sampling Quality to High.

  c. Set Filter Size to **3**.

  d. Set Filter Type to Gaussian.

Leave Fill Texture Seams at 1 and the remaining three check boxes (Ignore Mirrored Faces, Flip U, and Flip V) deselected. Click Bake and Close to complete the tool. The settings are shown in Figure 9.30.

Sometimes maps do not transfer properly. Errors usually look like solid pools of color. Often this is caused by the geometry not matching properly. To fix this, you can adjust the search envelope Maya uses to extract the differences between the models. The search envelope specifies the volume of space that Maya uses to search when creating the transfer map. Maya compares the target geometry (the low-resolution map) with the source geometry (the high-resolution map) and records the difference between the two as color values in the normal map. The search envelope sets the limits of the distance Maya will search when creating the map. The envelope itself is a duplicate of the target geometry that's offset from the original. The offset distance is specified by the Search Envelope slider in the Target Meshes section of the Transfer Maps tool. What's more, you can edit the Target Mesh geometry itself to improve the results of the final map.

NOTE   Normal maps can take a while to calculate, so it's a good idea to create a few test maps at lower quality and then raise the quality settings once you're satisfied that the map is free of errors.

New!   You can bake out the rest of the UV shells by selecting each group and swapping their placement into the 0 to 1 texture space. In the toolbar of the UV Texture Editor are controls for shifting a selected group of UV shells. You can select all of the shells that reside in the positive V space and shift them over a block using the right arrow (see Figure 9.31).

FIGURE 9.31
Use the arrows in the UV Texture Editor to relocate blocks of UV shells.

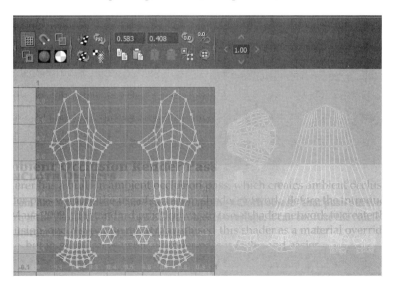

Some third-party applications like Mudbox read outside the 0 to 1 texture space and can transfer all the maps in one operation instead of your having to move the UV shell groups.

When the maps are finished, you can close the scene without saving, since no adjustments were made. The next exercise takes you through the process of applying the normal maps.

The Transfer In option has three choices: World Space, Object Space, and UV Space. These specify how the map will be calculated and transferred from the high-resolution version to the low-resolution version. If the models were different sizes, then the World Space option would be appropriate, and the models would need to be directly on top of each other. The objects used in this exercise are the same size and very similar except for their resolutions and level of detail, so the Object Space option is more appropriate. The UV Space option works best for objects of fairly similar but not exactly the same shape, such as a female human character and a male human character.

Applying Normal Maps

Normal maps are applied to an object's shader in the Bump channel, and they can be viewed in the perspective window. In this section, you'll see how the map looks when it's applied to the model, as well as a few suggestions for fixing problems.

1. Open the `giraffeUV_v07.ma` file from the `chapter9\scenes` folder at the book's web page.

2. Open the Hypershade window (Window ➤ Rendering Editors ➤ Hypershade).

3. Select the giraffe head_Mat shader, and open its Attribute Editor.

4. Click the checkered box next to the Bump Mapping channel, and choose File from the Create Render Node pop-up.

5. When you add the file node, the Attribute Editor will open to the bump2d node. Set the Use As option to Tangent Space Normals. This tells Maya that the texture you're applying is a normal map and not a bump map. You can leave the Bump Depth at 1; it has no effect on the strength of the normal map.

6. Switch to the file1 node, and click the folder next to the Image Name field.

7. Browse your computer's file folder, and find the `giraffeHead_Nrml.exr` file; it should be in the `sourceimages` folder (if you get an error when loading the image, make sure the OpenEXRLoader plug-in is selected in the preferences).

   Once the file is loaded, you should see a preview in the texture sample icon. The texture should appear mostly blue and purple. If it is completely flat blue, then there was an error during the creation process—most likely the source mesh was not selected in the Transfer Maps options, so you'll need to remake the map.

8. In the perspective view, choose High Quality Rendering from the Renderer menu at the top of the panel. After a few seconds, you should see a preview of the normal map in the perspective view. (Make sure that you have Texture Shaded activated; press the **6** key to switch to this mode.)

The normal map should make the low-resolution model look very similar to the high-resolution model. You can see in the silhouette of the geometry that the blockiness of the profile indicates that the geometry is still low resolution, but those areas facing the camera look highly detailed. This workflow is useful for creating game models. The models end up looking much more realistic and detailed without taxing the processor of the game console.

9. Apply the rest of the maps in the same manner. Figure 9.32 shows the giraffe with all of its normal maps applied.

FIGURE 9.32
The low-resolution model with its normal maps applied.

10. Inspect the model for errors in the texture.

Most likely you'll find some errors around the lips, ears, and eyes. If large portions of the model look wrong, you'll need to try creating the map again. Sometimes, just editing the geometry of the search envelope can fix the errors when you regenerate the map. At other times, you may need to change the actual generation settings, such as the Search Method and Max Search Depth values in the Advanced settings.

Normal maps are difficult but not impossible to edit in a 2D paint program such as Photoshop. If the normal map has just a few small glitches, you can open them in Photoshop and paint each Color channel (Red, Green, and Blue) separately to clean up the maps. This can be faster than trying to regenerate a whole new map just to fix a tiny spot.

For a completed version of the scene, open the `giraffeNormalMaps_v01.ma` file from the `chapter9\scenes` folder at the book's web page.

Displacement Mapping

Displacement maps are like bump maps in that they use a grayscale texture to add detail to a model. However, rather than just perturb the normal of the surface, displacement maps alter the geometry at render time. Unlike normal and bump maps, the silhouette of the geometry reflects the detail in the map. Displacement maps can be used with NURBS, polygon, and subdivision surfaces and can be rendered in both mental ray and Maya Software. The best results are usually achieved by rendering displacement maps on a polygon surface in mental ray using mental ray's Approximation Editor to subdivide the surface appropriately during render.

NOTE Displacement maps can be viewed only in a software render; they can't be previewed in the perspective window.

Displacement maps are tricky to use and require some practice to master; however, the results are often worth the time invested. Recent advances in digital sculpting programs, such as ZBrush and Mudbox, have enabled modelers to bring an unprecedented amount of realism and detail to digital characters. The detail created in these high-density meshes is often brought into Maya in the form of displacement maps or normal maps.

ZBrush Displacement Maps

By default, textures created in ZBrush are upside down when imported into Maya and therefore must be flipped. Because ZBrush interprets dark and light values in a different way than Maya, you'll need to make sure that the value for the texture's Alpha Offset is –0.5 times the Alpha Gain setting. This ensures that dark values on the displacement map push inward and lighter areas push outward.

If your object looks bloated or distorted, double-check the Alpha Gain and Alpha Offset settings for the file texture used for the displacement. Furthermore, make sure Alpha Is Luminance is checked.

In addition to aiding in creating detail on creatures, displacement maps have a wide variety of creative applications and innovations. You can use animated displacements to simulate rolling waves on an ocean surface, fissures opening in the earth, or veins crawling beneath the skin. In this section, you will apply displacement maps to the giraffe.

The Transfer Maps tool also allows for the creation of displacement maps. Generating a workable displacement map using this tool takes a little more work than if you used a third-party application, and the Transfer Maps tool generally falls short of third-party products' precision. Through trial and error, you need to establish the proper displacement height. The low-resolution geometry needs to be smoothed to avoid low-resolution shading (see Figure 9.33). In addition, I do not recommend that you use the EXR format to transfer the maps. The best format to use for transferring displacement maps is the native IFF format in Maya.

FIGURE 9.33
This map was transferred without first smoothing the surface on the low-polygon version.

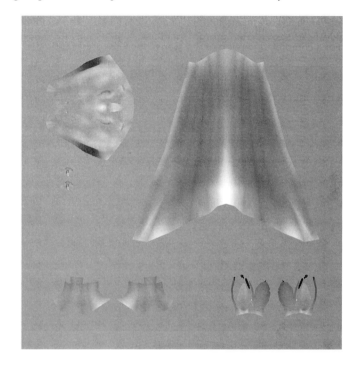

The only difference between the settings in transferring normal maps and displacement maps is the Maximum Value attribute, which controls the range of values on which the displacement is gauged. With the giraffe, a smaller value increases the contrast between low and high areas (see Figure 9.34).

FIGURE 9.34
The options used for transferring displacement.

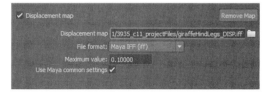

If you decide you want actual geometry to be created from the displacement, you can convert the displacement to a polygon object. It might be helpful as a stand-in object if you need to position objects in the scene near the displaced plane or if you want to model terrain using a procedural texture.

1. Select the plane, and choose Modify ➤ Convert ➤ Displacement To Polygons. There are no options for this action. A second object will be created based on the original displaced plane. Any animation of the texture will not be reflected in the converted object; it derives its displacement from the current state of the displacing texture.

2. To increase the resolution of the converted object, increase the subdivisions in Height and Width on the original plane. The conversion will take longer to calculate, and the resulting geometry will be denser.

Vector displacement maps use height and direction to offset geometry. This allows complex detail, like undercuts or overhangs, to be reproduced on low-resolution geometry. The best way to generate a vector displacement map is to use a digital sculpting program such as ZBrush or Mudbox. Although it involves learning another application, the results are excellent. This is the workflow of choice for many studios. The maps must be generated as 32-bit floating-point maps in the EXR or TIF file format. In this exercise, mental ray's Approximation Editor is used in conjunction with a vector displacement map to reproduce sculpted detail onto the giraffe. The vector displacement maps were generated using Mudbox.

1. Open the `giraffeDisp_v01.ma` scene from the `chapter9\scenes` folder at the book's web page.

   The giraffe has all of its UV texture coordinates set for applying the vector displacement maps. The giraffe's head is framed in the viewport. You will add a vector displacement to the head first.

2. Select the giraffe, and create an approximation node. Choose Window ➤ Rendering Editors ➤ mental ray ➤ Approximation Editor (if mental ray does not appear in the list, you'll need to load the `Mayatomr.mll` plug-in—`Mayatomr.bundle` on the Mac—using the Plug-in Manager).

3. In the Approximation Editor, click the Create button in the Subdivisions (Polygon And Subd. Surfaces) section. You do not need to create a displacement approximation node; the subdivision approximation provides enough geometry for displacement and smoothes the surface.

4. In the Attribute Editor for the mentalRaySubdivApprox1 node, change the parameters to match those shown in Figure 9.35.

FIGURE 9.35
The settings used for the subdivision approximation node.

This subdivides the model so that the detail created by the displacement texture is more refined. Higher values allow more of the detail in the map to come through but also to add more triangles. The Length/Distance/Angle efficiently adds triangles where they are needed the most.

5. Set the renderer to mental ray. Create a test render of the giraffe. It should look nice and smooth (see Figure 9.36).

FIGURE 9.36
A close-up of the giraffe's head rendered with a subdivision approximation node

6. In the Hypershade, select giraffeHead_Mat and choose Graph ➢ Input And Output Connections, or click its icon.

7. Open Blinn1SG in the Attribute Editor.

8. Click the checkered box next to Displacement Mat. The Create Render Node window is displayed. Choose Displacement from the left column and then Displacement from the right column. A displacement shader is added to the Blinn shading group node.

9. Open displacementShader2's Attribute Editor. The settings are shown in Figure 9.37.

FIGURE 9.37
The Displacement attributes

Make sure the proper vector space is being used. You set this in a program like Mudbox when you extract the map. In the case of the giraffe, object space was used; therefore no changes need to be made. Click the Create Node icon for vector displacement, and then click File to add a texture node. Browse your computer's chapter9\sourceimages folder and find the giraffeHead_VDisp.exr file.

10. Render the giraffe's head. Watch the Output window as it renders. The giraffe renders exactly as it was sculpted, reproducing even the smallest details (see Figure 9.38).

FIGURE 9.38
The giraffe rendered with vector displacement

11. Notice that you get numerous warnings in the Output window. Figure 9.39 is a snapshot of the feedback.

FIGURE 9.39
Warnings from the Output window

These errors can slow down your render significantly. To correct them, you need to decrease the default mental ray Maximum Displace setting. Select the giraffe and open its Attribute Editor.

12. Choose the giraffeMedResShape tab. Open the mental ray section. At the bottom of the section, check Override Maximum Displace and set the value to **0.027** (see Figure 9.40).

FIGURE 9.40
Changing the
Maximum Displace
value

You can obtain the Maximum Displace value by looking for the highest value listed in the Output window. Round that number up.

To see a finished version of the giraffe with all of its displacement maps connected, open the `giraffeDisplace_v02.ma` file from the `chapter9\scenes` folder at the book's web page.

Subsurface Scattering

Subsurface scattering (SSS) refers to the phenomenon of light rays bouncing around just beneath the surface of a material before being reflected back into the environment. It's the translucent quality seen in objects such as jade, candle wax, and human skin. (Actually, almost every material except metal has some amount of subsurface scattering.) Subsurface scattering adds an amazing level of realism to CG objects and characters.

Fast, Simple Skin-Shader Setup

In Maya, there are several ways to create the look of subsurface scattering, ranging from the simple to the complex. The Translucence, Translucence Depth, and Translucence Focus sliders included on standard Maya shaders offer the simplest way to create translucency. These sliders work fine for an object made of a single material, such as candle wax. Likewise, the Scatter Radius slider and related attributes in the mental ray section of Maya shaders add a quick-and-dirty subsurface quality to simple objects. However, these options fall far short when you're trying to create a complex material such as human skin.

New!   mental ray's layering shaders include a new implementation of subsurface scattering. Simplified and more accurate, the scatter layer mimics how physical scattering works to achieve convincing results. Scatter layers allow for multithreading and do not require the old style of lightmapping. The following exercise uses mental ray's layering shaders to add subsurface scatter to the giraffe.

1. Open the `giraffeSSS_v01.ma` scene from the `chapter9\scenes` folder at the book's web page.

2. Switch to the persp camera, and do a quick test render.

3. Store the image in the render view so that you can compare it with the subsurface scattering renders.

The character has a Blinn texture applied along with the skin and displacement textures used in previous sections. These same file textures (along with a few others) will be plugged into the skin shader (see Figure 9.41).

FIGURE 9.41
The giraffe rendered without subsurface scattering

4. Open the Hypershade and, on the left side, switch to the Create mental ray Nodes section.

5. From the Materials section, create a mila material shader. Name the shader **giraffeHeadSSS_Mat**.

6. Right-click giraffeHead_Mat, and choose Select Objects With Material from the marking menu. All the assigned faces are selected.

7. Right-click giraffeHeadSSS_Mat, and choose Assign Material To Selection from the marking menu. The parts of the giraffe assigned to the mila material turn a solid color in the perspective view (depending on your graphics card, the color will vary), and that's okay. Maya just can't preview some of the mental ray nodes using hardware rendering.

8. Right-click giraffeHeadSSS_Mat again, and choose Graph Network. You'll see that Maya has automatically created a layer node and a diffuse layer.

9. Select giraffeHeadSSS_Mat, and open its Attribute Editor. Change Base Component to Diffuse (Scatter). The subsurface scattering attributes are added to the Base rollout.

10. Choose the create render node for Color. This is also considered the Tint. Add a file node and browse to `chapter9\sourceimages` and add `giraffeHead_DIFF.tif`.

11. Graph giraffeHeadSSS_Mat in the Hypershade and select mila_mix_subsurface_scatter1 from the graphed shading network. The Color attribute from the material component section is the same attribute located at the top of the scatter layer. Do a test render to see the results of the scatter layer (see Figure 9.42).

FIGURE 9.42

The subsurface scattering is applied to the giraffe's head and neck.

12. The scale of the giraffe is that 1 centimeter is equal to 1 meter. Subsurface scattering is calculated based on meters. Therefore, you must convert the scale of the giraffe. This can be done easily within the shader. Change Scale Conversion to **100** to multiply 1 centimeter by 100, effectively converting it to meters.

Create another test render (see Figure 9.43).

13. In the Materials tab of the Hypershade, find displacementShader5. MMB-drag this shader on top of the shading group labeled mila_material1SG, and choose Default. These are the same displacement node, file texture, and settings created earlier in the chapter (see Figure 9.44).

FIGURE 9.43
The shader renders correctly, with the proper scale conversion.

FIGURE 9.44
The shading network for the subsurface scattering shader

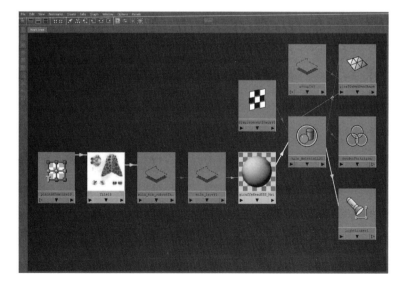

14. Create a test render to see how the giraffe looks so far.

The giraffe is close to its final look. Too much light is being back scattered. You can see around the edges of the head and neck a strong orange tint.

Back scattering is used to create the reddish color seen as light passes through thin skin. The default Back Weight and Back Color values are usually pretty good for earth-born animals as opposed to an animal from another world. Back Depth, however, needs a value. By default it is set to 0.0, which doesn't put a limit on how far light can travel through the surface. Change the Back Depth value to **1.0**.

15. Create another test render. Compare the render with the previously stored version; notice how the colors are more balanced.

16. Save your scene.

To see a version of the scene up to this point, open the `giraffeSSS_v02.ma` file from the `chapter9\scenes` folder at the book's web page. Figure 9.45 shows the render.

FIGURE 9.45
At this point, a render of the giraffe looks good but lacks specular highlights.

Subsurface Specularity

Specularity controls how the skin of your character reflects the lights in the scene. The giraffe is covered in fur. It still has specularity, but it reacts very differently than bare skin. The giraffe's specularity needs to be muted. It also needs to be broken up to give the appearance of a fur texture on the giraffe's surface. Adding a specular layer on top of the scatter layer allows you to control the specularity as well as add a bump to its effects. The following steps take you through the process.

1. Open the `giraffeSSS_v02.ma` scene from the `chapter9\scenes` folder at the book's web page. The scene picks up where the last exercise left off.

2. Part of achieving realism is adding a bump to the specular highlights of your character. First, let's add a bump map to the material. A scatter layer cannot take a bump map; therefore, it must be added to a different layer. Select giraffeHeadSSS_Mat and graph its input and output connections in the Hypershade.

3. Open giraffeHeadSSS_Mat's Attribute Editor. Click +Layer and add a Weighted Diffuse Reflection layer.

4. With a weight of 1.0, the diffuse layer overrides the lower scatter layer with its default color. Drag the `giraffeHead_DIFF.tif` texture from the Hypershade to the Color channel of the diffuse layer. Set the Weight value to **0.2**.

5. You now have the option to add a bump map to the diffuse layer or to the Overall Bump channel of the material. Eventually you will add more layers to the giraffe's material, so let's add it to the Overall Bump channel. To do so, click the Create Render Node icon for the Overall Bump channel on the Material Properties rollout (see Figure 9.46).

FIGURE 9.46
Add a bump map to the layered material.

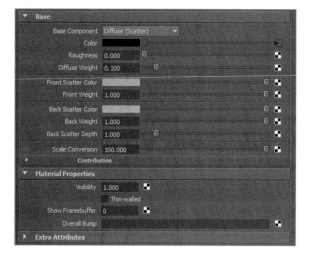

6. The bump2d node is not automatically added. In the Create Render Node window, click Utilities in the Maya section on the left side. Select Bump2D from the right side.

7. Assign a file texture to the Bump Value of the bump2d node. Use `giraffeHead_Bump.tif` for the image.

8. Create a test render and save the image (see Figure 9.47).

9. Add a weighted Glossy Reflection layer by clicking the +Layer button in the giraffeHeadSSS_Mat node. The glossy reflection becomes the uppermost layer. Create a test render using the defaults (see Figure 9.48).

FIGURE 9.47
A bump map
is added to the
giraffe's head.

FIGURE 9.48
The glossy layer is
set to 1, creating
dramatic specular
highlights.

10. Drag the `giraffeHead_DIFF.tif` texture from the Hypershade to the Color channel of the Glossy Reflection layer. Set Weight to **0.2**. Create another test render.

11. The specular value is too intense. To soften its intensity, set Roughness to **0.9**. Increasing the Roughness value creates a broader specular highlight (see Figure 9.49).

FIGURE 9.49
Setting Roughness to 0.9 softens the intensity of the specular highlight.

12. Add the same layering shader and appropriate textures to the rest of the giraffe. To simplify the process, you can choose Edit ➢ Duplicate ➢ Shading Network and replace the textures to match the different body parts.

To see a completed version of the model, open the `giraffeSSS_v03.ma` scene from the chapter9\scenes folder at the book's web page. Compare the image (shown in Figure 9.50) with the render from Figure 9.41. Subsurface scattering does a great deal toward adding realism to a character.

 **Real World Scenario**

BAKING SUBSURFACE SCATTERING

Making characters look photorealistic for real-time environments is extremely difficult. Suppose you're building characters for a new game engine, and you want to improve their overall look. Your resources are limited; you can support only a few texture maps and cannot implement any fancy shaders. In addition to normal maps, you wanted to have some type of subsurface scattering on the characters. Since shaders aren't an option, you decide to bake the rendered look of the layering shaders into the character's color or diffuse maps. Here is the process:

1. Create a mila material with scatter layers and all the appropriate maps, and assign it to the character.

2. In the Transfer Maps options window, choose Custom for the output map.

3. Enter the exact name of the mila material in the Custom Shader field. When you enter the correct name, the Create button at the end of the field changes to Edit.

4. Set the rest of the standard output options, and click Bake And Close.

5. The baked map looks good only from the camera's perspective, so you can bake multiple angles and piece them together in Photoshop to get a complete subsurface scattered texture map.

FIGURE 9.50
The final render of the giraffe with displacements, painted skin textures, and subsurface scattering

Viewport 2.0

Viewport 2.0 is the default high-performance scene viewer in Maya. It takes advantage of 64-bit architectures and makes use of GPU memory. Viewport 2.0 works with OpenGL and DirectX11.

Among other features, Viewport 2.0 allows you to visually interact with normal maps, ambient occlusion, and gamma correction. Its greatest power, however, resides in its ability to work with High-Level Shading Language (HLSL). Maya comes with a custom shader called the ubershader. As its name implies, the ubershader allows you to work with almost every type of shading effect with real-time interactivity. The ubershader is supported only under DirectX11.

DIRECTX11

DirectX11 is the rendering engine by default. If Maya cannot detect it, it will switch to OpenGL. To manually choose your rendering engine, choose Window ➤ Settings/Preferences ➤ Preferences. Choose Display in the Categories section of the Preferences window. You can then select from the available rendering engines under the Viewport 2.0 heading.

If you are using Mac OS X, your system will need to support OpenGL 4 in order to use the features of Viewport 2.0. In addition, Viewport 2.0 does not support the ATI Radeon X1900 card on Mac OS X.

Maya includes a material called the DX11Shader. The ubershader is connected to the DX11Shader by default. The following steps take you through the process of using the features of the ubershader using Viewport 2.0:

1. Open the `giraffeUber_v01.ma` scene from the `chapter9\scenes` folder at the book's web page. You'll see the giraffe standing on a primitive polygon plane.

2. In the perspective viewport, set Renderer to Viewport 2.0.

3. Open the Hypershade. Choose Create ➤ Materials ➤ DirectX 11 Shader. The new shader is added to the Hypershade window.

4. The giraffe is already textured and using the basic diffuse textures used earlier in the chapter. This makes it easy to assign the giraffe's UV shells to the new DX11Shader. In the Hypershade, RMB-click on giraffeBody_MAT and choose Select Objects With Material from the marking menu. The faces using the body texture are highlighted.

5. With the faces of the giraffe's body selected, RMB-click on DX11Shader1 and choose Assign Material To Selection from the marking menu.

6. Open DX11Shader1's Attribute Editor. Scroll to the Diffuse rollout. Change Diffuse Model to Blended Normal (Skin).

   This changes the shading model to simulate the look of skin or subsurface scattering.

7. Click the Create Render Node icon in the Diffuse Map channel and load the `giraffe-Body_DIFF.tif` file.

8. The map does not show up in the viewport yet. Click the Diffuse Map attribute to turn it on. Figure 9.51 shows the settings from the Diffuse rollout.

9. Click the Create Render Node icon for IBL 2D Map. Load an HDRI image for the texture. Chapter 7, "Lighting with mental ray," covers image-based lighting (IBL) and explains where to find useful HDRI images. In this example, we use the `rnl_probe.hdr` image.

10. Change IBL Type to 2D LatLong and check IBL Map. Press **7** on the keyboard to see the lighting results in Viewport 2.0 (Figure 9.52).

Figure 9.51
Load the giraffe's body texture and alter the settings to enable the image in Viewport 2.0.

Figure 9.52
The giraffe's body is lit using image-based lighting.

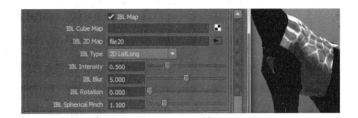

11. Repeat steps 3 through 8 for the rest of the giraffe's body parts.

DISPLACEMENTS

Vector displacement and standard displacement maps are also supported with Viewport 2.0. After choosing the displacement model, grayscale, or tangent vector, and assigning your texture, you must turn on the Tesselation parameter to see the results. The Tesselation parameter is located at the top of the ubershader's Attribute Editor.

To see a completed version, open the `giraffeUber_v02.ma` scene from the `chapter9\scenes` folder at the book's web page.

The Bottom Line

Create UV texture coordinates. UV texture coordinates are a crucial element of any polygon or subdivision surface model. If a model has well-organized UVs, painting texture and displacement maps is easy and error-free.

Master It Map UV texture coordinates on the giraffe's body.

Work with bump, normal, and displacement maps. Bump, normal, and displacement maps are ways to add detail to a model. Bump maps are great for fine detail, such as pores; normal maps allow you to transfer detail from a high-resolution mesh to a low-resolution version of the same model and offer superior shading and faster rendering than bump maps. Displacement maps alter the geometry.

Master It Create high-resolution and low-resolution versions of the model, and try creating a normal map using the Transfer Maps tool. See whether you can bake the bump map into the normal map.

Create a subsurface scattering layering shader. The subsurface scattering layering shader can create extremely realistic-looking skin.

Master It Bake the subsurface scattering shader into texture maps. Map the baked textures to the original Blinn shaders on the giraffe, and compare its look to the rendered subsurface scattering look.

Work with Viewport 2.0. Viewport 2.0 offers the ability to use advanced shaders in real time. Furthermore, high-end lighting can be combined without sacrificing interactivity.

Master It Using the DirectX11 ubershader, add normal, specular, and vector displacement maps to the `giraffeUber_v02.ma` scene file.

Chapter 10

Paint Effects

Paint Effects is a special Autodesk® Maya® module designed to allow artists to build, animate, and render large amounts of organic and natural detail quickly. Trees, grass, flowers, clouds, blood vessels, vines, rocks, and even small towns can be interactively painted into a scene in three dimensions. Paint Effects is both a dynamic particle-based system and a procedural modeling tool. There are many options for rendering the objects that you create using Paint Effects, giving you an astonishing amount of creative flexibility when incorporating natural elements into your projects.

Paint Effects is also part of the Toon Shading system, which is used to simulate the look of hand-drawn cartoons when rendering 3D animations. This chapter looks at how Paint Effects works through several short, experimental projects. By the end of the chapter, you'll understand how to design and apply your own custom Paint Effects objects in a scene.

In this chapter, you will learn to:

◆ Use the Paint Effects canvas

◆ Paint on 3D objects

◆ Understand strokes

◆ Design brushes

◆ Create complexity by adding strokes to a curve

◆ Shape strokes with behavior controls

◆ Animate strokes

◆ Render Paint Effects strokes

Using the Paint Effects Canvas

Maya contains a 2D paint program that you can use to paint illustrations, create textures, or experiment with Paint Effects brushes. The Paint Effects canvas works like a simplified version of a digital paint program such as Corel Painter. You can paint on the canvas using any of the Paint Effects brushes; it's a great way to test a brush before applying it in a 3D scene.

USING A TABLET

You don't have to use a digital tablet and pen to work with Paint Effects, but it makes things much easier. In this chapter, we assume that you'll be using a digital tablet. If you are using a mouse, please understand that, to paint with Paint Effects, you can left-click and drag to apply a stroke. If you're using a digital tablet, you can drag the pen across the tablet to apply a stroke to the Paint Effects canvas or to a 3D scene.

The Paint Effects Window

The Paint Effects window is like a mini–digital paint program inside Maya. In this section, you'll experiment with basic controls to create simple images on the canvas:

1. Create a new scene in Maya.

2. In the View panel, choose Panels ➤ Panel ➤ Paint Effects to open the Paint Effects window.

OPENING THE PAINT EFFECTS WINDOW

You can open Paint Effects in a number of ways. You can use the panel menu in a viewport, you can choose Window ➤ Paint Effects, or you can press **8** on the numeric keypad of your keyboard.

The viewport now appears white with some icons at the top. This white area is the Paint Effects canvas. If you see a 3D scene instead, choose Paint ➤ Paint Canvas (see Figure 10.1).

FIGURE 10.1
Choosing Paint Canvas from the Paint menu switches Paint Effects to 2D paint mode.

3. Click and drag on the canvas; you'll see a black line resembling ink appear wherever you paint on the canvas. If you are using a digital pressure-sensitive tablet, it varies the pressure as you paint: the line becomes thinner when less pressure is applied and thicker when more pressure is applied.

NAVIGATING THE PAINT EFFECTS WINDOW

You can use the same controls that you use in a 3D scene to zoom and pan while Paint Effects is open. To zoom, hold down Alt/Option and RMB-drag. To pan, hold down Alt/Option and MMB-drag. Since the canvas is two-dimensional, holding down Alt/Option and LMB-dragging doesn't rotate the canvas but instead serves as another way to pan.

4. Click the color swatch next to the *C* on the Paint Effects menu bar. This opens the Color Chooser. You can use this tool to change the color of the brush (see Figure 10.2).

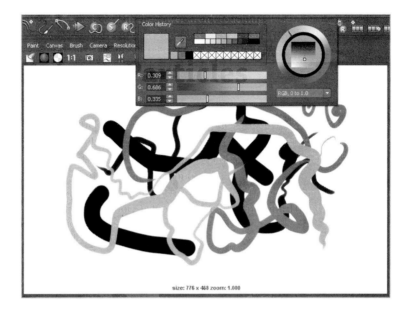

5. Move the slider to the right of the color swatch to change the Value (brightness) of the paintbrush color.

6. The color swatch labeled with a *T* and the slider next to it controls the transparency of the current stroke (see Figure 10.3) by changing color and transparency as you paint on the canvas.

Check out the other icons on the panel, from left to right, as shown in Figure 10.3:

◆ The *eraser* icon clears the canvas.

◆ The *color* icon displays the RGB channels (color) of the canvas.

◆ The *white circle* icon displays the alpha channel of the strokes on the canvas.

◆ The *1:1* icon displays the actual size of the canvas.

◆ The *camera* icon saves a snapshot of the canvas.

◆ The *editor* icon opens the Paint Effects Brush Settings dialog box for the current brush.

♦ The *double paintbrush* icon opens the Visor, which displays the available Brush presets.

♦ The *computer disk and brush* icon opens the Save Image dialog box to the sourceimages folder. When this button is active, every time you make a change to the canvas, the image will be automatically saved. The first time you activate the button, you'll be prompted to choose a location on disk to save the image.

♦ The *sideways arrow* allows the brush to wrap horizontally around the canvas. As you paint off one side of the canvas, this stroke is continued on the opposite side. This is useful when you want to create seamless tiling textures.

♦ The *down arrow* enables the brush to wrap vertically around the canvas. Strokes that you paint off the top or bottom of the canvas are continued on the opposite side.

♦ The *branching stroke* icon enables tube painting. This will be discussed in more detail later in this chapter.

♦ The *diagonally split* icon flips the tube direction. We will discuss this along with tubes.

7. Click the eraser icon to clear the canvas.

8. Click the double brush icon to open the Visor (or choose Window ➤ General Editors ➤ Visor).

9. In the Visor, make sure the Paint Effects tab is selected at the top. From the list of folders on the left side, open the flesh folder and select hands.mel. This switches the current brush to the hands brush—you'll see the current brush highlighted in yellow in the Visor (see Figure 10.4).

FIGURE 10.4
Select the hands.mel brush from the Visor.

THE VISOR

The Visor is a central library within Maya that allows you to access presets, example files, and other assets. The tabs at the top of the Visor let you browse and then choose the various types of assets. Much of the time you'll use the Visor to select a Paint Effects brush.

10. Paint some strokes on the canvas. Instead of an inky line, you'll see numerous hands appear as you paint. The hands vary in color while you apply them to the canvas (see Figure 10.5). You can control the amount of color variation under the Tube Shading rollout. You can read about these settings later in this chapter in the "Shading Strokes and Tubes" section.

FIGURE 10.5
When the hands
.mel brush is
selected, painting on
the canvas produces a
number of images of
human hands.

To change the size of the hands interactively as you paint, hold down the **b** key and drag left or right on the canvas; you'll see the circular brush icon grow as you drag to the right and shrink as you drag to the left.

If you want to change the background color of the canvas, choose Canvas ➤ Clear ➤ Options and change the Clear color. Clear the canvas. This removes strokes painted on the canvas and changes the background color at the same time.

11. Open the Visor, select some other brushes, and make a mess on the canvas. Try the defaultSmear.mel brush found in the airbrush folder. When you paint on the canvas, the brush smears the strokes already painted.

Some Paint Effects brushes create colors and images, whereas others alter the colors and images painted on the canvas. Some, such as the smearColor.mel brush, smear the strokes and apply color at the same time (see Figure 10.6).

Painting in Scene Mode

You can use Paint Effects brushes to paint in 3D. The strokes produce three-dimensional images that are incorporated into the scene. While in the Paint Effects window, you can preview what strokes will look like in a 3D scene.

FIGURE 10.6
Some brushes, such as the smearColor .mel brush, alter the strokes painted on the canvas.

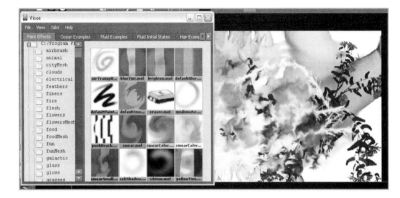

1. In the Paint Effects window, choose Paint ➤ Paint Scene. Maya will prompt you to save or discard the current image on the canvas. You can click No to discard the image or Yes if you're proud of it.

   The Paint Effects window now displays a perspective view, but notice that the Paint Effects menu is still at the top of the canvas. You are now in scene mode of the Paint Effects window. You can switch cameras using the Panels menu in the Paint Effects menu bar.

2. Open the Visor, and choose the hands.mel brush from the flesh folder. Paint some strokes on the grid.

3. The grid quickly becomes littered with dismembered hands (see Figure 10.7). Rotate the view of the scene. The hands switch to wireframe mode to help improve performance while you are changing the view. If you'd like the hands to remain visible, choose Stroke Refresh ➤ Rendered. Whenever you stop moving the camera, the strokes on the grid will reappear.

FIGURE 10.7
Painting in scene mode allows you to paint strokes directly in a 3D scene.

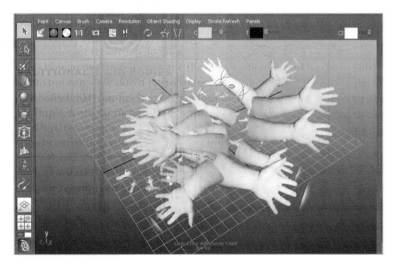

Notice that the brush icon appears as a 3D wireframe sphere. You can change its size interactively by holding down the **b** key and dragging left or right in the perspective view.

Painting on 3D Objects

Once you are comfortable selecting and applying Paint Effects brushes, you're ready to paint on some 3D objects. Both NURBS and polygon objects can be painted on the canvas using Paint Effects. You can add grass and flowers to rolling fields, clouds in the sky, and whiskers on an old man's chin.

You're not limited to using the Paint Effects window when adding Paint Effects strokes to a scene. You can apply Paint Effects while working in any camera view in a standard Maya scene. However, if you'd like to see a more accurate preview of what the stroke will look like when rendered, then use the Paint Effects window in scene mode. For these exercises, you'll paint strokes in a scene using the standard Maya viewports.

In this scene, there is a simple NURBS plane named waterSurface, which was created by lofting a surface between two dynamic hair curves. The hair system provides a gentle, fluid-like motion. Hair systems are covered in Chapter 14, "Hair and Clothing," in the section "Adding Hair to a Character." There's also a rock created from a polygon mesh (see Figure 10.8).

FIGURE 10.8
The waterPlant_v01 .ma scene contains a NURBS plane and a polygon rock.

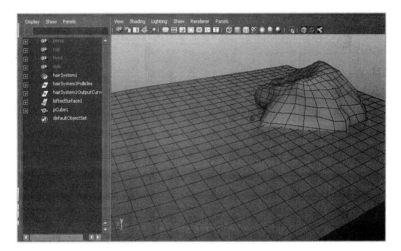

To paint on 3D objects, they must be made "paintable." Otherwise, any strokes you paint will appear on the grid and not on the objects. Furthermore, polygon objects must have UV texture coordinates that are nonoverlapping and that lie within the 0 to 1 range in the UV texture editor. (For more information on creating UV coordinates, consult Chapter 9, "Texture Mapping.")

1. Open the waterPlant_v01.ma scene from the chapter10\scenes directory at the book's web page (www.sybex.com/go/masteringmaya2015).

2. Select waterSurface, and Shift+click the rock mesh.

3. Switch to the Rendering menu set, and choose Paint Effects ➢ Make Paintable.

4. Choose Paint Effects ➢ Paint Effects Tool. Draw a stroke that starts on the rock and moves across the water surface, as shown in Figure 10.9.

FIGURE 10.9
A Paint Effects
stroke is painted
across two objects.

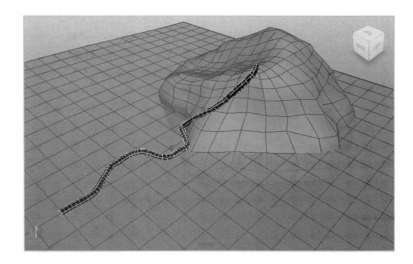

5. Rewind and play the scene. The part of the stroke that is on the water surface moves with the surface.

6. Save the scene as **paintOnObjects.ma**. To see a version of the scene, open the paintOnObjects.ma scene in the chapter10\scenes folder at the book's web page.

CORRECTING UNUSUAL BEHAVIOR

A single stroke can be painted across multiple objects as long as they are paintable. If you experience unusual behavior when painting on objects, double-check the UVs on surfaces made from polygons; also, check to see which way the normals of the object are facing, which can affect how some strokes behave. As you paint on the surfaces, be mindful of your viewing angle in the viewport window. Some angles will confuse Maya and cause strokes to become misplaced and stretched.

ATTACH TO A CURVE

Another way to add a stroke to a 3D object is to attach the stroke to an existing NURBS curve. To do this, select the brush you want in the Visor to load it as the current brush. Then select the curve, and choose Paint Effects ➤ Curve Utilities ➤ Attach To Curve. The stroke appears on the curve without the need to paint it in the scene. Multiple strokes can be attached to the same curve.

Understanding Strokes

When you create a Paint Effects stroke in a scene, several nodes are automatically created and connected. Some of the nodes are visible, and some are not. These nodes work together to produce the strokes you see in the scene.

The Anatomy of a Paint Effects Stroke

In this section, you'll look at the nodes created when you add a Paint Effects stroke to a scene. Some of these nodes you will most likely ignore; some of the nodes you will use to edit and animate the strokes.

1. Open the waterPlant_v01.ma scene from the chapter10\scenes directory at the book's web page.

2. Switch to the Rendering menu set. Select the rock object, and choose Paint Effects ➤ Make Paintable.

3. To open the Visor, choose Window ➤ General Editors ➤ Visor.

4. Choose the grasses folder, and select the astroturf.mel brush; the icon turns yellow in the Visor.

5. Zoom in to the rock, and start painting grass on it. Paint exactly three strokes. Each time you release the mouse button (or the pen from the tablet), a stroke node is added in the Outliner (see Figure 10.10).

FIGURE 10.10
Astroturf is painted on the surface of the rock.

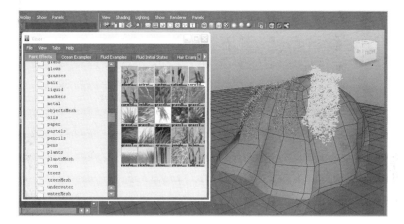

6. Once you have three strokes applied, look in the Outliner. You'll see that a stroke node was created each time you painted on a paintable surface.

MAKING AN OBJECT PAINTABLE

The rock does not have to be selected for you to paint on it, but it must be made paintable. Choose Paint Effects ➤ Make Paintable, as you did in step 2 of this exercise.

Each stroke has a transform node and a shape node. Figure 10.11 shows the Outliner with one of the stroke nodes expanded so you can see that the stroke's shape node is parented to the stroke's transform node. (For more about transform and shape nodes, consult Chapter 1, "Working in Autodesk Maya.")

FIGURE 10.11
The Astroturf
nodes appear in the
Outliner for each
stroke painted on the
rock. Each stroke has
a transform node and
a shape node.

The transform node contains information about the stroke's position, scale, and rotation. Most likely, you'll almost never edit the transform node's attributes except perhaps to hide the node by changing its Visibility attribute.

The shape node has a number of attributes specific to how the node appears and behaves:

1. Select the strokeAstroturf1 node, and open the Attribute Editor. You'll see a tab for the transform node labeled strokeAstroturf1.

2. Open the Attribute Editor for the shape node by clicking the strokeShapeAstroturf1 tab in the Attribute Editor.

   The strokeShapeAstroturf1 node has attributes that control how the stroke is displayed in the scene, how it renders, the pressure settings, and other settings specific to the individual stroke (see Figure 10.12).

3. In the Attribute Editor, switch to the astroturf1 tab. This tab contains settings for the astroturf1 brush. Editing these settings also changes the way the stroke appears in the scene.

FIGURE 10.12
The strokeShapeAstroturf1 tab contains settings that control the stroke in the scene.

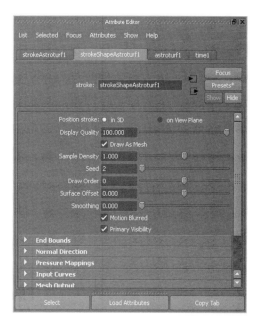

UNDERSTANDING THE CONNECTION BETWEEN THE SHAPE NODE AND THE BRUSH NODE

The relationship between the shape node (strokeShapeAstroturf1) and the brush node (astroturf1) can be a little confusing at first. Think of it this way: If you draw on a wall with a crayon, the mark on the wall is the stroke, and the shape node controls the appearance of that particular stroke. The crayon you used to make the mark on the wall is the brush (using Paint Effects terminology). Changing the settings on the brush would be like changing the crayon itself, which would affect the appearance and behavior of the strokes themselves. However, unlike in the real world where changing the crayon affects only each subsequent mark made by the crayon, there is a construction history connection between the stroke and the brush that made the stroke. Changing the settings on the brush causes a change in the strokes already created by that brush in the scene.

4. In the astroturf1 tab of the Attribute Editor, set Global Scale to **0.1**. The size of strokeAstroturf1 shrinks. Notice that the other strokes are not affected (see Figure 10.13).

FIGURE 10.13
Changing the Global Scale setting in the astroturf1 brush node affects only the size of one of the strokes painted on the rock.

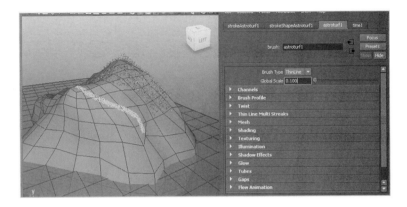

Brush Sharing

Another aspect of the relationship between the brush node (astroturf1) and the shape node (strokeShapeAstroturf1) is that, even though you have the same brush selected when you create multiple astroturf strokes on an object, Maya creates a new brush node for each stroke. It's as if you had a box of identical crayons, and each time you make a mark on the wall, you switch to a new crayon. This is confusing at first, but it means that you have more options for varying strokes in a Maya scene. To understand this relationship further, let's take a closer look at the nodes in the scene:

1. In the Outliner, expand the Display menu and turn off DAG Objects Only. This causes the Outliner to display all the nodes in the scene (for more on DAG nodes, consult Chapter 1).

   In the Outliner, you'll see several astroturf brush nodes (the nodes with the brush icon; in some cases, one of the nodes may be listed with the other astroturf nodes). These nodes are labeled astroturf, astroturf1, astroturf2, and astroturf3.

   The first astroturf node is really an instance of the currently selected brush. If you change your current brush selection to a different brush, the node changes to match the name of the new brush. Think of this as a placeholder for the current brush settings. Each time a stroke is created in the scene, a copy of this node is created and associated with the stroke. Figure 10.14 shows how the node name changes when the grassOrnament brush is selected in the Visor (middle image); if the scene is reloaded in Maya, the brush is relabeled brush1.

FIGURE 10.14
The name of the first brush node changes depending on the brush currently selected in the Visor.

2. Select astroturf2, and open the Attribute Editor to the astroturf2 node. Making a change to the settings—such as the Global Scale—affects only the associated stroke (in this case, strokeAstroTurf2).

   The ability to change the brush settings associated with each stroke means that you can easily create variations of the brushes within the scene. However, let's say you have 200 brush strokes that all use the same brush, and you need to change a setting, such as the Global Scale, for all of them or maybe even just 99 of them. Instead of changing each brush stroke individually, you can enable Brush Sharing so that the same brush node affects all the associated strokes.

3. Clear your selection and, in the Outliner, Shift+click strokeAstroturf1, strokeAstroturf2, and strokeAstroturf3.

4. Choose Paint Effects ➢ Share One Brush. After a couple seconds, all of the brushes adopt the same Global Scale setting.

   If you look in the Outliner, only one brush node is labeled astroturf3. The strokes adopt the brush settings of the last selected brush.

5. Select the astroturf3 node in the Outliner, and change its Global Scale slider. All three strokes update as you make the change.

6. Select the three strokeAstroturf nodes in the Outliner, and choose Paint Effects ➢ Remove Brush Sharing. At the bottom of the Outliner, you'll see the three astroturf brush nodes reappear. (The numbering of the brushes may change when you remove brush sharing.) Now you can return to editing each brush individually.

7. Save the scene as **grassOnRock.ma**. To see a version of the scene, open the grassOnRock .ma file from the chapter10\scenes folder at the book's web page.

Note that turning on brush sharing applies only to changes made to the settings in the brush node. Each individual brush still has its own shape node. The settings in the shape node can't be shared among multiple brushes. We'll discuss this further in the "Designing Brushes" section later in this chapter.

Understanding Brush Curve Nodes

When you paint a Paint Effects stroke in a scene, the stroke is attached to a curve that determines the overall shape of the stroke. The curve node itself may be visible or not depending on how the stroke is created. If you paint directly on the grid (Paint Effects ➢ Paint On View Plane), Maya creates a curve in the scene. The curve node is visible in the Outliner.

If you select a NURBS object, choose Paint Effects ➢ Make Paintable, and then paint on the surface, Maya creates a curveOnSurface node. You can see the curve on the surface if you hide or delete the stroke node after creating it. The curveOnSurface node is parented to the shape node of the NURBS surface, and you can also see the connection to this node by selecting the stroke and graphing it in the Hypergraph (Windows ➢ Hypergraph: Connections), as shown in Figure 10.15.

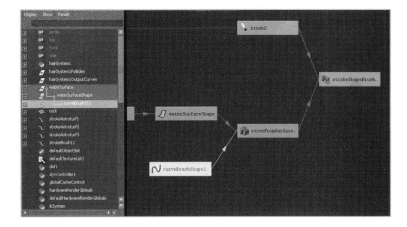

When you paint on a polygon surface, Maya creates a curveFromMeshCoM node, which allows Maya to draw a curve on a polygon surface. When you graph a stroke painted on a polygon, you can see both the curve node and the curveFromMeshCoM node. You can also see the curves parented to the shape node of the polygon geometry in the Outliner (see Figure 10.16).

FIGURE 10.16
A stroke painted on
a polygon surface
creates a curve node
and a curveFrom-
MeshCoM node.

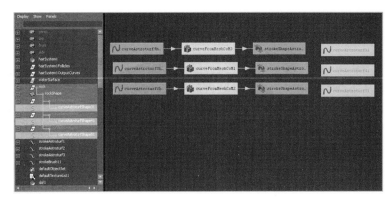

You may not be immediately concerned with the curve nodes Maya creates when you paint a stroke on a surface; however, a situation may arise in which you need to access the curve nodes to make some kind of change to the connection (for instance, if you decide you want to transfer a stroke from a regular curve to a dynamic hair curve). In these situations, it's good to have a basic understanding of how the paintbrushes are applied to 3D objects.

Designing Brushes

There's no better way to learn how to use Paint Effects than to get some hands-on training designing a custom brush. Once you have practical experience working with the many settings available for Paint Effects brushes, you'll have a much easier time working with the brushes listed in the Visor.

When you create your own brushes, most of the time you'll start with one of the existing brushes available in the Visor and then edit its settings until you get the look and the behavior you want. For instance, if you want to create a creepy nerve growing in a test tube, you may start with a brush preset that looks similar to what you want, such as a tree branch, and then experiment with the settings in the Attribute Editor until the branch looks and acts like a creepy nerve.

Paint Effects is a procedural modeling and animation workflow, meaning that the objects created by Paint Effects and the animation applied to the models are derived from mathematical algorithms (as opposed to pushing and pulling vertices). The math involved is beneath the hood. However, this does mean that you'll be working with a lot of interconnected sliders, settings, and controls. It's a very experimental process. Changing one setting affects a number of others. There's no particular order in how you edit the settings either; in fact, you'll find yourself bouncing around among the various controls and nodes in the Attribute Editor. Although this may seem overwhelming at first, after some practice you'll see that there's a lot to discover in Paint Effects, and you can create many unusual and unexpected things, which is always a lot of fun.

Paint Effects is most famous for creating plant life. The underlying technology that drives Paint Effects is based on L-systems, which are mathematical algorithms often used to simulate living systems such as plants. Most recently, Paint Effects was used to create large parts of the alien jungles of Pandora in the movie *Avatar*. In the next few sections of this chapter, the exercises will show you how you can design your own alien plant life and have it react to elements within a scene.

L-SYSTEMS

L-systems were developed by the 20th-century Hungarian biologist Aristid Lindenmayer as a way to describe the growth patterns of organisms, such as yeast and algae, mathematically. L-systems are composed of simple rules that determine branching growth patterns. More complex L-systems lead to fractal-like patterns. L-systems have been a strong influence in the development of computer graphics and artificial life.

Starting from Scratch

You'll start by painting with the default paintbrush on the surface of the water in the waterPlant scene. Gradually you'll develop the look of the brush until it resembles an alien plant that floats on the surface like a water lily or lotus flower. The only reason you'll be starting with the default stroke, as opposed to one of the presets in the Visor, is so that you can get some practice designing a stroke from the beginning. This is the best way to learn how Paint Effects works.

1. Open the `waterPlant_v01.ma` scene from the `chapter10\scenes` directory at the book's web page.

2. In the Outliner, select waterSurface. Switch to the Rendering menu set, and choose Paint Effects ➢ Make Paintable.

3. To make sure you are starting with the default brush, choose Paint Effects ➤ Reset Template Brush.

4. Choose Paint Effects ➤ Paint Effects Tool.

5. Paint a meandering line across the water surface, as shown in Figure 10.17.

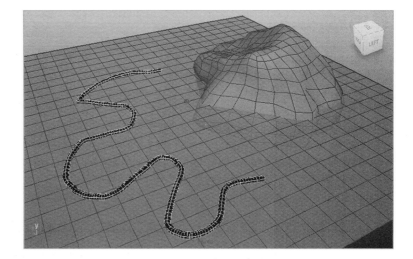

6. Select the newly painted brush stroke in the Outliner, and open the Attribute Editor.

7. Switch to the tab labeled "brush" (it may have a number such as brush1 or brush2, depending on how many strokes have been painted in the scene).

The first setting is Brush Type, which determines how the brush will render and affect other rendered objects in the scene:

Paint Type Brush   The Paint type brush creates strokes that are a series of dots stamped along the path of the stroke. The strokes look much smoother when a higher number of dots are used.

Smear and Blur Type Brushes   Smear and Blur type brushes distort or soften (respectively) the appearance of paint strokes applied to the canvas or objects in the scene. You can use them to create some interesting effects. For instance, objects behind the strokes in 3D space will appear smeared when rendered (see Figure 10.18). To see an example, open the smearBrush.ma scene from the chapter10/scenes folder at the book's web page.

Erase Type Brush   The Erase type brush creates a black hole in the alpha channel of a scene. It can be used to paint holes in the rendered image.

ThinLine or Thin Line MultiStreak Type Brushes   ThinLine/MultiStreak type brushes render strokes as groups of thin lines. They work well for hair and whisker effects.

Mesh Type Brush The Mesh type brush actually creates geometry from the stroke. This type of brush works well for hard-edge objects that appear close to the camera, such as trees or buildings. There are several folders in the Visor that contain Mesh type brush strokes. Using the Mesh type stroke is not the same as converting a stroke to polygons. Mesh type strokes, like all the other types, will not render in the mental ray® software.

8. Save the scene as `waterPlant_v02.ma`.

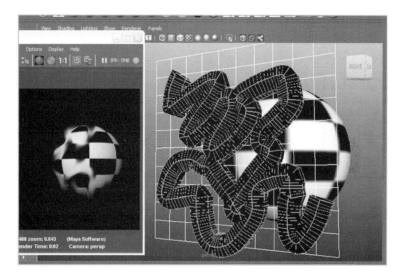

Figure 10.18
A Smear type brush is painted on a transparent plane; objects behind the brush stroke appear smeared when rendered.

RENDERING BRUSH TYPES

Paint Effects brush strokes render only in the Maya Software Renderer. There are some workarounds that allow you to render Paint Effects in mental ray. These include converting the strokes to geometry (polygons or NURBS). However, this won't work for all brush types. For instance, the Smear type brush will not smear pixels when converted to geometry.

The Global Scale slider adjusts the overall size of the stroke relative to other objects and strokes in the scene.

Adjusting the Brush Width value, under the Brush Profile section, changes the size of the area covered by the brush stroke. For simple strokes, such as the default stroke, it appears as though changing the Brush Width value is similar to changing the Global Scale value. However, with more complex brushes that use tubes (described in the following section), changing the Brush Width value changes the amount of area covered by the tubes. For instance, paint a stroke using the astroturf brush; the Brush Width value changes the width of the area covered by the grass. Changing the Global Scale value changes the overall size of the stroke, including the size of each blade of grass, as shown in Figure 10.19.

Increasing the brush's Softness value creates a fuzzy edge to the rendered stroke. Negative Softness values create an unusual-looking brush.

The default Paint brush is a rounded tube. Increasing the Flatness 1 setting makes the brush appear as a flat strip. You can then use the Twist controls (under the Twist rollout panel a little further down in the Attribute Editor) to rotate the stroke around its path curve. Increasing Twist Rate twists the stroke like a ribbon. Flatness 2 is available only for strokes that use tubes (tubes are discussed later in this chapter).

Stamp Density controls how many dots are used to create the stroke when Type is set to Paint. Increasing this setting creates a smoother stroke; decreasing the setting breaks the stroke into visible dots.

If you want the brush size to remain constant regardless of how close the camera is to the stroke, you can use the Screenspace Width controls. These controls are useful when you are working with toon lines. You can find more information on this book's web page.

Tubes

So, how do you get a flowering plant from a simple black line drawn on a surface? The answer is tubes. *Tubes* are smaller brush strokes that radiate from the center of the area defined by the brush width. Using tubes, you can create a series of crawling vines as opposed to the long singular strands created by brushes that don't use tubes (like the default brush). The tubes themselves can grow branches, twigs, leaves, and flowers. A complex brush using tubes can create a row of trees. Each tree can have its own branches and leaves.

Tubes have a lot of controls. Rather than describe what every control does, this section uses hands-on exercises to get you accustomed to using the controls. The Maya documentation has descriptions for every control available for Paint Effects. Go to the help files, and enter **Paint Effects** in the Search field. The page listed as Paint Effects Brush Settings provides you with brief descriptions of all the controls found in the brush node for a Paint Effects stroke. The following steps show you how to add tubes along a curve quickly:

1. Continue with the scene from the previous section, or open the `waterPlant_v02.ma` scene from the `chapter10\scenes` folder at the book's web page.

2. In the Outliner, select the strokeBrush11 node and open the Attribute Editor.

3. Switch to the brush2 tab. Scroll down to the Tubes rollout panel. Expand it, and select the Tubes check box.

The snaking black line now becomes a series of lines that shoot out from the original Paint Effects stroke (see Figure 10.20). The Tube Completion setting adjusts how the tubes behave toward the end of the painted stroke. When Tube Completion is off, tubes near the end of a Paint Effect stroke are not complete, just as younger branches at the top of a tree may be shorter than older branches toward the bottom.

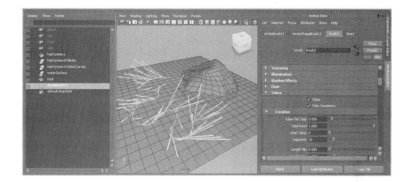

FIGURE 10.20
When Tubes are turned on, the snaking black line becomes a series of spikes.

4. Leave Tubes Completion on. Expand the Creation rollout panel, and set Tubes Per Step to **0.1**. This setting determines how many tubes will be created along the length of the stroke.

The brush you are creating will have a series of flowers along the length of the stroke. Each flower will grow on a tube. So, at this point you're establishing the placement of the flowers along the stroke using the settings in the Creation rollout panel.

5. Set Tube Rand to **0.5** and Start Tubes to **0**.

Tube Rand randomizes the placement of tubes along the stroke. Start Tubes is useful if you want a single tube or a clump of tubes to appear at the start of the stroke. The value determines the number of tubes placed at the start of the stroke. If you wanted to create a starburst effect, you can set Tubes Per Step to **0** and increase the Start Tubes value.

It will be easier to see how the other settings in the Creation rollout panel work once you have some flowers growing along the stroke.

REVERSED TUBES

If you encounter a situation where you have painted a single stroke across multiple surfaces and the tubes on one surface seem to face the opposite direction of the tubes on the other surface, you need to reverse the normals of one of the surfaces. This means going to the Polygons menu set and choosing Normals ➤ Reverse. If a NURBS surface is causing the problem, then open the Surfaces menu set and choose Edit NURBS ➤ Reverse Surface Direction. Unfortunately, doing so may adversely affect your painted strokes. You may have to delete the strokes and repaint them across the reversed surfaces.

Growing Flowers

The controls in the Growth section of the brush settings allow you to add flowers, leaves, branches, and buds to your strokes:

1. Expand the Growth rollout panel, and select Flowers. You'll see flowers appear at the end of the tubes.

   At this point, it would be nice if the flowers were resting on the surface of the water, more or less pointing upward; right now the flowers are pointing in the direction of the tubes. There are a few ways to fix this. The easiest way is to adjust the Tube Direction sliders under Creation ➢ Width Scale Settings.

   The sliders in the Tube Direction section control the overall direction in which the tubes point. As you develop your own custom brushes, you're likely to return to this section a lot because changes further along in the process may require you to tweak the tube direction.

   You'll experiment constantly with these controls as you work, but it's good to have an understanding of what the controls do:

   Tube Direction to Along Normal Setting Tube Direction to Along Normal makes the tubes point in a direction based on the normal of the path curve. Usually this means perpendicular to the curve itself.

   Tube Direction to Along Path Setting Tube Direction to Along Path means the tubes point in the direction of the path.

   Elevation Elevation refers to the direction the tubes point up and down, relative to the path (see the top of Figure 10.21). If you were lifting a flagpole to position it in the ground, the elevation of the pole at 0 would mean the flagpole is lying on the ground, and an elevation of 1 would mean that the flagpole is sticking straight up out of the ground. Values greater than 1 push the flagpole over in the opposite direction.

   Azimuth Azimuth refers to the direction the tubes point as they rotate around their origin on the path (see the bottom of Figure 10.21). If you pointed a flashlight straight in front of you, the azimuth of the light beam would be 1. If you pointed it 90 degrees to the side, the azimuth would be 0.5. At 1.5, the flashlight would point in the opposite direction from 0.5.

   Together the sliders can be used to define a range of elevation and azimuth for the tubes. How these sliders work is affected by the setting used in Tube Direction. Keep in mind that if Elevation Min and Elevation Max are both set to 1, changing the azimuth will have no effect.

2. Scroll up to the Width Scale settings in the Attribute Editor, and enter the following settings:

   Tube Direction: **Along Path**

   Elevation Min: **0**

   Elevation Max: **0.15**

Azimuth Min: **−0.086**

Azimuth Max: **0.15**

FIGURE 10.21
The top image dem-
onstrates changes in
the elevation of a 3D
arrow. The bottom
image demonstrates
changes in the azi-
muth of a 3D arrow.

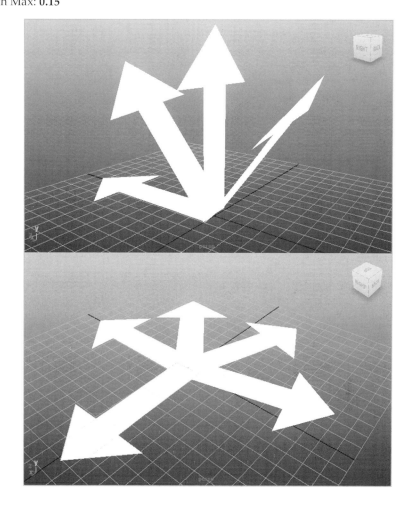

FIGURE 10.21
The top image demonstrates changes in the elevation of a 3D arrow. The bottom image demonstrates changes in the azimuth of a 3D arrow.

3. Scroll up to Length Max in the Creation settings. Set this value to **0.01** so that the flowers rest on the water (see Figure 10.22).

At this point, you can focus on changing the look of the flowers.

4. In the Attribute Editor, scroll back down to the Flowers rollout panel and enter the following settings:

Petals In Flower: **6**

Num Flowers: **1**

Petal Dropout: **0.17**

FIGURE 10.22
After you adjust the
Tube Direction and
Length Max settings,
the flowers rest on the
surface of the water.

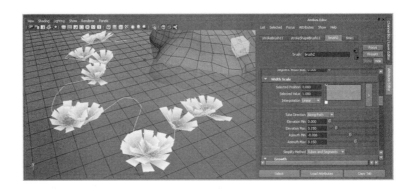

Petals In Flower determines how many petals each flower will have. Num Flowers determines how many flowers exist along the tube. Since the tubes in this stroke are very short, increasing this value would appear to add more petals to the flowers; in actuality, what is happening is that several flowers are stacked up on top of each other because the tubes' lengths are very short. You can use this to your advantage to customize the look of the flower.

Petal Dropout prunes petals from the flowers to help randomize the look of each flower. If this setting is at 0, every flower has exactly the same number of petals. If the setting is at 1, then all petals are pruned.

5. Enter additional settings:

   Petal Length: **0.18**

   Petal Base Width: **0.17**

   Petal Tip Width: **0**

   These settings help you establish a general shape for the flower petals. Making the Petal Tip Width value smaller than the Petal Base Width creates a tapered end to the petals.

6. Using the petalWidthScale ramp at the top of the Petal Width Scale section, you can further refine the shape of the petals. Try adding points to the ramp. Set the Interpolation menu to Spline for each point that you add. Doing so helps round the shape of the petals.

Think of the petalWidthScale ramp as a cross section of the petal. Click the arrow to the right of the ramp to open a larger view in a pop-up window (see Figure 10.23).

Flower Start is much like Start Tubes; it sets the location along the length of the tube where the first flowers appear. Flower Angle 1 and Flower Angle 2 determine a range for the angle of the flowers as they tilt inward from the tube. If you move Flower Angle 1, you'll see the petals tilt, but Flower Angle 2 appears to do nothing. This is because, at the moment, there is just a single flower coming out of the end of each tube. If you had a longer tube with a series of flowers growing along its length, you'd see that Flower Angle 1 sets the angle for the first flower on the branch and Flower Angle 2 sets the angle for the last flower (see Figure 10.24). Flowers in between will use angles in the range between the two settings. But you want to use these settings in a creative way to design a unique flower. To do so, you can overlap multiple flowers to create a more complex-looking plant:

1. Scroll back up to the top of the Flowers settings, and set Num Flowers to 6.

2. Go back down below Petal Width Scale, and enter the following settings:

   Flower Start: **1**

   Flower Angle 1: **70**

   Flower Angle 2: **2**

FIGURE 10.23
The petalWidth Scale ramp can be used to shape the flower petals.

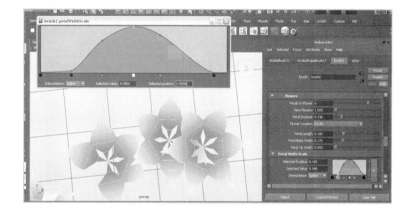

FIGURE 10.24
Flower Angle 1 and Flower Angle 2 set a range of angles for the flower petals along the length of the tube.

3. Set Flower Twist to **0.6**. Flower Twist will rotate the flowers along the length of the tube.

4. Set Petal Bend to **–0.34**. Petal Bend bends the petals toward or away from the center (see Figure 10.25).

FIGURE 10.25
The flower shape is further refined using the angle, twist, and bend settings.

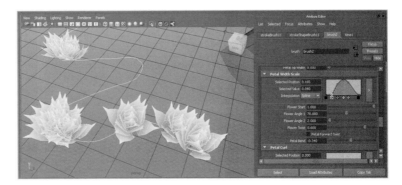

At this point you should have a nice-looking flower developing.

5. Save the scene as **waterPlant_v03.ma**.

To see a version of the scene up to this point, open the waterPlant_v03.ma scene from the chapter10\scenes folder at the book's web page.

You can use the settings in the Petal Curl section to give the petals more volume. To see best how this works, you can add geometry resolution to the petals by increasing the Petal Segments setting:

1. Set Petal Segments to **12**.

Petal Twirl rotates the petals around their base. Decreasing Petal Flatness adds volume to the petals, making them more three-dimensional. Decreasing Flower Size Decay decreases the size of the petals toward the end of the tubes. When Flower Size Decay is set to 1, all petals are the same size. Moving the setting beyond 1 inverts the effect so that petals toward the end of the tubes are larger than those at the bottom.

2. To create a more alien-looking flower, try these settings:

Petal Twirl: **0.156**

Petal Flatness: **0.7**

Flower Size Decay: **1.7**

Flower Size Random: **0.15**

UNDERSTANDING THE FLOWER FACES SUN SETTING

Some aspects of Paint Effects strokes can be made to simulate what's known in botany as phototropism—that is, the tendency for a plant to face a light source. The Flower Face Sun setting sets the strength of this force:

♦ A value of 1 causes the flower petals to face the Sun Direction.

♦ A value of 0 has no effect.

The Sun Direction setting is a vector value found in the Growth rollout panel. A similar setting can also be used to control the direction of leaves. The Sun Direction vector can be animated.

Before moving on to leaves, you can set the color for the petals of the flowers. We'll return to the Flower Translucence and Flower Specular settings when we discuss illuminating strokes later in the chapter.

3. Set Petal Color 1 to a pinkish red color and Petal Color 2 to a pale purple.

4. The Flower Hue Rand, Sat Rand, and Val Rand settings add variation to the color by randomizing hue, saturation, and value, respectively. Enter the following settings:

Flower Hue Rand: **0.027**

Flower Sat Rand: **0.095**

Flower Val Rand: **0.034**

5. Save the scene as `waterPlant_v04.ma`.

To see a version of the scene up to this point, open the `waterPlant_v04.ma` scene from the `chapter10\scenes` folder at the book's web page.

Adding Leaves

The process for adding leaves to Paint Effects is similar to adding flowers. One way you can add realism to Paint Effects strokes is to use a texture to shade the leaf geometry.

1. Continue with the scene from the previous section, or open the `waterPlant_v04.ma` scene from the `chapter10\scenes` folder at the book's web page.

2. Select the stroke in the Outliner, and open the Attribute Editor to the brush2 tab.

3. Under the Tubes rollout, expand Growth and select the Leaves option.

4. Expand the Leaves rollout panel in the Growth section, and use the following settings:

Leaves In Cluster: **4**

Num Leaf Clusters: **3**

Leaf Dropout: **0.415**

Leaf Length: **0.17**

Leaf Base Width: **0.1**

Leaf Tip Width: **0.1**

Under the Leaf Width Scale rollout:

Leaf Start: **1**

Leaf Angle 1: **90**

Leaf Angle 2: **80**

Leaf Twist: **0.65**

Leaf Bend: **−0.068**

Under the Leaf Curl rollout:

Leaf Twirl: **−1**

Leaf Segments: **14**

Leaf Flatness: **1**

Leaf Size Decay: **0.5**

Leaf Size Random: **0.2**

5. You can add a curl to the tip of the leaves by adjusting the leafCurl ramp. The default setting is 0.5; by raising or lowering points on the ramp, the leaves will curl in one direction
   or the other. The right side corresponds to the tip of the leaf, and the left side corresponds
   to the base. Try adjusting the ramp as shown in Figure 10.26.

FIGURE 10.26
The leafCurl ramp
adds curl to the
ends of the leaves.

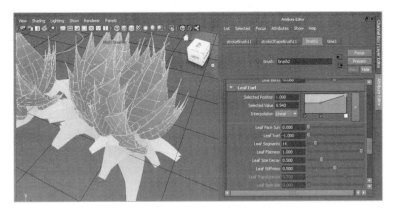

6. Set Leaf Color 1 and Leaf Color 2 to light greenish/yellow colors.

7. Enter the following settings:

    Leaf Hue Rand: **0.034**

    Leaf Sat Rand: **0.061**

    Leaf Val Rand: **0.259**

8. Turn off the Leaf Use Branch Tex option; this makes the Image Name field available.

9. Click the folder to the right of the field, and choose the `leaf.tif` image from the `chapter10\sourceimages` folder.

    The leaf image will be visible when the scene is rendered using the Maya Software Renderer.

10. Choose Window ➢ Rendering Editors ➢ Render View.

11. Set the Renderer option to Maya Software using the menu in the top bar of the Render View window.

12. Zoom into one of the flowers in the perspective view. In the Render View window, choose Render ➢ Render ➢ Persp. In the rendered image, you can see how the leaf texture has been applied to the leaves (see Figure 10.27).

FIGURE 10.27
A file texture can add realism to the leaves of Paint Effects strokes.

13. Save the scene as **`waterPlant_v05.ma`**.

File textures, and images created outside of Maya, can also be used for flower petals. Strategic use of file textures can create realistic plants and other objects with Paint Effects.

To see a version of the scene up to this point, open the `waterPlant_v05.ma` scene from the `chapter10\scenes` folder at the book's web page.

LEAF RENDER QUALITY

If you notice that the edges of the leaf image look a little jagged, you can improve the render quality by opening the Render Settings window. On the Maya Software tab, you can scroll to the bottom, expand the Paint Effects Rendering Options, and select the Oversample check box.

 Real World Scenario

PAINT EFFECTS CARDS

You may be required, at some point in your career, to create a dense forest or a crowd of people that will fill the background of a scene. To maximize rendering efficiency, it's common practice to map images to flat pieces of geometry. These *flats* (also known as *billboards*) can be placed in the background to fill in spaces in the render. If they are far from the camera, in most cases no one will notice that they are not actually 3D objects. You can use Paint Effects to paint these flats into the scene quickly. Here are the steps to accomplish this:

1. Create a stroke in the scene. Paint it in the area where you want the flats to appear.

2. Select Tubes and Tube Completion for the stroke.

3. In the Stroke Profile section, set both Flatness 1 and Flatness 2 to **1**.

4. In the Creation section, set Segments to **1**.

5. Lower the Tubes Per Step value to increase the amount of space between flats.

6. Set Tube Direction to Along Normal. Set Elevation Min and Max and Azimuth Min and Max to **1**.

7. Make the tubes match the proportions of the image you want to map to the flats. Set Length Min and Length Max to the height value and TubeWidth1 and TubeWidth2 to the same value.

8. In the Texturing options, activate Map Color and Map Opacity.

9. Set Texture Type to File, and use the Image Name field to select the image file. Use a file texture that has an alpha channel.

10. In the Twist controls, activate Forward Twist. This ensures that the tubes rotate to face the camera. Note that the automatic rotation occurs around only a single axis of the flats.

11. In the Tube Shading section, you can add a slight randomization to the Hue, Saturation, and Value of the images to increase variety. Create several similar brushes that use different images, and overlap brush strokes to create a dense forest or thick crowd.

Open the pfxFlatForest.ma scene from the chapter10\scenes folder at the book's web page to see an example of this technique.

Create Complexity by Adding Strokes to a Curve

You can increase the complexity of your plant life by attaching different strokes to the same curve.

Now you can try adding tendrils that drop below the surface of the water beneath each flower. A simple way to do this is to add a stroke to the same curve and then manipulate its settings in order to achieve the effect. Branches can be used to split the tubes into dense thickets.

1. Continue with the scene from the previous section, or open the `waterPlant_v05.ma` scene from the `chapter10` folder at the book's web page.

   To add a stroke to the original curve, duplicate the flower stroke and its input connections.

2. Select the strokeBrush11 stroke in the Outliner, and choose Edit ➢ Duplicate Special ➢ Options.

3. In the Duplicate Special Options dialog box, set Group Under to World, and select Duplicate Input Connections; make sure Number Of Copies is set to 1.

4. Click Duplicate Special to duplicate the stroke.

   The duplicate stroke looks exactly like the original, which is fine; you'll change that in a second.

5. Select strokeBrush11, and rename it **flowers**; select the new stroke, and rename it **tendrils**.

6. In the Outliner window, use the Display menu to turn on the visibility of the shape nodes (Display ➢ Shapes).

7. Expand the flowers node, and rename its shape node **flowerShape**. Rename the shape node for the tendril stroke to **tendrilShape**. Taking the time to do this will help avoid confusion when you're working in the Attribute Editor.

8. Select the tendrils stroke, open its Attribute Editor, and switch to the brush3 tab.

9. Scroll down to the Growth section under Tubes, deselect Flowers and Leaves, and select Branches.

10. Scroll up to the Creation settings, and set Length Min to **0.53** and Length Max to **1**. The flowers and leaves have disappeared, and now each flower has what appears to be sticks coming out of the top (see Figure 10.28). These sticks will become the tendrils.

    By duplicating the original stroke, you've ensured that the tubes of the second stroke are placed at the same position as the original; of course, now you need to find a way to get them to point downward into the water. The reason you're duplicating the stroke rather than just activating branches on the original is because doing the latter would change the number of flowers and thus mess up your carefully constructed plant.

11. In the Attribute Editor, switch to the tendrilShape tab. Expand the Normal Direction rollout panel, and select Use Normal.

FIGURE 10.28
The duplicated stroke
appears as sticks
coming out of the top
of each flower.

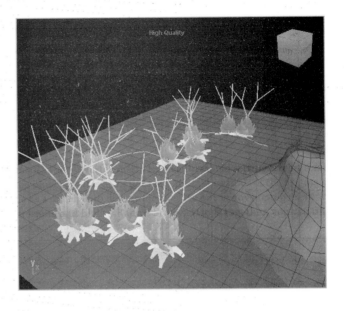

12. Set the Normal Direction fields to **0, –1, 0** (see Figure 10.29). This points the tubes downward along the negative y-axis.

FIGURE 10.29
Use the Normal
Direction settings
on the stroke's
Shape tab to con-
trol the direction
of the tubes.

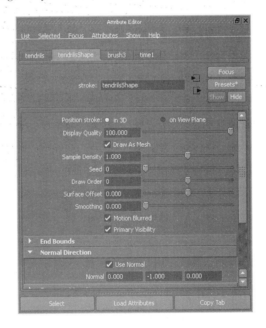

13. Switch back to the brush3 tab, and use the following settings to make the tubes look more like twisted tendrils:

UNDER CREATION	**UNDER BRANCHES**
Tubes Per Step: 0.1	Start Branches: 0
Segments: 20	Num Branches: 3
Tube Width 1: 0.025	Split Max Depth: 2
Tube Width 2: 0.005	Branch Dropout: 0
Tube Direction: Along Path	Split Rand: 0.204
Elevation Min: 0.172	Split Angle: 19.5
Elevation Max: 0.119	Split Twist: 0.1
Azimuth Min: 0.073	Split Size Decay: 0.602
Azimuth Max: −0.007	Split Bias: −0.633

These settings were arrived at through an experimental process and certainly not in the order in which they are listed. Once you become more comfortable with working with Paint Effects, you'll be able to design your own brushes through experimentation as well. Figure 10.30 shows the results of the settings.

FIGURE 10.30
The branches are shaped into tendrils that drop into the water.

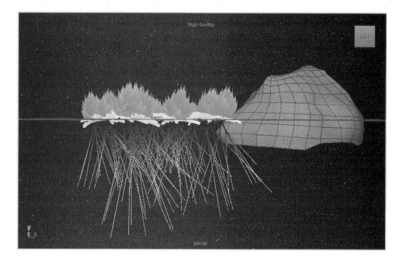

Middle Branch, located under the Branches rollout, adds a branch at the center of each branch split.

Twigs are similar in concept to branches, and their controls are similar to those used in the Creation section of the Attribute Editor. Experiment using twigs with and without branches. Sometimes they can be used to extend branches; sometimes they work well as an alternative to branches.

Buds are tiny tubes that are placed at the ends of branches and leaves.

14. Save the scene as `waterPlant_v06.ma`.

To see a version of the scene up to this point, open the `waterPlant_v06.ma` scene from the `chapter10\scenes` folder at the book's web page.

PAINT EFFECTS DISPLAY CONTROLS

As you add more elements to the scene, it may slow down the performance of Maya. You can reduce the display quality of the strokes in the scene or disable Display As Mesh. This makes working in the scene much more responsive.

You can find the display quality controls on the shape node of each stroke—not in the brush controls. Thus you need to set each one individually. However, if you have a lot of strokes in the scene, you can Shift+click them all in the Outliner and then change the display settings in the SHAPES section of the Channel Box.

Reducing the Display Percent makes it look as though parts of the stroke are being removed, but this will not affect how the stroke looks when rendered. Turning off Draw As Mesh makes the brush appear as a curve in the scene.

Shaping Strokes with Behavior Controls

The controls found in the Behavior section of the brush attributes are similar to deformers that you apply to models. You can use behaviors to shape the strokes and control how they appear in the scene.

Applying Forces

The order in which these settings are placed in the Attribute Editor is not exactly intuitive. Displacements are listed above Forces, but you may find that it's easier to work with the Forces settings first to establish a shape to the strokes and then use the Displacement settings to add detail to the shape of the strokes.

The various controls in the Forces rollout panel offer different ways of pushing and pulling the strokes. They can be used separately or in combination. Once again, applying these settings is an experimental process.

Path Follow Path Follow causes the strokes to grow along the length of the path used to define the stroke. A setting of 1 causes the strokes to cling to the original path. A negative value makes the strokes grow in the opposite direction. This option can be used to make tangled vines or twisted rope grow along the length of a stroke.

Path Attract Path Attract causes the original stroke to influence the growth of the tubes and branches. Increasing this value makes the tubes bend toward the path; decreasing the value makes the tubes bend away.

Curve Follow and Curve Attract   The Curve Follow and Curve Attract settings work the same way as Path Follow and Path Attract; however, they use a separate control curve rather than the original path curve. If there is no control curve present, these settings have no effect. To add a control curve, follow these steps:

1. Draw a curve in the scene.

2. Select the strokes in the Outliner and the curve.

3. Choose Paint Effects ➢ Curve Utilities ➢ Set Control Curves.

More than one curve can be used. The Curve Max Dist slider sets a maximum distance for the influence the control curve has on the stroke. A control curve can be attached to an animated object or character so that, when the character comes close to the strokes, they bend away from or toward the character. Control curves can be used to define the overall shape of the strokes more precisely. For instance, if you need ivy to grow in a specific way over the arched doorway of a building, you can use multiple control curves to shape the ivy strokes.

In the case of our waterPlant scene, a simple Gravity force can be used to make the tendrils droop in the water:

1. Continue with the scene from the previous section, or open the waterPlant_v06.ma scene from the chapter10\scenes folder at the book's web page.

2. Select the tendrils stroke, and open the Attribute Editor.

3. Switch to the brush3 tab. Toward the bottom, you'll find the Behavior rollout.

4. Expand Behaviors and then the Forces rollout panel. Set Gravity to **0.5**.

    The Uniform Force and Gravity controls apply a force to the strokes along a specified axis. You can define the axis of influence by entering numeric values in the Uniform Force fields. By increasing the Gravity slider, you ensure that the force is applied in the negative Y direction.

5. To add a more root-like appearance, set Random to **0.42**.

Deflection is used to keep strokes from going through the surface on which they are painted. In this case, it's not needed, but it can be useful if you find that your strokes are penetrating surfaces.

The Length Flex setting allows the tubes to stretch in response to forces like gravity. Momentum is used when stroke animation is enabled; stroke animation is discussed a little later, in the "Animating Strokes" section.

Displacement, Spiral, and Bend

You can add details to the stroke shape using the sliders in the Displacement section. It is sometimes easier to add displacements after adding forces.

Displacement Delay causes the changes made with the Displacement controls to be stronger toward the ends of the tubes. Setting this value to 0 means that displacements are applied along the length of the tube.

The Noise, Wiggle, and Curl sliders add tiny bends to the tubes and branches to create randomness. A larger Frequency value adds more detail to the changes. The Offset sliders are used when animating these attributes. Keyframing the offset over time will make the strokes appear to wiggle, curl, or move randomly, which can be great when you're creating animated creatures using Paint Effects. The following example shows how you can change the shape of the strokes using Displacement, Spiral, and Bend:

1. Try the following settings on the tendrils stroke:

   Displacement Delay: **0.2**

   Noise: **0.5**

   Noise Frequency: **0.109**

   Wiggle: **0.3**

   Wiggle Frequency: **8**

   Curl: **0.5**

   Curl Frequency: **2**

   Figure 10.31 shows the result.

FIGURE 10.31
Displacement settings are used to add detail to the strokes.

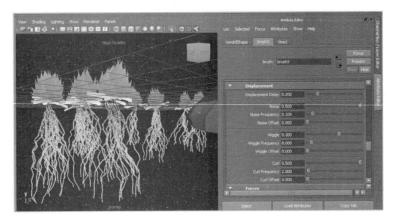

Spiral and Bend are similar to each other except that increasing the Spiral attribute creates a curve in the tubes, leaves, and flowers that bends the stroke around the stroke normal, whereas increasing the Bend attribute curves the stroke bend along the direction of the path. Once again, the best way to understand these behaviors is through experimentation.

2. Now try these settings:

   Spiral Min: **−0.741**

   Spiral Max: **0.510**

Spiral Decay: **0.027**

Positive Spiral Decay values create tighter spirals; negative values create looser spirals.

3. Set Bend to **–1.156** and Bend Bias to **0.224**. This spreads out the ends of the tendrils (see Figure 10.32).

FIGURE 10.32
The tendrils are bent and twisted around after the Spiral and Bend settings are applied.

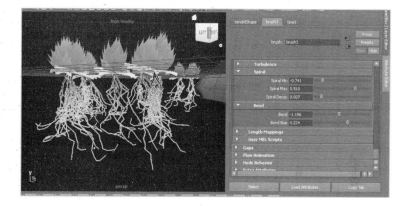

Bend Bias determines where along the length of the tube the bend starts. A Bias value of 0 makes the bend start at the base. Higher values cause the bend to be closer to the tip.

LEAF STIFFNESS

If you find that the Displacement settings distort the shape of the leaves, you can increase the Leaf Stiffness setting in the Leaf Curl controls to force the leaves back into their original shapes.

---

4. Save the scene as **waterPlant_v07.ma**.

To see a version of the scene up to this point, open the waterPlant_v07.ma scene from the chapter10\scenes folder at the book's web page.

Animating Strokes

Paint Effects strokes can be animated in a number of ways. Animation creates the sense that the strokes are alive and organic. Even a small amount of animation can have a major impact on the mood of a scene. In this section, you'll learn some of the techniques that are available for animating Paint Effects.

PRESSURE MAPPINGS

When you paint strokes in a scene using a digital tablet as an input device, variations in pressure are recorded as you paint the stroke. You can edit these recorded pressure values in the Attribute Editor for each stroke's shape node, and change which attributes are affected by pressure after the stroke has been painted.

In the shape node for a Paint Effects stroke, the recorded pressure values are listed in a table found under Pressure Mappings ➤ Pressure in the Attribute Editor. When you expand this list, you can select values and change them by typing in new values. To scroll down the list, select the lowest displayed value, and press the down-arrow key on the keyboard.

You can select up to three stroke attributes that can be controlled by the recorded pressure values. Select the stroke attribute you want pressure to affect from the menu next to Pressure Map 1, 2, and 3.

The Pressure Scale section provides you with a ramp curve that can be used to fine-tune how the pressure modifies the stroke attribute values.

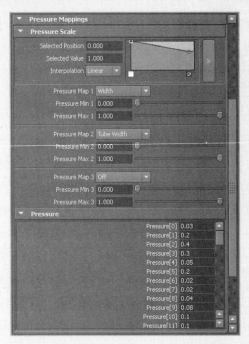

You can use the Pressure Mappings section to refine the shape and the animation of a brush stroke further. Note that, since the Pressure Mappings are part of the stroke shape node, they are not included when Brush Sharing is selected.

Animating Attribute Values

As you have no doubt noticed, a Paint Effects brush has a large number of attributes. Almost every single one of these can be animated using keyframes, expressions, driven keys, and textures. There's almost no limit to the number of wild effects that you can achieve by animating attribute values. This section demonstrates some creative ways to keyframe the attributes:

1. Continue with the scene from the previous section, or open the waterPlant_v07.ma scene from the chapter10\scenes directory at the book's web page.

2. Select the tendrils stroke in the Outliner, and open the Attribute Editor to the brush3 tab.

3. Scroll down to the bottom of the Attributes section, and expand the Behavior controls in the Tubes rollout.

4. In the Displacement rollout, in the field next to Wiggle Offset, type **=time;**. This creates a simple expression that sets the Wiggle Offset value equal to the current time (in seconds), as shown in Figure 10.33.

FIGURE 10.33
Add a simple expression to the Wiggle Offset attribute.

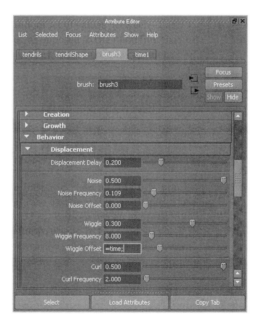

5. Set the timeline to **200**, and play the animation. The tendrils wiggle as a sinusoidal pattern moves along the length of the stroke.

Adding Turbulence

Paint Effects strokes have built-in *Turbulence* controls that are similar to the fields used with a dynamic system, such as nCloth and nParticles. You can choose among several types of turbulence.

Turbulence as a *force* causes the ends of the tubes to move back and forth as though the turbulence is moving laterally through a field of tubes. Turbulence as a *displacement* causes the tubes to bob up and down so that the strokes are being displaced based on the normal of the stroke.

The Turbulence Type options (Figure 10.34) are Off, Local Force, World Force, Local Displacement, World Displacement, Grass Wind, and Tree Wind. You can choose to have the turbulence force or displacement applied in local or world space. World space is generally a better option if you want a number of separate strokes to appear as though they are all affected by the same turbulence.

FIGURE 10.34
You can choose from a number of types of turbulence.

Grass Wind and Tree Wind are similar in that the turbulence affects the ends of the tubes more than the roots, so it appears as though the strokes are blowing in the wind. Grass Wind affects the tips of the tubes; Tree Wind affects the tips of branches. Both forces are applied using world space coordinates.

The Interpolation setting (also shown in Figure 10.34) adjusts the quality of the turbulence. A Linear setting causes a jerkier, random motion; Smooth Over Time and Smooth Over Time And Space create a more natural motion. Smooth Over Time And Space offers the highest quality, whereas Linear and Smooth Over Time work better for higher turbulence speeds.

Adding turbulence is simple:

1. Select the tendrils stroke in the Outliner, and open the Attribute Editor to the brush3 tab.

2. In the Displacement section under Behavior, right-click the Wiggle Offset field, choose Delete Expression, and set this value to **1**.

3. Expand the Turbulence rollout panel underneath Forces. Take a look at the options in the Turbulence Type menu.

4. Set Turbulence Type to Grass Wind and Interpolation to Smooth Over Time And Space.

5. Enter the following settings:

   Turbulence: **1**

   Frequency: **0.884**

   Turbulence Speed: **0.809**

   The Turbulence Offset shifts the position of the turbulence based on X, Y, and Z values. Leave this set to 0.0.

6. Play the animation. To get a sense of how the branches behave, create a playblast.

7. Save the scene as **waterPlant_v08.ma**.

Animating Growth

The most interesting way to animate a stroke is to animate its growth using the Flow Animation controls. Flow animation animates the growth of tubes, branches, leaves, twigs, and flowers along the path of the stroke.

1. Continue with the scene from the previous section, or open the `waterPlant_v08.ma` scene from the `chapter10\scenes` directory at the book's web page.

2. Select the tendrils stroke in the Outliner, and open the Attribute Editor to the brush3 tab.

3. In the Turbulence settings, set Turbulence to **0.1**. Reducing the turbulence will allow you to see how the flow animation affects the tendril stroke better.

4. Scroll to the bottom of the attribute list, and expand the Flow Animation controls. Set Flow Speed to **1**.

5. Select the Stroke Time and Time Clip options.

6. Deselect Texture Flow.

   ◆ If Stroke Time is selected, the tubes at the start of the stroke will grow first, and the tubes at the end of the stroke will grow last so that the growth moves along the path of the stroke. If Stroke Time is deselected, all the tubes grow at the same time.

   ◆ Time Clip enables the growth animation. If this option is deselected, the strokes will not grow. However, if Texture Flow is selected and Time Clip is not, textures applied in the Texturing section appear to move along the tubes. Applying textures to tubes is covered later in the chapter.

ABOUT TIME CLIP

When Time Clip is selected, the display of the strokes automatically converts to wireframe; this does not affect how the strokes appear in the render.

   ◆ Time Clip uses the Start Time and End Time values to establish the beginning and end of the animation. These values refer to seconds. Thus if your animation is set to 24 frames per second and you enter **2** for the start time, the growth will not begin until frame 48 (24 × 2).

   ◆ The End time is usually set to a high value, but you can create interesting effects by lowering this setting. If the End time is within the range of the animation, the strokes will appear to fly off the path as they disappear from the root of each tube. This is great for creating the look of fireworks or solar flares.

7. Select the flowers stroke in the Outliner.

8. Switch to the brush2 tab in the Attribute Editor, and apply the same settings to its Flow Animation.

9. Create a playblast of the animation to see the tendrils grow and the flowers bloom. They will be represented as wireframes during the animation.

10. Try setting the End Time value to **1** for both strokes, and create another playblast.

11. Save the scene as **waterPlant_v09.ma**.

To see a version of the scene up to this point, open the waterPlant_v09.ma scene from the chapter10\scenes folder at the book's web page.

END BOUNDS

You can also animate the growth of strokes by keyframing the Min and Max Clip attributes found in the End Bounds controls in the Attribute Editor of the stroke's shape node.

Modifiers

Modifiers can be used to affect specified regions of a stroke or an entire stroke. A modifier appears as a sphere or a cube. The modifier's position, rotation, and scale can be animated. Modifiers can be used to change specific attributes of a stroke. When they come within proximity of the stroke, they will take effect. In Maya 2015 you can use a modifier Occupation Surface or Volume attribute to simulate realistic plant growth. This works by using a space colonization algorithm that makes the strokes grow in unoccupied space instead of overlapping and interpenetrating.

To add a modifier, follow these steps:

1. Select one or more strokes.

2. Choose Paint Effects ➢ Create Modifier.

3. In the Attribute Editor for the modifier, set the range and falloff for the modifier as well as which stroke attributes are affected by the modifier.

4. Use the Occupation Volume rollout to control how the stroke occupies the volume.

Surface Collisions

Since Maya 2014 it has been possible to add real collisions between strokes and geometry. Collisions take place at the point of contact, allowing for complex interactions even with the most detailed strokes. In addition, strokes obey surface contours, giving you the ability to snap to a surface or be attracted to a surface. The following exercise explores these new features:

1. Open the fieldGrass_v01.ma scene from the chapter10\scenes directory at the book's web page.

2. Select the polygon plane and choose Paint Effects ➢ Make Paintable.

3. Choose Paint Effects ➢ Get Brush. From the Visor, choose the Grasses folder and select the fieldGrass brush.

4. Paint a stroke across the full length of the surface, from one low-lying area to the other (see Figure 10.35).

FIGURE 10.35
Add some field grass to the polygon surface.

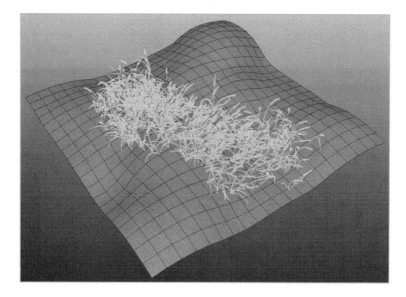

5. Open the stroke's Attribute Editor and select the fieldGrass1 tab.

6. Take a look under the polygon surface. You will notice the brush penetrates through the surface in several areas. This is visible from on top of the surface as well but less noticeable due to the complexity of the brush. By selecting Surface Snap, you force the tubes' starting position to snap to the closest point of the polygon shape. Expand the Tubes ➢ Creation rollout. At the bottom of the Creation section, click Surface Snap. Figure 10.36 shows the before-and-after results of using the Surface Snap option.

FIGURE 10.36
The left image shows the stroke before you apply Surface Snap; the right shows the after result.

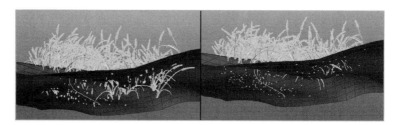

7. You can also have the tubes collide directly with the surface they have been painted on. To activate surface collisions, expand the Tubes ➢ Behavior ➢ Forces rollout and click Surface Collide.

Surface collision can take place on the inside, outside, or on both sides of the surface. The Collide Method, located under Surface Collide, contains these preferences.

8. Surface Attract can be used to pull tubes down to the surface or repel them. Enter a value of **5** for Surface Attract to give the field grass a dead or dying look (see Figure 10.37). This is effective since the stroke is colliding with the surface.

FIGURE 10.37
Surface Attract is used to make the field grass look like it is dying.

To see a version of the final scene, open the `fieldGrass_v02.ma` scene from the `chapter10\` scenes folder at the book's web page.

You can make Paint Effect strokes collide with any geometry. The surface does not need to have a painted stroke attached to it. To create a collision, select your geometry and stroke and choose Paint Effects ➤ Make Collide. Any surface type will work, but polygons calculate the fastest.

Rendering Paint Effects

When Maya renders Paint Effects strokes, they are added to the image after the rest of the image has been created. This is known as *postprocess*. Because the strokes are rendered after the rest of the scene elements have been rendered, complex Paint Effects objects can render quickly. However, it takes a little work to integrate Paint Effects smoothly into a realistic rendering.

Paint Effects are rendered normally using the Maya Software Renderer. At the bottom of the Maya Software tab in the Render Settings window are a number of options specific to Paint Effects. Strokes will not render unless Stroke Rendering is enabled. You can improve the quality of rendered strokes by selecting Oversampling, and you can also choose to render only the strokes by themselves.

Illumination

There are two ways to light Paint Effects strokes in the scene: You can use the scene lights or a default Paint Effects light. In the Illumination section of the Brush attributes, you'll find the controls for these options.

If the Illumination option is not selected, the strokes render as a flat color using the color specified in the Shading options of the Brush attributes. If the Real Lights option is not selected, you can specify the direction of the default Paint Effects lights numerically using the Light Direction fields. If Real Lights is selected, the strokes will be lit using the lights in the scene, which can add to render time.

The Lighting Based Width option alters the width of the tubes based on the amount of light they receive.

A number of options, including Flower Translucence and Flower Specular, affect the shading of the strokes and tubes when they are lit (see Figure 10.38). These attributes are covered in greater detail in Chapter 8, "mental ray Shading Techniques," in the "Shading Concepts" section.

FIGURE 10.38

The Illumination options determine how strokes react to lighting.

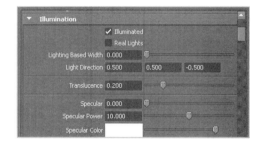

Shadow Effects

Paint Effects strokes can cast shadows in a number of ways. The options are set in the Shadow Effects controls in the Brush attributes.

If you want the shadows to be cast based on the actual lights in the scene, select Real Lights in the Illumination options, set the Fake Shadow option to None, and select the Cast Shadows option at the bottom of the Shadow Effects section. To change the quality of the shadows, you should use the Shadow controls for the lights in the scene (see Figure 10.39). The other options in the Shadow Effects section of the Brush attributes will have no effect on this particular render. Make sure shadows are enabled for the shadow-casting light. Paint Effects works only with Depth Map shadows (shadows are covered in Chapter 7, "Lighting with mental ray").

FIGURE 10.39

To cast shadows from scene lights, make sure Real Lights (under the Illumination rollout; see Figure 10.38) and Cast Shadows are both selected.

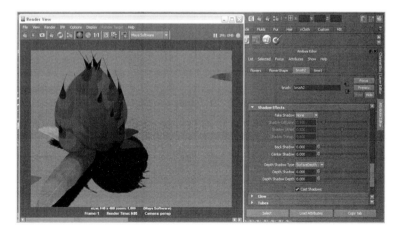

LIGHT LINKING AND PAINT EFFECTS

Light Linking will not work with Paint Effects. If you want only specific lights to illuminate Paint Effects strokes, use render layers to separate the strokes and shadows from the other scene elements, and then use compositing software to merge the passes. Render layer techniques are discussed further in Chapter 11, "Rendering for Compositing."

Paint Effects also has a number of controls for creating fake shadows. You can use 2D Offset to create a simple drop shadow, much like a drop-shadow effect created in a paint program such as Adobe Photoshop. You can also create fake 3D cast shadows. When you select 3D Cast in the Fake Shadow menu, Paint Effects creates an invisible plane beneath the surface of the stroke. Shadows are cast onto this plane and rendered in the scene (see Figure 10.40).

FIGURE 10.40
These two strokes demonstrate the difference between the two types of fake shadows. The top stroke uses 2D Offset; the bottom uses 3D Cast.

The options available include the following:

Shadow Diffusion   Increasing this setting softens the edge of the shadows.

Shadow Offset   This setting determines the distance between the stroke and the 2D Offset fake shadow type. This option is not available for 3D cast shadows.

Shadow Transparency   Increasing this value makes the fake shadow more transparent.

Back Shadow   This option darkens the areas of the stroke that faces away from the light source.

Center Shadow   You'll find this option useful when painting a clump of strokes, such as tall grass. The areas inside the clump are shaded darker than the areas that are more exposed to light. This makes a clump of strokes look more realistic.

Depth Shadow   This setting darkens the tube based on its distance from the surface or path. When you increase this setting, you can fine-tune the look by choosing Path Dist or Surface Depth from the Depth Shadow Type menu. Path Dist darkens the parts of the stroke that are closer to the path; Surface Depth darkens parts of the stroke that are close to the surface.

Depth Shadow Depth   If the distance between the stroke and the shadow-receiving surface is greater than this setting, the shadow will not appear.

Shading Strokes and Tubes

The controls in the Shading section of a brush's Attribute Editor control how colors and textures are applied to strokes and tubes. As we discussed earlier in the chapter, flower petals and leaves are shaded separately using controls in the Growth section.

1. Open the waterPlant_v09.ma scene from the chapter10\scenes folder. Rewind the scene.

    In this version of the scene, the strokes are animated using the Flow Animation controls, so most likely they are not visible at the start of the animation.

2. Open the Attribute Editor for each stroke, switch to its brush tab, and deselect Stroke Time and Time Clip in the Flow Animation section to make the strokes visible again.

3. Select the tendrils stroke, and open its Attribute Editor.

4. Switch to the brush3 tab. Scroll to the shading section, and expand the Shading rollout panel.

    There are two sets of controls: the Shading controls for the stroke and the Tube Shading controls that affect tubes and branches.

    Shading Controls   The Shading controls are very simple. The Color 1 slider applies a flat color to the stroke. This color is mixed with the color chosen in the Incandescence control. When the Transparency 1 slider is increased, the incandescence has a stronger influence on the shading of the stroke. A transparent stroke with a bright incandescence setting creates a nice neon glow or laser beam effect.

    Tube Shading Controls   The controls in the Tube Shading section are listed as Color 2, Incandescence 2, and Transparency 2. When you adjust these controls for a stroke that has tubes, it will shade the tips of tubes and branches. Thus a gradient between the Color 1 color and the Color 2 color is created along the length of the tube (see Figure 10.41). The same goes for Incandescence and Transparency.

FIGURE 10.41
Setting different colors for the Shading and Tube Shading controls creates a gradient along the length of the tubes.

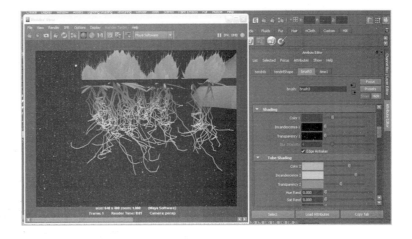

Just for fun, we'll see what happens when glow is applied to the plant tendrils toward the tips.

5. In the Shading section, enter the following settings:

Color 1: **Dark green**

Incandescence 1: **Black**

Transparency 1: **Black**

6. In the Tube Shading section, enter the following settings:

Color 2: **Light green**

Incandescence 2: **Bright green**

Transparency 2: **Dark gray**

7. Create a test render of the scene in the Render Preview window using Maya Software.

The Hue, Sat, Val, and Brightness Rand sliders can be used to add random variation to the tube shading. Root Fade and Tip Fade will make the ends transparent.

8. Scroll down to the Glow section below Shadow Effects, and enter the following settings:

Glow: **0.318**

Glow Color: **Pale yellow**

Glow Spread: **1.7**

Shader Glow: **0.2**

9. Create a test render.

The Glow settings are useful when you want to create effects such as lightning or neon tubes. Glow is applied to the whole stroke, including leaves and flower petals (see Figure 10.42).

FIGURE 10.42
The Glow settings
can add glowing
effects to strokes
and tubes.

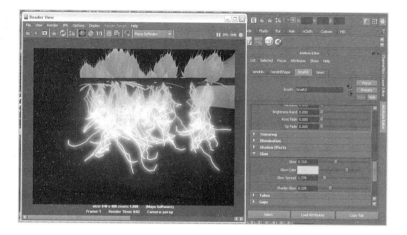

WORKING WITH THE SHADER GLOW NODE

To fine-tune the look of a glowing stroke, set the value for the Shader Glow slider above 0, and select the shaderGlow node in the Hypershade. The shaderGlow node is a global control for all glowing shaders and strokes in the scene. You can spend a fair amount of time working with these settings to produce glowing effects. Be aware that when you render an animation that has glowing shaders, you may see a noticeable flickering. To remove the flickering, deselect the Auto Exposure setting. When you do this, the glows will appear blown out. You can lower the Glow Intensity slider in the Glow Attributes to eliminate the blown-out look in the render.

Texturing Strokes

To create variation in the surface of a stroke, you can apply textures to the color, opacity, and even the displacement of the strokes.

1. Continuing with the settings on the brush3 tab of the Attribute Editor, in the Glow section set Glow to **0** and Shader Glow to **0** to turn off the glow.

2. In the Tube Shading section, set Incandescence 2 to **black**.

3. Scroll down to the Texturing section and select Map Color.

4. Set Tex Color Scale to **0** and Tex Color Offset to **0**.

5. Scroll down and set Texture Type to Fractal and Map Method to Full View. Set Repeat U and Repeat V to **2**.

6. Toward the bottom of the section, set Fractal Amplitude to **1**.

7. Create a test render in the Render View window using the Maya Software Renderer (see Figure 10.43).

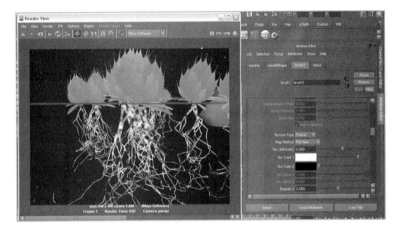

8. To bring back the green color of the tubes, increase the Tex Color Scale slider. Tex Color Offset can be used to brighten the fractal texture. You can also use the Tex Color 1 and Tex Color 2 sliders to adjust the colors used in the fractal texture.

The Map Method setting controls how the texture is applied to the strokes. Both the Tube 2D and Tube 3D methods wrap the texture around the stroke. However, when Map 2D is used the texture is always centered on the stroke. This eliminates any visible seam as the texture wraps around the stroke. Using the Map 3D method may give better results if the view of the stroke is animated.

Using Full View maps the texture across the entire view scene in the viewport.

9. Set Texture Type to File.

10. Scroll down and click the folder next to Image Name.

11. Use the File Browser dialog box to select the metalPlate.tif file from the chapter10\
sourceimages directory at the book's web page. Figure 10.44 shows the image.

FIGURE 10.44
The metal plate
texture that will be
applied to the stroke

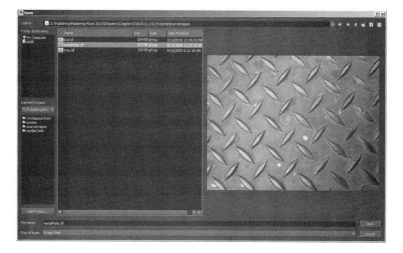

12. Set Map Method to Full View and Tex Color Scale to **0**.

13. Create a test render. The image is revealed in the tendrils. The image fills the viewable
area. If this stroke covered most of the screen, you would see the entire metalPlate image
(see Figure 10.45).

FIGURE 10.45
Full View maps the
texture to the stroke
based on the viewable
area of the scene.

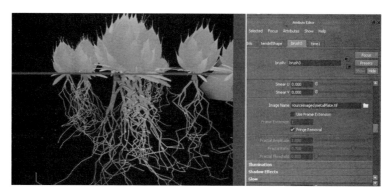

ANIMATING A LOGO

One possible use for this mapping method would be to animate a logo reveal by mapping an image
file of a logo to the stroke using the Full View method. The stroke could then be animated by drawing on the screen to reveal the logo.

The Brush Start method works similarly to the Full View method. However, the image is scaled to fit within the viewable area defined by the stroke.

You can map a texture to the opacity of the stroke and use a texture as a displacement. When you are using a displacement, you should set Stroke Type to Mesh, and you may need to increase the Tube Sections and Sub Segments settings in the Mesh controls. Setting Softness to 0 helps make the displacement more obvious. At this point, you can see how designing strokes involves a lot of moving back and forth among settings in the Attribute Editor.

14. Deselect Map Color, and select Map Displacement.

15. Scroll up to the top of the Attribute Editor, and set Brush Type to Mesh. Set Softness to **0**.

16. In the Mesh rollout panel, set Tube Sections to **30** and Sub Segments to **20**.

17. Scroll back down to the Texturing section, and enter the following settings:

    Texture Type: **Fractal**

    Repeat U: **4**

    Repeat V: **4**

18. At the bottom of the Texturing rollout panel, set Fractal Amplitude to **1**.

19. Expand the Illumination settings just below the Texturing rollout panel, and select Illuminated and Real Lights.

20. Set Lighting Based Width to **0.68**. This causes lighter areas of the stroke to become thinner.

21. Create a test render. You can see that the fractal texture displaces the stroke, making it appear lumpy (see Figure 10.46).

FIGURE 10.46
Applying a fractal texture as a displacement makes the surface of the stroke appear lumpy.

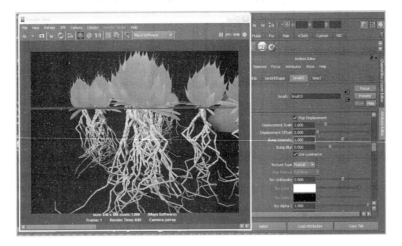

22. Save the scene as **waterPlant_v10.ma**.

To see a version of the scene up to this point, open the waterPlant_v10.ma scene from the chapter10\scenes directory at the book's web page.

CONVERTING DISPLACED STROKES TO POLYGONS

The displacement created by the texture persists even when you convert the Paint Effects stroke to polygons (Modify ➤ Convert ➤ Paint Effects To Polygons). Converting strokes is covered next.

Converting Strokes to Geometry

If you need to render Paint Effects strokes using mental ray, the best way to accomplish this is to convert the Paint Effects strokes into geometry. You can convert strokes into polygons or NURBS geometry. When you do this, Maya automatically creates a shader and applies it to the converted surface. The shader attempts to replicate any shading and texturing applied to the stroke in the Brush panel. File textures used for leaves and petals will be transferred to the newly created shaders. However, you'll most likely need to tweak the shader a little (or replace the shader with one of your own) to get the best results. A new shader is created for each stroke, so if you have a grass lawn made up of 30 strokes, Maya creates 30 identical shaders. You may want to apply one shader to all the strokes and then delete the unused shaders.

When you convert strokes to polygons, there is a limit to the number of polygons that Maya can generate. You can adjust this limit in the options for Convert ➤ Paint Effects To Polygons. If the conversion exceeds the polygon limit, you'll see a warning and the resulting geometry will be incomplete.

To convert the stroke to NURBS, select the stroke and choose Modify ➤ Convert ➤ Paint Effects To NURBS. The resulting geometry will be created from a group of NURBS surfaces.

When converting Paint Effects to geometry, you can choose to hide the original strokes in the scene; this option is selected by default. There is a history connection between the converted stroke and the geometry, so any animation applied to the stroke will be carried over to the geometry.

If you convert a stroke that uses flow animation into polygons, you may find that at some point during the growth of the stroke the polygon limit is exceeded. To avoid this, set the timeline to the end of the stroke's growth when it has reached its full length, and then convert the Paint Effects to polygons. You'll get a warning if the limit is exceeded. You can then take measures such as reducing the number of tubes or re-creating the animation using a number of shorter strokes.

1. Continue with the scene from the previous section, or open the waterPlant_v10.ma scene from the chapter10\scenes folder at the book's web page.

2. Select the flowers stroke in the Outliner, and choose Modify ➤ Convert ➤ Paint Effects To Polygons. After a few moments, the flower petals and leaves will be converted to polygons. You'll notice that the leaf texture now appears in the viewport window applied to the leaves.

3. In the Outliner, expand the brush2MainGroup node and you'll see separate nodes created from brush2Main, brush2Leaf, and brush2Flower.

   If you select any of these nodes and open the Attribute Editor, you'll find a tab for brush2. The settings here will affect the polygon geometry as long as history is not deleted on any of the geometry nodes.

4. Select the tendrils node, and open its Attribute Editor to the brush3 tab.

5. In the Mesh section, set Tube Sections to **8** and Sub Segments to **2**. If these settings are too high, you may encounter problems when converting to geometry.

6. Select Tendrils in the Outliner, and choose Modify ➢ Convert ➢ Paint Effects To NURBS. In the Outliner, you'll see a new group node named tendrilsShapeSurfaces; parented to this node is another group containing all the NURBS surfaces for the tendrils.

CONVERTING PAINT EFFECTS TO GEOMETRY

There are many advantages to converting Paint Effects to geometry. You can apply complex shaders to the converted strokes and take advantage of mental ray shaders, which can be much more realistic than a Maya Software render. You can also use modeling techniques to refine the converted geometry further, thus using Paint Effects as a way to start organic models such as trees and grass.

Be mindful that the geometry you create with Paint Effects can be quite heavy, which can lead to a slowdown in performance and longer render times. Many artists choose to create complex scenes using a combination of Paint Effects strokes and strokes that have been converted to geometry.

---

7. In the Outliner, expand the brush2Mesh group and select the brush2Flower node.

8. Switch to the Polygon menu set, and choose Mesh ➢ Smooth. After a few moments, you'll see that the geometry has been subdivided and smoothed.

9. Open the Render View window, set the Render Using menu to mental ray, and create a test render (see Figure 10.47).

FIGURE 10.47
After converting strokes to geometry, you can render the Paint Effects strokes using mental ray.

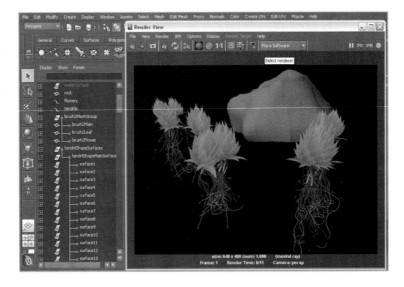

10. Save the scene as `waterPlant_v11.ma`.

To see a finished version of the scene, open the `waterPlant_v11.ma` scene from the `chapter10\scenes` folder at the book's web page.

The Bottom Line

Use the Paint Effects canvas.   The Paint Effects canvas can be used to test Paint Effects strokes or as a 2D paint program for creating images.

Master It   Create a tiling texture map using the Paint Effects canvas.

Paint on 3D objects.   Paint Effects brushes can be used to paint directly on 3D objects as long as the objects are either NURBS or polygon geometry. Paint Effects brushes require that all polygon geometry have mapped UV texture coordinates.

Master It   Create a small garden or jungle using Paint Effects brushes.

Understand strokes.   Many nodes are associated with a Paint Effects stroke. Each has its own set of capabilities.

Master It   Create a stroke and then manually move control vertices on the Paint Effects curve to alter the brush's placement.

Design brushes.   Custom Paint Effects brushes can be created by using a preset brush as a starting point. You can alter the settings on the brush node to produce the desired look for the brush.

Master It   Design a brush to look like a laser beam.

Create complexity by adding strokes to a curve.   Duplicating a Paint Effects curve allows you to add an additional effect to an existing stroke.

Master It   Choose a flower brush from the Visor and add grass around it.

Shape strokes with behavior controls.   Behaviors are settings that can be used to shape strokes and tubes, giving them wiggling, curling, and spiraling qualities. You can animate behaviors to bring strokes to life.

Master It   Add tendrils to a squashed sphere to create a simple jellyfish.

Animate strokes.   Paint Effects strokes can be animated by applying keyframes, expressions, or animated textures directly to stroke attributes. You can animate the growth of strokes by using the Time Clip settings in the Flow Animation section of the Brush attributes.

Master It   Animate blood vessels growing across a surface. Animate the movement of blood within the vessels.

Render Paint Effects strokes.   Paint Effects strokes are rendered as a postprocess using the Maya Software Renderer. To render with the mental ray software, you should convert the strokes to geometry.

Master It   Render an animated Paint Effects tree in mental ray.

Chapter 11

Rendering for Compositing

The Autodesk® Maya® software offers a number of options for dividing the individual elements of a render into separate passes. These passes can then be reassembled and processed with additional effects using compositing software such as Adobe After Effects or The Foundry Nuke. In this chapter, you'll learn how to use the render layers in Maya and render passes with the mental ray® renderer to split rendered images into elements that can then be used in your compositing software.

For best results when working on the project files in this chapter, you should copy the chapter11 project folder to your local drive and make sure that it is the current project by choosing File ➢ Set Project. Doing so will ensure that links to textures and Final Gathering maps remain intact and that the scenes render correctly.

In this chapter, you will learn to:

- ◆ Use render layers
- ◆ Use render passes
- ◆ Perform batch renders
- ◆ Use mental ray quality settings

Render Layers

Render layers are best used to isolate geometry, shaders, and lighting to create different versions of the same animation. Render layers can be used to create a balance between efficiency and flexibility. You have an enormous amount of creative flexibility when using render layers. This chapter explains the typical workflow; however, you may develop your own way of using render layers over time.

You can create and manage render layers using the Layer Editor in Render mode (called the Render Layer Editor). You can access the Layer Editor in the lower-right corner of the interface layout, just below the Channel Box.

Besides Render mode, the Layer Editor has Display and Animation modes. These three modes are the three types of layers that you can create in Maya. You change the mode by clicking one of the tabs at the top of the Layer Editor. Figure 11.1 shows the Render Layer Editor with a scene that has two custom render layers and the default render layer.

By default, every Maya scene has at least one render layer labeled masterLayer. All the lights and geometry of the scene are included in masterLayer. When you create a new render layer, you can specify precisely which lights and objects are included in that layer. As you add render layers, you can create alternate lights for each layer, use different shaders on each piece of geometry, render one layer using mental ray and another using Maya Software, use indirect lighting effects on one layer and not on another, and so on. A render layer can be rendered using any camera, or you can specify which camera renders which layer. In this section, you'll use many of these techniques to render different versions of the same scene.

FIGURE 11.1
The Render Layer Editor is a mode of the Layer Editor, which is found below the Channel Box on the lower right of the default interface.

Creating Render Layers

In this exercise, you'll render the bicycle model in a studio environment and in an outdoor setting. Furthermore, the bike is rendered using a different shader on the frame for each layer.

Start by opening the `bikeComposite_v01.ma` scene from the `chapter11\scenes` folder at the book's web page (`www.sybex.com/go/masteringmaya2015`).

The scene is set up in a studio environment. The lighting consists of two point lights that have mental ray Physical Light shaders applied. These lights create the shadows and are reflected in the frame of the bike. An Area light and a Directional light are used as simple fill lights.

The renderCam camera has a lens shader applied to correct the exposure of the image. As you learned in Chapter 8, "mental ray Shading Techniques," mia materials and physical lights are physically accurate, which means their range of values does not always look correct when displayed on a computer screen. The mia_exposure_simple lens shader is applied to the camera to make sure the scene looks acceptable when rendered.

To create two alternative versions of the scene, you'll want to use two separate render layers:

◆ The first render layer will look exactly like the current scene.

◆ The second render layer will use a different shader for the bike body and the Physical Sun and Sky network to create the look of outdoor lighting.

Generally, when you start to add render layers, the master layer is not rendered; only the layers that you add to the scene are used for rendering.

The first step is to create a new render layer for the scene:

1. In the bikeComposite_v01.ma scene, open the Render View window, and create a test render using the renderCam camera. It may take a minute or so to create the render (see Figure 11.2).

FIGURE 11.2

The scene shows a typical studio lighting and bike-Composite_v01.ma shading arrangement for the bike.

2. Set the Layer Editor mode to Render.

3. You can quickly add all the scene elements to a new layer by simply copying the layer:

    a. Select the masterLayer label in the Layer Editor.

    b. Right-click, and choose Copy Layer.

This creates a duplicate of the layer called defaultRenderLayer1 in the editor using all the same settings. See the upper-left segment of Figure 11.3.

4. In the Layer Editor, double-click the label for the new layer and rename it **studioLighting**. This is shown in the top-right image in Figure 11.3.

5. In the menu bar for the Render Layer Editor, select Options, and make sure Render All Layers is not selected. This is shown in the bottom-left part of Figure 11.3.

Right now you're interested in rendering only a single layer at a time. If this option is on, Maya will render all the layers each time you create a test render in the render view.

FIGURE 11.3
Copy masterLayer (top-left portion of this image) and rename it studio-Lighting (top right). Deselect the Render All Layers option (bottom left) and the masterLayer render option (bottom right).

6. By masterLayer, click the leftmost icon—the clapboard—so that a red *X* appears. Doing so deactivates this render layer so that it is not renderable. This is shown in the bottom-right portion of Figure 11.3.

7. Select the studioLighting layer in the Layer Editor so that it is highlighted in blue.

8. Open the Render View window, and create a test render using the renderCam camera. It should look exactly the same as the render from step 1.

9. Save the scene as **bikeComposite_v02.ma**.

Copying a layer is a fast and easy way to create a new render layer. You can instead create an empty layer as follows:

1. Choose Create Empty Layer from the Layers menu in the Layer Editor when in Render mode.

2. Select objects in the scene.

3. Right-click the new layer.

4. Choose Add Selected Objects from the context menu.

Another way to create a new layer is to select objects in the scene, and choose Create Layer From Selected from the Layers menu. A new render layer containing all the selected objects is created.

You can add new objects at any time by right-clicking the render layer and choosing Add Selected Objects. Likewise, you can remove objects by selecting the objects and choosing

Remove Selected Objects. You can delete a render layer by right-clicking the layer and choosing Delete Layer. This does not delete the objects, lights, or shaders in the scene, but just the layer itself.

To see a version of the scene up to this point, open the `bikeComposite_v02.ma` scene from the `chapter11\scenes` folder at the book's web page.

An object's visibility can be on for one render layer and off for another. Likewise, if an object is on a display layer and a render layer, the display layer's visibility affects whether the object is visible in the render layer. This is easy to forget, and you may find yourself unable to figure out why an object that has been added to a render layer is not visible. Remember to double-check the settings in the Layer Editor's Display mode if you can't see a particular object.

You can use the Relationship Editor to see the layers to which an object belongs. Choose Window ➢ Relationship Editors ➢ Render Layers.

Render Layer Overrides

To create a different lighting and shading setup for a second layer, you'll use render layer overrides. An override changes an attribute for a specific layer. So, for example, if you wanted Final Gathering to calculate on one layer but not another, you would create an override in the Render Settings window from the Final Gathering attribute. To create an override, right-click next to an attribute and choose Create Layer Override. As long as you are working in a particular layer that has an override enabled for an attribute, you'll see the label of the attribute highlighted in orange. Settings created in the master layer apply to all other layers unless there is an override.

This next exercise shows you how to use overrides as you create a new layer for the outdoor lighting of the bike:

1. Continue with the scene from the previous section, or open the `bikeComposite_v02.ma` scene from the `chapter11\scenes` folder at the book's web page.

2. In the Outliner, select the bicycle group.

3. Shift+click the ground object.

4. In the Render Layer Editor, choose Layers ➢ Create Layer From Selected.

5. Select the new layer so that it is highlighted in blue, and rename it **outdoorLighting**.

   If a group such as the bicycle group is added to a render layer, all of its children are part of that layer. If you want to add just a part, such as the wheels, select the geometry (or subgroup) and add that to the render layer rather than the entire group.

   Currently this layer has no lighting so, if you render it, the layer will appear dark (the default light in the render settings is off). That's fine because at this point you want to create a Physical Sun and Sky network for this layer.

6. Make sure that the outdoorLighting layer is selected in the Render Layer Editor. This ensures that you are currently in this layer and that any changes you make to the lighting or shading will appear in this layer.

7. In the Render Layer Editor, click the Render Settings icon (of the three icons, it's the farthest to the right), which opens the Render Settings window for the current layer.

In the Render Settings window, you'll notice outdoorLighting is selected in the Render Layer menu at the top. You can use this menu to switch between settings for the different layers.

8. Switch to the Indirect Lighting tab, and click the Create button for the Physical Sun and Sky.

This button creates a series of nodes, including the Sun Direction light, the Physical Sky node, and the mia_exposure lens shader, for all the lights in the scene. It also enables Final Gathering in the Render Settings window.

9. In the Render Settings window, RMB-click the label Final Gathering and choose Create Layer Override (see Figure 11.4). You'll see that the Final Gathering label turns orange, letting you know this setting has an override for the current layer (outdoorLighting).

FIGURE 11.4
Create a layer override for Final Gathering in the Render Settings window for the outdoorLighting layer.

10. You want Final Gathering only for the outdoorLighting layer. In the Render Settings window, select masterLayer from the Render Layer drop-down menu at the top of the window. Turn off Final Gathering while this layer is selected.

11. Select the studioLighting layer from the Render Layer menu in the Render Settings window. Final Gathering should now be off for this layer as well.

12. Select outdoorLighting, and you'll see that Final Gathering is enabled and the label is still orange.

This is the basic workflow for creating a render layer override. How do you know which settings can be overridden? Most attributes related to lighting and shading can be overridden on most nodes. You can always right-click next to the attribute layer and see whether the Create Layer Override setting is available.

13. In the Render View window, create a test render, but make sure outdoorLighting is still the selected render layer. The render will take 4 or 5 minutes (depending on your computer's speed and available RAM).

The render is obviously quite different from the render created for the studioLighting layer (see Figure 11.5).

14. Store the render in the Render View window (from the File menu in the Render View window, choose Keep Image In Render View).

15. In Render mode of the Layer Editor, select the studioLighting layer, and create another test render.

Figure 11.5

The lighting in the outdoorLighting layer is very different from the lighting in the studioLighting layer.

Something has gone wrong; the lighting has changed for this layer. Final Gathering is not calculating, but you'll see that the render takes a long time and the lighting no longer matches the original studioLighting render. This is not because of render layers per se, but because of the Physical Sun and Sky network that was added to the scene. Remember from Chapter 7, "Lighting with mental ray," that when you add a Physical Sun and Sky network, a number of nodes are added to the scene, including the renderable cameras. Normally this feature saves time and work, but in this case it's working against the scene.

The easiest way to fix the problem is to create a duplicate render camera. One camera can be used to render the studioLighting layer; the other can be used to render the outdoorLighting layer. You can make sure that the correct lens shaders are applied to both cameras. You can use overrides to specify which camera is available from which layer.

1. Select the renderCam camera in the Outliner. Rename it **outdoorCam**.

2. Duplicate outdoorCam, and rename the duplicate **studioCam**.

3. Open the Attribute Editor for studioCam.

4. Switch to the studioCamShape tab, and expand the mental ray section.

   You'll see that there are no lens or environment shaders attached to the studioCam camera. If you switch to the outdoorCam camera, you'll see the mia_physicalsky1 shader in the Environment Shader slot and the mia_exposure_simple2 shader in the Lens Shader slot. The original renderCam camera had a mia_exposure_simple1 node in the Lens Shader slot, but this was replaced by mia_exposure_simple2 when the Physical Sun and Sky network was added to the scene. The solution here is to reattach the mia_exposure_simple1 node to the lens shader of studioCam.

5. Open the Hypershade window, and switch to the Utilities tab.

6. MMB-drag mia_exposure_simple1 (you can see the full name if you hold the mouse pointer over the icon) down to the Lens Shader slot for studioCam (see Figure 11.6).

FIGURE 11.6
Attach the mia_
exposure_simple1
node to the Lens
Shader slot of
studioCam.

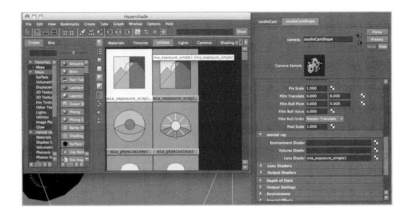

7. In the Hypershade, select the mia_physicalsky1 node on the Utilities tab, and open its Attribute Editor to the mia_physicalsky1 tab.

8. Right-click the check box next to the On attribute, and choose Create Layer Override. The attribute label should turn orange.

9. After adding the override, deselect the check box for this attribute to turn it off for this layer.

10. Create a test render in the Render View window, and make sure that studioCam is chosen as the rendering camera. The render now looks like it did at the start of the section.

11. Save the scene as **bikeComposite_v03.ma**.

To see a version of the scene up to this point, open the bikeComposite_v03.ma scene from the chapter11\scenes folder at the book's web page.

ANIMATED CAMERAS

You can use a parent constraint to attach the duplicate camera to the original if the original camera is animated. To do this, follow these steps:

1. Select the original camera.

2. Shift+click the duplicate.

3. Switch to the Animation menu.

4. Choose Constrain ➤ Parent ➤ Options.

5. In the options, deselect Maintain Offset, and select All for both Translate and Rotate.

Animation constraints are covered in Chapter 6, "Animation Techniques."

Creating Overrides for Rendering Cameras

Notice that you do not need to add cameras to render layers when you add them to a scene. You can if you want, but it makes no difference. The cameras that render the scene are listed on the Common tab of the Render Settings window.

If you're rendering an animated sequence using two cameras with different settings as in the bikeComposite example, you'll want to use overrides so that you don't render more images than you need.

1. Continue with the scene from the previous section, or open the bikeComposite_v03.ma scene from the chapter11\scenes folder at the book's web page.

2. Open the Render Settings window.

3. Make sure that the Render Layer menu at the top of the Render Settings window is set to studioLighting.

4. Switch to the Common tab, and expand the Renderable Cameras rollout.

5. Use the Renderable Camera menu to choose the studioCam camera.

6. Right-click on Renderable Camera, and choose Create Layer Override (see Figure 11.7).

FIGURE 11.7
Create a layer override for the rendering camera on the studio-Lighting layer.

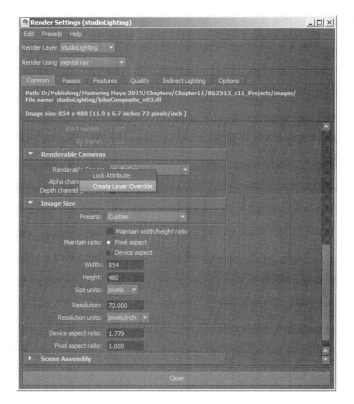

7. Set the Render Layer drop-down list at the top of the Render Settings window to outdoorLighting.

8. From the Renderable Camera menu, choose outdoorCam.

9. Right-click next to the menu, and choose Create Layer Override. (In some cases, Maya creates the override for you if you already have an override for the same setting on another layer.)

10. Switch between the studioLighting layer and the outdoorLighting layer, and make sure that the correct camera is selected for each layer.

    It is important to take these steps to ensure that the right camera will render the correct layer; otherwise, you may waste time rendering images from the wrong camera.

11. Save the scene as **bikeComposite_v04.ma**.

To see a version of the scene up to this point, open the bikeComposite_v04.ma scene from the chapter11\scenes folder at the book's web page.

After you create the overrides for the cameras, it is still possible to render with either camera in the render view. The overrides ensure that the correct camera is used for each layer during a batch render.

Material Overrides

A material override applies a material to all the objects within a particular layer. To create a material override, right-click one of the layers in the Render Layer Editor, and choose Overrides ➤ Create New Material Override. You can then select a new material to be created from the list.

Render Layer Blend Modes

Render layers can use blend modes, which combine the results of the render to form a composite. You can preview the composite in the Render View window. Typically, you render each layer separately, import the render sequences into compositing software (such as Adobe After Effects or The Foundry Nuke), and then apply the blend modes using the controls in the compositing software. Maya gives you the option of creating a simple composite using render layers, which you can view in the Render View window.

Blend modes use simple algorithms to combine the numeric color values of each pixel to create a composite. A composite is created by layering two or more images on top of each other. The image on top is blended with the image below. If both images are rendered as Normal, then the top image covers the bottom image, except where the top layer is transparent due to alpha. If the blend mode is set to Multiply, then the light pixels in the top image are transparent, and the darker pixels of the top image darken the pixels in the bottom image. This technique is often used to add shadowing to a composite. If the blend mode of the top image is set to Screen, then the darker pixels are transparent, and the lighter pixels brighten the pixels of the lower image. You can use this to composite glowing effects.

The blend modes available in Maya are as follows:

Lighten This mode compares the layered images and uses the lightest pixel value of the two layers to determine the resulting color. For example, the lower-layer image has a pixel in a particular spot with an RGB value of 0, 125, 255, and the pixel at the same location in the top-layer image has an RGB value of 0, 115, 235. The resulting RGB value for that pixel will be 0, 125, 255.

Darken   This mode is the opposite of Lighten, and the darker value is used. In the example cited previously, the resulting RGB value for the pixel would be 0, 115, 235.

Multiply   The pixel values of the top-layer image are multiplied by the pixel values of the bottom image and then divided by 255 to keep the values within the range of 0 to 255. The lighter pixels in the top-layer image are semitransparent, and the darker values of the top-layer image result in a darkening of the lower image.

Screen   A slightly more complex algorithm is used for this mode. The formula is 255 – [(255 – *top color RGB pixel value*) × (255 – *bottom color RGB pixel value*) ÷ 255] = blended RGB pixel value. This has the effect of making darker pixels in the top image semitransparent and lighter, resulting in a lightening of the lower image.

Overlay   This mode combines Multiply and Screen modes so that the lighter pixels of the top-layer image brighten the bottom-layer image, and the darker pixels of the top-layer image darken the bottom-layer image.

In this exercise, you'll use blend modes to create soft shadows for the render of the bike in the studio lighting scenario.

This scene shows the bike in the studio lighting scenario. A single render layer exists already. Using the technique in this exercise, you'll eliminate the harsh cast shadows that appear on the ground in the rendered image (shown earlier, in Figure 11.2) and replace them with soft shadows created using an ambient occlusion shader. First, you'll remove the shadows cast on the ground by the physical lights in the scene (note that physical lights always cast shadows; there is no option for turning shadows off when you use these lights).

1. Open the `bikeComposite_v05.ma` scene from the `chapter11\scenes` folder at the book's web page.

2. Select the ground object in the Outliner.

3. Open its Attribute Editor, and switch to the groundShape tab.

4. Expand the Render Stats section in the Attribute Editor, and deselect Receive Shadows (see Figure 11.8).

FIGURE 11.8
Deselect Receive Shadows for the ground surface.

Note that for some attributes, changing a setting on a render layer automatically creates a layer override.

5. Select the studioLighting layer, and create a test render in the Render View window using the renderCam camera (see Figure 11.9).

6. In the Outliner, Shift+click the bicycle group and the ground surface.

7. In the Render Layer Editor, choose Layers ➤ Create Layer From Selected. Name the new layer **AOShadow**.

8. Open the Hypershade window. Make sure the AOShadow layer is selected in the Render Layer Editor.

9. Create two new surface shaders in the Hypershade (from the Hypershade menu, choose Create ➤ Materials ➤ Surface Shader).

10. Name one of the surface shaders **shadowShader** and the other **whiteMask**.

11. In the Outliner, select the bicycle group, and apply the whiteMask shader to this group.

12. Select the ground object, and apply shadowShader to this surface.

13. Open the Attribute Editor for the whiteMask node, and set Out Color to white.

14. Open the Attribute Editor for shadowShader.

15. Click the checkered box to the right of Out Color. In the Create Render Node window, select Textures under mental ray. Choose the mib_amb_occlusion texture from the node list (Figure 11.10).

16. Open the Attribute Editor for the mib_amb_occlusion1 node, and set Samples to **64**.

17. Make sure AOShadow is selected in the Render Layer Editor; then create a test render using the renderCam camera.

The bike appears as flat white, but you can see the soft shadows created on the ground by the ambient occlusion node (see Figure 11.11). Later in this chapter, you'll learn more about how ambient occlusion textures create shadows.

FIGURE 11.10
Create an ambient occlusion texture for the shadow-Shader's Out Color channel.

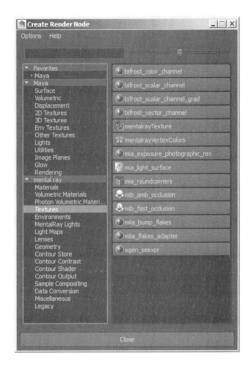

FIGURE 11.11
The soft shadows created by the ambient occlusion texture appear on the ground while the bike is masked in flat white.

18. Now you are ready to preview the composite in the Render View window. In the Render Layer Editor, set the blend mode of the AOShadow layer to Multiply (see Figure 11.12).

FIGURE 11.12
Set the blend
mode of the
AOShadow layer
to Multiply.

Because the bike in this render layer is flat white, when the pixels of the AOShadow layer are multiplied by the pixels of the studioLight layer only the soft shadows appear in the composite.

19. In the Render Layer Editor, choose Options ➤ Render All Layers ➤ Options. In the Render All Layers Options dialog box, set Keep Image Mode to Composite Layers.

There are three choices in the Render All Layers Options dialog box: Composite Layers, Composite And Keep Layers, and Keep Layers.

◆ Composite Layers renders both layers and then composites them in the Render View window.

◆ Composite And Keep Layers creates the composite, but it also keeps the rendered image of each individual layer available in the Render View window.

◆ Keep Layers does not composite the layers; instead, it renders all renderable layers and keeps them as individual images in the Render View window.

20. After choosing the Composite Layers option, click Apply And Close.

21. Make sure Render All Layers is now selected in the Options menu of the Render Layer Editor (see Figure 11.13).

FIGURE 11.13
Select the Render
All Layers option in
the Options menu.

22. In the Render Layer Editor, make sure the red *X* appears on the clapboard icon of master-Layer, indicating that this layer will not render. A green check box should appear next to the studioLighting and AOShadow layers, indicating that they will be rendered.

23. Open the Render View window, and create a test render using the renderCam camera. You'll see the studioLighting layer render first, and then the AOShadow layer will render on top of it. Figure 11.14 shows the composited image.

FIGURE 11.14
The two images composited in the Render View window

24. Save the scene as **bikeComposite_v06.ma**.

To see a finished version of the scene, open bikeComposite_v06.ma from the chapter11\ scenes folder at the book's web page.

This is a good way to preview basic composites; however, in practice you will most likely want more control over how the layers are composited. To do this, you should use more advanced compositing software such as Adobe Photoshop (for still images) or Adobe After Effects, or The Foundry Nuke (for animations).

Real World Scenario

COMPOSITE HARDWARE PARTICLES USING RENDER LAYERS

If you have a scene that involves a large number of nParticles, you may want to use hardware rendering to reduce the render time. If the scene also contains geometry that you want to render with Maya Software or mental ray, you can use render layers to composite the hardware-rendered nParticles with the software-rendered geometry in Maya. A workflow for doing this would be as follows:

1. In your scene, create a new render layer and add the geometry to this new layer. Name the layer **geometryRL**.

2. Create a second render layer above the geometry layer; then add the nParticles and the geometry to this layer. Name the layer **nParticlesRL**.

3. Open the Render Settings window for geometryRL, and set Render Using to mental ray.

4. Open the Render Settings window for nParticlesRL.

5. Right-click Render Using, and choose Create Layer Override.

6. Set the Render Using menu to Maya Hardware.

continues

continued

7. In the Maya Hardware tab of the Render Settings window, select Enable Geometry Mask.

8. In the Render Layer Editor, make sure that both the nParticlesRL and the geometryRL layers are set to Renderable.

9. In the Options menu, select Render All Layers.

10. Set the mode of the nParticlesRL layer to Screen.

11. Create a test render of a frame in which nParticles and the geometry are visible.

Using particle sprites (covered in Bonus Chapter 1, "Scripting with MEL and Python," on this book's web page) requires hardware rendering, so it's great to have a render layer set up that allows you to render all of your detailed geometry and particles within a single scene file using two different rendering engines (mental ray and Maya Hardware).

Render Passes

Render passes divide the output created by a render layer into separate images or image sequences. Using render passes, you can separate the reflections, shadows, diffuse color, ambient occlusion, specular highlights, and so on into images or image sequences, which can then be reassembled in compositing software. By separating things such as the reflections from the diffuse color, you can then exert maximum creative control over how the different images work together in the composite. This approach also allows you to make changes or variations easily or fix problems in individual elements rather than re-rendering the entire image or sequence every time you make a change.

Render passes replace the technique of using multiple render layers to separate things like reflections and shadows in older versions of Maya. (Render passes also replace the layer presets; more on this in a moment.) Each layer can be split into any number of render passes. When render passes are created, each layer is rendered once, and the passes are taken from data stored in the frame buffer. This means that each layer needs to render only once to create all the necessary passes. Render time for each layer increases as you add more passes.

THE FRAME BUFFER

When Maya renders an image, it collects data from the scene and stores it in a temporary image known as the frame buffer. When rendering is complete, the data from the frame buffer is written to disk as the rendered image. The images created by render passes are extracted from the render buffer, which is why the layer needs to render only once to create a number of render passes.

A typical workflow using passes is to separate the scene into one or more render layers, as demonstrated in the first part of this chapter, and then assign any number of render passes to each render layer. When you create a batch render, the passes are stored in subfolders in the images folder of the current project. You can then import the images created by render passes into compositing software and assemble them into layers to create the final composite.

Render passes work only with mental ray; they are not available for any other renderer (Maya Software or Maya Hardware). It's also crucial to understand that at this point not all materials will work with render passes. If you find that objects in your scene are not rendering correctly, double-check that you are using a material compliant with render passes.

The materials that work with render passes are as follows:

Anisotropic

Blinn

Lambert

Phong

Phong E

Env Fog

Fluid Shape

Light Fog

Particle Cloud

Volume Fog

Volume Shader

Hair Tube Shader

Ocean Shader

Ramp Shader

Hair

Fur

Image Plane

Layered Shader

Shading Map

Surface Shader

Use Background

mi_metallic_paint_x_passes

mi_car_paint_phen_x_passes

mia_material_x_passes

misss_fast_shader_x_passes

mila_material

Also, each shader does not necessarily work with every type of render pass listed in the render pass interface. For more information about specific shaders, consult the Maya documentation.

Upgrading Materials for Rendering Passes

The decision to render a scene in passes for compositing is going to affect what type of lighting and materials you use on the surfaces in your scene. As noted earlier, not all materials work with render passes. In addition, light shaders, such as the mia-physical light shader, can behave unpredictably with certain types of passes.

Generally speaking, any of the mental ray shaders that end with the "_passes" suffix are a good choice to use when rendering passes. If you have already applied the mia_material or mia_material_x shader to objects in the scene, you can easily upgrade these shaders to the mia_material_x_passes shader. The same is true for the mi_car_paint, mi_metallic_paint, and misss_fast_shader materials.

BE CONSISTENT WITH MATERIALS

The best way to minimize errors and confusion when rendering is to keep consistent with your material types: whenever possible, within a single render layer avoid using combinations of mia materials and standard Maya shaders.

The following example illustrates how to upgrade the mia_material_x shader to the mia_material_x_passes shader in order to prepare for the creation of render passes.

This scene uses an HDR image to create reflections on the surface of the metal. To render the scene correctly, we will be using the building_probe.hdr image from Paul Debevec's website at http://ict.debevec.org/~debevec/Probes/. This image is connected to the mentalrayIbl1 node in the coffeeMakerComposite_v01.ma scene. For more information on using the mentalrayIbl node, consult Chapter 7.

1. Open the coffeeMakerComposite_v01.ma scene from the chapter11\scenes folder at the book's web page.

2. Open the Hypershade window, and select brushedAluminum_MAT. This is a mia_material_x. Open the Attribute Editor, and scroll down to the Upgrade Shader rollout toward the bottom.

3. Click the Upgrade Shader To mia_material_x_passes button (see Figure 11.15).

4. Repeat this process to upgrade groundShader, matteBlackPlastic_MAT, readout_MAT, shinyBlackPlastic, thickGlass_MAT, and thinGlass_MAT.

5. Save the scene as **coffeeMakerComposite_v02.ma**.

To see a version of the scene, open the coffeeMakerComposite_v02.ma scene from the chapter11\scenes folder at the book's web page.

FIGURE 11.15
Upgrade the shader
to mia_material_x_
passes.

USE DEPTH PASSES TO CREATE DEPTH OF FIELD

Depth passes are particularly helpful in compositing. They can be used to add, among other things, camera depth of field in the composite. For example, using the Adobe After Effects Lens Blur filter, you can apply a depth pass to control the focal region of the render based on the luminance of the depth pass. Alternately, The Foundry Nuke includes the ZDefocus node, which also places a depth-of-field blur based on the values of a depth channel. Using a depth pass for depth of field in After Effects or Nuke dramatically reduces Maya render times, because mental ray's depth of field can take a long time to calculate.

Furthermore, any changes you make to the depth of field, such as the focal region, are done in the compositing program and do not require re-rendering the entire scene. The same is true for motion blur. You can create a 2D or 3D motion vector pass and then use a plug-in such as ReelSmart Motion Blur or use Nuke's VectorBlur node to add motion blur in the composite rather than in the initial render. This is a huge time-saver.

Rendering Multiple Passes from a Single Render Layer

**CERT
OBJECTIVE**

In this example, you'll create multiple passes for reflection, specular, depth, and shadow using the coffeemaker scene:

1. Continue with the scene from the previous section, or open the coffeeMakerComposite_v02.ma scene from the chapter11\scenes folder at the book's web page.

2. In the Render Layer Editor, select the coffeeMaker layer.

3. Click the Render Settings icon in the Render Layer Editor to open the Render Settings window, and choose the Passes tab.

4. Click the icon at the top of the stack of icons in the upper right. This opens the Create Render Passes window.

5. From Pass List, select the Camera Depth pass, and click the Create button at the bottom of the window.

6. Use the same steps to create Reflection, Shadow, and Specular passes (see Figure 11.16).

FIGURE 11.16
Render passes are created and listed in the Scene Passes section on the Passes tab for the coffeeMaker render layer.

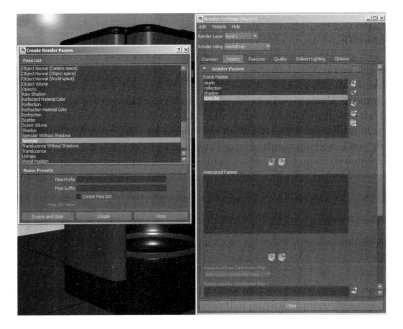

The passes have been created, but at the moment they are not associated with a render layer. You can create as many render passes as you like and then associate them with any combination of render layers in the scene—as long as those render layers are rendered using mental ray.

Once the pass is associated with the current layer, it is included in the frame buffer when the scene renders and saved as a separate image after rendering is complete. The Scene Passes and Associated Passes interface is a little confusing at first; just remember that only the passes listed in the Associated Passes section will be rendered for the current render layer. If you switch to another render layer, you'll see all the passes listed in the Scene Passes section.

7. Close the Create Render Pass window.

8. In the Passes tab of the Render Settings window, Shift+click the depth, reflection, shadow, and specular passes in the Scene Passes section.

9. Make sure that the Render Layer menu at the top of the Passes section of the Render Settings window is set to coffeeMaker.

10. Click the clapboard icon with the linked chain (between the Scene Passes and Associated passes sections). This moves the selected scene passes to the Associated Passes section, which means that the coffeeMaker render layer will now render the passes you've created.

    To disassociate a pass from a render layer, follow these steps:

    a. Select the pass in the Associated Passes section.

    b. Click the clapboard icon with the broken link between the two sections.

    This moves the pass back to the Scene Passes section. To delete a pass from either section, follow these steps:

    a. Select the pass.

    b. Press the Delete key.

11. Double-click the depth pass in the Associated Passes list; this causes its Attribute Editor to open.

12. Turn on Remap Depth Values, and set Far Clipping Plane to **18** (see Figure 11.17).

FIGURE 11.17
Edit the settings for the Depth pass in the Attribute Editor.

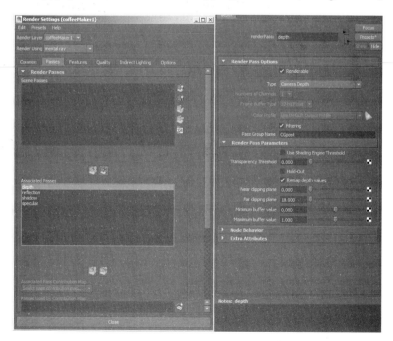

The scene size for this scene is 18 units in Z; when you set Far Clipping Plane to 18, any parts of a surface beyond 18 units are clipped to a luminance value of 1 (meaning they are white).

13. Double-click reflection to open its settings in the Attribute Editor.

14. Raise Maximum Reflection Level to **10**.

15. Create a test render from the Render View window using the renderCam camera.

You won't notice anything special about the render; the render passes have already been saved to disk in a subfolder of the project's Images folder, but they are not visible in the Render View window.

16. In the Render View window, choose File ➢ Load Render Pass ➢ Reflection (see Figure 11.18). Doing so opens the IMF_Display application.

FIGURE 11.18
Use the File menu in the Render View window to open the render-pass images in IMF_Display.

Sometimes this application opens behind the Maya interface, so you may need to minimize Maya to see it. On the Mac, an imf_disp or IMF_display icon appears on the Dock or within the Applications/Autodesk/maya2015/mentalray/bin folder.

17. Save the scene as **coffeeMakerComposite_v03.ma**.

The reflection pass shows only the reflections on the surface of the objects; the other parts of the image are dark. Thus the reflections are isolated. You can view the other passes using the File menu in the Render View window. Figure 11.19 shows each pass.

TONE MAPPING

Note that render passes are not tone-mapped; in other words, lens shaders applied to adjust the exposure of the image in the render view are not applied to the passes. IMF_display allows you to view the tone-mapped image by choosing the Tone Map option in the View menu. For more about tone mapping and lens shaders, consult Chapters 7 and 8.

The shadow pass will appear inverted in IMF_display. When you import this image into your compositing program, you can invert the colors and adjust as needed to create the effect you want.

FIGURE 11.19
Clockwise from the upper left: Reflection, Shadow, Depth, and Specular render passes as seen in IMF_display. The elements of the passes appear dark because they have been separated and rendered against black.

To see a finished version of the scene, open the coffeeMakerComposite_v03.ma scene from the chapter11\scenes folder at the book's web page.

You can add render passes to a render layer in the Render Layer Editor. To do so, follow these steps:

1. Right-click the layer.

2. Choose Add New Render Pass (see Figure 11.20).

3. Choose the type of pass from the pop-up list.

   The pass then automatically appears in the Associated Passes section in the Passes tab of the Render Settings window.

To remove a pass from a render layer, follow these steps:

1. Open the Render Settings window.

2. Switch to the Passes tab for the selected render layer.

3. Click the clapboard icon with the small red *X* between the Scene Passes and the Associated Passes sections.

Creating an Ambient Occlusion Render Pass

The mental ray renderer has a built-in ambient occlusion pass, which creates ambient occlusion shadowing in a render pass without the use of a custom shader network. Before the introduction of render passes in Maya 2009, the standard practice was to use a shader network to create the look of ambient occlusion, and a separate render layer used this shader as a material override. This can still be done, but in many cases using a render pass is faster and easier.

FIGURE 11.20
You can add render
passes to a render
layer by right-clicking
the layer in the
Render Layer Editor.

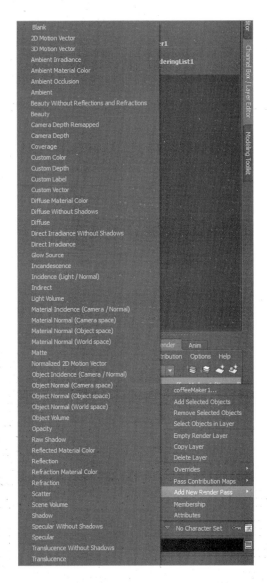

FIGURE 11.20
You can add render
passes to a render
layer by right-clicking
the layer in the
Render Layer Editor.

As explained in Chapter 7, ambient occlusion is a type of shadowing that occurs when indirect light rays are prevented from reaching a surface. Ambient occlusion is a soft and subtle type of shadowing. It's usually found in the cracks and crevices of objects in diffuse lighting.

To create ambient occlusion shadowing, mental ray uses raytracing to determine how the shading of a surface is colored. When a ray from the camera intersects with geometry, a number of secondary rays are shot from the point of intersection on the surface back into the scene. Imagine all the secondary rays as a hemisphere above each point on the surface that receives an initial ray from the camera. If the secondary ray detects another object (or part of the same object) within a given distance from the original surface, that point on the original surface has the dark color applied (which by default is black). If no other nearby surfaces are detected, then the bright color is applied (which by default is white). The proportion of dark to bright color is determined by the proximity of nearby surfaces.

In this section, you'll practice creating an ambient occlusion pass for the coffeemaker scene.

The scene has a single render layer named coffeeMaker. This layer is a duplicate of the master layer. You can create render passes for the master layer, but for the sake of simulating a production workflow, you'll use a render layer in this demonstration.

1. Open the `coffeeMakerComposite_v03.ma` scene from the `chapter11\scenes` folder at the book's web page.

2. Open the Render Settings window, and choose the Passes tab. At the top of the Render Settings window, make sure Render Layer is set to coffeeMaker1.

3. Click the top icon to the right of the Scene Passes section to open the Create Render Passes window.

4. From Pass List, select Ambient Occlusion (see Figure 11.21).

FIGURE 11.21
Select the Ambient Occlusion preset from the list of available render pass presets.

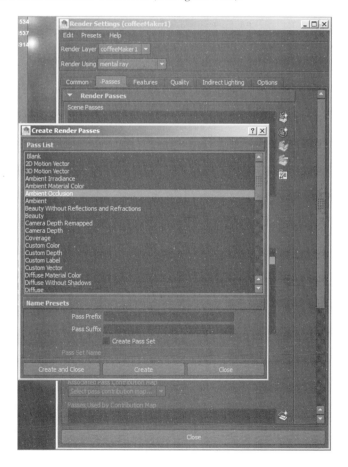

5. Click Create And Close to add the pass to the Scene Passes section.

6. You'll now see the Ambient Occlusion (AO) pass listed in the Scene Passes section as AO. Select the AO pass, and open the Attribute Editor. (If the pass settings don't appear in the Attribute Editor, double-click AO on the Passes tab of the Render Settings window.)

The settings for the pass are listed in the Attribute Editor. These include the following:

♦ The number of channels used for the pass

♦ The bit depth

The available settings may differ, depending on the selected pass preset:

♦ When Channels is set to 3, the pass will contain the red, green, and blue (RGB) channels.

♦ When Channels is set to 4, an alpha channel is also included along with the RGB channels.

7. Set Number Of Channels to 4 so that the alpha channel is included in the rendered image.

8. As opposed to using the global settings, you are going to tune the look of the ambient occlusion pass in the local AO settings. Scroll down to the lower section of the Attribute Editor, and select Use Local AO Settings.

GLOBAL AMBIENT OCCLUSION SETTINGS

In the Indirect Lighting tab of the Render Settings window, there is an Ambient Occlusion rollout that controls the global settings for creating ambient occlusion passes. These settings are bypassed when you select Use Local AO Settings in the Ambient Occlusion render pass attributes. Leave the Ambient Occlusion check box selected in the Render Settings window regardless of whether you are using local or global settings.

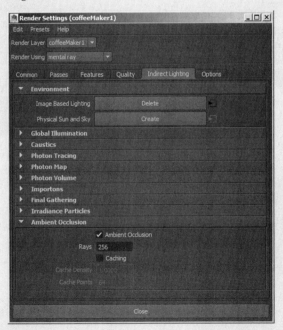

9. The Rays attribute adjusts the overall quality of the ambient occlusion shading. Increasing this setting improves quality but also increases render times. Leave this at 64, which is a good setting for testing.

   Bright and Dark Colors   The bright and dark colors determine how a surface is shaded based on the proximity of other surfaces or parts of the same surface. If you reverse these colors, you'll see the negative image of the ambient occlusion shadowing. For most compositions, it's fine to leave these as black and white. The values can easily be edited in compositing software after rendering.

   Spread   Spread determines the distance of the shading effect across the surface. Think of this as the size of the shadow. Higher values produce tighter areas of shadowing on the surface; lower values produce broader, softer shadows.

   Maximum Distance   The Maximum Distance attribute determines how much of the scene is sampled. Think of this as the distance the secondary rays travel in the scene as they search out nearby surfaces. If a nearby object is beyond the Maximum Distance setting, then it will not affect how ambient occlusion is calculated because the secondary rays will never reach it. When Maximum Distance is set to 0, the entire scene is sampled; Max Distance is essentially infinite.

   One of the best ways to increase efficiency in the scene is to establish a value for Maximum Distance. This decreases the render time and improves the look of the image. Determining the proper value for Maximum Distance often takes a little experimentation and a few test renders. You want to find the value that offers the type of shadowing you need within a reasonable render time.

10. Set Maximum Distance to **4**. Leave Spread at 0 (see Figure 11.22).

    At this point, these settings should produce a nice-looking ambient occlusion pass for this scene. Now you need to associate this pass with the coffeeMaker render layer. To save some render time for this exercise, the other render passes created earlier in the chapter can be de-associated.

11. On the Passes tab of the Render Settings window for the coffeeMaker layer, select AO in the Scene Passes section, and click the icon with the linked chain to move it down to the Associated Passes section.

12. Shift+click the depth, diffuse, reflection, shadow, and specular passes in the Associated Passes section so that they are highlighted in blue.

13. Click the icon with the broken chain to move them back to the Scene Passes section. This means that they will not be calculated when the coffeeMaker render layer is rendered (see Figure 11.23).

    Even though you have set up the AO layer and associated it with the coffeeMaker render layer, the ambient occlusion will not calculate correctly until you select Ambient Occlusion in the Features section of the Render Settings window. This is an easy thing to forget!

14. Click the Features tab of the Render Settings window.

15. Under Secondary Effects, select the Ambient Occlusion option (see Figure 11.24).

FIGURE 11.22
The Use Local AO Settings feature allows you to adjust how the ambient occlusion will look when the AO render pass for the coffee-Maker layer is created.

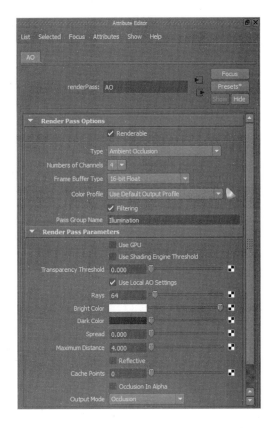

16. Open the Render View window, and create a render using the renderCam camera. You won't see any ambient occlusion in this render; however, it is being calculated and stored as a separate image.

The pass is stored in a temporary folder in the project's Images folder. If the scene uses layers, each layer has its own subfolder where the passes are stored.

17. To see the Ambient Occlusion pass, use the File menu in the Render View window. Choose File ➤ Load Render Pass ➤ AO. The image opens in a separate image view window (see Figure 11.25).

18. Save the scene as **coffeeMakerComposite_v04.ma**.

To see a finished version of the scene, open the coffeeMakerComposite_v04.ma scene from the chapter11\scenes folder at the book's web page.

FIGURE 11.23
Calculation of the
other render passes
is disabled by mov-
ing them from the
Associated Render
Pass section up to the
Scene Passes section.

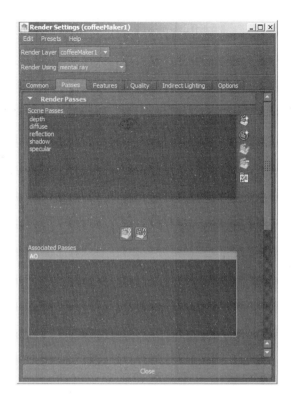

FIGURE 11.24
Select Ambient
Occlusion on
the Features tab
of the Render
Settings window.

FIGURE 11.25
The ambient occlusion pass as it appears in IMF_display.

Setting Up a Render with mental ray

Rendering is the process of translating a Maya animation into a sequence of images. The images are processed and saved to disk. The rendered image sequences can then be brought into a compositing software, where they can be layered together, edited, color-corrected, combined with live footage, and have additional effects applied. The composite can then be converted to a movie file or a sequence of images for distribution or imported to editing software for further processing.

Generally, you want to render a sequence of images from Maya. You can render directly to a movie file, but this usually is not a good idea. If the render stops while rendering directly to a movie file, it may corrupt the movie, and you will need to restart the whole render. When you render a sequence of images and the render stops, you can easily restart the render without re-creating any of the images that have already been saved to disk.

When you set up a batch render, you can specify how the image sequence will be labeled and numbered. You also set the image format of the final render, which render layers and passes will be included and where they will be stored, and other aspects related to the rendered sequences. You can use the Render Settings window to determine these properties or perform a command-line render using your operating system's terminal. In this section, you'll learn important features of both methods.

Batch rendering is also accomplished using render-farm software, such as the Autodesk® Backburner™ software, which is included with Maya. This allows you to distribute the render across multiple computers. Consult the help documents on how to use Backburner, since this subject is beyond the scope of this book.

AMBIENT OCCLUSION PASSES AND BUMP/DISPLACEMENT TEXTURES

Displacement maps applied to objects via shaders will be included in the ambient occlusion render pass regardless of the type of shader that is applied to the object. However, this is not true for bump maps. The details you create using a texture connected to the object's shader may not appear in the ambient occlusion pass if you're using a standard Maya material such as a Blinn or Lambert. If you're using the mental ray mia_material_x_passes shader, and a bump texture is connected to the shader's Standard Bump channel, then you'll see the details of the bump texture in the ambient occlusion pass.

In the images shown here, you can see that the two cubes at the top-left quadrant have a fractal texture applied to the bump channel of a standard Lambert shader. These details do not appear in the ambient occlusion pass (on the top right). The cubes at the bottom use a mia_material_x_passes shader, and you can clearly see the bump texture in the ambient occlusion pass (on the bottom right).

COLOR PROFILE MANAGEMENT

You can specify a color profile if you need to match a specific color space in your compositing software or if you need to match footage that requires a specific setting. A color profile can be assigned to individual textures and render passes. Many nodes throughout Maya now support the assignment of color profiles. For example, when you create a file texture node for use in a shader, you'll see a drop-down menu that gives you options for assigning a color profile (under the File Name field in the File node's Attribute Editor).

It is crucial to understand that, unless you select Color Management on the Common tab of the Render Settings window, any color profiles you assign to textures or render passes will not work.

File Tokens

File tokens are a way to automate the organization of your renders. If your scene has a lot of layers, cameras, and passes, you can use tokens to specify where all the image sequences will be placed on your computer's hard drive, as well as how they are named.

The image sequences created with a batch render are placed in the `images` folder of the current project or whichever folder is specified in the Project Settings window (see Chapter 1, "Working in Autodesk Maya," for information regarding project settings). Tokens are placed in the File Name Prefix field found on the Common tab of the Render Settings window. If this field is left blank, the scene name is used to label the rendered images (see Figure 11.26).

FIGURE 11.26

The File Name Prefix field on the Common tab of the Render Settings window is where you specify the image name and tokens.

By default, if the scene has more than one render layer, Maya creates a subfolder for each layer. If the scene has more than one camera, a subfolder is created for each camera. For scenes with multiple render layers and multiple cameras, Maya creates a subfolder for each camera within the subfolder for each layer.

You can specify any folder you want by typing the folder names into the File Name Prefix field. For example, if you want your image sequences to be named `marshmallow` and placed in a folder named `chocolateSauce`, you can type **chocolateSauce/marshmallow** in the File Name Prefix field. However, explicitly naming a file sequence lacks the flexibility of using tokens and runs the risk of allowing you to overwrite file sequences by mistake when rendering. You can see a preview of how the images will be named in the upper portion of the Render Settings window (see Figure 11.27).

FIGURE 11.27

A preview of the image name appears at the top of the Common tab of the Render Settings window.

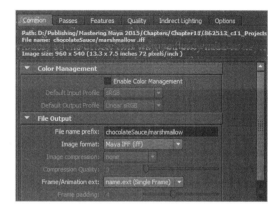

The whole point of tokens is to allow you to change the default behavior and specify how subfolders will be created dynamically for a scene. To use a token to specify a folder, place a slash after the token name. For example, to create a subfolder named after each camera, type **<camera>/** in the File Name Prefix field. To use a token to name the images, omit the slash. For example, typing **<scene>/<camera>** results in a folder named after the scene containing a sequence of images named `camera.iff`.

Here are some common tokens:

<Scene>   This token names the images or subfolder after the scene name.

<Camera>   This token names the images or subfolders after the camera. For example, in a scene with two cameras named renderCam1 and renderCam2, <Scene>/<Camera>/<Camera> creates a single folder named after the scene, within which are two subfolders named renderCam1 and renderCam2. In each of these folders is a sequence named `renderCam1.ext` and `renderCam2.ext`.

<RenderLayer>   This token creates a subfolder or sequence named after each render layer. If there are passes associated with the layer, then the pass names are appended to the layer name. For example, if you have a layer named spurtsOfBlood and an associated specular pass, the folder or image sequence would automatically be named `spurtsOfBlood_specular`.

<RenderPass>   This token creates a subfolder or sequence named after the render pass. Since render passes are available only for mental ray renders, this token applies only when using mental ray.

<RenderPassType>   This token is similar to <RenderPass> except that it abbreviates the name of the render pass. A reflection pass, for example, would be abbreviated as REFL.

<RenderPassFileGroup>   This token adds the name of the render-pass file group. The pass group name is set in the Attribute Editor of the render-pass node. Render pass file groups are assigned by mental ray, but you can create your own name for the group by typing it in the Pass Group Name field of the render pass node (see Figure 11.28).

FIGURE 11.28
You can set the render pass group name in the Attribute Editor of the render pass node.

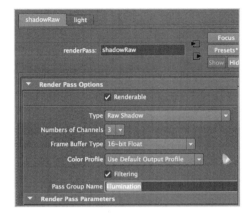

<**Extension**> This token adds the file format extension. It is usually added to the end of the filename automatically, but you can also use this token to label a folder based on the image format.

<**Version**> This token adds a custom label specified by the Version Label field in the Render Settings window (see Figure 11.29).

FIGURE 11.29
The <Version> token adds the label specified in the Version Label field in the Render Settings window.

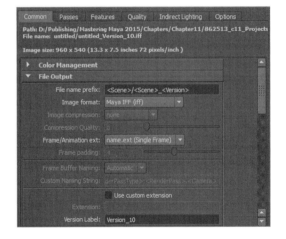

Note that the capitalization of the token name does matter. If you had a scene named chocolateSauce that has a render layer named banana that uses a specular and diffuse pass with two cameras named shot1 and shot2 and you wanted to add the version label v05, the following tokens specified in the File Name Prefix field,

```
<Scene>/<RenderLayer>/<Camera>/<RenderPass>/<RenderPass>_<Version>
```

would create a file structure that looks like this:

```
chocolateSauce/banana/shot1/specular/specular_v05.#.ext
chocolateSauce/banana/shot1/diffuse/diffuse_v05.#.ext
chocolateSauce/banana/shot2/specular/specular_v05.#.ext
chocolateSauce/banana/shot2/diffuse/diffuse_v05.#.ext
```

TOKENS FOR OPENEXR FILES

The OpenEXR format can create multiple additional channels within a single image. Each channel can contain an image created from a render pass. If a scene has one or more render passes and you choose the OpenEXR image format, you can use the Frame Buffer Naming field to specify the name of each pass. This feature is available only when OpenEXR is chosen as the file format and the scene has one or more render passes. You can use the automatic naming setting or enable the Custom option in the Frame Buffer Naming drop-down menu. You can then use the Custom Naming String field to choose the token you want to use.

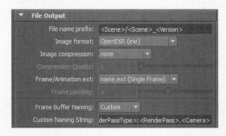

Use underscores or hyphens when combining tokens in the folder or image name. Avoid using periods.

You can right-click the File Name Prefix field to access a list of commonly used token keywords. This is a handy way to save a little typing.

Specifying Frame Range

For multiframe animations, you have a number of options for specifying the frame range and the syntax for the filenames in the sequence. These settings are found on the Common tab of the Render Settings window. To enable multiframe rendering, choose one of the presets from the Frame/Animation Ext drop-down list in the File output rollout. When rendering animation sequences, the safest choice is usually the *name*. #. ext option. This names the images in the sequence by placing a dot between the image name and the image number and another dot between the image number and the file extension. The Frame Padding option allows you to specify a number of digits in the image number, and it will insert zeros as needed. So a sequence named marshmallow using the Maya IFF format with a Frame Padding of 4 would be marshmallow.0001.iff.

The Frame Range settings specify which frames in the animation will be rendered. The By Frame setting allows you to render each frame (using a setting of 1), skip frames (using a setting higher than 1), or render twice as many frames (using a setting of 0.5, which renders essentially at half speed). You can also set Skip Existing Frames to have Maya automatically find frames that have already been rendered and skip over them.

It is possible to render backward by specifying a higher frame number for the Start Frame value than the End Frame value and using a negative number for By Frame. You would then want to use the Renumber Frames option so that the frame numbers move upward incrementally.

The Renumber Frames option allows you to customize the labeling of the image sequence numbers.

Renderable Cameras

The rendering cameras are specified in the Renderable Cameras list. To add a camera, expand the Renderable Cameras list and choose Add Renderable Camera (see Figure 11.30). To remove a rendering camera, click the trashcan icon next to the renderable camera. As noted earlier in the chapter, you can use a layer override to include a specific camera with a render layer.

FIGURE 11.30

You can add
and remove
renderable
cameras using
the Renderable
Camera menu.

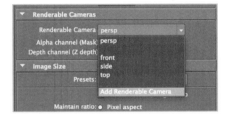

Each camera has the option of rendering alpha and Z-depth channels. The Z-depth channel stores information about the depth in the scene. This is included as an extra channel in the image (only a few formats, such as Maya IFF and OpenEXR, support this extra channel). Not all compositing software supports the Maya Z-depth channel. You may find it easier to create a camera depth pass using the custom passes (passes are described earlier in this chapter). The render depth pass can be imported into your compositing software and used with a filter to create depth-of-field effects.

File Formats and the Frame Buffer

When Maya renders a scene, the data stored in the frame buffer is converted into the native IFF format and then translated to the file type specified in the Image Format menu. Thus if you specify the TIFF format, for example, Maya translates the TIFF image from the native IFF format.

Many compositing packages (such as Adobe After Effects, Autodesk Composite, and The Foundry Nuke) support the IFF format, so it's generally safe to render to this file format. The IFF format uses four 16-bit channels by default, which is adequate for most viewing purposes. If you need to change the file to a different bit depth or a different number of channels, you can choose one of the options from the Data Type menu in the Framebuffer section of the Quality tab. This is where you will also find the output options, such as Premultiply (see Figure 11.31).

FIGURE 11.31

Specify bit depth
and other output
options using
the Framebuffer
settings on the
Quality tab
of the Render
Settings window.

Render passes use the secondary frame buffer to store the image data. You can specify the bit depth of this secondary buffer in the Attribute Editor for each render pass.

A complete list of supported image formats is available in the Maya documentation. Note that Maya Software and mental ray may support different file formats.

Starting a Batch Render

When you are satisfied that your animation is ready to render, and all the settings have been specified in the Render Settings window, you're ready to start a batch render. To start a batch render, set the main Maya menu set to Rendering and choose Render ➢ Batch Render ➢ Options. If you are rendering with mental ray, you can specify memory limits and multithreading, as well as local and network rendering.

One of the most useful options is Verbosity Level. This refers to the level of detail of the messages displayed in the Maya Output window as the render takes place. (This works only when you are using Maya with Windows.) You can use these messages to monitor the progress of the render as well as diagnose problems that may occur while rendering. The Progress Messages setting (Figure 11.32) is the most useful option in most situations.

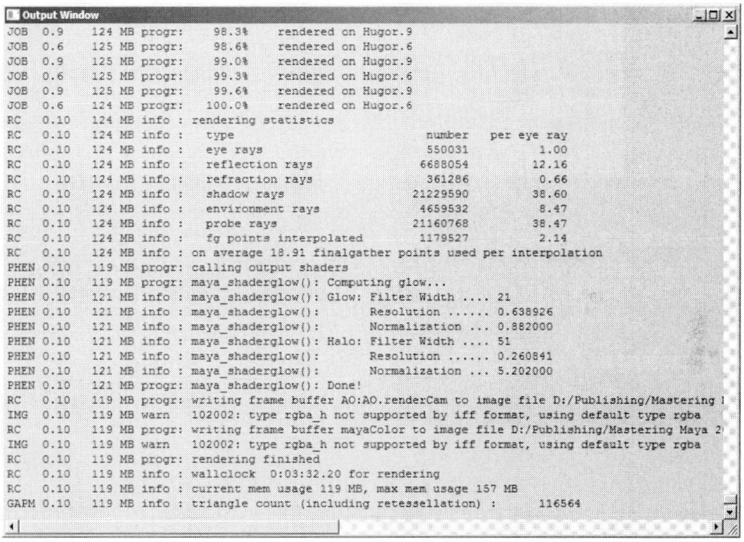

FIGURE 11.32
Detailed progress messages for each frame can be displayed in the Output window.

To start the render, click the Batch Render (or the Batch Render And Close) button. As the batch render takes place, you'll see the Script Editor update. For detailed information on the progress of each frame, you can monitor the progress in the Output window.

To stop a batch render, choose Render ➢ Cancel Batch Render. To see how the current frame in the batch render looks, choose Render ➢ Show Batch Render.

When the render is complete, you'll see a message in the Script Editor that says Rendering Completed. You can then use FCheck to view the sequence (File ➢ View Sequence) or import the sequence into your compositing software.

MONITORING A RENDER IN THE SCRIPT EDITOR

The Script Editor is not always completely reliable when it comes to monitoring the progress of a render. If the messages stop updating as the render progresses, it may or may not indicate that the render has stopped. Before assuming that the render has stopped, browse to the current image folder and double-check to see whether images are still being written to disk. This is especially true when using Maya on a Mac.

Command-Line Rendering

A batch render can be initiated using a command prompt (Windows) or Terminal window (Mac). This is known as a *command-line render*. A command-line render takes the form of a series of commands typed into the command prompt. These commands include information about the location of the Maya scene to be rendered, the location of the rendered image sequence, the rendering cameras, the image size, the frame range, and many other options similar to the settings found in the Render Settings window.

Command-line renders tend to be more stable than batch renders initiated from the Maya interface. This is because when the Maya application is closed, more of your computer's RAM is available for the render. You can start a command-line render regardless of whether Maya is running. In fact, to maximize system resources, it's best to close Maya when starting a command-line render. In this example, you can keep Maya open.

In this exercise, you'll see how you can start a batch render on both a Windows computer and a Mac. You'll use the solarSystem_v01.ma scene, which is a simple animation showing two planets orbiting a glowing sun.

Open the solarSystem_v01.ma scene from the chapter11\scenes folder at the book's web page.

This scene has a masterLayer render layer, which should not be rendered, and two additional layers:

♦ The solarSystem layer contains the sun and planets, which have been shaded. It uses the mental ray renderer. If you open the Render Settings window to the Passes tab, you'll see that this scene uses two render passes: diffuse and incandescence.

♦ The second layer is named orbitPaths. It contains Paint Effects strokes that illustrate the orbit paths of the two planets (see Figure 11.33).

On the Common tab of the Render Settings window, no filename prefix has been specified, and a frame range has not been set. Maya will use the default file structure when rendering the scene, and the frame range will be set in the options for the command line.

WINDOWS COMMAND-LINE RENDER

The first example starts a command-line render using Windows 7:

1. Click the Windows Start menu button. In the Search Programs And Files field, type **Command Prompt** or **cmd**. Click the Command Prompt icon that appears at the top of the search. (Note that you may need to RMB-click and choose Run As Administrator if the system security settings are restrictive.)

2. Use Windows Explorer to browse to the path of your scenes folder: right-click the Start button, and choose Open Windows Explorer.

3. Open the scenes folder in your current project where you placed the solarSystem_v01 .ma scene.

4. RMB-click the Explorer address bar, and choose Copy Address As Text to copy the path to the scenes folder to the clipboard.

5. At the command prompt, type **cd ..\..** and press Enter. Doing so goes back two directories and sets the command prompt to the root folder.

6. Type **cd** and then a space; right-click the command line and select Paste. This pastes the path to the scenes folder in the command prompt.

7. Press the Enter key to set the current folder to the scenes folder.

FIGURE 11.33
The solar
System_v01.ma
scene has been
prepared for
rendering.

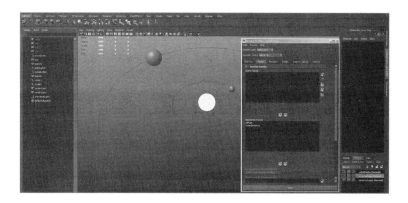

When starting a batch render, you can either specify the path to the scenes folder in the command-line options or set the command prompt to the folder that contains the scene.

To start a batch render, use the render command in the command prompt, followed by option flags and the name of the scene you want to render. The option flags are preceded by a hyphen. The flags are followed by a space and then the flag setting. For example, to start a scene using the mental ray renderer, you would type **render -r mr myscene.ma**. The render command starts the batch renderer, the -r flag specifies the renderer, and mr sets the -r flag to mental ray. The command ends with the name of the scene (or the folder path to the scene if you're not already in the folder with the scene).

If render is not recognized as a command, and the command line produces an error, the render executable was not given a proper global variable at the time of installation. You can sidestep this error by executing the render command from the Maya program bin folder. For example, in the Command Prompt window, navigate to the C:\Program Files\Autodesk\ Maya2015\bin folder before launching the batch render.

There are many options, but you don't need to use them, except if you want to specify an option that's different from what is used in the scene. If you want all the layers to render using mental ray regardless of the layer setting in the scene, then you specify mental ray using the `-r mr` flag. If you omit the `-r` flag, Maya uses the default renderer, which is Maya Software. If you have a scene with several layers that use different renderers (as in the case of the solar-System_v01.ma scene), you would type **-r file**. This sets the renderer to whatever is specified in the file, including what is specified for each layer.

Other common flags include the following:

`-s <float>` sets the start frame. (It replaces `<float>` with the starting frame; for example, `-s 120` would set the start frame to 120. A float is a number with a decimal point.)

`-e <float>` sets the end frame.

`-x <int>` sets the X resolution of the image. (An integer is a whole number without a decimal point.)

`-y <int>` sets the Y resolution of the image.

`- cam <name>` sets the camera.

`-rd <path>` specifies the folder for the images. (If this is not used, the folder in the project settings is used.)

`-im <filename>` sets the name of the rendered image.

`-of <format>` sets the image format.

There is a complete list of the flags in the Maya documentation. You can also print a description of commands by typing **render -help**. To see mental ray–specific commands, type **render -help -r mr**.

For example, if you want to render the scene using renderCam1, starting on frame 1 and ending on frame 24, type the following at the command prompt:

```
render -r file -s 1 -e 24 -cam renderCam1 solarSystem_v01.ma
```

You'll see the render execute in the command prompt. When it's finished, you can use FCheck to view each sequence. In the Images folder, you'll see two directories named after the layers in the scene. The orbitPath folder has the Paint Effects orbit paths rendered with Maya Software. The solarSystem folder has the rendered sequence of the planets and sun as well as subdirectories for the diffuse, incandescence, and MasterBeauty passes. (The MasterBeauty pass is created by default when you add passes to a scene.)

Let's say you want to render only the orbitPaths layer using renderCam2 for the frame range 16 to 48. You want to specify Maya Software as the renderer. You may want to name the sequence after the camera as well. Type the following at the command prompt (use a single line with no returns):

```
render -r sw -s 16 -e 48 -rl orbitPaths -cam renderCam2 ↵
 -im solarSystemCam2 solarSystem_v01.ma
```

Mac Command-Line Render

For a Mac, the Maya command-line render workflow is similar except that, instead of the command prompt, you use a special Terminal window that is included when you install Maya.

This is an application called `Maya Terminal.term`, and it's found in the `Applications\Autodesk\maya2015` folder. It's probably a good idea to add this application to the Dock so that you can easily open it whenever you need to run a batch render.

You need to navigate in the terminal to the `scenes` folder that contains the scene you want to render:

1. Copy the `solarSystem_v01.ma` scene from the book's web page to the `scenes` folder of your current project on your computer's hard drive.

2. In the Finder, open the current project folder.

3. Start the Maya Terminal application, and type **cd** at the prompt.

4. In the Finder, drag the `scenes` folder from the current project on top of the Maya Terminal. This places the path to the `scenes` folder in the Terminal.

5. Press the Enter key. The Terminal window is now set to the project's `scenes` folder, which contains the `solarSystem_v01.ma` scene.

The commands for rendering on a Mac are the same as they are for Windows. From here, you can take up with step 6 from the previous exercise.

mental ray Quality Settings

The quality of your render is determined by a number of related settings, some of which appear in the Render Settings window and some of which appear in the Attribute Editor of nodes within the scene. Tessellation, antialiasing, sampling, and filtering all play a part in how good the final render looks. You will always have to strike a balance between render quality and render time. As you raise the level of quality, you should test your renders and make a note of how long they take. Five minutes to render a single frame may not seem like much until you're dealing with a multilayered animation that is several thousand frames long. Remember that you will almost always have to render a sequence more than once as changes are requested by the director or client (even when you are sure it is the absolute final render!).

In this section, you'll learn how to use the settings on the Quality tab as well as other settings to improve the look of the final render.

ALWAYS TEST SHORT SEQUENCES

A single rendered frame may not reveal all of the quality problems in a scene. Remember to test a short sequence of rendered frames for problems such as flickering or crawling textures before starting a full batch render. For scenes with dynamic lighting or complex action you can render by skipping a specific frame amount.

Tessellation and Approximation Nodes

At render time, all the geometry in the scene, regardless of whether it is NURBS, polygons, or subdivision surfaces, is converted to polygon triangles by the renderer. *Tessellation* refers to the number and placement of the triangles on the surface when the scene is rendered. Objects that have a low tessellation will look blocky when compared to those with a high tessellation (see Figure 11.34). However, low-tessellation objects take less time to render than high-tessellation objects. Tessellation settings can be found in the shape nodes of surfaces. In Chapter 3, "Hard Surface Modeling," the settings for NURBS surface tessellation are discussed. The easiest way to set tessellation for NURBS surfaces is to use the Tessellation controls in the shape node of the surface. Additionally, you can set tessellation for multiple surfaces at the same time by opening the Attribute Spreadsheet (Window ➤ General Editors ➤ Attribute Spread Sheet) to the Tessellation tab.

FIGURE 11.34
The sphere on the left has a low-tessellation setting. The sphere on the right was rendered with a high-tessellation setting.

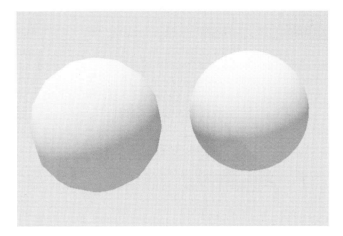

You can also create an approximation node that can set the tessellation for various types of surfaces. To create an approximation node, select the surface and choose Window ➤ Rendering Editors ➤ mental ray ➤ Approximation Editor.

The editor allows you to create approximation nodes for NURBS surfaces, displacements (when using a texture for geometry displacement), and subdivision surfaces.

To create a node, click the Create button. To assign the node to a surface, select the surface, and select the node from the drop-down menu in the Approximation Editor; then click the Assign button. The Unassign button allows you to break the connection between the node and the surface. The Edit button allows you to edit the node's settings in the Attribute Editor, and the Delete button removes the node from the scene (see Figure 11.35).

FIGURE 11.35
The Approximation Editor allows you to create and assign approximation nodes.

You can assign a subdivision surface approximation node to a polygon object so that the polygons are rendered as subdivision surfaces, giving them a smooth appearance similar to a smooth mesh or subdivision surface. In Figure 11.36, a polygon cube has been duplicated twice. The cube on the far left has a subdivision approximation node assigned to it. The center cube is a smooth mesh. (The cube is converted to a smooth mesh by pressing the **3** key. Smooth mesh polygon surfaces are covered in Chapter 4, "Organic Modeling.") The cube on the far right has been converted to a subdivision surface (Modify ➤ Convert ➤ Polygons To Subdiv). When the scene is rendered using mental ray, the three cubes are almost identical. This demonstrates the various options available for rendering smooth polygon surfaces.

FIGURE 11.36
Three duplicate cubes are rendered as smooth surfaces using an approximation node, a smooth mesh, and a subdivision surface.

When editing the settings for the subdivision approximation node, the Parametric Method option is the simplest to use. You can use the N Subdivisions setting to set the smoothness of the render. Each time you increase the number of subdivisions, the polygons are multiplied by a factor of 4. A setting of 3 means that each polygon face on the original object is divided 12 times.

Unified Sampling

Unified Sampling offers a simplified approach to your primary sampling settings. Instead of setting individual antialiasing and sampling settings, Unified Sampling uses a single Quality slider. The Quality slider employs enhanced sampling to avoid a lot of the common artifacts. For instance, Unified Sampling removes moiré patterns in your render.

Another advantage to Unified Sampling is the ability to use progressive rendering with the Interactive Photorealistic Render (IPR). When in IPR Progressive Mode, the rendered image starts with a low sample rate and is refined with more samples until it achieves the final result. The amount of sampling is derived from your Unified Sampling quality.

Progressive rendering allows you to see an initial preview of your render. Although low quality, the initial rendering provides quick feedback for your render settings, light position, and other attributes that would otherwise take minutes to hours to render. Detecting problems in your render early on enables you to stop the render before wasting time on calculating expensive antialiasing or other quality settings that may not have any bearing on your current refinements.

Filtering

Filtering occurs after sampling as the image is translated in the frame buffer. You can apply a number of filters, which are found in the menu in the Multi-Pixel Filtering section of the Render Settings window's Quality tab. Some filters blur the image, whereas others sharpen the image. The Filter Size fields determine the height and width of the filter as it expands from the center of the sample across neighboring pixels. A setting of 1×1 covers a single pixel, and a setting of 2×2 covers four pixels. Most of the time, the default setting for each filter type is the best one to use.

Box Filter   Applies the filter evenly across the image's height and width.

Triangle and Gauss Filters   Adds a small amount of blurring to the pixels, whereas Mitchell and Lanczos both sharpen the image.

Jitter Option   Reduces flickering or banding artifacts. Jittering offsets the sample location for a given sample block in a random fashion. Disabled with Unified Sampling.

Sample Lock Option   Locks the sampling pattern. This reduces flickering by forcing mental ray to sample the scene the same way for each frame. It can be useful in animated sequences and when using motion blur. If Sample Lock does not reduce flickering, try Jitter as an alternative.

The Bottom Line

Use render layers.   Render layers can be used to separate the elements of a single scene into different versions or into different layers of a composite. Each layer can have its own shaders, lights, and settings. Using overrides, you can change the way each layer renders.

> **Master It**   Use render layers to set up alternate versions of the coffeemaker. Try applying contour rendering on one layer and Final Gathering on another.

Use render passes.   Render passes allow you to separate material properties into different images. These passes are derived from calculations stored in the frame buffer. Each pass can be used in compositing software to rebuild the rendered scene efficiently. Render pass contribution maps define which objects and lights are included in a render pass.

> **Master It**   Create an Ambient Occlusion pass for the bicycle scene.

Perform batch renders.   Batch renders automate the process of rendering a sequence of images. You can use the Batch Render options in the Maya interface, or choose Batch Render from the command prompt (or Terminal) when Maya is closed. A batch script can be used to render multiple scenes.

> **Master It**   Create a batch script to render five fictional scenes. Each scene uses layers with different render settings. Set the frame range for each scene to render frames 20 through 50. The scenes are named `myScene1.ma` through `myScene5.ma`.

Use mental ray quality settings.   Controlling the quality of your renders is a joint venture between using approximation nodes and render settings. Unified Sampling offers a simplified approach to adjusting the quality of your renders. Combine this with progressive IPR, and you can quickly refine your renders.

> **Master It**   Set up an IPR render of the `coffeeMakerComposite_v04.ma` scene. Focus in on half of the coffeemaker and force the render to last only 20 seconds. Adjust the quality for the best results.

Chapter 12

Introducing nParticles

This chapter introduces nParticle dynamics in the Autodesk® Maya® program and shows you how you can use them creatively to produce a wide variety of visual effects. The example scenes demonstrate the fundamentals of working with and rendering particles. The subsequent chapters on Maya dynamics build on these techniques.

nParticles are connected to the Nucleus solver system, a difference from traditional Maya particles. Nucleus is a unified dynamic system that is part of nCloth. The Nucleus solver is the brain behind the nDynamic systems in Maya.

In this chapter, you will learn to:

◆ Create nParticles

◆ Make nParticles collide

◆ Create liquid simulations

◆ Emit nParticles from a texture

◆ Move nParticles with Nucleus wind

◆ Use force fields

Creating nParticles

A *particle* is a point in space that can react to the simulated dynamic forces generated by Maya. These dynamic forces allow you to create animated effects in a way that would be difficult or impossible to create with standard keyframe animation. When you create a *particle object*, points are created in the scene. You can then attach force fields to the particles to push them around and make them fall, swarm, float, or perform any number of other behaviors without the need for keyframes.

Maya particle dynamics have been part of Maya since the earliest versions of the software. In Maya 2009, Autodesk introduced *nParticles*, which have all the capabilities of the older, traditional particles, plus additional attributes that make them easier to use and more powerful. Unlike traditional particles, nParticles can collide and influence the behavior of other nParticles. nParticle collisions occur when two or more nParticles come within a specified distance, causing them to bounce off one another or, in some cases, stick together. Very complex behaviors can be created by adjusting the settings in the nParticle's Attribute Editor. In this chapter you'll learn how you can create effects by adjusting these settings. Since nParticles can do just about everything traditional particles can do and then some, this chapter will cover nParticles only and not traditional Maya particles.

An *nCloth object* is a piece of polygon geometry that can also react to dynamic forces. Each vertex in an nCloth object has the properties of an nParticle, and these nParticles are connected by invisible virtual springs, which means nCloth objects can collide with, and influence the behavior of, other nCloth objects and nParticles. In this chapter, you'll get a taste of working with nCloth; Chapter 13, "Dynamic Effects," demonstrates more advanced nCloth and nParticle effects.

When you create an nParticle object or an nCloth object (or both) in a scene, a *Nucleus solver* is created. The Nucleus solver is a node in Maya that acts as an engine for all the dynamic effects. The Nucleus solver determines global settings for the dynamics, such as the strength and direction of gravity, the air density, the wind direction, and the quality of the dynamics simulation (for example, how many times per frame the simulation is calculated). The same Nucleus solver is used to calculate the dynamics and interactions within the nParticle system and the nCloth system. A scene can have more than one Nucleus solver, but nDynamic systems using two different solvers can't directly interact. However, two separate nParticle objects using the same Nucleus solver can interact.

Traditional Maya dynamics use a much simpler solver node that does not take into account interactions between different dynamic objects. Traditional particle objects are completely self-contained, so two particle objects in a Maya scene are not aware of each other's existence (so to speak).

The following exercises take you through the process of using the different nParticle-creation methods and introduce you to working with the Nucleus solver.

NDYNAMICS

The *Nucleus dynamic systems (nDynamics)* are distinguished from the traditional dynamic systems by the letter *n*. So, *nParticles*, *nCloth*, and *nRigids* are part of the nDynamics system, and particles and rigid bodies are part of traditional Maya dynamics.

Drawing nParticles Using the nParticle Tool

You can create nParticles in a scene in a number of ways. You can draw them on the grid, use an emitter to spawn them into a scene, use a surface as an emitter, or fill a volume with nParticles. When you create an nParticle object, you also need to specify the nParticle's style.

Choosing a style activates one of a number of presets for the nParticle's attributes, all of which can be altered after you add the nParticle object to the scene. The nParticle styles include Balls, Points, Cloud, Thick Cloud, and Water.

The simplest way to create nParticles is to draw them on the grid using the nParticle tool, as follows:

1. Create a new scene in Maya. Switch to the nDynamics menu.

2. Choose nParticles ➤ Create nParticles, and set the style to Balls (see Figure 12.1).

3. Choose nParticles ➤ Create nParticles ➤ nParticle Tool. Click six or seven times on the grid to place individual particles.

4. Press the Enter key to create the particles.

   You'll see several circles on the grid. The ball-type nParticle style automatically creates blobby surface particles. Blobby surfaces are spheres rendered using the Maya Software or mental ray® program. Blobby surfaces use standard Maya shaders when rendered, and they can be blended together to form a gooey surface.

FIGURE 12.1
Using the nParticle menu to specify the nParticle style.

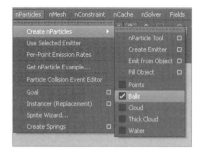

5. Set the length of the timeline to **600**. Rewind and play the animation. The particles will fall in space.

6. Open the Attribute Editor for the nParticle1 object, and switch to the nucleus1 tab. The settings on this tab control the Nucleus solver, which sets the overall dynamic attributes of the connected nDynamic systems (see Figure 12.2).

FIGURE 12.2
The settings on the nucleus1 tab define the behavior of the environment for all connected nDynamic nodes.

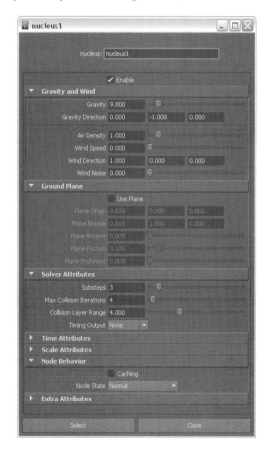

7. By default, a Nucleus solver has Gravity enabled. Select Use Plane in the Ground Plane settings (see Figure 12.3). This creates an invisible floor on which the nParticles can rest. Set the Plane Origin's Translate Y to **–1**.

FIGURE 12.3
The Use Plane parameter creates an invisible floor that keeps the nParticles from falling.

8. The Nucleus solver also has wind settings. Set Wind Speed to **3** and Wind Noise to **4**. By default, Wind Direction is set to 1, 0, 0 (see Figure 12.4). The fields correspond to the x-, y-, and z-axes, so this means that the nParticles will be blown along the positive x-axis. Rewind and play the animation. Now the nParticles are moving along with the wind, and a small amount of turbulence is applied.

FIGURE 12.4
You can find the settings for Air Density, Wind Speed, Wind Direction, and Wind Noise under the Nucleus solver's attributes.

By increasing the Air Density value, you adjust the atmosphere of the environment. A very high setting is a good way to simulate an underwater environment. Using wind in combination with a high air density pushes the nParticles with more force; this makes sense because the air is denser.

The Solver Attributes section of the nParticle menu sets the quality of the solver. The Substeps setting specifies how many times per frame the solver calculates nDynamics. Higher settings are more accurate but can slow down performance. Increasing the Substeps value may alter some of the ways in which nDynamics behave, such as how they collide with each other and with other objects. Thus when you increase this value, be aware that you may need to adjust other settings on your nDynamic nodes.

The Time Attributes section allows you to set the start time for the solver. This is useful if you have an nCloth object that does not need to do anything until a certain frame within your animation. Inversely, you can start the simulation prior to the beginning of your animation to give your nCloth object time to simulate to the desired position. Frame Jump Limit is good for previewing your simulations. Instead of having to simulate each frame, with a Frame Jump Limit value of 1.0 you can increase the limit, enabling the solver to skip over frames without error. Having a value greater than 1 will not produce an accurate simulation but will give you an idea of the final solution.

The Scale Attributes section has Time Scale and Space Scale sliders. Use Time Scale to speed up or slow down the solver. Values less than 1 slow down the simulation; higher values speed it up. If you increase Time Scale, you should increase the number of substeps in the

Solver Attributes section to ensure that the simulation is still accurate. One creative example of Time Scale would be to keyframe a change in its value to simulate the "bullet time" effect made famous in *The Matrix* movies.

Space Scale scales the environment of the simulation. By default, nDynamics are calculated in meters even if the Maya scene unit is set to centimeters. You should set this to **0.1** if you need your nDynamics simulation to behave appropriately when the Maya scene units are set to centimeters. This is more noticeable when working with large simulations. You can also use this setting creatively to exaggerate effects or when using more than one Nucleus solver in a scene. Most of the time, it's safe to leave this at the default setting of 1. For the following examples, leave Space Scale set to 1.

Spawning nParticles from an Emitter

An emitter shoots nParticles into the scene, like a sprinkler shooting water onto a lawn. When a particle is emitted into a scene, it is "born" at that moment and all calculations based on its age begin from the moment it is born.

1. Continue with the scene from the previous section. Add an emitter to the scene by choosing nParticles ➤ Create nParticles ➤ Create Emitter. An emitter appears at the center of the grid.

2. Open the Attribute Editor for the emitter1 object, and set Rate (Particles/Sec) to **10**. Set Emitter Type to Omni.

NPARTICLE COUNT

You can turn on Particle Count to display the number of particles in your scene. Choose Display ➤ Heads Up Display ➤ Particle Count.

---

3. Rewind and play the scene. The Omni emitter spawns particles from a point at the center of the grid. Note that after the particles are born, they collide with the ground plane and are pushed by the Nucleus wind in the same direction as the other particles (see Figure 12.5).

   The new nParticles are connected to the same Nucleus solver. If you open the Attribute Editor for the nParticle2 object, you'll see the tabs for nucleus1 and nParticle2, as well as the tab for nParticle1. If you change the settings on the nucleus1 tab, both nParticle1 and nParticle2 are affected.

NPARTICLE TABS IN THE ATTRIBUTE EDITOR

The tabs for each nParticle connected to a Nucleus solver appear at the same time at the top of the Attribute Editor. Thus it is easy to make the mistake of editing the settings for the wrong nParticle object. To avoid this mistake, pay attention to which nParticle object is listed on the tab at the top of the Attribute Editor while you are changing settings.

FIGURE 12.5

A second nParticle system is spawned from an emitter. These nParticles also collide with the ground plane and are pushed by the wind.

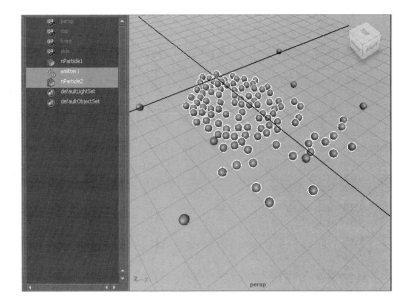

4. Select nParticle2, and choose nSolver ➤ Assign Solver ➤ New Solver. Rewind and play the scene. nParticle2 now falls in space, whereas nParticle1 continues to slide on the ground plane.

5. Open the Outliner and, in the Outliner's Display menu, deselect DAG Objects Only. This allows you to see all the nodes in the scene. If you scroll down, you'll see nucleus1 and nucleus2 nodes (see Figure 12.6).

FIGURE 12.6

The Nucleus nodes are visible in the Outliner.

6. Select nParticle2, and choose nSolver ➤ Assign Solver ➤ nucleus1. This reconnects nParticle2 with nucleus1.

7. Select emitter1, and in the Attribute Editor for emitter1, set Emitter Type to Volume.

8. Set Volume Shape in the Volume Emitter Attributes section to Sphere.

9. Use the Move tool to position the emitter above the ground plane. The emitter is now a volume, which you can scale up in size using the Scale tool (hot key = **r**). nParticles are born from random locations within the sphere (see Figure 12.7).

FIGURE 12.7
Volume emitters spawn nParticles from random locations within the volume.

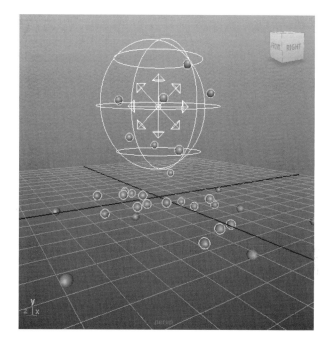

The directional emitter is similar to the omni and volume emitters in that it shoots nParticles into a scene. The directional emitter emits the nParticles in a straight line. The range of the directional emitter can be altered using the Spread slider, causing it to behave more like a sprinkler or fountain.

10. Open the Attribute Editor to the nParticleShape2 tab. This is where you'll find the attributes that control particle behavior, and there are a lot of them.

11. As an experiment, expand the Force Field Generation rollout panel, and set the Point Force Field to Worldspace.

12. Rewind and play the animation.

As the emitter spawns particles in the scene, a few nParticles from nParticle2 will bunch up in the space between nParticle1. nParticle1 is emitting a force field that pushes away individual nParticles from nParticle2. If you set Point Field Magnitude to a negative number, nParticle1 will attract some of the particles from nParticle1. You can also make the nParticles attract themselves by increasing the Self Attract slider (see Figure 12.8).

This is an example of how the Nucleus solver allows particles from two different particle objects to interact. The Force Field settings will be explored further in the section "Working with Force Fields" later in this chapter. If you switch nParticle2 to the nucleus2 solver, you will lose this behavior; only nParticles that share a solver can be attracted to each other. Be careful when using force fields on large numbers of nParticles (more than 10,000), because this will slow the performance of Maya significantly. See the nParticles_v01.ma scene in the chapter12 chapter12\scenes folder at the book's web page (www.sybex.com/go/masteringmaya2015) for an example of nParticle force fields.

FIGURE 12.8
The Force Field settings cause one nParticle object to push away other nDynamic systems.

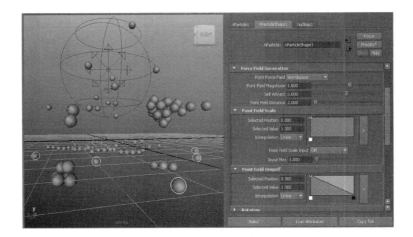

Emitting nParticles from a Surface

You can use polygon and NURBS surfaces to generate nParticles as well:

1. Create a new Maya scene. Create a polygon plane (Create ➤ Polygon Primitives ➤ Plane).

2. Scale the plane 25 units in X and Z.

3. Switch to the nDynamics menu. Set the nParticle style to Balls (nParticles ➤ Create nParticles ➤ Balls).

4. Select the plane. Choose nParticles ➤ Create nParticles ➤ Emit From Object ➤ Options. In the Emitter Options dialog box, set Emitter Type to Surface and Rate to **10**. Set Speed to **0**. Click Create to make the emitter. Figure 12.9 shows the options for the surface emitter.

5. Set the timeline to **600**.

6. Open the Attribute Editor to the nucleus1 tab, and set Gravity to **0**.

SURFACE EMITTERS

When you create a surface emitter, the emitter node is parented to the emitting geometry in the Outliner.

---

7. Rewind and play the animation. Particles appear randomly on the surface.

8. Open the Attribute Editor to the nParticleShape1 tab. Expand the Particle Size rollout panel. Set Radius to **1**.

9. Click the right side of the Radius Scale ramp to add a point. Adjust the position of the point on the left side of the ramp edit curve for Radius Scale so that it's at 0 on the left side, and it moves up to 1 on the right side (see Figure 12.10).

FIGURE 12.9

The options for creating a surface emitter.

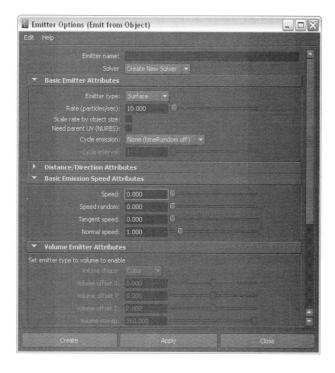

FIGURE 12.10

The Radius Scale ramp curve adjusts the radius of the nParticles

10. Rewind and play the animation. The particles now scale up as they are born (by default, Radius Scale Input is set to Age). Notice that adjacent particles push each other as they grow. The ball-style particle has Self Collision on by default, so the particles will bump into each other (see Figure 12.11).

RADIUS SCALE INPUT

The Radius Scale has several different inputs apart from age. You can base the scale of the nParticles on their speed or acceleration. You can also use nParticle ID. The ID is a unique value generated at the birth of each nParticle.

FIGURE 12.11
The balls scale up as
they are born and
push each other as
they grow.

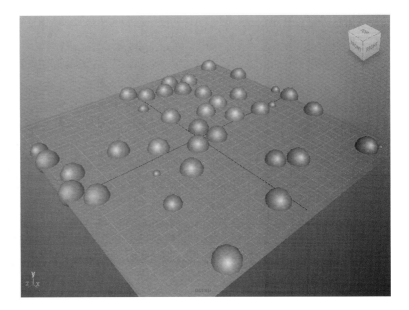

11. Set Radius Scale Randomize to **0.5**. The balls each have a random size. By increasing this slider, you increase the random range for the maximum radius size of each nParticle.

12. Set Input Max to **3**. This sets the maximum range along the x-axis of the Radius Scale ramp. Since Radius Scale Input is set to Time, this means that each nParticle takes 3 seconds to achieve its maximum radius, so they slowly grow in size.

See the nParticles_v02.ma scene in the chapter12\scenes folder at the book's web page for an example of an nParticle emitted from a surface.

Filling an Object with nParticles

An object can be instantly filled with particles. Any modeled polygon mesh can hold the nParticles as long as it has some kind of depression in it. A flat plane, on the other hand, can't be used.

1. Open the forge_v01.ma scene from the chapter12\scenes folder at the book's web page. You'll see a simple scene consisting of a tub on a stand. A bucket is in front of the tub. The tub will be used to pour molten metal into the bucket.

2. Set the nParticle style to Water by choosing nParticles ➢ Create nParticles ➢ Water.

3. Select the tub object, and choose nParticles ➢ Create nParticles ➢ Fill Object ➢ Options (see Figure 12.12). In the options, turn on Close Packing and click the Particle Fill button.

IF NO NPARTICLES ARE CREATED

If no nParticles are created at all, open the options for the Particle Fill command, reset the options, and make sure Close Packing is on. The problem occurs when Maya can't figure out how to fill the surface. You can verify that nParticles do exist by switching to wireframe mode, or you can look for a new nParticle node in the Outliner.

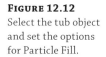

Figure 12.12
Select the tub object and set the options for Particle Fill.

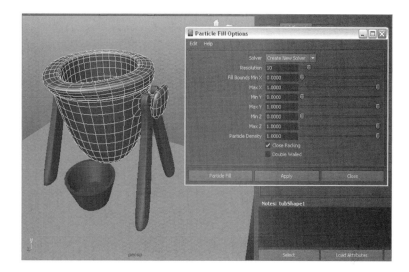

4. Set the display to Wireframe. You'll see a few particles stuck in the rim of the tub. If you play the scene, the particles fall through space.

   There are two problems:

   ◆ The object has been built with a thick wall, so Maya is trying to fill the inside of the surface with particles rather than the well in the tub.

   ◆ The tub is not set as a collision surface (see Figure 12.13).

5. Select the nParticle1 object in the Outliner, and delete it. Note that this does not delete the nucleus1 solver created with the particle, and that's okay; the next nParticle object you create will be automatically connected to this same solver.

This problem has a couple of solutions. When you create the nParticle object, you can choose Double Walled in the Fill Object options, which in many cases solves the problem for objects that have a simple shape, such as a glass. For more convoluted shapes, the nParticles may try to fill different parts of the object. For instance, in the case of the tub, as long as the Resolution setting in the options is at 10 or lower, the tub will fill with nParticles just fine (increasing Resolution increases the number of nParticles that will fill the volume). However, if you create a higher-resolution nParticle, you'll find that nParticles are placed within the walls of the tub and inside the handles where the frame holds the tub.

Another solution is to split the polygons that make up the object so that only the parts of the tub that actually collide with the nParticles are used to calculate how the nParticles fill the object:

1. Switch to shaded view. Select the tub object, and move the view so that you can see the bottom of its interior.

2. Choose the Paint Selection tool, right-click the tub, and choose Face to switch to face selection. Use the Paint Selection tool to select the faces at the very bottom of the tub (see Figure 12.14).

FIGURE 12.13
The nParticles lodge
within the thick
walls of the tub.

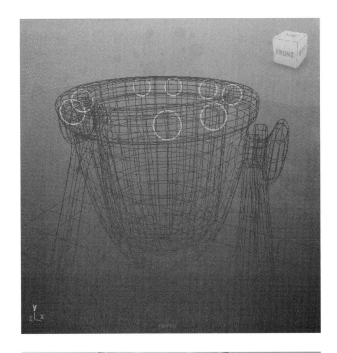

FIGURE 12.14
Select the faces at
the bottom of the
tub with the Paint
Selection tool.

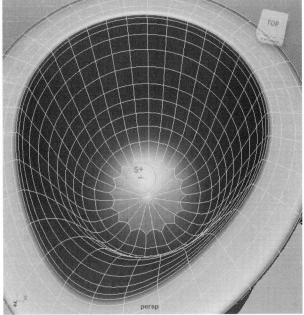

3. Hold the Shift key, and press the > key on the keyboard to expand the selection. Keep holding the Shift key while repeatedly pressing the > key until all the interior polygons are selected, up to the edge of the tub's rim (see Figure 12.15).

FIGURE 12.15

Expand the selection to include all the faces up to the rim of the tub.

4. Switch to wireframe mode, and make sure none of the polygons on the outside of the tub have been selected by accident. Hold the Ctrl key, and select any unwanted polygons to deselect them.

5. Switch to the Polygons menu, and choose Mesh ➤ Extract. This splits the model into two parts. The selected polygon becomes a separate mesh from the deselected polygons. In the Outliner, you'll see that the tub1 object is now a group with two nodes: polySurface1 and polySurface2 (see Figure 12.16).

6. Select the polySurface1 and polySurface2 nodes, and choose Edit ➤ Delete By Type ➤ History.

7. Name the interior mesh **insideTub** and the exterior mesh **outsideTub**.

8. Switch to the nDynamics menu. Select the insideTub mesh, and choose nParticles ➤ Create nParticles ➤ Fill Object ➤ Options.

9. In the options, set Solver to nucleus1 and set Resolution to **15**.

   The Fill Bounds settings determine the minimum and maximum boundaries within the volume that will be filled. In other words, if you want to fill a glass from the middle of the glass to the top, leaving the bottom half of the glass empty, set the minimum in Y to **0.5** and the maximum to **1**. (The nParticles would still drop to the bottom of the glass if Gravity was enabled, but for a split second you would confuse both optimists and pessimists.)

10. Leave all the Fill Bounds settings at the default. Deselect Double Walled and Close Packing. Click Particle Fill to apply it. After a couple of seconds, you'll see the tub filled with little blue spheres (see Figure 12.17).

FIGURE 12.16
Split the tub into two separate mesh objects using the Extract command.

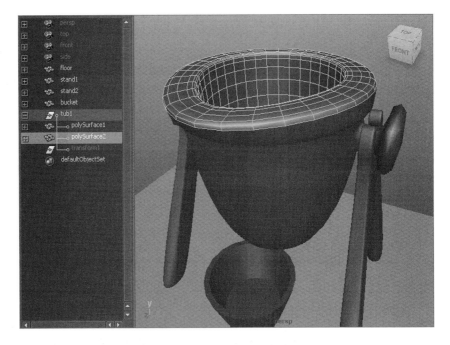

FIGURE 12.17
The inside of the tub is filled with nParticles.

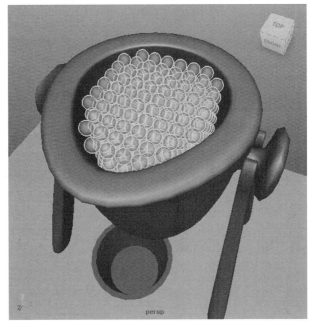

11. Rewind and play the animation. The spheres drop through the bottom of the tub. To make them stay within the tub, you'll need to create a collision surface.

Making nParticles Collide with nRigids

nParticles collide with nCloth objects, passive collision surfaces, and other nParticle objects. They can also be made to self-collide; in fact, when the ball-style nParticle is chosen, Self Collision is on by default. To make an nParticle collide with an ordinary rigid object, you need to convert the collision surface into a passive collider. The passive collider can be animated as well.

Passive Collision Objects

Passive collision objects, also known as *nRigids*, are automatically connected to the current Nucleus solver when they are created.

1. Rewind the animation, and select the insideTub mesh.

2. Choose nMesh ➤ Create Passive Collider. By default the object is assigned to the current Nucleus solver. If you want to assign a different solver, use the options for Create Passive Collider.

3. Play the animation. You'll see the nParticles drop down and collide with the bottom of the tub. They'll slosh around for a while and eventually settle.

CREATING NRIGID OBJECTS

When you create a passive collider object (nRigid object), any new nDynamic system you add to the scene that is connected to the same Nucleus solver will collide with the nRigid, as long as the new nDynamic node has Collisions enabled.

When creating a collision between an nParticle and a passive collision surface, there are two sets of controls that you can tune to adjust the way the collision happens:

◆ Collision settings on the nParticle shape control how the nParticle reacts when colliding with surfaces.

◆ Collision settings on the passive object control how objects react when they collide with it.

For example, if you dumped a bunch of basketballs and ping-pong balls on a granite table and a sofa, you would see that the table and the sofa have their own collision behavior based on their physical properties, and the ping-pong balls and basketballs also have their own collision behavior based on their physical properties. When a collision event occurs between a ping-pong ball and the sofa, the physical properties of both objects are factored together to determine the behavior of the ping-pong ball at the moment of collision. Likewise, the basketballs have their own physical properties that are factored in with the same sofa properties when a collision occurs between the sofa and a basketball.

The nDynamic systems have a variety of ways to calculate collisions as well as ways to visualize and control the collisions between elements in the system:

1. Select the nRigid1 node in the Outliner, and switch to the nRigidShape1 tab in the Attribute Editor. Expand the Collisions rollout panel.

The Collide option turns collisions on or off for the surface. It's sometimes useful to disable collisions temporarily when working on animating objects in a scene using nDynamics. Likewise, the Enable option above the Collisions rollout panel disables all nDynamics for the surface when it is deselected. It's possible to keyframe this attribute by switching to the Channel Box and to keyframe the Is Dynamic channel for the rigidShape node.

2. Set the Solver Display option to Collision Thickness. Choosing this setting creates an interactive display so that you can see how the collisions for this surface are calculated (see Figure 12.18).

FIGURE 12.18
You can display the collision surface thickness using the controls in the nRigid body shape node.

3. Switch to wireframe view (hot key = **4**). Move the Thickness slider back and forth, and the envelope grows and shrinks, indicating how thick the surface will seem when the dynamics are calculated.

The thickness will not change its appearance when rendered, but only how the nParticles will collide with the object. A very high Thickness value makes it seem as though there is an invisible force field around the object.

4. Switch back to smooth shaded view (hot key = **5**). Collision Flag is set to Face by default, meaning that collisions are calculated based on the faces of the collision object. This is the most accurate but slowest way to calculate collisions.

5. Set Collision Flag to Vertex. Rewind and play the animation. You'll see the thickness envelope drawn around each vertex of the collision surface.

The nParticles fall through the bottom of the surface, and some may collide with the envelopes around the vertices on their way through the bottom. The calculation of the dynamics is faster, though. This setting may work well for dense meshes, and it will calculate much faster than the Face method.

6. Set Collision Flag to Edge; rewind and play the animation. The envelope is now drawn around each edge of the collision surface, creating a wireframe network (see Figure 12.19).

COLLISION FLAG: FACE VS. EDGE

The calculation is much faster than when Collision Flag is set to Face but the nParticles stay within the tub. You may notice some bumping as the nParticles collide with the wireframe. Many times this may not be noticeable at all, which makes the Edge method useful for calculating collisions.

FIGURE 12.19
When Collision Flag
is set to Vertex, the
nParticles collide
with each vertex of
the collision surface,
allowing some to fall
through the bottom.
When the flag is set to
Edge, the nParticles
collide with the edges,
and the calculation
speed improves.

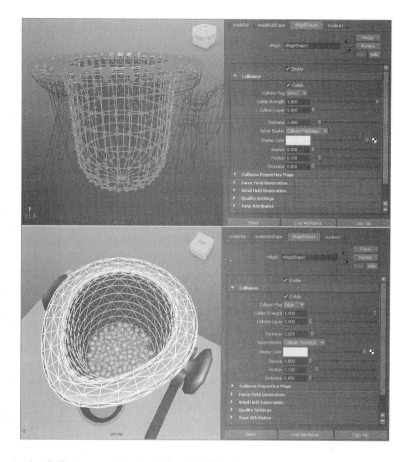

Other settings in the Collisions section include the following:

Bounce   This setting controls how high the nParticles bounce off the surface. Think of the
ping-pong balls hitting the granite table and the sofa. The sofa would have a much lower
Bounce setting than the granite table.

Friction   A smooth surface has a much lower Friction setting than a rough one. nParticles
will slide off a smooth surface more easily. If the sofa were made of suede, the friction would
be higher than for the smooth granite table.

Stickiness   This setting is pretty self-explanatory—if the granite table were covered in
honey, the ping-pong balls would stick to it more than to the sofa, even if the friction is lower
on the granite table. The behavior of the nParticles sticking to the surface may be different if
Collision Flag is set to Face than if it is set to Edge or Vertex.

You can use the display settings within the nParticle's Attribute Editor to visualize the collision width of each nParticle; this can help you determine the best collision width setting for
your nParticles.

1. Make sure that Collision Flag is set to Edge and that Bounce, Friction, and Stickiness are set to **0**. Set Thickness to **0.05**.

2. Select the nParticle1 object, and open the Attribute Editor to the nParticleShape1 tab. Expand the Collisions rollout panel for the nParticle1 object. These control how the nParticles collide with collision objects in the scene.

3. Click the Display Color swatch to open the Color Chooser, and pick a red color. Set Solver Display to Collision Thickness. Now each nParticle has a red envelope around it. Changing the color of the display makes it easier to distinguish from the nRigid collision surface display.

4. Set Collide Width Scale to **0.25**. The envelope becomes a dot inside each nParticle. The nParticles have not changed size, but if you rewind and play the animation, you'll see that they fall through the space between the edges of the collision surface (see Figure 12.20).

FIGURE 12.20
Reducing the Collide Width Scale value of the nParticles causes them to fall through the spaces between the edges of the nRigid object.

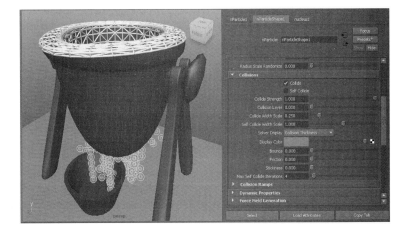

5. Scroll down to the Liquid Simulation rollout, and deselect Enable Liquid Simulation. This makes it easier to see how the nParticles behave when Self Collision is on. The Liquid Simulation settings alter the behavior of nParticles; this is covered later in the chapter.

6. Select Self Collide under the Collisions rollout, and set Solver Display to Self Collision Thickness.

7. Set Collide Width Scale to **1** and Self Collide Width Scale to **0.1**. Turn on wireframe view (hot key = **4**), and play the animation; watch it from a side view.

The nParticles have separate Collision Thickness settings for collision surfaces and self-collisions. Self Collide Width Scale is relative to Collide Width Scale. Increasing Collide Width Scale also increases Self Collide Width Scale (see Figure 12.21).

FIGURE 12.21
Reducing the Self Collide Width Scale value causes the nParticles to overlap as they collide.

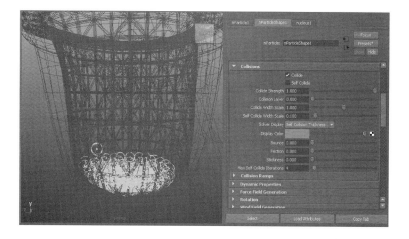

8. Scroll up to the Particle Size settings, and change Radius to **0.8**. Both Collide Width Scale and Self Collide Width Scale are relative to the radius of the nParticles. Increasing the radius can cause the nParticles to pop out of the top of the tub.

9. Set Radius to **0.4** and Collide Width Scale to **1**. Deselect Self Collide and click Enable Liquid Simulation to turn it back on.

10. Save the scene as **forge_v02.ma**.

To see a version of the scene up to this point, open forge_v02.ma from the chapter12\ scenes folder at the book's web page.

The nParticles also have their own Bounce, Friction, and Stickiness settings. The Max Self Collide Iterations slider sets a limit on the number of calculated self-collisions per substep when Self Collide is on. This prevents the nParticles from locking up or the system from slowing down too much. If you have a lot of self-colliding nParticles in a simulation, lowering this value can improve performance.

The Collision Layer setting sets a priority for collision events. If two nDynamic objects using the same Nucleus solver are set to the same Collision Layer value, they will collide normally. If they have different layer settings, those with lower values will receive higher priority. In other words, they will be calculated first in a chain of collision events. Both nCloth and passive objects will collide with nParticles in the same or higher collision layers. So if the passive collision object has a Collision Layer setting of 10, an nParticle with a Collision Layer setting of 3 will pass right through it, but an nParticle with a Collision Layer value of 12 won't.

Collide Strength and Collision Ramps

There are several ways to control how nParticles collide with rigid surfaces and other nParticles. You can use the Collide Strength attribute to dampen the collision effect between nParticles or between nParticles and other surfaces. At a strength of 1, collisions will be at 100 percent, meaning that nParticles will collide at full force. A setting of 0 turns off collisions completely for the nParticle object. Values between 0 and 1 create a dampening effect for the collision.

Using Collision Strength becomes more interesting when you modify Collide Strength using the Collide Strength Scale ramp. The ramp allows you to determine the strength of collisions on a per-particle basis using a number of attributes such as Age, Randomized ID, Speed, and others as the input for the ramp. Try this exercise to see how this works:

1. Open the collisionStrength.ma scene from the chapter12\scenes directory at the book's web page. This scene has a spherical volume emitter shooting out ball-type nParticles. There is a simple polygon object named pSolid1 within the scene as well.

2. Select the pSolid1 polygon object, and turn it into a collision object by switching to the nDynamics menu and choosing nMesh ➢ Create Passive Collider.

3. Rewind and play the scene; the nParticles collide with the pSolid object as you might expect.

4. Select the nParticle1 node, and open its Attribute Editor.

5. Play the scene, and try adjusting the Collision Strength slider while the scene is playing. Observe the behavior of the nParticles. Try setting the slider to a value of **10**. The collisions become very strong.

6. Set Collision Strength to **8**.

7. Expand the Collide Strength Scale ramp in the Collision Ramps rollout panel.

8. Edit the ramp so that the value on the left side is at **0.1** and the value on the right is at **1**, and set Collide Strength Scale Input to Randomized ID (see Figure 12.22).

9. Rewind and play the animation. You'll see the strength of collisions is randomized; some collisions are weak, whereas others are exaggerated.

   Other collision attributes can also be controlled with ramps. These include Bounce, Scale, and Stickiness. Remember that these scales act as multipliers for the values that are set in the Collisions section.

   nRigid objects also have a Collision Strength setting; however, they do not have a collision ramp.

10. In the Collisions section, set Collide Strength to **1**. Set Stickiness to **50**.

11. Expand the Stickiness Scale rollout.

12. Set the input to Age and Input Max to **3**. Adjust the ramp so that it slopes down from the left to the right (see Figure 12.23).

13. Increase the emitter rate to **50**. Rewind and play the scene. The nParticles stick to the wall and gradually lose their stickiness over time (see Figure 12.24).

14. Scroll to the top, and expand the Particle Size section. Try setting the Radius Scale Input option of the nParticles to Randomized ID. Adjust the radius scale to create random variation in the size of the nParticles. Then set an attribute, such as Friction, to use Radius as the scale input (see Figure 12.25). See whether you can make larger nParticles have more

friction than smaller ones. Remember to set the Friction attribute in the Collision section to a high value such as **100**.

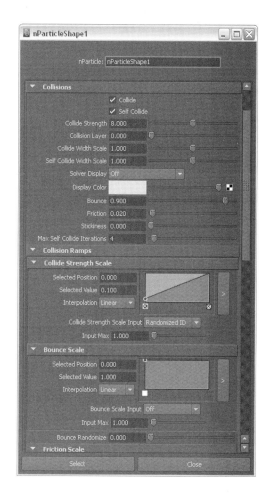

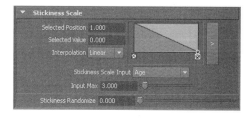

FIGURE 12.24
The nParticles lose stickiness over time and slide down the walls of the collision object.

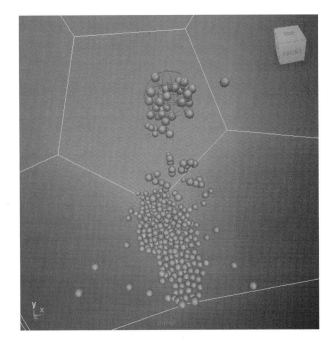

FIGURE 12.25
The Friction Scale Input option is set to Radius, and the ramp is adjusted so that larger nParticles have more friction than smaller ones.

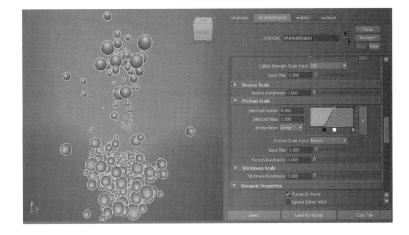

Using nParticles to Simulate Liquids

You can make nParticles simulate the behavior of fluids by enabling the Liquid Simulation attribute in the particle's shape node or by creating the nParticle as a water object. In this exercise, you'll use a tub filled with nParticles. The tub will be animated to pour out the nParticles, and their behavior will be modified to resemble hot molten metal.

Creating Liquid Behavior

Liquid simulations have unique properties that differ from other styles of nParticle behavior. This behavior is amazingly easy to set up and control:

1. Continue with the scene from the previous section, or open the `forge_v02.ma` scene from the `chapter12\scenes` folder at the book's web page. In this scene, the tub has already been filled with particles, and collisions have been enabled.

2. Select nParticle1 in the Outliner, and name it **moltenMetal**.

3. Open its Attribute Editor to the moltenMetalShape tab, and expand the Liquid Simulation rollout panel (see Figure 12.26).

FIGURE 12.26

Selecting Enable Liquid Simulation causes the nParticles to behave like water.

Liquid simulation has already been enabled because the nParticle style was set to Water when the nParticles were created. If you need to remove the liquid behavior from the nParticle, you can deselect the Enable Liquid Simulation check box; for the moment, leave it selected.

4. Switch to a side view, and turn on wireframe mode.

5. Play the animation, and observe the behavior of the nParticles.

   If you look at the Collisions settings for moltenMetal, you'll see that the Self Collide attribute is off but the nParticles are clearly colliding with each other. This type of collision is part of the liquid behavior defined by the Incompressibility attribute (this attribute is discussed a little later in the chapter).

6. Play the animation back several times; notice the behavior in these conditions:

   Enable Liquid Simulation is off.

   Self Collide is on (set Self Collide Width Scale to **0.7**).

   Both Enable Liquid Simulation and Self Collide are enabled.

7. Turn Enable Liquid Simulation back on, and deselect Self Collide.

8. Open the Particle Size rollout panel, and set Radius to **0.25**; then play the animation. There seems to be much less fluid for the same number of particles when the radius size is lowered.

9. Play the animation for about 140 frames until all the nParticles settle.

10. With the moltenMetal shape selected, choose nSolver ➤ Initial State ➤ Set From Current (see Figure 12.27).

FIGURE 12.27
Setting Initial State
makes the nParticles
start out from their
settled position.

11. Rewind and play the animation; the particles start out as settled in the well of the tub.

12. Select moltenMetal. At the top of the Attribute Editor, deselect Enable to disable the nParticle simulation temporarily so that you can easily animate the tub.

13. Select the tub1 group in the Outliner, and switch to the side view.

14. Select the Move tool (hot key = **w**). Hold down the **d** key on the keyboard, and move the pivot for tub1 so that it's aligned with the center of the handles that hold it in the frame (see Figure 12.28).

FIGURE 12.28
Align the pivot point
for the tub group
with the handles
from the side view.

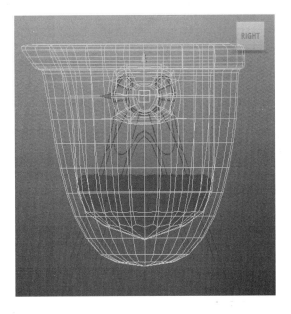

15. Set the timeline to frame **20**.

16. In the Channel Box, select the Rotate X channel for the tub1 group node, right-click, and set a keyframe.

17. Set the timeline to frame **100**.

18. Set the value of tub1's Rotate X channel to **85**, and set another keyframe.

19. Move the timeline to frame **250**, and set another keyframe.

20. Set the timeline to **330**, set Rotate X to **0**, and set a fourth key.

21. Select moltenMetal and, in the Attribute Editor, select the Enable check box.

22. Rewind the animation and play it. The nParticles pour out of the tub like water (see Figure 12.29).

FIGURE 12.29

When you animate the tub, the nParticles pour out of it like water.

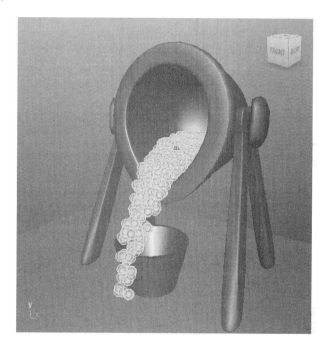

23. Switch to the perspective view. When you play the animation, the water goes through the bucket and the floor.

24. Select the bucket, and choose nMesh ➤ Create Passive Collider.

25. Switch to the nucleus1 tab, and select Use Plane.

26. Set the PlaneOrigin's Translate Y to **−4.11** to match the position of the floor. Now when you play the animation, the nParticles land in the bucket and on the floor.

SET THE COLLISION FLAG TO EDGE

You can improve the performance speed of the playback by selecting the nRigid node connected to the bucket and setting Collision Flag to Edge instead of Face.

27. By default, the liquid simulation settings (Figure 12.30) approximate the behavior of water. To create a more molten metal–like quality, increase Viscosity to **10**. Viscosity sets the liquid's resistance to flow. Sticky, gooey, or oily substances have a higher viscosity.

Viscosity and Solver Substeps

Increasing the number of substeps on the Nucleus solver will magnify viscosity.

---

28. Set Liquid Radius Scale to **0.5**. This sets the amount of overlap between nParticles when Liquid Simulation is enabled. Lower values create more overlap. By lowering this setting, you make the fluid look more like a cohesive surface.

You can use the other settings in the Liquid Simulation rollout panel to alter the behavior of the liquid:

Incompressibility   This setting determines the degree to which the nParticles resist compression. Most fluids use a low value (between 0.1 and 0.5). If you set this value to 0, all the nParticles will lie at the bottom of the tub in the same area, much like a nonliquid nParticle with Self Collide turned off.

Rest Density   This sets the overlapping arrangement of the nParticles when they are at rest. It can affect how "chunky" the nParticles look when the simulation is running. The default value of 2 works well for most liquids, but compare a setting of 1 to a setting of 5. At 1, fewer nParticles overlap and they flow out of the tub more easily than when Rest Density is set to 5.

Surface Tension   Surface tension simulates the attractive force within fluids that tend to hold them together. Think of how a drop of water forms a surface as it rests on wax paper or how beads of water form when condensing on a cold pipe.

29. To complete the behavior of molten metal, set Rest Density to **2** and Incompressibility to **0.5**.

30. In the Collisions rollout panel, set Friction to **0.5** and Stickiness to **0.25**.

31. Expand the Dynamic Properties rollout panel, and increase Mass to **6**. Note that you may want to reset the initial state after changing the settings because the nParticles will now collapse into a smaller area (as in Figure 12.30).

32. Save the scene as **forge_v03.ma**.

To see a version of the scene up to this point, open forge_v03.ma from the chapter12\ scenes folder.

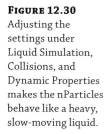

FIGURE 12.30
Adjusting the settings under Liquid Simulation, Collisions, and Dynamic Properties makes the nParticles behave like a heavy, slow-moving liquid.

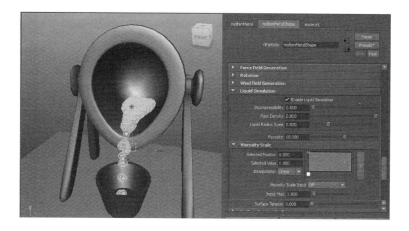

VISCOSITY SCALE AND SURFACE TENSION RAMP

You can now fine-tune the behavior of your liquid simulations using Viscosity Scale and Surface Tension Ramp.

You can use the viscosity scale to modify the viscosity over time. To do this, set Viscosity Scale Input to Age and adjust the ramp. You can also use other inputs such as Randomized ID and Radius to determine how viscosity is applied to the liquid.

The Surface Tension Scale Ramp setting allows you to scale the surface tension value based on an input such as the age of the particle, a randomized ID, the radius, and more using settings similar to the other ramps.

Converting nParticles to Polygons

You can convert nParticles into a polygon mesh. The mesh updates with the particle motion to create a smooth blob or liquid-like appearance, which is perfect for rendering fluids. In these steps, you'll convert the liquid nParticles created in the previous section into a mesh to make a more convincing molten metal effect:

1. Continue with the scene from the previous section, or open the forge_v03.ma scene from the chapter12\scenes folder at the book's web page.

2. Play the animation to about frame 230.

3. Select the moltenMetal object in the Outliner, and choose Modify ➢ Convert ➢ nParticle To Polygons.

   The nParticles have disappeared, and a polygon mesh has been added to the scene. You'll notice that the mesh is a lot smaller than the original nParticle simulation; this can be changed after converting the nParticle to a mesh. You can adjust the quality of this mesh in the Attribute Editor of the nParticle object used to generate the mesh.

4. Select the new polySurface1 object in the Outliner, and open the Attribute Editor to the moltenMetalShape tab.

5. Expand the Output Mesh section. Set Threshold to **0.8** and Blobby Radius Scale to **2.1**.

FINE-TUNING THE MESH

The settings in step 5 smooth the converted mesh. Higher Threshold settings create a smoother but thinner mesh. Increasing Blobby Radius Scale does not affect the radius of the original nParticles; rather, it uses this value as a multiple to determine the size of the enveloping mesh around each nParticle. Using the Threshold and Blobby Radius Scale settings together, you can fine-tune the look of the converted mesh.

---

6. Set Motion Streak to **0.5**. This stretches the moving areas of the mesh in the direction of the motion to create a more fluid-like behavior.

7. Mesh Triangle Size determines the resolution of the mesh. Lowering this value increases the smoothness of the mesh but also slows down the simulation. Set this value to **0.3** for now, as shown in Figure 12.31. Once you're happy with the overall look of the animation, you can set it to a lower value. This way, the animation continues to update at a reasonable pace.

FIGURE 12.31
Adjust the quality of the mesh in the Output Mesh section of the nParticle's shape node attributes.

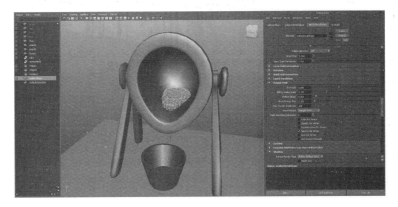

Max Triangle Resolution sets a limit on the number of triangles used in the nParticle mesh. If the number is exceeded during the simulation, Max Triangle Size is raised automatically to compensate.

ADJUST MAX TRIANGLE SIZE NUMERICALLY

Be careful when using the slider for Mesh Triangle Size. It's easy to move the slider to a low value by accident, and then you'll have to wait for Maya to update, which can be frustrating. Use numeric input for this attribute, and reduce the value by 0.05 at a time until you're happy with the look of the mesh.

Mesh Method determines the shape of the polygons that make up the surface of the mesh. The choices are Cubes, Tetrahedra, Acute Tetrahedra, and Quad Mesh. After setting the Mesh Method option, you can create a smoother mesh around the nParticles by increasing the Max Smoothing Iterations slider. For example, if you want to create a smoother mesh that uses four-sided polygons, set Mesh Method to Quads and increase the Max Smoothing Iterations slider. By default, the slider goes up to 10. If a value of 10 is not high enough, you can type values greater than 10 into the field.

Shading the nParticle Mesh

To create the look of molten metal, you can use a simple Ramp shader as a starting point:

1. Select the polySurface1 node in the Outliner. Rename it **metalMesh**.

2. Right-click the metalMesh object in the viewport. Use the context menu to assign a ramp material. Choose Assign New Material. A pop-up window will appear; choose Ramp Shader from the list (see Figure 12.32).

FIGURE 12.32
Assign a Ramp shader to the metalMesh object.

3. Open the Attribute Editor for the new Ramp shader. In the Common Material Attributes section, set Color Input to Facing Angle.

4. Click the color swatch, and use the Color Chooser to pick a bright orange color.

5. Click the right side of the ramp to add a second color. Make it a reddish orange.

6. Create a similar but darker ramp for the Incandescence channel.

RAMP SHADER COLOR INPUT SETTINGS

Each of the color channels that uses a ramp will use the same Color Input setting as the Color rollout panel. So, in the case of this ramp, Incandescence will also use Facing Angle as the input.

---

7. Set Specularity to **0.24** and the specular color to a bright yellow.

8. Increase the Glow intensity in the Special Effects rollout panel to **0.15**.

9. Back in the moltenMetal particle Attribute Editor, decrease Mesh Triangle Size to **0.1** (it will take a couple minutes to update), and render a test frame using mental ray. Set the Quality preset on the Quality tab to Production.

10. Save the scene as **forge_v04.ma**.

To see a version of the finished scene, open forge_v04.ma from the chapter12\scenes folder at the book's web page (see Figure 12.33).

FIGURE 12.33
Render the molten metal in mental ray.

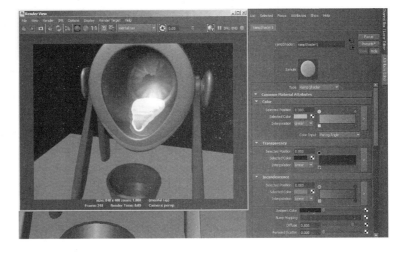

Emit nParticles Using a Texture

The behavior of nParticles is often determined by their many dynamic properties. These properties control how the nParticles react to the settings in the Nucleus solver as well as fields, collision objects, and other nParticle systems. In the following section, you'll get more practice working with these settings.

Surface Emission

In this exercise, you'll use nParticles to create the effect of flames licking the base of a space capsule as it reenters the atmosphere. You'll start by emitting nParticles from the base of the capsule and use a texture to randomize the generation of the nParticles on the surface.

1. Open the capsule_v01.ma scene from the chapter12\scenes directory at the book's web page. You'll see a simple polygon capsule model. The capsule is contained in a group named spaceCapsule. In the group, there is another surface named *capsule emitter*. This will serve as the surface emitter for the flames (see Figure 12.34).

FIGURE 12.34

The capsule group consists of two polygon meshes. The base of the capsule has been duplicated to serve as an emitter surface.

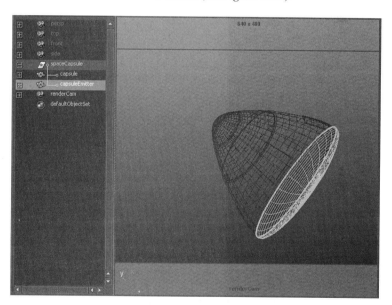

CREATING AN EMITTER SURFACE FROM A MODEL

The capsule emitter geometry was created by selecting the faces on the base of the capsule and duplicating them (Edit Mesh ➤ Duplicate Face). A slight offset was added to the duplicate face operation to move it away from the capsule surface. The idea is to have the nParticles generated by the bottom of the capsule. By creating an object separate from the bottom of the model, you can make the process much easier and faster.

2. Set a camera to the RenderCam. Play the animation. The capsule has expressions that randomize the movement of the capsule to make it vibrate. The expressions are applied to the Translate channels of the group node. To see the expressions, do the following:

   a. Open the Expression Editor (Window ➤ Animation Editors ➤ Expression Editor).

   b. Choose Select Filter ➤ By Expression Name.

   c. Select expression1, expression2, or expression3.

   You'll see the expression in the box at the bottom of the editor (see Figure 12.35).

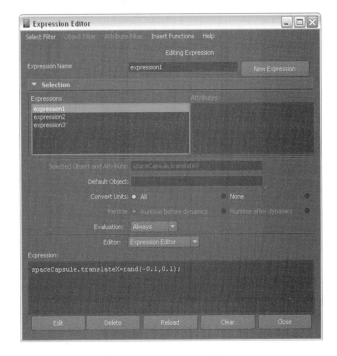

FIGURE 12.35
Create the vibration of the capsule using random function expressions applied to each of the translation channels of the capsule.

3. In the viewport, choose to look through the renderCam. The camera has been set up so that the capsule looks as though it's entering the atmosphere at an angle.

4. In the Outliner, expand the spaceCapsule and choose the capsuleEmitter object.

5. Switch to the nDynamics menu, and choose nParticles ➤ Create nParticles ➤ Points to set the nParticle style to Points.

6. Select the capsuleEmitter, and choose nParticles ➤ Create nParticles ➤ Emit From Object ➤ Options.

7. In the options, choose Edit ➤ Reset Settings to clear any settings that remain from previous Maya sessions.

8. Set Emitter Name to flameGenerator. Set Emitter Type to Surface and Rate (particles/sec) to **150**. Leave the rest of the settings at their defaults, and click the Apply button to create the emitter.

9. Rewind and play the animation. The nParticles are born on the emitter and then start falling through the air. This is because the Nucleus solver has Gravity activated by default. For now this is fine; leave the settings on the Nucleus solver where they are.

To randomize the generation of the nParticles, you can use a texture. To help visualize how the texture creates the particles, you can apply the texture to the surface emitter:

1. Select the capsuleEmitter, and open the UV Texture Editor (Window ➤ UV Texture Editor). The base already has UVs projected on the surface.

2. Select the capsuleEmitter, right-click the surface in the viewport, and use the context menu to create a new Lambert texture for the capsuleEmitter surface. Name the shader **flameGenShader**.

3. Open the Attribute Editor for flameGenShader, and click the checkered box to the right of the Color channel to create a new render node for color.

4. In the Create Render Node window, click Ramp to create a ramp texture.

5. In the Attribute Editor for the ramp (it should open automatically when you create the ramp), name the ramp **flameRamp**. Make sure texture view is on in the viewport so that you can see the ramp on the capsuleEmitter surface (hot key = **6**).

6. Set the ramp's type to Circular Ramp, and set Interpolation to None.

7. Remove the blue color from the top of the ramp by clicking the blue box at the right side at the top of the ramp. Click the color swatch, and use the Color Chooser to change the green color to white and then the red color to black.

8. Set Noise to **0.5** and Noise Freq to **0.3** to add some variation to the pattern (see Figure 12.36).

FIGURE 12.36
Apply the ramp to the shader on the base capsuleEmitter object.

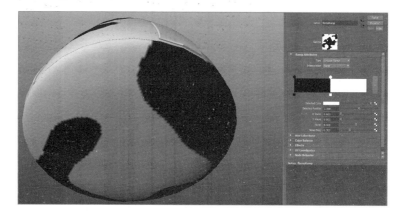

9. In the Outliner, select the nParticle node and hide it (hot key = **Ctrl+h**) so that you can animate the ramp without having the nParticle simulation slow down the playback. Set the renderer to High Quality display.

10. Select the flameRamp node, and open it in the Attribute Editor. (Select the node by choosing it from the Textures area of the Hypershade.)

11. Rewind the animation, and drag the white color marker on the ramp down toward the bottom. Its Selected Position should be at **0.05**.

12. Right-click Selected Position, and choose Set Key (see Figure 12.37).

FIGURE 12.37
Position the white color marker at the bottom of the ramp and keyframe it.

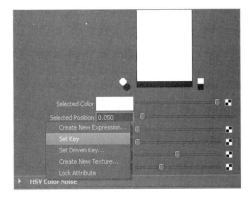

13. Set the timeline to frame **100**, move the white color marker to the top of the ramp, and set another key for the Selected Position.

14. Play the animation; you'll see the dark areas on the ramp grow over the course of 100 frames.

15. Open the Graph Editor (Window ➤ Animation Editors ➤ Graph Editor). Click the Select button at the bottom of the ramp's Attribute Editor to select the node; you'll see the animation curve appear in the Graph Editor.

16. Select the curve, switch to the Insert Keys tool, and add some keyframes to the curve.

17. Use the Move tool to reposition the keys to create an erratic motion to the ramp's animation (see Figure 12.38).

18. In the Outliner, select the capsuleEmitter node and expand it.

19. Select the flameGenerator emitter node, and open its Attribute Editor.

20. Scroll to the bottom of the editor, and expand Texture Emission Attributes.

21. Open the Hypershade to the Textures tab.

FIGURE 12.38
Add keyframes to
the ramp's anima-
tion on the Graph
Editor to make a
more erratic motion.

ANIMATE U WAVE AND V WAVE WITH EXPRESSIONS

To add some variation to the ramp's animation, you can animate the U and V Wave values or create an expression. In the U Wave field, type `=0.5+(0.5*noise(time));`. The `noise(time)` part of the expression creates a random set of values between –1 and 1 over time. `noise` creates a smooth curve of randomness values, as opposed to the `rand` function, which creates a discontinuous string of random values (as seen in the vibration of the capsule).

By dividing the result in half and then adding 0.5, you keep the range of values between 0 and 1. To speed up the rate of the noise, multiply `time` by 5 so that the expression is `=0.5+(0.5*noise(time*5));`. You can use an expression to make the V Wave the same as the U Wave; just type `=flameRamp.uWave` in the field for the V Wave attribute. When you play the animation, you'll see a more varied growth of the color over the course of the animation.

22. MMB-drag flameRamp from the Textures area onto the color swatch for Texture Rate to connect the ramp to the emitter (see Figure 12.39).

23. Select Enable Texture Rate and Emit From Dark.

24. Increase Rate to **2400**, unhide the nParticle1 node, and play the animation. You'll see that the nParticles are now emitted from the dark part of the ramp.

FIGURE 12.39
Drag the ramp texture with the MMB from the Hypershade onto the Texture Rate color swatch to make a connection.

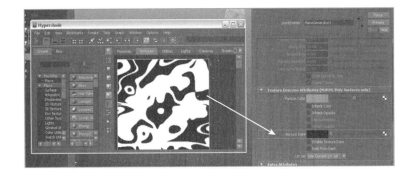

INHERIT COLOR AND OPACITY

You can make the particles inherit the color of the texture or use the color to control opacity. To do this, first switch to the particle's shape node attributes, expand the Add Dynamic Attributes rollout panel in the particle's shape tab, and click Opacity or Color. Then choose Add Per Particle from the pop-up window. Switch to the emitter's attributes, place the texture in the Particle Color swatch in the Texture Emission Attributes, and then select Inherit Color or Inherit Opacity or both.

You can also have particles inherit color and opacity from any type of emitter. You must first break the Opacity PP and RGB PP channels in the Per Particle (Array) Attributes section of the nParticle node. Once you've disconnected those channels, you can check the appropriate attributes and change the particle color on the emitter node.

---

25. Select the capsuleEmitter node, and hide it. Save the scene as **capsule_v02.ma**.

To see a version of the scene up to this point, open capsule_v02.ma from the chapter12\ scenes folder at the book's web page.

Using Wind

The Nucleus solver contains settings to create wind and turbulence. You can use these settings with nParticles to create snow blowing in the air, bubbles rising in water, or flames flying from a careening spacecraft.

Now that you have the basic settings for the particle emission, the next task is to make the particles flow upward rather than fall. You can do this using either an air field or the Wind settings on the Nucleus solver. Using the Wind settings on the Nucleus solver applies wind to all nDynamic nodes (nCloth, nRigid, and nParticles) connected to the solver. In these steps, you'll use the Nucleus solver. Fields will be discussed later in this chapter.

1. Continue with the scene from the previous section, or open the capsule_v02.ma file from the chapter12\scenes directory.

2. Select the nParticle1 object in the Outliner. Rename it **flames**.

3. Open the Attribute Editor, and choose the nucleus1 tab.

4. Set Gravity to **0**, and play the animation. The particles emerge from the base of the capsule and stop after a short distance. This is because by default the nParticles have a Drag value of 0.01 set in their Dynamic Properties settings.

5. Switch to the flamesShape tab, expand the Dynamic Properties rollout panel, and set Drag to **0**. Play the animation, and the nParticles emerge and continue to travel at a steady rate.

6. Switch back to the nucleus1 tab:

   a. Set the Wind Direction fields to **0, 1, 0** so that the wind is blowing straight up along the y-axis.

   b. Set Wind Speed to **5** (see Figure 12.40).

FIGURE 12.40

The settings for the wind on the nucleus1 tab

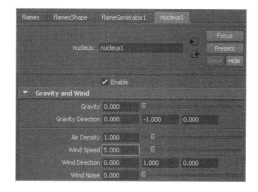

   c. Play the animation.

   There's no change; the nParticles don't seem affected by the wind.

   For the Wind settings in the Nucleus solver to work, the nParticle needs to have a Drag value, even a small one. This is why all the nParticle styles except Water have drag applied by default. If you create a Water-style particle and add a Wind setting, it won't affect the water until you set the Drag field above 0. Think of drag as a friction setting for the wind. In fact, the higher the Drag setting, the more the wind can grab the particle and push it along, so it actually has a stronger pull on the nParticle.

7. Switch to the tab for the flamesShape, set the Drag value to **0.01**, and play the animation. The particles now emerge and then move upward through the capsule.

8. Switch to the nucleus1 tab; set Air Density to **5** and Wind Speed to **25**. The Air Density setting also controls, among other things, how much influence the wind has on the particles.

   A very high air density acts like a liquid, and a high wind speed acts like a current in the water. It depends on what you're trying to achieve in your particular effect, but you can use drag or air density or a combination to set how much influence the Wind settings have on the nParticle. Another attribute to consider is the particle's mass. Since these are flames, presumably the mass will be very low.

9. Set Air Density to **1**. Rewind and play the animation. The particles start out slowly but gain speed as the wind pushes them along.

10. Set the Mass attribute in the Dynamic Properties section to **0.01**. The particles are again moving quickly through the capsule (see Figure 12.41).

FIGURE 12.41
Set the Mass and Drag attributes to a low value, enabling the nParticle flames to be pushed by the wind on the Nucleus solver.

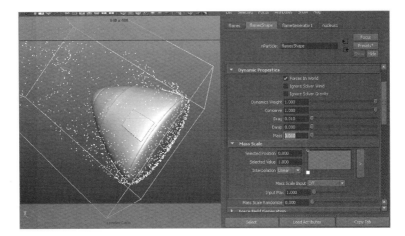

11. Switch to the nucleus1 tab, and set Wind Noise to **10**. Because the particles are moving fast, Wind Noise needs to be set to a high value before there's any noticeable difference in the movement. Wind noise adds turbulence to the movement of the particles as they are pushed by the wind.

SOLVER SUBSTEPS

The Substeps setting on the Nucleus tab sets the number of times per frame the nDynamics are calculated. Increasing this value increases the accuracy of the simulation but also slows down performance. It can also change how some aspects of nDynamics behave. If you change the Substeps setting, you may need to adjust Wind Speed, Noise, Mass, and other settings.

---

12. To make the nParticles collide with the capsule, select the capsule node, and choose nMesh ➤ Create Passive Collider. The nParticles now move around the capsule.

13. Select the nRigid1 node in the Outliner, and name it **flameCollide**.

14. Expand the Wind Field Generation settings in the flameCollideShape node. Set Air Push Distance to **0.5** and Air Push Vorticity to **1.5** (see Figure 12.42).

FIGURE 12.42
The Wind Field Generation settings on the flameCol-lideShape node

15. Save the scene as **capsule_v03.ma**.

To see a version of the scene up to this point, open capsule_v03.ma from the chapter12\ scenes folder at the book's web page.

A passive object can generate wind as it moves through particles or nCloth objects to create the effect of air displacement. In this case, the capsule is just bouncing around, so the Air Push Distance setting helps jostle the particles once they have been created. If you were creating the look of a submarine moving through murky waters with particulate matter, the Air Push Distance setting could help create the look of the particles being pushed away by the submarine, and the Air Push Vorticity setting could create a swirling motion in the particles that have been pushed aside. In the case of the capsule animation, it adds more turbulence to the nParticle flames.

The Wind Shadow Distance and Diffusion settings block the effect of the Nucleus solver's Wind setting on nParticles or nCloth objects on the side of the passive object opposite the direction of the wind. The Wind Shadow Diffusion attribute sets the degree to which the wind curls around the passive object.

Air Push Distance is more processor-intensive than Wind Shadow Distance, and the Maya documentation recommends that you not combine Air Push Distance and Wind Shadow Distance.

nParticles have these settings as well. You can make an nParticle system influence an nCloth object using the Air Push Distance setting.

Shading nParticles and Using Hardware Rendering to Create Flame Effects

Once you have created your nParticle simulation, you'll have to decide how to render the nParticles in order to best achieve the effect you want. The first decision you'll have to make is how to shade the nParticles—how they will be colored and what rendering style will best suit your needs. Maya makes this process fairly easy because there are several rendering styles to choose from, including Point, MultiPoint, Blobby Surface, Streak, MultiStreak, and Cloud. Any one of these styles will change the appearance of the individual nParticles and thus influence the way the nParticle effect looks in the final rendered image.

To make coloring the nParticles easy, Maya provides you with a number of colored ramps that control the nParticles' color, opacity, and incandescence over time. You can choose different attributes, such as Age, Acceleration, Randomized ID, and so on, to control the way the color ramps are applied to the nParticles. You can find all of these attributes in the Shading section of the nParticle's Attribute Editor.

Most of the time, you'll want to render nParticles as a separate pass from the rest of the scene and then composite the rendered nParticle image sequence together with the rest of the rendered scene in your compositing program. This is so that you can easily isolate the nParticles and apply effects such as blurring, glows, and color correction separately from the other elements of the scene. You have a choice how you can render the nParticles. This can be done using mental ray, Maya Software, Maya Hardware, or the Hardware Render Buffer. This section demonstrates how to render using the Hardware Render Buffer. Later in the chapter you'll learn how to render nParticles using mental ray.

Shading nParticles to Simulate Flames

Color and opacity attributes can be easily edited using the ramps in the nParticle's Attribute Editor. In these steps, you'll use these ramps to make the nParticles look more like flames:

1. Continue with the same scene from the previous section, or open `capsule_v03.ma` from the `chapter12\scenes` folder at the book's web page.

2. Select the flames nParticle node in the Outliner, and open the Attribute Editor to the flamesShape node. Expand the Lifespan rollout panel, and set Lifespan Mode to Random Range. Set Lifespan to **3** and Lifespan Random to **3**.

   This setting makes the average life span for each nParticle 3 seconds, with a variation of half the Lifespan Random setting in either direction. In this case, the nParticles will live anywhere between 0.5 and 4.5 seconds.

3. Scroll down to the Shading rollout panel, and expand it; set Particle Render Type to MultiStreak. This makes each nParticle a group of streaks and activates attributes specific to this render type.

4. Set Multi Count to **5**, Multi Radius to **0.8**, and Tail Size to **0.5** (see Figure 12.43).

FIGURE 12.43
Change Particle Render Type to MultiStreak to better simulate flames.

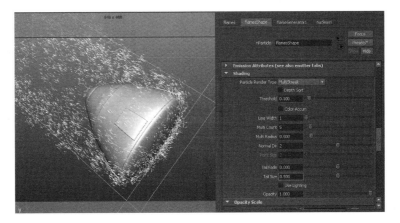

5. In the Opacity Scale section, set Opacity Scale Input to Age. Click the right side of the Opacity Scale ramp curve to add an edit point. Drag this point down. This creates a ramp where the nParticle fades out over the course of its life (see Figure 12.44).

   If you've used standard particles in older versions of Maya, you know that you normally have to create a per-particle Opacity attribute and connect it to a ramp. If you scroll down to the Per Particle Array Attributes section, you'll see that Maya has automatically added the Opacity attribute and connected it to the ramp curve.

FLASHING NPARTICLE COLORS

If the opacity of your nParticles seems to be behaving strangely or the nParticles are flashing different colors, make sure that the renderer in the viewport is not set to Legacy High Quality Viewport. Setting it to Legacy Default Viewport should fix the problem.

FIGURE 12.44
The opacity and
color ramps in the
nParticle's attribute
replace the need
to connect ramps
manually.

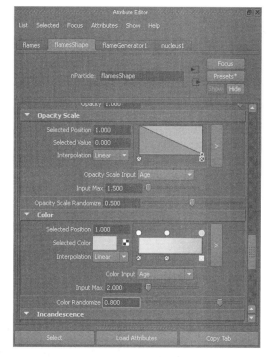

6. Set Input Max to **1.5**. This sets the maximum range along the x-axis of the Opacity Scale ramp. Since Opacity Scale Input is set to Age, this means that each nParticle takes 1.5 seconds to become transparent, so the nParticles are visible for a longer period of time.

INPUT MAX VALUE

If the Input Max value is larger than the particle's life span, it will die before it reaches zero opacity, making it disappear rather than fade out. This is fine for flame effects, but you should be aware of this behavior when creating an effect. If Opacity Scale Input is set to Normalized Age, then Input Max has no effect.

---

7. To randomize the opacity scale for the opacity, set Opacity Scale Randomize to **0.5**.

8. Expand the Color rollout panel. Set Color Input to Age. Click the ramp just to the right of the color marker to add a new color to the ramp. Click the color swatch, and change the color to yellow.

9. Add a third color marker to the right end of the ramp, and set its color to orange.

10. Set Input Max to **2** and Color Randomize to **0.8**, as in Figure 12.44.

11. In the Shading section, enable Color Accum. This creates an additive color effect, where denser areas of overlapping particles appear brighter.

12. Save the scene as **capsule_v04.ma**.

To see a version of the scene up to this point, open capsule_v04.ma from the chapter12\ scenes folder at the book's web page.

Creating an nCache

Before rendering, it's always a good idea to create a cache to ensure that the scene renders correctly.

1. Continue with the scene from the previous section, or open the capsule_v04.ma file from the chapter12\scenes folder at the book's web page.

2. Set the timeline to **200** frames.

3. In the Outliner, expand the capsuleEmitter group and select the flameGenerator emitter. Increase Rate (Particle/Sec) to **25000**. This will create a much more believable flame effect.

4. Select the flames node in the Outliner. Switch to the nDynamics menu, and choose nCache ➢ Create New Cache ➢ Options. In the options, you can choose a name for the cache or use the default, which is the name of the selected node (flamesShape in this example). You can also specify the directory for the cache, which is usually the project's data directory. Leave File Distribution set to One File Per Frame and Cache Time Range to Time Slider. Click Create to make the cache (see Figure 12.45).

FIGURE 12.45
The options for creating an nCache

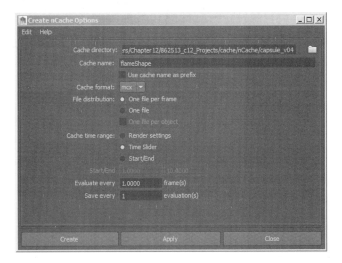

The scene will play through, and the cache file will be written to disk. It will take a fair amount of time to create the cache—anywhere from 5 to 10 minutes, depending on the speed of your machine.

5. Open the Attribute Editor for the flamesShape tab, and uncheck the Enable button so that the nParticle is disabled. This prevents Maya from calculating the nParticle dynamics while using an nCache.

POST CACHE RAMP EVALUATION

The Post Cache Ramp Evaluation attribute, located in the nParticle's Attribute Editor under the Caching rollout, allows you to use cached ramp data (when the box is checked) or the current ramp input. When the box is unchecked, you can alter the shading ramps (opacity, color, or incandescence) regardless of the cached data.

6. Play the animation, and you'll see the nParticles play back even though they have been disabled.

The playback is much faster now since the dynamics do not have to be calculated. If you make any changes to the dynamics of the nParticles, you'll have to delete or disable the existing cache before you'll see the changes take effect.

By default, only the Position and Velocity attributes of the nParticle are stored when you create an nCache. If you have a more complex simulation in which other attributes change over time (such as mass, stickiness, rotation, and so on), then open the Caching rollout panel in the nParticle's Attribute Editor, set Cacheable Attributes to All, and create a new nCache (see Figure 12.46). It is a fairly common mistake to forget to do this and, if you do not cache all of the attributes, you'll notice that the nParticles do not behave as expected when you play back from the nCache or when you render the animation. The nCache file will be much larger when you change the Cacheable Attributes setting.

FIGURE 12.46

Set Cacheable Attributes to All when you want to cache attributes other than just Position and Velocity.

You can use the options in the nCache menu to attach an existing cache file to an nParticle or to delete, append, merge, or replace caches.

PARTICLE DISK CACHE

nParticles do not use the Particle Disk Cache settings in the Dynamics menu. A normal particle disk cache works only for standard particles. Create an nCache for nParticles and any other nDynamic system.

Using the Hardware Render Buffer

One of the fastest and easiest ways to render flames in Maya is to use the Hardware Render Buffer. The results may need a little extra tweaking in a compositing program, but overall it does a decent job of rendering convincing flames. The performance of the Hardware Render Buffer depends on the type of graphics card installed in your machine. If you're using an Autodesk-approved graphics card, you should be in good shape.

THE HARDWARE RENDER BUFFER VS. MAYA HARDWARE

There are two ways to hardware-render in Maya: you can use the Hardware Render Buffer, which takes a screenshot of each rendered frame directly from the interface, or you can batch-render with Maya Hardware (chosen from the Render Settings window). The Hardware Render Buffer uses its own interface. There can be some differences in the way that the final render looks depending on the hardware rendering method you choose. You may want to test each method to see which one produces the best results.

The Blobby Surface, Cloud, and Tube nParticle render styles can be rendered only using software (Maya Software or mental ray). All nParticle types can be rendered in mental ray, although the results may be different than those rendered using the Hardware Render Buffer or Maya Hardware. The following steps explain how you use the Hardware Render Buffer to render particles.

NETWORK RENDERING WITH HARDWARE

If you are rendering using a farm, the render nodes on the farm may not have graphics cards, so using either the Hardware Render Buffer or Maya Hardware won't work. You'll have to render the scene locally.

---

1. Continue from the previous section. To render using the Hardware Render Buffer, choose Window ➤ Rendering Editors ➤ Hardware Render Buffer. A new window opens showing a wireframe display of the scene. Use the Cameras menu in the buffer to switch to the renderCam camera.

2. To set the render attributes in the Hardware Render Buffer, choose Render ➤ Attributes. The settings for the buffer appear in the Attribute Editor.

   The render buffer renders each frame of the sequence and then takes a screenshot of the screen. It's important to deactivate screen savers and keep other interface or application windows from overlapping the render buffer.

3. For Filename, type **capsuleFlameRender**, and for Extension, enter **name.0001.ext**.

4. Set Start Frame to **1** and End Frame to **200**. Keep By Frame set to 1.

   Keep Image Format set to Maya IFF. This file format is compatible with compositing programs such as Adobe After Effects.

5. To change the resolution, you can manually replace the numbers in the Resolution field or click the Select button to choose a preset. Click this button, and choose the 640 × 480 preset.

6. In the viewport window, you may want to turn off the display of the resolution or film gate. The view in the Hardware Render Buffer updates automatically.

7. Under Render Modes, select Full Image Resolution and Geometry Mask. Geometry Mask renders all the geometry as a solid black mask so that only the nParticles will render. You can composite the rendered particles over a separate pass of the software-rendered version of the geometry.

8. To create the soft look of the frames, expand the Multi-Pass Render Options rollout panel. Select Multi Pass Rendering, and set Render Passes to **36**. This means the buffer will take 36 snapshots of the frame and slightly jitter the position of the nParticles in each pass. The passes will then be blended together to create the look of the flame. For flame effects, this actually works better than the buffer's Motion Blur option. Leave Motion Blur at 0 (see Figure 12.47).

FIGURE 12.47
The settings for the Hardware Render Buffer

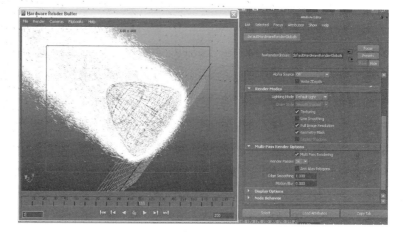

9. Rewind and play the animation to about frame 45.

10. In the Hardware Render Buffer, click the clapboard icon to see a preview of how the render will look (see Figure 12.48).

11. If you're happy with the look, choose Render ➢ Render Sequence to render the 200-frame sequence. It should take 5 to 10 minutes depending on your machine. You'll see the buffer render each frame.

12. When the sequence is finished, choose Flipbooks ➢ capsuleFlameRender1-200 to see the sequence play in FCheck.

13. Save the scene as **capsule_v05.ma**.

To see a version of the scene up to this point, open the capsule_v05.ma scene from the chapter12\scenes directory at the book's web page.

To finalize the look of flames, you can apply additional effects such as glow and blur in your compositing program. Take a look at the capsuleReentry movie in the chapter12 folder at the book's web page to see a finished movie made using the techniques described in this section.

nParticles and Fields

The behavior of nParticles is most often controlled by using fields. There are three ways to generate a field for an nParticles system. First, you can connect one or more of the many fields listed in the Fields menu. These include Air, Gravity, Newton, Turbulence, Vortex, and Volume Axis Curve. Second, you can use the fields built into the Nucleus solver—these are the Gravity and Wind forces that are applied to all nDynamic systems connected to the solver. Finally, you can use the Force field and the Air Push fields that are built into nDynamic objects. In this section, you'll experiment with using all of these types of fields to control nParticles.

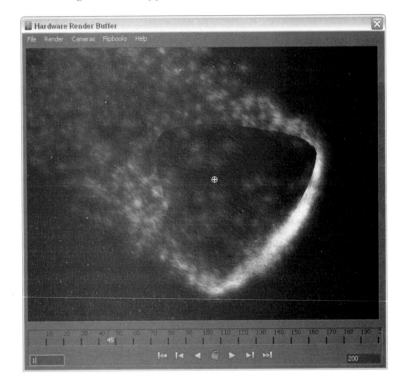

Using Multiple Emitters

When you create the emitter, an nParticle object is added and connected to the emitter. An nParticle can be connected to more than one emitter, as you'll see in this exercise:

1. Open the generator_v01.ma scene in the chapter12\scenes folder at the book's web page. You'll see a device built out of polygons. This will act as your experimental lab as you learn how to control nParticles with fields.

2. Switch to the nDynamics menu, and choose nParticles ➤ Create nParticles ➤ Cloud to set the nParticle style to Cloud.

3. Choose nParticles ➤ Create nParticles ➤ Create Emitter ➤ Options.

4. In the options, type **energyGenerator** in the Emitter Name field. Leave Solver set to Create New Solver. Set Emitter Type to Volume and Rate (Particles/Sec) to **200**.

5. In the Volume Emitter Attributes rollout panel, set Volume Shape to Sphere. You can leave the rest of the settings at the defaults. Click Create to make the emitter (see Figure 12.49).

FIGURE 12.49

The settings for the volume emitter

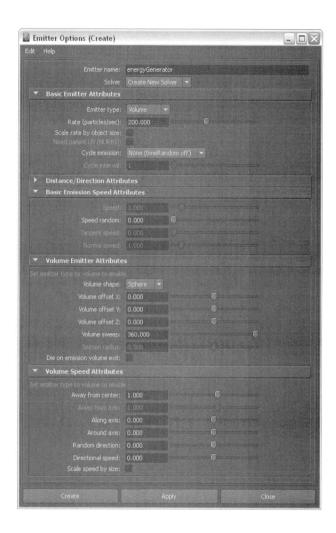

6. Select the energyGenerator1 emitter in the Outliner. Use the Move tool (hot key = **w**) to position the emitter around one of the balls at the end of the generators in the glass chamber. You may want to scale it up to about 1.25 (Figure 12.50).

7. Set the timeline to **800**, and play the animation. The nParticles are born and fly out of the emitter.

   Notice that the nParticles do not fall even though Gravity is enabled in the Nucleus solver and the nParticle has a mass of 1. This is because in the Dynamic properties for the Cloud style of nParticle, the Ignore Solver Gravity check box is selected.

8. Select the energyGenerator1 emitter, and duplicate it (hot key = **Ctrl/Cmd+d**). Use the Move tool to position this second emitter over the ball on the opposite generator.

If you play the animation, the second emitter creates no nParticles. This is because duplicating the emitter did not create a second nParticle object, but that's okay; you're going to connect the same nParticle object to both emitters.

FIGURE 12.50
Place the volume emitter over one of the balls inside the generator device.

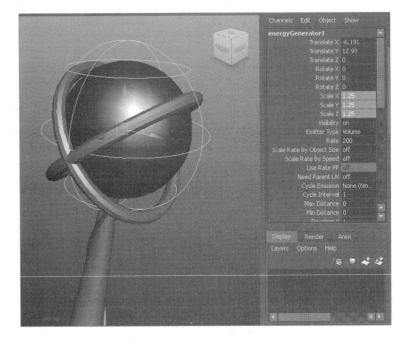

9. Select nParticle1 in the Outliner, and rename it **energy**.

10. Select energy, and choose Window ➢ Relationship Editors ➢ Dynamic Relationships. A window opens showing the objects in the scene; energy is selected on the left side.

11. On the right side, click the Emitters radio button to switch to a list of the emitters in the scene. energyGenerator1 is highlighted, indicating that the energy nParticle is connected to it.

12. Select energyGenerator2 so that both emitters are highlighted (see Figure 12.51).

13. Close the Dynamic Relationships Editor, and rewind and play the animation. You'll see both emitters now generate nParticles—the same nParticle object.

14. Select the energy object, and open the Attribute Editor. Switch to the Nucleus tab, and set Gravity to **1**.

15. In the energyShape tab, expand the Dynamic Properties rollout panel, and deselect Ignore Solver Gravity so that the energy nParticles slowly fall after they are emitted from the two generator poles (see Figure 12.52).

FIGURE 12.51
Use the Dynamic
Relationships
Editor to connect
the energy nParticle
to both emitters.

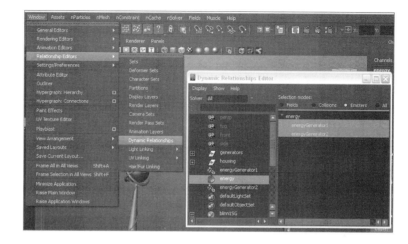

FIGURE 12.52
The energy nPar-
ticles are emitted
from both emitters.
Gravity is set to a
low value, causing
the nParticles to
fall slowly.

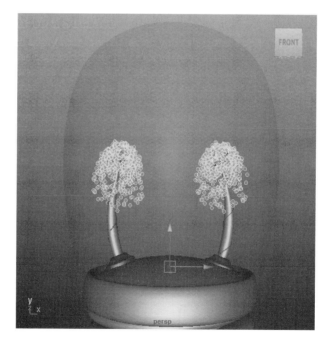

Volume Axis Curve

Volume Axis Curve is a versatile dynamic field that can be controlled using a NURBS curve.
You can use this field with any of the dynamic systems (traditional and nDynamic) in Maya.
In this section, you'll perform some tricks using the field inside a model of an experimental
vacuum chamber.

1. Select the energy nParticle node in the Outliner. In the Attribute Editor, open the Lifespan rollout panel and set the Lifespan mode to Random Range.

2. Set Lifespan to **6** and Lifespan Random to **4**. The nParticles will now live between 4 and 8 seconds each.

3. With the energy nParticle selected, choose Fields ➢ Volume Curve. Creating the field with the nParticle selected ensures that the field is automatically connected.

DYNAMIC RELATIONSHIPS EDITOR

You can use the Dynamic Relationships Editor to connect fields to nParticles and other dynamic systems. Review the previous section on using multiple emitters to see how the Dynamic Relationships Editor works.

---

4. Select curve1 in the Outliner, and use the Move tool to position it between the generators. The field consists of a curve surrounded by a tubular field.

5. Use the Show menu to disable the display of polygons so that the glass case is not in the way.

6. Select curve1 in the Outliner, and right-click the curve; choose CVs to edit the curve's control vertices.

7. Use the Move tool to position the CVs at the end of the curve inside each generator ball, and then add some bends to the curve (see Figure 12.53).

FIGURE 12.53
Position the CVs of the Volume Axis curve to add bends to the curve. The field surrounds the curve, forming a tube.

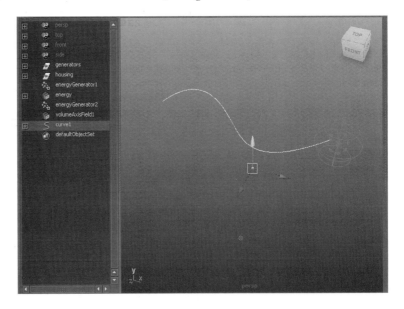

8. Rewind and play the animation. A few of the nParticles will be pushed along the curve. So far, it's not very exciting.

9. Select the volumeAxisField1 node in the Outliner, and open its Attribute Editor. Use the following settings:

    a. The default Magnitude and Attenuation settings (5 and 0) are fine for the moment.

    b. In the Distance rollout panel, leave Use Max Distance deselected.

    c. In the Volume Control Attributes rollout panel, set Section Radius to **3**.

    d. Set Trap Inside to **0.8**. This keeps most of the nParticles inside the area defined by the volume radius (the Trap Inside attribute is available for other types of fields such as the Radial field).

    e. Leave Trap Radius set to **2**. This defines the radius around the field within which the nParticles are trapped.

    f. Edit the Axial Magnitude ramp so that each end is at about **0.5** and the middle is at **1**, as shown in Figure 12.54. Set the interpolation of each point to Spline. This means that the area at the center of the curve has a stronger influence on the nParticles than the areas at either end of the curve.

FIGURE 12.54
The settings for the Volume Axis Curve field

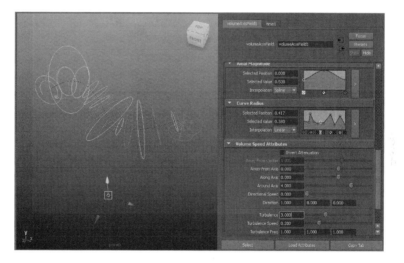

    g. Edit the Curve Radius ramp: add some points to the curve, and drag them up and down in a random jagged pattern. You'll see the display of the field update; this creates an interesting shape for the curve.

    h. In the Volume Speed Attributes rollout panel, set Away From Axis and Along Axis to **0**, and set Around Axis to **4**. This means that the nParticles are pushed in a circular motion around the curve rather than along or away from it. If you zoom into the field, you'll see an arrow icon at the end of the field indicating its direction. Positive numbers make the field go clockwise; negative numbers make it go counterclockwise.

    i. Set Turbulence to **3**, and leave Turbulence Speed at 0.2. This adds noise to the field, causing some nParticles to fly off.

10. Play the animation. You'll see the nParticles move around within the field. Faster-moving particles fly out of the field.

This effect is interesting, but it can be improved to create a more dynamic look.

11. In the Attribute Editor for the Volume Axis Curve field, remove the edit points from the Curve Radius ramp.

12. Edit the curve so that it has three points. The points at either end should have a value of **1**; the point at the center should have a value of **0.1**.

13. Select the edit point at the center and, in the Selected Position field, type `=0.5+(0.5*(noise(time*4)));`. This is similar to the expression that was applied to the ramp in the "Surface Emission" section earlier in this chapter. In this case, it moves the center point back and forth along the curve, creating a moving shape for the field (see Figure 12.55).

FIGURE 12.55

Create an expression to control the Selected Position attribute of the Curve Radius ramp's center point. The numeric field is not large enough to display the entire expression.

14. Save the scene as `generator_v02.ma`.

To see a version of the scene up to this point, open the `generator_v02.ma` scene from the `chapter12\scenes` folder at the book's web page. This version uses a Dynamic Hair curve to control the field. To learn how to use this technique, refer to the sidebar "Using a Dynamic Hair Curve with a Volume Axis Curve."

USING A DYNAMIC HAIR CURVE WITH A VOLUME AXIS CURVE

For an even more dynamic look, you can animate the curve itself using hair dynamics (as shown here). Hair is discussed in Chapter 14, "Hair and Clothing," but here is a quick walkthrough to show you how to set this up. In addition to making the volume curve dynamic, this workflow demonstrates how to change the input curve source for the volume curve.

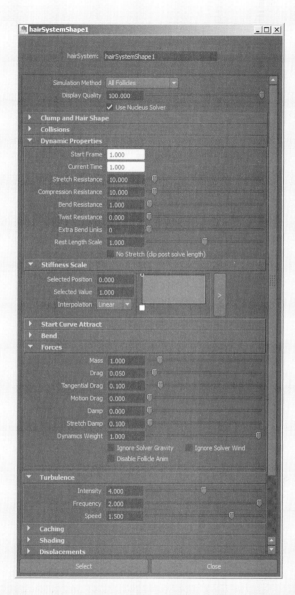

1. Select the curve1 object in the Outliner. Switch to the nDynamics menu, and choose nHair ➤ Make Selected Curves Dynamic.

2. Open the Attribute Editor for the hairsystem1 node, and switch to the hairSystemShape1 tab.

3. In the Dynamics rollout panel, set Stiffness to **0** and Length Flex to **0.5**.

continues

(continued)

4. In the Forces rollout panel, set Gravity to **0**.

5. In the Turbulence rollout panel, set Intensity to **4**, Frequency to **2**, and Speed to **1.5**.

   If you play the animation, you'll see two curves; the original Volume Axis curve is unchanged, but a second curve is now moving dynamically. You need to switch the input curve for the Volume Axis curve from the original curve to the Dynamic Hair curve.

6. In the Outliner, expand the hairSystem1OutputCurves group, and select the curveShape2 node. Open the Connection Editor (Window ➤ General Editors ➤ Connection Editor), as shown here. The curveShape2 node should be loaded on the left side.

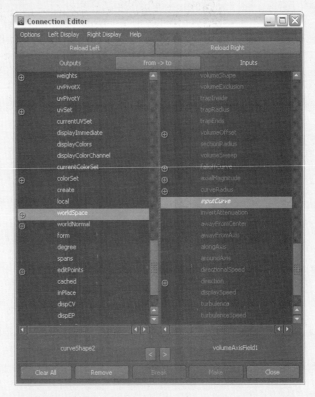

7. In the Outliner, select the VolumeAxisField1 and click Reload Right in the Connection Editor.

8. Select worldSpace from the list on the left and inputCurve from the list on the right to connect the Dynamic Hair curve to the Volume Axis field.

9. Play the animation; the Volume Axis field now animates in a very dynamic way.

You can use this technique to swap any curve you create for the input of the Volume Axis field.

You can use the Hypergraph to view connections between nodes (as shown here). In your animations, you may need to do some detective work to figure out how to make connections like this. If you graph the Volume Axis field in the Hypergraph, you can hold your mouse over the connection between curveShape2 and the Volume Axis field to see how the worldSpace attribute of the curve is connected to the input curve of the field. It's a simple matter of making the same connection between the shape node of a different curve to the Volume Axis field to replace the input curve for the field.

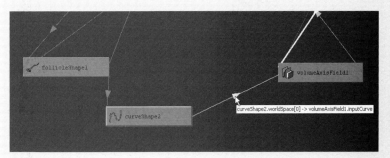

Working with hair curves is discussed in detail in Chapter 14.

Real World Scenario

ANIMATING BLOOD CELLS

A common challenge facing many animators is blood cells flowing through a tubular-shaped blood vessel. In early versions of Maya, the solution had been to use the Curve Flow Effect, which uses a series of goals, or emitters, placed along the length of a curve.

To create this effect, follow these steps:

1. Add an Omni emitter and an nParticle to a scene using the Water nParticle style.
2. Draw a curve that defines the shape of the blood vessel.
3. Extrude a NURBS circle along the length of the curve to form the outside walls of the vessel.
4. Place the emitter inside the blood vessel at one end of the curve.
5. Select the nParticle, and add a Volume Axis Curve field.
6. Use the Connection Editor to attach the worldSpace attribute of the blood vessel curve's shape node to the inputCurve attribute of the Volume Axis Curve field.
7. In the Volume Axis Curve field's attributes, set Trapped to **1** and define the trapped radius so that it fits within the radius of the vessel.
8. Adjust the Along Axis and Around Axis attributes until the nParticles start to flow along the length of the curve.
9. Adjust the Drag attribute of the nParticles to adjust the speed of the flow.
10. Set the life span of the nParticles so that they die just before reaching the end of the blood vessel.

You can use the Blobby Surface render type to make the nParticles look like globular surfaces or try instancing modeled blood cells to the nParticles. Instancing is covered in Chapter 13.

Working with Force Fields

nParticles, nCloth, and passive collision objects (also known as *nRigids*) can all emit force fields that affect themselves and other nDynamic systems attached to the same Nucleus node. In this example, the surface of the glass that contains the particle emitters will create a field that controls the nParticle's behavior:

1. Continue with the scene from the previous section, or open the generator_v02.ma scene from the chapter12\scenes folder at the book's web page.

2. Expand the housing group in the Outliner. Select the dome object, and choose nMesh ➢ Create Passive Collider.

3. In the Outliner, rename the nRigid1 node to **domeCollider**.

4. To keep the particles from escaping the chamber, you'll also need to convert the seal and base objects to passive collision objects:

   a. Select the seal object, and choose nMesh ➢ Create Passive Collider.

   b. Name the new nRigid1 node **sealCollide**.

   c. Do the same for the base, and name it **baseCollide**.

5. Play the animation. Because some of the nParticles are thrown from the Volume Axis Curve field, they are now contained within the glass chamber (see Figure 12.56).

FIGURE 12.56
Parts of the generator device are converted to collision objects, trapping the nParticles inside.

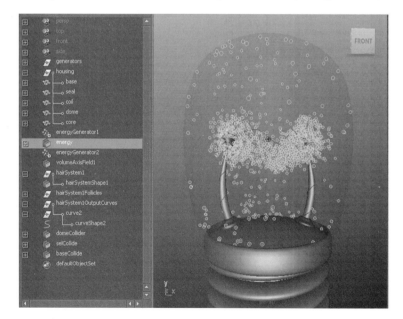

6. Open the settings for the energyShape node in the Attribute Editor. In the Particle Size rollout panel, make sure that Radius Scale Input is set to Age.

7. Edit the Radius Scale ramp so that it slopes up from 0 on the left to 1 in the middle and back down to 0 on the left.

8. Set Interpolation to Spline for all points along the curve.

9. Set Input Max to **3** and Radius Scale Randomize to **0.5** (see Figure 12.57).

FIGURE 12.57
Edit the Radius
Scale settings to
create a more ran-
domized radius
for the nParticles.

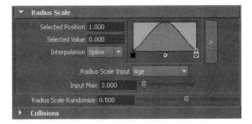

10. Select the domeCollider node, and open the Attribute Editor to the domeColliderShape tab.

11. Expand the Force Field Generation settings, and set Force Field to Single Sided. This generates a force field based on the positive normal direction of the collision surface.

Along Normal generates the field along the surface normals of the collision object. In this case, the difference between Along Normal and Single Sided is not noticeable. Double Sided generates the field based on both sides of the collision surface.

12. The normals for the dome shape are actually pointing outward. You can see this if you choose Display ➢ Polygons ➢ Face Normals. To reverse the surface, switch to the Polygons menu set, and choose Normals ➢ Reverse (see Figure 12.58).

13. Back in the Force Field Generation settings for the domeColliderShape node, set Field Magnitude to **100** and Field Distance to **4**, and play the animation. The particles are repelled from the sides of the dome when they are within 4 field units of the collision surface. A lower field magnitude will repel the particles with a weaker force, allowing them to collide with the dome before being pushed back to the center. If you set Magnitude to 1000, the nParticles never reach the collision surface.

14. Set Field Magnitude to **–100**. The nParticles are now pulled to the sides of the dome when they are within 4 field units of the collision surface, much like a magnet. Setting a value of –1000 causes them to stick to the sides.

The Field Scale Edit ramp controls the strength of the field within the distance set by the Field Distance value. The right side of the ramp is the leading edge of the field—in this case, 4 field units in from the surface of the dome. The left side represents the scale of the force field on the actual collision surface.

You can create some interesting effects by editing this curve. If Field Magnitude is at a value of –100 and you reverse the curve, the nParticles are sucked to the dome quickly when they are within 4 units of the surface. However, they do not stick very strongly to the side, so they bounce around a little within the 4-unit area. Experiment with creating different shapes for the curve, and see how the curve affects the behavior of the nParticles. By adding variation to the center of the curve, you get more of a wobble as the nParticle is attracted to the surface.

FIGURE 12.58
Reverse the normals for the dome surface so that they point inward.

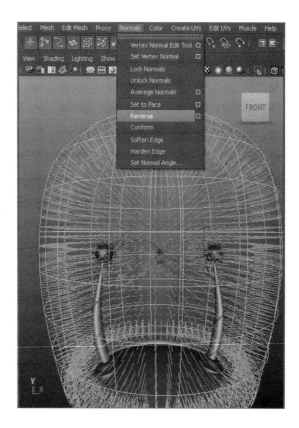

15. Save the scene as **generator_v03.ma**.

To see a version of the scene to this point, open the generator_v03.ma scene from the chapter12\scenes folder at the book's web page.

Painting Field Maps

The strength of the force field can be controlled by a texture. The texture itself can be painted onto the collision surface.

1. Continue with the scene from the previous section, or open the generator_v03.ma scene from the chapter12\scenes folder at the book's web page.

2. In the Attribute Editor for domeCollider, set the Field Scale ramp so that it's a straight line across the top of the curve editor. Set Field Magnitude to **1**.

3. Select the dome object, and choose nMesh ➢ Paint Texture Properties ➢ Field Magnitude. The dome turns white, and the Artisan Brush tool is activated. If the Dome turns black, open the Flood controls in the Artisan Tool options, and click the Flood button to fill the surface with a value of 1 for the Field Strength attribute.

4. Open the tools options for the Artisan Brush. The color should be set to black, and Paint Operation should be set to Paint.

5. Use the brush to paint a pattern on the surface of the dome. Make large, solid lines on the surface; so that the end result is clear, avoid blurring the edges (see Figure 12.59).

FIGURE 12.59
Use the Artisan Brush tool to paint a pattern for the field magnitude on the collision surface.

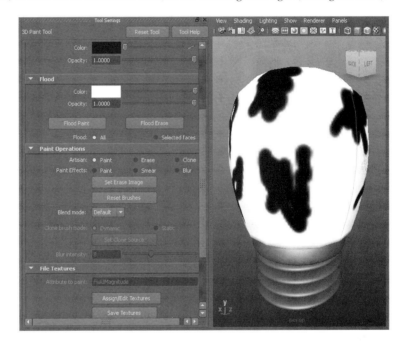

6. When you've finished, click the Select tool in the toolbox to close the Artisan Brush options.

7. Open the Hypershade. On the Textures tab, you'll see the texture map you just created. You can also use file textures or even animated sequences for the map source.

8. Select the dome in the scene. In the Work Area of the Hypershade, right-click and choose Graph ➤ Graph Materials On Selected Objects.

9. MMB-drag the file1 texture from the texture area of the Hypershade down onto the shader and choose Color. Connecting the texture to the color does not affect how the field works, but it will help you visualize how the map works (see Figure 12.60).

If you play the animation, you won't see much of a result. The reason is that the values of the map are too weak and the movement of the nParticles is too fast to be affected by the field.

10. In the Hypershade, select the file1 texture and open its Attribute Editor. The outAlpha of the texture is connected to the field magnitude of the collision surface. You can see this when you graph the network in the Hypershade.

11. To increase the strength of the map, expand the Color Balance section. Set Alpha Gain to **1000** and Alpha Offset to **−500**. Chapter 16, "Scene Management and Virtual Filmmaking," has a detailed explanation of how the Alpha Gain and Alpha Offset attributes work. Essentially this means that the light areas of the texture cause the force field magnitude to be at a value of 500, and the dark areas cause it to be at −500.

FIGURE 12.60
Connect the newly painted texture to the color of the dome shader.

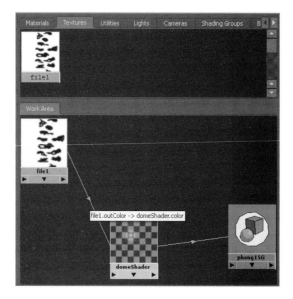

12. Play the animation. You'll see that most of the nParticles stay in the center of the dome, but occasionally one or two nParticles will fly out and stick to the side. They stick to the areas where the texture is dark (see Figure 12.61).

TEXTURE MAPS FOR DYNAMIC ATTRIBUTES

You can create texture maps for other attributes of the collision surface, including stickiness, friction, bounce, and collision thickness.

Vertex maps assign values to the vertices of the surface using the colors painted by the brush; texture maps use a file texture. One may work better than the other depending on the situation. You can paint vertex maps by choosing nMesh ➤ Paint Vertex

Properties. In the Map properties, set Map Type to Vertex or Texture, depending on which one you are using.

FIGURE 12.61
The painted force field texture causes most of the nParticles to remain hovering around the center, but a few manage to stick to the dark areas.

When using a texture or vertex map for the force field, the Force Field Magnitude setting acts as a multiplier for the strength of the map.

13. Back in the domeCollider node, set Field Magnitude to **10** and play the animation. You'll see more nParticles stick to the surface where the texture has been painted. To smooth their motion, you can adjust the Field Scale ramp.

14. Save the scene as **generator_v04.ma**.

To see a version of the scene up to this point, open generator_v04.ma from the chapter12\ scenes folder at the book's web page.

Using Dynamic Fields

The traditional set of dynamic fields is found in the Fields menu. They have been included as part of Maya since version 1.

Fields such as Air and Gravity are similar to the wind and gravity forces that are part of the Nucleus system. But that is not to say you can't use them in combination with the Nucleus forces to create a specific effect.

Drag is similar to the Drag attribute of nParticles; it applies a force that, in some cases, slows an nParticle down; in other cases, it actually pulls the nParticle in a direction determined by the force.

You can use the Inherit Transform slider on the Drag field to create wavelike effects in a cloud of particles, similar to the wind field generation on nDynamic objects.

Radial fields are similar to force fields emitted by nRigids and nParticles; they push or pull particles, depending on their Magnitude settings.

A Uniform force is similar to Gravity because it pushes a particle in a particular direction. The Volume Axis field is similar to the Volume Axis curve used earlier in the chapter. It has a built-in turbulence and affects particles within a given volume shape (by default).

ATTENUATION AND MAX DISTANCE IN DYNAMIC FIELDS

Attenuation with dynamic fields can be a little difficult to wrap your head around when you start using fields with dynamic simulations. This is because many fields have both Attenuation and a Max Distance falloff curve, which at first glance appear to do very similar things.

The Maya documentation defines Attenuation with regard to an air field as a value that "sets how much the strength of the field diminishes as distance to the affected object increases". The rate of change is exponential with distance; the Attenuation is the exponent. If you set Attenuation to 0, the force remains constant over distance. Negative numbers are not valid. Before you break out the calculator, you can get a visual guide of how Attenuation affects the application of a field by using the Show Manipulators tool on a field. Try this experiment:

1. Start a new scene in Maya.

2. Switch to the nDynamics menu, and set the nParticle type to Balls.

3. Choose Create nParticles ➤ nParticle Tool ➤ Options.

4. In the options, select the Create Particle Grid check box and With Text Fields under Placement.

5. In the Placement options, set the Minimum Corner X, Y, and Z values to **−10**, **0**, and **−10** and the Maximum Corner X, Y, and Z values to **10**, **0**, and **10**, as shown here. Press Enter on the numeric keypad to make the grid.

6. Select the nParticle grid, and choose Fields ➤ Air. An air field is placed at the center of the grid. On the Nucleus tab, set Gravity to **0**.

7. Select the air field, and open the Attribute Editor (as shown here). You'll see that the air field is at the default settings where Magnitude is 4, the air field is applied along the y-axis (Direction = 0, 1, 0), and Attenuation is set to 1. Under the Distance settings, Use Max Distance is selected, and Max Distance is set to **20**.

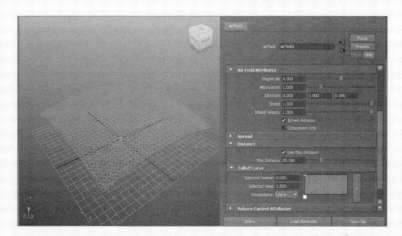

8. Play the animation, and you'll see the grid move upward; the strength of the air field is stronger at the center than at the edges, creating a semispherical shape as the particles move up. You may need to extend the length of the timeline to something like 500 frames to see the motion of the particles.

9. Rewind the animation, deselect Use Max Distance, and play the animation again. Now the entire grid moves uniformly. For air fields, Attenuation has no effect when Use Max Distance is off.

10. Rewind the animation. Select Use Max Distance again.

11. Select the air field, and choose the Show Manipulators tool from the toolbox.

12. Drag the blue dot connected to the attenuation manipulator handle in toward the center of the manipulator, and play the animation. You'll see that the shape of the field resembles the attenuation curve on the manipulator:

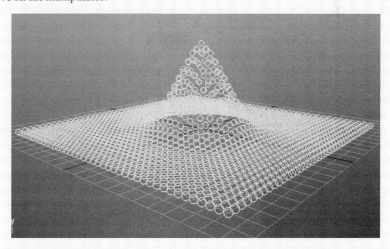

continues

(continued)

13. If you deselect Use Max Distance, you'll see the Attenuation slider flatten out because it no longer affects the field.

14. Select Use Max Distance, and set Attenuation to **0**.

15. In the Attribute Editor, find the falloff curve for the air field. Click at the top-left corner of the falloff curve to add a control point.

16. Drag the new control point downward, and play the animation. The falloff curve appears to work much like Attenuation. You can create interesting shapes in the field motion by adding and moving points on the falloff curve, and you can also change the interpolation of the points on the curve, as shown here:

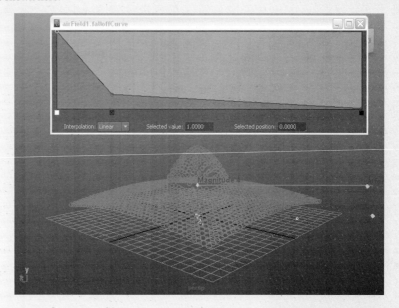

The difference between Attenuation and the Max Distance falloff curve is often subtle in practice. Think of it this way: attenuation affects how the force of the field is applied; the falloff curve defines how the maximum distance is applied to the force. It's a little easier to see when you lower the Conserve value of the nParticle. By default Conserve is at 1, meaning that particles do not lose any energy or momentum as they travel. Lowering Conserve even a little (say to a value of 0.95) causes the nParticle to lose energy or momentum as it travels; the effect is that the nParticle slows down when it reaches the boundary of the force. In practice, the best approach is to set Attenuation to **0** when you first apply the field to a particle system and then adjust Attenuation and/or the Max Distance setting and falloff until you get the behavior you want.

Some fields have unique properties that affect how they react to Attenuation settings. With some fields, such as Turbulence, the Attenuation attribute will affect the dynamic simulation even when Use Max Distance is not selected. Once again, it's a good idea to start with Attenuation at **0** and then add it if needed.

The behavior of Attenuation and Max Distance is the same for both nDynamic systems and traditional Maya dynamics.

The Turbulence field creates a noise pattern, and the Vortex field creates a swirling motion. Newton fields create a Newtonian attraction to dynamic objects.

1. Open the generator_v04.ma scene from the chapter12\scenes folder at the book's web page.

2. Select the energy nParticle group, and choose Fields ➢ Turbulence to connect a Turbulence field to the nParticle.

3. In the Attribute Editor for the Turbulence field, set Magnitude to **100**, Attenuation to **0**, and Frequency to **0.5**.

4. In the Dynamic Properties section of the nParticle's Attribute Editor, set Drag to **0.1**. This can help tone down the movement of the nParticles if they get a little too crazy. An alternative technique is to lower the conserve a little.

5. To see the particles behave properly, you'll probably want to create a playblast. Set the timeline to 300, and choose Window ➢ Playblast. A flip-book will be created and played in FCheck.

6. Save the scene as **generator_v05.ma**.

To see a version of the scene up to this point, open generator_v05.ma from the chapter12\ scenes folder at the book's web page.

Rendering Particles with mental ray

All particle types can be rendered using mental ray software rendering, and particles will appear in reflections and refractions. In this section, you'll see how easy it is to render different nParticle types using mental ray.

In this exercise, you'll render the nParticles created in the generator scene:

1. Open the generator_v05.ma scene from the chapter12\scenes folder at the book's web page or continue from the previous section.

2. Select the energy nParticle node in the Outliner, and open its Attribute Editor to the energyShape tab.

3. Expand the Shading attributes in the bottom of the editor. Set Opacity to **0.8**.

4. Set Color Input to Age. Make the left side of the ramp bright green and the right side a slightly dimmer green.

5. Set Incandescence Input to Age. Edit the ramp so the far-left side is white, followed closely by bright green. Make the center a dimmer green and the right side completely black (see Figure 12.62).

6. Select each of the emitter nodes, and raise the Rate value to **1000**.

7. Select the domeShader node in the Hypershade, and break the connection between the color and the file texture. (Don't delete the file texture—it still controls the force field magnitude.)

FIGURE 12.62
The shading
attributes for the
energy nParticle

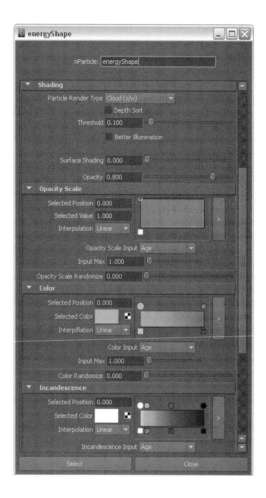

8. Set the color of the domeShader node to a dark gray.

9. Play the animation for about 80 frames.

10. Open the render settings, and set the renderer to mental ray.

11. From the Presets menu, choose Load Preset ➤ Production.

12. Select the energy nParticle and, in the Render Stats section of the energyShape tab, select the boxes for Visible in Reflections and Refractions.

13. Create a test render of the scene. You can see in the glass of the chamber and the metal base that the nParticles are reflected.

14. Open the Hypershade, and select the metal shader. Increase Reflectivity in the Attribute Editor to **0.8**. The nParticles are more visible in the reflection on the base.

15. Select the domeShader node, and in its Attribute Editor under Raytrace Options, select Refractions and set Refractive Index to **1.2**.

16. Under the Specular Shading rollout panel, increase Reflectivity to **0.8**.

17. Create another test render. You can see the effect refraction has on the nParticles. Figure 12.63 shows both reflections and refractions.

FIGURE 12.63
The nParticles are visible in reflections and refractions on the surfaces.

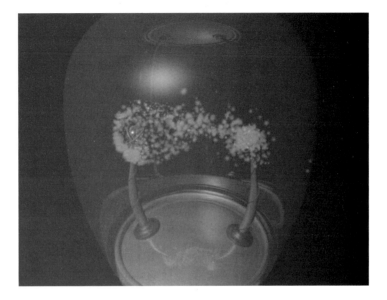

You can render the Point, MultiPoint, Streak, and MultiStreak render types using mental ray. They will appear in reflections and refractions as well; however, you'll notice that in the Render Stats section for these nParticle types, the options for Reflections and Refractions are unavailable.

18. In the Hypershade, select the npCloudVolume shader. This shader is created with the nParticle. Graph the network in the Hypershade Work Area (see Figure 12.64).

You can see that a particleSamplerInfo node is automatically connected to the volume shader. This node transfers the settings you create in the nParticle's Attribute Editor for color, opacity, and transparency to the shader. An npCloudBlinn shader is also created. This shader is applied when you switch Particle Type to Points. You can further refine the look of the nParticles by adjusting the settings in the npCloudVolume shader's Attribute Editor.

You can add a shader glow to the particles by increasing Glow Intensity in the npCloud-Volume shader; however, the glow does not appear behind refractive surfaces with standard Maya shaders.

19. When you are happy with the look of the render, you can create an nCache for the energy nParticle and render the sequence using mental ray.

20. Save the scene as `generator_v06.ma`.

To see a finished version of the scene, open the `generator_v06.ma` file from the `chapter12\` scenes directory.

FIGURE 12.64
Shaders are automatically created for the nParticles. The particleSamplerInfo node connects the attributes of the nParticle to the shader.

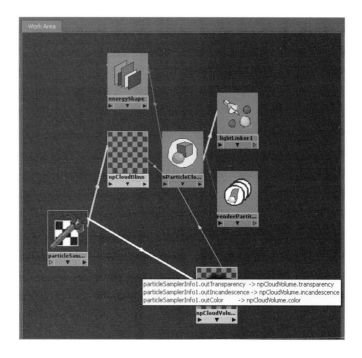

FURTHER READING

There is no limit to the number of creative effects you can achieve using nParticles. This chapter is but a brief introduction. If you have enjoyed working through these examples, you can continue your nParticle education by reading my *Maya Studio Projects: Dynamics* (Sybex, 2009), which covers a variety of effects using many of the dynamic tools.

The Bottom Line

Create nParticles.   nParticles can be added to a scene in a number of ways. They can be drawn using the tool or spawned from an emitter, or they can fill an object.

   Master It   Create a spiral shape using nParticles.

Make nParticles collide.   nParticles can collide with themselves, other nParticles, and polygon surfaces.

   Master It   Make nParticles pop out of the top of an animated volume.

Create liquid simulations.   Enabling Liquid Simulations changes the behavior of nParticles so that they act like water or other fluids.

   Master It   Create a flowing stream of nParticles that ends in a waterfall.

Emit nParticles from a texture.   The emission rate of an nParticle can be controlled using a texture.

    Master It   Create your own name in nParticles.

Move nParticles with Nucleus wind.   The wind force on the Nucleus node can be used to push nParticles.

    Master It   Blow nParticles off a surface using wind.

Use force fields.   Force fields can be emitted by nParticles and collision objects, creating interesting types of behavior in your scenes.

    Master It   Add a second nParticle object emitted from the base of the generator. Enable its force field so that it attracts some of the original energy nParticle.

Chapter 13

Dynamic Effects

The nCloth system in the Autodesk® Maya® software was originally designed to make dynamic cloth simulation for characters easier to create and animate. The Nucleus dynamics solver, which you learned about in Chapter 12, "Introducing nParticles," is at the heart of nCloth simulations. (The *n* in *nCloth* stands for "nucleus.") nCloth has evolved into a dynamic system that goes well beyond simply simulating clothing. Creative use of nCloth in combination with nParticles yields nearly limitless possibilities for interesting effects, as you'll see when you go through the exercises in this chapter.

You'll delve deeper into Maya dynamics to understand how the various dynamic systems, such as nCloth, nParticles, and rigid bodies, can be used together to create spectacular effects. You'll also use particle expressions to control the motion of particle instances.

In this chapter, you will learn to:

◆ Use nCloth

◆ Combine nCloth and nParticles

◆ Use Maya rigid body dynamics

◆ Use nParticles to drive instanced geometry

◆ Create nParticle expressions

◆ Create a soft body simulation with Bullet

Creating nCloth Objects

Typically, nCloth is used to make polygon geometry behave like clothing, but nCloth can be used to simulate the behavior of a wide variety of materials. Everything from concrete to water balloons can be achieved by adjusting the attributes of the nCloth object. nCloth uses the same dynamic system as nParticles and applies it to the vertices of a piece of geometry. An nCloth object is simply a polygon object that has had its vertices converted to nParticles. A system of virtual springs connects the nParticles and helps maintain the shape of nCloth objects. nCloth objects automatically collide with other nDynamic systems (such as nParticles and nRigids) that are connected to the same Nucleus solver, and an nCloth object collides with itself.

In this section, you'll see how to get up and running fast with nCloth using the presets that ship with Maya as well as get some background on how the Nucleus solver works. The examples in this chapter illustrate a few of the ways nCloth and nParticles can be used together to create interesting effects. These examples are only the beginning; there are so many possible applications and uses for nCloth that a single chapter barely scratches the surface. The goal of this chapter is to give you a starting place so that you feel comfortable designing your own unique effects. Chapter 14, "Hair and Clothing," demonstrates techniques for using nCloth to make clothing for an animated character.

Making a Polygon Mesh Dynamic

Any polygon mesh you model in Maya can be converted into a dynamic nCloth object (also known as an *nDynamic object*); there's nothing special about the way the polygon object needs to be prepared. The only restriction is that only polygon objects can be used. NURBS and subdivision surfaces can't be converted to nCloth.

CERT OBJECTIVE

There are essentially two types of nCloth objects: active and passive. *Active nCloth objects* are the ones that behave like cloth. They are the soft, squishy, or bouncy objects. *Passive nCloth objects* are solid pieces of geometry that react with active objects. For example, to simulate a tablecloth sliding off a table, the tablecloth would be the active nCloth object, and the table would be the passive nCloth object. The table prevents the tablecloth from falling in space. You can animate a passive object, and the active object will react to the animation. Thus you can keyframe the table tilting, and the tablecloth will slide off the table based on its dynamic settings.

The first exercise in this chapter shows you how to create the effect of a dividing cell using two nCloth objects:

1. Open `cellDivide_v01.ma` from the `chapter13\scenes` folder at the book's web page (www.sybex.com/go/masteringmaya2015). The scene contains two polygon hemispheres.

2. Switch to the nDynamics menu. Select both objects, and choose nMesh ➤ Create nCloth. In the Outliner, you'll see that two nCloth nodes have been added.

3. Switch to wireframe mode, and select nCloth1. One of the cell halves turns purple, indicating the nCloth node is an input connection to that particular piece of geometry.

4. Rename the nCloth1 and nCloth2 nodes **cellLeftCloth** and **cellRightCloth** according to which piece of geometry they are connected to (see Figure 13.1).

FIGURE 13.1
Add two nCloth nodes to the Outliner, one for each side of the cell, and rename them cellLeftCloth and cellRightCloth.

5. Set the timeline to 400 frames, and play the scene. You'll see that both pieces of geometry fall in space. This is because Gravity is turned on by default in the Nucleus solver.

When you create an nCloth object or any nCloth dynamic system (nParticles, nRigids), several additional nodes are created and connected. You can see this when you graph the cellLeftShape node on the Hypergraph, as shown in Figure 13.2.

FIGURE 13.2
The input and output connections for the cellLeft-Shape node are graphed on the Hypergraph.

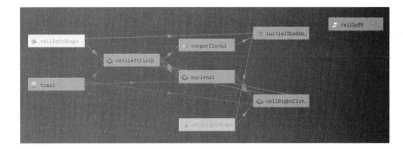

Each nCloth object consists of the original geometry, the nCloth node, and the Nucleus solver. By default, any additional nDynamic objects you create are attached to the same Nucleus solver. Additional nodes include the original cellLeftShape node, which is connected as the inputMesh to the cellLeftClothShape node. This determines the original starting shape of the nCloth object.

6. Select the cellLeftCloth node, and open the Attribute Editor.

7. Switch to the cellLeftClothShape tab, as shown in Figure 13.3. This node was originally named nCloth1. The tabs found in the Attribute Editor include the following:

cellLeftCloth   This tab contains the settings for the nCloth1 transform node. Most of the time you won't have a reason to change these settings.

cellLeftClothShape   This tab contains the settings that control the dynamics of the nCloth object. There are a lot of settings on this tab, and this is where you will spend most of your time adjusting the settings for this particular nCloth object.

nucleus1   This tab contains all the global settings for the Nucleus solver. These include the overall solver quality settings but also the Gravity and Air Density settings. If you select the cellRightCloth node in the Outliner, you'll notice that it also has a nucleus1 tab. In fact, this is the same node as attached to the cellLeftCloth object.

It's possible to create different Nucleus solvers for different nDynamic objects, but unless the nDynamic objects are connected to the same Nucleus solver, they will not directly interact.

NAME YOUR nCLOTH NODES

Because the nCloth objects are connected to the same Nucleus solver, when you open the Attribute Editor for the nucleus node, you'll see tabs for each node that are connected to the solver. To reduce confusion over which nCloth object is being edited, always give each nCloth node a descriptive name as soon as the node is created.

FIGURE 13.3
The Attribute
Editor for the
cellLeftClothShape
node has tabs for
the transform and
shape nodes as well
as the nucleus1
solver.

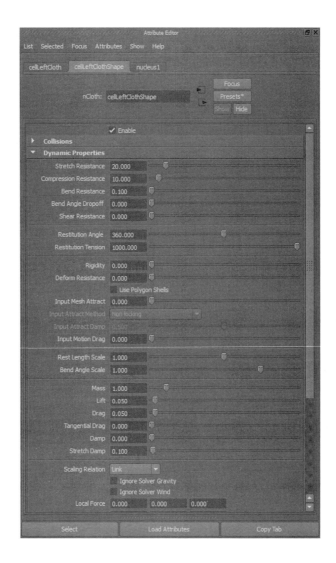

8. Choose the cellLeftClothShape tab. Under the Dynamic Properties section, change Input Motion Drag to **1.0**.

Input Motion Drag controls how much the nCloth object follows its input mesh. Increasing it to 1.0 causes the simulated motion of the nCloth hemisphere to be blended with its stationary input mesh. By default, the input mesh or, in this case, the cellLeftShape node, is set to Intermediate Object under its Object Display settings. You can toggle its visibility by unchecking Intermediate Object or by choosing nMesh ➤ Display Input Mesh.

9. Choose the cellRightClothShape tab. Change its Input Motion Drag to **1.0** as well.

When you rewind and play the scene, the cells slowly descend under the influence of gravity and their input meshes.

Applying nCloth Presets

The concept behind this particular example is that both halves of the cell together form a single circular spherical shape. To make the cells separate, you'll adjust the nDynamic settings so that each half of the cell inflates and pushes against the other half, moving them in opposite directions. Creating the correct settings to achieve this action can be daunting simply because there is a bewildering array of available settings on each nCloth shape node. To help you get started, Maya includes a number of presets that can act as templates. You can apply a preset to the nCloth objects and then adjust a few settings until you get the effect you want.

MAYA PRESETS

You can create a preset and save it for any Maya node. For instance, you can change the settings on the nucleus1 node to simulate dynamic interactions on the moon and then save those settings as a preset named **moonGravity**. This preset will be available for any Maya session. Some nodes, such as nCloth and fur nodes, have presets already built in when you start Maya. These presets are created by Autodesk and other Maya users and can be shared between users. You'll often find new presets available on the Autodesk Area website (http://area.autodesk.com).

To apply a preset to more than one object, select all the objects, select the preset from the list, and choose Replace All Selected.

---

1. Continue with the scene from the previous section.

2. Select the cellLeftCloth node, and open the Attribute Editor to the cellLeftClothShape node.

3. At the top of the editor, click and hold the Presets button in the upper right. The asterisk by the button label means that there are saved presets available for use.

4. From the list of presets, scroll down to find the waterBalloon preset. A small pop-up appears; from this pop-up, choose Replace (see Figure 13.4). You'll see the settings in the Attribute Editor change, indicating the preset has been loaded.

5. Repeat steps 2 through 4 for the cellRightCloth node.

6. Rewind and play the animation. Immediately, you have a decent cell division.

OVERLAPPING nCLOTH OBJECTS

Initially it might seem like a good idea to have two overlapping nCloth objects that push out from the center. However, if the geometry of the two nCloth objects overlaps, it can confuse the Nucleus solver and make it harder to achieve a predictable result.

FIGURE 13.4
Using a preset selected from the Presets list is a quick way to start a custom nCloth material.

The next task is to create a more realistic behavior by adjusting the setting on the nCloth objects:

1. Switch to the nucleus1 tab, and set Air Density to **35** (see Figure 13.5). This makes the cells look like they are in a thick medium, such as water.

FIGURE 13.5
Increasing the Air Density setting on the nucleus1 tab makes it appear as though the cells are in a thick medium.

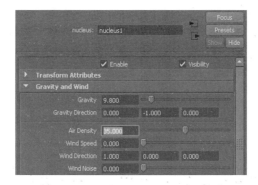

2. You can blend settings from other presets together to create your own unique look. Select cellLeftCloth and, in its shape node tab, click and hold the Presets button in the upper right.

3. Choose Honey ➤ Blend 10%. Do the same for the cellRightCloth.

4. Play the animation. The two cells separate more slowly.

5. You can save these settings as your own preset so that it will be available in other Maya sessions. From the Presets menu, choose Save nCloth Preset. In the dialog box, name the preset **cell**.

6. Save the scene as `cellDivide_v02.ma`.

SAVING MAYA PRESETS

When you save a Maya preset, it is stored in the subfolder `maya\2015\presets\attrPresets`. Your custom nCloth presets will appear in the nCloth subfolder as a MEL script file. You can save to this folder nCloth presets created by other users, and they will appear in the Presets list. If you save a preset using the same name as an existing preset, Maya will ask you if you want to overwrite the existing preset.

Making Surfaces Sticky

At this point, you can start to adjust some of the settings on the nCloth tabs to create a more interesting effect. To make the cells stick together as they divide, you can increase the Stickiness attribute:

1. Continue with the scene from the previous section, or open the `cellDivide_v02.ma` scene from the `chapter13\scenes` folder at the book's web page.

2. Select the cellLeftCloth node, and open the Attribute Editor to its shape node tab.

3. Expand the Collisions rollout, and set Stickiness to **1** (see Figure 13.6). Do the same for the cellRight object.

FIGURE 13.6
Increase the Stickiness attribute in the cellLeft-ClothShape tab of the Attribute Editor.

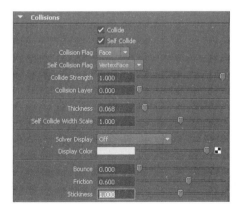

Notice that many of the settings in the Collision rollout are the same as the nParticle Collision settings. For a more detailed discussion of how nucleus collisions work, consult Chapter 12.

4. Play the animation; the cells remain stuck as they inflate. By adjusting the strength of the Stickiness attribute, you can tune the effect so that the cells eventually come apart. Shift+click both the cellLeftCloth and cellRightCloth nodes in the Outliner. Open the Channel Box, and, with both nodes selected, set Stickiness to **0.4**.

EDIT MULTIPLE OBJECTS USING THE CHANNEL BOX

By using the Channel Box, you can set the value for the same attribute on multiple objects at the same time. This can't be done using the Attribute Editor.

---

5. We will manually move the right cell away from the left cell to get them to separate. To do so, it is best to turn off the Nucleus solver to prevent it from solving. Select nucleus1, and open its Attribute Editor.

6. Deselect Enable, effectively stopping the cells from being simulated.

7. Select cellRight, and keyframe its position at frame 10 for its translation and rotation.

8. Move to frame 100 on the timeline, and change the following attributes:

Translate Y: **7.0**

Translate Z: **-8.0**

Rotate X: **-50**

You will not see the geometry move unless you display the cell's input mesh.

9. Return to frame 1, and enable the Nucleus solver. Play the simulation to see the results (see Figure 13.7).

FIGURE 13.7
The stickiness tries to keep the cells together as they move away from one another.

10. Save the nCloth settings as **stickyCell**. Save the scene as `cellDivide_v03.ma`.

CREATE PLAYBLASTS OFTEN

It's difficult to gauge how the dynamics in the scene work using just the playback in Maya. You may want to create a playblast of the scene after you make adjustments to the dynamics so that you can see the effectiveness of your changes. For more information on creating playblasts, consult Chapter 6, "Animation Techniques."

Creating nConstraints

nConstraints can be used to attach nCloth objects together. The constraints themselves can be broken depending on how much force is applied. In this example, nConstraints will be used as an alternative technique to the Stickiness attribute. There are some unique properties of nConstraints that can allow for more creativity in this effect.

1. Open the `cellDivide_v03.ma` scene from the `chapter13\scenes` folder at the book's web page.

2. Switch to the side view. In the Outliner, Shift+click the cellLeft and cellRight polygon nodes. Set the selection mode to Component. By default, the vertices on both objects should appear.

3. Drag a selection down the middle of the two objects so that the vertices along the center line are selected (see Figure 13.8).

FIGURE 13.8
Create nConstraints between the vertices along the flattened side of each cell.

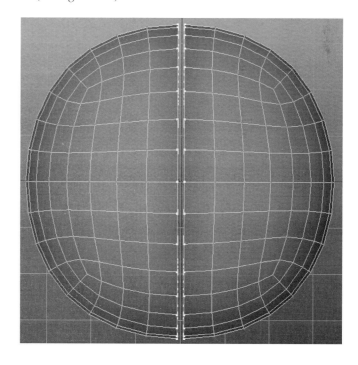

4. In the nDynamics menu, choose nConstraint ➤ Component To Component. Doing so creates a series of springs that connect the two objects.

5. Rewind and play the scene. The two sides of the cell are stuck together.

6. In the Outliner, a new node named dynamicConstraint1 has been created. Select this node, and open the Attribute Editor.

TRANSFORM CONSTRAINTS

A transform node can be created between nCloth objects and the transform node of a piece of geometry. You can create the constraint between the vertices and another object, such as a locator. Then you can animate the locator and have it drag the nCloth objects around in the scene by the nConstraint attached to the selected vertices.

A wide variety of settings are available in the Attribute Editor for the dynamicConstraint node; each one is described in detail in the Maya documentation. For the moment, your main concern is adjusting the constraint strength.

7. Strength determines the overall strength of the constraint. Tangent Strength creates a resistance to the tangential motion of the constraint. In this example, you can leave Strength at 20 and set Tangent Strength to **0**.

8. Glue Strength is the setting that determines whether the constraint will break when force is applied. It is calculated in world space based on the size of the objects. A value of 1 means the constraint can't be broken; a value of 0 turns the constraint off altogether. Set this attribute to **0.25**.

9. Glue Strength Scale modifies the Glue Strength based on the world space distance between the constraints. Set this value to **0.6**.

10. Rewind and play the animation. The two sides of the cell start to separate but fail to part completely.

    The Force attribute determines the level of attraction between the constraints. Positive values cause the constraints to repel each other after they break; negative values cause the constraints to attract each other. In this scene, very small values can create a big difference.

11. Set the Force attribute on the dynamic constraint node to **0.01**. Rewind and play the scene.

12. The cells now push each other apart and keep going. To halt their motion after separation, adjust the Dropoff Distance value. Set this to **3**.

13. Adjust the Strength Dropoff curve so that there is a sharp decline to 0 on the right side of the curve. The strength of the force drops to 0 as the distance between the constraints approaches 3 units (see Figure 13.9).

FIGURE 13.9
Add a small value
to the Force attri-
bute, and lower the
Dropoff Distance
to a value of 3.
By adjusting the
Strength Dropoff
ramp, you can fine-
tune the effect.

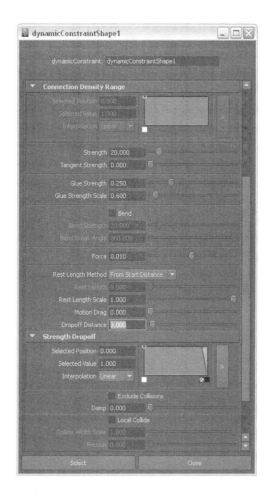

14. You can fine-tune the effect by adding a small amount of motion drag. Set Motion Drag to **0.01**. If the cells can't quite separate, try raising Force by small increments until you get a result you like.

THE CONSTRAINT FORCE ATTRIBUTE

Using the Force attribute, you can make constraints repel each other after they break. This would work well for a situation like a shirt splitting under pressure as buttons fly off. Setting the Force attribute to a small negative value causes the constraints to attract each other. This works well for gelatinous or gooey substances that re-form after being sliced by a passive collision object.

Working with nDynamics becomes an experimental process much like cooking; you adjust the sliders and season to taste until the effect looks like what you want. Since many of the attributes are interconnected, it's best to adjust one at a time and test as you go. You can move an nCloth object after it has been constrained. However, the results of the simulation might not behave the way you expect. It's best to make sure your nCloth objects and their constraints are positioned where you want them. Avoid setting keyframes on the translation or rotation of the nCloth object.

Rest Length attributes significantly affect how the simulation behaves. *Rest length* refers to the length of each constraint when no tension is applied. (Imagine an unattached spring sitting on a table; its length at rest is its rest length.) If Rest Length Method is set to From Start Distance, then the rest length of each constraint is equal to its length at the first frame of the animation. If this option is set to Constant, the rest length is determined using the Rest Length numeric input.

Rest Length Scale applies a scaling factor to the constraints. If this is set to 1 and Rest Length Method is set to From Start Distance, then the constraints have no initial tension. In other words, at frame 1 the scale is equal to the rest length. Lowering this value increases the tension on the constraint and makes it harder to break.

1. Rewind the animation, and set Rest Length Scale to **0.5**.

2. Play the animation to frame 40, and set a keyframe on Rest Length Scale.

3. Play the animation to 50, and set Rest Length Scale to **1**.

4. Set another keyframe. Rewind and play the animation. This is one way in which you can control the timing of the cell division. You can also control this attribute using an expression or Set Driven Key. The cells may not separate completely at this point—that's okay, because in the next section you'll add pressure to complete the division effect.

5. Save the scene as **cellDivide_v04.ma**.

REST LENGTH SCALE

The nCloth nodes also have a Rest Length Scale attribute that you can adjust to alter the behavior of the cells. The stickyCell preset created by blending the waterBalloon and Honey presets has a Rest Length Scale of 0.73. Lowering this value causes the cells to push against each other with more force. Setting this value to 1 reduces the tension, making the cells more relaxed and less likely to divide.

To see a version of the scene up to this point, open the cellDivide_v04.ma scene from the chapter13\scenes folder at the book's web page.

 **Real World Scenario**

CONNECTING NCLOTH OBJECTS TO DYNAMIC CURVES

In a scientific animation created for Harvard Medical School, a contributor to a previous edition of this book attached a chromosome made of an nCloth object to a spindle fiber created from a dynamic curve. The technique he used involved these steps:

1. Create a standard CV curve. This will be used to drag the nCloth chromosome around the scene.

2. Select the curve, and switch to the Dynamics menu.

3. Choose Hair ➤ Make Selected Curves Dynamic. When you convert a curve to a dynamic curve, a duplicate of the original curve is created. This curve is contained within a group named hairSystem1OutputCurves. Dynamic curves are discussed in detail in Chapter 15, "Maya Fluids."

4. Attach a locator to the output curve of the hair system using a motion path.

5. In the options for the motion path, set Time Range to Start.

6. Delete the keyframes on the motion path's U Value, and set the U Value so that the locator is at one end of the curve. This way, the locator is attached to the curve.

7. Use a transform nConstraint to attach the vertices at the center of the nCloth chromosome (known in biology circles as the *centromere* of the chromosome) to the locator.

Once this setup is complete, you can use the hair curve to drag the nCloth object all over the scene.

Making nCloth Objects Expand Using Pressure

Using pressure, you can inflate a piece of geometry like a balloon or, in the case of this example, make it appear as though the geometry is filled with fluid.

There are two ways to calculate pressure:

Manual Pressure Setting Manual Pressure Setting is simple—the Pressure slider and Pressure Damping slider are the only two controls (see Figure 13.10). These can be keyframed to make it appear as though the nCloth object is being filled with air. If you set Pressure to 0 and create a keyframe, and then play the animation to frame 100, set Pressure to 1, and set another keyframe, the nCloth object will grow in size over those frames as if it were being inflated.

FIGURE 13.10
Manual Pressure Setting has simple controls for adding internal pressure to nCloth objects.

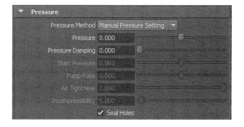

Volume Tracking Model Volume Tracking Model, which is used by the waterBalloon preset originally applied to the cell geometry, is a more accurate method for calculating volume and has more controls (see Figure 13.11).

When Volume Tracking Model is selected as the pressure method, you have access to additional controls, such as Pump Rate, Air Tightness, and Incompressibility. The Pump Rate value determines the rate at which air is added within the volume. Positive values continue to pump air into the volume; negative values suck the air out. The Start Pressure value sets the initial pressure of the air inside the volume at the start of the animation.

FIGURE 13.11
Volume Tracking
Model has more
controls and
produces a more
accurate internal
pressure simulation
for nCloth objects.

The Air Tightness value determines the permeability of the nCloth object. Lower settings allow the air to escape the volume. The Incompressibility setting refers to the air within the volume. A lower value means the air is more compressible, which slows down the inflation effect of the cell. Activating Seal Holes causes the solver to ignore openings in the geometry.

As you may have noticed, after the cells divide in the example scene, they don't quite return to the size of the original dividing cell. You can use the Pump Rate attribute to inflate the cells:

1. Continue with the scene from the previous section, or open the `cellDivide_v04.ma` scene from the `chapter13\scenes` folder at the book's web page.

2. Select the cellLeftCloth shape, and open its Attribute Editor.

3. Expand the Pressure settings. Note that Pressure Method is already set to Volume Tracking Model. These settings were determined by the waterBalloon preset originally used to create the effect.

4. Set Pump Rate to **50** for each cell, and play the animation (see Figure 13.12). Each cell starts to grow immediately and continues to grow after the cell divides.

FIGURE 13.12
Setting Pump
Rate to 50 on the
cellLeftCloth object
causes it to grow as
it separates from
the right side.

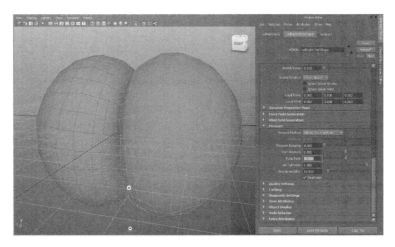

5. Try setting keyframes on the start Pump Rate of both cells so that at frame 15 Pump Rate is **0**, at frame 50 it's **50**, and at frame 100 it's **0**.

6. To give an additional kick at the start of the animation, set Start Pressure to **0.25**.

CONNECT ATTRIBUTES USING THE CONNECTION EDITOR

You can save some time by using the Connection Editor to connect the Pressure attributes of one of the cells to the same attributes of the other. This way, you only need to keyframe the attributes of the first cell. For more information on using the Connection Editor, consult Chapter 1, "Working in Autodesk Maya."

Additional Techniques

To finish the animation, here are additional techniques you can use to add some style to the behavior of the cells:

1. In the Collisions rollout, increase the Stickiness attribute of each cell to a value of **0.5**. You can also try painting a Stickiness texture map. To do so, select the cells and choose nMesh ➤ Paint Texture Properties ➤ Stickiness. This activates the Artisan Brush, which allows you to paint specific areas of stickiness on the cell surface. (Refer to Chapter 12 to see how a similar technique is used to paint the strength of a force field on geometry.)

2. If you want the objects to start out solid and become soft at a certain point in time, set keyframes on each cell's Input Mesh Attract attribute. The input mesh is the original geometry that was converted into the nCloth object. Setting the Input Mesh Attract attribute to 1 or higher causes the nCloth objects to assume the shape of the original geometry. As this value is lowered, the influence of the nucleus dynamics increases, causing the objects to become soft.

To see a finished version of the scene, open the `cellDivide_v05.ma` scene from the `chapter13\scenes` folder at the book's web page.

COMBINE TECHNIQUES

In practice, you'll most likely find that the best solution when creating a complex effect is to combine techniques as much as possible. Use Dynamic Fields, Force, Wind, nConstraints, Air Density, Stickiness, and Pressure together to make a spectacular nCloth effect.

Creating an nCache

At this point, you'll want to cache the dynamics so that playback speed is improved and the motion of the cells is the same every time you play the animation. Doing so also ensures that when you render the scene, the dynamics are consistent when using multiple processors.

DISTRIBUTED SIMULATION

You can use the power of multiple computers to cache your simulations if you are using the Maya Entertainment Creation Suite. Backburner™, which is part of the suite, must be installed and turned on. The distSim.py plug-in must also be loaded. You can then choose nCache ➤ Send To Server Farm from the nDynamics menu. Distributed simulation allows you to create variants of a single simulation and monitor its progress.

---

1. Shift+click the cellLeft and cellRight objects in the Outliner.

2. Choose nCache ➤ Create New Cache ➤ Options.

   In the options, you can specify where the cache will be placed. By default, the cache is created in a subfolder of the current project's Data folder. If the scene is going to be rendered on a network, make sure that the cache is in a subfolder that can be accessed by all the computers on the network.

   In the options, you can specify whether you want to create a separate cache file for each frame or a single cache file. You can also create a separate cache for each geometry object; this is not always necessary when you have more than one nCloth object in a scene (see Figure 13.13). However, caching objects individually is preferred when dealing with complex simulations. Having individual caches enables you to make isolated adjustments.

FIGURE 13.13
The options for creating an nCache

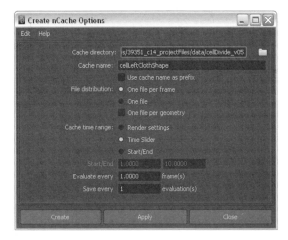

3. The default settings should work well for this scene. Click the Create button to create the cache. Maya will play through the scene.

   After the nCache has been created, it is important that you disable the nCloth objects so that Maya does not calculate dynamics for objects that are cached. This is especially important for large scenes with complex nDynamics.

4. In the Attribute Editor for cellLeftClothShape, scroll to the top, and uncheck the Enable box to disable the nCloth calculation. Do the same for cellRightClothShape.

DELETE NCACHE BEFORE MAKING CHANGES

When the cache is complete, the scene will play much faster. If you make changes to the nCloth settings, you won't see the changes reflected in the animation until you delete or disable the nCache (nCache ➤ Delete nCache). Even though the geometry is using a cache, you should not delete the nCloth nodes. This would disable the animation.

---

5. You can select the cellLeft and cellRight objects and move them so that they overlap at the center at the start of the scene. This removes the seam in the middle and makes it look as though there is a single object dividing into two copies.

6. You can also select the cellLeft and cellRight objects and smooth them using Polygon ➤ Mesh ➤ Smooth, or you can simply select the nCloth object and activate Smooth Mesh Preview by pressing the **3** key on the keyboard.

CACHEABLE ATTRIBUTES

The specific attributes that are included in the nCache are set using the Cacheable Attributes menu in the Caching rollout found in the Attribute Editor for each nCloth object. You can use this menu to cache just the position or the position and velocity of each vertex from frame to frame. You also have the choice to cache the dynamic state of the nCloth object from frame to frame.

Caching the dynamic state means that the internal dynamic properties of the nCloth object are stored in the cache along with the position and velocity of each vertex. This means that if you decide to add more frames to the cache using the Append To Cache option in the nCache menu, you're more likely to get an accurate simulation. This is because Maya will have more information about what's going on inside the nCloth object (things such as pressure, collision settings, and so on) and will do a better job picking up from where the original cache left off. This does mean that Maya will require more space on your hard drive to store this extra information.

Creating nCloth and nParticle Interactions

Creating dynamic interaction between nParticles and nCloth objects is quite easy because both systems can share the same Nucleus solver. Effects that were extremely difficult to create in previous versions of Maya are now simple to create, thanks to the collision properties of nDynamics. Before continuing with this section, review Chapter 12 so that you understand the basics of working with nParticles.

In this section, you'll see how you can use nParticles to affect the behavior of nCloth objects. nCloth objects can be used to attract nParticles, nParticles can fill nCloth objects and cause them to tear open, and many interesting effects can be created by using nParticles and nCloth objects together.

Creating an nParticle Goal

Goal objects attract nParticles like a magnet. A goal can be a locator, a piece of geometry (including nCloth), or even another nParticle. In Chapter 12, you worked with force fields, which are similar to goals in some respects, in that they attract nParticles dynamically. Deciding whether you need to use a goal or a force field generated by an nDynamic object (or a combination of the two) depends on the effect you want to create and usually involves some experimentation. This section will demonstrate some uses of goal objects with some simple examples.

1. Create a new, empty scene in Maya.

2. Create a locator (Create ➤ Locator).

3. Switch to the nDynamics menu, and choose nParticles ➤ Create nParticles ➤ Balls to set the nParticle style to Balls.

4. Choose nParticles ➤ Create nParticles ➤ Create Emitter. By default, an omni emitter is created at the center of the scene.

5. Use the Move tool to position the emitter away from the locator (set Translate X, Y, and Z to **20**).

6. Set the length of the timeline to **300**.

7. Play the animation. Balls are emitted and fall through space because of the Gravity settings on the nucleus node.

8. Select the nParticle object, and Ctrl/Command+click locator1. Choose nParticles ➤ Goal ➤ Options.

9. In the options, set Goal Weight to **1** (see Figure 13.14).

FIGURE 13.14
Convert the locator into a goal for the nParticles.

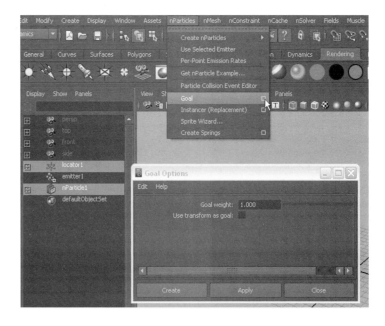

10. Rewind and play the scene.

The nParticles appear on the locator and bunch up over time. Since Goal Weight is set to 1, the goal is at maximum strength, and the nParticles move so quickly between the emitter and the goal object that they cannot be seen until they land on the goal. Since the Balls-style nParticles have Collision on by default, they stack up as they land on the goal.

11. Select the nParticle object. In the Channel Box, set Goal Weight to **0.25**. Play the animation. You can see the nParticles drawn toward the locator. They move past the goal and then move back toward it, where they bunch up and start to collide, creating a swarm (see Figure 13.15).

FIGURE 13.15
Lower the Goal Weight for the nParticle in the Channel Box, causing the nParticles to swarm around the locator.

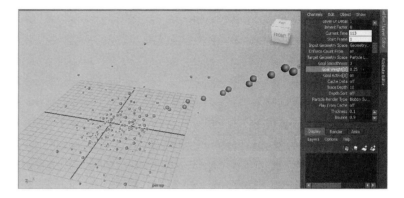

12. Create a second locator. Position locator2 10 units above locator1.

13. Select the nParticle and Ctrl/Command+click locator2. Make it a goal with a weight of **0.25** as well.

14. Play the scene. The nParticles swarm between the two goals.

MULTIPLE GOALS

As goals are added to an nParticle, they are numbered according to the order in which they are added. The numbering starts at 0, so the first goal is referred to as Goal Weight[0], the second goal is referred to as Goal Weight[1], and so on. It's a little confusing; sometimes it's best to name the goal objects themselves using the same numbering convention. Name the first goal locator **locatorGoal0**, and name the second **locatorGoal1**. When adding expressions or when creating MEL scripts, this technique will help you keep everything clear.

---

15. Select one of the locators, and choose nSolver ➤ Interactive Playback. You can move the locator in the scene while it's playing and watch the nParticles follow. They are always drawn to the midpoint between the two goals (see Figure 13.16).

FIGURE 13.16
Using Interactive
Playback, you can
move the goals
around and watch
the nParticles
follow.

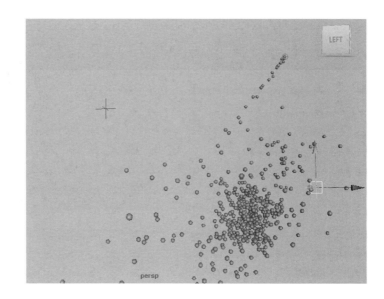

16. Open the Attribute Editor for the nParticle, and switch to the nParticleShape1 tab. Try lowering the Conserve value on the nParticles. This causes the nParticles to lose energy as they fly through the scene.

17. Try these settings:

    Conserve: **0.98**

    Drag: **0.05**

    Wind Speed on the Nucleus tab: **8**

    Wind Noise: **25**

    You can edit these settings in the Attribute Editor or in the Channel Box for the nParticle-Shape1 node. Suddenly a swarm of particles buzzes between the goal. By animating the position of the goals, you control where the swarm goes.

18. Enter the following settings:

    Point Force Field on the nParticle node: World Space

    Self Attract: **-10**

    Point Field Distance: **10**

    Now the motion of the nParticles is controlled by the goals, gravity, wind, wind noise, and a force field generated by the nParticles themselves. You can quickly create complex behavior without the need for a single expression (see Figure 13.17).

FIGURE 13.17
FIGURE 13.17
Combining goals,
forces, dynamic
attributes, and
wind noise creates
some complex
nParticle behaviors.

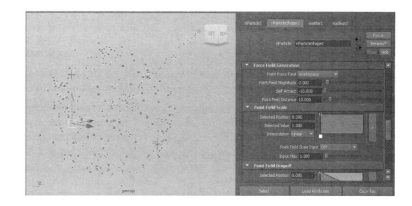

To see an example version of this scene, open the `swarm.ma` file from the `chapter13\scenes` folder at the book's web page. To see another example of the use of goals, open the `nClothGoal.ma` scene from the same location.

Controlling Collision Events

Using the Collision Event Editor, you can specify what happens when a collision between an nParticle and a goal object occurs.

1. Open the `nClothGoal.ma` scene from the `chapter13\scenes` folder.

2. Select the nParticle, and choose nParticles ➤ Particle Collision Event Editor.

3. In the Editor window, select the nParticle. Leave the All Collisions check box selected.

4. Set Event Type to Emit.

SPLIT VS. EMIT

The difference between Emit and Split is fairly subtle, but when Emit is selected, new particles are emitted from the point of collision, and you can specify that the original colliding nParticle dies. When you choose Split, the option for killing the original nParticle is unavailable.

---

5. Enter the following settings:

Num Particles: **5**

Spread: **0.5**

Inherit Velocity: **0.5**

Select the Original Particle Dies option. Click Create Event to create the event (see Figure 13.18).

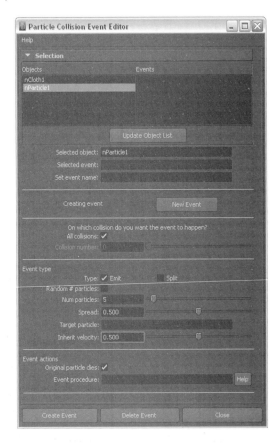

Note that the collision event will create a new nParticle object.

6. Rewind and play the scene.

It may be difficult to distinguish the new nParticles that are created by the collision event from the original colliding nParticles. To fix this, continue with these steps:

7. Select nParticle2 in the Outliner, and open its Attribute Editor.

8. In the Particle Size rollout, set Radius to **0.05**.

9. In the Shading rollout, set Color Ramp to a solid yellow.

10. Rewind and play the scene.

Each time an nParticle hits the nCloth object, it dies and emits three new nParticles. The nParticle2 node in the Outliner controls the behavior of and settings for the new nParticles. To see an example of this scene, open the collisionEvents.ma scene from the chapter13\scenes folder at the book's web page.

Bursting an Object Open Using Tearable nConstraints

This short example demonstrates how to create a bursting surface using nParticles and an nCloth surface:

1. In a new Maya scene, create a polygon cube at the center of the grid. The cube should have one subdivision in width, height, and depth.

2. Scale the cube up 8 units in each axis.

3. Select the cube, switch to the Polygon menu, and choose Mesh ➢ Smooth.

4. In the Channel Box, select the polySmoothFace1 node, and set Divisions to **3**.

5. Select the cube, and switch to the nDynamics menu.

6. Choose nMesh ➢ Create nCloth to make the object an nCloth.

7. Open the Attribute Editor for the nCloth object, and use the Presets menu to apply the rubberSheet preset to the nCloth object.

8. Switch to the nucleus1 tab, and set Gravity to **0**.

9. Choose nParticles ➢ Create nParticles ➢ Balls to set the nParticle style to Balls.

10. Choose nParticles ➢ Create nParticles ➢ Create Emitter to create a new emitter. By default, the emitter is placed at the origin inside the nCloth object.

11. Select the nParticles; in the Attribute Editor for the nParticleShape1 tab, expand the Particle Size rollout and set Radius to **0.5**.

12. Set the length of the timeline to **800**.

13. Rewind and play the animation. The nParticles start to fill up the surface, causing it to expand (see Figure 13.19). If some nParticles are passing through the surface, switch to the Nucleus solver and raise the Substeps value to **8**.

FIGURE 13.19
Placing the emitter inside the nCloth object causes it to fill with nParticles.

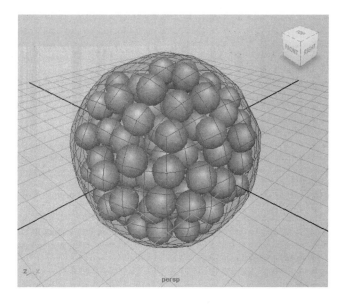

14. Create a new shader, and apply it to the nCloth object.

15. Set the transparency of the shader to a light gray so that you can see the nParticles inside the nCloth object.

16. Select the pCube1 object in the Outliner.

17. Choose nConstraint ➤ Tearable Surface. This applies a new nConstraint to the surface.

18. If you play the scene, you'll see the surface burst open (see Figure 13.20). Open the Attribute Editor for the nDynamic constraint. Set Glue Strength to **0.3** and Glue Strength Scale to **0.8**; this will make the nConstraint more difficult to tear, so the bursting will not occur until around frame 500.

FIGURE 13.20
Adding a Tearable Surface nConstraint allows the surface to rip when a certain amount of force is applied.

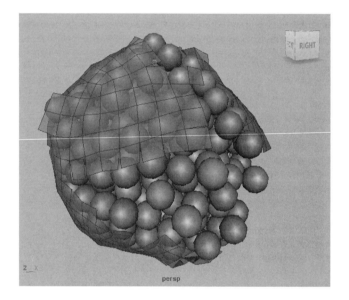

To see two examples of Tearable Surface nConstraints, open burst.ma and burst2.ma from the chapter13\scenes folder at the book's web page.

DESIGNING TEARING SURFACES

You can specify exactly where you'd like the tearing to occur on a surface by selecting specific vertices before applying the Tearable Surface nConstraint.

Rigid Body Dynamics

Rigid body dynamics are the interactions of hard surfaces, such as the balls on a pool table, collapsing buildings, and links in a chain. The rigid body dynamic system in Maya has been part of the software since long before the introduction of nDynamics. In this section, you'll learn how to set up a rigid body simulation and see how it can be used with nParticles to create the effect of a small tower exploding.

Creating an Exploding Tower

The example scene has a small tower of bricks on a hill. You'll use a rigid body simulation to make the bricks of the tower explode outward on one side. Later, you'll add nParticles to the simulation to create an explosion.

The scene is designed so that only one side of the tower will explode. Only a few stone bricks will be pushed out from the explosion; these bricks have been placed in the active group. The bricks in the passive group will be converted to passive colliders; they won't move, but they will support the active brick. The bricks in the static group will be left alone. Since they won't participate in the explosion, they won't be active or passive, just plain geometry. This will increase the efficiency and the performance of the scene.

1. Open the `tower_v01.ma` scene in the `chapter13\scenes` folder, expand the active group that's inside the tower node, and select all the brick nodes in this group.

2. Switch to the Dynamics menu (not the nDynamics menu), and choose Soft/Rigid Bodies ➢ Create Active Rigid Body.

3. Expand the passive group, Shift+click all the bricks in this group, and choose Soft/Rigid Bodies ➢ Create Passive Rigid Body.

4. Select the ground, and choose Soft/Rigid Bodies ➢ Create Passive Rigid Body.

   By default, there is no gravity attached to the active rigid bodies; to add gravity, you need to create a gravity field.

5. Shift+click all the members of the active group, and choose Fields ➢ Gravity.

   If you play the scene, you'll see the active bricks sag slightly. You actually don't want them to move until the explosion occurs. To fix this, you can keyframe their dynamic state.

6. To animate their dynamic state, rewind the scene, Shift+click the members of the active group, and set the Active attribute in the Channel Box to Off (see Figure 13.21).

FIGURE 13.21
You can keyframe the Active state of the rigid bodies.

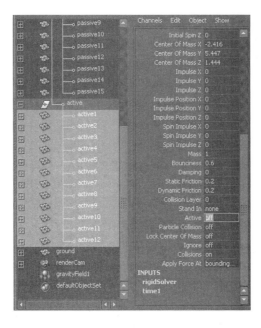

7. Move the Time Slider to frame 19, right-click the Active channel, and choose Key Selected from the pop-up context menu.

8. Move the timeline to frame 20, set Active to On, and set another keyframe.

CERT OBJECTIVE

9. To make the bricks explode, select the members of the active group, and add a radial field.

10. Position the radial field behind the active bricks, and enter the following settings:

    Magnitude: **400**

    Attenuation: **0.5**

    Max Distance: **5**

11. Select the active bricks, and set their Mass value to **20** (see Figure 13.22).

When you play the scene, the bricks fly out at frame 20.

INTERPENETRATION ERRORS

Interpenetration errors occur when two pieces of geometry pass through each other in such a way as to confuse Maya. Only one side of the surface is actually used in the calculation based on the direction of the surface normals—there are no double-sided rigid bodies. The surface of two colliding rigid bodies (active + active or active + passive) need to have their normals pointing at each other to calculate correctly.

To fix these errors, you can increase the Tessellation Factor value in the Performance Attributes rollout of each of the rigid body objects.

Also, you will notice that the bricks in the tower aren't touching. When you model objects for a rigid body simulation, you'll want to make sure that they all have some "breathing room" at the start so that the slightest movement won't accidentally cause interpenetration.

FIGURE 13.22
Increase the Mass value of the rigid bodies to make the bricks appear heavier.

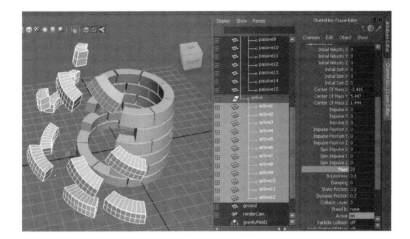

Tuning the Rigid Body Simulation

You can tune the simulation by editing the settings on the active rigid bodies. The easiest way to do this for multiple objects is to select them all in the Outliner and then edit the settings in the Channel Box. For this example, you can decrease the amount of bouncing and sliding in the motion of the bricks by adjusting the bounciness and friction settings. There are two kinds of friction:

Static Friction Static Friction sets the level of resistance for a resting dynamic object against another dynamic object. In other words, if an object is stationary, this setting determines how much it resists starting to move once a force is applied.

Dynamic Friction Dynamic Friction sets how much a moving dynamic object resists another dynamic object, such as a book sliding across a table.

Other settings to note include Damping and Collision Layer. Damping slows down the movement of the dynamic objects. If the simulation takes place under water, you can raise this setting to make it look as though the objects are being slowed down by the density of the environment. Collision Layer specifies which objects collide with other objects. By default, all rigid bodies are on collision layer 0. However, if you set just the active bricks to collision layer 1, they react only with each other and not the ground or the passive bricks, which would still be on collision layer 0. The following steps take you through the process.

1. Select the ground plane, and set both the Static and Dynamic Friction attributes in the Channel Box to **1**.

2. Shift+click the active bricks and, in the Channel Box, set Dynamic Friction to **0.5**. Lower Bounciness to **0.1**.

RIGID BODY SOLVING METHODS

Rigid bodies use the Rigid Solver node to calculate the dynamics. This node appears as a tab in the Attribute Editor when you select one of the rigid body objects, such as the bricks in the active group. The rigid solver uses one of three methods to calculate the dynamics: Mid-Point, Runge Kutta, and Runge Kutta Adaptive. Mid-Point is the fastest but least accurate, Runge Kutta is more accurate and slower, and Runge Kutta Adaptive is the most accurate and slowest method. In most cases, you can leave the setting on Runge Kutta Adaptive.

---

3. Save the scene as **`rigidBodyTower_v01.ma`**.

To see a version of the scene up to this point, open `rigidBodyTower_v01.ma` from the `chapter13\scenes` folder.

COMMON RIGID BODY PITFALLS

Moving objects with dynamics is very different than working with keyframed movement. For instance, you'll notice that you can't scrub through the timeline and see the motion properly update. This is because for the solver to function properly, it needs to calculate every frame and it can't be rushed through the process. Because of this, you'll want to make sure that you always have the playback speed of your scene set to Play Every Frame (right-click the timeline, and select Playback Speed ➤ Play Every Frame, Max Real-Time).

In addition, you need to be careful when you group active rigid bodies. It makes sense at times to organize rigid bodies into groups, such as grouping the active body bricks in the tower. However, be careful not to transform these groups since the solver will become confused when it tries to move dynamic objects that have been scaled or moved around by a parent group.

Baking the Simulation

It's common practice to bake the motion of traditional rigid bodies into keyframes once you're satisfied that the simulation is working the way you want. This improves the performance of the scene and allows you to adjust parts of the animation by tweaking the keyframes on the Graph Editor.

1. In the Outliner, Shift+click the active bricks and choose Edit ➤ Keys ➤ Bake Simulation ➤ Options.

2. In the Channel Box, Shift+click the Translate and Rotate channels.

3. In the Bake Simulation Options section, set Time Range to Time Slider.

4. Set the Channels option to From Channel Box. Keyframes are created for just the channels currently selected in the Channel Box. This eliminates the creation of extra, unnecessary keys.

5. Turn on Smart Bake. This setting tells Maya to create keyframes only where the animation requires it instead of creating a keyframe on every frame of the animation.

The Increase Fidelity option improves the accuracy of the smart bake. Fidelity Keys Tolerance specifies the baking tolerance in terms of a percentage. Higher percentages produce fewer keyframes but also allow for more deviation from the original simulation.

Other important options include the following:

Keep Unbaked Keys   Keeps any key outside the baked range.

Sparse Curve Bake   Keeps the shape of connected animation curves when baking. Since the bricks are using dynamics, this option does not apply.

Disable Implicit Control   This option is useful when the object's animation is being driven by Inverse Kinematic handles and other controls. This is not applicable when baking rigid body dynamics.

6. Select Increase Fidelity, and set Fidelity Keys Tolerance to **1** percent (see Figure 13.23).

FIGURE 13.23
The options for baking keyframes

7. Click the Bake button to bake the simulation into keyframes. The animation will play through as the keys are baked.

8. When the animation is finished, select Edit ➢ Delete All By Type ➢ Rigid Bodies to remove the rigid body nodes.

9. Select the active bricks, and open the Graph Editor (Window ➢ Animation Editors ➢ Graph Editor) to see the baked animation curves for the bricks (see Figure 13.24).

FIGURE 13.24
The Graph Editor shows the animation curves for the baked simulation of the active bricks.

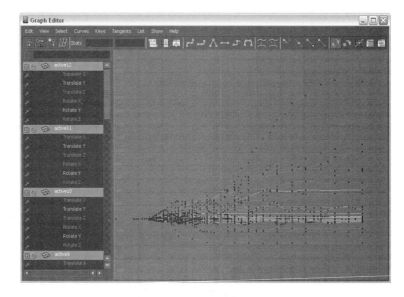

10. If any of the bricks continue to wobble after landing on the ground, you can edit their motion on the Graph Editor by deleting the "wobbly" keyframes.

11. Save the scene as `rigidBodyTower_v02.ma`.

To see an example of the scene that uses traditional rigid bodies, open the `rigidBodyTower_v02.ma` scene from the `chapter13\scenes` folder at the book's web page.

DUPLICATING TRADITIONAL RIGID BODIES

When duplicating rigid bodies that have fields connected, do not use Duplicate Special ➢ Duplicate Input Connections or Duplicate Input Graph. These options do not work well with rigid bodies. Instead, duplicate the object, convert it to an active rigid body, and then use the Relationship Editor to make the connection between the rigid bodies and the fields.

Crumbling Tower

nCloth objects can also be made into rigid objects. The advantage of doing this is that it allows you to make the nCloth objects semi-rigid. In addition, the setup can be easier. Maya 2013 added the ability to simulate polygon shells—combined geometry made into a single node—as if they were separate objects. The next project takes you through the steps.

1. Open the `tower_v01.ma` scene in the `chapter13\scenes` folder.

2. Select a few well-chosen bricks from the tower and delete them (see Figure 13.25).

3. Select the tower node, and choose Mesh ➤ Combine from the Polygons menu set.

4. Delete the history, and rename the combined node back to **tower**.

5. Switch to the nDynamics menu, and choose nMesh ➤ Create nCloth.

6. Open nCloth1's Attribute Editor.

7. Under Dynamic Properties, set Rigidity to **10.0** and check Use Polygon Shells (see Figure 13.26).

8. Under the Collisions section, change Self Collision Flag to VertexEdge.

9. Select ground.

10. Choose nMesh Create Passive Collider.

11. Play the simulation, and watch the tower crumble (see Figure 13.27).

FIGURE 13.27
The tower crumbles.

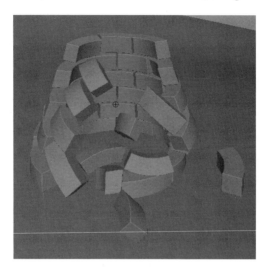

Try modifying the attributes to get the individual bricks to lose their shape as well. *Hint*: Use a low Deform Resistance value instead of Rigidity, and set Restitution Angle to **0.0**.

Soft Body Dynamics

Soft body dynamics assign particles to each vertex of a polygon or NURBS object. The particles can be influenced by normal dynamic fields, such as air and gravity, as well as rigid bodies. When influenced, the particles cause the vertices to follow, deforming the geometry.

There are two options for creating a soft body object. The first method is to make the geometry soft, which simply adds particles to every vertex. This allows the geometry to deform freely, never returning to its original shape. The second option is to make a duplicate, with one of the objects becoming a goal for the other. This method allows the geometry to return to its original shape. Using a goal is useful for creating objects that jiggle, like fat or gelatin.

Use the following steps to create and adjust a soft body object:

1. Select a polygon or NURBS object.

2. Choose Soft/Rigid Bodies ➤ Create Soft Body.

3. Set the Creation options to Duplicate and Make Copy Soft, and select Make Non-Soft A Goal. Click Create.

With the soft body selected, you can add any field to influence the particles. Moving the original object will cause the soft body to follow. You can adjust the Goal Smoothness and Goal Weight values on the particle node to alter the soft body's behavior.

Creating Flying Debris Using nParticle Instancing

nParticle instancing attaches one or more specified pieces of geometry to a particle system. The instanced geometry then inherits the motion and much of the behavior of the particle system. For this example, you'll instance debris and shrapnel to a particle system and add it to the current explosion animation. In addition, you'll control how the instance geometry behaves through expressions and fields.

The goal for the exercises in this section is to add bits of flying debris to the explosion that behave realistically. This means that you'll want debris of various sizes flying at different speeds and rotating as the particles move through the air. The first step is to add an nParticle system to the scene that behaves like debris flying through the air.

Adding nParticles to the Scene

The first step in creating the explosion effect is to add nParticles to the scene and make sure that they are interacting with the ground and the bricks of the tower. It's a good idea to be efficient in your approach to doing this so that Maya is not bogged down in unnecessary calculations. To begin, you'll add a volume emitter at the center of the tower.

1. Open the `rigidBodyTower_v02.ma` scene from the `chapter13\scenes` folder. In this scene, the rigid body simulation has been baked into keyframes.

2. Switch to the nDynamics menu, and choose nParticles ➢ Create nParticles ➢ Balls, to set the nParticle style to Balls.

3. Choose nParticles ➢ Create nParticles ➢ Create Emitter ➢ Options.

4. In the options, set Emitter Type to Volume and Rate to **800**.

5. In the Distance/Direction Attributes rollout, set Direction X and Direction Z to **0** and Direction Y to **1** so that the nParticles initially move upward.

6. In the Volume Emitter Attributes rollout, set Volume Shape to Cylinder.

7. In the Volume Speed Attributes rollout, enter the following settings:

   Away From Axis: **1**

   Along Axis: **0.5**

   Random Direction: **1**

   Directional Speed: **4**

8. Click Create to create the emitter (see Figure 13.28).

FIGURE 13.28
The options for the
volume emitter

9. Switch to wireframe mode. Select emitter1 in the Outliner, and use the Move and Scale tools to position the emitter at the center of the stone tower.

10. Set Translate Y to **3.1** and all three Scale channels to **2**.

11. Rewind and play the animation.

   The nParticles start pouring out of the emitter. They pass through the bricks and the ground.

12. Select the ground, and choose nMesh ➤ Create Passive Collider.

13. Shift+click the bricks in the passive group, and convert them to passive colliders; do the same for the bricks in the active group.

   The nParticles still pass through the static bricks at the back of the tower. You can convert the static bricks to passive colliders; however, this adds a large number of new nRigid nodes to the scene, which may slow down the performance of the scene. You can conserve some of the energy Maya spends on collision detection by creating a single, simple collider object to interact with the nParticles that hit the back of the tower. This object can be hidden in the render.

14. Switch to the Polygon menu, and choose Create ➢ Polygon Primitives ➢ Cylinder.

15. Select the nParticle1 node and, in the Attribute Editor for the shape nodes, set Enable to Off to disable the calculations of the nParticle temporarily while you create the collision object.

16. Set the timeline to frame 100 so that you can easily see the opening in the exploded tower.

17. Set the scale and position of the cylinder so that it blocks the nParticles from passing through the back of the tower. Set the following:

Translate Y: **2.639**

Scale X and Scale Z: **2.34**

Scale Y: **3.5**

18. Select the cylinder, and switch to face selection mode; delete the faces on the top and bottom of the cylinder and in the opening of the exploded tower (see Figure 13.29).

FIGURE 13.29
Delete the faces on the top and bottom of the cylinder, as well as the faces near the opening of the exploded tower.

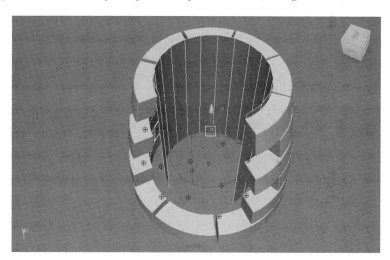

19. Rename the cylinder **collider**. Switch to the nDynamics menu set, and choose nMesh ➢ Create Passive Collider.

20. Select the nParticles, and turn Enable back on.

21. Rewind and play the animation; the nParticles now spill out of the front of the tower once it breaks open (see Figure 13.30).

22. Save the scene as `explodingTower_v01.ma`.

To see a version of the scene up to this point, open the `explodingTower_v01.ma` scene from the `chapter13\scenes` folder at the book's web page.

FIGURE 13.30
With the collision surface in place, the nParticles pour out of the opening in the front of the stone tower.

Sending the Debris Flying Using a Field

So far, the effects look like a popcorn popper gone bad. To make it look as though the nParticles are expelled from the source of the explosion, you can connect the radial field to the nParticle.

1. Continue with the scene from the previous section, or open `explodingTower_v01.ma` from the `chapter13\scenes` folder at the book's web page. Select nParticle1, and rename it **particleDebris**.

2. Open the Attribute Editor for particleDebris. Switch to the nucleus1 tab.

3. In the Time Attributes rollout, set Start Frame to **20** so that the emission of the nParticles is in sync with the exploding brick.

   It's not necessary to have the debris continually spewing from the tower. You need only a certain number of nParticles. You can either set keyframes on the emitter's rate or set a limit to the number of nParticles created by the emitter. The latter method is easier to do and to edit later.

4. In the Attribute Editor for particleDebrisShape, expand the Emission Attributes rollout. Max Count is set to –1 by default, meaning that the emitter can produce an infinite number of nParticles. Set this value to **1200** (see Figure 13.31).

5. After the number of nParticles reaches 1200, the emitter stops creating new nParticles. Select the emitter, and set the rate to **2400**. This means that the emitter will create 1,200 nParticles in half a second, making the explosion faster and more realistic.

FIGURE 13.31
Set Max Count to
1200, limiting the
number of nPar-
ticles created by the
emitter.

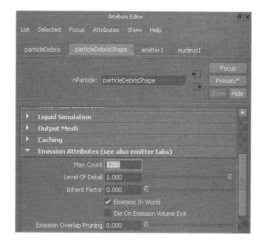

6. You can connect the particleDebris node to the existing radial field that was used to push out the bricks. To connect the radial field to the particleDebris node, select the particle-Debris node and Ctrl/Command+click radialField1 in the Outliner. Choose Fields ➤ Affect Selected Object(s).

7. Rewind and play the animation. Not all the nParticles make it out of the tower; many of the nParticles are pushed down on the ground and toward the back of the collider object. To fix this, reposition the radial field.

8. Set the Translate X of the field to **1.347** and the Translate Y to **0.364** (see Figure 13.32).

9. Save the scene as **explodingTower_v02.ma**.

To see a version of the scene up to this point, open the explodingTower_v02.ma scene from the chapter13\scenes folder at the book's web page.

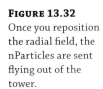

FIGURE 13.32
Once you reposition the radial field, the nParticles are sent flying out of the tower.

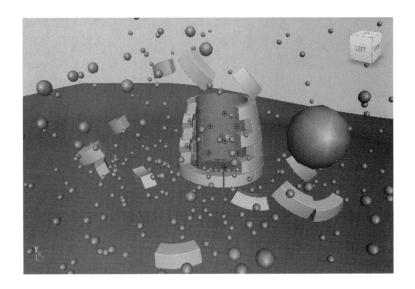

Creating a More Convincing Explosion by Adjusting nParticle Mass

Next, to create a more convincing behavior for the nParticles, you can randomize the mass. This means that there will be random variation in how the nParticles move through the air as they are launched by the radial field.

1. Select the particleDebris node in the Outliner, and open its shape node in the Attribute Editor.

2. Under the Dynamic Properties rollout, you can leave Mass at a value of 1. In the Mass Scale settings, set Mass Scale Input to Randomized ID. This randomizes the mass of each nParticle using its ID number as a seed value to generate the random value.

3. If you play the animation, the mass does not seem all that random. To create a range of values, add a point to the Mass Scale ramp on the right side, and bring it down to a value of **0.1**.

    When Mass Scale Input is set to Randomized ID, you can alter the range of variation by adjusting the Input Max slider. If you think of the Mass Scale ramp as representing possible random ranges, lowering Input Max shrinks the available number of random values to the randomize function, thus forcing the randomizer to have more "contrast" between values. Increasing Input Max makes more data points available to the randomize function, making a smoother variation between random values and producing less contrast (see Figure 13.33).

FIGURE 13.33

Mass Scale sets a range for the mass for each nParticle. The Input Max value is used to add contrast to the values generated by the ramp.

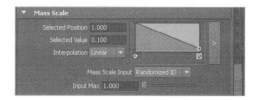

4. Set the Input Max slider to **0.5**.

    The Input Max slider is part of the Mass Scale Input options. The slider is an additional randomization value that is multiplied against the initial mass value. You can further set the Mass Scale Input to read the speed, age, or acceleration of the particle. Or you can use the slider to add some random variation to the mass. You don't need to use this slider if the Mass Scale input is set to Randomized ID, and sometimes it can result in creating random values so close to 0 that the nParticles end up getting stuck in the air.

5. Create a playblast of the scene so that you can see how the simulation is working so far.

    The nParticles are sliding along the ground in a strange way. To make them stop, you can increase the stickiness and friction of the ground.

6. Select the ground geometry, and open its Attribute Editor.

7. Switch to the nRigidShape1 tab. Under the Collisions rollout, set Stickiness to **1** and Friction to **0.2**.

8. Save the scene as `explodingTower_v03.ma`.

To see a version of the scene, open `explodingTower_v03.ma` from the `chapter13\scenes` folder at the book's web page.

Instancing Geometry

The debris is currently in the shape of round balls, which is not very realistic. To create the effect of flying shrapnel, you'll need to instance some premade geometry to each nParticle. This means that a copy of each piece of geometry will follow the motion of each nParticle.

1. Continue using the scene from the previous section, or open the `explodingTower_v03` `.ma` scene from the `chapter13\scenes` folder.

2. The debris is contained in a separate file, which will be imported into the scene. Choose File ➢ Import, and select the `debris.ma` scene from the `chapter13\scenes` folder at the book's web page.

The debris scene is simply a group of seven polygon objects in the shape of shards.

3. Expand the debris:debris group in the Outliner, Shift+click all the members of the group, and choose nParticles ➢ Instancer (Replacement) ➢ Options.

In the Options window, all the debris objects are listed in the order in which they were selected in the Outliner. Notice that each one has a number to the left in the list. This number is the index value of the instance. The numbering starts with 0.

4. In the Particle Object To Instance drop-down menu, choose the particleDebrisShape object. This sets the instance to the correct nDynamic object (see Figure 13.34).

FIGURE 13.34
The selected objects appear in the Instanced Objects list. Select the particleDebrisShape node in the Particle Object To Instance options.

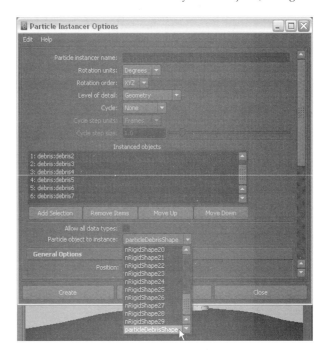

5. Leave the rest of the settings at their defaults, and choose Create to instance the nParticles. In the Outliner, a new node named instance1 has been created.

6. Play the scene. Switch to wireframe mode, and zoom in closely to the nParticles so that you can see what's going on.

7. Save the scene as **explodingTower_v04.ma**.

To see a version of the scene up to this point, open the explodingTower_v04.ma scene from the chapter13\scenes folder at the book's web page.

When playing the scene, you'll notice that each nParticle has the same piece of geometry instanced to it, and they are all oriented the same way (see Figure 13.35). To randomize which objects are instanced to the nParticles and their size and orientation, you'll need to create some expressions. In the next section, you'll learn how to assign the different objects in the imported debris group randomly to each nParticle as well as how to make them rotate as they fly through the air. You will also learn how to use each nParticle's mass to determine the size of the instanced geometry. All of this leads to a much more realistic-looking explosion.

FIGURE 13.35
Each nParticle has the same piece of geometry instanced to it.

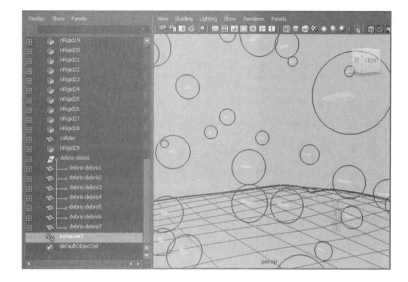

TIPS FOR WORKING WITH NPARTICLE INSTANCES

Geometry that is instanced to nParticles inherits the position and orientation of the original geometry. If you place keyframes on the original geometry, this is inherited by the instanced copies.

If you're animating flying debris, it's a better idea to animate the motion of the instances using expressions and the dynamics of the nParticles rather than setting keyframes of the rotation or translation of the original instanced geometry. This approach makes animation simpler and allows for more control when editing the effect.

It's also best to place the geometry you want to instance at the origin and place its pivot at the center of the geometry. You'll also want to freeze transformations on the geometry to initialize its translation, rotation, and scale attributes.

In some special cases, you may want to offset the pivot of the instanced geometry. To do this, position the geometry away from the origin of the grid, place the pivot at the origin, and freeze transformations.

If you are animating crawling bugs or the flapping wings of an insect, you can animate the original geometry you want to instance, or you can create a sequence of objects and use the Cycle feature in the instance options. The Cycle feature causes the instance to progress through a sequence of geometry based on the index number assigned to the instanced geometry. The Cycle feature offers more flexibility than simply animating the instanced geometry. You can use expressions to randomize the start point of the cycle on a per-particle basis. nParticle expressions are covered in the next section.

You can add more objects to the Instanced Objects list after creating the instance using the options in the Attribute Editor for the instance node.

Animating Instances Using nParticle Expressions

nParticles allow you to create more interesting particle effects than in previous versions of Maya without relying on expressions. However, in some situations, expressions are still required to achieve a believable effect. If you've never used particle expressions, they can be a little intimidating at first, and the workflow is not entirely intuitive. Once you understand how to create expressions, you can unleash an amazing level of creative potential; combine them with the power of the Nucleus solver, and there's almost no effect you can't create. Expressions work the same way for both nParticles and traditional Maya particles.

Randomizing Instance Index

The first expression you'll create will randomize which instance is copied to which nParticle. To do this, you'll need to create a custom attribute. This custom attribute will assign a random value between 0 and 6 for each nParticle, and this value will be used to determine the index number of the instance copied to that particular particle.

1. Select the particleDebris node in the Outliner, and open its Attribute Editor to the particleDebrisShape tab.

2. Scroll down and expand the Add Dynamic Attributes rollout.

3. Click the General button; a pop-up dialog box appears (see Figure 13.36). This dialog box offers you options to determine what type of attribute will be added to the particle shape.

FIGURE 13.36
The General button in the Add Dynamic Attributes section allows you to create your own custom attributes.

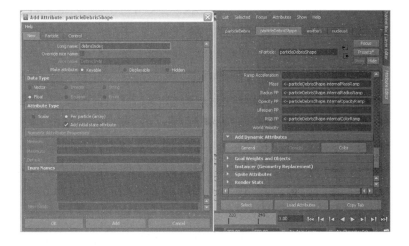

4. In the Long Name field, type **debrisIndex**. This is the name of the attribute that will be added to the nParticle.

NAMING AN ATTRIBUTE

You can name an attribute anything you want (as long as the name does not conflict with a preexisting attribute name). It's best to use concise names that make it obvious what the attribute does.

---

5. Set Data Type to Float. A float is a single numeric value that can have a decimal. Numbers like 3, 18.7, and −0.314 are examples of floats.

6. Set Attribute Type to Per Particle (Array).

PER PARTICLE VS. SCALAR ATTRIBUTES

A per-particle attribute contains a different value for each particle in the particle object. This is opposed to a scalar attribute, which applies the same value for all the particles in the particle object. For example, if an nParticle object represented an American president, a per-particle attribute would be something like the age of each president when elected. A scalar attribute would be something like the nationality of the presidents, which would be American for all of them.

---

7. Click OK to add the attribute.

Now that you have an attribute, you need to create the expression to determine its value:

1. Expand the Per Particle (Array) Attributes rollout, and you'll see Debris Index listed.

2. Right-click the field next to Debris Index, and choose Creation Expression (see Figure 13.37).

FIGURE 13.37
The new Debris Index attribute appears in the Per Particle (Array) Attributes list. To create an expression, right-click and choose Creation Expression.

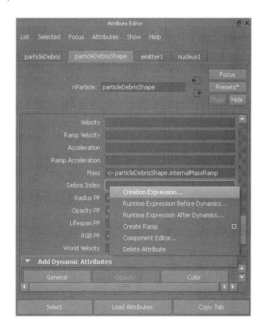

The Expression Editor opens, and debrisIndex is selected in the Attributes list. Notice that the Particle mode is automatically set to Creation.

3. In the Expression field, type **debrisIndex=rand(0,6);** (see Figure 13.38). Remember that the list of instanced objects contains seven objects, but the index list starts with 0 and goes to 6.

FIGURE 13.38
Add an expression to randomize the value of the debrisIndex attribute for each nParticle.

This adds a random function that assigns a number between 0 and 6 to the debrisIndex attribute of each nParticle. The semicolon at the end of the expression is typical scripting syntax and acts like a period at the end of a sentence.

4. Click the Create button to create the expression.

5. Rewind and play the animation.

Nothing has changed at this point—the same piece of debris is assigned to all the nParticles. This is because, even though you have a custom attribute with a random value, you haven't told Maya how to apply the attribute to the particle.

6. Expand the Instancer (Geometry Replacement) rollout in the Attribute Editor of particleDebrisShape.

7. In the General Options section, expand the Object Index menu and choose debrisIndex from the list (see Figure 13.39).

Now when you rewind and play the animation, you'll see a different piece of geometry assigned to each nParticle.

8. Save the scene as **explodingTower_v05.ma**.

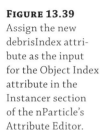

FIGURE 13.39
Assign the new debrisIndex attribute as the input for the Object Index attribute in the Instancer section of the nParticle's Attribute Editor.

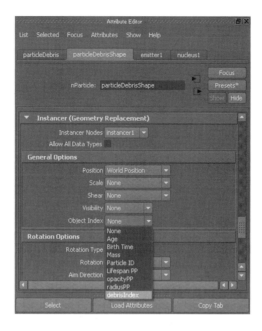

To see a version of the scene up to this point, open the `explodingTower_v05.ma` scene from the `chapter13\scenes` folder at the book's web page.

CREATION VS. RUNTIME EXPRESSIONS

There are two types of expressions you can create for a particle object: creation and runtime. The difference between creation and runtime is that creation expressions evaluate once when the particles are created (or at the start of the animation for particles that are not spawned from an emitter), and runtime expressions evaluate on each frame of the animation for as long as they are in the scene.

A good way to think of this is that a creation expression is like a trait determined by your DNA. When you're born, your DNA may state something like "Your maximum height will be 6 feet, 4 inches." So, your creation expression for height would be "maximum height = 6 feet, 4 inches." This has been set at the moment you are created and will remain so throughout your life unless something changes.

Think of a runtime expression as an event in your life. It's calculated each moment of your life. If for some reason during the course of your life your legs were replaced with bionic extend-o-legs that give you the ability to change your height automatically whenever you want, this would be enabled using a runtime expression. It happens after you have been born and can override the creation expression. Thus, at any given moment (or frame in the case of particles), your height could be 5 feet or 25 feet, thanks to your bionic extend-o-legs.

If you write a creation expression for the particles that says radius = 2, each particle will have a radius of 2, unless something changes. If you then add a runtime expression that says something like "If the Y position of a particle is greater than 10, then radius = 4," any particle that goes beyond 10 units in Y will instantly grow to a radius of 4 units. The runtime expression overrides the creation expression and is calculated at least once per frame as long as the animation is playing.

Connecting Instance Size to nParticle Mass

Next you'll create an expression that determines the size of each nParticle based on its mass. Small pieces of debris that have a low mass will float down through the air. Larger pieces that have a higher mass will be shot through the air with greater force. The size of instances is determined by their Scale X, Scale Y, and Scale Z attributes, much like a typical piece of geometry that you work with when modeling in Maya. This is different from a Balls-type nParticle that uses a single radius value to determine its size.

The size attributes for instanced geometry are contained in a vector. A vector is an attribute with a three-dimensional value, as opposed to an integer or a float, which has only a single-dimensional value.

1. Select the particleDebris object and, in the shape node's Attribute Editor, under Add Dynamic Attributes click the General button to create a new attribute.

2. Set the Long Name value to **debrisScale**.

3. Set Data Type to Vector and Attribute Type to Per Particle (Array), and click OK to create the attribute (see Figure 13.40).

FIGURE 13.40
Create another attribute, and name it debrisScale; this time set Data Type to Vector.

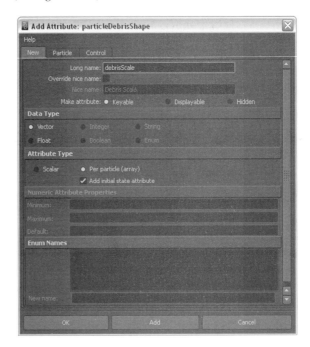

4. In the Per Particle (Array) Attributes section, right-click the field next to debrisScale, and choose to create a creation expression.

REFRESH THE ATTRIBUTE LIST

If the new attribute does not appear in the list, click the Load Attributes button at the bottom of the Attribute Editor to refresh the list.

In the Expression field of the Expression Editor, you'll see the debrisIndex expression. Note that the name debrisIndex has been expanded; it now says `particleDebrisShape` `.debrisIndex=rand(0,6);`. Maya does this automatically when you create the expression.

5. Below the debrisIndex expression, type **debrisScale=<<mass,mass,mass>>;**. Click Edit to add this to the expression (see Figure 13.41).

FIGURE 13.41
Set the debris-Scale attribute to be equivalent to the mass of each nParticle. Add the expression in the Expression Editor.

The double brackets are the syntax used when specifying vector values. Using mass as the input value for each dimension of the vector ensures that the pieces of debris are uniformly scaled.

6. In the Instancer (Geometry Replacement) attributes of the particleDebris object, set the Scale menu to debrisScale (see Figure 13.42).

7. Rewind and play the animation.

The pieces of debris are now sized based on the mass of the nParticles, but of course the mass of some of the particles is so small that the instanced particles are invisible. To fix this, you can edit the expression, as follows:

1. In the Per-Particle (Array) Attributes section, right-click debrisScale, and choose Creation Expression to open the Expression Editor.

2. In the Expression field, add the following text above the debris scale expression:

```
float $massScale = mass*3;
```

3. Now edit the original debrisScale expression, as shown in Figure 13.43, so it reads as follows:

```
debrisScale = <<$massScale, $massScale, $massScale>>;
```

By using the `float` command in the Expression Editor, you're creating a local variable that is available to be used only in the creation expressions used by the nParticle. This variable is local, meaning that, since it was created in the Creation expression box, it's available only for creation expressions. If you use this variable in a runtime expression, Maya gives you an error message. The variable is preceded by a dollar sign. The $massScale variable is assigned the mass multiplied by 3.

4. Click Edit to implement the changes to the expression.

5. Rewind and play the animation.

It's an improvement; some debris pieces are definitely much bigger, but some are still too small. You can fix this by adding a clamp function. *clamp* sets an upper and lower limit to the values generated by the expression. The syntax is clamp(lower limit, upper limit, input);. Make sure you click the Edit button in the editor after typing the expression.

FIGURE 13.43
Edit the expression so that the size of each nParticle is equal to the mass multiplied by 3.

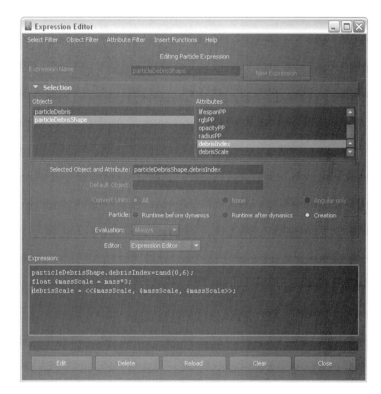

6. Edit the expression for the massScale variable so that it reads float $massScale=clamp(1,5,mass*5);. Again, make sure that you click the Edit button in the editor after typing the expression.

7. Play the animation.

Now you have a reasonable range of sizes for the debris, and they are all based on the mass on the particles (see Figure 13.44).

FIGURE 13.44
After you add the clamp expression, the range of size for the debris is more reasonable.

CERT OBJECTIVE

8. In the Attribute Editor for the particleDebris, scroll to the Shading section and set Particle Render Type to Points so that you can see the instanced geometry more easily.

9. Save the scene as **explodingTower_v06.ma**.

To see a version of the scene, open the explodingTower_v06.ma scene from the chapter13\ scenes folder at the book's web page.

Controlling the Rotation of nParticles

Rotation attributes are calculated per particle and can be used to control the rotation of geometry instanced to the nParticles. In addition, the Rotation Friction and Rotation Damp attributes can be used to fine-tune the quality of the rotation. In this exercise, you'll add rotation to the debris:

1. Continue with the scene from the previous section, or open the explodingTower_v06.ma scene from the chapter13\scenes folder at the book's web page.

2. Select the particleDebris node in the Outliner, and open its Attribute Editor to the particleDebrisShape tab.

3. Expand the Rotation tab, and turn on Compute Rotation (see Figure 13.45). This automatically adds a new attribute to the Per Particle Array Attributes list. However, you won't need to create any expressions in order to make the nParticle rotate.

4. Scroll down to the Instancer (Geometry Replacement) settings. In the Rotation Options, set the Rotation menu to rotationPP.

FIGURE 13.45
Turn on Compute
Rotation in order
to add per-particle
rotation attributes
to the nParticles.

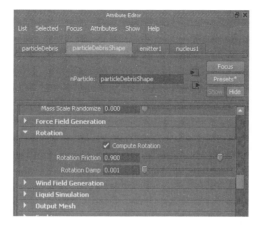

FIGURE 13.45
Turn on Compute
Rotation in order
to add per-particle
rotation attributes
to the nParticles.

5. Create a playblast of the scene.

6. You may notice that some of the debris rotates a bit too quickly as it falls to Earth. To adjust this, scroll up to the Rotation section, and set Rotation Damp to **0.01**. Try making another playblast.

7. Save the scene as `explodingTower_v07.ma`.

Rotation Friction and Rotation Damp are per-particle attributes, which can be used in per-particle expressions to drive other attributes:

Rotation Friction This attribute determines how likely an nParticle will rotate based on its collision with other nDynamic objects and self-collisions (inter-particle collisions within the same nParticle shape). Setting Rotation Friction to 0 turns off rotation.

Rotation Damp This attribute causes the rotation of nParticles to slow down after collisions with other nDynamic objects and self-collisions.

To see a version of the scene, open the `explodingTower_v07.ma` scene from the `chapter13\` scenes folder at the book's web page.

CACHING INSTANCED NPARTICLES

When creating an nCache for nParticles that have geometry instanced to them or any nParticle with custom attributes and expressions, be sure to set the Cacheable Attributes menu (in the Caching rollout of the nParticle's Attribute Editor) to All. Otherwise, the cache will store only position and velocity data, and the motion of the nParticles will not look correct when you render the scene.

Bullet Physics

Bullet physics is based on the open source Bullet Physics Library. Bullet is a plug-in to Maya and is available only for 64-bit versions. Using Bullet, you can create realistic dynamic simulations on a large scale. Bullet supports rigid bodies, rigid body constraints, and soft bodies. In addition, you can create rigid body kinematics or ragdoll effects. The following exercise takes you through the process of creating a rigid body simulation.

1. Load the Bullet plug-in. Choose Window ➢ Settings/Preferences ➢ Plug-in Manager. Find `bullet.mll` (`bullet.bundle` on the Mac), and select Loaded and Auto Load.

2. Open the `wreckingBall_v01.ma` scene from the `chapter13\scenes` folder at the book's web page.

3. Select the wreckingBall node in the Outliner.

4. Choose Bullet ➢ Create Active Rigid Body. A collision box is placed around the wrecking ball (see Figure 13.46). This is a new shape node called bulletRigidBodyShape1.

FIGURE 13.46
Create an active rigid body from the wrecking ball.

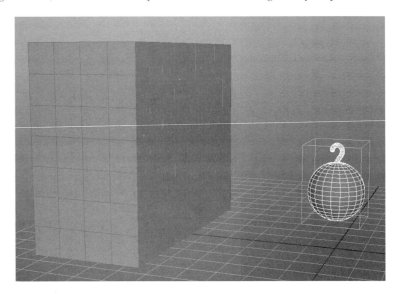

5. Open the Attribute Editor for bulletRigidBodyShape1. The wrecking ball's rigid body properties are controlled through this node. Expand the Collider Properties rollout. Set the Collider Shape Type to Sphere, as Figure 13.47 shows.

6. Click play to watch the simulation. The wrecking ball falls into infinite space. To get the ball to swing you will first need to add a constraint. With the wrecking ball selected, choose Bullet ➢ Create Rigid Body Constraint.

7. All of the rigid body constraints share the same attributes. Open the Attribute Editor for bulletRigidBodyConstraint1. At the top of the editor is the Constraint Type option. You can change this setting at any point when constructing your simulation. Leave Constraint Type set to Point.

FIGURE 13.47
Change the colli-
sion box to match
the shape of the
wrecking ball.

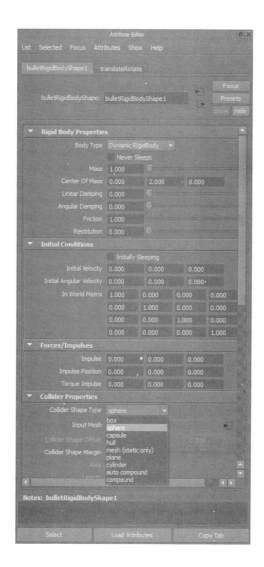

8. Translate the constraint to 9.0 units in the Translate Y. The manipulator will move but the actual constraint does not update until the simulation is refreshed. Click Play to refresh the simulation. The wrecking ball no longer falls.

9. To give the wrecking ball motion, you need to add some velocity. Open the wrecking ball's Attribute Editor. Choose the bulletRigidBodyShape1 tab.

10. Under the Initial Conditions rollout, set the Initial Velocity to **-20.0**.

11. The wrecking ball now spins around its constraint during the simulation. Let's give it something to hit. Select all of the cubes in the scene. Make sure you are selecting the actual nodes and not the group node they are parented to.

12. With all 252 blocks selected, choose Bullet ➢ Create Active Rigid Body. Click Play to watch the simulation (Figure 13.48).

FIGURE 13.48
The wrecking ball
hits the falling
blocks.

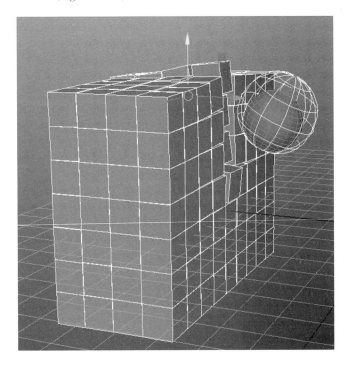

13. The simulation is working but not as explosive as we would like. The blocks fall through space just like the wrecking ball prior to adding its constraint. You do not want to restrict the blocks' movement with a constraint. Instead, you want to add a floor. Choose Bullet ➢ Select Solver.

14. Under the bulletSolverShape1 tab in the Attribute Editor, select Ground Plane from the Solver Properties rollout.

15. Watch the simulation again. The cubes rest on the artificial ground plane. The wrecking ball, however, barely makes a dent. Select the wrecking ball and open its rigid body properties in the Attribute Editor. Change Mass to **100**. Click Play to see the results (see Figure 13.49).

16. The wrecking ball moves too much. Under the Mass attribute change Linear Damping to **0.5**. The motion is now less erratic.

FIGURE 13.49
The increased
mass makes a huge
impact on the
blocks.

FIGURE 13.49
The increased
mass makes a huge
impact on the
blocks.

17. Although Linear Damping helped, the ball wobbles quite a bit. Choose Bullet ➤ Select Solver. Change Internal Fixed Frame Rate to **240Hz**. This speeds up the simulation calculations, resulting in smoother motion.

18. Save the scene as `wreckingBall_v02.ma`.

To see a version of the scene, open the `wreckingBall_v02.ma` scene from the `chapter13\` `scenes` folder at the book's web page.

RAGDOLL

In addition to rigid and soft body simulations, you can create rigid body kinematics or ragdoll effects. These steps take you through the process:

1. Create a skeleton of a human character.

2. Make sure each joint is uniquely named. Bullet uses the names of your joints to create rigid capsules. If any of the names are duplicates, the capsules cannot be generated.

3. Select the root joint of your skeleton. Choose Bullet ➤ Create Ragdoll From Skeleton.

4. Create a primitive plane at the skeleton's feet. Choose Bullet ➤ Create Passive Rigid Body.

5. Click the Play button on the timeline to watch the simulation.

The Bottom Line

Use nCloth. nCloth can be used to make polygon geometry behave dynamically to simulate a wide variety of materials. Using the presets that come with Maya, you can design your own materials and create your own presets for use in your animations.

Master It Create the effect of a cube of gelatinous material rolling down the stairs.

Combine nCloth and nParticles. Because nCloth and nParticles use the same dynamic systems, they can be combined easily to create amazing simulations.

Master It Make a water balloon burst as it hits the ground.

Use Maya rigid body dynamics. Rigid body dynamics are not quite as powerful as nCloth objects, but they do calculate much faster and work better for simulations involving a large number of interacting pieces.

Master It Animate a series of dominoes falling over.

Use nParticles to drive instanced geometry. Modeled geometry can be instanced to nParticles to create a wide variety of effects.

Master It Create the effect of a swarm of insects attacking a beach ball.

Create nParticle expressions. nParticle expressions can be used to further extend the power of nParticles. Using expressions to automate instanced geometry simulations is just one of the ways in which expressions can be used.

Master It Improve the animation of the insects attacking the beach ball by adding different types of insects to the swarm. Randomize their size, and create expressions so that larger insects move more slowly.

Create a soft body simulation with Bullet. Bullet physics are fast and accurate. In addition to creating rigid body simulations, you can use Bullet to create clothlike effects with its soft bodies.

Master It Drape a tablecloth over a table using soft body physics.

Chapter 14

Hair and Clothing

The Autodesk® Maya® software offers a number of tools for adding fur, hair, and clothing to characters. Creative use of these tools adds believability and originality to your animated characters. In addition, many of these tools can be used to create engaging visual effects.

In this chapter, you will learn to:

◆ Add XGen descriptions to characters

◆ Create dynamic curves

◆ Add hair to characters

◆ Style hair

◆ Paint nCloth properties

Understanding XGen

New!

XGen is an arbitrary primitive generator. With XGen you can place any number of primitive objects in a scene. Regardless of the type of object you use, XGen gives you the ability to control attributes such as size and shape. Using XGen, you can create grass, hair, or even an entire forest.

XGen works by creating primitives. A primitive can be a spline, sphere, card, or archive. (An archive is a polygon object that has been saved previously.) Primitives cannot be manipulated individually. Instead you control primitives through guides, attributes, and expressions. This allows you to make changes to thousands, even millions, of primitives at once. Figure 14.1 shows the window used for controlling XGen.

There are four major components to XGen:

Descriptions These are the core of any XGen endeavor. A description is used to define everything about the look of the primitive. Multiple descriptions can be added to a polygon surface. They can also be saved and reused on different objects.

Patches Patches are attached to polygon faces and let the description know where and how to place the primitives. Patches are identified with a magenta X that is placed in the center of the polygon face it is connected to. There are no attributes you can modify in a patch.

Collections   Descriptions are always placed within a collection, and collections are used to organize your descriptions. They create external folders in your project directory to keep the numerous associated description files from conflicting with other descriptions.

Guides   Guides are representations of what your primitive objects will look like. Some guides can be selected and shaped. Shaping the guide is preferable when dealing with long hair.

XGen uses Ptex texture maps to store attribute information about your description. Most importantly, it uses Ptex texture maps to place your primitives on a polygon surface. As a result, your geometry does not need UVs to work with an XGen description.

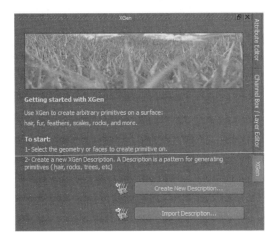

Creating an XGen Description

The first step in using XGen is to create a description. Descriptions can be added to polygon surfaces or selected faces. In this exercise, you'll build a description to define hair for a character's head.

1. Open the `hairstyle_v01.ma` scene from the `chapter14\scenes` folder at the book's web page, `www.sybex.com/go/masteringmaya2015`.

2. Select all the faces of the character's scalp. Use Figure 14.2 as reference.

3. With the faces selected, choose XGen ➢ Open The XGen Window. Alternatively, you could choose XGen ➢ Create Description to go directly to the creation options. You will need to work in the XGen window, so it makes sense to open the window.

4. In the XGen window, click Create New Description.

5. Name the description **shortHair** and create a new collection named **female**. Refer to Figure 14.3 for the rest of the settings.

6. The Grooming Tools tab is automatically selected because of the description you chose. Under the Settings rollout, increase the Density parameter to increase the number of groomable guides. Set Density to **50.0** (see Figure 14.4).

Figure 14.2
Select faces for the
character's scalp.

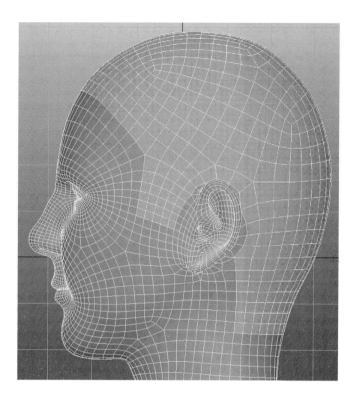

Figure 14.3
The settings for
creating a new
description

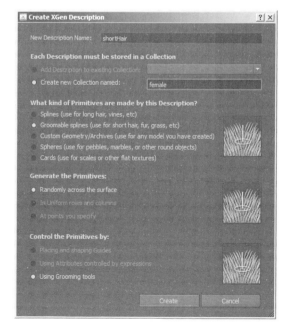

FIGURE 14.4
FIGURE 14.4
Additional guides
are added to the
description based
on the Density
parameter.

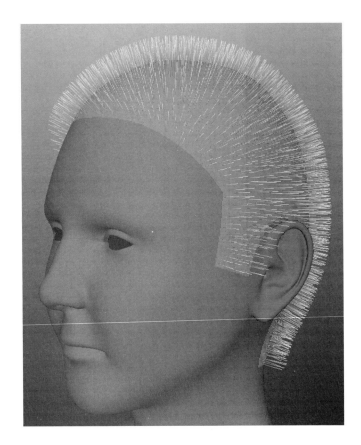

THE SYNC CHECK BOX

At the end of the Density slider is a check box for Sync. When it's selected, the density of the primitives generated matches the density value of the groomable guides.

---

7. When you're creating a hairstyle, it's best to start with the length. You can always increase or decrease the length as you work, but starting with the longest length mimics the way a hairstyle is cut in the real world. In the Settings rollout, change Length to **1.6** to increase the length of the hair uniformly.

8. Choose the Length brush from the Brush rollout. To paint length, you first establish a goal length. In this case, you want to trim the length of the hair. By default, the goal is set to 5.0 cm. Change Goal Length to **0.5**. This value now represents the shortest possible

length of hair. Set the Increment to **–0.1** to gradually cut the hair's length. Paint the sideburns area to shorten the hair length.

REMOVING HAIR

To create bald patches or to remove hair, use a Goal Length of 0.0.

---

9. Choose the Smooth brush. Paint the transitional area between the two different lengths of hair you painted in step 8. The Smooth brush changes the hair length to make a gradual transition (see Figure 14.5).

FIGURE 14.5
The Smooth brush can be used to soften the transition between hair attributes.

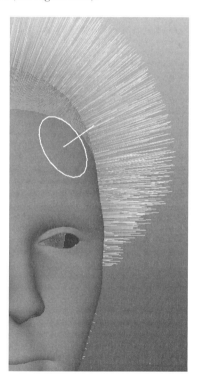

10. Under the Edit rollout, choose Flip To Right to mirror the changes you made to the other side of the head.

11. Choose the Pose brush, which is a combination of the Orient and Bend brushes. Posing the hair is a bit like brushing and curling your hair at the same time. Use the brush to

comb half of the hair down. At this point, you need to comb only one side of the character's head (see Figure 14.6).

12. Choose Flip To Right to mirror the combed hair to the other side of the character's head.
You can mirror your changes as often as needed.

FIGURE 14.6
Use the Pose brush
like a comb to style
and shape the hair.

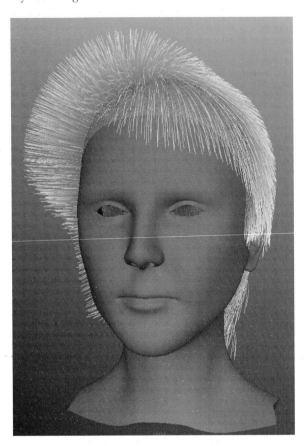

13. With the hair flattened to the character's head, you can begin to see problems with the
hair's length. Choose the Length brush and trim along the sides to taper the length.

14. Use the Smooth brush to even out the length of the hair. If you find that you cut too
much, switch to the Length brush. Increase the Goal Length value and flip Increment
from negative to positive to extend the hair's length.

15. Use the Pose brush to style the hair. Start at the root of the hair and drag the brush in the
direction you want the hair to go.

16. The hair guides do not automatically detect the surface underneath it. If hairs are pushed below the scalp surface, use the Elevation brush to lift them back up. Remember that you can mirror your changes to the other side of the character's head at any time.

17. The Attract brush pulls hairs toward the brush. This can give the effect of wet or gelled hair. Use the Attract brush to create several clumped areas to give the haircut some style (see Figure 14.7). Use a small brush size to avoid clumping too many hairs together.

FIGURE 14.7
Use the Attract brush to create clumps of hair.

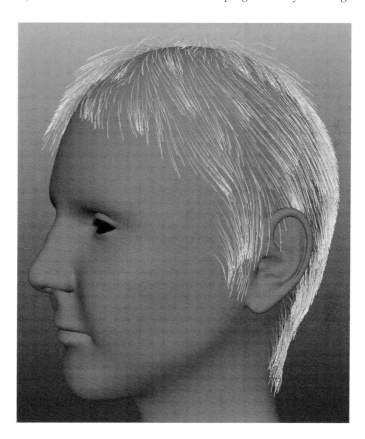

18. Hair is never perfect. Adding noise increases the realism of any hair design. Select the Noise brush. Increase the Middle attribute to **0.2** to disrupt the position of the hair from its root to its middle. Increase the Tip value to **0.435**. Apply the brush sparingly to the character's hair (see Figure 14.8).

19. Save the scene as `hairstyle_v02.ma`.

To see a version of the scene, open the `hairstyle_v02.ma` scene from the `chapter14\scenes` folder.

FIGURE 14.8
Add noise to
give the hair a
more realistic
appearance.

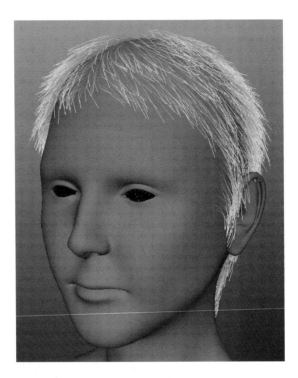

Rendering an XGen Description

When a description is created, Maya automatically assigns a mental ray® shading network. Before visualizing the shader, you want to make sure you have enough primitives to render. The next exercise takes you through the steps to render your character's hairstyle.

1. Continue with your scene or open the hairstyle_v02.ma scene from the chapter14\ scenes folder.

2. In the toolbar of the XGen window is an eyeball icon. Below the eyeball is a yellow triangle with an exclamation mark. The icon is the preview button for displaying your primitives. Click the button to force XGen to update the primitives to match your groomed guides.

3. The eyeball icon or preview button changes and a green check appears under the eye. You will also notice that primitive splines now cover the character's head (see Figure 14.9).

   The splines match the guide's shape and position. However, they do not match the width. Under the Settings rollout, change Width to **0.01**. Click the Preview button to see your changes.

PREVIEWING AUTOMATICALLY

Next to the Preview button is an arrow that when clicked exposes preview options. You can set XGen to update the preview automatically. This works well when you have a low number of primitives. With a large number, you may find yourself waiting for the preview to update in between brush strokes or attribute changes.

4. Zoom close in to a few primitive strands of hair. The splines are tubular. Their start width is the same as their end width. To taper the hair, choose the Primitives tab. Under the Primitives Attributes rollout, set Taper to **0.7** and Taper Start to **0.5**. Update the preview to see the results (Figure 14.10).

FIGURE 14.9
Primitive splines are added among the guides.

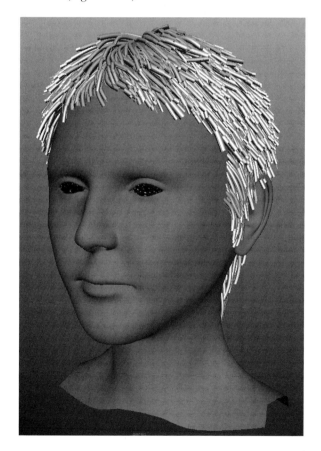

FIGURE 14.10
Taper the width
of the primitive
splines.

5. Choose the Grooming tab. Under the Settings rollout, deselect Visibility to turn off the guides. The hair looks pretty sparse. You can increase the density of your primitives through the Density attribute since Sync is checked. However, at this point any additional hairs will be added with default settings. That means the new hairs will not be groomed like the old hairs. To prevent this, choose Interp from the Sampling attribute.

6. Change Density to **400**. The hairs are blended with the existing groomed hairs.

7. Render a version of the hair. Figure 14.11 shows the result.

FIGURE 14.11
A render of the cur-
rent state of the
hair

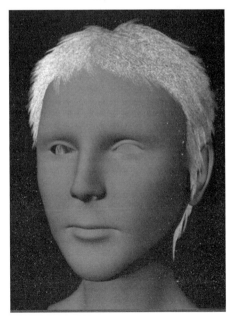

8. Select xgen_hair_phen from the Hypershade and open its Attribute Editor. Change Diffuse Color to match the following settings:

   Hue: **46.347**

   Saturation: **0.388**

   Value: **1.0**

9. Turn on Final Gather and turn off the Default light. Change the Background Color setting of the perspective camera's environment to a sky blue. Add a back light and render the scene (see Figure 14.12).

FIGURE 14.12
The hair is colored, lit, and rendered.

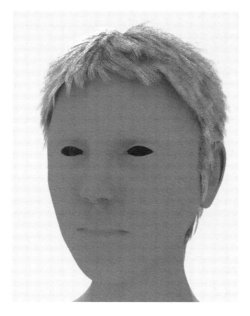

To see a version of the scene, open the `hairstyle_v03.ma` scene from the `chapter14\scenes` folder.

Animating Using Dynamic Curves

Dynamic curves are NURBS curves driven by the Nucleus dynamic simulation framework. The primary use of dynamic curves is to drive the dynamics of nHair systems applied to characters. They can also be used to drive fur. However, the usefulness of dynamic curves goes far beyond creating hair motion. Curves used to loft or extrude surfaces, curves used for Paint Effects strokes, curves projected on NURBS surfaces, curves used as IK splines, curves used as particle emitters, and so on can be made dynamic, thus opening up a large number of possibilities for creating additional dynamic effects in Maya. While working through the scenes in this chapter, you may want to set the timeline preferences to loop so that you can see the hair update continuously as you adjust its settings. To do so, follow these steps:

1. Choose Window ➤ Settings/Preferences ➤ Preferences.

2. Choose the Time Slider category in the Preferences dialog box.

3. Set Looping to Continuous.

Using Dynamic Curves with IK Splines

In Chapter 5, "Rigging and Muscle Systems," you learned about the IK Spline tool, which uses a curve to control the inverse kinematics (IK) of a joint chain. The curve itself can be converted into a dynamic curve that can be used to drive the IK Spline tool. This is a great way to add dynamic motion to a rig used for tails or tentacles.

In this example, you'll use a dynamic curve to control a segmented armored tail. The armored tail consists of polygon pieces, each of which has been parent-constrained to a joint in a chain. The first step is to create a curve (see Figure 14.13).

FIGURE 14.13
The armored tail consists of polygon pieces constrained to a joint chain.

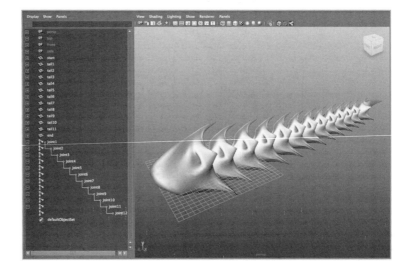

1. Open the armoredTail_v01.ma scene from the chapter14\scenes folder at the book's web page.

2. Switch to a side view, and select Snap To Points.

3. In the viewport's Show menu, turn off the visibility of polygons so that only the joints are visible.

4. Choose Create ➢ EP Curve Tool. Click the first joint in the chain on the far-left side and the last joint in the chain on the far-right side.

5. Press Enter to complete the curve.

The EP Curve tool creates a curve that has four CVs. Using the EP Curve tool is an easy way to create a straight curve. If you want to add more vertices, you can use the Edit

Curves ➤ Rebuild Curve command. In the options, specify how many spans you want to add to the curve. In this example, the curve should work fine with only four CVs.

6. Switch to the perspective view. Turn off the visibility of Joints in the Show menu so that only the curve is visible.

7. Switch to the nDynamics menu. Select curve1, and choose nHair ➤ Make Selected Curves Dynamic. In the Outliner, a new hairSystem1 node is created, as are two groups: hairSystem1Follicles and hairSystem1OutputCurves (see Figure 14.14).

FIGURE 14.14
A number of nodes are added to the scene when a curve is made dynamic.

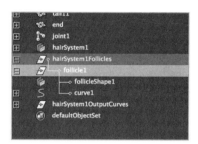

UNDERSTANDING DYNAMIC HAIR CURVE NODES

The hairSystem1 node controls the dynamics of the curve.

The hairSystem1Follicles group contains the follicle1 node and the original curve1. The follicle node contains settings to control the dynamics of the individual follicles. Some of these settings can override the hairSystem settings. If you selected a number of curves before issuing the Make Selected Curves Dynamic command, the hairSystem1Follicles group would contain a follicle node for each curve. This is explored later on this chapter in the section "Adding Hair to a Character."

The hairSystem1OutputCurves group creates a duplicate curve named curve2. This curve is a duplicate of the original curve. The output curve is the dynamic curve; the curve in the follicle group is the original, nondynamic curve. The purpose of the nondynamic curve is to serve as an attractor for the dynamic curve if needed. The dynamic curve gets its shape from the follicle curve.

---

8. Set the timeline to **200**, and click the Play button. You'll see the dynamic curve move a little. (It can be a little hard to see; this will be more obvious in the next step.)

9. Stop the playback, and switch to the hairSystem1 tab.

10. In the Stiffness Scale rollout panel under Dynamics Properties, set the Selected value to **0**, and play the scene. You'll see the dynamic curve droop a little. As the scene is playing, set the Stretch Resistance value under the Dynamic Properties rollout to **0.1**.

The Stiffness setting controls the rigidity of the curve. A higher Stiffness setting makes the curve less flexible. Lowering the Stiffness value makes the curve bend easily.

As you decrease the Stretch Resistance value, the curve stretches as much as it needs to in order to accommodate the dynamic forces applied to the curve. You'll notice the curve droop downward, indicating that it has weight. The Nucleus solver controls the gravity, as discussed in Chapter 12, "Introducing nParticles."

You'll notice that both ends of the curve appear to be attached to the original curve (see Figure 14.15).

FIGURE 14.15
The dynamic curve droops as if it is attached at both ends to the original curve.

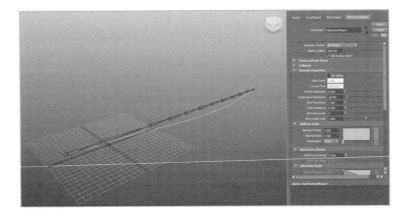

11. Stop the playback, and rewind the animation.

12. Set Stiffness Scale Selected Value to **1.0** and Bend Resistance to **0.5**.

13. Select the follicle1 node in the Outliner, and switch to the Move tool (turn off Snap To Grids or Snap To Points if it is still on).

14. Choose Solvers ➢ Interactive Playback. The animation starts playing automatically. As it is playing, move the follicle around in the scene; you'll see the dynamic curve follow the movements.

15. Stop the animation, and switch to the follicleShape1 tab in the Attribute Editor.

16. Set the Point Lock menu to Base. Turn on Interactive Playback, and move the follicle around again. You'll see that the dynamic curve is attached at only one end.

    If you wanted the curve to be attached to the other end, you'd set Point Lock to Tip. To detach the curve entirely, set Point Lock to No Attach.

17. Stop the animation, and rewind the playback.

KEYFRAME POINT LOCK

The Point Lock attribute can be keyframed in the Channel Box for the follicle node. To animate a dynamic curve detaching from one end, follow these steps:

1. Set Point Lock to Both Ends.

2. Create a keyframe by right-clicking the Point Lock channel in the Channel Box and choosing Key Selected.

3. Change the current frame on the timeline.

4. Set Point Lock to Tip or Base (the opposite end will become detached).

5. Set another keyframe.

This is a good way to create the effect of a cable or rope snapping.

---

18. Select the follicle1 node, and set the Translate channels to **0** to return the curve to its start position.

19. With the follicle selected, select Snap To Points.

20. Hold the **d** key, and use the Move tool to move the pivot point of the follicle to the end of the curve on the side where the dynamic curve is still attached, as shown in Figure 14.16.

FIGURE 14.16
Move the pivot point of the follicle to the end of the curve.

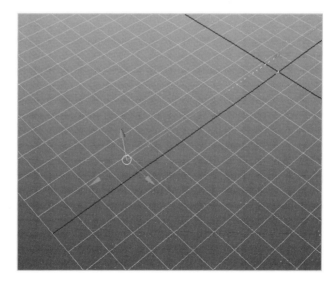

TIPS FOR MOVING THE PIVOT POINT

As you move the pivot point, the curve should not move; sometimes it takes a couple of tries to get Maya to switch properly to move pivot mode. An alternative to the **d** hot key is to press the **Insert** key on a PC or the **Home** key on a Mac on the keyboard while the Move tool is activated—not every keyboard has an Insert key, however. Another alternative is while holding **d**, press **w**, and then let go of both to lock the move pivot. Repeat the command to unlock the move pivot.

---

21. When the pivot point is repositioned, Shift+click the Translate and Rotate channels in the Channel Box, right-click, and choose Key Selected from the pop-up context menu.

22. Select Auto Keyframe; go to various points in the animation, and move and rotate the follicle.

While Auto Keyframe is selected, a keyframe is placed on all the Translate and Rotate channels as you make changes to the position of the follicle. The dynamic curve may not update correctly as you make changes; don't worry about that at the moment.

You want to create an animation where the curve moves around in the scene like a sword slashing through the air.

23. Rewind and play the animation; you'll see the dynamic curve follow the movements of the follicle as it moves through the air.

24. Save the scene as `armoredTail_v02.ma`.

To see a version of the scene, open the `armoredTail_v02.ma` scene from the `chapter14\` scenes folder.

Creating an IK Spline Handle from the Dynamic Curve

In this section, you'll create an IK spline handle for the armored tail and attach it to the dynamic curve. The dynamics of the curve will be edited to change the behavior of the tail.

1. Continue with the scene from the previous section, or open the `armoredTail_v02.ma` scene from the `chapter14\scenes` folder.

2. In the perspective view, turn on the visibility of joints in the Show menu.

3. In the Outliner, select and hide the follicle1 node. This prevents you from selecting the wrong curve when creating the IK spline handle.

4. Switch to the Animation menu, and choose Skeleton ➢ IK Spline Handle Tool ➢ Options.

5. In the Tool Settings dialog box, make sure Auto Create Curve and Root On Curve are both deselected.

6. With the IK Spline Handle tool active, select the first joint in the chain and the last joint in the chain.

7. Zoom in closely, and carefully select the blue curve that runs down the center of the chain.

If the operation is successful, you'll see the ikHandle1 node appear in the Outliner. The Dynamic curve (curve4) will move out of the hairSystem1OutputCurves group. That should not affect how the curve behaves.

8. Rewind and play the scene. The joints follow the motion of the curves.

9. In the Show menu of the perspective view, turn the visibility of polygons back on and play the scene. The armored tail thrashes around when you play the animation.

10. In the Outliner, select the hairSystem1 node and open its Attribute Editor to the hairSystemShape1 tab.

11. Scroll down and expand the Dynamics section.

    The Stiffness Scale edit curve changes the stiffness of the curve along the length of the curve. The left side of the curve corresponds to the stiffness at the base; the right side of the curve corresponds to the stiffness at the tip.

12. Add a point to the Stiffness Scale edit curve by clicking the left side of the curve and dragging downward.

13. Play the animation, and you'll see the end of the tail lag behind the motion more than the front of the tail. You should be able to edit the curve while the animation is playing and observe the changes (see Figure 14.17).

FIGURE 14.17
Editing the Stiffness Scale curve changes the stiffness along the length of the dynamic hair.

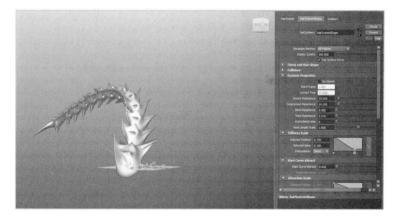

14. Save the scene as **armoredTail_v03.ma**.

The Stiffness setting creates the overall stiffness value for the dynamic curve. Stiffness Scale modifies that value along the length of the curve. Both settings, like almost all of the dynamic curve settings, can be animated.

To see a version of the scene, open the armoredTail_v03.ma file from the chapter14\scenes folder.

Using Forces

The settings in the Forces section add levels of control for the curve's motion. Play the animation in the armoredTail_v03.ma scene, and adjust these settings while the scene loops so that you can see how they affect the motion of the tail.

Mass   Affects the motion of the curve only when additional fields (created from the Dynamics menu) are applied to the curve—for example, a Turbulence or a Drag field. Mass does not change how the curve responds to forces created in the hairSystem1 shape node. Increasing Mass increases the simulated weight of each CV on the curve as the curve moves through a dynamic field.

Drag   Creates friction between the dynamic curve and the air. Increasing this value is a good way to simulate the motion of hair in thick fluids.

Tangential Drag   Applies a resistance along the direction of the hair curve shape. Increasing this value is also a good way to simulate the motion of hair in thick fluids.

Motion Drag   Similar to Drag. However, Motion Drag is affected by the Stiffness Scale attribute. In other words, the Drag setting creates a drag in the motion across the length of the dynamic curve, whereas Motion Drag creates a drag along the length of the curve that is influenced by the Stiffness Scale curve. This setting can be used to fine-tune the motion of the dynamic curve.

Damp   Used most often to control erratic motion of dynamic curves. Higher Damp values decrease the momentum of the curve as it follows the motion of the follicle.

Stretch Damp   Used most often to control erratic motion of dynamic curves. Higher Damp values decrease the momentum of the curve as it follows the motion of the follicle.

Dynamics Weight   Controls the amount of overall influence external dynamic fields (such as Turbulence and Drag) have over the dynamic curve. It does not influence how the Forces settings in the hairSystem node affect the dynamic curve.

 **Real World Scenario**

DYNAMIC CURVES

The opening sequence to my movie series *Living Flesh* required venetian blinds to be blowing in the wind in front of a shattered window. Animating the subtleness of a gentle breeze can be difficult. An additional challenge is that venetian blinds do not sway uniformly. One side of the blinds can move at a different speed than the other. To achieve the effect, I bound the model of the blinds to two different skeletons that were positioned on either side of the model. I added a Spline IK handle to each of the skeletons. Then I made the curve generated from the spline IK handle into a dynamic curve. Using the Nucleus solver, I added wind, thus providing a uniform breeze to the blinds. To get the two sides to move at irregular intervals, I increased the stiffness scale on the left side, causing it to lag behind the right side.

Adding Hair to a Character

Maya offers two methods for adding hair to a character, XGen and nHair. If you plan on animating the hair, you will have to connect your XGen guides to an nHair system. This section focuses on using nHair to build a head of hair. To learn how to use XGen for creating hair, watch the movies in the chapter14\movies folder. You should complete this section before creating XGen hair.

Hair is created by attaching follicle nodes to a surface. Each follicle node controls a number of hairs. The follicles themselves are styled using a combination of control curves and forces. Follicles and control curves are connected to a hair system node. A single hair system node can control hair connected to any number of surfaces, and a single surface can be attached to multiple hair systems.

When you create hair, you have to consider how you plan to render it. You have the choice of creating Paint Effects strokes for the hair or curves that can be used to render in third-party engines such as Pixar's RenderMan®, or creating both Paint Effects strokes and curves. Even though hair uses Paint Effects, it renders using mental ray without the need to convert the hair to polygons.

You can still use Classic Hair, located under nHair ➤ Classic Hair, to build and style your character's hair. Once nHair is created, you can toggle between Classic Hair and the Nucleus solver from within the hair system shape node's Attribute Editor. In this section, you'll create and style hair for a character using nHair and the Nucleus framework.

Applying Hair to a Surface

When you want to apply hair to a character, you can either apply the hair uniformly to the entire surface or paint the hair selectively on parts of the surface.

It is common practice to create a nonrendering scalp surface that can be parented to a character's head and then apply the hair to the scalp surface rather than directly to the character's head. This approach allows flexibility because scalp surfaces and their attached hair can easily be swapped between characters. It also speeds up playback in the animation because the hair dynamics are not factored into the calculations required to deform the character's surface if it has been skinned to a skeleton or to other deformers.

Some animators like to apply separate hair systems to each part of the scalp to control the various sections of a particular hairstyle. For instance, one hair system may be applied to the bangs that hang over the character's forehead, whereas another system may be used for the hair on the back of the head. In this exercise, you'll keep things simple by using a single hair system for the character's hairstyle. Both methods are valid, and as you become comfortable working with hair, you may want to experiment with different techniques to see which approach works best for you.

The following procedure uses a rigged character head. The head is rigged to a series of joints. You can select and rotate the headCtrl curves above the head to change the position of the head. A scalp surface has been created by duplicating part of the head geometry. This scalp geometry is parent-constrained to one of the joints in the head rig.

You can apply hair to NURBS or polygon surfaces. When you use polygon surfaces, the UV texture coordinates must be mapped so that none of the UVs overlap and the coordinates fit within the 0 to 1 range in the UV Texture Editor. As with fur, you'll get better results from your hair system if the UV coordinates have been carefully mapped. Remember to delete history for the surface once you have created UV texture coordinates to keep the coordinates (and attached hair) from moving unpredictably during animation.

1. Open the nancyHair_v01.ma scene from the chapter14\scenes folder.

2. In the Outliner, select the scalp surface and open its Attribute Editor.

3. In the scalpShape tab, expand the Render Stats section; then deselect Casts Shadows, Receive Shadows, Motion Blur, and Primary Visibility so that the surface will not render or affect any other geometry in the render.

For the scalp, you'll create a simple grid and then add follicles if needed later.

ADDING HAIR TO A SURFACE

You can add hair to a surface in a number of ways. You can paint hair on the surface using the Artisan Brush interface, you can select faces on polygons or surface points on NURBS surfaces and apply hair to the selected components, or you can create a uniform grid of follicles on a surface. Once you attach follicles to a surface, you can add more follicles later to fill in blank areas by painting them on the surface.

---

4. Make sure the scalp surface is selected, switch to the nDynamics menu, and choose nHair ➢ Create Hair ➢ Options.

5. In the Create Hair Options dialog box, choose Edit ➢ Reset Settings to reset the options to the default settings.

6. Set the Output to Paint Effects, and choose the Grid option. Use the following settings:

U and V Count: **24**

Passive Fill: **0**

Randomization: **0.1**

UNDERSTANDING FOLLICLE TYPES

Follicles can be dynamic, passive, or static:

Dynamic Follicles   Dynamic follicles react to forces and dynamic fields based on the settings in the hairSystem node or on any dynamic overrides created in the follicle shape node. Dynamic follicles can collide with surfaces.

Passive Follicles   Passive follicles inherit the dynamic motion of nearby dynamic follicles, which can reduce computational overhead, especially when collisions are involved.

Static Follicles   Static follicles have no dynamic motion but can be used to style parts of the hair. You can change the mode of a follicle after creating the hair system if you decide to make a passive follicle dynamic, make a dynamic follicle static, and so on.

The Randomization setting randomizes the arrangement of the grid to make the hair placement look less even.

By increasing the Passive Fill option, a number of the follicles created when the hair is attached to the surface will be passive rather than dynamic. If the Passive Fill option is set to 1, every other row and column of the follicles based on the settings for U and V Count will be passive follicles. If the setting is 2, every two rows and every two columns of follicles will be passive.

When you first create a hair system, you can create a number of passive follicles using this setting. This speeds up the dynamics as you create the initial hairstyle. Later you can convert the follicles to dynamic or static follicles as needed.

7. Select the Edge Bounded and Equalize options.

When the Grid method is used, the follicles are placed uniformly on the surface based on the U and V coordinates. If Edge Bounded is on, the follicles are placed up to and including the edge of the UV coordinates. In the case of the example, this means that hairs are placed along the edge of the scalp surface. The Equalize option evens out the spacing of the follicle placement to compensate for areas of the U and V coordinates that may be stretched or squashed.

8. Set Points Per Hair to **20** and Length to **5**.

Hairs that have more points per curve are more flexible and have more detail in their motion as they respond to dynamics; they also slow down the playback speed of Maya in the scene. The Length attribute can be modified after creation.

The Place Hairs Into option should be set to New Hair System. If a hair system exists in the scene already, you can use this option to add the newly created hairs into the existing system by selecting it from the list. Figure 14.18 shows the settings for the new hair.

FIGURE 14.18
The Create Hair
Options area

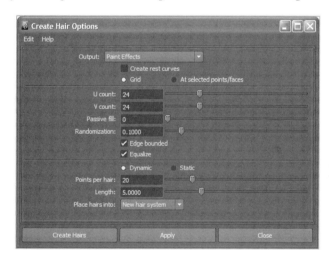

9. Click Create Hairs to make the hair. The hairs appear as long spikes coming out of the head (see Figure 14.19).

10. Select the nancy head geometry. Choose nMesh ➤ Create Passive Collider.

11. Click Play, and the hairs start to fall. After a few moments, the hairs start to settle.

12. Save the scene as **nancyHair_v02.ma**.

To see a version of the scene, open the nancyHair_v02.ma scene from the chapter14\scenes folder.

In the next section, you'll learn how to style the hair.

FIGURE 14.19
The hairs appear as long spikes on the top of the head. When you click the Play button, the hairs fall and settle into a basic hair shape.

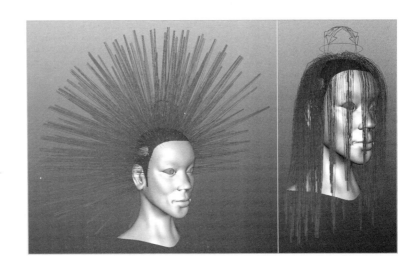

HAIR TRANSPLANTS

You can move an existing hair system from one surface to another using the Transplant command. To use this command, follow these steps:

1. Select the hair system you want to move.

2. Ctrl/Cmd+click the destination surface.

3. From the Dynamics menu, choose nHair ➤ Transplant Hair.

If the surfaces have very similar UV texture coordinates, you can choose to move the hair based on the UV coordinates in the Transplant options. Otherwise, you can choose to move the hair based on the closest points in the surface. In this case, make sure that the destination surface is placed and scaled to match the existing hair system and its source.

Determining Hair Shape

A number of settings in the hair system node determine the look of the hair. These are found in the Clump and Hair Shape section of the hair system's attributes.

1. Continue with your scene or open the nancyHair_v03.ma scene from the chapter14\ scenes folder.

2. Select hairSystem1, and open its Attribute Editor to the hairSystemShape1 tab.

DISPLAY QUALITY

You can decrease the Display Quality of the nHair to improve performance while working in the scene. Keep in mind, though, this means you will not be viewing the actual amount of hair on the head.

---

3. The hair appears as groups bunched around long spikes that shoot out from the scalp. Each group of hairs is a clump. The movement of each clump of hair is driven by the movement of the follicles. This way, Maya can create dynamics for thousands of hairs using a much smaller number of follicles. The hair remains as long spikes until you play the simulation and let the hair fall down. For the moment, leave the animation at frame 1. It's easier to see how the clumps work when the hair is in its spiky state. In the Clump and Hair Shape section, increase the Hairs Per Clump number to **60** to increase the fullness of the hair.

4. Play the animation until frame 20, and then stop the animation.

5. Zoom in to the end of a clump, and move the Bend Follow slider back and forth.

When Bend Follow is at 0, the end of the clump appears flat if the follicle is curved. When Bend Follow is 1, the clump shape is more tubular toward the end of the clump. This attribute should be used to fine-tune the look of your hair as you develop the overall shape.

6. Rewind the animation, and set Clump Width to **0.7**. This expands the overall width of the clumps, which helps fill out the hairstyle without the need to add more follicles.

In the Clump and Hair Shape rollout, you can use the following settings to determine the look of the hair:

Baldness Map The Baldness Map field allows you to apply a texture to control where the hair grows on the head. The texture must be a black-and-white 2D texture. The texture itself does not need to be baked as it does with fur. Just like with fur, black areas of the map indicate no hair (or baldness), and white areas indicate places where the hair grows. Texture maps can also be used, much like the texture maps created for fur baldness.

Sub Segments Use this setting to improve the details of the hair (such as curls and kinks) when rendered. Increasing this setting does not affect the dynamics of the hair.

Thinning Higher values decrease the number of hairs per clump to create a thin and wispy look to the hair.

Clump Twist This setting rotates each clump around the base of the follicle. Positive values rotate the clump in one direction; negative values rotate it in the opposite direction. Twisting the clump rotates all of the hairs uniformly. If you like the way the hair looks on one side of the clump, you can use the clump twist to rotate the preferred side toward the camera.

Bend Follow This setting determines how closely the rotation of the clump affects the shape of the hair clumps. This is most noticeable at the end of each clump.

Hair Width Hair Width adjusts the width of the hairs. This setting can be used to thicken or thin the hair. The effect of changing hair width is seen when the hair is rendered. This is a setting you'll probably want to return to when you are setting up your hair for a render.

Below the Clump and Hair Shape setting sliders are a number of edit curves that can be used to further refine the hair shape. The left side of each curve represents the area of the clump closest to the root; the right side represents the area closest to the tip. Each scale uses the setting in the sliders in the Clump And Hair Shape section as a starting point, so each scale is a modifier for the settings you have already created. The following describes how each ramp affects the look of the hair:

Clump and Hair Width Scale You can exaggerate or reduce the amount of tapering in the clumps by changing the Clump Width Scale edit curve. Hair Width Scale modifies the width of the hairs based on the setting in the Hair Width slider.

Clump Curl The Clump Curl edit curve can be used to twist the clumps around the central axis of the follicle. By default, the graph is set so that the value of the curling is at 0.5. By moving a point on the curve up or down (moving up creates values closer to 1; moving down creates values closer to 0), the curling twists in one direction or the other (see Figure 14.20).

FIGURE 14.20
Adding and moving points along the various edit curves can shape the overall look of the hair.

Clump Flatness The Clump Flatness scale can be used to make the clumps appear as flat planks of hair. Higher values along the curve flatten out the clumps. This setting works well for creating the shape of wet hair.

The final two settings in this section are sliders labeled Clump Interpolation and Interpolation Range:

Clump Interpolation Increasing the Clump Interpolation slider spreads the hair out between clumps. This slider can be used to even out the shape of the hair so that the clumping is much less obvious. Dynamics are calculated based on the position of each clump. If you set a high Clump Interpolation value, you may find that hairs do not appear to collide correctly. This is because the interpolation can push hairs outside the boundary of the original clump width, and thus their placement exceeds the collision width of their clump.

Interpolation Range   Interpolation Range sets the limits for how far a hair can move out of the width of the clump when Clump Interpolation is increased. The value set in Interpolation Range is multiplied against the Clump Width setting.

7. Play the animation to frame 50 and stop.

8. Remove any extra points you may have placed on the Clump Width Scale and Clump Curl so that there are only two points on the scales, one on the far right and one on the far left.

9. Set the value of the point on the left side of the Clump Width Scale to **1**; set the point on the far right to **0.32**.

10. Set the point on the far right of the Clump Curl curve to **0.6**.

11. Set the point on the far left of the Clump Flatness scale to **0.5**. Add a point to the far right side of Clump Flatness, and move it to **0.7**. This helps the roots of the hair to lie closer to the head, creating less of a "poufy" shape.

12. Set Clump Interpolation to **0.3**. Leave Interpolation Range set to the default value of **8**.

13. Rewind and play the animation, and make any changes you'd like to the shape of the hair. The length, color, and other properties are further defined in the next section. Rewind and play the animation.

14. Save the scene as **nancyHair_v03.ma**.

To see a version of the scene, open the nancyHair_v03.ma scene from the chapter14/scenes folder.

FOLLICLE OVERRIDES

Many of the settings found in the hairSystemShape node are also found on the nodes for individual follicles in the Per Follicle Overrides section of each follicle's Attribute Editor. You can use these overrides to refine the hair shape for individual follicles. Dynamic overrides are available only for dynamic follicles; these settings are grayed out for passive or static follicles.

Styling Hair

Once the hair has been set up, you can use a number of tools to style it. You can use dynamic fields as a hair-styling tool, paint follicle properties on the hair, or even manipulate the CVs of control curves.

Start and Rest Positions

Before styling the hair properly, you should create a start position for the hair so that the animation does not start with the hair sticking straight out of the head. Doing so makes styling much easier.

The start position represents the shape of the hair at the start of the simulation. The rest position represents the hair's shape when no forces are acting upon it. These are very similar, but you can distinguish between the two by thinking of it like this: Imagine an animation where a character is jumping up and down and then stops. The animation starts with the character in midair. You want to set the start position to represent what the hair looks like when the character is in midair. Once the character stops jumping and the hair settles, the hair assumes its rest position. For some animations the start and rest positions may look exactly the same; at other times, such as in the example described, the start and rest positions look different.

1. Continue using the scene from the previous section, or open the nancyHair_v03.ma scene from the chapter14\scenes folder.

2. Play the animation until the hair has completely settled (see Figure 14.21).

FIGURE 14.21
Establish the basic shape of the hair using the settings in the hairSystem1 node.

3. Once the hair has settled, expand the hairSystem1Follicles group in the Outliner and Shift+click all of the follicle nodes.

4. Choose nHair ➤ Set Start Position ➤ From Current.

5. Set the rest position by choosing nHair ➤ Set Rest Position ➤ From Current.

6. Rewind the animation. The hair should now be down and relatively motionless at the start of the animation.

The start and rest positions are determined by two sets of curves that drive the follicles. You can activate the visibility of these curves in the Perspective window.

7. In the Viewport menu, use the Show menu to turn off the visibility of Strokes. This hides the Paint Effects hair.

HAIRSTYLE PRESETS

Maya comes with a number of preset hairstyles in the Visor, as shown here. You can open these by choosing (from the nDynamics menu) nHair ➤ Get Hair Example. To use a hairstyle, right-click one of the icons and choose to import the file into your scene. Each preset style comes with hair-line geometry that can be parented to your character's head. Or you can copy the style using the Transplant Hair option.

> **SETTING THE START AND REST POSITIONS**
>
> Notice that you can set the start position from the rest position, and vice versa. You can change these positions at any time as you continue to work on the hair and any animations. Notice also that the start and rest positions are applied to the follicles themselves, rather than to the hair system. This means that you can set start and rest positions for individual follicles if needed.

8. Select the hairSystem1 node, and choose nHair ➢ Display ➢ Start Position. A series of curves appears in blue, representing the hair's start position.

9. Choose nHair ➢ Display ➢ Rest Position. The rest position curves appear in red. If the start and rest positions for the hair system are different, each set of curves will have a different shape.

10. Choose nHair ➢ Display ➢ Start Position. Save the scene as **nancyHair_v04.ma**.

To see a version of the scene, open the nancyHair_v04.ma scene from the chapter14\scenes folder at the book's web page.

Painting Follicle Attributes

Using the Artisan Brush interface, you can paint follicle attributes. Before doing this, you must make sure that the hair is in its rest or start position. Some attributes, such as Inclination, require that the animation be on frame1.

1. Continue with the scene from the previous section, or open the nancyHair_v04.ma scene from the chapter14\scenes folder.

2. Select the hairSystem1 node or the scalp surface.

3. From the nDynamics menu, choose nHair ➢ Paint Hair Follicles.

The Tool Options area for the Artisan Brush interface opens as well as the Paint Hair Follicles Settings pop-up box.

4. Set Paint Mode to Trim Hairs. This setting allows you to reduce the length of the hair as you paint across the follicles.

For the dynamics to remain consistent, you must adjust the number of points on the hair as you paint. When you created the hair originally, the Points Per Hair attribute was set to 10, so to trim the length of a hair by half, set Points Per Hair to **5**. The Points Per Hair setting determines how the hair will be trimmed. When you set Points Per Hair to 5, the hair will be trimmed to half the original length regardless of the Hair Length setting.

5. Set Points Per Hair to **5**, and paint across the follicles in the front of the scalp to create bangs for the nancy character (see Figure 14.22).

6. Once you have trimmed the hair, select the follicles in the Outliner (it's easiest just to Shift+click all the follicles rather than figure out which ones were painted), and choose Hair ➢ Set Rest Position ➢ From Current.

7. To extend the hair, set Paint Mode to Extend Hairs, and increase Points Per Hair to a number larger than 10. Remember to reset the rest and start positions after extending the hair.

You can use the nHair ➢ Scale Hair tool to apply global scaling to the hair. To use this tool, select it from the nHair menu, and drag left or right. This tool will scale all aspects of the hair, so some adjustment to the shape and dynamics settings may be required after using the tool.

FIGURE 14.22
Trim the hair at the front of the head using the Paint Hair Follicles tool.

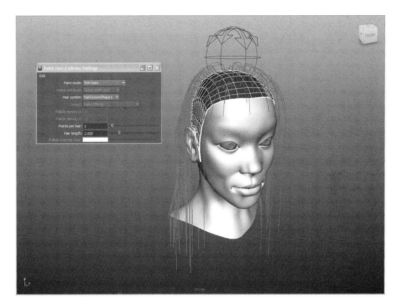

QUICK SELECT FOLLICLES

Repeatedly selecting all the follicles or certain follicles whenever you need to set the rest or start position gets tedious rather quickly. You can speed up the process by creating a quick selection set for the follicles.

1. Shift+click the follicles in the Outliner.

2. Choose Create ➢ Sets ➢ Quick Select Set.

3. Name the set **NancyFolliclesAll**.

4. You have the option to create a shelf button for this set. To do this, click Add Shelf Button.

   The button appears in the shelf. Every time you need to select all the follicles, just click the button.

5. If you want the button to appear on the shelf the next time you start Maya, click the down-facing black triangle next to the shelf, and choose Shelf ➢ Save All Shelves.

Be aware that this selection set is specific to this scene. If you click the button in another scene, you will get an error.

If you want to take it a step further, try writing a MEL script that selects the follicles and sets the rest and/or start position all in one click. Creating MEL scripts is discussed in Bonus Chapter 1, "Scripting with MEL and Python," on this book's web page.

To paint other attributes, set Paint Mode to Edit Follicle Attributes and choose an attribute from the Follicle Attribute menu. When painting these attributes, the Value setting in the Brush Options area determines the value painted on the follicles.

8. Save the scene as **nancyHair_v05.ma**.

To see a version of the scene, open the nancyHair_v05.ma scene from the chapter14\scenes folder.

Modifying Curves

You can modify curves directly by moving their CVs or by using the tools in the Hair ➢ Modify Curves menu. By modifying curves directly, you can fine-tune a style.

You can modify only start or rest curves. To do this, use the Show menu in the viewport window to disable the visibility of strokes in the scene, and choose nHair ➢ Display Rest Position (or Start Position). Select the curve (or right-click the curve and choose Control Vertex to work just on selected CVs), and apply one of the actions listed in the nHair ➢ Modify Curves menu. You can also edit the shape of the curve directly using the Move tool to change the position of CVs on the curve (see Figure 14.23).

FIGURE 14.23
Modify the CVs of a start curve using the Move tool.

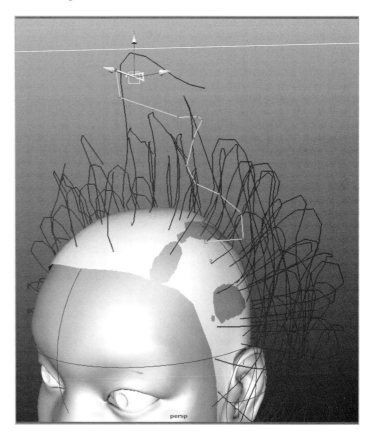

As you are editing the curve, you can lock the length so that the changes you make do not stretch the curve beyond its original length. Select the curve, and choose nHair ➤ Lock Length (or use the l hot key). Conversely, you can unlock the curve if you want to change its length.

Curling, Noise, Sub Clumping, and Braids

Curling, Noise, and Braids all work best when the Sub Segments attribute in the Clump and Hair Shape section of the hair system node is increased. You can find the Curling and Noise settings in the Displacement section of the hair system node.

The Sub Clumping setting causes the hair within clumps to bunch together. This helps when you are creating wet or kinky hair.

The Braid option is available as an attribute for individual hair follicle nodes. For a braid to work successfully, you may need to alter the clump shape and the hairs per clump. It may be a good idea to use a separate hair system to create a detailed braid.

DELETING HAIR SYSTEMS

Maya allows you to delete specific parts of your hair system. This works for hair curves and Paint Effects hair. Deleting nHair is useful if you wish to retain hair curves or the hair system nodes in order to reuse them in other hair simulations. Select the curves you want to delete and choose nHair ➤ Delete Hair.

Rendering Hair

Rendering hair can be done using Maya Software or mental ray. The hair should be either Paint Effects strokes or Paint Effects strokes converted to geometry. Paint Effects strokes are discussed in detail in Chapter 10, "Paint Effects."

COLORING HAIR

If you decide to render hair as Paint Effects strokes, you can change the Hair Color, Translucence, and Specular properties using the settings in the hairSystemShape tab's Shading section.

Rendering hair is a straightforward process. If you're not familiar with Paint Effects, you should review Chapter 10 before reading this section.

When you convert hair to geometry, the Hair Tube shader is automatically applied. You can render Paint Effects hair using mental ray without the need to convert the hair to geometry.

When you are ready to render the hair, you'll want to increase the Hair Sub Segments setting in the hairSystem node's Attribute Editor, as well as Hairs Per Clump, Hair Width, and Hair Width Scale, in order to create fuller hair. You can always add follicles as well using the Paint Follicles tool.

In the Render Stats section of the hairSystem node, you can enable Receive Shadows, Visible In Reflections, and Visible In Refractions when rendering with mental ray. If the hair will not render using mental ray, make sure the Render Fur/Hair setting is selected on the Features tab of the mental ray Rendering section.

In this scene, the `dreads.mel` preset, found on the Hair Examples tab of the Visor, is applied to the nancy model. The `hairLights.mel` file has also been imported from the Visor and applied to the scene.

1. Open the `renderHair.ma` scene from the `chapter14\scenes` folder at the book's web page.

2. Switch to the quarterSide camera, and create a test render in the Render View window.

The scene is set up to render using mental ray. The render will take a couple of minutes. Figure 14.24 shows the results (shadows have been enabled for the lights in the image).

FIGURE 14.24
Apply the dreadlocks preset hair to the nancy model, and render it with mental ray.

Most standard lights will render hair nicely. When you're testing the look of the hair, using the `hairLights.mel` preset makes it easy to see how the hair will look when rendered.

Creating Clothing for Characters

In this section, you'll explore techniques for using nCloth to add dynamic motion to a character's clothes. The example files are simple, but you can use the same techniques for more complex characters and models.

The Nucleus solver divides its computations into multiple threads for self-colliding surfaces and stretch resistance. Additional threading is also used to speed up playback of simulations with multiple nCloth objects on the same solver. Before starting this section, you should review Chapter 12 ("Introducing nParticles") and Chapter 13 ("Dynamic Effects") so that you understand how nDynamics and the Nucleus solver work.

Modeling Clothes for nCloth

The models you create for use with nCloth must be polygon meshes. Beyond that, there is nothing special about how you model your clothing. Smooth mesh polygons work just as well as standard polygons. You'll start by taking a look at an example scene.

This scene has a simple cartoon character that has been rigged and animated. The character has a shirt and pants that have been created using standard polygon modeling techniques. Both objects are currently smooth mesh polygons. The scene has been arranged so that the display layers contain the major components of the model and the animation rig.

1. Open the `simpleMan_v01.ma` scene from the `chapter14\scenes` folder at the book's web page (see Figure 14.25).

FIGURE 14.25
The `simpleMan_v01`
`.ma` scene contains a
simple cartoon char-
acter. Clothes have
been modeled using
polygons.

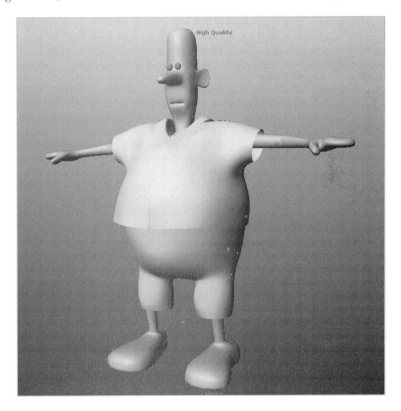

2. Switch to the nDynamics menu.

3. Select the pants, and choose nMesh ➢ Create nCloth. The pants switch to standard polygon mode.

4. Select the pants, and press the **3** key to switch to smooth mesh polygons.

5. Play the scene. You'll see the pants fall down. (This kind of thing can be embarrassing, but it happens a lot to cartoon characters; see Figure 14.26.)

FIGURE 14.26
When you play the scene, the character's pants fall down.

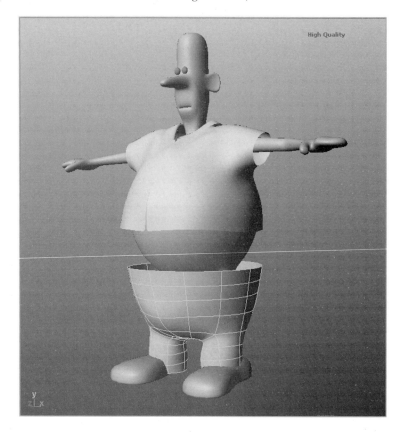

The first step in preventing the pants from falling is to make the character's body a Passive Collider object. It does not matter that the character is already rigged and animated. However, it's a good idea to convert the polygons to nCloth objects (both nCloth and Passive Collider objects) when the character is in the default pose and there are no intersections between the nCloth and Passive Collider geometry.

1. Rewind the animation.

2. In the Display Layer Editor, click the R next to the MAN layer to turn off Reference mode so that you can directly select the man geometry.

3. Select the man geometry, and choose nMesh ➤ Create Passive Collider.

SIMPLE VS. COMPLEX GEOMETRY

The geometry used for the man is fairly simple. If you have a complex character, you may want to use a lower-resolution copy of the geometry as a collision object. This lower-resolution copy should have its Primary Visibility setting turned off in the Render Stats section of its Attribute Editor, and the geometry should be skinned to joints or deformers in a way that matches the deformations of the higher-resolution objects.

---

4. Make sure that you are starting at frame 0 and play the scene. The pants still fall down, but the character's feet stop them from falling indefinitely.

5. Save the scene as **simpleMan_v02.ma**.

To see a version of the scene, open the simpleMan_v02.ma scene from the chapter14\scenes folder.

In the next section, you'll create a constraint that will keep a character's pants from falling down.

Using Constraints

The simplest way to keep the character's pants on is to create a transform constraint. A transform constraint attaches the selected vertices on an nCloth object to the pivot point of another object without affecting the position of the nCloth vertices. When the constraining object is translated or rotated, the vertices follow along, dragging the rest of the nCloth object with them.

1. Continue with the scene from the previous section, or open the simpleMan_v02.ma scene from the chapter14\scenes folder at the book's web page.

2. Turn off the visibility of the MAN layer, and turn on the visibility of the JOINTS layer.

   At the center of the pelvis, you'll see a locator. This is the rootCtrl locator used to animate the character's skeleton. You can use this locator as the constraining object for the nCloth pants.

3. Right-click the pants, and choose Edge to switch to edge selection mode.

4. Double-click one of the edges at the top of the pants. Doing so selects all the edges that run around the top of the pants (left image, Figure 14.27).

5. Hold the mouse over the selected edges, press the Ctrl/Cmd key, and RMB-drag to the left.

6. Select the To Vertices label from the marking menu. This converts the selection to vertices (center image, Figure 14.27).

7. With the vertices selected (they should be highlighted in yellow) in the Outliner, Ctrl/Cmd+click the rootCtrl locator, and choose nConstraint ➢ Transform. The vertices should

turn green, indicating that they are constrained. In the Outliner, you'll see a new dynamicConstraint1 node has been created.

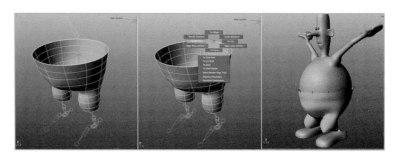

8. Turn the visibility of the MAN layer back on, and play the animation. The pants should now stay in place, and when the man starts moving, they should collide with the character's legs (right image, Figure 14.27).

9. Save the scene as **simpleMan_v03.ma**.

To see a version of the scene, open the simpleMan_v03.ma scene from the chapter14\scenes folder at the book's web page.

You can also constrain objects to components of nCloth objects, such as vertices. Using this technique, you can easily simulate the effect of buttons holding a shirt together.

1. Continue with the scene from the previous section, or open the simpleMan_v03.ma scene from the chapter14\scenes folder.

2. In the Display Layer Editor, turn on the visibility of the SHIRT layer.

3. Before converting the shirt to an nCloth object, make sure that it does not intersect with the pants. Rotate the view so that you can see the back of the character; here you can see that the shirt is intersecting the pants (left image, Figure 14.28).

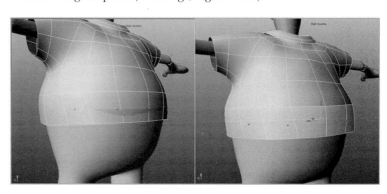

4. Right-click the faces near the intersection, and choose Faces.

5. Use the Move tool to move the faces outward just enough that they do not intersect the pants (right image, Figure 14.28).

6. Select the shirt, and choose nMesh ➤ Create nCloth. The shirt switches back to standard polygon mode; select the shirt, and press the **3** key to return to smooth mesh.

7. Rewind and play the animation. The shirt falls until it collides with the character geometry. It moves as the character moves; however, you can see the front of the shirt fly open (see Figure 14.29).

FIGURE 14.29
As the character moves, the front of the shirt flies open.

8. Zoom in to the front of the shirt, and turn off the visibility of the MAN and PANTS display layers.

9. Right-click the shirt, and choose Vertex.

10. Switch to wireframe mode. Select the two vertices at the top of the shirt close to the collar (see Figure 14.30, left image).

11. Choose nConstraints ➤ Component To Component. This creates a constraint between the two vertices.

12. Repeat steps 10 and 11 to create constraints for the other three pairs of vertices running down the shirt. You don't need to constrain the two at the very bottom. You should end

up with four constraints running down the front of the shirt (see Figure 14.30, right image).

FIGURE 14.30
Select vertices near the collar, and turn them into a constraint (left image). Then create four pairs of constraints on the front of the shirt (right image).

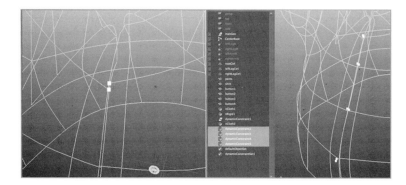

13. Switch to shaded mode, turn on the MAN and PANTS layers, and rewind and play the scene. The front of the shirt is now bound as if it has buttons (see Figure 14.31).

FIGURE 14.31
When you play the animation, the shirt stays closed as if it has buttons.

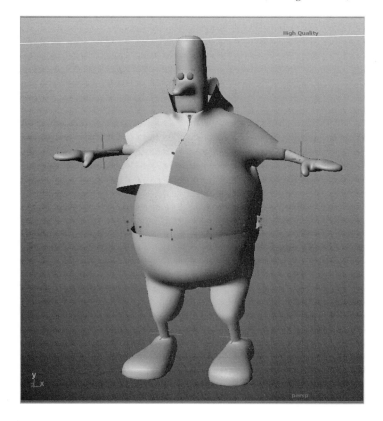

14. Save the scene as **simpleMan_v04.ma**.

To see a version of the scene, open the `simpleMan_v04.ma` scene from the `chapter14\scenes` folder at the book's web page.

---

nConstraint Membership

You can add, replace, or remove vertices from an nConstraint interactively using the nConstraint Membership Tool. You can also manually select the vertices and select the specific tool from the nConstraint drop-down menu.

Maya 2014 added a new type of constraint called simply Component. The Component constraint differs from the Component To Component constraint you just used; you can use it to replace nCloth's internal Stretch constraints. As a result, you gain a high level of individual control. The following steps demonstrate the process and the potential for the Component constraint:

1. Continue with the scene from the previous section, or open the `simpleMan_v04.ma` scene from the `chapter14\scenes` folder.

2. Select all of the vertices of the man's shirt except for his sleeves (see Figure 14.32).

FIGURE 14.32
Select the vertices of the shirt minus the sleeves.

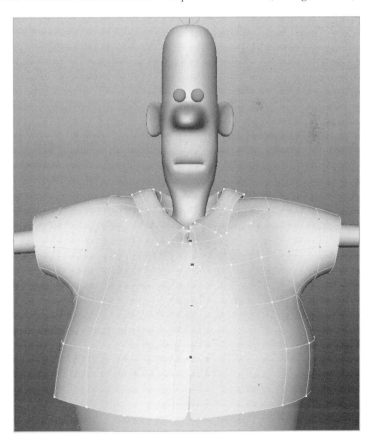

3. Open the tool options for nConstraint ➤ Component. Make sure you are using the defaults by resetting the tool. Click Apply to add the constraint (see Figure 14.33).

FIGURE 14.33
The default
attributes of
the Component
constraint

SINGLE EDGE

The Single Edge parameter lets you specify how the edges receive the constraint. Leaving the setting at its default of 0 causes all of the edges to have a constraint. A value of 1 adds the constraint to the edges in only one direction, whereas 2 adds them orthogonally to the first row of constraining edges. Adding the constraint in this manner gives you individual control over each of the surface's directions. By decreasing the Rest Length Scale parameter on the constraint itself, you can cause sleeves to roll up or stretch independently with gravity.

---

4. The Component constraint now controls the stretch values of the edges. Open the nCloth's Attribute Editor. Set the Stretch Resistance value to **0.0**.

Click the Play button to see the effects. The shirt holds together well where the constraint was added, but the sleeves slink down with gravity since they have no stretch resistance (see Figure 14.34).

5. Return to frame 1. Select the two end loops of vertices from each sleeve and choose nConstraint ➤ Component. The same options from step 3 are applied.

6. Click the Play button to see the effects of the two constraints. Compare these to how the simulation worked without them. The sleeves are allowed to stretch more since there are no cross links holding back the garment's ability to stretch. There is no need to save the scene file to continue.

Connecting Buttons to the Shirt

You can connect buttons to the shirt geometry using the Point On Poly constraint:

1. Continue with the scene from the previous section, or open the `simpleMan_v04.ma` scene from the `chapter14\scenes` folder at the book's web page.

2. In the Outliner, select button1. The button is located at the origin, so currently it is in the center of the character. Use the Move tool to move the button close to the top of the shirt. Enter the following settings:

    Translate X: **0.115**

    Translate Y: **3.576**

    Translate Z: **2.295**

FIGURE 14.34
Without any resistance, the sleeves stretch with gravity.

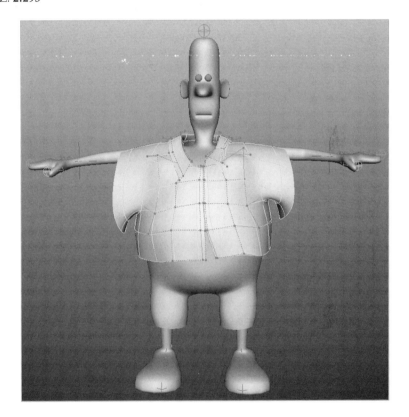

3. Right-click the shirt geometry, and choose Vertex to switch to vertex selection mode.

4. Select one of the vertices toward the top of the shirt on the inside edge (see Figure 14.35). Shift+click the button1 node.

5. Switch to the Animation menu, and choose Constrain ➤ Point On Poly. The button will snap to the geometry. Most likely, the position and the rotation will be off.

6. In the Outliner, select the button1 object, expand it, and select the button1_pointOnPoly-Constraint1 node.

FIGURE 14.35
Select the vertices
toward the top of
the shirt, and then
Shift+click the
button.

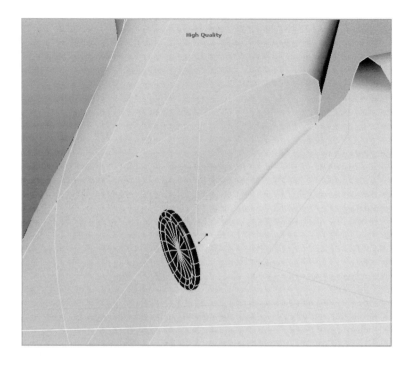

7. Open the Channel Box, and MMB-drag the field for Offset Rotate X to rotate the button to a better position; try a value of **75**. You can use the other Offset fields to fine-tune the rotation and position of the button (see Figure 14.36).

FIGURE 14.36
The Offset fields
are used to rotate
and translate the
constrained but-
ton into the correct
position.

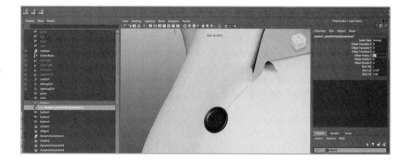

8. Repeat the process to constrain the other three buttons in the Outliner to the shirt.

9. Save the scene as **simpleMan_v05.ma**.

To see a version of the scene, open the simpleMan_v05.ma scene from the chapter14\scenes folder at the book's web page.

You can also select a face of a polygon object and use the Point On Poly constraint to attach an object to a polygon face.

Applying Forces

You can use wind or a directional force to move an nCloth object. You can assign these locally, affecting the object and leaving all other nCloth objects unaffected. This feature can be useful to give elements such as capes a cinematic feel. The settings to modify a local force or local wind are located on the nCloth shape node (see Figure 14.37).

FIGURE 14.37

The Local Force and
Local Wind settings

Painting nCloth Properties

nCloth properties can be painted to gain detail in your simulation. You can paint properties such as Bounce, Stretch, and Wrinkle onto an nCloth object. All the properties can be painted as vertex maps or texture maps.

When you paint a vertex property map, you paint property values directly onto the vertices of the object, similar to painting smooth skin weights for joints. The more vertices you have in your object, the more detail you can create for your vertex property map. The vertex map values are saved with the object, so you do not need to link to external map files.

Texture property maps are independent of the number of vertices in the object, but they do require that UVs are properly created for the object, meaning that the UVs do not overlap and do remain within the 0 to 1 range in the UV Texture Editor. Texture property maps for nCloth objects are similar to texture property maps created for fur. However, you do not need to bake the maps after applying them.

When you paint a vertex or texture map, the map is listed in the Attribute field in the Dynamic Properties section of the nCloth shape node's Attribute Editor.

In this example, you'll paint Wrinkle attributes for the simple man character's pants. A wrinkle map displaces an nCloth object to create folds in the surface. You can paint detailed wrinkles into objects with a lot of vertices. In this example, you'll use the wrinkle map to add cartoonish embellishments to the pants, which have a fairly low number of vertices.

When applying a Wrinkle attribute, positive values push the nCloth outward, while negative values push it inward. There are a few peculiarities about painting Wrinkle values, which you'll explore in this exercise:

1. Continue with the scene from the previous section, or open the `simpleMan_v05.ma` scene from the `chapter14\scenes` folder.

2. Turn off the visibility of the SHIRT and JOINTS layers.

3. Rewind and play the animation. The pants maintain their shape until they start to collide.

4. Rewind the animation again; select the pants object, and from the nDynamics menu choose nMesh ➢ Paint Vertex Properties ➢ Wrinkle ➢ Options.

   The pants turn white, indicating that a value of 1 is applied to the vertices of the pants for the Wrinkle property. Make sure the Renderer in the Viewport menu is set to Default Render Quality so that you can see the color values painted onto the pants geometry.

5. Rewind and play the animation. The pants suddenly bloat outward even though you have not made any changes (see the top image in Figure 14.38). What just happened?

FIGURE 14.38
When you create the wrinkle map and play the animation, the pants bloat outward. When you apply the value 0 to all the vertices, the pants turn black and the shape returns to normal.

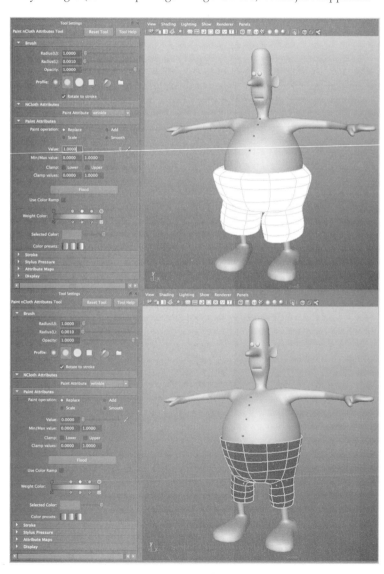

When you start to create the wrinkle map, Maya applies a value of 1 to all the vertices of the object at the moment the map is created. Prior to creating the wrinkle map, no Wrinkle value is applied to the pants, so they do not bloat outward until the map is made. This behavior is specific to the wrinkle map.

6. In the Tool Settings dialog box, set the value to **0**. Make sure that the Paint Attributes menu in the nCloth Attributes rollout panel of the Tool settings is set to Wrinkle.

7. Click the Flood button, and rewind the animation.

The pants turn black, and the bloating disappears. The wrinkle values are now set to 0 for all the vertices of the pants geometry (see bottom image in Figure 14.38).

At this point, you'll paint the area where the pant legs emerge from the pants with a value of **-0.2** so that the pant legs shrink inward. Notice, however, that the Value slider in the Artisan Tool options goes only from 0 to 1.

8. In the Tool Settings dialog box, look at the Min/Max value fields. Set the first field, which is the Min Value, to **-1**, and the second field, which is the Max Value, to **1**.

Now it is possible to paint negative numbers, but you'll notice that since the black color on the pants indicates a value of 0, there is no color feedback for negative numbers. This can be changed as well.

9. Scroll down to the bottom of the Tool Settings dialog box, and expand the Display rollout panel. Make sure Color Feedback is on. Set Min Color to **-1** and Max Color to **1** (see Figure 14.39).

FIGURE 14.39
You can adjust the Min/Max value fields to allow for a wider range of values for the Paint nCloth Attributes tool. Adjusting the Min Color and Max Color sliders lets you visualize the new values painted on the surface.

The pants turn gray, indicating that the current value applied to the vertices (0) is in the middle range of colors between black and white. As you paint negative values on the pants, you'll see darker areas appear.

10. Set the Value slider to **-0.2**, and paint around the area where the pant legs meet the pants.

11. Rewind and play the scene. You'll see the tops of the pant legs shrink in a little.

12. To create flares (flares on shorts are apparently all the rage now), set the value to **0.4**, and paint the cuffs of the pants (see Figure 14.40).

FIGURE 14.40
Paint a value of -0.2 around the belt area of the pants. Paint positive values near the pant cuffs to create flares.

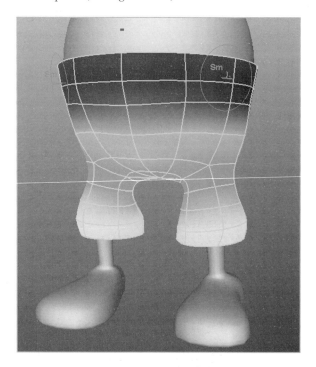

13. To create the impression of a drawstring, paint a value of **-1** around the area of the pants where a belt would go.

14. Press the **q** hot key to switch to the Select tool. Doing so will close the Artisan tool; the pants return to green.

15. Rewind and play the animation. Experiment making more changes by painting various Wrinkle values on the pants.

16. Save the scene as **simpleMan_v06.ma**.

To see a version of the scene, open the simpleMan_v06.ma scene from the chapter14\scenes folder.

To learn more about fur, hair, and nCloth, check out *Maya Studio Projects*: *Photorealistic Characters* (Sybex, 2011).

The Bottom Line

Add XGen descriptions to characters. XGen is a primitive generator that adds realistic short hairs to the surface of character. The placement, length, and other attributes of the hairs can be controlled by painting on the surface using the XGen grooming tools.

    Master It Create eyebrows for the head used at the beginning of this chapter.

Create dynamic curves. A standard Maya curve can be made dynamic by using the Make Dynamic Curves action in the Hair menu. A copy of the curve is created that will respond to dynamic motion and forces. The curve can be used in skeletons for IK Spline tools, as a source for Paint Effects strokes, as a modeling tool, or for any other effect that requires curves.

    Master It Create a flag using dynamic curves.

Add hair to characters. Hair is created using Paint Effects strokes that are controlled by follicles. The follicles are dynamic curves that respond to forces and movement. Follicles can be applied to polygon or NURBS surfaces as a grid or by painting on the surface. The Visor contains a number of hair presets that can be imported into a scene.

    Master It Add hair to the top of the giraffe's head from Chapter 9.

Style hair. Hair can be styled by painting attribute values on follicles or by directly editing the CVs of start or rest curves.

    Master It Create an avant-garde hairdo for the nancy character by painting attributes.

Paint nCloth properties. Properties such as Bounce, Stretch, and Wrinkle can be painted onto nCloth objects using either texture or vertex painting techniques. When painting properties, you may need to alter the Min and Max Value ranges in the Artisan interface to allow for values beyond the range of 0 to 1. Vertex maps have the advantage that the values are not stored in an external texture file.

    Master It Add starch to the simple man's shirt by painting a Rigidity value on the shirt geometry.

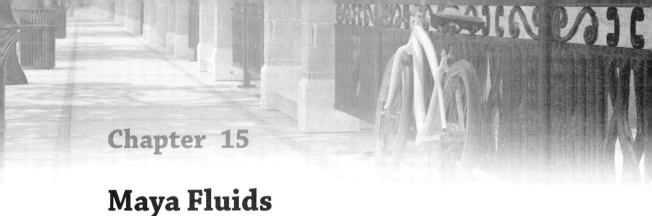

Chapter 15

Maya Fluids

In the Autodesk® Maya® software, Maya Fluids is a suite of tools designed to create a number of fluid-based effects. The tools available in Maya Fluids consist of containers and emitters, which are designed to simulate gaseous effects such as clouds, smoke, flames, explosions, galactic nebulae, and so on. Maya Fluids also include dynamic geometry deformers and shaders, which can be used to simulate rolling ocean waves, ripples in ponds, and wakes created by boats. In addition, Maya controls and features enhance the realism of the effects you can create using fluids.

In this chapter, you will learn to:

- ◆ Use fluid containers
- ◆ Create a reaction
- ◆ Render fluid containers
- ◆ Use fluids with nParticles
- ◆ Create an ocean

Using Fluid Containers

Fluid containers can be thought of as mini-scenes within a Maya scene. They are best used for gaseous and plasma effects such as clouds, flames, and explosions. The effect itself can exist only within the container. You can generate fluids inside the container by using an emitter or by painting the fluid inside the container. Dynamic forces then act on the fluid within the container to create the effect.

There are two types of containers: 2D and 3D. They work the same way. Two-dimensional containers are flat planes that generally calculate faster than 3D containers, which are cubical volumes. If you do not need an object to fly through a fluid effect or if the camera angle does not change in relation to the fluid, you might want to try a 2D container instead of a 3D container. Using a 2D container can save a lot of calculation and render time. Two-dimensional containers are also a great way to generate an image sequence that can be used as a texture on a surface.

Real World Scenario

FLUIDS VS. NPARTICLES

When should you use fluids, and when should you use nParticles? There's no hard-and-fast rule for choosing one over the other. However, if you need to create a dense cloud and you find yourself setting the rate of an nParticle emitter greater than 100,000 nParticles per second, you should consider switching to fluids. Fluids and nParticles can work together as well, as you'll see later in this chapter.

Fluids are not part of the Nucleus system, so they are not influenced by settings on the Nucleus solver. However, fluids are cached using the nCache caching system and share the same options. nParticles and the Nucleus solver are covered in Chapter 12, "Introducing nParticles," and Chapter 13, "Dynamic Effects."

Using 2D Containers

In this first exercise, you'll work with fluid basics to create a simple but interesting effect using 2D containers. When you set up a container, you can choose to add an emitter that generates the fluid within the container, or you can place the fluid inside the container using the Artisan Brush interface. You'll start your experimentation using the latter method.

1. Create a new scene in Maya. Switch to the Dynamics menu.

2. Choose Fluid Effects ➤ Create 2D Container. A simple plane appears on the scene.

   The simple plane is the 2D container. If you play the scene, nothing happens because currently there are no fluids within the container. In the Outliner, you'll see a new node named fluid1. The fluid1 object, like many Maya objects, consists of a transform node (named fluid1) and a shape node (fluidShape1).

3. Select fluid1, and choose Fluid Effects ➤ Add/Edit Contents ➤ Paint Fluids Tool.

4. Click the Tool settings icon in the upper right of the interface to open the settings for the Artisan Brush interface.

5. Under the Paint Attributes rollout, make sure Paintable Attributes is set to Density and Value is set to 1.

6. Paint a few strokes on the container. Clumps of green dots appear if you are in wireframe mode.

7. Press the **5** key on the keyboard to switch to shaded mode. The clumps appear as soft, blurry blobs (see Figure 15.1).

8. Set the length of the timeline to **200**.

9. Rewind and play the scene. The fuzzy blobs rise and distort like small clouds. They mix together and appear trapped by the edges of the container.

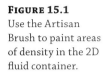

FIGURE 15.1
Use the Artisan Brush to paint areas of density in the 2D fluid container.

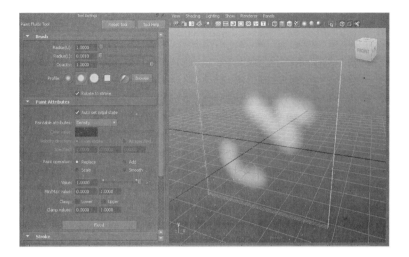

PLAYING FLUID SIMULATIONS

Like many dynamics modules in Maya, the Fluids module evaluates each frame based on what occurs in the previous frame. Therefore, you need to have your playback preferences set to Every Frame in order for Fluids to calculate correctly.

The properties that govern how the fluid exists within the container and how it behaves are controlled using the settings on the fluidShape1 node. When you painted in the container using the Paint Fluid tools, you painted the density of the fluid. By creating areas of density, you position the fluid in an otherwise empty container.

You can paint various attributes in a container using the Artisan Brush. Some attributes can be painted simultaneously, like Density And Color or Density And Fuel. Other attributes, like Velocity and Temperature, are painted singularly. As you work through the exercises in this chapter, you'll learn how these attributes affect your fluid simulations.

Adding an Emitter

Another way to generate a fluid within a fluid container is to use a *fluid emitter*. Fluid emitters are similar to particle emitters in that they consist of a point or area in 3D space that generates fluids at a rate you can control. The main difference between fluids and particles is that the fluids created by an emitter can exist only within the confines of the fluid container.

Fluid emitter types include omni, volume, surface, and curve:

♦ An omni emitter is a point in space that emits in all directions.

♦ A volume emitter creates fluids within a predefined area that can be in the form of a simple primitive such as a sphere or a cube.

♦ Surface emitters create fluids from the surface of a 3D object.

♦ Curve emitters create fluids along the length of a NURBS curve.

Maya fluid emission maps can control the emission of a fluid's density, heat, and fuel using a texture.

FLUID EMISSION

Although Maya uses terms like *heat* and *fuel* for its emission names, their functionality can differ. For instance, adding fuel to a container does not mean that it will automatically catch fire when heat is introduced. Fuel is merely a reactive element, and when combined with heat, it can cause a change in the properties of the fluid. The changes caused by fuel and heat combining can be anything from adding color to a rapid dissipation of the fluid.

This opens up a lot of possibilities for creating interesting effects. In this exercise, you'll map a file texture to the fluid's density attribute:

1. Continue with the scene from the previous section. Rewind the scene. In the options for the Artisan Brush, set Value to 0 and click the Flood button. This clears the container of any existing fluid density.

2. Create a NURBS plane (choose Create ➤ NURBS Primitives ➤ Plane). Rotate the plane 90 degrees on the x-axis, and scale the plane so that it fits within the 2D container (see Figure 15.2).

FIGURE 15.2
A NURBS plane is placed within the 2D fluid container.

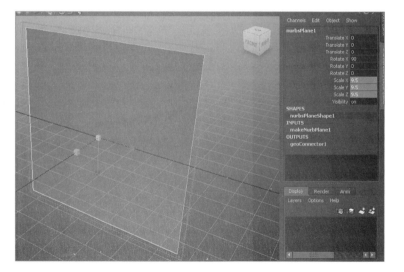

3. Select the plane, and then Shift+click the fluid1 node. Choose Fluid Effects ➤ Add/Edit Contents ➤ Emit From Object ➤ Options. In the options, make sure Emitter Type is set to Surface. You can leave the rest of the settings at their default values (see Figure 15.3).

FIGURE 15.3
The options for the
fluid emitter

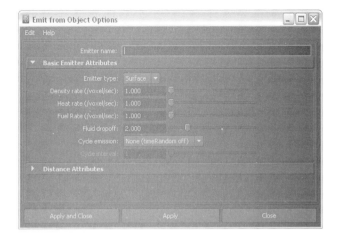

4. Rewind and play the animation; you'll see a cloud appear around the plane. To get a better idea of what's going on, use the Show menu in the viewport to disable the display of NURBS surfaces. This should not affect the simulation.

5. In the Outliner, expand the nurbsPlane1 object and select fluidEmitter1.

6. Open its Attribute Editor, and expand the Fluid Attributes rollout panel.

7. Click the checkered icon to the right of Density Emission Map (see Figure 15.4). This opens the Create Texture Node window. Select File from the 2D Textures section.

FIGURE 15.4
You can find the
Density Emission
Map settings in the
Attribute Editor for
the Fluid Emitter
node.

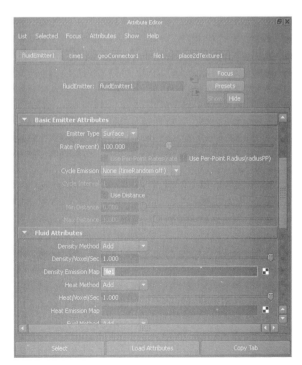

8. When you select the file texture type, a new node called file1 is added. The Attribute Editor for file1 should open automatically when you create the node; if it doesn't, open it now.

9. Click the folder icon to the right of the Image Name field. Browse your computer, and find the jollyRoger.tif file in the chapter15\sourceimages folder at the book's web page (www.sybex.com/go/masteringmaya2015).

10. Rewind and play the scene. You'll see a cloud appear in the form of the skull and cross-bones. After a few moments, it will rise to the top of the fluid container.

11. In the Outliner, select fluid1 and open its Attribute Editor.

12. To improve the look of the cloud, you can increase the Base Resolution setting of the fluid container. Set Base Resolution to **120**. This will slow down the playback of the scene, but the image will be much clearer (see Figure 15.5).

FIGURE 15.5
Increasing the Base Resolution setting will result in a clearer image created from the texture map.

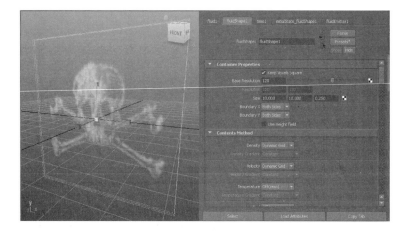

13. Save the scene as **jollyRoger_v01.ma**.

To see a version of the scene, open the jollyRoger_v01.ma scene from the chapter15\scenes folder at the book's web page. Create a playblast of the animation to see how the image acts as an emitter for the fluid.

Fluid containers are subdivided into a grid. Each subdivision is known as a *voxel*. When Maya calculates fluids, it looks at each voxel and how the fluid particles in one voxel affect the particles in the next voxel. As you increase the resolution of a fluid container, you increase the number of voxels and the number of calculations Maya has to perform in the simulation.

The Base Resolution slider is a single control that you can use to adjust the resolution of the fluid container along both the x- and y-axes as long as the Keep Voxels Square option is selected. If you decide you want to create rectangular voxels, you can deselect this option and then set the X and Y resolution independently. This can result in a stretched appearance for the fluid voxels. Generally speaking, square voxels will result in a better appearance for your fluid simulations.

The nice thing about 2D containers is that you can use a fairly high-resolution setting (such as 120) and get decent playback results. Three-dimensional containers take much longer to calculate because of the added dimension, so higher settings can result in really slow playback.

When using 2D or 3D containers, it's a good idea to start with the default Base Resolution setting and then move the resolution upward incrementally as you work on refining the effect.

EMISSION TEXTURE MAPS

Emission texture maps work only with surface and volume fluid emitters.

Using Fields with Fluids

Fluids can be controlled using dynamic fields such as Turbulence, Volume Axis, Drag, and Vortex. In this section, you'll distort the image of the Jolly Roger using a Volume Axis field.

As demonstrated in the previous section, when you play the Jolly Roger scene, the image forms and then starts to rise to the top of the container like a gas that is lighter than air. In this exercise, you want the image to remain motionless until a dynamic field is applied to the fluid. To do this, you'll need to change the Buoyancy property of the fluid and then set the initial state of the fluid container so that the image of the skull and crossbones is present when the animation starts.

1. Continue with the scene from the previous section, or open the jollyRoger_v01.ma scene from the chapter15\scenes folder at the book's web page.

2. In the Outliner, select the fluidShape1 node and open the Attribute Editor.

3. Scroll down to the Contents Details rollout panel, and expand the Density section.

4. Set Density Scale to **2**. Set Buoyancy to **0**. This can create a clearer image from the smoke without having to increase the fluid resolution (see Figure 15.6).

FIGURE 15.6
You set the Buoyancy option of the fluid so that the gas will not rise when the simulation is played.

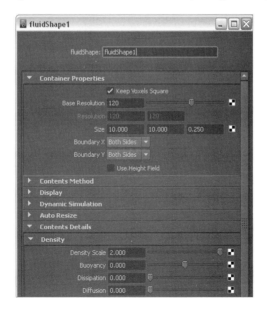

5. Rewind and play the animation. The image of the Jolly Roger should remain motionless as it forms.

6. Play the animation to frame 30, at which point you should see the image fairly clearly.

7. Select fluid1, and choose Fluid Effects ➤ Set Initial State.

8. Switch to the fluidEmitter1 tab in the Attribute Editor, and set Rate (percent) to **0** so that the emitter is no longer adding fluid to the container.

9. Rewind and play the animation.

You should see the image of the skull and crossbones clearly at the start of the animation, and it should remain motionless as the animation plays.

CHANGING THE DYNAMIC PROPERTIES OF A SIMULATION

If you set the initial state of a fluid but then decide to make changes to the dynamic properties of the simulation, first delete the initial state (Fluid Effects ➤ Clear Initial State) and then make your changes. Otherwise, the simulation may not update properly.

---

10. Select fluid1, and choose Fields ➤ Volume Axis. By selecting fluid1 before creating a field, you ensure that the field and the fluid are automatically connected.

In this exercise, imagine that the field is a cannonball moving through the ghostly image of the skull and crossbones.

11. Open the Attribute Editor for volumeAxisField1. Use the following settings:

Magnitude: **100**

Attenuation: **0**

Use Max Distance: **on**

Max Distance: **1**

Volume Shape: **Sphere**

Away From Center: **10**

12. On frame 1 of the animation, set the Translate Z of the Volume Axis field to **5**, and set a keyframe.

13. Set the timeline to frame **50**. Set the Translate Z of the Volume Axis field to **-5**, and set another keyframe.

14. Set Translate X to **1.3** and Translate Y to **2**.

15. Rewind and play the animation (or create a playblast). As the Volume Axis field passes through the container, it pushes the fluid outward like a cannonball moving through smoke (see Figure 15.7).

FIGURE 15.7
The Volume Axis
field pushes the
smoke as it moves
through the field.

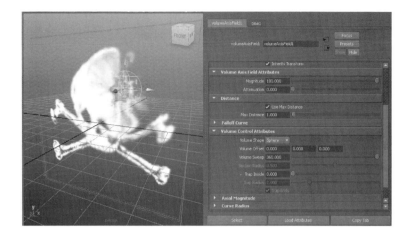

FLUID EXAMPLES

Maya comes with a number of fluid examples located in the Visor. To use one of these examples, choose Fluid Effects ➢ Get Fluid Example. You can find the fluid examples on the Ocean Examples, Fluid Examples, and Fluid Initial States tabs (as shown here). To use an example, RMB-click its icon and choose Import Into Maya Scene. Information about the examples is stored in the Notes section of the fluid shape node's Attribute Editor. These notes explain how the example was created and how it can be edited. Much of the information in the notes will make more sense after you have some experience using fluids.

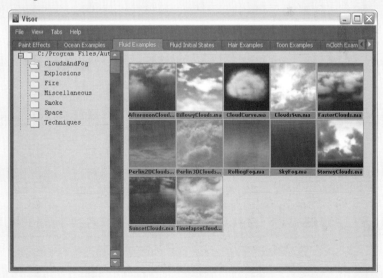

16. Add two more Volume Axis fields to the container, with the same settings. Position them so that they pass through the image at different locations and at different frames on the timeline.

17. Create a playblast of the scene. Watch it forward and backward in FCheck.

18. Save the scene as `jollyRoger_v02.ma`.

To see a version of the scene up to this point, open the `jollyRoger_v02.ma` scene from the `chapter15\scenes` folder at the book's web page. You will need to create a new cache for this scene in order to see the effect.

If you decide to try rendering this scene, make sure the Primary Visibility setting of the NURBS plane is turned off in Render Stats of the plane's Attribute Editor; otherwise, the plane will be visible in the render.

Now that you have had a little practice working with containers, the next section explores some of the settings more deeply as you create an effect using 3D fluid containers and emitters.

Using 3D Containers

Three-dimensional fluid containers work just like 2D containers, except they have depth as well as width and height. Therefore, they are computationally much more expensive. If you double the resolution in X and Y for a 2D container, the number of voxels increases by a factor of 4 (2×2); if you double the resolution of a 3D container, the number of voxels increases by a factor of 8 ($2 \times 2 \times 2$). A good practice for working with 3D containers is to start at a low resolution, such as $20 \times 20 \times 20$, and increase the resolution gradually as you develop the effect.

1. Start a new Maya scene, and switch to the Dynamics menu.

2. Choose Fluid Effects ➢ Create 3D Container.

You'll see the 3D container appear in the scene. On the bottom of the container you'll see a small grid. The size of the squares in the grid indicates the resolution (in X and Z) of the container.

3. Select the fluidShape1 node in the Outliner, and open its Attribute Editor.

4. Expand the Display section on the fluidShape1 tab. Set Boundary Draw to Reduced. This shows the voxel grid along the x-, y-, and z-axes (see Figure 15.8). The grid is not drawn on the parts of the container closest to the camera, so it's easier to see what's going on in the container.

At the top of the Container Properties rollout for the fluidShape1 node, you'll see that the Keep Square Voxels option is selected. As long as this option is on, you can change the resolution of the 3D grid for all three axes using the Base Resolution slider. If Keep Voxels Square is off, you can use the Resolution fields to set the resolution along each axis independently.

You'll also see three fields that can be used to determine the size of the 3D grid. You can use the Scale tool to resize the fluid container, but it's a better idea to use the Size setting in the fluid's shape node. This Size setting affects how dynamic properties (such as Mass and Gravity) are calculated within the fluid. Using the Scale tool does not affect these calculations, so increasing the scale of the fluid using the Scale tool may not give you the results you want. It depends on what you're trying to accomplish, of course. If you look at the `Blast.ma` example in the Visor, you'll see that the explosion effect is actually created by animating the Scale X, Y, and Z channels of the fluid container.

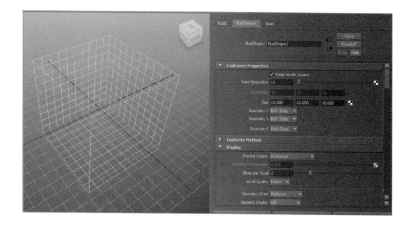

Fluid Interactions

There's no better way to gain an understanding of how fluids work than by designing an effect directly. In this section, you'll learn how emitters and fluid settings work together to create flame and smoke. You can simulate a reaction within the 3D container as if it were a miniature chemistry lab.

Emitting Fluids from a Surface

In the first part of this section, you'll use a polygon plane to emit fuel into a container. A second surface, a polygon sphere, is also introduced and used to emit heat into the same container as the fuel.

1. Start a new Maya scene. Choose Fluid Effects ➤ Create 3D Container.

2. Create a primitive polygon plane, and rename it **fuelPlane**. Set its transforms using the following values:

   Translate Y: **-4.5**

   Scale X: **10**

   Scale Y: **10**

   Scale Z: **10**

3. Select fuelPlane and fluid1. Choose Fluid Effects ➤ Add/Edit Contents ➤ Emit From Object. The plane can now emit fluids.

4. Expand fuelPlane in the Outliner. Select fluidEmitter1. Rename it **fuelEmitter**.

5. Open fuelEmitter's Attribute Editor.

6. Under the Fluid Attributes rollout, set Density Method and Heat Method to No Emission. Without Density, the emitted fuel cannot be seen presently in the viewport.

7. Open the fluid container's Attribute Editor (fluid1). Under the Contents Method rollout, change Fuel to Dynamic Grid.

8. Expand the Display rollout and change Shading Display to Fuel.

9. Play the simulation. The results at frame 40 are shown Figure 15.9.

FIGURE 15.9
Fuel is emitted into
the container from
the plane.

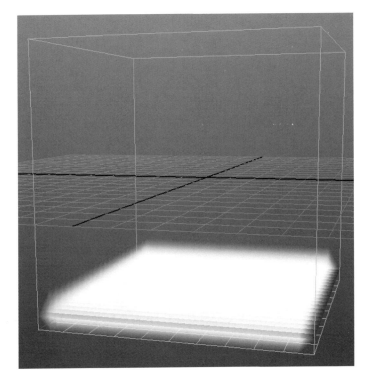

This creates an explosive situation. To complete the effect, drop a dynamically driven sphere emitting temperature onto the plane.

10. Create a primitive polygon sphere. Set its transforms using the following values:

Translate Y: **3.0**

Scale X: **0.25**

Scale Y: **0.25**

Scale Z: **0.25**

THREE OPTIONS FOR ADDING CONTENT

You have three options for adding content (density, velocity, temperature, or fuel) to a 3D container: Static Grid, Dynamic Grid, and Gradient. If you don't need to calculate density, temperature, or other content, you can set these options to Off.

Static Grid This option is used for elements of the simulation that are placed within the container using the Paint tool or emitters. The values created for these elements are not changed by the simulation. For example, if you wanted to create a simple cloud, you could set Density to Static Grid, paint the cloud in the container, and then animate the container moving across the sky.

Dynamic Grid Use this option when you know the element and its values will change over time as a result of the simulation. Most of the examples in this section use dynamic grids.

Gradient This option creates a static range of values between 0 and 1. The values affect the simulation but are not changed by it. For example, a container can be set so that the velocity at one end is higher than the velocity at the other end, which causes the fluid to move steadily faster as it approaches the higher range of values in the gradient. When you choose the Gradient option, a menu becomes available that allows you to determine the direction of the gradient.

11. Delete the sphere's history and freeze its transformations.

12. Choose Soft/Rigid Bodies ➤ Create Active Rigid Body.

13. With the sphere still selected, choose Fields ➤ Gravity.

14. The sphere that is now affected by gravity needs to collide with the fuel plane. Select fuelPlane, and choose Soft/Rigid Bodies ➤ Create Passive Rigid Body.

15. Set the end of the playback range to **200**.

16. Select the sphere and fluid1. Choose Fluid Effects ➤ Add/Edit Contents ➤ Emit From Object.

17. Open the Attribute Editor for the fluid emitter on the sphere. Use the values in Figure 15.10 to set the fluid attributes.

FIGURE 15.10
The Fluid Attributes rollout

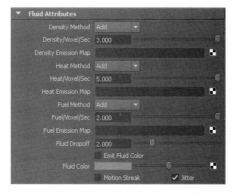

18. Save the scene as `gasolineFire_v01.ma`.

To see a version of the scene up to this point, open the `gasolineFire_v01.ma` scene from the `chapter15\scenes` folder at the book's web page.

USING MULTIPLE EMITTERS

The contents that you can inject into a container by a fluid emitter are density, fuel, and temperature. You can use an emitter to inject any combination of the three. The settings on the fluid container's shape node determine how these contents behave within the container. You can use more than one emitter within a container and create reactions via the interaction of anything within the container. For instance, you can use one emitter to add fuel and another to add temperature. Note that the contents of two separate fluid containers can't interact.

Making Flames

To get the density to take on the look of flames, you need to add heat. By emitting temperature into the container, you can use it to drive the incandescence of the fluid. The next steps take you through the process:

1. Continue with the scene from the previous section, or open the gasolineFire_v01.ma scene from the chapter15\scenes folder at the book's web page.

2. Select fluid1, and open its Attribute Editor.

3. Under Container Properties, change Base Resolution to **30**.

4. Under Contents Method, set Temperature to Dynamic Grid.

5. Open the Display rollout, and change Shaded Display to As Render.

6. Expand the Contents Details rollout and then the Temperature rollout.

7. Use the values from Figure 15.11 for the Temperature settings.

FIGURE 15.11
The Temperature settings

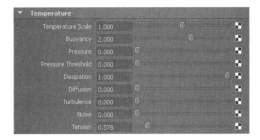

8. Scroll down and open the Shading rollout. Change the Selected Color to black. The color represents smoke or what the fire looks like when it loses all of its heat. Play the simulation to see the effects (Figure 15.12).

9. The Incandescence parameters can be used to make flames. Change the color graph and related attributes to match Figure 15.13. The left side of the Incandescence ramp is used to color lower temperatures; the right side colors higher temperatures. Set the key all the way to the right, at the 1.0 position, using the following values:

Hue: **18.0**

Saturation: **0.871**

Value: **20.0**

FIGURE 15.12
The fluid fades to
black around its
edges.

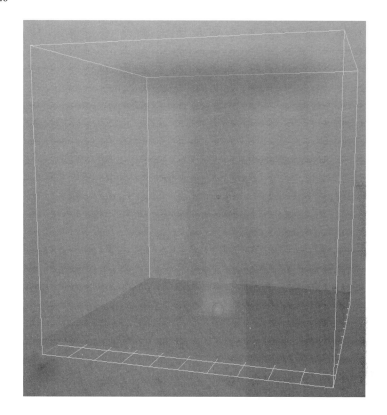

FIGURE 15.13
The Incandescence
parameters

10. Under the Opacity rollout, change Opacity Input to Temperature.

You can edit the Opacity ramp by adding points to the curve. Just like the Incandescence ramp, the left side of the curve controls opacity based on lower temperatures, whereas the right side controls the opacity of higher temperatures. You can experiment with this ramp to shape the way the flames look.

11. Scroll up toward Contents Details, and open the Velocity rollout. Change Swirl to **5** and Noise to **0.343**. This makes the flame waver and flicker.

Velocity pushes fluids around within a container. You can add velocity as a constant force to push fluids in a particular direction, or you can use an emitter. The Swirl setting adds rolling and swirling motion to the contents of a container. In the current example, the flames are already rising to the top of the container because of the Buoyancy setting, so you'll use Velocity to add swirl.

12. Save the scene as **gasolineFire_v02.ma**.

VELOCITY DRAW

You can activate the Velocity Draw option in the Display rollout panel of the fluid shape node. This creates a number of arrows within the container that indicate the direction of the fluid velocity, as shown here. Longer arrows indicate areas of faster motion.

To see a version of the scene up to this point, open the gasolineFire_v02.ma scene from the chapter15\scenes folder at the book's web page.

Igniting the Fuel

Reactions can cause several things to happen. In this example, you want the fuel to appear as if it has caught on fire. This is achieved by using the ignited fuel to add heat and color to the fluid.

1. Continue with the scene from the previous section, or open the `gasolineFire_v02.ma` scene from the `chapter15\scenes` folder at the book's web page.

2. Select fluid1, and open its Attribute Editor.

3. Expand the Contents Details ➢ Fuel rollout. Use the values from Figure 15.14 for the Fuel settings.

FIGURE 15.14
The Fuel settings

Press the **6** key to switch to shaded mode. Play the simulation. Shortly after the ball hits the ground plane, the fuel is ignited (see Figure 15.15).

FIGURE 15.15
Frame 120 of the simulation

You can think of the fuel emitter as a gas leak inside the container. As the temperature and the fuel come within close proximity to each other, a reaction takes place. The fuel burns until the fuel is exhausted or the temperature is lowered. Since the fuel is being emitted from the plane into the container, the flame keeps burning.

You can alter how the fuel ignites and burns by adjusting the fuel attributes. Here is an explanation of some of the parameters:

Reaction Speed   Determines how fast the reaction takes place once the heat ignites the fuel. Higher values produce faster reactions.

Air/Fuel Ratio   Fire needs air to burn. This setting increases the amount of air in the container, causing the fuel to burn in a different manner. Gasoline requires 15 times more air than fuel. To simulate a gas fire, use a value of **15**.

Ignition Temperature   This option sets the minimum temperature required to ignite the fuel. If you want to create a reaction that occurs regardless of temperature, set this value to a negative number such as **-0.1**.

Heat Released   This option causes the reaction to add more temperature to the fluid container.

Light Released   This option adds a value to the current Incandescent value of the fluid, which causes the fluid to glow brightly when rendered.

Light Color   This option specifies the color of the light to be released. You can easily add a blue tinge to the flame by changing the light color.

Try experimenting with the various parameters to see their effects on the simulation.

You'll notice that, as the simulation plays, the flame and smoke appear trapped within the walls of the 3D container. This is because, by default, containers have boundaries on all sides. You can remove these boundaries to let the contents escape. Be aware that, as the contents leave the container, they will disappear since fluid simulations cannot exist outside the fluid container (2D or 3D).

4. In the Container Properties section at the top of the fluidShape1 tab, set the Boundary Y option to –Y Side. This means that there is a boundary on the bottom of the container but not on the top.

5. Save the scene as `gasolineFire_v03.ma`.

To see a version of the scene up to this point, open the `gasolineFire_v03.ma` scene from the `chapter15\scenes` folder at the book's web page.

Filling Objects

Fluids can interact directly with polygon and NURBS surfaces in several ways. In the "Emitting Fluids from a Surface" section earlier, a plane was used to emit fluid. You can also use a surface to give a fluid its initial shape. In the next example, you will fill a polygon model in the shape of ice cream to create a melting ice cream effect. To further enhance the effect, a modeled ice cream cone will be used as a collision object for the melting ice cream.

1. Open the `iceCreamCone_v01.ma` scene from the `chapter15\scenes` folder at the book's web page. You are presented with two separate models—the ice cream and the cone—each on its own layer (see Figure 15.16).

2. Choose Fluid Effects ➢ Create 3D Container. The default container is created in the center of the world.

FIGURE 15.16
Set the size of the
fluid container.

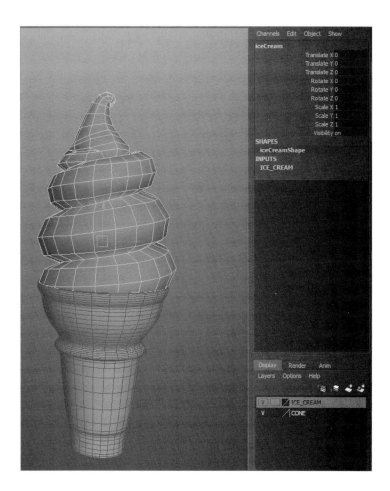

3. Open the fluid container's Attribute Editor. Change the Base Resolution setting to **100** and the size parameters to **12**, **20**, and **12**, which are the x-, y-, and z-axes, respectively (see Figure 15.17).

FIGURE 15.17
Change the size and
resolution of the
fluid container.

4. Select the geometry and the fluid container. Choose Fluid Effects ➤ Add/Edit Contents ➤ Emit From Object. Use the default settings.

5. The surface now emits the fluid when you play the simulation; however, the goal is to have the fluid take on the shape of the ice cream. To make this happen, select the emitter and select Fill Object under the Basic Emitter Attributes rollout (see Figure 15.18).

FIGURE 15.18
Select Fill Object on the fluid's emitter node.

Turn off the visibility of the ICE_CREAM layer; then click the Play button to see the fluid take the shape of the geometry. Figure 15.19 shows the results.

FIGURE 15.19
The fluid fills the shape of the ice cream geometry.

6. The fluid looks more like cotton candy than ice cream at this point. Open the fluid's Attribute Editor. Expand the Surface rollout. Choose Surface Render and Soft Surface to give the fluid the desired look (see Figure 15.20).

FIGURE 15.20
Change the fluid to
Surface Render and
Soft Surface.

7. The ice cream is starting to take shape. To get it to look as if it is melting, you need to change a couple of the density details. In the fluid's Attribute Editor, expand the Density rollout under Content Details. Set Buoyancy to **-5.0** and Diffusion to **0.2**. Figure 15.21 shows the results of the new density values.

FIGURE 15.21
The ice cream
begins to melt.

8. Save the scene as `iceCreamCone_v02.ma`.

To see a version of the scene up to this point, open the `iceCreamCone_v02.ma` scene from the `chapter15\scenes` folder at the book's web page.

9. Continue with the scene from step 8, or open the `iceCreamCone_v02.ma` scene from the `chapter15\scenes` folder at the book's web page.

10. The ice cream fluid has transparency. To remove it, expand the Shading rollout and set Transparency to black.

11. The fluid takes a couple of frames before it completely fills the ice cream surface. To have it filled immediately, open the emitter's Attribute Editor, and under the Basic Emitter Attributes rollout, set Start Frame Emission to Start Frame Only. In addition, change Rate (Percent) to **500.0** (see Figure 15.22).

FIGURE 15.22
Change the emit-
ter's emissions.

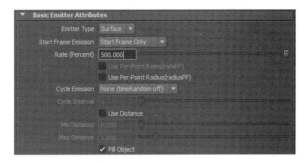

12. To further enhance the shape of the ice cream fluid, set Density Method, under the Fluid Attributes rollout on the emitter, to Replace. Figure 15.23 shows the results of the fluid.

FIGURE 15.23
The ice cream at its
initial frame

13. The ice cream needs to collide with the cone to create the impression of the ice cream melting downward. Select the fluid container and the cone geometry. Choose Fluid Effects ➤ Make Collide.

14. The simulation runs a little slow at its present resolution. To increase the speed without sacrificing quality, enable Auto Resize under the Fluid Shape node.

15. To finish the effect, select Enable Liquid Simulation under the Liquids rollout in the fluid's Attribute Editor. Set Liquid Mist Fall to **0.5**. Figure 15.24 shows the melted ice cream.

FIGURE 15.24
The ice cream fluid melting

USING LIQUID ATTRIBUTES

Enabling Liquid simulation allows access to several attributes. Each is described here:

Liquid Method Maya uses two methods for creating liquid simulations: Liquid And Air and Density Based Mass. The Liquid And Air method divides the fluid density into a liquid or as air based on the Liquid Min Density attribute. The Density Based Mass method makes denser areas of fluid heavier. The Mass Range sets the maximum mass.

Liquid Mist Fall Areas of the fluid that have a lower density than the value of the Liquid Min Density attribute receive a downward force based on the Liquid Mist Fall setting.

Density Tension Density Tension causes the fluid to form round clusters. Density Tension is also located under the Density rollout under Content Details and is not restricted to liquid simulations.

Tension Force This setting adds a small amount of velocity to the fluid affected by Density Tension. Tension Force is also located under the Density rollout under Content Details, and it is not restricted to liquid simulations.

Density Pressure This setting tries to conserve the fluid volume to avoid any loss of density. Density Pressure is also located under the Density rollout under Content Details and is not restricted to liquid simulations.

Density Pressure Threshold Any density value lower than the threshold does not receive any density pressure. Density Pressure Threshold is also located under the Density rollout under Content Details, and it is not restricted to liquid simulations.

16. Save the scene as **iceCreamCone_v03.ma**.

To see a version of the scene up to this point, open the iceCreamCone_v03.ma scene from the chapter15\scenes folder at the book's web page.

Rendering Fluid Containers

Fluid simulations can be rendered using Maya Software or mental ray®, with identical results for the most part. Because fluids have an incandescent value, they can be used as light-emitting objects when rendering with Final Gathering. If you want the fluid to appear in reflections and refractions, you need to turn on the Visible In Reflections and Visible In Refractions options in the Render Stats section of the fluid's shape node.

This section demonstrates some ways in which the detail and the shading of fluids can be improved when rendered.

Fluids can react to lighting in the scene, and you can apply self-shadowing to increase the realism. As an example of how to light fluids, a scene with simple clouds has been created for you to experiment with:

1. Open the simpleCloud_v01.ma scene from the chapter15\scenes folder at the book's web page.

2. Play the animation to frame 100. A simple cloud appears in the center of the scene.

The scene contains a fluid container, an emitter, a plane, and a light. The scene is already set to render using mental ray at production quality.

3. Open the Render View window, and render the scene from the perspective camera. A puffy white cloud appears in the render. Store the render in the Render View window (see Figure 15.25, left image).

FIGURE 15.25
Render the cloud with built-in lights (left image). Enable Self Shadows (center image). Then render the cloud using a directional light that casts raytrace shadows (right image).

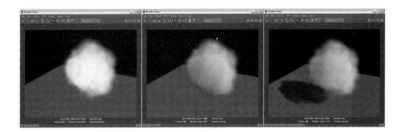

4. Select the fluid1 node, and open the Attribute Editor to the fluidShape1 tab. Scroll down to the Lighting section at the bottom of the editor.

The Lighting section contains two main settings: Self Shadow and Real Lights. When Real Lights is off, the fluids are lit from a built-in light. Maya has three Light Type options when using an internal light: Directional, Point, and Diagonal. Using an internal light will make rendering faster than using a real light.

When using a Directional internal light type, you can use the three fields labeled Directional Light to aim the light. The Diagonal internal light is the simplest option; it creates lighting that moves diagonally through the x- and y-axes of the fluid. The Point internal light is similar to using an actual point light; it even lets you specify the position of the light and has options for light decay just like a regular point light. These options are No Decay, Linear, Quadratic, and Cubic. For more information on light decay, consult Chapter 7, "Lighting with mental ray."

You can use the options for Light Color, Brightness, and Ambient Brightness to modify the look of the light. Ambient Diffusion will affect the look of the cloud regardless of whether you use internal or real lights. Ambient Diffusion controls how the light spreads through the fluid and can add detail to shadowed areas.

5. Turn on Self Shadow. You'll see that the cloud now has dark areas at the bottom in the perspective view. The Shadow Opacity slider controls the darkness of the shadows.

6. Create a test render, and store the render in the Render View window (see Figure 15.25, middle image).

   Shadow Diffusion controls the softness of self-shadowing, simulating light scattering. Unfortunately, it can be seen only in the viewport. This effect will not appear when rendering with software (Maya Software or mental ray). The documentation recommends that, if you'd like to use Shadow Diffusion, you render a playblast and then composite the results with the rest of your rendered images using your compositing program.

7. In the Outliner, select the directional light and open its Attribute Editor. Under Shadows, select Use Raytrace Shadows.

8. Select fluid1 and, in the Lighting section under the fluidShape1 tab, deselect Self Shadow and select Real Lights.

9. In the Render Stats section, make sure Casts and Receive Shadows are on.

10. Create another test render from the perspective camera (see Figure 15.25, right image).

11. Save the scene as **simpleCloud_v02.ma**.

When you render using Real Lights, the fluid casts shadows onto other objects as well as itself. When rendering using real shadow-casting lights, make sure that Self Shadow is disabled to avoid calculating the shadows twice. You can see that rendering with Real Lights does take significantly longer than using the built-in lighting and shadowing. Take this into consideration when rendering fluid simulations.

VIEWING FLUIDS WITH VIEWPORT 2.0

You can improve the visual quality of your fluid by turning on Floating Point Render Target under the Common tab. Enabling this setting reduces banding and makes the fluid appear smoother.

To see a version of the final scene, open the `simpleCloud_v02.ma` scene from the `chapter15\` scenes folder at the book's web page.

Create Fluids and nParticle Interactions

Fluids and nParticles can work together in combination to create a near-limitless number of interesting effects. You can use nParticles as fluid emitters, and you can also use a fluid to affect the movement of nParticles as if it were a field. Next, we'll cover two quick examples that show you how to make the systems work together.

Emitting Fluids from nParticles

In this section, you'll see how you can emit fluids into a 3D container using nParticles, and you'll learn about the Auto Resize feature that can help you optimize calculations for fluids.

1. Open the `rockWall_v01.ma` scene from the `chapter15\scenes` folder at the book's web page. Rewind and play the scene.

   In this scene, nParticles are emitted from a volume emitter. A rock wall has been modeled and turned into a collision object. If you watch the animation from camera1, you'll see that the scene resembles the wall of a volcanic mountain during an eruption.

2. Stop the animation, and switch to the perspective camera.

3. Switch to the Dynamics menu, and choose Fluid Effects ➤ Create 3D container to add a container to the scene (see Figure 15.26).

FIGURE 15.26
A 3D fluid container is added to the scene and positioned over the polygon wall.

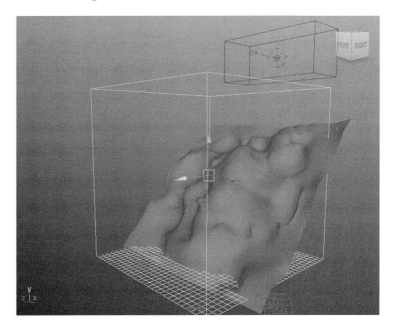

4. Set Translate Y of the container to **1.26** and Translate Z to **1.97**.

5. Open the Attribute Editor for the fluid1 node. Switch to the fluidShape1 tab, and set Base Resolution to **30**.

6. In the Outliner, select the nParticle1 node and Ctrl/Cmd+click the fluid1 node.

7. Choose Fluid Effects ➤ Add/Edit Contents ➤ Emit From Object ➤ Options.

8. In the options, use the following settings:

   Emitter Type: **Surface**

   Density: **10**

   Heat Rate and Fuel Rate: **0**

9. Click Apply to create the emitter. The new fluid emitter is parented to the nParticle1 node.

10. Rewind and play the scene. As the nParticles enter the fluid container, they leave a trail of smoke that rises and gathers at the top of the container (Figure 15.27).

FIGURE 15.27
The nParticles emit fluids as they enter the container.

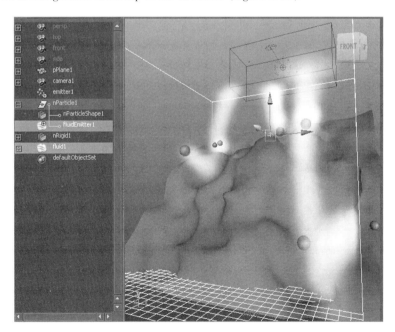

11. Open the Attribute Editor for the fluid1 node. Set Boundary X, Boundary Y, and Boundary Z to None. This will keep the fluid from becoming trapped at the sides of the container.

12. Scroll down to the Auto Resize rollout panel. Expand this, and select Auto Resize.

13. Rewind and play the simulation.

Auto Resize causes the fluid container to change its shape automatically to accommodate the fluid (see Figure 15.28). The Max Resolution slider sets a limit to the resolution. When you use Auto Resize, be mindful of the maximum size of the entire simulation; think about what will be within the rendered frame and what will be outside of it. You don't want to waste resources calculating fluid dynamics that will never be seen in the final render.

FIGURE 15.28
The fluid container automatically resizes to accommodate the emitted density.

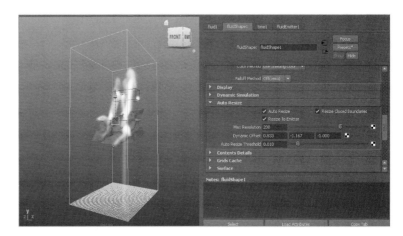

AUTO RESIZE AND DENSITY

Auto Resize for fluid containers is calculated based on the density of the fluid within the container. If none of the emitters within a container emits fluid density, the Auto Resize feature will not function correctly.

The problem with this setup is that, as the nParticles fall off the bottom edge of the rock-Wall collision object, the fluid container stretches downward to accommodate their position. Also, as the fluid rises, the container stretches upward to contain the fluid. There are a couple of strategies you can use so that the Auto Resize feature does not stretch the container too far, discussed in the following steps.

14. Open the Attribute Editor for the fluid1 node. In the Contents Detail section, expand the Density rollout panel.

15. Set Buoyancy to **0.25** and Dissipation to **1**.

These settings will keep the fluid from rising indefinitely, which will limit stretching of the fluid in the upward direction. They also help to keep the smoke trails left by the bouncing nParticles a little more defined.

To keep the fluid1 container from stretching downward forever, you can kill the nParticles as they fall off the bottom edge of the rockWall collision object. One way to do this is to lower the life span; however, this strategy can backfire because some of the nParticles that take longer to bounce down the wall may disappear within the camera view, which can ruin the effect. A better solution is to write an expression that kills the nParticles when they fall below a certain point on the y-axis.

16. Select the nParticle1 object in the Outliner, and open its Attribute Editor.

17. In the Lifespan rollout panel toward the top, set Lifespan Mode to LifespanPP Only.

18. Scroll down to the Per Particle (Array) Attributes section. Right-click the field next to Lifespan PP, and choose Creation Expression.

19. In the Expression field, type **lifespanPP=8;**.

This creation expression creates an overall lifespanPP so that each nParticle that is born will have a maximum life span of 8 seconds. This should be enough time so that slower-moving nParticles don't die before leaving the frame.

20. In the Expression Editor, click the Runtime Before Dynamics radio button. Runtime expressions calculate every frame of the simulation and can override the settings established by the creation expression.

21. Type the following into the Expression field:

```
vector $pPos = position;
float $yPos = $pPos.y;
if($yPos<-4)
{
lifespanPP=0;
}
```

This expression says that if the Y position of the nParticle is less than –4, then the nParticle's life span is 0 and the nParticle dies. You need to jump through a few small hoops to get this to work properly. First, you need to access the Y position of the nParticle—which, because of the expression syntax in Maya, cannot be done directly. In other words, you can't just say if(position.y<-4). Instead, you have to set up some variables to get to the Y position. That's just a quirk of the expression syntax. Thus the first line of the expression creates a vector variable called $pPos that holds the position of the nParticle. The second line creates a float variable called $yPos that retrieves the Y value of the $pPos vector variable. Now you can use $yPos in the if statement as a way to access the Y position of each nParticle. In Figure 15.29 you can see the setup of two different expressions applied to the same attribute. The expression on the left is applied at the particle's creation while the expression on the right is applied at runtime before dynamics. For more information on nParticle expressions, consult Chapter 12.

FIGURE 15.29
Per-particle expressions are created to kill the nParticles when they fall below –4 units on the y-axis.

22. Click Create to make the expression. If there are no syntax errors, rewind and play the scene. The nParticles should die off as they leave the bottom of the rockWall.

23. Save the scene as `rockWall_v02.ma`.

To see a version of the scene up to this point, open `rockWall_v02.ma` from the `chapter15\` scenes folder at the book's web page.

Creating Flaming Trails

To finish the look, you can edit the fluid settings so that the trails left by the nParticles look like flames.

1. Continue with the scene from the previous section, or open the `rockWall_v02.ma` scene from the `chapter15\scenes` folder at the book's web page.

2. Play the scene for about 40 frames.

3. Select the fluid1 node, and open its Attribute Editor.

4. In the Contents Method section, set Temperature and Fuel to Dynamic Grid.

5. Scroll down to the Content Details section and, in the Temperature section, set Buoyancy to **0.25** and Dissipation to **0.5**.

6. In the Fuel section, use the following settings:

Reaction Speed: **0**

Ignition Temperature: **–1**

Max Temperature: **1**

Heat Released: **1**

Since Ignition Temperature is at –1, a reaction should occur regardless of how much temperature is released.

7. In the Shading section, set Transparency to a dark gray, and set Glow Intensity to **0.1**.

GLOW INTENSITY

The Glow Intensity attribute works exactly like the Glow Intensity slider found in the Special Effects section of the standard Maya shaders. This boosts the incandescent values of the fluid as a post-render effect, making the fluid appear to glow. Just like all glow effects in the scene, the quality of the glow is controlled using the shaderGlow1 node found in the Hypershade.

When rendering a sequence using a glow, you should always deselect the Auto Exposure setting in the shaderGlow1 node to eliminate flickering that may occur when the animation is rendered.

8. In the Color section, click the color swatch and set the color to black.

9. The Incandescence ramp should be set to Temperature already. If not, choose Temperature from the menu next to Incandescence Input.

10. In the Outliner, expand the nParticle1 node, select the fluidEmitter1 node, and open its Attribute Editor.

11. Under Fluid Attributes, use the following settings:

Heat Method: **Add**

Heat/Voxels/Sec: **100**

Fuel Method: **Add**

Fuel/Voxels/Sec: **100**

12. Rewind and play the animation. You should see flaming trails left behind each nParticle (see Figure 15.30).

You can improve the look by experimenting with the settings, as well as by increasing the Base Resolution and Max Resolution settings in the Auto Resize section.

13. Save the scene as `rockWall_v03.ma`.

To see a version of the scene up to this point, open the `rockWall_v03.ma` scene from the `chapter15\scenes` folder at the book's web page.

FIGURE 15.30
The nParticles leave flaming trails as they bounce down the side of the rock wall.

Creating Water Effects

New!

Creating believable water or liquid effects in the past required a mixture of particle and fluid simulations. This was a difficult process that fell short on functionality and realism. To solve this problem, Maya 2015 introduced Bifrost, a procedural engine specifically designed for liquid effects. Bifrost's predecessor was Exotic Matter's Naiad. Autodesk acquired the Naiad fluid-simulation software in 2012.

Bifrost Liquid Simulation

The Bifrost engine differs from Maya Fluids and particle simulations by using a FLIP solver. A FLIP solver is a hybrid of sorts, using features from both particle systems and fluid simulations. As a result, water volume and splashing effects are handled with the same solver. The resulting liquid simulation is stable and highly accurate.

There are several components to a Bifrost liquid. Here is an explanation of the nodes and attributes required for a simulation:

bifrost The bifrost node is the root of the simulation. It controls the display of the liquid in the viewport and is the conduit for all of the other nodes and attributes. The bifrost node is represented by a bounding box based on the overall size of your liquid (see Figure 15.31). As the dimensions of your liquid change, so does the size of the bifrost node.

bifrostLiquid This is the actual container for the liquid. Each container has its own solver settings allowing for independent control over start frame and gravity. The bifrostLiquid node is where you control the resolution or voxel size of the liquid. Figure 15.32 shows the bifrostLiquid icon.

FIGURE 15.31
The bifrost node is the box surrounding the sphere.

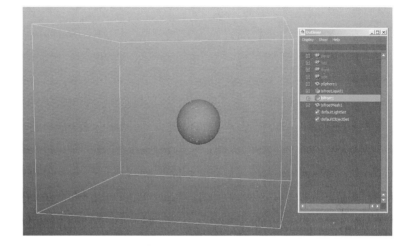

FIGURE 15.32
The bifrostLiquid node is represented by a single icon of two perpendicular circles and a red locator.

bifrostMesh   The bifrostMesh node exists so the liquid can be converted to polygon geometry. Rendering the liquid as a mesh allows for advanced shading features not available in its particle or voxel form. You can turn the mesh on or off at any point during the simulation from within the bifrost node (see Figure 15.33).

bifrost emitter   A liquid simulation cannot be created without an emitter. Any polygon geometry can be an emitter. When a mesh is used as an emitter, a new bifrost rollout is added to its shape node. Figure 15.34 shows the additional attributes.

FIGURE 15.33
The bifrost liquid has a built-in meshing feature to convert the simulation to polygons.

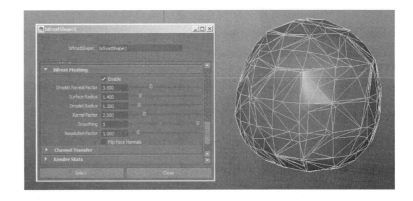

FIGURE 15.34
A bifrost rollout is added to objects being used as emitters.

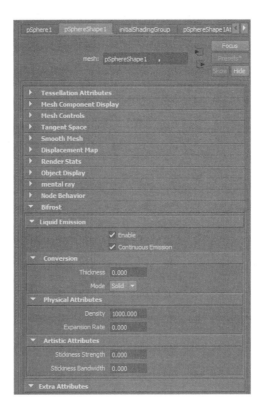

Liquid simulation with Bifrost requires very little effort since the solver handles all the intricacies of the liquid's motion. Furthermore, Bifrost is multithreaded and can take full advantage of your computer's hardware. The following exercise takes you through the process of creating a Bifrost liquid simulation:

1. Open the pool_v01.ma scene from the chapter15\scenes folder at the book's web page. The scene contains a diving platform, a container, a ball, and a pool. The pool is on a layer with its visibility turned off. The ball is a rigid-body simulation and designed to drop into the pool.

2. Select the container and choose Bifrost ➤ Create Liquid. The container is filled with a liquid represented by particle points (see Figure 15.35).

FIGURE 15.35
Create a liquid
from the container
geometry.

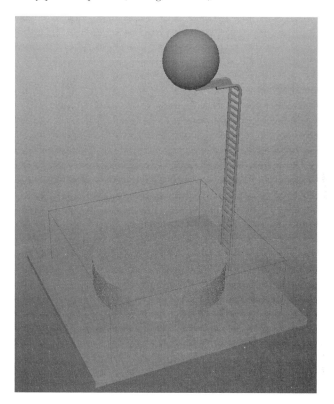

LIQUID DISPLAY

You can change the way liquids are displayed through the bifrost shape node. There are two initial choices: Particles and Voxels. You can choose either or use both simultaneously. You can alter attributes such as point size and color for specific channels.

---

3. Turn the visibility off for the CONTAINER layer and turn the visibility on for the POOL layer.

4. Make the liquid collide with the pool, ground, and ball. With bifrost1 selected, Shift+click the pool, ground, and ball. Choose Bifrost ➤ Add Collider. The objects now collide with the liquid.

5. Select bifrost1. Notice the green bar at frame 1 in the timeline. Click Play. Two things happen. First, the animation plays based on the values in the Time Slider. A yellow bar fills the timeline as the animation progresses. This bar signifies the uncached frames of the liquid simulation. The second thing is that the liquid begins to cache. The cached frames are represented by a green bar in the timeline that overlaps the yellow bar. If playback is set to Continuous, every loop of the animation will show more and more of the finished simulation. At any point, you can click the Stop button in the lower-right corner of the interface. The progress of the simulation is also displayed here (see Figure 15.36).

FIGURE 15.36

The liquid simulation is cached during playback.

Liquid simulations are saved to a scratch cache. This allows you to watch the simulation at a decent frame rate. When you make a change to one of the bifrost nodes, the scratch cache is removed. Playing the simulation will generate a new scratch cache. Making changes to a secondary object, like a collider, does not cause the scratch to be removed. You can manually remove the scratch cache by choosing Bifrost ➤ Flush Scratch Cache.

6. During the simulation, the liquids spill onto the ground object and flow into empty space. Figure 15.37 shows the liquids at frame 210.

   Liquid falling into the open air unnecessarily complicates the simulation. To prevent the liquid from traveling too far or off camera, you can introduce a kill plane. Select bifrost1 and choose Bifrost ➤ Add Killplane.

7. Scale bifrostKillplane1 uniformly to **22.0** units and translate it to **-1.0** in the y-axis. The actual scale of the kill plane is irrelevant. Increasing its scale simply makes it easier to see and select. Click Play to re-create the scratch cache. Figure 15.38 shows the results at frame 210.

FIGURE 15.37
The liquid falls over the edge of the ground object.

FIGURE 15.38
The kill plane prevents the liquids from falling.

8. The scale of the pool water looks too large. You can decrease the voxel size in order to increase the resolution of your liquid. Doing so effectively reduces the scale of the liquid. Go to frame 1 and select bifrostLiquid1. In the Channel Box, set Master Voxel Size to **0.20**. Depending on the speed of your computer, the lower voxel size may take hours to solve.

SOLVER START FRAME

If you want to make changes to a simulation, your current frame needs to be set to the solver's start frame. By default, this is frame 1. You can change the start frame under the Liquid Solver Attributes rollout in the bifrostLiquidContainer node.

---

9. The smaller voxel size makes the liquid more reactive to forces applied against it. In this case, that means the falling ball is going to make a much bigger splash. This may not always be the desired result. To tame the results, you can increase the gravity. Change Gravity Magnitude to **17.6** (see Figure 15.39)

FIGURE 15.39
Changing the gravity magnitude helps reduce the effects of forces on the liquid.

BIFROST SCALE

Bifrost liquid simulation is internally measured in meters. Maya uses centimeters as its default unit of measurement. Therefore, 1cm is seen as 1 meter by the bifrost solver. It is a good practice to keep this ratio and model your environments based on this conversion. You can then adjust the gravity to match.

---

10. Instead of using the scratch cache, create a permanent cache file. This will prevent any accidental loss of the cache. Choose the Bifrost ➤ Compute and Cache To Disk options.

11. Choose a cache directory and give the cache a name. Set the range to be cached and click Create.

12. Save the scene as **pool_v02.ma**.

To see a version of the scene up to this point, open the pool_v02.ma scene from the chapter15\scenes folder.

Shading Bifrost Liquids

You can render the liquid simulation in two ways. Voxel rendering is the default method. This is similar to how Maya Fluids render. As with Maya Fluids you can also convert the simulation data into a polygon mesh. Mesh nodes are created along with the liquid; therefore, a separate conversion is not necessary. You can enable the mesh for a liquid at any point.

The Bifrost liquid is automatically assigned a shader. The liquid material is similar to mental ray's mia_material shader Enabling the mesh option for the liquid allows you to take full advantage of the shader's features and different rendering techniques. The following example takes you through the steps to render a realistic-looking liquid:

1. Continue with the scene from the previous section, or open the pool_v02.ma scene from the chapter15\scenes folder at the book's web page.

2. Select bifrost1. In the Channel Box, set Mesh Enable to On. A polygon mesh is created, matching the particle volume.

   With the mesh turned on, your simulation will run slower. However, the liquid is already cached. That means you can skip frames to see the results of the mesh.

3. Go to frame 90. The mesh will update accordingly. The ball, however, will not since it is an uncached bullet simulation (see Figure 15.40).

FIGURE 15.40
Create a polygon mesh by enabling meshing on the bifrost node.

4. Create a layer named **BIFROST**. Add bifrost1 and turn off the visibility for the layer.

5. With bifrost1 still selected, change Meshing Surface Radius to **1.0**. The smaller surface radius reduces the volume of the polygon mesh—in this case, giving the water finer details. Compare Figure 15.41 with 15.40.

FIGURE 15.41
Decrease the surface radius to 1.0.

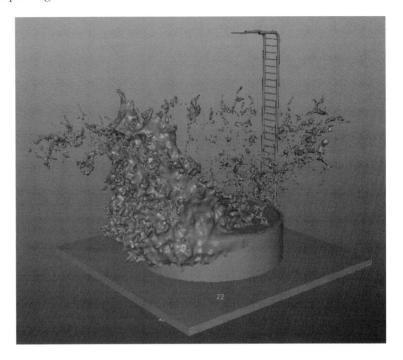

6. Open the Hypershade and choose bifrostLiquidMaterial1. Open its Attribute Editor.

7. The liquid material is similar in design to the mia_material shader. Most of the default values of the liquid material are already set for a convincing water look. Open the Reflection rollout. Reflection Color is pure white and Reflection Weight is set to 1.0. These are good settings; however, the scene does not have an environment to reflect.

   Select the Perspective camera and open its Attribute Editor. Choose the perspShape tab and expand the Environment rollout. Change Background Color to a sky blue. Render a test frame to see the water reflect the blue sky (see Figure 15.42).

8. Under the Refraction rollout, change the Refraction Color value to **0.85** and Transparency to **1.0** (see Figure 15.43).

9. Expand the mental ray rollout and the subsequent Advanced Refraction rollout. Select Max Distance and set the Max Distance value to **10.0**. Using a maximum distance for the refraction causes the water to fade to black at the distance value.

FIGURE 15.42
The water mesh reflects its environment.

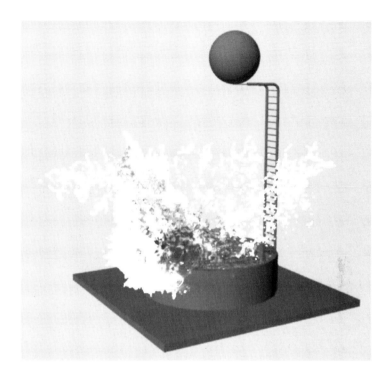

FIGURE 15.43
Add transparency to the water.

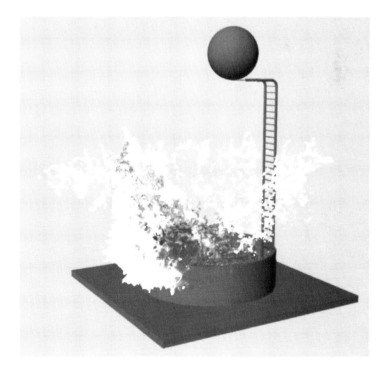

10. Select the option Use Color At Max Distance. Adding a color for the water to fade to gives the liquid more visual depth. Use the following parameters to set the color value:

    Hue: **200.0**

    Saturation: **0.298**

    Value: **0.146**

11. When water gets agitated, it bubbles and reflects more light. We identify this as foam. Currently, the foam effect is too extreme and the water turns white. Expand the Foam Remap rollout. Cut the intensity of the foam weight by lowering the last key in the Foam Weight Remap graph to **0.5**. Figure 15.44 shows the water with its new foam attributes.

FIGURE 15.44
Adding foam com-
pletes the look of
the water.

REMAPPING COLOR CHANNELS

The Bifrost liquid material allows you to map a solid color to a color ramp. The values of the color ramp are driven by the velocity and vorticity channels of the liquid simulation.

---

12. The water is very clear. Let's make it blue. Expand the Diffuse Remap rollout. Deselect the Diffuse Color Remap Enable option. Turning this off reverts to the solid color shown for Diffuse Color. Figure 15.45 shows the final look of the water.

13. Save the scene as **pool_v03.ma**.

To see a version of the scene, open the pool_v03.ma scene from the chapter15\scenes folder at the book's web page. You can also watch the rendered version of the simulation from the chapter15\movies folder.

Creating an Ocean

The ocean fluid effect uses a surface and a special Ocean shader to create a realistic ocean surface that can behave dynamically. The Ocean shader uses an animated displacement map to create the water surface. Ocean surfaces can take a while to render, so you should consider this when planning your scene.

You can find all the controls needed to create the ocean on the Ocean shader node. This node is created and applied automatically when you create an ocean. In this example, you'll create the effect of a space capsule floating on the surface of the ocean:

1. Open the capsule_v01.ma scene from the chapter15\scenes folder at the book's web page. This scene has the simple space capsule model used in Chapter 12.

2. Switch to the Dynamics menu, and choose Fluid Effects ➢ Ocean ➢ Create Ocean.

PREVIEW PLANES

When you create an ocean, you'll see a large NURBS surface appear. This represents the surface of the ocean. At the center is a preview plane, which approximates how the ocean will behave when the scene is played.

---

3. Rewind and play the scene. You'll see the preview plane move up and down. This demonstrates the default behavior of the ocean (see Figure 15.46).

FIGURE 15.46
The ocean effect
uses a preview
plane to indicate
the behavior of the
ocean.

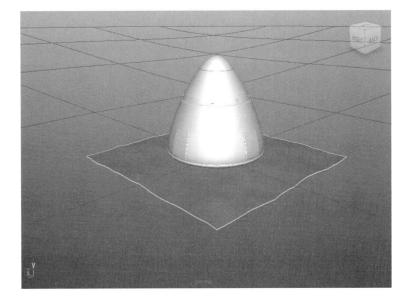

4. In the Outliner, select the Transform1 node and open the Attribute Editor. Switch to the Ocean Shader tab.

You'll find all the controls you need to change the way the ocean looks and behaves in the Ocean Shader controls. Each control is described in the Maya documentation, but many of the controls are self-explanatory.

5. Expand the Ocean Attributes rollout panel. To slow down the ocean, set Wave Speed to **0.8**. You can use Observer Speed to simulate the effect of the ocean moving past the camera without the need to animate the ocean or the camera. Leave this setting at 0.

6. To make the ocean waves seem larger, increase Wave Length Max to **6**. The wavelength units are measured in meters.

To make the ocean seem a little rougher, you can adjust the Wave Height edit curve. The Wave Height edit curve changes the wave height relative to the wavelength. If you edit the curve so that it slopes up to the right, the waves with longer wavelengths will be proportionally taller than the waves with shorter wavelengths. A value of 1 means that the wave is half as tall as it is long. When you edit this curve, you can see the results in the preview plane.

Wave Turbulence works the same way, so by making the curve slope up to the right, longer waves will have a higher turbulence frequency.

Wave Peaking creates crests on top of areas that have more turbulence. Turbulence must be a nonzero value for wave peaking to have an effect.

7. Experiment with different settings for the Wave Height, Wave Turbulence, and Wave Peaking edit curves (see Figure 15.47). Create a test render from the perspective camera to see how these changes affect the look of the ocean.

FIGURE 15.47
You can shape the ocean by editing the Wave Height, Wave Turbulence, and Wave Peaking edit curves.

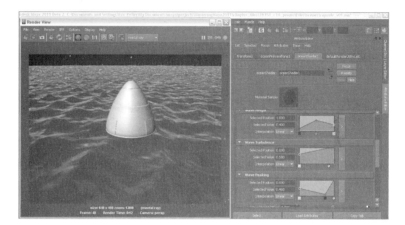

8. To make the capsule float in the water, select the capsule and choose Fluid Effects ➤ Ocean ➤ Float Selected Objects.

9. In the Outliner, select Locator1 and open its Attribute Editor.

10. In the Extra Attributes section, set Buoyancy to **0.01** and Start Y to **–3**.

11. Select the capsule, and rotate it a little so that it does not bob straight up and down.

12. Select the transform1 node, and open the Attribute Editor to the Ocean Shader tab.

13. In the Common Material Attributes section, set Transparency to a dark gray color. This allows you to see some of the submerged parts of the capsule through the water. The oceanShader already has a refraction index of 1.3, so the water will refract light.

14. Set Foam Emission to **0.355**. This shades the peaks of the ocean with a light color, suggesting whitecaps.

15. Create a test render of the scene from the perspective camera (see Figure 15.48).

FIGURE 15.48
Render the capsule
floating in the
water.

16. Save the scene as **capsule_v02.ma**.

To see a finished version of the scene, open the capsule_v02.ma scene from the chapter15\
scenes folder at the book's web page.

This is a good start to creating a realistic ocean. Take a look at some of the ocean examples in
the Visor to see more advanced effects.

The Bottom Line

Use fluid containers. Fluid containers are used to create self-contained fluid effects. Fluid
simulations use a special type of particle that is generated in the small subunits (called *voxels*)
of a fluid container. Fluid containers can be 2D or 3D. Two-dimensional containers take less
time to calculate and can be used in many cases to generate realistic fluid effects.

Master It Create a logo animation that dissolves like ink in water.

Create a reaction. A reaction can be simulated in a 3D container by combining temperature
with fuel. Surfaces can be used as emitters within a fluid container.

Master It Create a chain reaction of explosions using the Paint Fluids tool.

Render fluid containers. Fluid containers can be rendered using Maya Software or mental
ray. The fluids can react to lighting, cast shadows, and self-shadow.

Master It   Render the `TurbulentFlame.ma` example in the Visor so that it emits light onto nearby surfaces.

Use fluids with nParticles.   Fluid simulations can interact with nParticles to create a large array of interesting effects.

Master It   nCloth objects use nParticles and springs to simulate the behavior of cloth. If fluids can affect nParticles, it stands to reason that they can also affect nCloth objects. Test this by creating a simulation where a fluid emitter pushes around an nCloth object.

Create an ocean.   Ocean effects are created and edited using the Ocean shader. Objects can float in the ocean using locators.

Master It   Create an ocean effect that resembles stormy seas. Add the capsule geometry as a floating object.

Chapter 16

Scene Management and Virtual Filmmaking

More and more computer-generated movies are being made. Every aspect of the production is created within the 3D world. This can be hundreds to even thousands of objects in a single scene. Often these objects are built by multiple artists. The Autodesk® Maya® software allows you to tackle large scenes and complex objects with a special set of tools, and makes it easy to work within a team.

When all of the assets are built, it's time to film. As with all filmmaking, the story is told through the camera. The camera is used to manipulate the elements of the scene, letting viewers know what they need to focus on and how they should feel about what is going on in the scene.

Although the technical aspects of using the cameras are not difficult to learn, mastering the art of virtual cinematography can take years of practice.

In this chapter, you will learn to:

◆ Use assets

◆ Create file references

◆ Determine the camera's image size and film speed

◆ Create and animate cameras

◆ Create custom camera rigs

◆ Use depth of field and motion blur

◆ Create orthographic and stereo cameras

◆ Use the Camera Sequencer

Organizing Complex Node Structures with Assets

A *production pipeline* consists of a number of artists with specialized tasks. Modelers, riggers, animators, lighters, technical directors (TDs), and many others work together to create an animation from a director's vision. Organizing a complex animation sequence from all the nodes in a scene can be a daunting task. *Assets* (collections of nodes you choose to group together for the purpose of organization) are designed to help a director separate the nodes in a scene and their many attributes into discrete interfaces so that each team of specialized artists can concern itself only with its individual part of the project.

An asset is not the same as a group node; assets do not have an associated transform node and do not appear in the viewport of a scene. For example, a model, its animation controls, and its shaders can all be placed in a single asset. This example demonstrates some of the ways you can create and work with assets.

Creating an Asset

In this example, you'll create an asset for the front wheels of a vehicle:

1. Open the `vehicle_v01.ma` file from the `chapter16\scenes` directory at the book's web page (`www.sybex.com/go/masteringmaya2015`). You'll see a three-wheeled vehicle. In the Outliner, the vehicle is grouped.

2. Expand the vehicle group in the Outliner. The group consists of subgroups for the two front wheels, the rear wheel, the chassis, the suspension, and a NURBS curve named steering.

3. Select the steering node in the Outliner. This is the animation control for the steering. Switch to the Rotate tool. Rotate the steering node on the y-axis. The front wheels match the arrow's orientation (see the left image in Figure 16.1).

FIGURE 16.1

The Y rotation of each front wheel is connected to the Y rotation of the steering control (left). The X rotation of each front wheel is connected to the Y translate of the steering control, giving the animator the ability to tilt the wheels if needed (right).

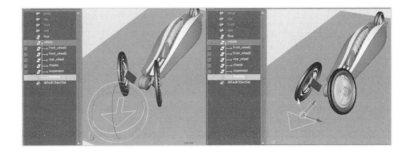

If you select one of the front_wheel groups in the Outliner, you'll see that its Rotate Y channel is colored yellow in the Channel Box, indicating it has an incoming connection. The steering curve's Y rotation is connected to both front_wheel groups' Y connection.

4. Select steering again, and switch to the Move tool.

5. Move steering up and down along the y-axis. The front wheels rotate on the x-axis based on the height of the steering object, making them tilt (see the right image in Figure 16.1).

If you look in the Channel Box for either of the front_wheel groups, you'll see that the Rotate X channel is colored orange, indicating that it has been keyframed. The Rotate channels of the group are using a *driven key* to determine their values. The keyframe's driver is the Y translation of the arrow group.

6. Select the vehicle group node.

7. Drag the red arrow of the Move tool to translate the vehicle back and forth along the x-axis. All three wheels rotate as the car moves.

If you expand the front_wheel1 group in the Outliner and select the wheel1Rotate child group node, you'll see that the Rotate Z channel is colored purple in the Channel Box, indicating an expression is controlling its z-axis rotation. You can open the Attribute Editor for the front_wheel1 group and switch to the expression4 tab to see the expression, as shown in Figure 16.2. (The field isn't large enough to display the entire expression; you can click the field and drag left or right to read the whole expression.)

FIGURE 16.2
The Z rotation of the wheels is controlled by an expression node. The expression node is a separate tab in the Attribute Editor.

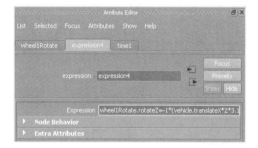

This model uses a simple rig, but already there are a lot of nodes connected to the vehicle geometry to help the job of the animator. To simplify, you can create an asset for just the wheels and their connected nodes so that the animator can focus on just this part of the model to do his or her job without having to hunt through all the different nodes grouped in the Outliner.

8. In the Outliner, expand the vehicle group and the two front_wheel groups.

9. Ctrl/Cmd+click front_wheel1, wheel1Rotate, front_wheel2, wheel2Rotate, and the steering curve node.

10. Open the Hypergraph in connections mode (Window ➤ Hypergraph: Connections).

11. In the Hypergraph menu, choose Graph ➤ Input And Output Connections. The selected nodes are graphed in the Hypergraph (see Figure 16.3).

FIGURE 16.3
The vehicle group is expanded, and several of the nodes related to the front wheels are selected and graphed on the Hypergraph.

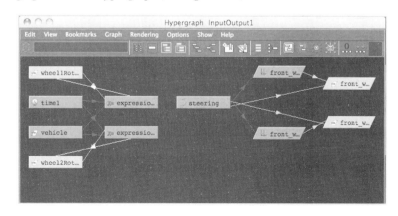

12. In the Hypergraph, select the node named time1 and the vehicle node, and drag them out of the way of the other nodes.

13. Drag a selection over all the nodes except time1 and vehicle. These nodes include the group nodes, keyframe nodes, and expression nodes, all related to controlling the rotation of the front_wheel groups.

14. In the Hypergraph menu, choose Edit ➤ Asset ➤ Advanced Assets ➤ Create ➤ Options. (Options is selected by clicking the small square to the right of the command list in the menu.)

15. In the Create Advanced Assets Options dialog box, type **front_wheels** in the Name field. Make sure all the settings under Include Options and Publish Options are deselected (see Figure 16.4). All of the keyframes and expressions are applied to the rotation of the wheel groups, not the geometry nodes contained in the groups, so you needn't worry about including the contents of the groups in the asset.

FIGURE 16.4
The options are set for the container that will hold all the selected nodes in the Hypergraph.

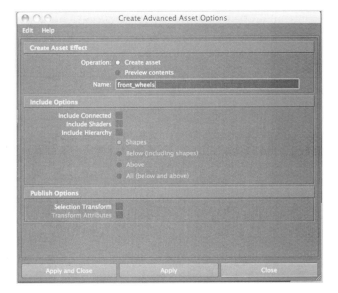

16. Choose the Create Asset option at the top of the dialog box.

PREVIEW THE ASSET CONTENTS

The Preview Contents option selects all the nodes that will be included in the asset when you click the Apply button, but it will not actually create the asset. This is so you can verify that you have all the nodes you want included in the asset before creating it.

---

17. Click Apply And Close to create the asset.

In the Hypergraph, you'll see a gray box labeled front_wheels; this box is also visible in the Outliner. The time1 and vehicle nodes are still visible in the Hypergraph. It may appear as though they have been disconnected, but that's not actually the case.

18. Select the front_wheels asset in the Hypergraph, and graph its input and output connections (Graph ➢ Input And Output Connections). The connections to the time1 and vehicle nodes are visible again.

19. Select the front_wheels asset in the Hypergraph, and click the Expand Selected Assets icon on the Hypergraph toolbar (or double-click the container). You will see the nodes within the container (Figure 16.5).

FIGURE 16.5
Expanding the view of a container in the Hypergraph makes the connections between nodes within the container visible.

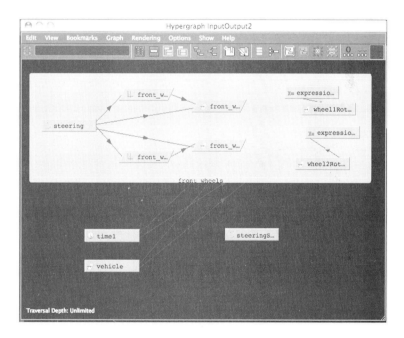

20. Double-click the thick border of the asset to collapse it, or click the Collapse Selected Assets icon at the top of the Hypergraph.

You can select a node inside the container and remove it from the container by right-clicking the node and choosing Remove From Container.

21. Save the scene as **vehicle_v02.ma**.

TIPS FOR WORKING WITH ASSETS

Here are some tips for working with assets:

◆ To delete an asset, select it and choose (from the Hypergraph menu) Edit ➢ Asset ➢ Remove Asset. Don't select the asset and delete it; deleting the asset will delete the contents from the scene as well.

◆ You can remove all the assets in a scene without deleting their contents by choosing Edit ➢ Delete By Type ➢ Assets from the main Maya menu.

◆ In the Outliner, you can expand the asset node to reveal the contents. Note that the wheel groups are no longer shown as children of the vehicle group but are now inside the asset group. The nodes themselves still behave as children of the vehicle group. If you change the position of the vehicle, the wheels will still rotate and move with the vehicle.

◆ Assets can be created in the Hypershade as well, and they can contain any type of node, including shaders and textures.

◆ You can create assets without going into the Hypershade. Just select the nodes in the scene, and use the options in the Assets menu.

◆ If you choose Set Current Asset from the Advanced Assets submenu, all new nodes created in the scene will automatically become part of the specified asset.

◆ You can use the Create Assets With Transform option in the Assets menu to create an asset with a selectable transform handle. Translating or rotating the asset will also translate and rotate the contents of the asset.

Publishing Asset Attributes

You can publish selected attributes of the container's nodes to the top level of the container. This means that the animator can select the asset node and have all the custom controls available in the Channel Box without having to hunt around the various nodes in the network. You can also template your asset for use with similar animation rigs.

In this exercise, you'll publish the attributes of the front_steering asset:

1. Continue with the file from the previous section, or open `vehicle_v02.ma` from the `chapter16\scenes` folder at the book's web page.

2. In the Outliner, select the front_wheels asset and expand the node by clicking the plus sign to the left of the node. Select the steering node from within the asset.

3. In the Channel Box, select the Translate Y channel and, from the Edit menu in the Channel Box, choose Publish To Asset ➢ Options.

4. In the Publish Attribute Options dialog box, choose both Selected Channel Box Attributes and Custom Name.

5. Type **wheelTilt** in the Custom String field. Click Apply, and then click Close (see Figure 16.6).

FIGURE 16.6

The Translate Y attribute of the steering node is published to the container under the name wheelTilt.

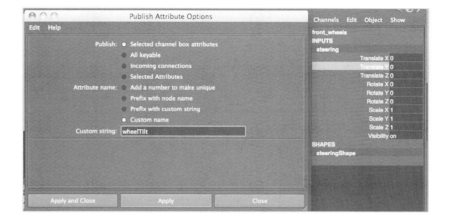

6. Select the front_wheels asset in the Outliner; you'll see the wheelTilt channel has been added in the Channel Box. If you change this value between –1 and 1, the arrow controller moves up and down and the front wheels tilt.

PUBLISH ATTRIBUTES FROM THE ATTRIBUTE EDITOR

If you need to publish a specific attribute that does not appear in the Channel Box, you can open the Attribute Editor for the appropriate node, right-click the attribute name, and choose the publish options from the pop-up menu.

Using the Asset Editor

The Asset Editor can help you further customize and manage your scene's assets. You can use it as another way to publish specific attributes of an asset.

1. Open the scene `vehicle_v03.ma` from the `chapter16\scenes` folder at the book's web page.

   In the Outliner, you'll see two containers, one named front_wheels and another named carPaint (which holds the blue paint shader applied to the car).

2. To open the Asset Editor, choose Assets ➢ Asset Editor. The editor is in two panels; on the left side you'll see all the assets in the scene.

   The Asset Editor opens in view mode. In the list of assets on the left, you can click the plus sign in the square to see the nodes within each container. You can see the attributes of each node listed by clicking the plus sign in the circle next to each node.

3. Select the front_wheels container, and click the pushpin icon above and to the right of the asset list to switch to edit mode. On the right side of the editor, you'll see the wheelTilt attribute you created in the previous section.

4. Select the arrow next to wheelTilt on the right panel, and the wheels asset expands to reveal the Translate channel of the steering node. This is the attribute originally published to the container as wheelTilt.

5. In the list on the left below the Translate channels, expand the Rotate attributes of the steering node. Select Rotate Y, and click the second icon from the top in the middle bar of the Asset Editor. This publishes the selected attribute to the container with a custom name.

6. A dialog box will open prompting you to name the selected attribute. Name it **steer** (see Figure 16.7).

FIGURE 16.7
Attributes can be published to the container from within the Asset Editor.

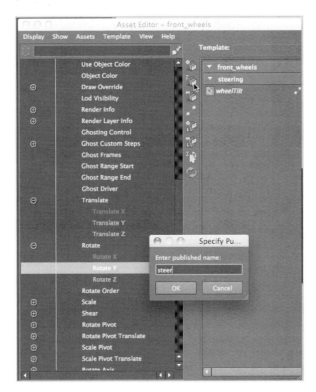

Note that steps 5 and 6 are just another way to publish an attribute; the end result is the same as when you published the wheelTilt attribute from the Channel Box in the previous section.

7. Steer now appears in the right side of the Asset Editor. The view on the right side of the Asset Editor shows the attributes grouped by node. If you want to see just the published attributes, choose View ➤ Mode ➤ Flat from the Asset Editor's menu bar.

8. Select the front_wheels asset in the Outliner, and open its Attribute Editor.

9. Expand the Asset Attributes rollout, and turn on Black Box (see Figure 16.8). (The Black Box option allows you to restrict access to an asset's attributes so that other artists working on the team can focus on just the attributes they need.) When you do this, the only attributes that appear in the Channel Box are the ones that have been published to the asset (wheelTilt and steer). Likewise, in the Outliner you can no longer expand the asset node.

FIGURE 16.8
Turning on Black Box restricts access to the container's contents and their attributes.

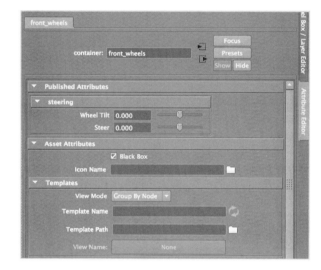

The Asset Editor has a number of advanced features, including the ability to create templates of complex assets that can be saved to disk and used in other scenes for similar assets.

Viewing Assets in the Node Editor

Published assets and their connections can be viewed in the Node Editor. Assets are shown as unique nodes. Their published attributes are shown with ports for connecting while their non-published attributes are hidden. However, connections for non-published attributes can be accessed through the superport of the asset node.

File References

File referencing is another workflow tool that can be used when a team of artists is working on the same scene. For example, by using file references, an animator can begin animating a scene while the modeler is still perfecting the model. This is also true for any of the other team members. A texture artist can work on textures for the same model at the same time. The animator and texture artist can import a reference of the model into their Maya scene, and each time the modeler saves a change, the model reference in the other scenes will update (when the animator or the texture artist reload either the scene or the reference).

FILE REFERENCING VS. IMPORTING

File referencing is not the same as importing a Maya scene into another Maya scene. When you import a Maya scene, all the imported nodes become fully integrated into the new scene and have no links to any external files. On the other hand, file references maintain a link to external files regardless of whether the referenced files are open or closed.

You can alter a referenced file in a scene, but doing so is not a great idea; it can break the link to the referenced file, and defeats the purpose of file referencing in the first place.

Referencing a File

In this example, you'll reference a model into a scene, animate it, and then make changes to the original reference, to get a basic idea of the file-referencing workflow:

1. Find the `vehicleReference_v01.ma` scene and the `street_v01.ma` scene in the `chapter16\scenes` directory at the book's web page. Copy both of these files to your local hard drive. I recommend that you put them in the `scenes` directory of your current project.

2. Open the scene `street_v01.ma` from the `scenes` directory of the current project (or wherever you placed the file on your local drive). The scene contains a simple street model. A locator named carAnimation is attached to a curve in the center of the street. If you play the animation, you'll see the locator zip along the curve.

3. To bring in a file reference, RMB-click in the Outliner and choose Reference ➤ Create Reference.

4. Find the `vehicleReference_v01.ma` scene that you copied to your local drive. Select it and choose Reference in the Reference dialog box. After a few moments, the car will appear in the scene (see Figure 16.9).

FIGURE 16.9
The referenced vehicle appears in the scene with its associated containers.

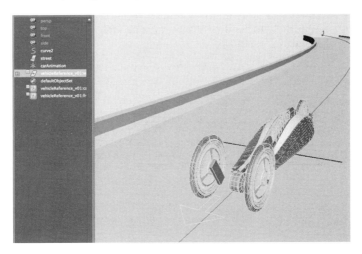

In the Outliner, you'll see the vehicleReference_v01:vehicle node, the vehicleReference_v01:front_wheels and carPaint container nodes, and the vehicleReference_v01RN node. (The container node is an asset with both the wheelTilt and steer attributes created in the previous section.) You can choose to display the reference node, or RN, by checking or unchecking it from the Outliner's Display menu.

REFERENCING MAYA SCENES

You don't need to do anything special to the scene you want to reference; it can be a standard Maya scene. When you reference a file in a scene, all of its associated nodes appear using the referenced file's scene name as a prefix. You can change this to a custom string using the options in the Create Reference tool.

---

5. In the Outliner, select the carAnimation locator, and then Ctrl/Cmd+click the vehicle-Reference_v01:vehicle node.

6. Switch to the Animation menu set, and choose Constrain ➤ Parent ➤ Options.

7. In the options for the Parent constraint, turn off Maintain Offset, make sure both Translate All and Rotate All are selected, and set the weight to **1**.

8. Click Add to make the constraint. The car is now constrained to the locator, and it will zip along the curve in the center of the street.

9. Try setting keyframes on the wheelTilt and steer attributes of the vehicleReference_v01:front_wheels node.

10. Save the scene to your local scenes directory as **street_v02.ma**.

11. Open the vehicleReference_v01.ma scene from the directory where you copied this file on your local drive.

12. Expand the vehicle group and the chassis subgroup.

13. Select the body subgroup. Set its Scale Y attribute to **0.73** and its Scale Z attribute to **1.5**. The Scale Y attribute is the second scale field in the Attribute Editor; the Scale Z attribute is the third scale field.

14. Open the Hypershade (Window ➤ Rendering Editors ➤ Hypershade), and select the blue-Paint material.

15. In the Attribute Editor for the bluePaint material, click the blue color swatch next to the color channel, and use the Color History to change the color to red.

16. Save the scene using the same name (**vehicleReference_v02.ma**).

17. Open the street_v02.ma scene. The scene is still referencing vehicleReference _v01.ma.

    If you had saved the changes to the vehicle with the same referenced scene filename, the changes would have shown up automatically when you opened the street_v02.ma scene.

However, since you changed the version of the scene filename, you will have to replace the reference. Select vehicleReference_v01RN in the Outliner. RMB-click in the Outliner, and choose Reference ➤ Replace. Browse for the `vehicleReference_v02.ma` scene. Select it and choose Reference in the Reference dialog box. The car is now updated with its wider, red body (see Figure 16.10). Play the animation or scrub on the Time Slider to see this.

FIGURE 16.10
The changes made to the body shape and color in the `vehicle-Reference_v02.ma` file are reflected in the referenced model in the street scene.

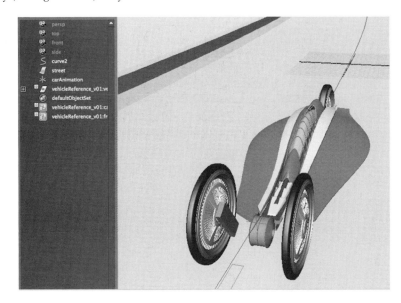

If the car had been animated in the referenced scene, you could make changes to its animation after it is loaded into your scene. Once the changes are made, you can export the reference as an offline file. Allow Referenced Animation Curves To Be Edited must be turned on in the Animation Preferences in order for this to work.

This is the basic file-referencing workflow; however, a file-referencing structure can be made much more complex to accommodate the needs of multiple teams. In addition, a referenced file can use other references so that a file-referencing tree can be constructed by layering several levels of file references. This kind of structure is best planned out and agreed upon at the beginning of a project in order to minimize confusion and keep a consistent workflow.

Bounding-Box Representations

Bounding-box representations allow you to use stand-ins for high-resolution objects, hierarchies, or animations. This can make dealing with large scenes a lot easier because the stand-ins improve performance and update faster in Maya as you work with all aspects of your scene.

Multiple versions of the model can be created and used as proxies to facilitate different needs in the scene. A proxy should be the same size and roughly the same shape as the referenced file.

1. Open the `street_v03.ma` scene from the `chapter16\scenes` directory at the book's web page. This scene has the same street as before, with the same animated locator.

2. Choose File ➤ Import. Select `vehicleReference_v01.ma` from the browser. The vehicle is imported into the scene.

3. From the Outliner, select vehicleReference_v01_vehicle. Choose Modify ➢ Convert ➢ Geometry To Bounding Box options. Set the options as shown in Figure 16.11. Make sure to check Keep Original.

FIGURE 16.11
In the Bounding Box options, represent the hierarchy as one bounding box per shape.

4. Click the Convert button. The car is replaced with bounding-box shapes and named vehicle_BBox.

5. Go to frame 100 on the timeline. In the Outliner, MMB-drag the vehicleReference_ v01:vehicle on top of the carAnimation locator. Do the same for vehicle_BBox.

6. Hide vehicleReference_v01:vehicle.

7. Play the animation to see how the car is now represented by boxes (see Figure 16.12).

FIGURE 16.12
The vehicleReference_v01RNlocator is parented to the carAnimation locator, and its geometry is now represented by bounding boxes.

Determining the Image Size and Film Speed of the Camera

When starting a new project in Maya, you should first determine the final size of the rendered image or image sequence, as well as the film speed (frames per second). These settings will affect every aspect of the project, including texture size, model tessellation, render time, how the shots are framed, and so on. You should raise this issue as soon as possible and make sure that every member of the team—from the producer to the art director, to the compositor, and to the editor—is aware of the final output of the animation. This includes the image size, resolution, frames per second, and any image cropping that may occur after rendering. Nothing is worse than having to redo a render or even an animation because of a miscommunication concerning details such as resolution settings or frames per second.

TAKING OVER A PROJECT

If you inherit a shot or a project from another animator, double-check that the resolution and camera settings are correct before proceeding. Never assume that the animation is set up properly. It's always possible that something has changed between the time the project started and the moment you took over someone else's scene files.

Setting the Size and Resolution of the Image

The settings for the image size and resolution are located in the Render Settings window under the Image Size rollout on the Common tab (shown in Figure 16.13). When you start a new scene, visit this section first to make sure the settings are what you need.

Image size refers to the number of pixels on the horizontal axis by the number of pixels on the vertical axis. Thus a setting of 640×480 means 640 pixels wide by 480 pixels tall.

Resolution refers to how many pixels fit within an inch (or centimeter, depending on the setting). Generally you'll use a resolution of 72 pixels per inch when rendering for animations displayed on computer screens, television screens, and film. Print resolution is much higher, usually between 300 and 600 pixels per inch.

You can create any settings you'd like for the image size and resolution, or you can use one of the Maya Image Size presets. The list of presets is divided so that common film and video presets are at the top of the list and common print settings are at the bottom of the list. In addition to the presets, there are fields that allow you to change the size and resolution units.

ADJUSTING SIZE FOR RENDER TEST PREVIEWS

If you need to create test renders at a smaller size, you can change the size of just the images you see in the Render Preview window by choosing a setting from the Render ➤ Test Resolution menu in the Rendering menu set. This option affects images only when they're displayed in the Render Preview window; it does not change the final output settings. When you render your final animation using a batch render, your images will use the size settings specified on the Common tab of the Render Settings window.

FIGURE 16.13
The Image Size roll-out in the Render Settings window is where you establish the image size and image resolution. Visit this panel when you start a new project.

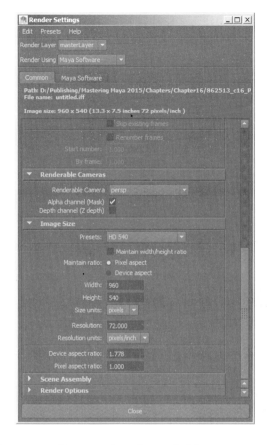

CERT OBJECTIVE

Resolution is expressed in a number of ways in Maya:

Image Aspect Ratio   The ratio of width over height. An image that is 1280×720 has a ratio of 1.778.

Pixel Aspect Ratio   The ratio of the actual pixel size. Computer monitors use square pixels: the height of the pixel is 1, and the width of the pixel is 1; thus, the pixel aspect ratio is 1.

Device Aspect Ratio   The image aspect ratio multiplied by the pixel aspect ratio. High definition displays have brought pixel aspect ratios of 1.0. Prior to HD, standard video had a pixel aspect ration of 0.9.

Film Aspect Ratio   The film aspect ratio is found in the Attribute Editor for the selected camera. For a typical 35mm video image, this would be 0.816 ÷ 0.612 = 1.333.

VIEWING NONSQUARE PIXELS ON A COMPUTER MONITOR

Viewing nonsquare pixels on a computer monitor makes the image look squished. With today's standards of high definition video, nonssquare pixels is a thing of the past. However if you find yourself working with older footage you would typically test-render your animation using a pixel aspect ratio of 1.0 with an image size of 720×540. When you are ready for final output, you can switch your resolution to a standard video resolution using a pixel aspect ratio of 0.9 and an image size of 720×486.

Setting the Film Speed

The film speed (also known as *transport speed*) is specified in frames per second. You can find this setting in the Maya Preferences window (Window ➤ Settings/Preferences ➤ Preferences). Under the Categories column on the left side of the window, choose Settings. In the Working Units area, use the Time drop-down list to specify the frames per second of the scene. You can change this setting after you've started animating, but it's a good idea to set it at the start of a project to avoid confusion or mistakes. When changing this setting on a scene that already has keyframed animation, you can choose to keep the keyframes at their current frame numbers or have Maya adjust the keyframe position automatically based on the new time setting (see Figure 16.14).

FIGURE 16.14
You set the animation speed (frames per second) in the Preferences window.

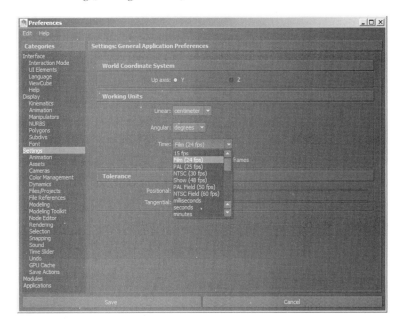

Creating and Animating Cameras

When you add a camera to a scene, you should think about how the shot will be composed and whether the camera will be animated. The composition of a shot affects the mood and tells the viewer which elements visible within the frame are most important to the story. The camera settings allow you to fine-tune the composition of the shot by controlling what is visible within the frame and how it appears.

Most of the attributes of a camera can be animated, allowing you to set the mood of a scene and create special camera effects. Three types of cameras offer different animation controls. These are the one-, two-, and three-node cameras. The controls available for each camera type are suited to different styles of camera movement. This section covers how to create different camera types for a scene and how to establish and animate the settings.

ANIMATICS

An *animatic* is a film-industry term referring to a rough animation designed to help plan a shot, like a moving storyboard. Typically, models in an animatic are low-resolution and untextured, with simple lighting. Animatics are used to plan both computer-generated (CG) and live-action shots. Camera work, timing, and the composition of elements within the frame are the most important aspects of an animatic.

Creating a Camera

Every new Maya scene has four preset cameras by default. These are the front, side, top, and perspective (persp) cameras. You can render a scene using any of these cameras; however, their main purpose is to navigate and view the 3D environment shown in the viewport. It's always a good idea to create new cameras in the scene for the purpose of rendering the animation. By keeping navigation and rendering cameras separate, you can avoid confusion when rendering.

1. Open the `chase_v01.ma` scene from the `chapter16/scenes` folder at the book's web page. You'll find that a simple animatic of a car racing down a track has been created.

2. Create a new camera (Create ➢ Cameras ➢ Camera). Open the Outliner, and select the new camera1 node. Double-click its transform node in the Outliner, and rename it **shotCam1** (see Figure 16.15).

FIGURE 16.15
A new camera is created and renamed in the Outliner.

3. In the Display tab of the Layer Editor, turn off the visibility of all the layers except the street layer to hide the unnecessary geometry in the scene.

4. Select shotCam1 in the Outliner, and press the **f** hot key to focus on this camera in the viewport.

The icon for the camera looks like a movie camera. It has a transform node and a shape node. The camera attributes are located on the shape node.

5. To move the camera up from the center of the grid to the level of the street, set the Translate X, Y, and Z channels to **1.382**, **4.138**, and −**3.45** in the Channel Box. Press **f** again to focus the view on the camera that should now be above the street.

6. Choose Modify ➢ Transformation Tools ➢ Show Manipulator Tool, or press the **t** hot key. If you zoom out in the viewport, you'll see the camera has a second positional icon; this manipulator can be used to aim the camera (see Figure 16.16). Grab the aim handle of the manipulator, and position it on the street so that the camera is looking up the road (toward the beginning of the track where the car starts).

FIGURE 16.16
The Show Manipulator tool displays a second handle, which can be used to aim the camera.

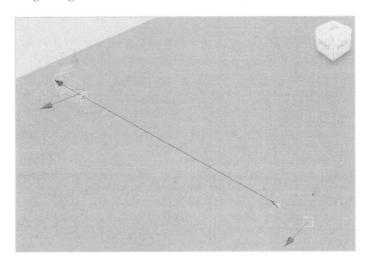

7. In the Viewport panel menu, choose Panels ➢ Look Through Selected (or Panels ➢ Perspective ➢ shotCam1). This will switch the view to shotCam1.

2D PAN/ZOOM TOOL

The 2D Pan/Zoom tool allows you to pan or zoom around the view of the current viewing camera without changing its position or rotation. This tool is designed to help you if you are working on a scene in which you are matching the animation of a model closely to footage projected on an image plane. To do this, you may need to zoom in or move the view to get a better look without disturbing the actual position of the camera. Follow these steps:

1. Switch to the camera that is viewing the scene and the footage on the image plane.

2. From the panel menu, choose View ➢ Camera Tools ➢ 2D Pan/Zoom Tool ➢ Options. The options should open in the Tool Settings. In the options, you can switch between 2D Pan and 2D Zoom modes.

3. Drag around in the viewport window to pan or zoom.

4. To toggle back to the actual camera view, use the 2D Pan/Zoom button in the panel menu bar or use the \ hot key.

In the Attribute Editor for the camera's shape node, you can enable rendering for the 2D Pan/Zoom view if needed under the Display Options rollout panel.

---

8. In the Display tab of the Layer Editor, turn on the visibility of the buildings layer so that the buildings are visible. Tumble around in the viewport so that you can see part of the large building to the left of the street.

9. From the panel menu, turn on the Resolution Gate display (the blue sphere on a white background icon). Click the Camera Attributes icon to open the Attribute Editor for shotCam1.

DISPLAY SETTINGS

These same settings appear in the Attribute Editor for the camera's shape node under the Display Options rollout. You can use these settings to change the opacity or the color of the gate mask. Turn on both the Resolution and Film Gate displays at the same time, and change the Overscan setting, which changes the amount of space between the gate and the edge of the viewport.

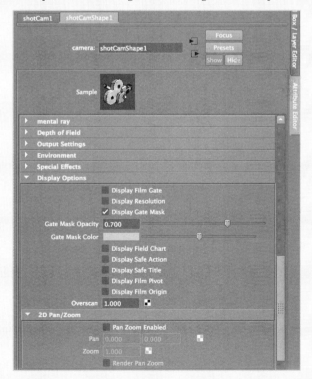

The image size of this scene is set to 1280×720, which is the HD 720 preset. You can see the image resolution at the top of the screen when the Resolution Gate is activated. Working with the Resolution Gate on is extremely helpful when you're establishing the composition of your shots (see Figure 16.17).

FIGURE 16.17
The Resolution Gate is a helpful tool when framing a shot.

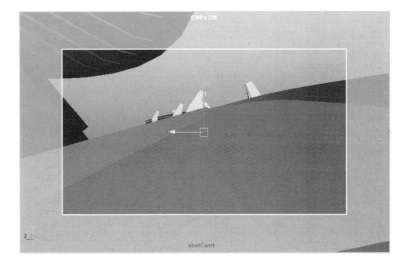

When you create a new camera to render the scene, you need to add it to the list of renderable cameras in Render Settings. You can render the scene using more than one camera.

10. Scroll down in the Attribute Editor for shotCam1, and expand the Output Settings rollout. Make sure the Renderable option is selected.

11. Open the Render Settings window. In the Renderable Cameras area, you'll see both the shotCam1 and persp cameras listed (see Figure 16.18). Remove the perspective camera from the list of renderable cameras by clicking the Trash Can to the right of the listing.

To change the renderable camera, choose a different camera from the list. To add another camera, choose Add Renderable Camera at the bottom of the list. The list shows all the available cameras in the scene.

Setting Camera Attributes

CERT OBJECTIVE

At the top of the Attribute Editor for the camera's shape node, you'll find the basic settings for the camera available in the Camera Attributes rollout panel.

Single-Node Camera   A single-node camera is just a plain camera like the perspective camera. You can change its rotation and translation by setting these channels in the Channel Box, by using the Move and Rotate tools, or by tumbling and tracking while looking through the camera.

Two-Node Camera   A *two-node camera* is a camera that has a separate aim control. The Camera and Aim controls are contained within a group. When you switch to this type of camera (or create this type of camera using the Create ➢ Cameras menu), the rotation of the camera is controlled by the position of the aim node, which is simply a locator. It works much like the Show Manipulators tool except that the locator has a transform node itself. This makes it easy to visualize where the camera is looking in the scene and makes doing animation easier. You can keyframe the position of the aim locator and the position of the camera separately and easily edit their animation curves on the Graph Editor.

Three-Node Camera   A *three-node camera* is created when you choose Camera, Aim, and Up from the Controls menu. This adds a third locator, which is used to control the camera's rotation around the z-axis. These controls and alternative arrangements will be explored later in the "Creating Custom Camera Rigs" section.

FIGURE 16.18
You can change or add cameras to the list of renderable cameras in the Render Settings window using the Renderable Cameras drop-down menu.

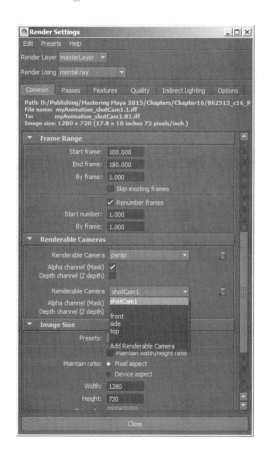

When working with two- or three-node cameras, resist the temptation to move or keyframe the position of the group node that contains both the camera and the aim locator. Instead, expand the group in the Outliner, and keyframe the camera and aim nodes separately. This will keep the animation simple and help avoid confusion when editing the animation. If you need to move the whole rig over a large distance, Shift+click both the camera and the aim locator and move them together. Moving the group node separately is asking for trouble.

CAMERA TWIST

The Camera and Aim type of rig has a twist attribute on the group node above the camera and aim nodes. The group node is labeled "Camera1_group," and it can be selected in the Outliner. Twist controls the Z rotation of the camera much like the Up control on the three-node camera. This is the only control on the group node that you may want to adjust or keyframe.

For most situations, a two-node camera is a good choice since you can easily manipulate the aim node to point the camera accurately at specific scene elements yet, at the same time, it doesn't have additional nodes, like the three-node camera, which can get in the way. In this example, you'll use a two-node camera to create an establishing shot for the car-chase scene.

The focal length of the camera has a big impact on the mood of the scene. Adjusting the focal length can exaggerate the perspective of the scene, creating more drama.

CERT OBJECTIVE

1. Select shotCam1, and open its Attribute Editor to the shotCam1Shape1 tab. In the Controls drop-down list, you have the option of switching to a camera with an aim node or to a camera with an Aim and an Up control. Set the camera to Camera And Aim (see Figure 16.19).

FIGURE 16.19
You can add other camera controls using the Controls menu in the Attribute Editor. The camera is then grouped in the Outliner with a separate Aim control.

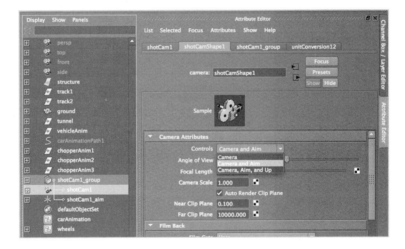

2. Expand the shotCam1_group node that now appears in the Outliner, and select the shot-Cam_aim node.

3. In the Channel Box, set its Translate X, Y, and Z settings to **–0.155**, **4.206**, **–2.884**. (The camera's node should still have its X, Y, and Z Translate settings at 1.382, 4.138, and –3.45.)

4. In the Display Layer menu, turn on the visibility of the car layer. Set the current frame to **60** so that the car is in view of the camera.

5. In the Attribute Editor for shotCam1, adjust the Angle Of View slider. Decreasing this setting flattens the perspective in the image and zooms in on the scene; increasing this setting exaggerates the perspective and zooms out.

6. With the camera still selected, switch to the Channel Box, and find the Focal Length setting under the shotCamShape1 node.

7. Highlight the Focal Length channel label, and MMB-drag left and right in the viewport window. Set Focal Length to **20** (see Figure 16.20).

FIGURE 16.20
The Angle Of View slider in the Attribute Editor and Focal Length attribute in the Channel Box both adjust the zoom of the camera.

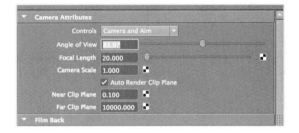

Adjusting the focal length of the camera has a similar effect on the camera as changing the angle of view; however, it is inversely related to the angle of view. Increasing the focal length zooms in on the scene, and decreasing it zooms out. The two settings are connected; they can't be set independently of each other.

RENDERING A PORTRAIT

When you want to render a close-up of a character, a short focal length can distort the features of your character's face. To achieve the best results, you want to push the camera back in the scene and then zoom in. This flattens the depth of the scene and creates a more accurate portrayal of the character. Try these steps:

1. In the Render Settings, create an image size suitable for a portrait—try something like 990 × 1220.

2. Create a new camera, and turn on the Resolution Gate display so that you can properly frame the face.

3. Set the camera to a focal length of **50**, dolly the camera back (Alt/Option+RMB), and frame the face.

continues

continued

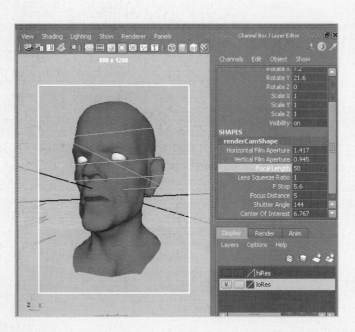

A good portrait should be slightly off-center. Divide the frame horizontally into thirds, and position the eyes at about the place where the top and middle thirds meet. You can always experiment with different camera positions relative to the subject to see how they affect the emotional impact of the image. Unless you want to create a confrontational image, try not to put the subject dead center in the frame. When rendering characters for a portfolio, I find that this setup creates a visually pleasing way to show off my work, which is not surprising since these techniques have been developed by portrait artists over the centuries.

In a real camera, as you adjust the focal length, you are essentially repositioning the lens in the camera so that the distance between the lens and the film gate (where the sensor is exposed to light) is increased or decreased. As you increase the focal length, objects appear larger in the frame. The camera zooms in on the subject. The viewable area also decreases—this is the angle of view. As you decrease the focal length, you move the lens back toward the film gate, increasing the viewable area in the scene and making objects in the frame appear smaller. You're essentially zooming out (see Figure 16.21).

By default, Maya cameras have a focal length of 35. Roughly speaking, the human eye has a focal length of about 50. A setting of 20 is a good way to increase drama in an action scene by exaggerating the perspective. Higher settings can flatten out the view, which creates a different type of mood; by reducing perspective distortion, you can make the elements of a scene feel large and distant.

FIGURE 16.21

Two Maya cameras seen from above. A longer focal length produces a smaller angle of view (the left camera); a shorter focal length produces a larger angle of view (the right camera).

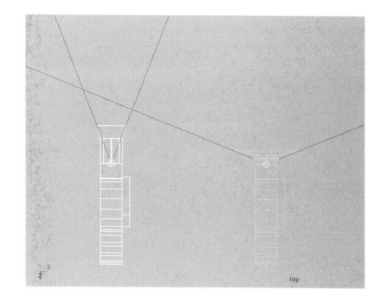

Limiting the Range of Renderable Objects with Clipping Planes

Clipping planes are used to determine the range of renderable objects in a scene. Objects that lie outside the clipping planes are not visible or renderable in the current camera. Clipping planes can affect the quality of the rendered image; if the ratio between the near clipping plane and the far clipping plane is too large, image quality can suffer. (If the near clipping plane is 0.1, the far clipping plane should be no more than 20,000.) Keep the far image plane just slightly beyond the farthest object that needs to be rendered in the scene, and keep the detail of distant objects fairly low.

The Auto Render Clip Plane option automatically determines the position of the clipping planes when rendering with Maya software. (This setting does not affect animations rendered with mental ray, Maya hardware, or vector renders.) It's always a good idea to turn off this option and set the clipping-plane values manually:

1. From the panel menu, choose Panels ➤ Layouts ➤ Two Panes Side By Side. Set the left pane to the perspective view and the right pane to shotCam1.

New!

2. Select shotCam1 and open its Attribute Editor. Expand the Frustrum Display Controls rollout. Check all three attributes to visually display the field of view or frustrum.

3. Press **t** to activate the Show Manipulator tool for shotCam1.

4. Zoom in on the shot cam in the perspective view, and click the blue manipulator switch twice (located just below the camera when the Show Manipulator tool is active) to switch to the clipping-plane display (see Figure 16.22). After you click the manipulator, it turns yellow.

FIGURE 16.22
Clicking the blue
switch below the
Show Manipulators
tool cycles through
the various actions
of the tool. Clicking
twice activates the
manipulators for
the clipping planes.

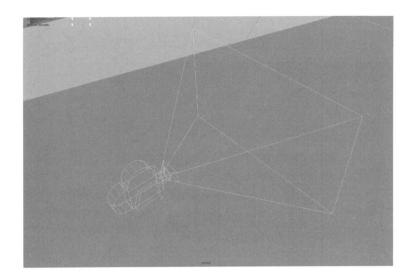

The clipping-plane manipulator consists of two blue rectangles connected by lines. The near clipping plane is a small rectangle close to the camera; the far clipping plane is large and far from the camera.

5. Zoom in close to shotCam1, and RMB- or MMB-drag the clipping-plane manipulator. You can set the position of this clipping plane interactively. Note that as you move the plane away from the camera, the geometry in the shotCam1 view is cut off. Any object between the camera and the near clipping plane will not render or will only partially render.

6. Zoom out until you can see the far clipping-plane manipulator.

7. MMB-drag this to bring it in closer to the camera. Objects beyond this clipping plane will not be rendered by the camera or will appear to be cut off.

8. In the Attribute Editor for the shotCamShape1 node, set Near Clip Plane to **0.05** and Far Clip Plane to **85** (the units for this scene are set to meters), as in Figure 16.23. This is a good starting place; if the positions of the planes need to change later, they can be adjusted.

9. Save the scene as `chase_v02.ma`.

To see a version of the scene to this point, open `chase_v02.ma` from the `chapter16/scenes` directory at the book's web page.

CLIPPING-PLANE PROBLEMS

Sometimes you may find that everything disappears in a scene when you change the working units in the Preferences dialog box or when you open a scene. This usually happens when the clipping planes have been set incorrectly or have changed. Try opening the Attribute Editor for the current viewing camera, and adjust the clipping-plane values. This is true for the front, side, and top cameras as well as the perspective camera.

FIGURE 16.23
The positions of the clipping planes are set for shotCam1.

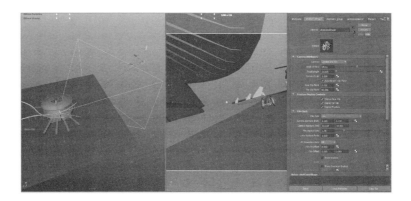

Composing the Shot Using the Film-Back Settings

In an actual film camera, the *film back* refers to the plate where the negative is placed when it is exposed to light. The size of the film determines the film-back setting, so 35mm film uses a 35mm film back. The *film gate* is the gate that holds the film to the film back. Unless you are trying to match actual footage in Maya, you shouldn't need to edit these settings.

Ideally you want the Film Gate and Resolution Gate to be the same size in the viewport. If you turn on the display of both the Film Gate and the Resolution in the camera's Display Options rollout panel (toward the bottom of the Attribute Editor—you can't turn on both the Film Gate and Resolution Gate using the icons in the panel menu bar), you may see that the Film Gate appears to be larger than the Resolution Gate in the viewport—the gates are displayed as boxes. You can fix this by adjusting the Film Aspect Ratio setting. Simply divide the resolution width by the resolution height (1280 ÷ 720 = 1.777777), and put this value in the Film Aspect Ratio setting (see Figure 16.24).

The Film Gate drop-down list has presets available that you can use to match footage if necessary. The presets will adjust the camera aperture, film aspect ratio, and lens squeeze ratio as needed. If you're not trying to match film, you can safely leave these settings at their defaults and concern yourself only with the Image Size and Resolution attributes in the Render Settings window.

The Film Fit Offset and Film Offset controls in the Film Back rollout can be useful in special circumstances when you need to change the center of the rendered area without altering the position of the camera. The parallax caused by the perspective of the 3D scene in the frame does not change even though the camera view has. Creating an offset in an animated camera can create a strange but stylistic look.

The Film Fit Offset value has no effect if Fit Resolution Gate is set to Fill or Overscan. If you set Fit Resolution Gate to Horizontal or Vertical and then adjust the Film Fit Offset, the offset will be either horizontal or vertical based on the Fit Resolution Gate setting. The Film Offset values accomplish the same thing; however, they don't depend on the setting of Fit Resolution Gate. The following steps demonstrate how to alter the Film Offset:

1. Continue with the scene from the previous section, or open the chase_v02.ma scene from the chapter16/scenes directory at the book's web page. Set the current camera in the viewport to shotCam1 and the timeline to frame 61.

2. In the Display tab of the Layer Editor, turn on the choppers layer so that the helicopter is visible in the shot.

FIGURE 16.24
In the top image, the boxes representing the Film Gate and Resolution do not match. In the bottom image, the Film Aspect Ratio setting has been changed so that Film Gate and Resolution do match.

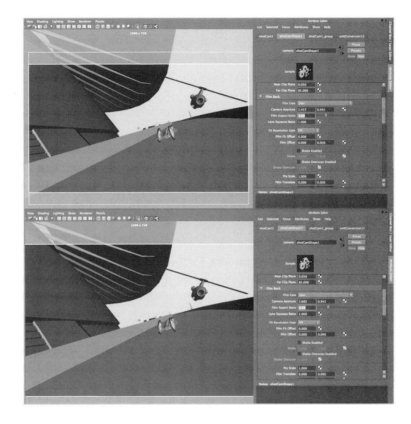

3. Open the Attribute Editor for shotCam1, and switch to the shape node (shotCamShape1) tab.

4. In the Film Back rollout panel, set Film Offset to **0.2** and **–0.05**. Notice how this change alters the composition of the frame. Even a small change can affect the emotional impact of a shot (see Figure 16.25).

FIGURE 16.25
Adjusting the Film Offset setting changes the framing of the shot without actually moving the camera or the perspective of the image.

Creating a Camera-Shake Effect

The Shake attribute is an easy way to add a shaky vibrating motion to a camera. The first field is the horizontal shake, and the second field is the vertical shake. The values you enter in the shake fields modify the current settings for Film Offset. When you are applying a shake, you're essentially shaking the film back, which is useful because this does not change how the camera itself is animated. You can apply expressions, keyframes, or animated textures to one or both of these fields. The Shake Enabled option allows you to turn the shaking on or off while working in Maya; it can't be keyframed. However, you can easily animate the amount of shaking over time.

In this example, you'll use an animated fractal texture to create the camera-shake effect. You can use an animated fractal texture any time you need to generate random noise values for an attribute. One advantage fractal textures have over mathematical expressions is that they are easier to animate over time.

1. Turn on the Shake Enabled option.

2. Right-click the first field in the Shake option, and choose Create New Texture from the context menu (see Figure 16.26).

FIGURE 16.26
Right-click the attribute field, and choose Create New Texture. The Create Render Node window will open.

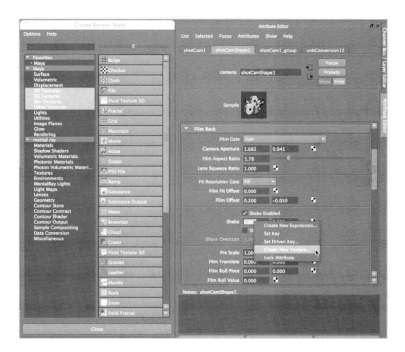

3. Under the Maya section in the node list on the left of the Create Render Node window, choose Fractal from the 2D Textures section. The camera view will move when you add the texture, and that's okay.

4. The attributes for the fractal texture will appear in the Attribute Editor. Set Amplitude to **0.1**.

5. Select the Animated check box to enable the animation of the texture, and rewind the animation.

6. Right-click the Time attribute, and choose Set Key (see Figure 16.27).

FIGURE 16.27
To animate a fractal
texture, turn on the
Animated option
and set keyframes
on the Time Slider.

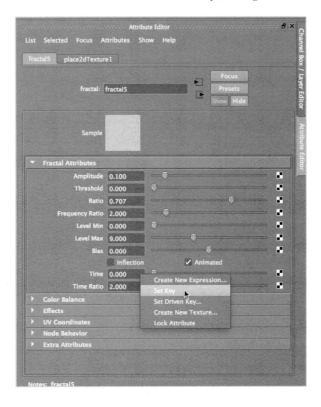

7. Set the timeline to frame 200. Set the Time attribute to **100**, and set another key.

8. Rewind and play the animation; you'll see the camera move back and forth.

9. Repeat steps 2 though 7 for the Vertical setting in Shake to add another animated fractal texture to this attribute. You want to have a different texture for each setting so that the horizontal and vertical shaking settings of the camera are not the same value; otherwise, the camera will appear to shake diagonally.

10. In the Attribute Editor for the second fractal texture, expand its UV Coordinates rollout panel, and click the arrow to the right of it to go to the fractal texture's place2dTexture2 node.

11. Set the Rotate UV value to **45**. This rotates the texture so that the output of this animated texture is different from the other, ensuring a more random motion.

You may notice that the shaking is nice and strong but that you've lost the original composition of the frame. To bring it back to where it was, adjust the range of values created by each texture. The Fractal Amplitude of both textures is set to 0.1, which means each texture is adding a random value between 0 and 0.1 to the film offset. You need to equalize these values by adjusting the Alpha Offset and Alpha Gain settings of the textures.

12. With the camera selected, open the Node Editor by choosing Window ➤ Node Editor.

13. Choose the Input and Output Connections icon from the Node Editor toolbar. In the Work Area, you'll see the two textures connected to the camera.

14. Hold the mouse over the line connecting one of the textures to the shotCamShape1 node. The pop-up label shows that the outAlpha attribute of the texture is connected to the vertical or horizontal shake of the camera. This means that you must adjust the outAlpha value to compensate for the change made to the camera's offset (see Figure 16.28).

FIGURE 16.28
The outAlpha value generated by the animated fractal texture is connected to the camera's horizontal shake.

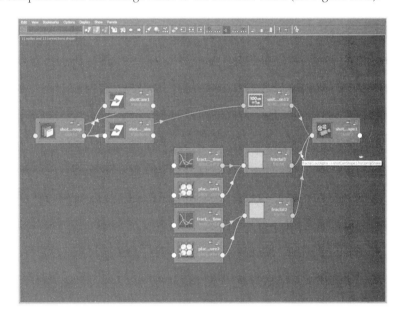

If you look at what's going on with the fractal texture, you'll see that when the Amplitude setting of the texture is 0, the outAlpha value is 0.5. (You can see this by switching to the shotCamShape1 tab and looking at the Horizontal Shake field.) The fractal texture itself is a flat gray color (value = 0.5). As you increase the Amplitude setting, the variation in the texture is amplified. At an Amplitude value of 1, the outAlpha attribute ranges from 0 to 1. You can see this in the values generated for the Shake attribute in the camera node. This is a large offset and causes the shaking of the camera to be extreme. You can set Amplitude to a low value, but this means the outAlpha value generated will remain close to 0.5, so as the shake values are added to the film offset, the composition of the frame is changed—the view shifts up to the right.

To fix this, you can adjust the Alpha Gain and Alpha Offset attributes found in the Color Balance rollout of each fractal texture. Alpha Gain is a scaling factor. When Alpha Gain is set to 0.5, the outAlpha values are cut in half; when Alpha Gain is set to 0, outAlpha is also 0, and thus the Shake values are set to 0 and the camera returns to its original position. If you want to shake the camera but keep it near its original position, it seems as though the best method is to adjust the Alpha Gain value of the fractal texture.

However, there is still one problem with this method. You want the outAlpha value of the fractal to produce both negative and positive values so that the camera shakes around its original position in all directions. If you set Alpha Gain to a positive or negative number, the values produced will be either positive or negative, which makes the view appear to shift in one direction or the other. To adjust the output of these values properly, you can use the Alpha Offset attribute to create a shift.

Set Alpha Offset to negative one-half of Alpha Gain to get a range of values that are both positive and negative; 0 will be in the middle of this range. Figure 16.29 shows how adjusting the Amplitude, Alpha Gain, and Alpha Offset attributes affects the range of values produced by the animated fractal texture.

FIGURE 16.29
You can adjust the range of values produced by the animated fractal texture using the Amplitude, Alpha Offset, and Alpha Gain attributes.

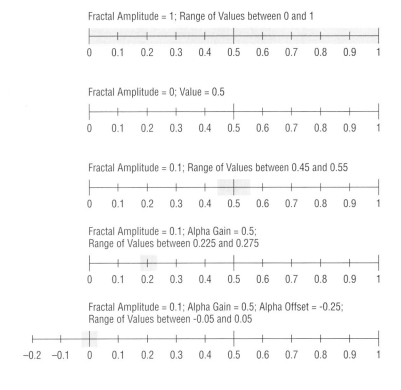

Using an Expression to Control Alpha Offset

You can reduce the number of controls needed to animate the camera shake by automating the Alpha Offset setting on the fractal node. The best way to set this up is to create a simple expression where Alpha Offset is multiplied by negative one-half of the Alpha Gain setting. You can use this technique any time you need to shift the range of the fractal texture's outAlpha to give both positive and negative values.

1. Select the fractal node that has been connected to the camera, and open its attributes in the Attribute Editor. Expand the Color Balance rollout panel, and set the Alpha Gain value of fractal1 to **0.25**.

2. In the field for Alpha Offset, type **=−0.5*fractal1.alphaGain;**. Then press the Enter key to enter the expression (see Figure 16.30). Note that the correct fractal node must be explicitly stated in the expression or you will get an error. If the node itself is named something other than fractal1, make sure that this is named in the expression accordingly. When in doubt, just look at the top of the Attribute Editor in the Fractal field.

FIGURE 16.30
An expression is created to set the Alpha Offset value of fractal1 automatically to negative one-half of the Alpha Gain value.

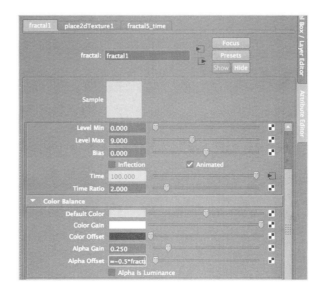

You can create the same setup for the fractal2 node. However, it might be a better idea to create a direct connection between the attributes of fractal1 and fractal2, so you need only adjust the Alpha Gain of fractal1, and all other values will update accordingly.

3. In the Node Editor, click the output port of fractal1, and choose Alpha Gain from the pop-up menu.

4. Extend the yellow wire to the input port of fractal2. Choose Alpha Gain from the pop-up menu to make the connection.

5. Repeat the procedure for the Alpha Offset and Amplitude to connect these two attributes as well (see Figure 16.31).

6. Play the animation, and you'll see the camera shake. To tone down the movement, reduce the Alpha Gain of fractal1.

FIGURE 16.31
The Node Editor is used to connect the Alpha Gain, Alpha Offset, and Amplitude of fractal2 to fractal1.

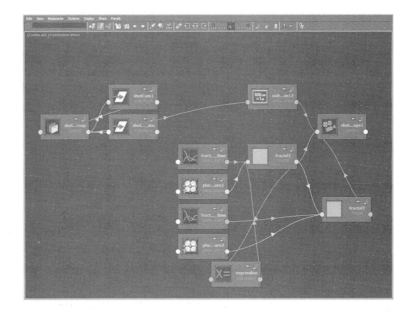

7. Set the timeline to frame 60, and set the Alpha Gain value of fractal1 to **0**. Right-click the Alpha Gain field, and choose Set Key.

8. Set the timeline to frame 65. Set the Alpha Gain value of fractal1 to **0.5**, and set another key.

9. Set the timeline to frame 90. Set the Alpha Gain value of fractal1 to **0**, and set a third key.

10. Play back the animation, and you'll see the camera shake as the car and helicopter fly by (make sure the playback speed in the Time Slider preferences is set to Real-time [24 fps]; otherwise, the shake will not appear at the proper speed in the view window as you play the animation).

11. Save the scene as **chase_v03.ma**.

To see a version of the scene to this point, open the chase_v03.ma scene from the chapter16\ scenes directory at the book's web page.

The Shake Overscan attribute moves the film back and forth on the z-axis of the camera as opposed to the Shake settings, which move the film back and forth horizontally and vertically. Try animating the Shake Overscan setting using a fractal texture to create some dramatic horror-movie effects.

SHAKING CAMERA ASSET

This camera arrangement is a good candidate for an asset. You can create an asset from nodes that have already been connected and animated. In the Outliner, turn off DAG Objects Only in the Display menu. From the list of nodes in the Outliner, select the camera's shape node, expression, and fractal textures, and create an asset. You can then use the Asset Editor to publish the Amplitude and Alpha Gain attributes of fractal1 to the container as custom attributes. (Give the attributes descriptive names, such as **shakeAmplitude** and **shakeScale**.) When you need to make changes to the animation of the shake, you can simply set keyframes on the published shakeScale attribute.

Creating Custom Camera Rigs

The three camera types in Maya (Camera, Camera and Aim, Camera Aim and Up) work well for many common animation situations. However, you'll find that sometimes a custom camera rig gives you more creative control over a shot. This section shows you how to create a custom camera rig for the car-chase scene. Use this example as a springboard for ideas to design your own custom camera rigs and controls.

Swivel Camera Rig

This rig involves attaching a camera to a NURBS circle so that it can easily swivel around a subject in a perfect arc:

1. Open the chase_v03.ma scene from the chapter16\scenes directory at the book's web page, or continue with the scene from the previous section. In the Display tab of the Layer Editor, turn off both the choppers and buildings layers.

2. Switch to the persp camera in the viewport.

3. Create a NURBS circle by choosing Create ➤ NURBS Primitives ➤ Circle. Name the circle **swivelCamRig**.

4. Create a new camera (Create ➤ Cameras ➤ Camera), and name it **swivelCam**.

5. Open the Attribute Editor for swivelCam to the swivelCamShape tab. Set Controls to Camera and Aim.

6. Expand the new swivelCam_group node in the Outliner. Select the swivelCam, and press the **f** hot key to focus on the camera in the viewport.

7. In the Outliner, select swivelCam, and Ctrl/Cmd+click the swivelCamRig circle.

8. Switch to the Animation menu set, and choose Animate ➤ Motion Paths ➤ Attach To Motion Path ➤ Options.

9. In the Attach To Motion Path Options dialog box, set Time Range to Start and uncheck Follow.

10. Click Attach to attach the camera to the circle (see Figure 16.32). You may get a warning in the Script Editor when you attach a camera to a curve stating that the camera may not evaluate as expected. You can safely ignore this warning.

FIGURE 16.32
The swivelCam is attached to the NURBS circle using the Attach To Motion Path command.

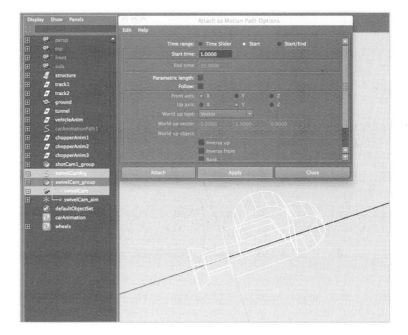

The camera is now attached to the circle via the motion path; the camera will stay in a fixed position on the circle curve. This is a fast and easy way to attach any object or other type of transform node (such as a group) to a curve.

11. Make sure the visibility of the street and car display layers is on, and rewind the animation.

12. Zoom out in the perspective viewport. In the Outliner, select swivelCamRig, and MMB-drag it up in the Outliner into the vehicleAnim group.

13. Expand the vehicleAnim group, and select the swivelCamRig.

14. Open the Channel Box, and set the Translate and Rotate channels to **0**. The circle will be repositioned around the car.

15. Select the swivelCam_aim locator from within the swivelCam_group.

16. In the Outliner, MMB-drag this up into the vehicleAnim group as well. Set its Translate and Rotate channels to **0**. This will move to the pivot point of the vehicleAnim group.

17. Select the swivelCamRig, and in the Channel Box set Translate Y to **0.4**. Set the Scale attributes to **0.5** (see Figure 16.33).

FIGURE 16.33
The NURBS circle (swivelCamRig) and the swivelCam_aim have been parented to the vehicleAnim group.

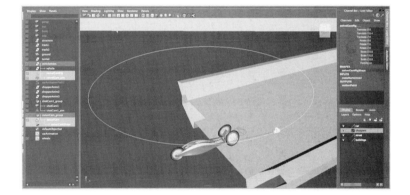

18. Set the viewport to the swivelCam, and turn on the Resolution Gate display.

19. Select the swivelCam node, and set its Focal Length to **20**. Play the animation. You'll see the camera follow along with the car as it drives down the road.

Swivel Camera Rig Asset

The camera follows the car, but things don't get interesting until you start to animate the attributes of the rig. To cut down on the number of node attributes that you need to hunt through to animate the rig, you'll create an asset for the camera and rig and publish attributes for easy access in the Channel Box.

1. In the Outliner, Ctrl/Cmd+click the swivelCam node, swivelCamShape, the swivelCam_aim locator, and the swivelCamRig node.

2. Choose Assets ➢ Advanced Assets ➢ Create ➢ Options.

3. Set Operation to Create Asset, and set the name to **swivelCamera**. Turn off Include Hierarchy so that only the nodes selected in the Outliner are included.

4. Click Apply And Close to create the asset (see Figure 16.34).

FIGURE 16.34
The Create
Advanced Asset
Options dialog box.

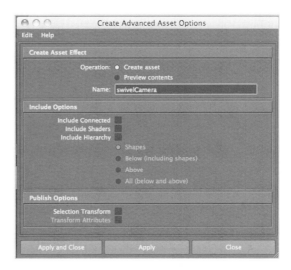

5. Choose Assets ➤ Asset Editor. On the left side of the Asset Editor, select the swivelCamera asset and click the pushpin icon to edit the asset.

6. Click the plus sign in the square to expand the swivelCamera asset, and then expand the swivelCam rig node (click the plus sign in the circle next to swivelCamRig).

7. From the list of attributes, scroll down to find the Translate attributes. Expand the Translate group by clicking the plus sign in the circle, and select the Translate Y attribute.

8. Click the second icon from the top at the center of the Asset Editor. Set the published name to **rise**.

9. Expand the Rotate group, select the Rotate Y attribute, and publish it using the name **swivel**. Expand the Scale group, select Scale Z, and publish it using the name **push**.

10. On the left side of the editor, expand the swivelCam_aim node, and select its Translate attribute.

11. Publish it using the name **aim** (see Figure 16.35). The three attributes, Aim X, Aim Y, and Aim Z, will be created at once. Maya will automatically capitalize these attributes in the Channel Box.

12. Expand the swivelCam (click the plus sign in the square) and the swivelCamShape nodes (click the plus sign in the circle).

13. Select the Focal Length attribute, and publish it using the name **zoom**.

14. Close the Asset Editor, and select the swivelCamera asset node in the Outliner. Try changing the values of the published attributes and playing the animation.

15. Open the Preferences panel (Window ➤ Settings/Preferences ➤ Preferences), and select Animation from the Settings category in the column on the left. Make sure Default In Tangent and Default Out Tangent are set to Clamped.

FIGURE 16.35
Various attributes are chosen from the nodes in the swivelCam asset and published to the Channel Box using the Asset Editor.

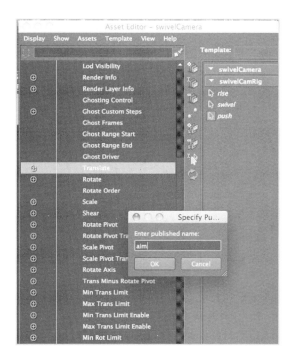

LOCK UNUSED ROTATION CHANNELS

To cut down on rotation problems, you'll want to lock the Rotate X and Rotate Z values of the swivelCameraRig. Select the nodes in the INPUTS section of the Channel Box, set the values to **0**, right-click these attributes, and choose Lock Selected. This keeps the rotation nice and simple.

16. Try setting the following keyframes to create a dramatic camera move using the rig (see Figure 16.36).

FRAME	RISE	SWIVEL	PUSH	AIM X	AIM Y	AIM Z
Frame 1	3.227	48.4116	0	0	0	0
Frame 41	0.06	134.265	0.3	0	0	0
Frame 92	0.06	246.507	0.3	0	0.091	0.046
Frame 145	0.13	290.819	0.8	0	0.167	−0.087
Frame 160	0	458.551	0.4	0	0.132	−0.15
Frame 200	0.093	495.166	0.4	0	0.132	−0.015

FIGURE 16.36
The attributes of the asset are selected and keyframed.

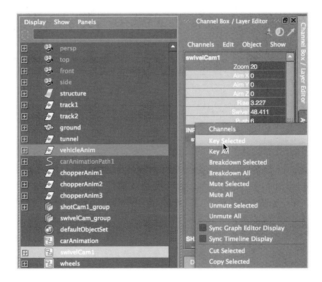

17. Make sure that the view in the perspective window is still set to swivelCam (Panels ➤ Perspective ➤ swivelCam).

18. Turn on all the display layers, and play the animation (see Figure 16.37). Save the scene as `chase_v04.ma`.

To see a finished version of the animation, open the `chase_v04.ma` scene from the `chapter16\scenes` directory at the book's web page.

Applying Depth of Field and Motion Blur

Depth of field and motion blur are two effects meant to replicate real-world camera phenomena. Both of these effects can increase the realism of a scene as well as the drama. However, they can both increase render times significantly, so it's important to learn how to apply them efficiently when rendering a scene. In this section, you'll learn how to activate these effects and the basics of how to work with them. Using both effects well is closely tied to render-quality issues.

FIGURE 16.37
A snapshot of the animation using our custom camera rig.

Rendering Using Depth of Field

The depth of field (DOF) settings in Maya simulate the photographic phenomena where some areas of an image are in focus and other areas are out of focus. Artistically this can greatly increase the drama of the scene, because it forces the viewers to focus their attention on a specific element in the composition of a frame.

Depth of field is a ray-traced effect and can be created using both Maya software and mental ray; however, the mental ray DOF feature is far superior to that of the Maya software. This section describes how to render depth of field using mental ray.

 **Real World Scenario**

DEPTH OF FIELD AND RENDER TIME

Depth of field adds a lot to render time, as you'll see from the examples in this section. When working on a project that is under time constraints, you will need to factor DOF rendering into your schedule. If a scene requires an animated depth of field, you'll most likely find yourself re-rendering the sequence a lot. As an alternative, you may want to create the DOF using compositing software after the sequence has been rendered. It may not be as physically accurate as mental ray's DOF, but it will render much faster, and you can easily animate the effect and make changes in the compositing stage. To do this, you can use the Camera Depth Render Pass preset to create a separate depth pass of the scene and then use the grayscale values of the depth-pass layer in conjunction with a blur effect to create DOF in your compositing software. Not only will the render take less time to create in Maya, but you'll be able to fine-tune and animate the effect quickly and efficiently in your compositing software.

There are two ways to apply the mental ray depth-of-field effect to a camera in a Maya scene:

◆ Activate the Depth Of Field option in the camera's Attribute Editor.

◆ Add a mental ray physical_lens_dof lens shader or the mia_lens_bokeh lens shader to the camera. (mental ray has special shaders for lights and cameras, as well as surface materials.)

Both methods produce the same effect. In fact, when you turn on the DOF option in the Camera Attributes settings, you're essentially applying the mental ray physical DOF lens shader to the camera. The mia_lens_bokeh lens shader is a more advanced DOF lens shader that has a few additional settings that can help improve the quality of the DOF render. For more on lens shaders, consult Chapter 8, "mental ray Shading Techniques."

The controls in the camera's Attribute Editor are easier to use than the controls in the physical DOF shader, so this example will describe only this method of applying DOF:

1. Open the chase_v05.ma scene from the chapter16/scenes directory at the book's web page.

2. In the viewport, switch to the DOF_cam camera. If you play the animation (which starts at frame 100 in this scene), you'll see the camera move from street level upward as two helicopters come into view.

3. In the panel menu bar, click the second icon from the left to open the DOF_cam's Attribute Editor.

4. Expand the Environment rollout, and click the Background Color swatch.

5. Use the Color Chooser to create a pale blue color for the background (see Figure 16.38).

FIGURE 16.38
A test render is created for frame 136.

6. Open the Render Settings dialog box, and make sure the Render Using drop-down list is set to mental ray.

7. Choose the Indirect Lighting tab and check Final Gather.

8. Switch to the Rendering menu set. Choose Render ➤ Test Resolution ➤ 50% Settings (640 × 360). This way, any test renders you create will be at half resolution, which will save a lot of time but will not affect the size of the batch-rendered images.

9. Set the timeline to frame 136, click in the viewport to set the rendering view, and Choose Render ➤ Render Current Frame to create a test render (refer back to Figure 16.38).

   As you can see from the test render, the composition of this frame is confusing to the eye and does not read very well. There are many conflicting shapes in the background and foreground. Using depth of field can help the eye separate background elements from foreground elements and sort out the overall composition.

10. In the Attribute Editor for the DOF_cam, expand the Depth Of Field rollout panel and activate Depth Of Field.

11. Store the current image in the Render Preview window (from the Render Preview window menu, choose File ➤ Keep Image In Render View). Click the viewport to set the render view, and then create another test render using the default DOF settings.

12. Use the scroll bar at the bottom of the Render View window to compare the images. There's almost no discernable difference. This is because the DOF settings need to be adjusted. There are only three settings:

    Focus Distance   This setting determines the area of the image that is in focus. Areas in front or behind this area will be out of focus.

    F Stop   This setting describes the relationship between the diameter of the aperture and the focal length of the lens. Essentially, it is the amount of blurriness seen in the rendered image. F Stop values used in Maya are based on real-world F stop values. The lower the value, the blurrier the areas will be beyond the focus distance. Changing the focal length of the lens will affect the amount of blur as well. If you are happy with a camera's DOF settings but then change the focal length or angle of view, you'll probably need to reset the F Stop setting. Typically, values range from 2.8 to about 12.

    Focus Region Scale   You can use this value to adjust the area in the scene that you want to stay in focus. Lowering this value will also increase the blurriness. Use this option to fine-tune the DOF effect once you have the Focus Distance and F Stop settings.

13. Select the DOF_cam, and set Focus Distance to **15**, F Stop to **2.8**, and Focus Region Scale to **0.1** and create another test render from the DOF_cam.

    The blurriness in the scene is much more obvious, and the composition is a little easier to understand. The blurring is grainy. You can improve this by adjusting the Quality slider in the Render Settings. For now you can leave the settings where they are as you adjust the DOF (see Figure 16.39).

FIGURE 16.39
Adding depth of
field can help sort
the elements of
a composition by
increasing the sense
of depth.

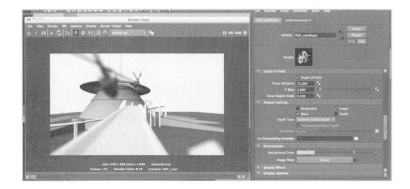

14. Save the scene as **chase_v06.ma**.

To see a version of the scene so far, open chase_v06.ma from the chapter16\scenes directory at the book's web page.

Creating a Rack Focus Rig

A *rack focus* refers to a depth of field that changes over time. It's a common technique used in cinematography as a storytelling aid. By changing the focus of the scene from elements in the background to the foreground (or vice versa), you control what the viewer looks at in the frame. In this section, you'll set up a camera rig that you can use to change the focus distance of the camera interactively.

1. Continue with the scene from the previous section, or open the chase_v06.ma file from the chapter16\scenes directory at the book's web page.

2. Switch to the perspective view. Choose Create ➢ Measure Tools ➢ Distance Tool, and click two different areas in the scene to create the tool. Two locators will appear with an annotation that displays the distance between the two locators in scene units (meters for this scene).

3. In the Outliner, rename locator1 to **camPosition**, and rename locator2 to **distToCam** (see Figure 16.40).

4. In the Outliner, expand the DOF_cam_group. MMB-drag camPosition on top of the DOF_cam node to parent the locator to the camera.

5. Open the Channel Box for the camPosition locator, and set all of its Translate and Rotate channels to **0**; this will snap camPosition to the center of the camera.

6. Ctrl/Cmd+click the fields for the camPosition's Translate and Rotate channels in the Channel Box, right-click the fields, and choose Lock Selected so that the locator can no longer be moved.

FIGURE 16.40
A measure tool,
consisting of two
locators, is created
on the grid.

7. In the Outliner, MMB-drag distToCam on top of the camPosition locator to parent dist-
ToCam to camPosition.

8. Select distToCam and, in the Channel Box, set its Translate X and Y channels to **0**, and
lock these two channels (see Figure 16.41). You should be able to move distToCam only
along the z-axis.

FIGURE 16.41
The Translate X and
Y channels of the
distToCam node are
locked so that it can
move only along the
z-axis.

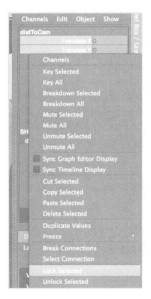

9. Open the Connection Editor by choosing Window ➢ General Editors ➢ Connection
Editor.

10. In the Outliner, select the distanceDimension1 node, and expand it so that you can select
the distanceDimensionShape1 node. (Make sure the Display menu in the Outliner is set
so that shape nodes are visible.)

11. Click the Reload Left button at the top of the Connection Editor to load this node.

12. Expand the DOF_cam node in the Outliner, and select DOF_camShape. Click Reload Right in the Connection Editor.

13. From the bottom of the list on the left, select distance. On the right side, select focus-Distance (see Figure 16.42).

FIGURE 16.42

The distance attribute of the distance DimensionShape1 node is linked to the focusDistance attribute of the DOF_camShape node using the Connection Editor.

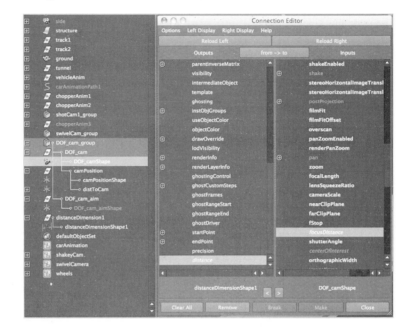

14. Look in the perspective view at the distance measured in the scene, select the distToCam locator, and move it so that the annotation reads about 5.5 units.

15. Select the DOF_camShape node, and look at its focusDistance attribute. If it says something like 550 units, then there is a conversion problem:

a. Select the distanceDimensionShape1 node in the Outliner, and open the Attribute Editor.

b. From the menu in the Attribute Editor, click Focus and select the node that reads unit-Conversion14. If you are having trouble finding the unit conversion node, turn off DAG Objects Only in the Outliner's Display menu and turn on Show Auxiliary Nodes in the Outliner's Show menu. You should see the unitConversion nodes at the bottom of the Outliner.

c. Select unitConversion14 to switch to the unitConversion node in the Attribute Editor, and set Conversion Factor to **1**.

Occasionally, when you create this rig and the scene size is set to something other than centimeters, Maya converts the units automatically and you end up with an incorrect number for the Focus Distance attribute of the camera. This node may not always be necessary when setting up this rig. If the value of the Focus Distance attribute of the camera matches the distance shown by the distanceDimension node, you don't need to adjust the unitConversion's Conversion Factor setting.

16. Set the timeline to frame 138. In the Perspective window, select the distToCam locator and move it along the z-axis until its position is near the position of the car (about –10.671 in the Channel Box).

17. In the Channel Box, right-click the Translate Z channel and choose Key Selected (see Figure 16.43).

FIGURE 16.43
The distToCam locator is moved near the position of the car on frame 138 and keyframed.

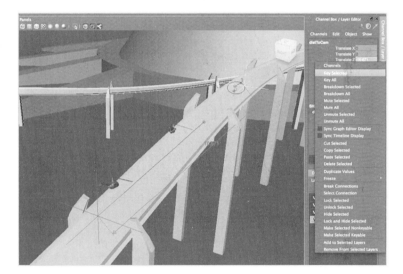

18. Switch to the DOF_cam in the viewport, and create a test render. The helicopters should be out of focus, and the area further up the street in the distance should be in focus.

19. Set the timeline to frame 160.

20. Move the distToCam node so that it is at about the same position as the closest helicopter (around –1.026).

21. Set another keyframe on its Z translation.

22. Switch back to the DOF_cam, and render another test frame.

The area around the helicopter is now in focus (see Figure 16.44).

FIGURE 16.44
The focus distance of the camera has been animated using the rig so that, at frame 160, the helicopter is in focus and the background is blurry.

If you render a sequence of this animation for the frame range between 120 and 180, you'll see the focus change over time. To see a finished version of the camera rig, open chase_v07.ma from the chapter16\scenes directory at the book's web page.

Adding Motion Blur to an Animation

If an object changes position while the shutter on a camera is open, this movement shows up as a blur. Maya cameras can simulate this effect using the Motion Blur settings found in the Render Settings as well as in the camera's Attribute Editor. Not only can motion blur help make an animation look more realistic, but it can also help smooth the motion in the animation.

Like depth of field, motion blur is expensive to render, meaning that it can take a long time. Also much like depth of field, there are techniques for adding motion blur in the compositing stage after the scene has been rendered. You can render a motion vector pass using mental ray's passes and then add the motion blur using the motion vector pass in your compositing software. For jobs that are on a short timeline and a strict budget, this is often the way to go. In this section, however, you'll learn how to create motion blur in Maya using mental ray.

There are many quality issues closely tied to rendering with motion blur. In this chapter, you'll learn the basics of how to apply the different types of motion blur.

MENTAL RAY MOTION BLUR

The mental ray Motion Blur setting supports all rendering features, such as textures, shadows (ray trace and depth map), reflections, refractions, and caustics.

You enable the Motion Blur setting in the Render Settings window so, unlike the Depth Of Field setting, which is activated per-camera, all cameras in the scene will render with motion blur once it has been turned on. Likewise, all objects in the scene have motion blur applied to them by default. You can, and should, turn off the Motion Blur setting for those objects that appear in the distance or do not otherwise need motion blur. If your scene involves a close-up of an asteroid whizzing by the camera while a planet looms in the distance surrounded by other slower-moving asteroids, you should disable the Motion Blur setting for those distant and slower-moving objects. Doing so will greatly reduce render time.

To disable the Motion Blur setting for a particular object, select the object, open its Attribute Editor to its Shape Node tab, expand the Render Stats rollout panel, and deselect the Motion Blur option. To disable the Motion Blur setting for a large number of objects at the same time, select the objects, and open the Attribute Spread Sheet (Window ➢ General Editors ➢ Attribute Spread Sheet). Switch to the Render tab, and select the Motion Blur header at the top of the column to select all the values in the column. Enter **0** to turn off the Motion Blur setting for all the selected objects (see Figure 16.45).

FIGURE 16.45
You can disable the Motion Blur setting for a single object in the Render Stats section of its Attribute Editor or for a large number of selected objects using the Attribute Spread Sheet.

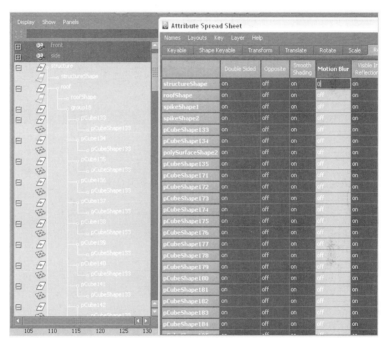

MOTION BLUR AND RENDER LAYERS

The Motion Blur setting can be active for an object on one render layer and disabled for the same object on another render layer using render-layer overrides. For more information on using render layers, consult Chapter 11, "Rendering for Compositing."

There are two types of motion blur in mental ray for Maya: No Deformation and Full. No Deformation calculates only the blur created by an object's transformation—meaning its transla- tion, rotation, and scale. A car moving past a camera or a helicopter blade should be rendered using No Deformation.

The Full setting calculates motion vectors for all of an object's vertices as they move over time. Full should be used when an object is being deformed, such as when a character's arm geometry is weighted to joints and animated moving past the camera. Using Full motion blur will give more accurate results for both deforming and nondeforming objects, but it will take a longer time to render than using No Deformation.

MOTION BLUR FOR MOVING CAMERAS

If a camera is moving by a stationary object, the object will be blurred just as if the object were moving by a stationary camera.

The following procedure shows how to render with motion blur:

1. Open the scene chase_v08.ma from the chapter16\scenes directory at the book's web page.

2. In the Display tab of the Layer Editor, right-click the buildings display layer and choose Select Objects.

3. Open the Attribute Spread Sheet (Window ➤ General Editors ➤ Attribute Spread Sheet), and switch to the Render tab.

4. Select the Motion Blur header to select all the values in the Motion Blur column, and type 0 and press Enter to turn the settings to Off (as shown in Figure 16.45). Do the same for the objects in the street layer.

5. Switch to the Rendering menu set. Choose Render ➤ Test Resolution ➤ Render Settings (1280×720). This will set the test render in the Render View window to 1280×720, the same as in the Render Settings window.

6. Switch to the shotCam1 camera in the viewport.

7. Set the timeline to frame 59, and open the Render View window (Window ➤ Rendering Editors ➤ Render View).

8. Create a test render of the current view. From the Render View panel, choose Render ➤ Render ➤ shotCam1. The scene will render.

9. In the Render View panel, drag a rectangle over the blue helicopter. To save time while working with motion blur, you'll render just this small area.

10. Open the Render Settings window. Choose Presets ➤ Load Preset ➤ Production.

11. Switch to the Quality tab. Expand the Motion Blur rollout panel, and set Motion Blur to No Deformation. Leave the settings at their defaults.

12. In the Render View panel, click the Render Region icon (second icon from the left) to render the selected region in the scene. When it's finished, store the image in the render view.

You can use the scroll bar at the bottom of the render view to compare stored images (see Figure 16.46).

FIGURE 16.46
The region around the helicopter is selected and rendered using motion blur.

In this case, the motion blur did not add a lot to the render time; however, consider that this scene has no textures, simple geometry, and default lighting. Once you start adding more complex models, textured objects, and realistic lighting, you'll find that the render times will increase dramatically.

OPTIMIZING MOTION BLUR

Clearly, optimizing Motion Blur is extremely important, and you should always consider balancing the quality of the final render with the amount of time it takes to render the sequence. Remember that, if an object is moving quickly in the frame, some amount of graininess may actually be unnoticeable to the viewer.

13. Switch back to the Quality tab, and take a look at the settings under Motion Blur:

Motion Blur By   This setting is a multiplier for the motion blur effect. A setting of 1 produces a realistic motion blur. Higher settings create more stylistic or exaggerated effects.

Displace Motion Factor   This setting adjusts the quality of motion-blurred objects that have been deformed by a displacement map. It effectively reduces geometry detail on those parts of the model that are moving past the camera, based on the amount of detail and the amount of motion as compared to a nonmoving version of the same object. Slower-moving objects should use higher values.

14. For the most part, Unified Sampling is taking care of the quality of the motion blur. If the blur is too grainy, increase the Quality value.

Using Orthographic and Stereo Cameras

Orthographic cameras are generally used for navigating a Maya scene and for modeling from specific views. A stereoscopic, or stereo, camera is a special rig that can be used for rendering stereoscopic 3D movies.

Orthographic Cameras

The front, top, and side cameras that are included in all Maya scenes are orthographic cameras. An *orthographic view* is one that lacks perspective. Think of a blueprint drawing, and you get the basic idea. There is no vanishing point in an orthographic view.

Any Maya camera can be turned into an orthographic camera. To do this, open the Attribute Editor for the camera and, in the Orthographic Views rollout panel, turn on the Orthographic option (see Figure 16.47). Once a camera is in orthographic mode, it appears in the Orthographic section of the viewport's Panels menu. You can render animations using orthographic cameras; just add the camera to the list of renderable cameras in the Render Settings window. The Orthographic Width is changed when you dolly an orthographic camera in or out.

FIGURE 16.47
The Orthographic option for the perspective camera is activated, flattening the image seen in the perspective view.

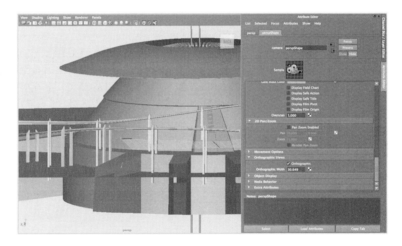

THE VIEWCUBE

You can use the ViewCube to view the objects in your scene from a variety of angles. This means that you are not limited to just the Perspective, Front, Side, and Top camera options. You can turn the ViewCube on through the Preferences window, under the Interface section. To change the view, simply click one of the faces of the ViewCube. When you have the cube set to an orthographic view, such as the bottom, the other faces of the ViewCube will not be visible. In this case, arrows appear outside of the ViewCube. You can click these arrows to rotate the ViewCube and thus change the viewing angle of the scene. Click the center of the ViewCube to zoom in, click an edge or corner of the ViewCube to see the scene from an oblique view, and click the house icon to return to your starting view. You can choose more options for the ViewCube by clicking the small arrow at the lower right of the ViewCube icon.

Stereo Cameras

You can use stereo cameras when rendering a movie that is meant to be watched using special 3D glasses. Follow the steps in this example to learn how to work with stereo cameras:

1. Create a new scene in Maya. From the Create menu, choose Cameras ➤ Stereo Camera. You'll see three cameras appear on the grid.

2. Switch the panel layout to Panels ➤ Saved Layouts ➤ Four View.

3. Set the upper-left panel to the perspective view and the upper-right to Panels ➤ Stereo ➤ stereoCamera.

4. Use the panel menu in the viewport to set the lower-left viewport to StereoCameraLeft and the lower-right viewport to StereoCameraRight.

5. Create a NURBS sphere (Create ➤ NURBS Primitives ➤ Sphere).

6. Position the sphere in front of the center camera of the rig, and set its Translate Z channel to –**10**.

7. In the perspective view, select the center camera and open the Attribute Editor to stereoCameraCenterCamShape.

   In the Stereo rollout panel, you can choose which type of stereo setup you want; this is dictated by how you plan to use the images in the compositing stage. Interaxial Separation adjusts the distance between the left and right cameras, and Zero Parallax defines the point on the z-axis (relative to the camera) at which an object directly in front of the camera appears in the same position in the left and right cameras.

8. In the Attribute Editor, under the Stereo Display Controls rollout panel, set Display Frustum to All. In the perspective view, you can see the overlapping angle of view for all three cameras.

9. Turn on Zero Parallax Plane. A semitransparent plane appears at the point defined by the Zero Parallax setting (see Figure 16.48).

10. Set the Stereo setting in the Stereo rollout panel to Converged.

11. Set the Zero Parallax attribute to **10**.

12. In the perspective view, switch to a top view and make sure that the NURBS sphere is directly in front of the center camera and at the same position as the Zero Parallax plane (Translate Z = –10).

    As you change the Zero Parallax value, the left and right cameras will rotate on their y-axes to adjust, and the Zero Parallax Plane will move back and forth depending on the setting.

13. In the top view, move the sphere back and forth, toward and away from the camera rig. Notice how the sphere appears in the same position in the frame in the left- and right-camera views when it is at the Zero Parallax plane. However, when it is in front of or behind the plane, it appears in different positions in the left and right views.

    If you hold a finger up in front of your eyes and focus on the finger, the position of the finger is at the Zero Parallax point. Keep your eyes focused on that point, but move your finger toward and away from your face. You see two fingers when it's before or behind the Zero Parallax point (more obvious when it's closer to your face). When a stereo camera rig is rendered and composited, the same effect is achieved and, with the help of 3D glasses, the image on the two-dimensional screen appears in three dimensions.

FIGURE 16.48
A stereo camera uses three cameras to render an image for 3D movies. The Zero Parallax plane is positioned at the point where objects in front of the center camera appear in the same position in the left and right cameras.

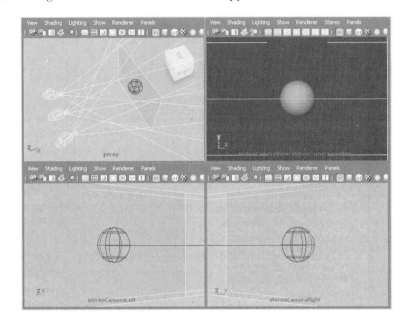

14. Select the center stereo camera, and turn on the Safe Viewing Volume option in the Attribute Editor. This displays the area in 3D space where the views in all three cameras overlap. Objects should remain within this volume in the animation so that they render correctly as a stereo image.

15. Open the Render Settings to the Common tab.

16. Under Renderable Cameras, you can choose to render each camera of the stereo rig separately, or you can select the Stereo Camera (Stereo Pair) option to add both the right and left cameras at the same time. Selecting the stereoCamera option renders the scene using the center camera in the stereo camera rig. This can be useful if you want to render a non-stereoscopic version of the animation.

The cameras will render as separate sequences, which can then be composited together in compositing software to create the final output for the stereo 3D movie.

You can preview the 3D effect in the Render View window by choosing Render ➤ Stereo Camera from the Render menu in the Render view. The Render View window will render the scene and combine the two images. You can then choose one of the options in the Display menu of the Render view by selecting Display ➤ Stereo Display menu to preview the image.

If you have a pair of red/green 3D glasses handy, choose the Anaglyph option and put on the glasses, and you'll be able to see how the image will look in 3D.

The upper-right viewport window has been set to StereoCamera, which enables a Stereo menu in the panel menu bar. This menu has a number of viewing options you can choose from when working in a stereo scene, including viewing through just the left or right camera. Set the shading mode to Smooth Shade All, and switch to Anaglyph mode to see the objects in the scene shaded red or green to correspond with the left or right camera. (This applies to objects that are in front or behind the Zero Parallax plane.)

Using the Camera Sequencer

The Camera Sequencer is a nonlinear editing interface that allows you to stitch together multiple camera views into a single sequence. The Camera Sequencer editing interface itself is similar to editing interfaces found in video editing and compositing programs, but instead of editing a sequence of images, the Camera Sequencer edits the animation of cameras in an existing 3D scene. This allows you to work out the timing of shots in a scene without having to render any images.

This exercise will demonstrate the basic functions of the Camera Sequencer:

1. Open the chase_v09.ma scene from the chapter16/scenes folder at the book's web page.

2. In the perspective viewport, choose Panels ➤ Saved Layouts ➤ Persp/Camera Sequencer (see Figure 16.49).

FIGURE 16.49
Choose the Persp/Camera Sequencer layout preset.

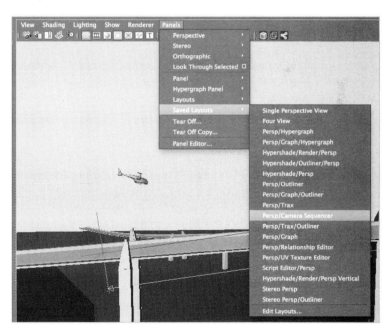

The Camera Sequencer interface appears at the bottom, below the persp view. Notice that it has its own timeline. When you work with the Camera Sequencer, you do not need to move the playhead on the main Time Slider; in fact, this can get a little confusing when you first start using the sequencer, so it is not a bad idea to hide the Time Slider.

3. From the main menu bar, choose Display ➤ UI Elements. Uncheck both Time Slider and Range Slider.

Now you can add a camera to the sequencer and start stitching together a sequence from all three cameras.

4. From the menu bar in the Camera Sequencer, choose Create ➤ Shot ➤ Options. Make sure shot1 is listed in the Name field. Set the Shot Camera menu to shotCam1. Set Start Time to **50** and End Time to **90**. Set New Shot Placement to Current Frame. Click the Create Shot button (see Figure 16.50).

FIGURE 16.50
The options for adding a shot to the Camera Sequencer.

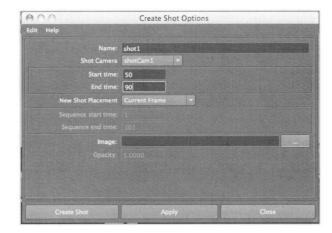

5. Hold the Alt key, and drag to the right in the sequencer so that you can see more of the timeline.

When you create the shot, a blue bar is added to the sequencer. This represents the range of shot1. Notice that the shot is placed at the start of the Time Slider in the sequencer even though the shot itself starts at frame 50 (see Figure 16.51).

FIGURE 16.51
shot1 has been added to the sequencer, indicated by a long blue bar.

6. Click the Playback Sequence button (the triangle pointed to the right) in the sequencer. The animation shows the car and the helicopter whizzing past the shaking camera.

7. Stop the animation, and rewind the playhead in the sequencer by clicking the double triangle button on the far left of the sequencer controls.

8. Choose Create ➤ Shot ➤ Options to create a second shot. In the Create Shot Options dialog box, set the shot name to **shot2**, set Shot Camera to swivelCam, and set Start Time to **40** and End Time to **150**. Leave New Shot Placement set to Current Frame. Click the Create Shot button.

A second blue bar appears in the Camera Sequencer editing interface below the shot1 bar on a new track. This is because New Shot Placement was set to Current Frame. You can add the shot to the same track as the original by choosing After Current Shot. I think it's easier to work with the shots if they are on separate tracks. As you'll see, you can easily move the tracks around in the Camera Sequencer Editing Interface.

9. In the Camera Sequencer Editing Interface, click the long blue bar in track 2 (turns yellow when selected) and drag it to the right so that the left end of shot2 is below the right end of shot1 (see Figure 16.52).

FIGURE 16.52

Move shot2 so that it is aligned with the end of shot1 in the Camera Sequencer Editing Interface.

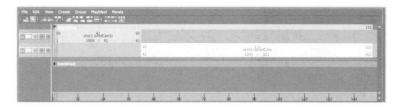

The numbers at either end of the track correspond to the frame numbers in the animation. The upper number is the frame of the original sequence. The lower number is the frame number in the Camera Sequencer Editing Interface. Look at the blue bar for shot1. The number 41 indicates that you're on frame 41 in the sequencer. The number 90 indicates that it is frame 90 of the actual animation. At the start of the bar for shot2 (the left end), the number 42 indicates that you're on frame 42 of the sequence and the number 40 indicates frame 40 of the actual animation.

10. Click the Playback Sequence button in the sequencer to play the animation. In spite of the fact that technically the animation is jumping backward from the end of shot1 to the start of shot2, it looks seamless. In fact, you could even drag shot1 so that it comes after shot2.

The shot at the top of the stack is what you'll see when the animation plays.

11. Stop the animation, rewind it, and use the Create menu to add a third shot. Name the shot **shot3**, and set Shot Camera to **DOF_camShape**, Start Time to **100**, and End Time to **150**. Leave New Shot Placement set to Current Frame so that the new shot creates a new track. Click the Create Shot button.

12. Drag the blue bar for shot3 to the right until the number in the lower-left corner of the bar reads 90. You may need to Alt+MMB-drag to pan the view of the sequencer. Drag the bar up and place it on the same track with shot1.

13. Play the sequence.

Now things are taking shape. With little effort, you're already editing a film before a single frame has been rendered!

14. Drag the double red vertical line (this is the playhead) until you're at frame 120 in the sequence. Select the bar for shot2 so that it turns yellow.

15. On the menu bar for the Camera Sequencer Editing Interface, click the fith icon from the left—the icon that looks like a pair of scissors. Doing so splits the selected shot at the playhead (see Figure 16.53).

16. Click a blank part of the sequencer to deselect the shots and then click the shorter end of the shot2 bar in the Camera Sequencer Editing Interface. Drag it to the right so that the left end is aligned with the right end of shot3.

17. Hold the mouse cursor over the frame number in the upper-right corner of shot2. The cursor looks like a brush. Drag this corner to the right to extend the shot. Drag it all the way until this number reads 200 (see Figure 16.54).

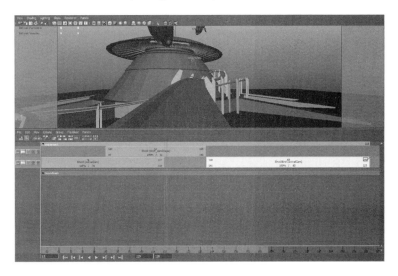

18. Play the sequence. Congratulations—you are on your way to becoming a virtual filmmaker!

19. Save the scene as **chase_v10.ma**. To see a version of this scene, open the chase_v10.ma scene chapter16/scenes directory at the book's web page.

The Camera Sequencer is a powerful tool. In addition to rearranging camera sequences in a nonlinear fashion, you can change the speed of the shots simply by dragging left or right on the frame number in the lower-left or lower-right corners of the shot bar. When you do this, you'll notice that the percentage value at the center of the bar updates. So if you extend the shot to 200 percent of its original length, the camera moves and the animation in the shot will be slowed down to half speed. If you try this for shot3, you'll see the blades of the helicopters rotate slower than in the original shot. However, the actual animation has not been changed. If you leave the Camera Sequencer as is, the original animation in the scene will not be altered.

You can create an Ubercam that incorporates all of the changes created in the Camera Sequencer into a single camera. To do this, choose Create ➤ Ubercam in the Camera Sequencer. The main caveat is that you cannot alter the duration of the shots in the camera sequence.

The Bottom Line

Use assets An asset is a way to organize the attributes of any number of specified nodes so that the attributes are easily accessible in the Channel Box. This means that members of each team in a pipeline only have to see and edit the attributes they need to get their job done, thus streamlining production.

> **Master It** Create an asset from the nodes in the miniGun_v04.ma scene in the chapter1\scenes folder. Make sure that only the Y rotation of the turret, the X rotation of the guns, and the Z rotation of the gun barrels are available to the animator.

Create file references File references can be used so that as part of the team works on a model, the other members of the team can use it in the scene. As changes to the original file are made, the referenced file in other scenes will update automatically.

> **Master It** Create a file reference for the miniGun_v04.ma scene; create a proxy from the miniGun_loRes.ma scene.

Determine the camera's image size and film speed You should determine the final image size of your render at the earliest possible stage in a project. The size will affect everything from texture resolution to render time. Maya has a number of presets that you can use to set the image resolution.

> **Master It** Set up an animation that will be rendered to be displayed on a high-definition progressive-scan television.

Create and animate cameras The settings in the Attribute Editor for a camera enable you to replicate real-world cameras as well as add effects such as camera shaking.

> **Master It** Create a camera setting where the film shakes back and forth in the camera. Set up a system where the amount of shaking can be animated over time.

Create custom camera rigs Dramatic camera moves are easier to create and animate when you build a custom camera rig.

> **Master It**   Create a camera in the car-chase scene that films from the point of view of chopperAnim3 but tracks the car as it moves along the road.

Use depth of field and motion blur   Depth of field and motion blur replicate real-world camera effects and can add a lot of drama to a scene. Both are expensive to render and therefore should be applied with care.

> **Master It**   Create a camera asset with a built-in focus distance control.

Create orthographic and stereo cameras   Orthographic cameras are used primarily for modeling because they lack a sense of depth or a vanishing point. A stereoscopic rig uses three cameras and special parallax controls that enable you to render 3D movies from Maya.

> **Master It**   Create a 3D movie from the point of view of the driver in the chase scene.

Use the Camera Sequencer   The Camera Sequencer can be used to edit together multiple camera shots within a single scene. This is useful when blocking out an animatic for review by a director or client.

> **Master It**   Add a fourth camera from the point of view of the car, and edit it into the camera sequence created in the section "Using the Camera Sequencer" in this chapter.

Appendix A

The Bottom Line

Each of The Bottom Line sections in the chapters suggests exercises to deepen skills and understanding. Sometimes there is only one possible solution, but often you are encouraged to use your skills and creativity to create something that builds on what you know and lets you explore one of many possibilities.

Chapter 1: Working in Autodesk Maya

Understand transform and shape nodes.   DAG nodes have both a transform node and a shape node. The transform node tells where an object is located; the shape node describes how it is made. Nodes can be parented to each other to form a hierarchy.

Master It   Arrange the nodes in the `miniGun_v03.ma` file in a hierarchical structure so that the barrels of the guns can rotate on their z-axis, the guns can be aimed independently, and the guns rotate with the turret.

Solution   In the Outliner, MMB-drag the left_gunBarrels node onto the left_housing node. MMB-drag the left_housing node onto left_mount, and then MMB-drag the left mount onto the turret node. Do the same for the right_gunBarrels, housing, and mount nodes. Graph the node structure on the Hypergraph, and examine the network.

Create a project.   Creating a project directory structure keeps Maya scene files and connected external files organized to ensure the animation project is efficient.

Master It   Create a new project named Test, but make sure the project has only the scene, source images, and data subfolders.

Solution   Use the New button in the Project Window dialog box to create a new project named **Test**; delete the text in all the fields except for Scenes, Source Images, and Data. Name the folders in these fields `scenes`, `sourceImages`, and `data`, respectively.

Chapter 2: Introduction to Animation

Use inverse kinematics.   Inverse kinematics creates a goal object, known as an end effector, for joints in a chain. The joints in the chain orient themselves based on the translation of the goal. The IK Handle tool is used to position the end effector.

Master It   Create an inverse kinematic control for a simple arm.

Solution   Create a simple arm using three joints—one for the upper arm, one for the forearm, and one for the wrist. Rotate the forearm slightly so that the IK solver understands which direction the joint should rotate. Freeze transformations on the joints. Activate the IK Handle tool, click the first joint (known as the root), and then click the wrist joint. Move around the IK Handle to bend the joint.

Animate with keyframes. A keyframe marks the state of a particular attribute at a point in time on the timeline. When a second keyframe is added to the attribute at a different point in time, Maya interpolates the values between the two keyframes, creating animation. There are a number of ways to edit keyframes using the timeline and the Channel Box.

Master It Create a number of keyframes for the Translate channels of a simple object. Copy the keyframes to a different point in time for the object. Try copying the keyframes to the Scale channels. Try copying the keys to the Translate channels of another object.

Solution After creating keys for the object, Shift-drag a selection on the timeline. Use the arrows in the selection box to move or scale the keys. Right-click the keys, and choose Copy. Move to a different point in time on the timeline, and paste the keys. Copying, pasting, and duplicating keys to another object can be accomplished by selecting the channels in the Channel Box and using the options that appear when you right-click the channels.

Use the Graph Editor. Sophisticated animation editing is available using the animation curve-editing tools on the Graph Editor.

Master It Create a looping animation for the mechanical bug model using as few keys as possible. The bug should leap up repeatedly and move forward with each leap.

Solution Create keyframes on the bug's Translate Y and Translate Z channels. Set four keys on the Translate Y channel so that the bug is stationary, then moves up along the y-axis, moves back down to 0, and then holds for a number of frames. In the Graph Editor, set the Post-Infinity option for the Translate Y channel to Cycle. Create a similar set of keyframes for the Translate Z channel on the same frames. Set the Post-Infinity option for Translate Z to Cycle With Offset.

Preview animations with a playblast. A playblast is a tool for viewing the animation as a flipbook without actually rendering the animation. FCheck is a utility program that is included with Maya. Playblasts can be viewed in FCheck.

Master it Create a playblast of the mechBugLayers_v04.ma scene.

Solution Open the mechBugLayers_v04.ma scene from the chapter2\scenes directory at the book's web page. Rewind the animation, and create a playblast by choosing Windows ➢ Playblast. Watch the playblast in FCheck.

Animate with motion paths. Motion paths allow you to attach an object to a curve. Over the course of the animation, the object slides along the curve based on the keyframes set on the motion path's U Value.

Master It Make the bug walk along a motion path. See whether you can automate a walk cycle based on the position along the path.

Solution Draw a curve in a scene with the fully rigged mechanical bug. Attach the bodyCtrl curve to the curve using Animate ➢ Attach To Motion Path. Create set-driven keys for the leg animation, but instead of using the Translate Z of the bodyCtrl curve, use the U Value of the motion path node.

Use animation layers. Using animation layers, you can add new motion that can override existing animation or be combined with it.

Master It Create animation layers for the flying bug in the `mechBug_v08.ma` scene in the `chapter2\scenes` folder at the book's web page. Create two layers: one for the bodyCtrl curve and one for the legsCtrl curve. Use layers to make the animation of the wings start with small movements and then flap at full strength.

Solution Open the `mechBug_v08.ma` scene. Select the bodyCtrl curve. In the animation layers, create an empty layer. Select the BaseAnimation layer, select the bodyCtrl curve, and choose Layers ➤ Extract Selected. Do the same for the legsCtrl curve and the wing motors. Set keyframes on the weight of the layer that contains the wing motors. Keyframe the weight from a value of 0 to a value of 1 over 20 frames.

Chapter 3: Hard-Surface Modeling

Understand polygon geometry. Polygon geometry consists of flat faces connected and shaped to form three-dimensional objects. You can edit the geometry by transforming the vertices, edges, and faces that make up the surface of the model.

Master It Examine the polygon primitives in the Create ➤ Polygon Primitives menu.

Solution Create an example of each primitive shown in the menu. Switch to vertex selection mode, and move the vertices of each primitive to create unique shapes.

Understand NURBS surfaces. NURBS surfaces can be created by lofting a surface across a series of curves. The curve and surface degree and parameterization affect the shape of the resulting surface.

Master It What is the difference between a one-degree (linear) surface, a three-degree (cubic) surface, and a five-degree surface?

Solution The degree of the surface is determined by the number of CVs per span minus one. Thus a one-degree surface has two CVs per span, a three-degree surface has four CVs per span, and a five-degree surface has six CVs per span. Linear and cubic surfaces are the ones used most frequently.

Understand subdivision surfaces. Any polygon object can be converted to a subdivision surface directly from its Attribute Editor. Maya offers three different methods for subdivision.

Master It Convert a polygon model to a subdivision surface model. Examine how the polygon object changes in shape.

Solution Create various polygon primitives. Open their Attribute Editor and expand the Smooth Mesh rollout. Deselect Use Global Subdivision Method. Change Subdivision Method to OpenSubdiv Catmull-Clark.

Employ image planes. Image planes can be used to position images for use as a modeling guide.

Master It Create image planes for side, front, and top views for use as a model guide.

Solution Create reference drawings or use photographs taken from each view. Save the images to your local disk. Create image planes for the front, side, and top views, and apply the corresponding reference images to each image plane. Use the settings in each image plane's Attribute Editor to position the image planes in the scene. Use display layers for each plane so that their visibility can be turned on and off easily.

Model with NURBS surfaces.   A variety of tools and techniques can be used to model surfaces with NURBS. Hard-surface/mechanical objects are well-suited subjects for NURBS surfaces.

Master It   Create the spokes of the bike.

Solution   Draw a cubic CV curve to the length of a single spoke. Extrude a circle along the curve to generate the spoke.

Model with polygons.   Booleans can be a great way to quickly cut holes into polygon surfaces. It is important, however, to establish a clean surface for the Boolean to cut into or intersect with. When you're using multiple objects, doing so becomes even more important.

Master It   Create the hub for all of the bicycle spokes to come into. Each spoke should have its own hole.

Solution   Create a polygon cylinder. Resize it to match the shape of the hub. Extrude a thin lip where all of the spokes come into the hub. Duplicate numerous cylinders where the spokes enter into the hub. Select all of the cylinders and the hub. Perform a Boolean Difference.

Chapter 4: Organic Modeling

Implement box modeling.   Box modeling allows you to start with a simple primitive that you can extrude to create a complex form.

Master It   Starting from a smoothed cube, use box modeling techniques to create a head.

Solution   Extrude the two adjacent faces on the bottom of the smoothed cube for the character's chin. Insert edge loops horizontally to define the center lines for the eyes, nose, and mouth. Extrude locally inside existing faces to create the eye and mouth loops.

Employ build-out modeling.   From a single polygon, you can extrude edges to create smaller sections of a larger object.

Master It   Use the build-out method to model an ear.

Solution   Create a polygon with the Create Polygon tool. Use the polygon for the outer loop of the ear. Extrude edges to complete the loop. Create a separate loop of polygons for the inner ear canal. Use Bridge to connect the two pieces.

Sculpt polygons.   Artisan is a brush-based modeling and editing toolset. Using Artisan, you can sculpt directly on the surface of geometry.

Master It   Use Artisan to sculpt dents into a surface.

Solution   Create a polygon surface with fairly dense geometry. Choose Polygons ➢ Sculpt Geometry to activate Artisan. Open the options for the tool while working, and then use the brush to make small dents in the surface of the geometry.

Use retopology tools.   Highly detailed, sculpted models are impractical to take through the production pipeline. Instead, the high-resolution model is *retopologized* to a lower, more manageable resolution.

> **Master It**   Use Quad Draw to create a low-polygon game model of the hand in hand_v01.ma.

> **Solution**   Make the hand a live surface. Choose Quad Draw from the Modeling Toolkit. Draw quads on the surface. Try to keep the overall polygon count to fewer than 500 triangles.

Chapter 5: Rigging and Muscle Systems

Create and organize joint hierarchies.   A joint hierarchy is a series of joint chains. Each joint in a chain is parented to another joint, back to the root of the chain. Each joint inherits the motion of its parent joint. Organizing the joint chains is accomplished by naming and labeling the joints. Proper orientation of the joints is essential for the joints to work properly.

> **Master It**   Create a joint hierarchy for a giraffe character. Orient the joints so that the x-axis points down the length of the joints.

> **Solution**   Draw joint chains for each appendage of the animal. Draw another joint chain for the giraffe's spine. Parent the root of each joint chain appendage to the appropriate joint on the spine.

Use Human Inverse Kinematics rigs.   Human Inverse Kinematics (HIK) creates IK Handles that control an entire bipedal or quadrupedal skeleton rather than using multiple IK chains on individual limbs.

> **Master It**   Define the giraffe skeleton, and apply the HIK system to it.

> **Solution**   Select the skeleton's root joint. Choose Skeleton ➢ HumanIK to open the Character Controls panel. Define the skeleton and then create the control rig.

Apply skin geometry.   Skinning geometry refers to the process in which geometry is bound to joints so that it deforms as the joints are moved and rotated. Each vertex of the geometry receives a certain amount of influence from the joints in the hierarchy. This can be controlled by painting the weights of the geometry on the skin.

> **Master It**   Paint weights on the giraffe model to get smooth-looking deformations on one side of the model. Mirror the weights to the other side.

> **Solution**   Select the giraffe geometry. Open Skin ➢ Edit Smooth Skin ➢ Paint Skin Weights Tool. Paint values on the geometry based on the proximity of the influencing joint. Use the smooth brush and the Weight Hammer to polish the look of the deformations. When done, choose Skin ➢ Edit Smooth ➢ Mirror Skin Weights.

Use Maya Muscle.   Maya Muscle is a series of tools designed to create more believable deformations and movement for objects skinned to joints. Capsules are used to replace

Maya joints. Muscles are NURBS surfaces that squash, stretch, and jiggle as they deform geometry.

Master It Use Maya Muscle to create muscles for the hind leg of the giraffe. Use the muscle system to cause skin bulging and sliding.

Solution Use Muscle ➢ Muscle/Bones ➢ Muscle Creator to generate the proper musculature. Shape the muscles to fit under the geometry. Paint different muscle weights to achieve various sliding effects.

Chapter 6: Animation Techniques

Work with deformers. Maya has a multitude of deformers that can be used to animate or model any object with control points. Deformers provide real-time results, making them easy and flexible to work with.

Master It Create a planet with a terrain filled with craters.

Solution Create a primitive polygon sphere. Add a texture deformer with the 3D Crater texture. Change Point Space to World and Direction to Normal. Increase the amount of geometry on the sphere through its polySphere1 construction history node until you achieve the desired effect.

Animate facial expressions. Animated facial expressions are a big part of character animation. It's common practice to use a blend shape deformer to create expressions from a large number of blend shape targets. The changes created in the targets can be mixed and matched by the deformer to create expressions and speech for a character.

Master It Create blend shape targets for the amanda character. Make an expression where the brows are up and another where the brows are down. Create a rig that animates each brow independently.

Solution Create two duplicates of the neutral amanda character. Use the modeling tools to model raised eyebrows on one copy and lowered eyebrows on the other. Add these targets to the amanda model. Use the Paint Blend Shape tool to make four additional targets: leftBrowUp, leftBrowDown, rightBrowUp, and rightBrowDown. Add these new targets to the amanda model. Create a custom control using the Curve tool. Connect the control to the Blend Shape controls using driven keys.

Animate nonlinear deformers. Nonlinear deformers apply simple changes to geometry. The deformers are controlled by animating the attributes of the deformer.

Master It Animate an eel swimming past the jellyfish you animated in this chapter.

Solution Model a simple eel using your favorite tools and techniques. Apply a sine deformer to the eel. Create an expression that animates the offset of the sine wave. Group the eel and the deformer, and animate the group moving past the jellyfish.

Add jiggle movement to an animation. Jiggle deformers add a simple jiggling motion to animated objects.

Master It Add a jiggling motion to the belly of a character.

Solution   Create a rotund character. Animate the character moving. Add a jiggle deformer to the character. Use the Paint Jiggle Weights tool to mask the jiggle weights on the entire character except for the belly.

Apply motion capture.   Maya comes with several motion-capture animations. You can access them through the Visor.

Master It   Switch between multiple motion-capture examples on the same character.

Solution   Import another motion-capture example into the `mocap_v01.ma` scene file. In the Character Controls window, change Source to the newly imported motion-capture animation.

Chapter 7: Lighting with mental ray

Use shadow-casting lights.   Lights can cast either depth map or raytrace shadows. Depth map shadows are created from an image projected from the shadow-casting light, which reads the depth information of the scene. Raytrace shadows are calculated by tracing rays from the light source to the rendering camera.

Master It   Compare mental ray depth map shadows to raytrace shadows. Render the `crystalGlobe.ma` scene using soft raytrace shadows.

Solution   Depth map shadows render faster and are softer than raytrace shadows. Raytrace shadows are more physically accurate. Create a light and aim it at the crystalGlobe. Enable Raytrace Shadows, and increase the Shadow Rays and the Light Radius settings.

Render with global illumination.   Global illumination simulates indirect lighting by emitting photons into a scene. Global illumination photons react with surfaces that have diffuse shaders. Caustics use photons that react to surfaces with reflective shaders. Global illumination works particularly well in indoor lighting situations.

Master It   Render the `rotunda_v01.ma` scene, found in the `chapter7\scenes` folder at the book's web page, using global illumination.

Solution   Create a photon-emitting area light, and place it near the opening in the top of the structure. Set its Intensity to **0**. Create a shadow-casting direct light, and place it outside the opening in the ceiling. Turn on Emit Photons for the area light, and enable Global Illumination in the Render Settings window. Increase Photon Intensity and the number of photons emitted as needed.

Render with Final Gathering.   Final Gathering is another method for creating indirect lighting. Final Gathering points are shot into the scene from the rendering camera. Final Gathering includes color bleeding and ambient occlusion shadowing as part of the indirect lighting. Final Gathering can be used on its own or in combination with global illumination.

Master It   Create a fluorescent lightbulb from geometry that can light a room.

Solution   Model a fluorescent lightbulb from a polygon cylinder. Position it above objects in a scene. Apply a Lambert shader to the bulb, and set the incandescent channel to white. Enable Final Gathering in the Render Settings window, increase the Scale value, and render the scene. Adjust the settings to increase the quality of the render.

Use image-based lighting. Image-based lighting (IBL) uses an image to create lighting in a scene. High dynamic range images (HDRIs) are usually the most effective source for IBL. There are three ways to render with IBL: Final Gathering, global illumination, and with the light shader. These can also be combined if needed.

Master It Render the bicycle scene using the Uffizi Gallery probe HDR image available at http://ict.debevec.org/~debevec/Probes.

Solution Create an IBL node in the bicycle scene using the settings in the Render Settings window. Download the Uffizi Gallery light probe image from http://ict .debevec.org/~debevec/Probes. Apply the image to the IBL node in the scene (use Angular mapping). Experiment using Final Gathering, global illumination, and the IBL light shader. Use these in combination to create a high-quality render.

Render using the Physical Sun and Sky network. The Physical Sun and Sky network creates realistic sunlight that's ideal for outdoor rendering.

Master It Render a short animation showing the street corner at different times of day.

Solution Add the Physical Sun and Sky network to the scene using the settings in the Render Settings window. Make sure Final Gathering is enabled. Keyframe the sun Direction light rotating on its x-axis over 100 frames. Render a sequence of the animation.

Understand mental ray area lights. mental ray area lights are activated in the mental ray section of an area light's shape node when the Use Light Shape option is enabled. mental ray area lights render realistic, soft raytrace shadows. The light created from mental ray area lights is emitted from a three-dimensional array of lights as opposed to an infinitely small point in space.

Master It Build a lamp model that realistically lights a scene using an area light.

Solution Build a small lamp with a round bulb. Create an area light, and place it at the center of the bulb. In the area light's shape node settings, enable Use Shape in the mental ray settings and set the shape's Type to Sphere. Scale down the light to fit within the bulb. Enable Raytrace Shadows, and render the scene.

Chapter 8: mental ray Shading Techniques

Understand shading concepts. Light rays are reflected, absorbed by, or transmitted through a surface. A rough surface diffuses the reflection of light by bouncing light rays in nearly random directions. Specular reflections occur on smooth surfaces; the angle at which rays bounce off a smooth surface is equivalent to the angle at which they strike the surface. Refraction occurs when light rays are bent as they are transmitted through the surface. A specular highlight is the reflection of a light source on a surface. In CG rendering, this effect is often controlled separately from reflection; in the real world, specular reflection and highlights are intrinsically related.

Master It Make a standard Blinn shader appear like glass refracting light in the jellybeans_v01.ma scene in the chapter8\scenes folder on the book's web page.

Solution Open the jellybeans_v01.ma scene in the chapter8\scenes folder on the book's web page. Open the Hypershade, and select the glass material—this is a standard Maya Blinn shader. In the Raytrace Options of the glass shader's Attribute Editor, turn on Refractions, and set Refractive Index to **1.1**. Create a test render.

Apply reflection and refraction blur.   Reflection and Refraction Blur are special mental ray options available on many standard Maya shading nodes. You can use these settings to create glossy reflections when rendering standard Maya shading nodes with mental ray.

Master It   Create the look of translucent plastic using a standard Maya Blinn shader.

Solution   Apply a Blinn shader to an object. Increase transparency and reflectivity. Enable Refractions in the Raytrace Options settings. In the mental ray section, increase the Mi Reflection and Mi Refraction settings. Render with mental ray.

Use mia materials.   The mia materials and nodes can be used together to create realistic materials that are always physically accurate. The mia materials come with a number of presets that can be used as a starting point for your own materials.

Master It   Create a realistic polished-wood material.

Solution   Create a mia_material_x shader for an object in a scene that uses physical sky and sun lighting. Use the Glossy finish as a starting place to create the material. In the Color channel of the Diffuse settings, add the Wood 3D texture from the standard Maya 3D texture nodes. Add glossiness to the reflections and the highlight. (Remember that lower settings spread out the reflection, whereas higher settings create a more defined reflection.)

Understand mila shading layers.   The layering shaders are separate components of a traditional shader that can easily be stacked and blended on top of one another. Layered shaders allow you to add an infinite amount of detail to a single shader.

Master It   Create a mix layer and blend two colored diffuse layers together.

Solution   Create a mila_material shader. Add a weighted Diffuse Reflection layer. Click +Mix to add another layer and mix its values with the first Diffuse Reflection layer. Change the color of the first layer to blue. Change the color of the second layer to red. The colors mix together to form purple.

Render contours.   mental ray has the ability to render contours of your models to create a cartoon drawing look for your animations. Rendering contours requires that options in the Render Settings window and in the shading group for the object be activated.

Master It   Render the coffeemaker using contours.

Solution   Open one of the versions of the coffeemaker scene in the `chapter8\scenes` folder. Apply a material to the coffeemaker geometry. Enable Contour Rendering in the material's shading group node and on the Features tab of the Render Settings window.

Chapter 9: Texture Mapping

Create UV texture coordinates.   UV texture coordinates are a crucial element of any polygon or subdivision surface model. If a model has well-organized UVs, painting texture and displacement maps is easy and error-free.

Master It   Map UV texture coordinates on the giraffe's body.

Solution   Select the faces making up the giraffe's body. Use a cylindrical projection to establish the UV shell. Smooth out the UVs with the Unfold and Smooth tools.

Work with bump, normal, and displacement maps.   Bump, normal, and displacement maps are ways to add detail to a model. Bump maps are great for fine detail, such as pores; normal maps allow you to transfer detail from a high-resolution mesh to a low-resolution version of the same model and offer superior shading and faster rendering than bump maps. Displacement maps alter the geometry.

Master It   Create high-resolution and low-resolution versions of the model, and try creating a normal map using the Transfer Maps tool. See whether you can bake the bump map into the normal map.

Solution   Open the Transfer Maps window. Load your low-resolution model to the Target Meshes rollout. Load your high-resolution model to the Source Meshes rollout. Select an Output Map, and change the settings to meet your specifications. Bake the map.

Create a subsurface scattering layering shader.   The subsurface scattering layering shader can create extremely realistic-looking skin.

Master It   Bake the subsurface scattering shader into texture maps. Map the baked textures to the original Blinn shaders on the giraffe, and compare its look to the rendered subsurface scattering look.

Solution   Open the Transfer Maps window. Load your low-resolution model to the Target Meshes rollout. Load your Sub-Surface Scattering mapped model to the Source Meshes rollout. Select the Custom output map. Enter the Sub-Surface Scattering shader's name into the Custom Shader field. Bake the map.

Work with Viewport 2.0.   Viewport 2.0 offers the ability to use advanced shaders in real time. Furthermore, high-end lighting can be combined without sacrificing interactivity.

Master It   Using the DirectX11 ubershader, add normal, specular, and vector displacement maps to the `giraffeUber_v02.ma` scene file.

Solution   Load the specific maps under the correct rollouts in the ubershader Attribute Editor. Be sure to click the check box for each shader to turn their effects on in Viewport 2.0.

Chapter 10: Paint Effects

Use the Paint Effects canvas.   The Paint Effects canvas can be used to test Paint Effects strokes or as a 2D paint program for creating images.

Master It   Create a tiling texture map using the Paint Effects canvas.

Solution   Choose a brush from the Visor, such as the `downRedFeathers.mel` brush from the `feathers` folder. On the canvas toolbar, select the Horizontal and Vertical Wrap options. Paint feathers across the canvas; strokes that go off the top or sides will wrap around to the opposite side. Save the image in the Maya IFF format, and try applying it to an object in a 3D scene.

Paint on 3D objects.   Paint Effects brushes can be used to paint directly on 3D objects as long as the objects are either NURBS or polygon geometry. Paint Effects brushes require that all polygon geometry have mapped UV texture coordinates.

Master It   Create a small garden or jungle using Paint Effects brushes.

Solution   Model a simple landscape using a polygon or NURBS plane. Create some small hills and valleys in the surface. Make the object paintable, and then experiment using the Brush presets available in the Visor. The `plants`, `plantsMesh`, `trees`, `treesMesh`, `flowers`, and `flowersMesh` folders all have presets that work well in a garden or jungle setting.

Understand strokes.   Many nodes are associated with a Paint Effects stroke. Each has its own set of capabilities.

Master It   Create a stroke and then manually move control vertices on the Paint Effects curve to alter the brush's placement.

Solution   Choose a brush from the Visor, such as the `brassTacks.mel` brush from the `objectsMesh` folder. Paint the stroke in a new scene. Open the Hypergraph and find the curve associated to the stroke. Turn on its visibility. Choose control vertices on the curve and transform them around the scene.

Design brushes.   Custom Paint Effects brushes can be created by using a preset brush as a starting point. You can alter the settings on the brush node to produce the desired look for the brush.

Master It   Design a brush to look like a laser beam.

Solution   Use one of the neonGlow brushes found in the `glows` folder in the Visor. Paint the brush in a 3D scene, paint as straight a line as possible, or attach the stroke to a straight curve using the options in the Paint Effects ➢ Curve Utilities menu. Open the Attribute Editor for the neon brush, and adjust the Color and Glow settings in the Shading section of the Brush attributes. Set the Stamp Density value in the Brush Profile section to a low value to create a series of glowing dots.

Create complexity by adding strokes to a curve.   Duplicating a Paint Effects curve allows you to add an additional effect to an existing stroke.

Master It   Choose a flower brush from the Visor and add grass around it.

Solution   Paint a stroke with several flowers on the grid plane. Select the stroke and duplicate it. Choose a grass brush from the Visor and apply it to the duplicated stroke.

Shape strokes with behavior controls.   Behaviors are settings that can be used to shape strokes and tubes, giving them wiggling, curling, and spiraling qualities. You can animate behaviors to bring strokes to life.

Master It   Add tendrils to a squashed sphere to create a simple jellyfish.

Solution   Use the slimeWeed brush in the `grasses` folder of the Visor. Paint on the bottom of the sphere. Adjust the look of the tendrils by modifying the Noise, Curl, Wiggle, and Gravity forces in the Behavior section of the Brush attributes.

Animate strokes.   Paint Effects strokes can be animated by applying keyframes, expressions, or animated textures directly to stroke attributes. You can animate the growth of strokes by using the Time Clip settings in the Flow Animation section of the Brush attributes.

Master It   Animate blood vessels growing across a surface. Animate the movement of blood within the vessels.

Solution Use any of the treeBare presets from the `Trees` folder in the Visor as a starting point for the blood vessels. Use the Shading attributes to add a red color. Animate the growth of the vessels by selecting Time Clip in the Flow Animation attributes. To animate the blood in the vessels, set Texture Type to Fractal for the color in the Texturing section and select Texture Flow in the Flow Animation attributes.

Render Paint Effects strokes. Paint Effects strokes are rendered as a postprocess using the Maya Software Renderer. To render with the mental ray software, you should convert the strokes to geometry.

Master It Render an animated Paint Effects tree in mental ray.

Solution Choose the Tree Sparse stroke from the `Trees` folder of the Visor. Draw the tree in the scene, and add animation using the Turbulence controls (choose Tree Wind turbulence). Convert the tree to polygons and render with mental ray.

Chapter 11: Rendering for Compositing

Use render layers. Render layers can be used to separate the elements of a single scene into different versions or into different layers of a composite. Each layer can have its own shaders, lights, and settings. Using overrides, you can change the way each layer renders.

Master It Use render layers to set up alternate versions of the coffeemaker. Try applying contour rendering on one layer and Final Gathering on another.

Solution In the Layer Editor, copy the masterLayer twice. Rename one copy for contour shading, and the other for Final Gathering. To create the layer for contour shading, make that layer active. Right-click the contour shading layer, and choose Overrides ➢ Create New Material Override. Select a new lambert shader to be created from the list. Enable contour rendering in the shading group of this new lambert. In the Features tab of the Render Settings window, enable contour rendering and click the Create Layer Override check box. To create the render layer with Final Gathering, make the Final Gathering layer active, go to the Indirect Lighting tab in the Render Settings window, turn on Final Gathering, and click the Create Layer Override check box.

Use render passes. Render passes allow you to separate material properties into different images. These passes are derived from calculations stored in the frame buffer. Each pass can be used in compositing software to rebuild the rendered scene efficiently. Render pass contribution maps define which objects and lights are included in a render pass.

Master It Create an Ambient Occlusion pass for the bicycle scene.

Solution In the Passes tab in the Render Settings window, click the Create New Render Pass icon. In the Create Render Passes window, select Ambient Occlusion from the Pass List.

Perform batch renders. Batch renders automate the process of rendering a sequence of images. You can use the Batch Render options in the Maya interface, or choose Batch Render from the command prompt (or Terminal) when Maya is closed. A batch script can be used to render multiple scenes.

Master It   Create a batch script to render five fictional scenes. Each scene uses layers with different render settings. Set the frame range for each scene to render frames 20 through 50. The scenes are named `myScene1.ma` through `myScene5.ma`.

Solution   You can use additional rendering flags, but the script should follow this basic template:

```
render -r mr -s 20 -e 50 -cam renderCam1 myScene1.mb
render -r mr -s 20 -e 50 -cam renderCam1 myScene2.mb
render -r mr -s 20 -e 50 -cam renderCam1 myScene3.mb
render -r mr -s 20 -e 50 -cam renderCam1 myScene4.mb
render -r mr -s 20 -e 50 -cam renderCam1 myScene5.mb
```

Use mental ray quality settings.   Controlling the quality of your renders is a joint venture between using approximation nodes and render settings. Unified Sampling offers a simplified approach to adjusting the quality of your renders. Combine this with progressive IPR, and you can quickly refine your renders.

Master It   Set up an IPR render of the `coffeeMakerComposite_v04.ma` scene. Focus in on half of the coffeemaker and force the render to last only 20 seconds. Adjust the quality for the best results.

Solution   Make sure Unified Sampling is turned on in your render settings. Choose Progressive Mode ➤ IPR Only. In your render view, choose IPR ➤ IPR Quality ➤ IPR Progressive Mode. Render an IPR image and then draw a region around half of the helmet. In the Render Settings, set the Max Time to 20.0.

Chapter 12: Introducing nParticles

Create nParticles.   nParticles can be added to a scene in a number of ways. They can be drawn using the tool or spawned from an emitter, or they can fill an object.

Master It   Create a spiral shape using nParticles.

Solution   Create a NURBS cylinder. Use a twist deformer to make the surface isoparms spiral. Choose Edit Curves ➤ Duplicate Surface Curves to extract a curve from the cylinder. Use the extracted curve as a volume curve field and emit nParticles into it.

Make nParticles collide.   nParticles can collide with themselves, other nParticles, and polygon surfaces.

Master It   Make nParticles pop out of the top of an animated volume.

Solution   Use the `forge_v02.ma` scene from the `chapter12\scenes` folder. Animate the scale X and Z of the insideTub node to push the nParticles out the top.

Create liquid simulations.   Enabling Liquid Simulations changes the behavior of nParticles so that they act like water or other fluids.

Master It   Create a flowing stream of nParticles that ends in a waterfall.

Solution   Emit water nParticles with a cylindrical volume. Use the Volume Speed settings to emit the nParticles along the axis of the cylinder. Create a polygon plane and make the nParticles collide against it. Move the emitter close to the edge of the plane to have the nParticles flow over the side.

Emit nParticles from a texture.   The emission rate of an nParticle can be controlled using a texture.

Master It   Create your own name in nParticles.

Solution   Create a texture with your name. Use the texture as the Texture Rate on a surface emitting nParticles.

Move nParticles with Nucleus wind.   The wind force on the Nucleus node can be used to push nParticles.

Master It   Blow nParticles off a surface using wind.

Solution   Sketch numerous nParticles onto a polygon plane with the nParticle tool. Make the plane a passive collider. Animate the wind parameters to move the nParticles across the plane slowly. Increase the wind rapidly to create a gust.

Use force fields.   Force fields can be emitted by nParticles and collision objects, creating interesting types of behavior in your scenes.

Master It   Add a second nParticle object emitted from the base of the generator. Enable its force field so that it attracts some of the original energy nParticle.

Solution   Create an emitter and move it under one of the conductors. Set the nParticles radius to **0.01**. Change its Point Field Magnitude value to **-0.01**.

Chapter 13: Dynamic Effects

Use nCloth.   nCloth can be used to make polygon geometry behave dynamically to simulate a wide variety of materials. Using the presets that come with Maya, you can design your own materials and create your own presets for use in your animations.

Master It   Create the effect of a cube of gelatinous material rolling down the stairs.

Solution   Create a polygon cube with a minimum of five subdivisions for the width and height. Make the cube an nCloth object. Use wind to blow the cube down the stairs. Alter the Compression Resistance on the nCloth node to achieve different effects.

Combine nCloth and nParticles.   Because nCloth and nParticles use the same dynamic systems, they can be combined easily to create amazing simulations.

Master It   Make a water balloon burst as it hits the ground.

Solution   Model a water balloon and convert it to nCloth. Assign the waterBalloon preset to the nCloth geometry. Fill the balloon with nParticles using the Fill Object settings. Use a tearable surface constraint on the nCloth balloon. Add a primitive plane to the scene, and have the balloon collide against it.

Use Maya rigid body dynamics.   Rigid body dynamics are not quite as powerful as nCloth objects, but they do calculate much faster and work better for simulations involving a large number of interacting pieces.

Master It   Animate a series of dominoes falling over.

Solution   Place modeled dominoes in a row. Make sure the distance between them is less than the overall height of the domino model. Make all of the dominoes active rigid bodies except for the first one in the row; make it a passive rigid body. Animate the passive rigid domino falling over to hit the others and cause the chain reaction.

Use nParticles to drive instanced geometry.   Modeled geometry can be instanced to nParticles to create a wide variety of effects.

Master It   Create the effect of a swarm of insects attacking a beach ball.

Solution   Create a simulation of nParticles. Replace the nParticles with instanced geometry of a small insect. Create a beach ball using nCloth. Make the nCloth beach ball a goal to the nParticles.

Create nParticle expressions.   nParticle expressions can be used to further extend the power of nParticles. Using expressions to automate instanced geometry simulations is just one of the ways in which expressions can be used.

Master It   Improve the animation of the insects attacking the beach ball by adding different types of insects to the swarm. Randomize their size, and create expressions so that larger insects move more slowly.

Solution   Use per-particle attributes and the Expression Editor to create a relationship between the insects' scale and the particle's velocity.

Create a soft body simulation with Bullet.   Bullet physics are fast and accurate. In addition to creating rigid body simulations, you can use Bullet to create clothlike effects with its soft bodies.

Master It   Drape a tablecloth over a table using soft body physics.

Solution   Model a basic table. Create a primitive plane and translate it a few units above the table. Convert the plane to a soft body. Increase the resolution of the plane to improve the look of the simulation.

Chapter 14: Hair and Clothing

Add XGen descriptions to characters.   XGen is a primitive generator that adds realistic short hairs to the surface of character. The placement, length, and other attributes of the hairs can be controlled by painting on the surface using the XGen grooming tools.

Master It   Create eyebrows for the head used at the beginning of this chapter.

Solution   Open the `hairstyle_v03.ma` scene from the `chapter14\scenes` folder at the book's web page. Add a new description to the female collection. Use the grooming brushes to remove hairs to get the shape of an eyebrow.

Create dynamic curves.   A standard Maya curve can be made dynamic by using the Make Dynamic Curves action in the Hair menu. A copy of the curve is created that will respond to dynamic motion and forces. The curve can be used in skeletons for IK Spline tools, as a source for Paint Effects strokes, as a modeling tool, or for any other effect that requires curves.

Master It   Create a flag using dynamic curves.

Solution   Create two parallel curves, and make both dynamic. Set the Point Lock attribute on both curves to Base. Loft a NURBS surface between the dynamic curves. Edit the dynamic properties of the curves, and apply fields to the curves to create a flapping motion for the flag.

Add hair to characters.   Hair is created using Paint Effects strokes that are controlled by follicles. The follicles are dynamic curves that respond to forces and movement. Follicles can be applied to polygon or NURBS surfaces as a grid or by painting on the surface. The Visor contains a number of hair presets that can be imported into a scene.

Master It   Add hair to the top of the giraffe's head from Chapter 9.

Solution   Open the `giraffeUV_v07.ma` scene from the `chapter9\scenes` folder at the book's web page. Create a scalp surface for the giraffe by duplicating selected faces on the head. Paint follicles on the head to suggest hair growing from the top of the head. Use Thinning and other hair properties to create the look of long and wispy hair.

Style hair.   Hair can be styled by painting attribute values on follicles or by directly editing the CVs of start or rest curves.

Master It   Create an avant-garde hairdo for the nancy character by painting attributes.

Solution   Open the `nancyHair_v06.ma` scene from the `chapter14\scenes` folder. Apply a turbulence field to the hairSystem1 node. Set Magnitude to a high value (**10** to **20**), and set Attenuation to **0**. Play the animation. When the hair achieves an interesting state, select the follicles and set the state as the hair's rest position (and start position). Delete the field, and increase the hair's start curve Attract attribute.

Paint nCloth properties.   Properties such as Bounce, Stretch, and Wrinkle can be painted onto nCloth objects using either texture or vertex painting techniques. When painting properties, you may need to alter the Min and Max Value ranges in the Artisan interface to allow for values beyond the range of 0 to 1. Vertex maps have the advantage that the values are not stored in an external texture file.

Master It   Add starch to the simple man's shirt by painting a Rigidity value on the shirt geometry.

Solution   Open the `simpleMan_v06.ma` scene from the `chapter14\scenes` folder. Select the surface, and paint a vertex map. Choose Rigidity as the property you want to paint. Set Max Value in the Artisan Tool options to **30**. Set the Max Color slider in the Artisan Display options to **30**. Set the Paint value to somewhere between **20** and **30**, and paint on the surface where you want the shirt to be stiff. Adjust the values as needed.

Chapter 15: Maya Fluids

Use fluid containers.   Fluid containers are used to create self-contained fluid effects. Fluid simulations use a special type of particle that is generated in the small subunits (called *voxels*) of a fluid container. Fluid containers can be 2D or 3D. Two-dimensional containers take less time to calculate and can be used in many cases to generate realistic fluid effects.

Master It   Create a logo animation that dissolves like ink in water.

Solution   Create a 2D fluid container. Add a surface emitter using a NURBS plane, and add an emission map for the diffusion attribute of the emitter. Use a file texture created from a logo. Set the Buoyancy value of the fluid to **0**. Use dynamic fields to push the logo to create the dissolving motion. Try using Turbulence, Drag, and Vortex fields on the logo.

Create a reaction.   A reaction can be simulated in a 3D container by combining temperature with fuel. Surfaces can be used as emitters within a fluid container.

Master It   Create a chain reaction of explosions using the Paint Fluids tool.

Solution   Create a 3D fluid container. Use the Paint Fluids tool to paint small blobs of fuel separated by short distances. The painted fuel blobs should be arranged so that they create a chain reaction when lit. Add an emitter that emits temperature, and place it below the first fuel blob in the container. Set the Ignition Temperature, Reaction Speed, and Heat Released attributes in the Fuel section of the container so that the fuel burns and emits heat when a certain temperature is reached. Set Shading to Temperature so that you can see the reaction.

Render fluid containers.   Fluid containers can be rendered using Maya Software or mental ray. The fluids can react to lighting, cast shadows, and self-shadow.

Master It   Render the `TurbulentFlame.ma` example in the Visor so that it emits light onto nearby surfaces.

Solution   Create a scene that has simple modeled surfaces such as a floor and some logs. Import the `TurbulentFlame.ma` scene from the `Fire` folder of the Visor (on the Fluid Examples tab). Set the renderer to mental ray. In the Indirect Lighting section, select Final Gathering. Increase the value of the HSV color on the Final Gathering Scale to **4**. Disable the Default Light under the Render Options rollout of the Common tab of the Render Settings window. Play the animation, and render a test frame when the fire is burning.

Use fluids with nParticles.   Fluid simulations can interact with nParticles to create a large array of interesting effects.

Master It   nCloth objects use nParticles and springs to simulate the behavior of cloth. If fluids can affect nParticles, it stands to reason that they can also affect nCloth objects. Test this by creating a simulation where a fluid emitter pushes around an nCloth object.

Solution   Create a 3D fluid container and an emitter that emits density and temperature. The fluid should rise in the container, and the Swirl attribute in Velocity should be set to **10** so that there is a turbulent motion. Create a polygon sphere, and place it inside the fluid container above the emitter. Convert the sphere to an nCloth object. Use the Silk preset for the nCloth object, and set Gravity in the Nucleus tab to **0.1**. Play the animation, and experiment with the settings in the fluid container and on the nCloth object until the fluid pushes the nCloth object around.

Create an ocean.   Ocean effects are created and edited using the Ocean shader. Objects can float in the ocean using locators.

Master It   Create an ocean effect that resembles stormy seas. Add the capsule geometry as a floating object.

Solution   Import the `WhiteCaps.ma` scene from the Ocean Examples tab of the Visor. Import the `capsule_v01.ma` scene from the `chapter15\scenes` folder at the book's web page. Use the Float Selected Objects command to make the capsule float on the surface of the water. Look at the settings in the Ocean shader node to see how the stormy sea effect was created.

Chapter 16: Scene Management and Virtual Filmmaking

Use assets   An asset is a way to organize the attributes of any number of specified nodes so that the attributes are easily accessible in the Channel Box. This means that members of each team in a pipeline only have to see and edit the attributes they need to get their job done, thus streamlining production.

Master It   Create an asset from the nodes in the `miniGun_v04.ma` scene in the `chapter1\scenes` folder. Make sure that only the Y rotation of the turret, the X rotation of the guns, and the Z rotation of the gun barrels are available to the animator.

Solution   Make a container that holds the turretAim and turret nodes (and their child nodes). Use the Asset Editor to publish the Rotate Y, Rotate X, and barrelSpin attributes of the turretAim curve node to the container. Set the container to Black Box mode so that the animator can't access any of the attributes of the contained nodes.

Create file references   File references can be used so that as part of the team works on a model, the other members of the team can use it in the scene. As changes to the original file are made, the referenced file in other scenes will update automatically.

Master It   Create a file reference for the `miniGun_v04.ma` scene; create a proxy from the `miniGun_loRes.ma` scene.

Solution   Create a new scene, and reference the `miniGun_v04.ma` file in the `chapter1\ scenes` directory. Use the Reference Editor to make a proxy from the `miniGun_loRes.ma` scene in the same folder at the book's web page.

Determine the camera's image size and film speed   You should determine the final image size of your render at the earliest possible stage in a project. The size will affect everything from texture resolution to render time. Maya has a number of presets that you can use to set the image resolution.

Master It   Set up an animation that will be rendered to be displayed on a high-definition progressive-scan television.

Solution   Open the Render Settings, and choose the HD 1080 preset under the Image Size rollout on the Common tab. Progressive scan means the image will not be interlaced (rendered as alternating fields), so you can render at 24 frames per second. Open the Preferences window, and set the Time value under Settings to Film (24 fps).

Create and animate cameras   The settings in the Attribute Editor for a camera enable you to replicate real-world cameras as well as add effects such as camera shaking.

Master It   Create a camera setting where the film shakes back and forth in the camera. Set up a system where the amount of shaking can be animated over time.

Solution   Enable the Shake Overscan attribute on a camera. Attach a fractal texture to the Shake Overscan attribute, and edit its Amplitude settings. Create an expression that sets the Alpha Offset to minus one-half the Alpha Gain setting. Set keyframes on Alpha Gain to animate the shaking of the Shake Overscan attribute over time.

Create custom camera rigs   Dramatic camera moves are easier to create and animate when you build a custom camera rig.

Master It   Create a camera in the car-chase scene that films from the point of view of chopperAnim3 but tracks the car as it moves along the road.

Solution   Create a two-node camera (Camera and Aim). Attach the camera to a NURBS curve using a motion path, and parent the curve to chopperAnim3. Parent the aim of the camera to the vehicleAnim group. Create an asset for the camera so that the position of the camera around the helicopter can be changed, as can the position of the aim node relative to the vehicleAnim group.

Use depth of field and motion blur   Depth of field and motion blur replicate real-world camera effects and can add a lot of drama to a scene. Both are expensive to render and therefore should be applied with care.

Master It   Create a camera asset with a built-in focus distance control.

Solution   Create the same camera and focus distance control as shown in this chapter. Select the camera, camera shape node, and distance controls, and place them within a container. Publish the Z Translation of the distToCam locator to the container. Publish the F Stop and Focus Region Scale attributes as well.

Create orthographic and stereo cameras   Orthographic cameras are used primarily for modeling because they lack a sense of depth or a vanishing point. A stereoscopic rig uses three cameras and special parallax controls that enable you to render 3D movies from Maya.

Master It   Create a 3D movie from the point of view of the driver in the chase scene.

Solution   Create a stereo camera rig, and parent it to the car in the chase scene. Use the center camera to position the rig above the car's cockpit.

Use the Camera Sequencer   The Camera Sequencer can be used to edit together multiple camera shots within a single scene. This is useful when blocking out an animatic for review by a director or client.

Master It   Add a fourth camera from the point of view of the car, and edit it into the camera sequence created in the section "Using the Camera Sequencer" in this chapter.

Solution   Create a new camera, and parent it to the car. Name the new camera `driverCam`. Position and aim driverCam so that it shows the point of view of the driver. In the Camera Sequencer, choose Create ➤ Create Shot ➤ Options to add a new shot. Set the Shot Camera menu to driverCam. Set Start Time to **130** and End Time to **160**. Use the Sequencer editor to position the new shot in the sequence.

Appendix B

Autodesk Maya 2015 Certification

Autodesk® certifications are industry-recognized credentials that can help you succeed in your career—providing benefits to both you and your employer. Getting certified is a reliable validation of skills and knowledge, and it can lead to accelerated professional development, improved productivity, and enhanced credibility.

This Autodesk Official Press book can be an effective component of your exam preparation for the Autodesk Maya 2015 Certified Professional exam or the Autodesk Maya 2015 Certified User exam. Autodesk highly recommends (and we agree!) that you schedule regular time to prepare; review the most current exam preparation roadmap available at www.autodesk.com/certification; use this book; take a class at an Authorized Training Center (find ATCs near you here: www.autodesk.com/atc); and use a variety of resources to prepare for your certification, including plenty of actual hands-on experience.

To help you focus your studies on the skills you'll need for this exam, the following table shows objectives that could appear on an exam and in what chapter you can find information on that topic—and when you go to that chapter, you'll find certification icons like the one in the margin here.

CERT OBJECTIVE

These Autodesk exam objectives were accurate at press time; please refer to www.autodesk.com/certification for the most current exam roadmap and objectives.

Good luck preparing for your certification!

TABLE B.1: Autodesk Maya 2015 Certified Professional Exam topics and objectives

TOPIC	LEARNING OBJECTIVE	CHAPTER
Animation	Create a path animation and evaluate an object along the path	2
	Edit animation curves using the Graph Editor	2
	List constraint types	2
	Identify a custom attribute added to a controller	5
	Locate the value of an animated attribute	1
Cameras	Differentiate camera types	16
	Identifying a camera's angle of view	16

TABLE B.1: Autodesk Maya 2015 Certified Professional Exam topics and objectives *(CONTINUED)*

TOPIC	LEARNING OBJECTIVE	CHAPTER
	Explain the Film Aspect ratio for your camera	16
	Identify camera attribute names or values	16
Data Management/ Interoperability	Use the import feature to import model data	4
Dynamics/Simulation	Identify and describe the behavior of a Soft Body	13
	Differentiate active and passive rigid bodies	13
	Describe a soft or rigid body	13
	Identify rigid body settings or properties	13
Effects	Identify and use physical fields	13
Lighting	Differentiate light types	7
	Identify the specular component of a light	7
	Differentiate types of light or lighting	7
	Identify the value of Raytrace shadow attributes	7
	Describe useful methods for placing lights in a scene	7
Materials/Shading	Identify the type of material assigned to geometry	8
	Identify the specified shading component in a render	11
Modeling	Identify the typical workflow for Subdivision surface modeling	3
	Identify the type of Boolean operation performed on the objects	3
	Use polygon modeling tools	3
	Identify the typical work flow when smoothing meshes	3
Rendering	Describe Raytrace/Scanline quality settings	7
	List and differentiate renderers	7, 10, 12
Rigging/Setup	Identify Bones	2
	Identify IK Handle bones or controls	2, 5

TABLE B.1: Autodesk Maya 2015 Certified User Exam topics and objectives *(CONTINUED)*

TOPIC	LEARNING OBJECTIVE	CHAPTER
Scene Assembly/ Pipeline Integration	Describe how to improve scene organization by using Search and Rename operations	5
	Describe the FBX translator/file format	4
UI/Object Management	Identify the purpose and benefits of freezing transformation data on objects	2
	Describe camera gates or regions	16
	Identify object details and Outliner features	1

TABLE B.2: Autodesk Maya 2015 Certified User Exam topics and objectives

TOPIC	LEARNING OBJECTIVE	CHAPTER
Animation	Keyframing Basics	2
	Creating Animation: Keyframing	2
	Editing Animation: Keyframing	2
	Editing Animation: Graph Editor	2
	Creating Animation: Motion Paths	2
Camera	Camera Types	16
	Camera Attributes	16
	Camera Settings	16
Lighting	Light Types	7
	Shadows	7
Materials / Shading	Shading UI	1
	Shading Components	1
	Material Attributes	8
	UV Texture Editor	9

TABLE B.2:   Autodesk Maya 2015 Certified User Exam topics and objectives   *(CONTINUED)*

TOPIC	LEARNING OBJECTIVE	CHAPTER
Modeling	Scene Setup/Layout	1
	2D NURBS Curve Tools	3
	Object Cloning	3
	Polygon Tools	3, 4
	Modeling Tools	3, 4
	Polygon Modeling Tools	3, 4
	Polygon Information	3, 4
	Polygon Surface Editing	3, 4
	Smooth Mesh in the Attribute Editor for Polygons	3, 4
	Polygon Components	3, 4
	Modeling Aids	3, 4
Rendering	Render Settings	8, 16
	Renderer	7, 10, 12
Rigging	Skeleton	2, 5
UI/Object Management	UI Elements	1
	Viewport Display Types	1
	Object Selection	1
	Pivots	1
	Object Organization	1, 16

Index

Note to the Reader: Throughout this index **boldfaced** page numbers indicate primary discussions of a topic. *Italicized* page numbers indicate illustrations.